THE OXFORD HANDBOOK OF

CHILDREN'S LITERATURE

THE OXFORD HANDBOOK OF

CHILDREN'S LITERATURE

Edited by

JULIA L. MICKENBERG AND LYNNE VALLONE

OXFORD

UNIVERSITY PRESS

OXFORD
UNIVERSITY PRESS

Oxford University Press, Inc., publishes works that further
Oxford University's objective of excellence
in research, scholarship, and education.

Oxford   New York
Auckland   Cape Town   Dar es Salaam   Hong Kong   Karachi
Kuala Lumpur   Madrid   Melbourne   Mexico City   Nairobi
New Delhi   Shanghai   Taipei   Toronto

With offices in
Argentina   Austria   Brazil   Chile   Czech Republic   France   Greece
Guatemala   Hungary   Italy   Japan   Poland   Portugal   Singapore
South Korea   Switzerland   Thailand   Turkey   Ukraine   Vietnam

Published by Oxford University Press, Inc.
198 Madison Avenue, New York, New York 10016

www.oup.com

Oxford is a registered trademark of Oxford University Press

Library of Congress Cataloging-in-Publication Data
The Oxford handbook of children's literature / edited by Julia L.
Mickenberg and Lynne Vallone.
p.   cm.—(Oxford handbooks)
Includes bibliographical references and index.
ISBN 978-0-19-537978-5
1. Children's literature, English—History and criticism.
2. Children's literature, American—History and criticism. I. Mickenberg,
Julia L. II. Vallone, Lynne.
PR990.O94   2011
820.99282—dc22   2010014848

3 5 7 9 8 6 4

Printed in the United States of America
on acid-free paper

Acknowledgments

....

IN addition to our talented contributors, we would like to thank several other individuals and institutions who assisted us in the creation of this book. First, thanks are due to the University of Texas College of Liberal Arts, which supported production of this book with a generous subvention grant that allowed us to include many wonderful children's book illustrations and otherwise to improve the book's production quality. We would also like to acknowledge our home departments, the Department of Childhood Studies at Rutgers University and the Department of American Studies at the University of Texas at Austin, both of which provided institutional support. The Institute for Research in the Humanities at the University of Wisconsin, where Julia was an Honorary Fellow during the 2009–10 academic year, provided facilities support during the period that this book was in its final months of completion. Special thanks to Peter Hunt for offering valuable comments on an early draft of the book's introduction. We also appreciate the authors, illustrators, and publishers who allowed us to reprint their work. Patrick Cox and Deborah Valentine, of the Department of Childhood Studies at Rutgers University, provided much-appreciated assistance with manuscript preparation. Thanks also to Philis Barragan, Amy Ware, Judith Plotz, Jack Zipes, and the students in Julia's summer 2009 Children's Literature and American Culture course, who offered useful input at various points in the process. Shannon McLachlan and Brendan O'Neill at Oxford University Press have been wonderful editors to work with. Finally, we would like to extend heartfelt thanks to Howard Marchitello, Dan Birkholz, Lena Birkholz, and Edie Birkholz for their camaraderie, good humor, and distractions throughout the process.

CONTENTS

....

About the Contributors, XI

Introduction, 3
Julia L. Mickenberg and Lynne Vallone

Chapter Abstracts, 23

PART I: ADULTS AND CHILDREN'S LITERATURE

1. The Fundamentals of Children's Literature Criticism: *Alice's Adventures in Wonderland* and *Through the Looking-Glass*, 35
   Peter Hunt

2. Randall Jarrell's *The Bat-Poet*: Poets, Children, and Readers in an Age of Prose, 53
   Richard Flynn

3. Arnold Lobel's *Frog and Toad Together* as a Primer for Critical Literacy, 71
   Teya Rosenberg

4. Blending Genres and Crossing Audiences: *Harry Potter* and the Future of Literary Fiction, 93
   Karin E. Westman

PART II: PICTURES AND POETICS

5. Wanda's Wonderland: Wanda Gág and Her *Millions of Cats*, 115
   Nathalie op de Beeck

6. A Cross-Written Harlem Renaissance: Langston Hughes's *The Dream Keeper*, 129
   Katharine Capshaw Smith

7. *Dumbo,* Disney, and Difference: Walt Disney Productions and Film as Children's Literature, 147
Nicholas Sammond

8. Redrawing the Comic-Strip Child: Charles M. Schulz's *Peanuts* as Cross-Writing, 167
Charles Hatfield

9. The Cat in the Hippie: Dr. Seuss, Nonsense, the Carnivalesque, and the Sixties Rebel, 189
Kevin Shortsleeve

10. Wild Things and Wolf Dreams: Maurice Sendak, Picture-Book Psychologist, 211
Kenneth Kidd

11. Reimagining the Monkey King in Comics: Gene Luen Yang's *American Born Chinese*, 231
Lan Dong

PART III: READING HISTORY/LEARNING RACE AND CLASS

12. *Froggy's Little Brother*: Nineteenth-Century Evangelical Writing for Children and the Politics of Poverty, 255
Kimberley Reynolds

13. History in Fiction: Contextualization as Interpretation in Robert Louis Stevenson's *Kidnapped*, 275
M. O. Grenby

14. *Tom Sawyer*, Audience, and American Indians, 293
Beverly Lyon Clark

15. Living with the Kings: Class, Taste, and Family Formation in *Five Little Peppers and How They Grew*, 313
Kelly Hager

16. A Daughter of the House: Discourses of Adoption in L. M. Montgomery's *Anne of Green Gables*, 329
Mavis Reimer

17. Where in America Are You, God?: Judy Blume, Margaret Simon, and
    American National Identity, 351
    June Cummins

18. Let Freedom Ring: Land, Liberty, Literacy, and Lore in Mildred
    Taylor's Logan Family Novels, 371
    Michelle H. Martin

19. "What Are Young People to Think?": The Subject of Immigration and
    the Immigrant Subject in Francisco Jiménez's *The Circuit*, 389
    Phillip Serrato

PART IV: INNOCENCE AND AGENCY

20. "My Book and Heart Shall Never Part": Reading, Printing, and
    Circulation in the *New England Primer*, 411
    Courtney Weikle-Mills

21. Castaways: *The Swiss Family Robinson,* Child Bookmakers, and the
    Possibilities of Literary Flotsam, 433
    Karen Sánchez-Eppler

22. Tom Brown and the Schoolboy Crush: Boyhood Desire, Hero
    Worship, and the Boys' School Story, 455
    Eric L. Tribunella

23. *Peter Pan* as Children's Theater: The Issue of Audience, 475
    Marah Gubar

24. *Jade* and the Tomboy Tradition, 497
    Claudia Nelson

25. Happily Ever After: *Free to Be . . . You and Me,* Second-Wave
    Feminism, and 1970s American Children's Culture, 519
    Leslie Paris

26. Paradise Refigured: Innocence and Experience in
    His Dark Materials, 539
    Naomi Wood

    Index, 561

About the Contributors

Beverly Lyon Clark is Professor of English at Wheaton College (Massachusetts). Her recent work includes *Kiddie Lit: The Cultural Construction of Children's Literature in America* (2004) and the Norton Critical Edition of *The Adventures of Tom Sawyer* (2006).

June Cummins is Associate Professor in the Department of English and Comparative Literature at San Diego State University, where she specializes in children's literature and Jewish American literature. She has published articles that incorporate a range of perspectives, including feminism, multiculturalism, consumerism, and American identity, and she writes about both American and British literature. She is currently working on a biography of Sydney Taylor, author of the All-of-a-Kind Family series.

Lan Dong is the author of *Reading Amy Tan* (2009), *Who's the Real Mulan: The Woman Warrior's Cross-Cultural Journey* (tentative title, forthcoming 2010), and several articles and book chapters on Asian and Asian American literature and films, children's literature, and comics. She is currently editing a collection of critical essays on transnational Asian American heroines and another volume on teaching graphic narratives in the literature classroom. She holds a PhD in Comparative Literature and is Assistant Professor of English at University of Illinois Springfield where she teaches Asian American literature and culture, world literature, and graphic narratives.

Richard Flynn is Professor of Literature at Georgia Southern University where he teaches children's and adolescent literature and modern and contemporary poetry. He has written extensively about children's poetry and about childhood in the works of Randall Jarrell, Gwendolyn Brooks, June Jordan, Robert Lowell, Elizabeth Bishop, and others. He edited the *Children's Literature Association Quarterly* from 2004 to 2009.

M. O. Grenby is the author of *The Child Reader 1700–1840* (forthcoming) and *Children's Literature* (2008) and is coeditor of *The Cambridge Companion to Children's Literature* (2009) and *Popular Children's Literature in Britain* (2008). He has also published several studies of late eighteenth-century culture, including *The Anti-Jacobin Novel: British Conservatism and the French Revolution* (2001). He is Reader in Children's Literature in the School of English Literature, Language and Linguistics at Newcastle University, U.K.

MARAH GUBAR is Associate Professor of English and Director of the Children's Literature Program at the University of Pittsburgh. Her book *Artful Dodgers: Reconceiving the Golden Age of Children's Literature* (OUP, 2009) was chosen as a *Times Higher Education* "Book of the Week." Her new book project is focused on Anglo-American children's theatre.

KELLY HAGER teaches Victorian literature and children's literature at Simmons College. She is the author of *Dickens and the Rise of Divorce: The Failed-Marriage Plot and the Novel Tradition* (2010) and a contributor to *Keywords for Children's Literature, The Oxford Encyclopedia of Children's Literature*, and *The American Child: A Cultural Studies Reader*.

CHARLES HATFIELD teaches comics and children's literature at California State University, Northridge. He is the author of *Alternative Comics: An Emerging Literature* (2005) and the forthcoming *Hand of Fire: The Narrative Art of Jack Kirby*, and serves on the executive committee for the MLA Discussion Group in Comics and Graphic Narratives.

PETER HUNT was the first specialist in children's literature to be appointed full Professor of English in a British University. He has written or edited twenty-four books, has written over 120 articles on the subject, and has edited *The Wind in the Willows, Treasure Island*, and *The Secret Garden* for Oxford World's Classics. In 2003 he won the Brothers Grimm Award for services to children's literature from the International Institute for Children's Literature, Osaka. His latest book is the four-volume *Children's Literature: Critical Concepts in Literary and Cultural Studies* (2006).

KENNETH KIDD is Associate Professor of English at the University of Florida, where he teaches seminars in children's literary and cultural studies. He is the author of *Making American Boys: Boyology and the Feral Tale* (2004) and coeditor of *Wild Things: Children's Culture and Ecocriticism* (2004).

MICHELLE H. MARTIN, Associate Professor of English at Clemson University in South Carolina, published *Brown Gold: Milestones of African-American Children's Picture Books, 1845–2002* in 2004 and coedited (with Claudia Nelson) *Sexual Pedagogies: Sex Education in Britain, Australia, and America, 1879–2000* (2003). Martin is currently working on a book-length critical examination of the collaborative and individual works that Arna Bontemps and Langston Hughes wrote for young people during their friendship and collaborative working relationship that lasted from the 1920s until the 1960s.

JULIA L. MICKENBERG is Associate Professor of American Studies, and an affiliate of the Center for Women and Gender Studies and the Center for Russian and Eastern European Studies at the University of Texas at Austin. She is the author of *Learning* *from the Left: Children's Literature, the Cold War, and Radical Politics in the United States* (OUP, 2006), which won several awards, including the Children's Literature Association Book Award. She is also coeditor (with Philip Nel) of *Tales for Little Rebels: A Collection of Radical Children's Literature* (2008). Her essays on children's literature have appeared in *American Literary History, American Quarterly, The Cambridge History of the Novel,* and elsewhere.

CLAUDIA NELSON is Professor of English and Affiliated Professor of Women's and Gender Studies at Texas A&M University. In addition to coediting three anthologies of critical articles, she is the author of four books, *Family Ties in Victorian England* (2007), *Little Strangers: Portrayals of Adoption in America, 1850–1929* (2003), *Invisible Men: Fatherhood in Victorian Periodicals, 1850–1910* (1995), and *Boys Will Be Girls: The Feminine Ethic and British Children's Fiction, 1857–1917* (1991).

NATHALIE OP DE BEECK is Associate Professor of English at Pacific Lutheran University, where she directs the program in children's literature. She writes on graphic narrative, and her projects include a critical facsimile edition of Mary Liddell's 1926 picture book, *Little Machinery.*

LESLIE PARIS is Associate Professor of History at the University of British Columbia. She is the author of *Children's Nature: The Rise of the American Summer Camp* (2008). She has also coedited volumes on Adirondack summer camps, vulnerable children in Canada and the United States, and American girls of the nineteenth and twentieth centuries. Currently, she is writing a history of American childhood from 1965 to 1980.

MAVIS REIMER is Canada Research Chair in the Culture of Childhood and Professor of English at the University of Winnipeg in Canada, where she directs the programs and activities of the Centre for Research in Young People's Texts and Cultures. She is coauthor of the third edition of *The Pleasures of Children's Literature* (2003), editor of the collection of essays, *Home Words: Discourses of Children's Literature in Canada* (2008), and lead editor of the journal *Jeunesse: Young People, Texts, Cultures.*

KIMBERLEY REYNOLDS is Professor of Children's Literature in the School of English Literature, Language, and Linguistics at Newcastle University in the U.K. She was President of the International Research Society for Children's Literature (2003–2007). Recent publications include *Radical Children's Literature: Future Visions and Aesthetic Transformations* (2007), which received the Children's Literature Association Book Award in 2009, and *Children's Literature Studies: A Handbook to Research* (coeditor, forthcoming 2010).

TEYA ROSENBERG teaches undergraduate and graduate courses in children's litera-ture, fantasy, magical realism, Canadian literature, and introductory critical theory and practice at Texas State University—San Marcos, where she is an associate pro-fessor in the Department of English. She has published articles on magical realism in children's literature and coedited *Diana Wynne Jones: An Exciting and Exacting Wisdom* (2002) and *Considering Children's Literature: A Reader* (2008).

NICHOLAS SAMMOND is Associate Professor in the Cinema Studies Institute and English Department at the University of Toronto. He is the author of *Babes in Tomorrowland: Walt Disney and the Making of the American Child, 1930–1960* (2005). He is currently working on the book *Biting the Invisible Hand: Blackface Minstrelsy and the Industrialization of American Animation* (forthcoming).

KAREN SÁNCHEZ-EPPLER is Professor of English and American Studies at Amherst College. The author of *Touching Liberty: Abolition, Feminism, and the Politics of the Body* (1993) and *Dependent States: The Child's Part in Nineteenth-Century American Culture* (2006), she is currently working on a book tentatively titled *The Unpub-lished Republic: Manuscript Cultures of the Mid-Nineteenth-Century US*, which will include a chapter on the Hale libraries. She is one of the founding editors of *The Journal of the History of Childhood and Youth*.

PHILLIP SERRATO is Assistant Professor of English and Comparative Literature at San Diego State University. A specialist in Chicano/a literary and cultural studies, his publications include essays on the *Personal Memoirs* of Juan Seguín, the chil-dren's television program *Dragon Tales*, and books for children by Chicano/a authors such as Luis J. Rodríguez and Gloria Anzaldúa.

KEVIN SHORTSLEEVE is Assistant Professor at Christopher Newport University in Virginia. He received his undergraduate degree from Emerson College in Boston, a Masters from The University of Florida, and PhD from Oxford. He has published academic work on the subjects of literary nonsense, Edward Gorey, and Walt Dis-ney. He is also the author of several children's books, including *Thirteen Monsters Who Should Be Avoided*.

KATHARINE CAPSHAW SMITH is Associate Professor of Children's Literature and Afri-can American Literature at the University of Connecticut. She is editor of *Children's Literature Association Quarterly* and author of *Children's Literature of the Harlem Renaissance* (2005), winner of the 2006 Children's Literature Association Book Award.

ERIC L. TRIBUNELLA is Associate Professor of English at the University of Southern Mississippi, where he teaches children's and young adult literature. He is the author of *Melancholia and Maturation: The Use of Trauma in American Children's Literature* (2010).

LYNNE VALLONE is Professor and Chair of Childhood Studies at Rutgers University. She is the author of a number of articles on children's literature and culture, two coedited anthologies of critical essays, as well as *Disciplines of Virtue: Girls' Culture in the Eighteenth and Nineteenth Centuries* (1995) and *Becoming Victoria* (2001). She is also a coassociate general editor of the *Norton Anthology of Children's Literature* (2005) and is currently writing a book on the miniature and gigantic in children's literature and culture.

COURTNEY WEIKLE-MILLS is Assistant Professor of Children's Literature and Early American Literature at the University of Pittsburgh. Her article, "'Learn to Love Your Book': The Child Reader and Affectionate Citizenship," appeared in volume 43 of *Early American Literature*. She is currently at work on a book manuscript tentatively titled *Imaginary Citizens: Child Readers and the Making of an American Literary Public, 1700–1868*.

KARIN E. WESTMAN is Associate Professor and Department Head of English at Kansas State University, where she teaches courses on modern and contemporary British literature, including children's literature. She has published *Pat Barker's Regeneration: A Reader's Guide* (2001) as well as essays on Virginia Woolf, Georgette Heyer, A. S. Byatt, Pat Barker, and J. K. Rowling; her forthcoming publications include *J. K. Rowling's Library: Harry Potter in Context*.

NAOMI WOOD is Associate Professor of English at Kansas State University, where she teaches graduate and undergraduate courses in children's and young adult literature. She has published articles on a range of fantasy writers from Charles Kingsley and George MacDonald in the nineteenth century, to E. Nesbit and C. S. Lewis in the twentieth, and to Philip Pullman and others in the twenty-first. She is working on a book about the theological and cultural work of children's fantasy fiction.

THE OXFORD HANDBOOK OF

CHILDREN'S LITERATURE

INTRODUCTION

JULIA L. MICKENBERG
AND LYNNE VALLONE

THE growing attention given to childhood as a category of analysis has infused the academic study of children's literature with new energy. It has also highlighted the exciting and innovative aspects of children's literature scholarship, which today benefits from the insights of historians, sociologists, psychologists, media studies scholars, political scientists, and legal scholars, as well as literary critics, education specialists, and library professionals. Focusing their analyses on children's texts and children's culture, contemporary scholars are producing theoretically sophisticated, politically engaged, and historicized yet wide-ranging work that marks this field as exceptionally dynamic. To mention only a few examples, recent work interrogating the roles of children and childhood in social, cultural and literary history includes studies of "boyology" and queer theory; child-rearing manuals and the Walt Disney company; radical children's literature or the radical possibilities of children's literature; African American children in slavery; the history of babysitting; postcolonial theory and American, Canadian, and Australian children's books; and the "hidden adult" in children's literature.[1] But even as the study of children's literature attracts new scholars in a range of fields and gains in academic prestige, scholars in the field nonetheless can find themselves on slippery ground, experts in something that, arguably, kids might know more about than they do.

Back in 1984, Jacqueline Rose's assertion in *The Case of Peter Pan, Or, the Impossibility of Children's Fiction* that children's literature was itself "impossible" startled children's literature scholars: written by adults for children, children's literature, she argued, is never "children's;" instead, it represents an adult projection of what childhood is or ought to be.[2] Rose's claim was not simply provocative; it also invited literary critics to presume grounds previously ceded to children were rightfully theirs. But many—laypeople and scholars alike—continue to believe that children's literature *is* for children. If that is the case, arguably, it must be simple, transparent, and hardly worthy of analysis, which is to say, might children's literature criticism itself be "impossible"?[3]

Although clearly the growing body of sophisticated children's literature criticism belies these assumptions, a scholar new to the field might understandably suspect that there is very little to know in order to read children's books critically or that this expertise ought to be easy to come by. Conversely, of course, he or she might find a children's book's apparent simplicity—or perhaps its unexpected complexity—baffling: how, and where, to begin approaching the children's text? We believe that if he or she is willing to leave preconceptions and prejudices about the complexity and literary value of children's literature behind, in reading children's literature critically a scholar new to the field is likely to discover unexpected richness in both children's literature itself and in the range of scholarship that addresses, analyzes, or incorporates it. Certainly, we hope that the *Oxford Handbook of Children's Literature* will help address the needs of this beginning scholar—as well as the interests of those well established in the field.

Thinking about the unexpected pleasures—and risks—taken when adults read and analyze children's literature, that is, when adults presume a higher order of expertise over a body of literature that has been codified (by design or by adoption) as "children's," one of this book's editors is reminded of a time she was seated in an airplane next to a child traveling alone. She tried to make small talk with him—to make him more comfortable (so she imagined). After looking up several times from his book to answer her questions, he finally said, with exasperation, "This is the brand new Harry Potter book, which I waited a long time to get, and I really just want to focus on reading it now. I hope you don't mind." Chastened, the adult so-called expert in children's literature was reminded not only of how easy it is to make assumptions about what children need but also of that almost holy bond that can be formed between child and book. In reading children's books critically, as many of the essays included in this handbook remind us, it is important to acknowledge the phantom child—implied, addressed, represented, assumed—always lurking, though perhaps never quite possible (as Rose would say). Although our interest in creating the *Oxford Handbook of Children's Literature* is scholarly rather than sentimental, anyone interested in exploring children's literature confronts the haunting presence of childhood and the child reader within every text written for or adopted by children.

We begin the discussion that follows by outlining this book's purposes and organization, and then we briefly review some of the field's history and highlight a number of key principles and important scholarly works. Finally, we turn to important issues related to four general rubrics under which we have grouped the essays that follow. These rubrics, which serve as the structuring apparatus for the book, emerged organically from the essays and point to key areas of inquiry in children's literature study: Adults and Children's Literature; Pictures and Poetics; Reading History/Learning Race and Class; and Innocence and Agency. Our discussion of these categories is designed not simply to introduce the essays that are grouped under each of these rubrics (chronologically within each thematic section) but also to situate the issues they raise within scholarship and literary history.

Organizing Principles: Canons, Contexts, and Classrooms

This handbook attempts to reveal the possibilities of children's literature criticism. In creating it we avoided replicating existing reference works that survey the various genres in children's literature, offer national literary histories, or define important terminology.[4] Our goal was to create an interdisciplinary book that uses literary texts to introduce theoretical, methodological, and critical approaches, as well historical, political, and sociological themes. This makes the book valuable both to those wishing to gain a basic introduction to the field and to scholars seeking clear models of interdisciplinary approaches that have been enriching the field. The essays address a representative sampling of texts, in various genres, from the colonial era to the present, and from Britain, the United States, and Canada, that regularly appear (or arguably ought to appear) on syllabi of children's literature or childhood studies courses. The contributors provided headnotes that introduce the individual authors discussed, as well as lists of further reading that point readers toward the broader implications of each essay. Taken together, all of these features make the handbook a practical companion for graduate and undergraduate courses in which literary texts themselves (not abstract theoretical paradigms, generic formulas, or historical rubrics) are the focus of study.

The essays collected here serve less to demarcate the field of children's literature than to push at the generic and gatekeeping boundaries that cordon off (and can marginalize) "children's literature" as a field of study. By introducing works that may not immediately spring to mind as "literature"—including film, children's writing, comics, and musical recordings—but that belong to children's culture more generally, we hope to expose all of the messy possibilities of children's literature scholarship and encourage readers to go beyond this handbook and make connections between children's literature and other cultural arenas.

As scholars who came to children's literature from different disciplines—Lynne Vallone from literary studies and childhood studies and Julia Mickenberg from American studies with training in cultural history—in approaching our task as editors, we have tried to make our disciplinary differences a virtue. These disciplinary differences affected how we initially sought to shape the volume, our choices about scholars whose work we hoped to include, and the topics we wanted to cover; they also had an effect upon what we brought to the editing process itself, in the sense that each of us encouraged contributors to think expansively and in interdisciplinary ways.

We approached some of the top scholars of children's literature to become contributors, also stretching the boundaries of the children's literature field to bring it into dialogue with exciting work being done in the broader area of childhood studies, a burgeoning interdisciplinary arena that incorporates work related to children and childhood from history, media studies, anthropology, sociology, psychology, legal studies, politics, literature, and other disciplines. Instead of giving contributors a predictable assignment typical of many reference works, for example, to characterize a genre (the school story; fantasy; primers) or a critical approach (feminist, Marxist, postcolonial), we let our contributors propose "wish lists" of accessible, in-print texts from the Anglo-American tradition that they felt were particularly "teachable" and flexible and that, if not readily classifiable as canonical, rightly deserved a place within the canon. We felt that if scholars were encouraged to write about a work about which they felt passionate, then exciting and perhaps unpredictable—in the best sense—scholarship would ensue, scholarship that organically addresses many of the forms, approaches, and issues that in a traditional handbook format might be explicated in a more mechanical fashion. What emerged confirms the value of our unconventional approach: a book of original, innovative essays that use individual texts of various genres, historical eras, and national traditions to model critical approaches to reading and analyzing children's literature or to explore historical and/or sociological themes.

This book was constructed with the notion of "canonical" children's literature as a guiding principle but also as something contributors should actively call into question. In asking contributors to choose a "canonical" text as the centerpiece of their essays, from which they could address larger issues and showcase various theoretical frameworks or methodological approaches, we operated on the assumption that canonical works—especially those that are taught at the college level and also assigned in primary schools—are thought to embody qualities worth preserving and/or attitudes worth refuting. As such, these texts may be particularly revealing of the culture from which they emerged, especially in terms of how childhood is constructed. But we also asked our contributors to think about neglected texts that were popular in their time, retain a following, or can be said to be worthy of inclusion in a canon.

Although many of the children's works considered in the following essays are widely accepted as canonical—*Alice's Adventures in Wonderland, Tom Sawyer,* and *Peter Pan,* for example—not all of the texts discussed continue to be "works for children" anymore: some are too far removed from the lives of contemporary children (the Evangelical best-seller *Froggy's Little Brother*) or have long ago fallen out of classroom use (the *New England Primer*). However, each of the works discussed in the handbook—whether novel, film, comic strip, picture book, poem, memoir, primer, or play—may lay claim to the status of the "classic" or deserve to be placed there. Certainly, one person's "classic" might be another's "trash," yet we felt that a classic children's book should be in print or readily available and embody qualities that had at one time communicated something essential to an understanding of childhood of a certain era.

Deborah Stevenson clarifies the qualities of a children's literature classic in this way: "a text need not be popular with a multitude of contemporary children in order to be a classic. It must, however, speak of childhood, not just of literature, to adults" (119). Some of the works analyzed in this handbook may be considered to have recently achieved "classic" status in the canon of children's literature—Charles Schulz's *Peanuts* cartoons, *Roll of Thunder, Hear My Cry* by Mildred Taylor, or the Frog and Toad books—and others may be classified as "classics-in-the-making" (the Harry Potter books or Gene Luen Yang's award-winning graphic novel, *American Born Chinese*). While the *Oxford Handbook of Children's Literature* does not attempt to create a canon of children's literature, it engages with many of the same questions of value, significance, and boundaries.

HISTORY AND APPROACHES TO CHILDREN'S LITERATURE

Children's literature has come rather late to the canon-formation game; it was not thought important enough to be included in the "high stakes" canon wars of the 1980s. Children's literature first began to be recognized as a specialty in some university English departments in the 1980s and 1990s; previously it tended to be taught only in schools with strong elementary education programs or in library schools. Anthologies of national literatures (e.g., *The Norton Anthology of American Literature*) still mostly ignore children's literature. If they do include works such as *Little Women* or *The Adventures of Huckleberry Finn*, these stories, as Beverly Lyon Clark has discussed in *Kiddie Lit: The Cultural Construction of Children's Literature in America* (2003), are no longer labeled "children's literature," for the term is still often viewed as something of an oxymoron in the context of Great Books. Even when children's literature is recognized within literary history it is often classed as a genre in and of itself: the forthcoming *Cambridge History of the American Novel*, for instance, has a single chapter on "the children's novel," even as it recognizes the generic diversity of novels for adults.

Although only recently has this study begun to earn serious recognition within the academy, the critical study of children's literature has a well-established history. Scholarly works on children's literature began to appear in the early to mid-twentieth century, in works such as F.J. Harvey Darton's *Children's Books in England: Five Centuries of Social Life* (1932) and Paul Hazard's *Books, Children, and Men* (published originally in French in 1944), which sought to place children's literature within a larger cultural context. Within literary studies, the study of children's literature gained a significant foothold in the 1970s: the British journal *Signal* was established in 1970; the U.S. journal *Children's Literature* was established in 1972; and the Children's Literature Association was formed in 1973, holding an annual conference beginning the following year and promoting scholarship in the field. And numerous colleges and universities developed programs in children's literature study, based in English departments, library schools, and schools of education. Foundational works published since the late 1970s have shaped the field in important ways, helping define its contours and unique qualities,[5] bringing theoretical perspectives to bear,[6] creating essential historical overviews,[7] highlighting the intersection between ideologies and politics,[8] opening the canon of nineteenth-century literature (and other time periods) to include works for children,[9] and attending to the child reader/writer.[10]

Beyond its academic history, children's literature has developed in conjunction with a long tradition of critical evaluation that followed the development of children's book publishing itself. Experts in the field have offered advice on what books to give to children since the late eighteenth century (see, for example, Sarah Trimmer's *The Guardian of Education* and Charlotte Yonge's influential three-part essay in *Macmillan's Magazine*, "Children's Literature of the Last Century"). "Treasuries" of children's stories and popular anthologies have appeared in Britain and the United States since the late eighteenth century as well.[11] With the advent of library services to children in the late nineteenth century—special reading rooms for the young, staffed by librarians (most of them among a new cadre of college-educated women) trained to select books for children—new standards of quality in the field developed. Librarians, booksellers, and critics began to publish regular lists of recommended children's books (*Booklist*, for example, began publication in 1905, and *The Horn Book*, devoted to the critical evaluation of children's books and scholarship in the field, first appeared in the United States in 1924). Macmillan established the first juvenile division in a U.S. publishing house in 1919, and most other publishers followed suit within the following two decades, continuing the field's professionalization. In Britain, which had a long legacy of children's book publishing going back to the printer John Newbery, the Puffin imprint of Penguin published its first children's books in 1940, thus inaugurating an Anglo-American tradition of high-quality but affordable children's books that would be continued in the United States with Little Golden Books.

Author and illustrator awards for children's books have grown in number and prestige in the United States, the United Kingdom, and Canada and have contributed to the process of canon formation in the field. Awards include the Newbery Medal (est. 1922) and the Caldecott Medal (est. 1937) in the United States and the British Carnegie Medal (est. 1937) and Kate Greenaway Medal (est. 1955). In Canada, the Governor General's Literary Award for Children's Literature and Illustrators was established in 1937. Peter Hunt's *Children's Literature: An Anthology 1801-1902* (2000) and the comprehensive *Norton Anthology of Children's Literature* (2005) point to the fact that children's literature, while perhaps not integrated within a larger literary canon, has certainly developed a canon of its own, a point that returns us to the essays in this volume, which are organized under the general rubrics discussed below.[12]

ADULTS AND CHILDREN'S LITERATURE

The creation of a children's literature canon interests literacy specialists, parents, librarians and scholars—not children, without whom there would be no "children's literature." The first part of the handbook explores both the differences as well as the surprising affinities between adult and child audiences that are fundamental to the very project of children's literature criticism. In narrating his responses to children's books of the 1960s and 1970s in his memoir *The Child That Books Built*, Francis Spufford makes a compelling case for the benefits of reading as a child and rereading children's literature as an adult: "The book becomes part of the history of our self-understanding. The stories that mean most to us join the process by which we come to be securely our own" (9). Like Spufford, a growing number of adults find themselves (often despite themselves) engrossed by children's fare—be it the Harry Potter series or the *Twilight* books or the Wes Anderson film adaptation of *Fantastic Mr. Fox*. The many reiterations of children's books in Western children's culture—in films (from *The Cat in the Hat* to *The Polar Express* to *The Golden Compass*), toys (Fancy Nancy dress-up kits, American Girl dolls, and Harry Potter trading cards), amusement park rides (think of much of Disneyland), cultural references ("down the rabbit hole," a "Grinch")—attest to the powerful presence that children's books hold in today's world. But this very ubiquity can make it harder to pin down just what we mean when we talk about children's books or children's literature. What might these terms mean today, and what have they meant in the past? What might "children's literature," variously defined, tell us about childhood(s) and culture(s)?

Peter Hunt's opening essay for the volume, centered on the *Alice* books, asks foundational questions about children's literature that help orient any scholar or adult reader of children's books, starting with the basic issue of defining "children's literature." Spufford suggests a children's book is whatever a child reads, whether it is *The Hobbit*, *To Kill a Mockingbird*, or *Where the Wild Things Are*, all touchstone books for him. Interestingly, all three of these books may be called works of "cross-writing" as described by U. C. Knoepflmacher and Mitzi Myers.[13] Put simply, cross-written books engage both the child and the adult, whether through dual readership or by reflecting the interplay of voices or images that either simultaneously or differently address both adults and children.

The "cross-written" nature and formative effects of children's literature—or at least many works of children's literature—make its study inherently interesting and also make a project such as ours especially difficult. As Spufford's memoir reminds us, all former book-loving children may be considered "experts" in children's literature and may bring this expertise to any new reading of a children's book. But this seeming easy access to children's books can produce stumbling blocks to critical reading—especially for students who have only recently left childhood behind. Yet, children's literature is well suited to introduce students to the pleasures of analyzing literature and culture because its texts tend to be readily accessible.

Bringing children's literature to the college-level classroom goes some way toward fulfilling Knoepflmacher's and Myers's prognostication about the fertility of reading children's books when readers, and critical practices, are all grown up: "Cultural studies itself, as most centrally the study of relationships within and between cultures, has to go back to how cultures produce and construct citizens and consumers" (xv). Knoepflmacher and Myers claim a kind of partnership between adults and children in cross-writing that might provide more nuanced and sophisticated views of children and childhood in literature and in life: "Cross-writing may even help us revise, once and for all, the notions of a 'Romantic' natural childhood which still tend to dominate most readings of children's literature and the child" (xvi). Indeed, the idea of cross-writing has proven to be instructive in many of the essays gathered here and is foundational to our purpose of bringing new scholarship on important children's works (as a means for highlighting significant historical, critical, theoretical, or methodological issues) to an adult audience of students and educators. Yet, although cross-written, or "cross-over," fiction, as Karin Westman calls the Harry Potter books in her essay for this volume, is not universally appreciated by some critics—she cites A. S. Byatt's now notorious *New York Times* editorial that denigrates the "childish adult" reader of Rowling's series— we agree with Westman that the increasing tendency of "children's literature" to attract adult readers and serious scholarship is indeed energizing, as the essays collected here indicate.

The first four essays in the handbook wrestle with the following fundamental issues in children's literature study: the meanings of "childhood," "children," and "children's literature" and the power dynamics inherent in these terms (Peter Hunt); the politics of children's literature and its analysis (Richard Flynn); the ways in which children's books can serve in the college classroom as primers for critical literacy (Teya Rosenberg); and the significance of children's literature's growing popularity with adults and increasing intertwining with consumer culture (Karin Westman).

PICTURES AND POETICS

We grouped together a seemingly diverse set of essays that discuss aspects of visual or poetic forms, both of which traffic in images, visual or verbal, to communicate information succinctly, often in playful ways, to a child audience. Visual imagery has special resonance for the field of children's literature. Most obviously, both illustrated books (in which pictures supplement the text but are not integral to it) and picture books (where the text, if any, is incomplete without reference to illustrations) are among the forms most likely to be labeled "children's books," and this has been the case for centuries: among the earliest Western texts published for children, such as Comenius's *Orbis Sensualium Pictus* (1658), illustrations were used to engage young readers' attention. Comenius wrote, "Pictures are the most intelligible books that children can look upon" (qtd. in Zipes et al. 1051). The picture book as we know it, with interdependent text and imagery, is primarily a twentieth-century form, and, as the essays by Nathalie op de Beeck and Kenneth Kidd suggest, relating picture books to modernism and psychoanalysis respectively, the history of the picture book cannot be separated from intellectual and artistic paradigms and practices that have helped define twentieth-century culture. Pictures provide an important mode of communication with preliterate children who can understand visual cues earlier than verbal ones. But visual images also distill a great deal of information. The old cliché that a picture tells a thousand words simultaneously suggests the form's appropriateness to children and childhood but also reminds us of visual imagery's beguiling complexity and the challenges of acquiring vocabulary sufficient to analyze it.

Discussing picture books' complex modes of communication, Perry Nodelman notes in *Words about Pictures* (1988):

> [Picture books] imply a viewer with a mastery of many skills and much knowledge. Yet for the most part they also imply a viewer who is innocent, unsophisticated—childlike. Picture books are clearly recognizable as children's books simply because they do speak to us of childlike qualities, of youthful simplicity and youthful exuberance; yet paradoxically, they do so in terms that imply a vast sophistication in regard to both visual and verbal codes. Indeed, it is part of the charm of many of the most interesting picture books that they so strangely combine the childlike and the sophisticated—that the viewer they imply is both very learned and very ingenuous. (21)[14]

The idea of cross-writing again becomes useful in thinking about how to approach picture books critically, for the picture books that become family, library, and classroom favorites are typically those that sustain a dual appeal, particularly given the fact that younger children, usually without purchasing power of their own, gain access to picture books through the various intercessions of adults and older readers who read aloud, select books, buy them, or check them out of the library. Thus, picture books often operate at several different levels that appeal differently to adults and children. Take, for example, the 1999 picture book written by Philomen Sturges and illustrated by Amy Walrod, *Little Red Hen Makes a Pizza*. Adapting the classic tale of the Little Red Hen who repeatedly seeks assistance in baking a loaf of bread but whose appeals fall on deaf ears until the bread is ready to be eaten, Sturges and Walrod upend the didactic imperative of the traditional tale with a laid-back urban hen who is happy to let her goofy animal friends (a duck wearing a bathing cap and inner tube, a beatnik cat wearing a beret and playing the saxophone, etc.) enjoy the fruits of her labor. Although the friends predictably are willing to help Hen eat the delicious pizza when it's done, they are also happy to clean up after dinner while the hen relaxes. In addition to revising the original plot with enough familiar details that children as well as adults will recognize the humorous aspects of the conscious revision, Sturges also plays with language in ways that adults will appreciate perhaps more than children. Even as the familiar "Not I!" refrain of the original story is retained, a new twist is added: when the hen realizes she has no pizza pan (and, later, flour and, still later, mozzarella cheese) she exclaims, in each instance, "Cluck!" ("I need a pizza pan" or flour or mozzarella cheese)—"fowl" language that is (hopefully) more likely to induce chuckles in adults than in young children. So too are adults more likely to see the humor in a beatnik cat or in the can of dolphin-safe tuna visible on the hen's pantry shelf.

Attention to visual imagery and iconography, along with an awareness of the sophisticated and multiple layers of address in works for children, is essential not simply because children's books often contain pictures but also because in our mass-mediated contemporary culture, the visual reigns supreme. This also means that any study of visual imagery in children's culture must move well beyond picture books. It is not only fruitful but also necessary to approach the category of "children's literature" as inclusively as possible to include all forms of media aimed at children, from children's books to films, television programs, comic strips, graphic novels, and even websites and video games. And as with picture books, these forms are also quite often cross-written to engage adult and child audiences, especially in the case of box office films that young children may attend only if there is an adult to take them to the theater.

Attending to these other forms of visual media, the handbook includes essays (not exclusively in the Picturebooks and Poetics section) that discuss children's film (Nicholas Sammond); comic strips (Charles Hatfield); graphic novels (Lan Dong); and the multimedia record album/television program/book, *Free to Be . . . You and Me* (Leslie Paris). Children's films, as Ian Wojcik-Andrews has discussed, operate in close dialog with children's literature, and thus critical frameworks developed by scholars of children's literature bring important insights to the studies of these films. Although comic strips are rarely understood as literature, Charles Hatfield argues in his essay on *Peanuts* that they represent an ideal example of cross-writing. And in a striking contrast to comics, the graphic novel—somewhere between a comic book and a novel—is increasingly recognized as an ascendant literary form that, once again, is difficult to classify in terms of audience but that tends to attract young readers in part by virtue of its visual codes.

The image as a structuring category encompasses not only visual texts but also poetry, which relies on the evocativeness of language to fashion carefully selected words into dense snapshots of meaning. A number of important works in the field of children's literature criticism such as Zohar Shavit's *The Poetics of Children's Literature* (1986) and Roni Natov's *The Poetics of Childhood* (2002) argue that both childhood and children's literature have associations with the notion of the poetic—that is, with creativity, innocence, fluidity, purity, or essence. Although such notions are hotly contested (much of the scholarly work in the field is devoted to challenging them), there is a great deal to be gained from investigating the very notion of poetry through the lens of childhood. Poetry and poetics figure into children's literature both in forms clearly demarcated as verse—as in Langston Hughes's *The Dream Keeper*, a collection of poetry for children, which Katharine Capshaw

Smith discusses in her essay here, or *The Bat-Poet,* which Richard Flynn discusses in an earlier section—and in rhyming, rhythmic, or metered texts such as Dr. Seuss's *The Cat in the Hat,* the vehicle for Kevin Shortsleeve's essay on the politics of nonsense.

READING HISTORY/LEARNING RACE AND CLASS

Covering a wide range of children's books, from historical fiction (Michelle H. Martin and M. O. Grenby) to autobiography (Phillip Serrato), from Evangelical "street arab fiction" (Kimberley Reynolds) to the domestic novel (Kelly Hager, Mavis Reimer, and Beverly Lyon Clark), to the coming-of-age story (June Cummins), the chapters in this section of the handbook are all concerned with how child characters are invited to belong, or are kept from belonging, to familial, class, racial, ethnic, religious, and/or national groups. Moreover, as "unwritten" or untainted by culture, and as the object of contrast or comparison with adults or "others" (who are often described as childlike), the child makes a natural figure upon which ideas of national and racial identities may be draped, as Mavis Reimer, Kelly Hager, Beverly Lyon Clark, and June Cummins discuss in their essays for this volume. Recent scholarship in childhood studies has, for example, brought to light the central placement of the figure of the child within social, political, scientific, and theoretical discourses of the nineteenth century. Claudia Castañeda, in her book *Figurations: Child, Bodies, Worlds* (2002), argues that the "child-body" functions as a potent "figuration" of development with significant implications for nineteenth-century European ideologies supporting racial hierarchies and imperialism. In scientific discourses such as Spencerian evolutionary biology and physiological psychology, the white, Western, middle-class adult male was viewed as the final standard of the completed, developed body and self, leaving children and racialized "others" behind. The child represented, for many, the savage past of human life, a position that put colonial and racial others at the bottom of social structures, outside of normalcy and into "pathology." In Herbert Spencer's published essays on education (collected in one volume in 1860 as *Education: Intellectual, Moral, and Physical*), he refers to a biological history of human development in which the physiological, emotional, and instinctive natures of the child are reflected in the savage: "During early years, every civilized man passes through that phase of character exhibited by the barbarous race from which he is descended. As the child's features—flat nose, forward-opening nostrils, large lips, wide-apart eyes, absent frontal sinus, &c.—resemble those of the savage, so too do his instincts. . ." (qtd. in Castañeda 21).

Such ideas about the relationship between the child and the childlike savage may be traced in nineteenth-century American constructions of childhood as well. In *Dependent States: The Child's Part in Nineteenth-Century American Culture* (2005), Karen Sánchez-Eppler comments, "Inchoate, children are often presented as not yet fully human, so that the figure of the child demarcates the boundaries of personhood, a limiting case for agency, voice, or enfranchisement. Hence, for people who are not male, or white, or American, or considered sufficiently sane or sufficiently rich, exclusion from civil rights has often been implemented through analogies to the child" (xxiv). Essays in this volume that focus on texts about immigrant or minority children directly confront the question of what it means to be socialized for citizenship and to retain a sense of personal dignity in a society in which they are likely to remain infantilized in the eyes of those who are part of the dominant culture.

In *Cradle of Liberty: Race, the Child, and National Belonging from Thomas Jefferson to W. E. B. DuBois* (2006), Caroline F. Levander illustrates the ways in which, in the conflict between righteous young colony and corrupt parent nation, notions of children and childhood played essential roles in young America's rhetoric of rebellion, rights, and liberty. Dependent, in part, on the same discourses of developmentalism and the importance of whiteness described in nineteenth-century evolutionary biology, the child, according to Levander, functions as central to "key political debates crystallizing national identity that enables the child to act as a persuasive vehicle through which individuals come to affiliate with the nation at pivotal moments in its development . . ." (12).

By the 1970s, when Mildred Taylor first began publishing the Logan family series of historical novels (discussed here in an essay by Michelle Martin) based on stories from her family, nineteenth-century discourses of "racial science" promoted in anthropometrical studies and in physiological psychology, and unconsciously influencing authors such as Twain, had been rethought and discarded. However, the United States continued to show deep racial divisions, and persistent racial intolerance threatened to overshadow the legal gains of the recent civil rights movement. Just as living children played an essential role in the civil rights movement itself—marching in Birmingham or serving as martyrs for the movement (in the latter instance as the cases of Emmett Till or the four girls who died in the Sixteenth Street Baptist Church in Birmingham make clear)—so multicultural children's literature has played an essential role in socializing the young to reject notions of white supremacy or narrow nationalist thought, as discussions in the handbook of Taylor's *Roll of Thunder, Hear My Cry*, Francisco Jiménez's *The Circuit*, and Gene Luen Yang's *American Born Chinese* suggest.

In addition to informing illuminating notions about the child within discussions of racial and national identity, the figure of the child provides a lens through which class identity can be interrogated. As Troy Boone argues in *Youth of Darkest England: Working-Class Children at the Heart of Victorian Empire* (2005), both the conflation of the working classes with the idea of the juvenile and working-class youth themselves were essential to the ideological enterprise of imperialist Victorian England, themes explored in other chapters in this section in essays by Kimberley Reynolds and Kelly Hager, respectively, on two nineteenth-century novels: the British Evangelical novel *Froggy's Little Brother* by "Brenda" and *Five Little Peppers and How They Grew* by Margaret Sidney.

Innocence and Agency

We have collected the final group of essays under the category "Innocence and Agency," two key terms in the study of childhood, children, and children's literature. Perhaps no concept related to childhood is more contested than the notion of children's innocence, understood both in terms of lack of knowledge and lack of sin. The idea of innocence as a defining feature of modern childhood forms a basis for innumerable programs and policies affecting children, including censorship, which has historically been undertaken under the guise of protecting children. As legal scholar Marjorie Heins demonstrates in *Not in Front of the Children: "Indecency," Censorship, and the Innocence of Youth* (2001), industry codes among producers of films, comic books, and television programming were established as a way for these producers to show their commitment to children's best interests and as a way to preempt censors.[15] The very category of children's literature comes not simply from the recognition that children are cognitively less developed than adults, not fully literate, and less experienced—and therefore in need of simpler materials that will be comprehensible and relevant to them—but also from the belief that certain material is inappropriate for the young: for example, explicit sexuality, violence, political exhortation, or discussions about drugs, rape, or murder.

But the idea of childhood innocence is relatively recent, a product of the romantic era. In what became a landmark if controversial text in the study of childhood, French art historian Philippe Ariès argued in *Centuries of Childhood: a Social History of Family Life* (1962) that the concept of childhood did not exist until the seventeenth century, and then only for the middle and upper classes. Although his historical evidence has been called into question, what remains striking about his findings, which others have corroborated, is the fact that until relatively recently, most children were not shielded from sex, death, or other realities, and they were expected to work and add to the family income from a very young age. In other words, the idea of childhood innocence is a distinctly modern phenomenon and not something inherent to the child's being.

The Puritans believed in infant depravity or the doctrine of original sin. As Courtney Weikle-Mills's essay on *The New England Primer* reminds us, the Puritans emphasized literacy in the young as an essential means for transmitting religious belief and for promoting penitence, prayer, and piety, all seen as keys to salvation. In a time when infant mortality rates were extremely high, children were taught repeatedly in the few reading materials to which they had access that death could come to them at any time. The danger was not simply the loss of life itself but, worse, the threat of eternal damnation if one had not been saved. The title of James Janeway's *A Token for Children: Being an Exact Account of the Conversion, Holy and Exemplary Lives and Joyful Deaths of Several Young Children* (1671) makes clear the emphasis on child death: this highly influential work remained in print in Britain and America for more than two hundred years and spurred imitations of triumphant child deathbed scenes into the Victorian era.

In *Pricing the Priceless Child: The Changing Social Value of Children* (1985), sociologist Viviana Zelizer's examination of life insurance policies helped her make the argument that children became emotionally priceless (i.e., valued in sentimental terms) as they became economically useless. This transformation of the child from performing important economic work to performing affective roles essential to a family's emotional well-being was completed for children of the working classes only in the late nineteenth and early twentieth centuries, after child labor was strictly curtailed and education mandated. This shift went hand in hand with the assumption that childhood was a unique and sacred stage of life that merited special protection, nurturance, and guidance. In *Childhood, Culture, and Class in Britain: Margaret Macmillan, 1860–1931* (1990), Carolyn Steedman emphasizes the reach of this change, as poor and working-class children, like their more affluent counterparts, were granted the "right to childhood."

With the movement toward a construction of the child as innocent—and a waning of patriarchal authority—came a shift in children's literature away from didactic and religious instruction and toward works written for children's enjoyment as much as for their edification. This process began in the eighteenth century, as educators and theorists of childhood ranging from John Locke to Jean Jacques Rousseau emphasized the pedagogical value of children's play and stressed that children would learn more if they were interested in what they read. Such thinking applied primarily to middle- and upper-class children, but as Karen Sánchez-Eppler's essay on *Swiss Family Robinson* and child book makers would suggest, it would filter into children's literature as well as educational practice. The idea that children's reading should be a pleasurable activity would dominate by the late nineteenth century.

As Eric Tribunella's reading of *Tom Brown's Schooldays* in terms of the "schoolboy crush" would suggest, ostensible innocence can grant a kind of agency—within bounds—to the child who can be seen as unaware of the sexual context in which he/she operates, thus marking those relationships as unthreatening. If *Peter Pan*, the topic of Marah Gubar's essay, has become a flashpoint for thinking about notions of childhood innocence, the long 1960s are often seen as a turning point in thinking about childhood innocence. Rising divorce rates, the questioning of authority, the women's movement (which some believed contributed to the breakdown of traditional family structures), as well as the sexual revolution itself all produced commentary in the 1970s and 1980s on "the disappearance of childhood"—a discourse that assumed the increasing intrusion of the "real world" upon children's lives constituted a threat to childhood.[16] Changing perceptions of childhood were manifest in transformations in children's literature, particularly as expectations about appropriate content for children's literature also shifted. Discussions of the sea change in children's literature brought about by the 1960s typically focus on the rise of adult themes in the ascendant genre of adolescent literature—themes such as drug abuse, divorce, rape, homosexuality, teenage pregnancy, masturbation, alcoholism, and gang violence—which would have been taboo in children's literature only a decade earlier.[17] Claudia Nelson's essay centering on the historical novel *Jade* and Leslie Paris's discussion of *Free to Be . . . You and Me* in different ways both come to grips with the impact of the sixties revolutions, particularly the sexual revolution, on children's literature and notions of child innocence and agency.

As suggested above, in the contemporary moment we seem to be at a point where the lines dividing children's literature and literature for adults often cannot easily be drawn, which may come down to the fact that without "innocence" as a clear demarcation of the line between childhood and adulthood, we are losing a sense of that boundary as well as the need for it. Exceptions remain, of course (the motion picture rating system is alive and well, as are Internet filtering devices and other vehicles for protecting children from media content considered by many to be inappropriate), but Phillip Pullman's *His Dark Materials* trilogy, the subject of the handbook's final essay (by Naomi Wood), is a good example of a set of works that engages both child and adult readers, in part by interrogating the very idea of childhood innocence.

Concluding Comments

Given the limitations of space and the fact that contributors were afforded significant leeway in their text selections, the final collection of essays is not comprehensive in terms of national traditions, historical periods, genres, social issues, theoretical traditions, or methodological practices. Still, we believe the handbook demonstrates the complexity and richness of scholarship in children's literature and points readers toward other important work in a range of fields. The four rubrics under which the essays are grouped not only highlight themes fundamental to the study of children's literature, but as categories they are also flexible enough to encompass a wide range of key issues, and the essays cover a diverse array of topics and genres (from children's writing to the history of the book to African American, Asian American, and Mexican American children's literature), theoretical/methodological approaches (including postcolonial, psychoanalytic, Marxist, feminist, and performance studies), and historical and sociological issues important to children and childhood (from religious indoctrination, modernism, child-rearing advice, consumerism, and the relationship of second-wave feminism to children's media in the 1970s).

In forming this handbook we have attempted to tackle some questions essential to understanding children's books, questions that both engage the phantom child and situate children's books within literary history and culture more generally: Where do children's books belong? How do children's books engage with and create culture? What makes children's books especially useful vehicles for understanding the past and the present? If this handbook does more to raise questions than to provide answers, it will have succeeded in its goal of demonstrating the richness of children's literature scholarship at a moment of great possibility within the field.

NOTES

1. See, in order, Kidd; Sammond; Mickenberg; Reynolds; Mitchell; Forman-Brunell; Bradford; Nodelman, *The Hidden Adult*. This list, of course, simply gestures at the richness of work being done on the topic of children and childhood and is not meant to convey the entirety of excellent recent work in literature, history, American studies, or childhood studies.

2. See Rose.

3. Karín Lesnick-Oberstein makes a related argument in *Children's Literature: Criticism and the Fictional Child*. She claims that children's literature criticism is based on a fictional construct, "the child," and by virtue of this fact, children's literature criticism in fact has no real ground to stand on.

4. See, for example, Hunt and Ray; Rudd; Zipes, *Oxford Encyclopedia*; Grenby and Immel; Nodelman and Reimer. See also comprehensive websites by academic librarians such as David K. Brown's site (from the University of Calgary, Canada), the Children's Literature Web Guide: http://www.ucalgary.ca/~dKbrown/aboutclwg.html, and Professor Emerita of Rutgers University Kay E. Vandergrift's Special Interest Page on Children's and Young Adult Literature: http://comminfo.rutgers.edu/professional-development/childlit/.

5. See Hunt, *Criticism, Theory, and Children's Literature*; Nodelman, *Words about Pictures*; Nikolajeva.

6. See Rose; Bradford; Dusinberre; Wall; Paul; Zipes, *Breaking the Magic Spell*.

7. See Avery; Pickering; MacCann.

8. See Stephens; Richards.

9. See Nelson; Griswold; Knoepflmacher, *Ventures into Childland*; MacLeod, *A Moral Tale*; Plotz.

10. See Steedman, *The Tidy House*; Wolf and Heath.

11. Some influential American examples include Charles Herbert Sylvester's multi-volume *Journeys through Bookland* and May Hill Arbuthnot's *Arbuthnot Anthology of Children's Literature*.

12. See also Stahl, Hanlon, and Keyser, which is a kind of hybrid anthology of primary texts and criticism.

13. Knoepflmacher returns to the topic of "generational dynamics" in children's books and discusses Sendak's *Where the Wild Things Are* (along with Mary Norton's *The Borrowers*) in particular—in "Children's Texts and the Grown-Up Reader."

14. See also the following scholarship on picture books, picture-book theory, and visual literacy: Bang; Doonan; Lewis; Nikolajeva and Scott; Sipe and Pantaleo.

15. See Gilbert for additional information on comic book censorship and youth.

16. See Postman and Polakow for further discussion of this topic.

17. See MacLeod, *American Childhood*, and Townsend.

WORKS CITED

Arbuthnot, May Hill. *The Arbuthnot Anthology of Children's Literature; Single-Volume Edition of Time for Poetry, Time for Fairy Tales and Time for True Tales. A Collection of Poems and Stories for Children, to be used in the Classroom, Home or Camp; especially Planned for College Classes in Children's Literature . . . Illustrated by Arthur Paul [and Others]*. Rev ed. Chicago: Scott, Foresman, 1961.

Ariès, Philippe. *Centuries of Childhood: a Social History of Family Life*. Translated from the French by Robert Baldick. New York: Knopf, 1962.

Avery, Gillian. *Behold the Child: American Children and Their Books, 1621–1922*. Baltimore, MD: Johns Hopkins UP, 1994.

Bang, Molly. *Picture This: How Pictures Work*. New York: SeaStar Books, 2000.

Boone, Troy. *Youth of Darkest England: Working-Class Children at the Heart of Victorian Empire*. New York: Routledge, 2005.

Bradford, Clare. *Reading Race: Aboriginality in Australian Children's Literature*. Carlton, Victoria: Melbourne UP, 2001.

Brown, David K. *Children's Literature Web Guide*. The Doucette Library of Teaching Resources at University of Calgary, Canada. April 22, 1998. Web. 22 January 2010. <http://people.ucalgary.ca/~dKbrown/>.

Byatt, A. S. "Harry Potter and the Childish Adult." *New York Times*, 7 July 2003.

Castañeda, Claudia. *Figurations: Child, Bodies, Worlds*. Durham NC: Duke UP, 2002.

Clark, Beverly Lyon. *Kiddie Lit: The Cultural Construction of Children's Literature in America*. Baltimore, MD; London: Johns Hopkins UP, 2003.

Darton, F. J. Harvey. *Children's Books in England: Five Centuries of Social Life*. Cambridge: Cambridge UP, 1932.

Doonan, Jane. *Looking at Pictures in Picture Books*. Stroud, UK: Thimble 1992.

Dusinberre, Juliet. *Alice to the Lighthouse: Children's Books and Radical Experiments in Art*. New York: St. Martin's Press, 1987.

Forman–Brunell, Miriam. *Babysitter: An American History*. New York: New York UP, 2009.

Gilbert, James Burkhart. *A Cycle of Outrage: America's Reaction to the Juvenile Delinquent in the 1950s*. New York: Oxford UP, 1986.

Grenby, M. O., and Andrea Immel. *The Cambridge Companion to Children's Literature*. Cambridge: Cambridge UP, 2009.

Griswold, Jerome. *Audacious Kids: Coming of Age in America's Classic Children's Books*. New York: Oxford UP, 1992.

Hazard, Paul. *Books, Children, and Men*. 5th ed. Boston: Horn Book, 1983.

Heins, Marjorie. *Not in Front of the Children: "Indecency," Censorship, and the Innocence of Youth*. New York: Hill and Wang, 2001.

Hughes, Langston. *The Dream Keeper and Other Poems*. New York: Knopf, 1932.

Hunt, Peter, and Sheila G. Bannister Ray. *International Companion Encyclopedia of Children's Literature*. London: Routledge, 1996.

Hunt, Peter. *Children's Literature: An Anthology, 1801–1902*. Oxford: Blackwell Publishers, 2000.

———. *Criticism, Theory, and Children's Literature*. Oxford, UK: B. Blackwell, 1991.

Janeway, James. *A Token for Children: Being an Exact Account of the Conversion, Holy and Exemplary Lives and Joyful Deaths of Several Young Children*. London: Printed for Dorman Newman, 1676.

Kidd, Kenneth B. *Making American Boys: Boyology and the Feral Tale*. Minneapolis: U of Minnesota P, 2004.

Knoepflmacher, U. C. *Ventures into Childland: Victorians, Fairy Tales, and Femininity*. Chicago: U of Chicago P, 1998.

———. "Children's Texts and the Grown-Up Reader." In *The Cambridge Companion to Children's Literature*, edited by M. O. Grenby and Andrea Immel, 159–73. Cambridge: Cambridge UP, 2009.

Knoepflmacher, U. C., and Mitzi Myers. "From the Editors: 'Cross-Writing' and the Reconceptualizing of Children's Literary Studies." *Children's Literature* 25 (1997): vii–xvii.

Lesnick-Oberstein, Karín. *Children's Literature: Criticism and the Fictional Child*. Oxford: Clarendon P, 1994.

Levander, Caroline Field. *Cradle of Liberty: Race, the Child, and National Belonging from Thomas Jefferson to W. E. B. Du Bois*. Durham, NC: Duke UP, 2006.

Lewis, David. *Reading Contemporary Picturebooks: Picturing Text*. London: Routledge/ Falmer, 2001.

MacCann, Donnarae. *White Supremacy in Children's Literature: Characterizations of African Americans, 1830–1900*. New York: Garland Publishing, 1998.

MacLeod, Anne. *American Childhood: Essays on Children's Literature of the Nineteenth and Twentieth Centuries*. Athens: U of Georgia P, 1994.

———. *A Moral Tale: Children's Fiction and American Culture, 1820–1860*. Hamden, CT: Archon Books, 1975.

Mickenberg, Julia L. *Learning from the Left: Children's Literature, the Cold War, and Radical Politics in the United States*. New York: Oxford UP, 2006.

Mitchell, Mary Niall. *Raising Freedom's Child: Black Children and Visions of the Future After Slavery*. New York: New York UP, 2008.

Natov, Roni. *The Poetics of Childhood*. New York: Routledge, 2002.

Nelson, Claudia. *Boys Will Be Girls: The Feminine Ethic and British Children's Fiction, 1857–1917*. New Brunswick, NJ: Rutgers UP, 1991.

Nikolajeva, Maria. *Children's Literature Comes of Age: Toward a New Aesthetic*. New York: Garland Publishing, 1996.

Nikolajeva, Maria, and Carole Scott. *How Picturebooks Work*. New York: Garland Publishing, 2001.

Nodelman, Perry, and Mavis Reimer. *The Pleasures of Children's Literature*. 3rd ed. Boston: Allyn and Bacon, 2003.

Nodelman, Perry. *The Hidden Adult: Defining Children's Literature*. Baltimore, MD: Johns Hopkins UP, 2008.

———. *Words about Pictures: The Narrative Art of Children's Picture Books*. Athens: U of Georgia P, 1988.

Paul, Lissa. *Reading Otherways*. Portland, ME: Calendar Islands, 1998.

Pickering, Samuel F. *John Locke and Children's Books in Eighteenth-Century England*. Knoxville: U of Tennessee P, 1981.

Plotz, Judith A. *Romanticism and the Vocation of Childhood*. New York: Palgrave, 2001.

Polakow, Valerie. *The Erosion of Childhood*. Chicago: U of Chicago P, 1992.

Postman, Neil. *The Disappearance of Childhood*. New York: Delacorte Press, 1982.

Reynolds, Kimberley. *Radical Children's Literature: Future Visions and Aesthetic Transformations in Children's Literature*. London: Palgrave Macmillan, 2007.

Richards, Jeffrey, ed. *Imperialism and Juvenile Literature*. New York: St. Martin's P, 1989.

Rose, Jacqueline. *The Case of Peter Pan, Or, the Impossibility of Children's Fiction*. London: Macmillan, 1984.

Rudd, David. *The Routledge Companion to Children's Literature*. New York: Routledge, 2010.

Sammond, Nicholas. *Babes in Tomorrowland: Walt Disney and the Making of the American Child, 1930–1960*. Durham, NC: Duke UP, 2005.

Sánchez-Eppler, Karen. *Dependent States: The Child's Part in Nineteenth-Century American Culture*. Chicago: U of Chicago P, 2005.

Shavit, Zohar. *Poetics of Children's Literature*. Athens: U of Georgia P, 1986.

Sipe, Lawrence R., and Sylvia Joyce Pantaleo. *Postmodern Picturebooks: Play, Parody, and Self-Referentiality*. New York: Routledge, 2008.

Spufford, Francis. *The Child That Books Built: A Life in Reading*. New York: Metropolitan Books, 2002.

Stahl, J. D., Tina L. Hanlon, and Elizabeth Lennox Keyser. *Crosscurrents of Children's Literature: An Anthology of Texts and Criticism*. New York: Oxford UP, 2007.

Steedman, Carolyn. *Childhood, Culture and Class in Britain: Margaret MacMillan, 1860–1931*. New Brunswick, NJ: Rutgers UP, 1990.

———. *The Tidy House: Little Girls Writing*. London: Virago, 1982.

Stephens, John. *Language and Ideology in Children's Fiction*. London: Longman, 1992.

Stevenson, Deborah. "Sentiment and Significance: The Impossibility of Recovery in the Children's Literature Canon, Or the Drowning of the Water Babies." *The Lion and the Unicorn* 21, no. 1 (1997): 112–30.

Stimpson, Carol R. "Reading for Love: Canons, Paracanons and Whistling Jo March." *New Literary History: A Journal of Theory and Interpretation* 21, no. 4 (1990): 957–76.

Sturges, Philomen, and Amy Walrod. *The Little Red Hen Makes a Pizza*. New York: Dutton Children's Books, 1999.

Sylvester, Charles Herbert. *Journeys through Bookland; a New and Original Plan for Reading, Applied to the World's Best Literature for Children*. Chicago: Bellows-Reeve Company, 1912.

Townsend, John Rowe. *Written for Children: An Outline of English-Language Children's Literature*. New York: HarperTrophy, 1992.

Trimmer, Sarah. *The Guardian of Education*. 5 vols. London, 1802–6.

Vandergrift, Kay E. *Kay E. Vandergrift's Special Interest Page*. 14 August 1995. Web. 22 January 2010. <http://comminfo.rutgers.edu/professional-development/childlit/>.

Wall, Barbara. *The Narrator's Voice: The Dilemma of Children's Fiction*. New York: St. Martin's Press, 1991.

Wojcik-Adrews, Ian. *Children's Films: History, Ideology, Pedagogy, Theory*, New York: Garland Publishing, 2000.

Wolf, Shelby Anne, and Shirley Brice Heath. *The Braid of Literature: Children's Worlds of Reading*. Cambridge, MA: Harvard UP, 1992.

Yonge, Charlotte. "Children's Literature of the Last Century." *Macmillan's Magazine* 20 (1869).

Zelizer, Viviana A. Rotman. *Pricing the Priceless Child: The Changing Social Value of Children*. New York: Basic Books, 1985.

Zipes, Jack. *Breaking the Magic Spell: Radical Theories of Folk and Fairy Tales*. Rev. and exp. ed. Lexington: UP of Kentucky, 2002.

———. *The Oxford Encyclopedia of Children's Literature*. 4 vols. Oxford: Oxford UP, 2006.

Zipes, Jack, Lissa Paul, Lynne Vallone, Peter Hunt, and Gillian Avery, eds. *The Norton Anthology of Children's Literature: The Traditions in English*. New York: W.W. Norton, 2005.

CHAPTER ABSTRACTS

CHAPTER 1: "THE FUNDAMENTALS OF CHILDREN'S LITERATURE CRITICISM: *ALICE'S ADVENTURES IN WONDERLAND* AND *THROUGH THE LOOKING-GLASS*" BY PETER HUNT

USING *Alice's Adventures in Wonderland* (1865) and *Through the Looking-Glass* (1871) as case studies, Hunt asks big questions about children's literature: how do "adult" and "child" readers make meanings from children's texts, and how is power exercised over those meanings? From the answers to these and other foundational questions, Hunt asks, can we deduce what we mean by a "book for children"—as opposed to any other book?

CHAPTER 2: "RANDALL JARRELL'S *THE BAT-POET*: POETS, CHILDREN, AND READERS IN AN AGE OF PROSE" BY RICHARD FLYNN

Flynn considers how *The Bat-Poet* (1964) may be used to explore the rich traditions of American children's poetry within a larger literary history encompassing both fiction and criticism. Part autobiography and part critical meditation, the essay is also a comment on the politics of New Criticism—a method associated with close reading—which in practice attempts to separate "the literary" from "the political."

CHAPTER 3: "ARNOLD LOBEL'S *FROG AND TOAD TOGETHER* AS A PRIMER FOR CRITICAL LITERACY" BY TEYA ROSENBERG

Rosenberg argues that the Frog and Toad books function as useful literary "primers," not just for young children, but for college students as well. Modeling a critical practice that could be applied to many "simple" books, Rosenberg argues that *Frog and Toad Together* (1972) offers an accessible introduction to critical reading practices and multiple theoretical paradigms.

CHAPTER 4: "BLENDING GENRES AND CROSSING AUDIENCES: *HARRY POTTER* AND THE FUTURE OF LITERARY FICTION" BY KARIN E. WESTMAN

Westman discusses the *Harry Potter* series' (1997-2007) generic hybridity, focusing on elements of the school story, *bildungsroman*, and fantasy in the texts. Westman argues that the books' boundary crossing and enormous appeal to both adults and children call the basic distinctions between children's and adult literature into question.

CHAPTER 5: "WANDA'S WONDERLAND: WANDA GÁG AND HER *MILLIONS OF CATS*" BY NATHALIE OP DE BEECK

This essay offers a model of how to analyze picture books. Situating her discussion of Gág's iconic *Millions of Cats* (1928) within the context of developments in publishing and in modernism, op de Beeck demonstrates ways in which Gág's use of folk motifs (in her written text, design, and pictures) speaks to the tension between atavism and industrial capitalism at the heart of modernist cultural production.

CHAPTER 6: "A CROSS-WRITTEN HARLEM RENAISSANCE: LANGSTON HUGHES'S *THE DREAM KEEPER*" BY KATHARINE CAPSHAW SMITH

Smith opens up the literary, aesthetic, and cultural contexts of the Harlem Renaissance by discussing how children were imagined within this movement and by examining in particular Hughes's *The Dream Keeper* (1932). Attending to the dynamics of literary production for African American writers in the 1920s and 1930s, she argues that both literature and children were crucial vehicles for social change.

CHAPTER 7: "*DUMBO*, DISNEY, AND DIFFERENCE: WALT DISNEY PRODUCTIONS AND FILM AS CHILDREN'S LITERATURE" BY NICHOLAS SAMMOND

Sammond explores ways in which Walt Disney created a cinematic empire by selling his creations as "good for children." He did so by linking them to classic children's literature and by incorporating popular child-rearing wisdom. Sammond analyzes ways in which the animated film *Dumbo* (1941) functioned both as a form of and in dialog with World War II–era child-rearing advice.

CHAPTER 8: "REDRAWING THE COMIC STRIP CHILD: CHARLES M. SCHULZ'S *PEANUTS* AS CROSS-WRITING" BY CHARLES HATFIELD

Hatfield describes the formal similarities and distinctions between comic strips and narrative children's books, exploring the historical development of the "comic-strip child," especially in the context of the *Peanuts* strip (1950–2000). Charles M. Schulz's vision and aesthetic in *Peanuts*, he argues, were fundamental to the construction of childhood in the postwar era.

CHAPTER 9: "THE CAT IN THE HIPPIE: DR. SEUSS, NONSENSE, THE CARNIVALESQUE, AND THE SIXTIES REBEL" BY KEVIN SHORTSLEEVE

Shortsleeve suggests that the works of Dr. Seuss, the most beloved bard (and artistic evoker) of children's nonsense—and especially *The Cat in the Hat* (1957)—can be read within the context of the dramatic cultural changes that prepared the way for and grew out of the rebellions of the 1960s. Seuss's anarchic nonsense, both verbal and visual, fostered a sensibility conducive to the New Left ideal of participatory democracy.

CHAPTER 10: "WILD THINGS AND WOLF DREAMS: MAURICE SENDAK, PICTURE-BOOK PSYCHOLOGIST" BY KENNETH KIDD

Kidd combines cultural history with the insights of psychoanalytic theory, reading Sendak's Caldecott-winning and controversial *Where the Wild Things Are* (1963) in relation to Sendak's larger *oeuvre*. Detailing Sendak's engagement with both Freudian psychoanalysis and progressive educational practice, Kidd rereads *Where the Wild Things Are* as a psychoanalytic treatise in picture-book form.

CHAPTER 11: "REIMAGINING THE MONKEY KING IN COMICS: GENE LUEN YANG'S *AMERICAN BORN CHINESE*" BY LAN DONG

Dong introduces the graphic novel, as well as Asian American children's literature more generally, through Yang's award-winning 2006 book. Dong discusses the importance of folklore to Yang's narrative and in so doing places ancient mythology in conversation with postmodern popular culture, highlighting ethnic stereotypes in order to call them into question.

CHAPTER 12: "FROGGY'S LITTLE BROTHER: NINETEENTH-CENTURY EVANGELICAL WRITING FOR CHILDREN AND THE POLITICS OF POVERTY" BY KIMBERLEY REYNOLDS

Reynolds reads *Froggy's Little Brother* (1875), a British nineteenth-century "street arab" novel about destitute London children, through the lens of postcolonial theory. She shows how fictional conventions magnifying the plight of the poor child helped focus the debate over the "politics of poverty" at issue in Victorian society.

CHAPTER 13: "HISTORY IN FICTION: CONTEXTUALIZATION AS INTERPRETATION IN ROBERT LOUIS STEVENSON'S *KIDNAPPED*" BY M. O. GRENBY

Grenby argues that attending to the various historical and geographical contexts that inform the setting of *Kidnapped* (1886) and the 1880s British milieu in which Stevenson wrote allows the novel to comment upon political and cultural debates of long-standing importance in British life.

CHAPTER 14: "TOM SAWYER, AUDIENCE, AND AMERICAN INDIANS" BY BEVERLY LYON CLARK

Clark reads Twain's *Tom Sawyer* (1876) in terms of the depiction of Indians and in relation to audience. Noting that the native figure is both emulated and despised in the book, Clark argues that Injun Joe performs an essential mediating function between adult and child, making the book safe for white children (and adults) both inside and outside the text by keeping the Native an outsider.

CHAPTER 15: "LIVING WITH THE KINGS: CLASS, TASTE, AND FAMILY FORMATION IN *FIVE LITTLE PEPPERS AND HOW THEY GREW*" BY KELLY HAGER

Hager uses Margaret Sidney's domestic novel *Five Little Peppers and How They Grew* (1881)—the first in a series—to reveal assumptions about social class, birth, and taste in late nineteenth-century America. Starting with the idea of this text as a "classic," Hager moves to the place of class within the classic, examining ways in which tensions between manner(s) and money illuminate popular notions about class and family.

CHAPTER 16: "A DAUGHTER OF THE HOUSE: DISCOURSES OF ADOPTION IN L. M. MONTGOMERY'S *ANNE OF GREEN GABLES*" BY MAVIS REIMER

Examining public discourses surrounding adoption at the turn of the century, Reimer reads documentary evidence against *Anne of Green Gables* (1908) to argue that the figure of the adopted (white, Canadian) child—and the British child emigrants and aboriginal Canadians who this figure erases—encapsulate ideas about belonging and acceptance within the home and within Canadian national identity.

CHAPTER 17: "WHERE IN AMERICA ARE YOU, GOD? JUDY BLUME, MARGARET SIMON, AND AMERICAN NATIONAL IDENTITY" BY JUNE CUMMINS

Cummins shifts the conversation about *Are You There, God? It's Me, Margaret* (1970) from the controversy over its discussions of puberty to the postwar debate over American identity engaged in by popular sociologists such as David Riesman. Cummins argues that Margaret's struggles with religious identity may be read as an early meditation on a post-ethnic identity widely embraced today.

Chapter 18: "Let Freedom Ring: Land, Liberty, Literacy, and Lore in Mildred Taylor's Logan Family Novels" by Michelle H. Martin

Martin argues that the Logan family novels (1975–2001) present a compelling longitudinal study of African American experience in the early to mid-twentieth century. Taylor, according to Martin, explores the meaning and process of attaining "true freedom" through economic and educational achievements and through respect for the traditions of the past, key themes in African American children's literature.

Chapter 19: "'What Are Young People to Think?' The Subject of Immigration and the Immigrant Subject in Francisco Jiménez's *The Circuit*" by Phillip Serrato

Drawing on U.S. immigration history and postcolonial theory, Serrato highlights Jiménez's effort to challenge media misrepresentations and xenophobic myths about undocumented workers. *The Circuit* (1997), Serrato argues, troubles naive notions of nationalism by placing the migrant child's life at the center of the national imaginary, marking a larger goal in much Mexican American children's literature.

Chapter 20: "'My Book and Heart Shall Never Part': Reading, Printing, and Circulation in the *New England Primer*" by Courtney Weikle-Mills

Examining multiple editions of the *New England Primer* (1688-90), Weikle-Mills argues that despite the *Primer*'s emphasis upon authority, as children were invited into unmediated communion with the text they gained a sense of themselves as agents with the power to shape both literary meaning and an interior realm of subjectivity. The *Primer*'s history thus reflects dramatic changes in childhood.

CHAPTER 21: "CASTAWAYS: *THE SWISS FAMILY ROBINSON,* CHILD BOOKMAKERS, AND THE POSSIBILITIES OF LITERARY FLOTSAM" BY KAREN SÁNCHEZ-EPPLER

Taking the history of Wyss's *Swiss Family Robinson* (1812, 1814) as her starting point, Sánchez-Eppler looks at the work of two generations of children in a Boston family who created their own books, many incorporating shipwreck narratives. Her essay is part book history and part methodological treatise upon the insights that can be gleaned about literary reception and history from children's writing.

CHAPTER 22: "TOM BROWN AND THE SCHOOLBOY CRUSH: BOYHOOD DESIRE, HERO WORSHIP, AND THE BOYS' SCHOOL STORY" BY ERIC L. TRIBUNELLA

Tribunella examines a classic boys' school story, Hughes's *Tom Brown's Schooldays* (1857) through the lenses of queer and postcolonial theory to suggest the ways in which homosocial networks and homosocial desire both upheld and threatened to destabilize the hegemony of the British empire as young people attending elite boarding schools—and reading stories about those schools—were socialized into norms of acceptable behavior.

CHAPTER 23: "*PETER PAN* AS CHILDREN'S THEATER: THE ISSUE OF AUDIENCE" BY MARAH GUBAR

By looking closely into the history of *Peter Pan* (1904) and relating it to nonprofessional children's theatricals, and by describing children's own responses to the play as audience members, Gubar reinscribes agency both to the performers of Barrie's play (and, by implication, to child performers in general) and to child audience members, whose responses are notoriously difficult to track.

CHAPTER 24: "*JADE* AND THE TOMBOY TRADITION" BY CLAUDIA NELSON

Nelson's essay engages questions of canonicity, asking why Sally Watson's popular 1969 novel, *Jade*, which enjoyed an almost cult-like following, never achieved critical recognition. Nelson suggests that Watson's tomboy characters, especially Jade, crossed a line in terms of their gender-bending performances, which, by the late 1960s, produced anxiety in adult critics, thus keeping *Jade* out of the canon.

CHAPTER 25: "HAPPILY EVER AFTER: *FREE TO BE . . . YOU AND ME*, SECOND-WAVE FEMINISM, AND 1970S AMERICAN CHILDREN'S CULTURE" BY LESLIE PARIS

Paris argues that the example of the enormously popular *Free to Be . . . You and Me* (1972), in contrast to the rather dark portrait of the 1970s in much of the historiography of the period, points to the ways in which childhood became a utopian space of liberation in large part because of the new possibilities that emerged from feminism's challenge to traditional gender norms.

CHAPTER 26: "PARADISE REFIGURED: INNOCENCE AND EXPERIENCE IN *HIS DARK MATERIALS*" BY NAOMI WOOD

Wood argues that through a radical retelling of the myth of the fall from Paradise in the *His Dark Materials* trilogy (1995–2000), Pullman replaces an old mythology of childhood and coming of age with a fresh version that does not privilege innocence over experience or adulthood over childhood. According to Wood, Pullman models a critical engagement with questions about self and other and one's place and meaning in the cosmos.

PART I

ADULTS AND CHILDREN'S LITERATURE

THE FUNDAMENTALS OF CHILDREN'S LITERATURE CRITICISM: *ALICE'S ADVENTURES IN WONDERLAND* AND *THROUGH THE LOOKING-GLASS*

PETER HUNT

THE *Reverend Charles Lutwidge Dodgson, who wrote books for children under the name "Lewis Carroll," was born in England on 27 January 1823. He became a Senior Student and Mathematical Lecturer at Christ Church, Oxford University, where he lived as a bachelor for the rest of his life, while financially supporting his unmarried sisters. He was ordained Deacon, although he did not proceed to Priest's orders, possibly because of his stammer and shyness. An active pamphleteer on local and national topics, he was a diarist and prolific letter writer with an obsessive personality—he kept a register of his correspondence totalling around one hundred thousand items. He published extensively on mathematics but is remembered for two of the classics of English and children's literature,* Alice's Adventures in Wonderland *(1865) and* Through the Looking-Glass *(1872), initially inspired by his friendship with Alice Liddell, the small daughter of the Dean of his college. They are among the most translated and most quoted books in the world and mark a change in attitude toward children in fiction. Carroll's surrealist poem,* The Hunting of the Snark *(1876)—perhaps only marginally for children—is regarded as a masterpiece, although his explicitly religious writing for children* (Sylvie and Bruno *1889, 1892) was not a success. He was a notable amateur photographer, especially of literary and theatrical personalities, but his interest in photographing young girls has been controversial. There have been more than twenty biographies, many concentrating on psychological speculation. He died on 14 January 1898.*

> "Would you tell me, please [said Alice to the Cheshire Cat], which way I ought to go from here?"
> "That depends a good deal on where you want to get to," said the Cat.
> (Carroll, *Alice's Adventures in Wonderland* 57)

> "There's glory for you!"
> "I don't know what you mean by 'glory,'" Alice said.
> Humpty Dumpty smiled contemptuously. "Of course you don't—till I tell you . . . When I use a word . . . it means just what I choose it to mean— neither more nor less."
> "The question is," said Alice, "whether you *can* make words mean so many different things."
> "The question is," said Humpty Dumpty, "which is to be master - that's all."
> (Carroll, *Through the Looking-Glass* 190)

In this chapter, we are hunting three elephants. Not the flower-probing elephants that briefly appear in *Through the Looking-Glass* (Carroll 148): these elephants are the ones in the literary living room. They are fundamental questions about children's literature—questions that are so big that we usually have to ignore them if the business of reading the books and talking about the books is to go on as usual. But they won't go away: they are about meaning and power, discrimination and control. They are:

- How do "adult" and "child" readers make meanings from —understand—a text written for children, and how is power exercised over those meanings?
- If the "children's book" is powerful, what is it doing to its audience, and how does this relate to its author?
- From the answers to these questions, can we deduce what we mean by "children's book" or a "book for children"—as opposed to any other book?

Without at least trying to answer these potentially difficult questions, which involve asking ourselves *why* we, as adults, are reading "children's books" at all, almost all other approaches to the subject rest on rather insecure foundations. Realizing how wide the disparity of meanings constructed from a text by different readers can be is a major step in appreciating the *value* of different meanings (if we are concerned primarily with adult-to-adult discussions) and a major help in mediating books to less-experienced readers (if we are concerned with adult-to-child discussions). Understanding that *intent* by the author and *effect* on the reader are not directly (and sometimes not even indirectly) related may clarify our political and ideological feelings about texts, even if it does not make a practical difference to how we handle them. And being able to distinguish between a "book for children/children's book" and a "book for adults" is not merely an administrative convenience. If you are working with books and children, the importance of such a distinction is directly proportional to the amount of time that you can spend with individual children; if you are not interested in practical applications but in the internal workings of the books, this is still an important distinction because the degree of "forness," as it were, radically changes content, texture, and technique. Either way, our value systems and judgments in relationship to both literature and childhood may be affected.

These are big elephants, and so how do we stalk them, pin them down, come to terms with them? One way is to look carefully at what happens when we read and interpret two of the most well-known children's books—two of the most well-known books— in the world: *Alice's Adventures in Wonderland* and *Through the Looking-Glass*. These books, chameleon-like, suffused with remorseless logic masquerading as nonsense, and nonsense masquerading as logic, are at their core about the relationship between adults and children. And as this is what most children's books and most of children's book studies are about, they are our ideal guides.

So, come with me down the rabbit hole of the study of children's literature where we will find that it is necessary to hold contradictory beliefs simultaneously. For our first elephant: every individual reading of a text is un-knowable but valuable, and yet we can generalize about the meanings made by large, largely undefinable groups called "adults" and "children"; for our second elephant, although the intention of the adult author is often, if not usually, shipwrecked on the uncertainty of the response, books *do* affect readers, and in quantifiable ways; and, for the third, while the meanings of "for" and "children" are infinitely fluid, we can recognize and find useful the term "books for children." And, as the Red Queen said in *Through the Looking-Glass*—"You may call it 'nonsense' if you like . . . but *I've* heard nonsense compared with which that would be as sensible as a dictionary" (Carroll 143).

If we are going to use *Alice's Adventures* and *Through the Looking-Glass* as our guidebooks, perhaps we should begin by working out just what they *are*. ("Begin," as the King said to the White Rabbit, "at the beginning, and go on till you come to the end: then stop" [Carroll 106].) What are the *facts* about them?

They are quintessential classics: part of world culture and among the most translated of all books. They can be read in hundreds of languages from Finnish (*Liisan seikkailut ihmemaailmassa*) to Welsh (*Anturiaethau Alys yng Ngwlad Hud*); Alis, Alisa, Alicja, Alicji, Alenka, Elenkine, Elisi, Elsje, or Else has her adventures *im Wunderland, du pays des merveilles, nel paese delle meraviglie, csodaországban, I eventyrland, w krainie czarów*, or, if you are in the Australian outback, *ngura tjukurtjarangka*, which is "in the dreamtime" in the native Australian language Pitjantjatjara.

They are in print, in English, in hundreds of editions from scholarly, annotated versions to pop-up cartoon books; there have been at least fourteen movies (three scheduled for release in 2010) and sixteen TV versions, and they are probably the most-quoted books: "wonderland" is synonymous with madness—in politics, art, and (recently) finance. Words and phrases from the books have entered the language ("chortled," "jam today," and "we're all mad here"); Alice and other characters are international icons, internationally marketable brands. The poem "Jabberwocky" in *Through the Looking-Glass* inspired Ed McBain's 87th Precinct novel, *The Frumious Bandersnatch* (2004); Graham Masterton's horror novel *Mirror* (1988) suggests that "Jabberwocky" holds the key to the return of the anti-Christ; and the characters in Desmond Davis's 1967 "swinging London" movie, *Smashing Time*, were named from the poem. Even more curiously ("curiouser and curiouser") Rev. Charles Dodgson, who wrote the books under the pseudonym "Lewis Carroll" (which name I shall use, for convenience—if not always appropriately—throughout this chapter), is almost as famous as his books: there have been at least twenty biographies of him—including a book "proving" that he was Jack the Ripper (Wallace 1996). Even the little girl, Alice Liddell, who *inspired* the books (and did little else of note in the wide world) has two biographies. Their story has inspired fictionalizations from a romantic semi-tragedy (*Still She Haunts Me* by Katie Roiphe, 2001) to a crime novel (*Belladonna: A Lewis Carroll Nightmare* by Donald Thomas, 1983).

There are libraries of books *about* the "Alice" books, analyzing them from, it seems, every theoretical, psychological, sociological, and historical viewpoint. There are societies, websites, and research archives relating to the books and their author across the world, in perhaps improbable places. The Harry Ransom Center, at the University of Texas at Austin, contains 2,525 items in the Warren Weaver and Byron Sewell collections (including one of twenty-three copies of the "suppressed" first edition of *Alice*—a collector's item because Carroll withdrew the first printing of the book because of its inferior quality); the Parrish Collection at Princeton has 992 Carroll-related items, from Carroll's own copy of the 1866 edition of *Alice's Adventures in Wonderland* to "Alice in Wonderland Characters in Soap by Spencer." And at a conservative estimate, every minute, somewhere in the world, another essay, paper, talk, or book joins the pile. *Alice's Adventures in Wonderland* and *Through the Looking-Glass* are among the very few books that have a place in both the adult canon and the children's canon; they are taught in university courses and adapted as plays for children.

At which point, we might ask whether this avalanche of facts makes any difference to the way we read? A skeptic might say that knowing that these are "classics" primes us to read with more attention, more respect, or even, perhaps, less expectation of pleasure than we get from other books. Or do all these facts mean that the "Alice" books have been so colonized by adults that they have become a literary and historical industry rather than texts "merely" to be enjoyed?

The most important question here is, does the reader who doesn't know all these facts (more likely to be a child, perhaps) read at a disadvantage? The assumption that all this peripheral information enriches our reading may be true in a certain way, but it is dangerous to assume that it will give us access to a *better*, more complete, and more *accurate* reading. That is especially dangerous for children's literature because it leads to the assumption that a child's reading is *necessarily* inferior—and is coupled with the idea that a child's reading *skills* will also be inferior. The fact that some child readers cannot (or do not) articulate their responses to texts very effectively is adduced as evidence to support this view—although, as David Lewis has said, "those who think that children can tell us nothing of any use about the books they read have simply not been listening" (238).

What other things (apart from mountains of facts) affect what readers make of texts like the "Alice" books? We are primed by the peritext—what surrounds the printed text physically (margins, dust jacket, illustrations)—and the cultural context of the text or its reading. Even if we found a copy of *Alice's Adventures* lying without a cover on a beach somewhere, and we had never heard of it, we would not have to be very experienced readers to find ourselves judging fairly accurately whether it was "quality literature" or "popular trash"—whether it was for adults or for children, old or new, even American or British—the paper, the typeface, even the smell, all speak to us. But, of course, that sort of unencumbered encounter with a book never happens: it is highly probable that readers new to the "Alices" in book form will have images in their heads from the ubiquitous marketing of the original John Tenniel illustrations or from the 1949 Walt Disney film (although Disney's animators "respectfully took a good deal of their inspiration from the original Tenniel drawings" (Mosley 206).

So we start reading, with our various levels of skills and knowledge, and we come across this exchange from chapter 5 of *Alice's Adventures*:

> The Caterpillar and Alice looked at each other for some time in silence: at last the Caterpillar took the hookah out of its mouth, and addressed her in a languid, sleepy voice.
> "Who are *you*?" said the Caterpillar.
> This was not an encouraging opening for a conversation. Alice replied, rather shyly, "I—I hardly know, Sir, just at present—at least I know who I *was* when I got up this morning, but I think I must have changed several times since then." (Carroll 41)

If we rid ourselves of the invidious ideas that there is a clear distinction (or opposition) between children and adults, that childhood is merely a less-informed and less-mature stepping stone to adulthood, or that it is a separate kingdom with its own laws, the complexity of the interaction with such a text for *all* readers should leap off the page. For the most important distinguishing factor in the meaning made is not knowledge or skill, but the *reason* for reading the text. (That reason is very likely to be controlled by the age of the reader, but age is not the determining factor.)

If we, as experienced readers, are reading a "peer" text—that is, one intended broadly for readers like ourselves or a text that *implies* a reader like ourselves—then we read in two usually overlapping ways: we read either for our personal enjoyment, pleasure, information (and so on), and/or we read (perhaps as a student of literature or education) in order to discuss the text with others. If we are reading a text "written for children," or a book that *implies* some kind of "child" reader—one who is less or differently experienced than us—then the reading process becomes much more complex. We may still be reading for ourselves, and in order to discuss the book with others—but we will also be reading in compliance with, or in tension with, the implied readership. In the case of Alice and the Caterpillar, the text implies a reader who will recognize the normality of Alice's shy and formally respectful reaction to an adult, who will understand what a hookah is and not have any judgmental views on it, and who will accept quite complex sentences and a particular kind of vocabulary. That audience is a conceptualized English Victorian child (if derived fairly directly from a real child), and so, depending on our experience, we can attempt to adopt that role or intellectually adjust to it, or accept it as (sometimes incomprehensibly) different or reject it as being incomprehensibly—or unacceptably—different. (Of course, we may simply reject the whole book because it is fantasy and *therefore* childish, but such a reaction is rather less probable now than it was thirty years ago [see Le Guin 40]).

In one sense, some of these choices may lead the experienced "adult" reader to read as, or attempt to read as, a "child"—that is, either their concept of a child in general or an approximation gained from close observation of how a specific child or children read or as they remember how they themselves read as a child. There has been a good deal of disagreement among critics over this process: some feel that these options (notably the last) are not possible (Nodelman 85) or even desirable (Alderson 53–55). Others argue that they are at least romantically and empathetically desirable (Hunt, *Criticism* 189–201) or genuinely practicable (Chambers 138–64). This undeniable complexity has been seen as making the whole project of adults-reading-children's-books (and writing them and criticizing them) inherently unviable (Rose 1–2, 137–40) or that which makes the study worthwhile and interesting (Rudd 1:29–43).

Most straightforwardly, the other way in which children's books might be read—and very commonly are—is *on behalf of* the child. Many adult/experienced readers are reading the children's book to fit the book to the child, to mediate, to protect. It is at this point that judgments about whether the actions or the language of the Caterpillar are comprehensible to or suitable for a particular child or children come in. For example, the word "hookah" might be judged as too difficult for an inexperienced reader (even if there is a picture to help); and, in any case, if the book is being read in a culture that (generally) frowns on smoking and that might be worried by a device associated with the Middle East and drugs, the question might arise: should this image be placed in the hands of susceptible readers? (Presumably, a reader in the Middle East might find the hookah the norm and other things, such as Alice's freedom of movement, troubling.) The fact that these judgments are made in the face of the almost intractable difficulties of understanding what another reader makes of a text, or of what effect a text may have, is, as we shall see, commonly ignored.

Thus the two key factors in approaching a text are *who* the reader is and *why* she/he is reading the text; and the only thing that might be confidently stated is that the "adult" reader is more likely than the "child" reader to have a purpose other than personal gratification in reading the text. Which of them, confronted by a

150-year-old book from a radically different culture, is going to have the easier, or more rewarding, read, is another matter.

Different kinds of experience need to be factored in as well. The closer to a recognizable world, the less fantastic the book will be. It has been speculated that for a girl like the real Alice, the world of the fictional Alice would not have been particularly surprising, or even interesting: what would have been interesting would have been Alice's reaction to it. Similarly, the further a reader is away from one's own worldview, the more difficult it is to imagine what meaning is being made.

This is the challenge of our first elephantine question: the challenge of realizing that understanding how different readers read (even two very generalized groups labeled "adults" and "children") is *not* to bring them to the *same* understanding, but to appreciate (and value) their *different* understandings. The "Alice" books are not instructions for flying an airplane or (if your beliefs so prompt you) a religious text, both of which (perhaps for similar reasons) require a convergence of understanding. As Lewis Carroll wrote of his surreal masterpiece *The Hunting of the Snark* in a letter (18 August 1884): "I'm very much afraid that I didn't mean anything but nonsense! Still, you know, words mean more than we mean to express when we use them: so a whole book ought to mean a great deal more than the writer meant" (Cohen 409). Consequently, we should beware of arrogance in valorizing one opinion over another. As Alice remarked, after reading "Jabberwocky," "Somehow it seems to fill my head with ideas—only I don't know exactly what they are!" (Carroll 156). It takes a genuine adult egghead to have the confidence that his interpretations are the *correct* ones:

> "Let's hear it," said Humpty Dumpty. "I can explain all the poems that ever were invented—and a good many that haven't been invented just yet." (Carroll 191)

Essentially, then, to shrink the first elephant, if not to make it disappear, we need to problematize the creation of meaning and the concepts of adulthood and childhood with regard to reading. If that happens, judgments of the value of reading "children's books" and of the books themselves may radically shift. But as long as adults (as commonly characterized) hang on tenaciously to the idea of the primacy of the "adult" interpretation of the text, the term "children's literature" will remain an oxymoron and the elephant will still be with us. We need to see that apparently benign opinions such as C. S. Lewis's much-quoted "I am almost inclined to set it up as a canon that a children's story which is enjoyed only by children is a bad children's story" (Lewis 1966, 24) disguise an adultist denigration of both readers and their texts.

And at this point we catch our first clear glimpse of our second elephant. What do the books *do* to their readers, and what should we do about it if we don't like it? This problem was born with the idea that children's books are (despite all the evidence to the contrary) innocent—and woe betide either the dirty-minded critic or the morally suspect author who would defile this ludic space. Adults who think this, it might be said, must either have had deprived literary childhoods or have short memories: or, more charitably, they are trying to create or recreate an oasis, a sanctuary for a new generation of children, in that uncomfortable place called childhood. Such thinking leads to the supposition that because the "Alice" books are obviously, manifestly, "children's books" they will be *suitable for* children who are what the adults wish the children ideally to be: innocent (and possibly ignorant), charming, playful, harmless, unfrightening, sexless, nonviolent, and religiously correct. Put like that, I hope it is obvious that a children's book can no more be these things than children can, except in certain minds—and the "Alice" books perhaps least of all. Even a cursory reading of them suggests that we cannot retreat to the position of the King in *Alice's Adventures*: "If there's no meaning in it, that saves a world of trouble, you know, as we needn't try to find any" (Carroll 107).

But what meanings are there to be seen? One of the most fascinating aspects of the "Alice" books is Carroll's technique of "layering" meanings as the books developed and the way in which, as a consequence, readers are included or excluded at various stages. The question of what meanings can be made, and (our second question/elephant) what effect those meanings might have becomes a matter of balancing the conscious and unconscious input of the author with the factual and emotional decoding by the readers. This must be true of all books, but the "Alices" provide a particularly well-documented example.

There is no doubt (although there was, as we will see, a good deal of myth-making about it) that *Alice's Adventures in Wonderland* began life as an oral story told to Alice Liddell and her sisters and that a version of that story was then written, as a manuscript present for Alice, as *Alice's Adventures under Ground* (1864). Carroll then prepared another version for publication, adding layers of mathematical, political, and philosophical jokes, and references to a wider world of Oxford academic squabbles and national personalities and concerns—in short, embedding in the book preoccupations of a singular and obsessive character and the natural furniture of the mind of a well-educated Victorian scholar and gentleman. And, as a result, the implied audience shifts.

A good example of the first conscious, personal level, using incidents, characters, and places familiar to the original Alice and her immediate circle is the brief episode during the mad tea party, when the Dormouse is encouraged to tell a story.

> "Once upon a time there were three little sisters," the Dormouse began in a great hurry; "and their names were Elsie, Lacie, and Tillie; and they lived at the bottom of a well—"
> "What did they live on?" said Alice, who always took a great interest in questions of eating and drinking.
> "They lived on treacle," said the Dormouse, after thinking a minute or two.
> "They couldn't have done that," Alice gently remarked. "They'd have been ill."
> "So they were," said the Dormouse; "*very* ill."
> Alice tried a little to fancy to herself what such an extraordinary way of living would be like, but it puzzled her too much: so she went on: "But why did they live at the bottom of a well?" . . .

The Dormouse took a minute or two to think about it, and then said "It was a treacle-well." (Carroll 65)

Nonsense, of course, and on the fairly reliable evidence of having watched my four (then small) daughters as this was read to them, and on the much less reliable evidence of my own memories of encountering this passage, *entertaining* nonsense. Reactions to stickiness, wells, and sweetness seem to be common to all ages, although possibly for differing reasons. Of course, there are language problems: the American Modern Library Classics edition of the "Alice" books finds it necessary to gloss "treacle" as "molasses" (which, in the United Kingdom is used primarily as animal feed) (Vallone 251). But this paragraph, accessible as it may seem to be to any audience, is in fact a texture of in-jokes for Alice and her sisters. The three "little" sisters is a pun on "Liddell" sisters; and their names are Elsie (from Lorinda Charlotte's initials), Lacie (an anagram of Alice) and Tillie (the pet name of Edith), and it seems likely that Alice's interest in eating and drinking is taken from life. Even the treacle well is not a nonsense invention: an early meaning of treacle was "balm" or "medicine/medicinal," and there are several medicinal or treacle wells in Oxfordshire. Alice would probably have known of such a well at St. Margaret's Church at Binsey, near Oxford, and would certainly have known the panel in the window of Christ Church Cathedral (which was virtually next door to her home) by Edward Burne-Jones, which shows pilgrims on their way to the well. (The most concise guide to these kinds of references, which, not quite incidentally, form the basis of a huge tourist industry is Mavis Batey's *The World of Alice*.)

The most that an uninformed reader (or outsider) might derive from the text (apart from enjoying—or not—the "nonsense") might be a feeling of the affection in the authorial voice: everything else is only accessible to those with special knowledge. The same is true of the contemporary political jokes (the dog that Alice meets in the garden is a Beagle with the face of the young Darwin), but there is a stratum of jokes that the author almost certainly intended to be accessible, notably the death jokes. Falling down the rabbit hole, Alice muses: "'After such a fall as this . . . why, I wouldn't say anything about it, even if I fell off the top of the house!' (Which was very likely true)" (Carroll 10). There is even, in *Through the Looking-Glass*, a discussion of the metaphysics of existence, when Alice comes across the sleeping Red King:

"He's dreaming now," said Tweedledee: "and what do you think he's dreaming about?"
Alice said: "Nobody can guess that."
"Why, about *you!*" Tweedledee exclaimed . . . "and if he left off dreaming about you, where do you suppose you'd be? . . . You'd be nowhere. Why, you're only a sort of thing in his dream!"
"If that there King was to wake," added Tweedledum, "you'd go out—bang!—just like a candle." (Carroll 168)

If your business with children's books involves mediating them to children (or policing a certain construct of childhood), then alarm bells might possibly start to ring: you may well regard that sort of material as potentially frightening and inappropriate—rather than as an invitation to philosophical speculation (as Carroll probably did). But in doing so, you will inevitably be subscribing to one of those impossible dualities—that, despite what we might believe about individual readers making individual meanings, the text still has the power to directly affect behavior. Suddenly, the things that adult critics see—often rejected as gratuitous and elitist— become valid and potentially toxic.

And what things they see! Far from being lighthearted pieces of harmless nonsense, the "Alice" books have long been seen by critics as reflecting a tormented soul: they are nightmares where there is no love (there is not a single kind character in the books) but only madness ("We're all mad here," observes the Cheshire Cat, one of the nicer characters); there is aggression, violence, and godlessness. Humphrey Carpenter in the chapter "Alice and the Mockery of God" sees a parody of the Christian Eucharist in the "Eat Me" and "Drink Me" references (66); Alice is the victim of a "mindless, Godless universe" (67), and the Victorians "needed his Anti-Religion, his act of destruction . . . Alice . . . provided a whole language, albeit a covert, coded one, for the much needed rejection of the old secure system of beliefs" (69). All of which might make holders of certain religious beliefs pause. And worse is to come.

J. D. Salinger's narrator, Buddy Glass, in *Seymour—an Introduction* (1964), reflects on the attraction of the more lurid aspects of writers' lives:

> I surely think . . . that it I were to ask the sixty odd girls (or, that is, the sixty-odd girls) in my two Writing for Publication courses—most of them seniors, all of them English majors—to quote a line, any line from "Ozymandias," or even just to tell me roughly what the poem is about, it is doubtful whether ten of them could do either, but I'd bet my unrisen tulips that some fifty of them could tell me that Shelley was all for free love, and had one wife who wrote "Frankenstein" another who drowned herself. (105–6)

And for every person who has read the "Alice" books there are probably ten thousand who know that its author was infamous for taking photographs of little girls in various stages of undress, and (as the editor of the Puffin children's book series informed her young readers in 1946):

> even when he set out alone on a journey by train, he took with him a supply of puzzles, games, and small toys in case he found a child in his compartment. Moreover, when he went to the seaside he kept a bunch of large safety pins in his pocket for the convenience of little girls who might want their frocks pinned up so that they could paddle more comfortably. (Graham 12)

We might read that with a very skeptical eye or perhaps with regret for a lost, innocent age—that age being the 1940s as much as the 1860s. Times change. Edward Ardizzone's picture book *Lucy Brown and Mr. Grimes* (1937) showed a small girl befriending an old man, a stranger, in a park: when it was reissued in 1970, the old man had become a family friend because of what Ardizzone described as "silly women librarians" (Tucker 1970, 24). And even ten years ago, British society would have allowed strangers to comfort distressed small children—and its schools were not fortified, as they are now, against spectral molesters. In 2008, a report, *Licensed to Hug*, was subtitled "How Child Protection Policies Are Poisoning the Relationship between the Generations" (Furedi and Bristow).

People censor children's books, it has been said, because they can, but this kind of reaction involves accepting a very simplistic idea of literary communication. How else is it that so many children's books (and in this context I use the term in its U.K. sense, covering both "children's" and "young adult" books) have been banned or censored for things that they do not explicitly say? Some novels, it is true, take overt stances—Judy Blume's *Forever* (1970) not only "shows" full-frontal sexual activity but also allows the characters to get away with it. But nowhere in the *Harry Potter* books, intended by their author (so she says) as innocent fantasies, is there any explicit antireligious propaganda or devil worshiping. This did not deter Pope Benedict XVI (when Cardinal Joseph Ratzinger) from seeing in the books "subtle seductions that are barely noticeable, and which act unnoticed and by this deeply distort Christianity in the soul before it can grow properly" (qtd. in Malvern). This is, of course, a different reaction to that of the priest in New Mexico who burned the *Harry Potter* books because, in Deuteronomy, "God says that witchcraft is an abomination" (ibid.), because one could hardly deny that the books are about witchcraft—although whether they are about the same kind of witchcraft is another (scarcely debatable) matter (and see Broad). It is interesting to speculate what critics with such a turn of mind might make of Jack Zipes's view that Harry occupies a "phallocentric world . . . and the test of a male's virtue is whether he will win contest after contest with his wand" (Zipes 183) because perhaps the worst of all the accusations that can be leveled against a "children's book" is sexual immorality: it is a problem that haunts children's literature.

It even haunts theorists. One of the most influential critical interventions in the discussion of children's literature is Jacqueline Rose's argument in *The Case of Peter Pan, or The Impossibility of Children's Fiction* that adults fundamentally create and manipulate the "child" audience in children's fiction in order, as Nodelman puts it, "to satisfy adult wants and needs" (Nodelman 161 and see 200–201). This has caused, over the years, a good deal of critical *angst* among children's literature critics (such as myself) who prefer to see the project of children's literature as essentially benign. But the problem with Rose's argument is that the idea of creating and manipulating an audience applies to *every* act of writing—probably to every act of communication. Why, then, should it prove so contentious a notion when applied to children's literature? It is that the idea of manipulating children carries a much stronger freight of sexual anxiety than any other: it is no less than potential violation.

But it haunts Lewis Carroll in particular. Even his most sympathetic biographers wrestle with this. Morton N. Cohen wrote: "We cannot know to what extent sexual urges lay behind Charles's preference for drawing and photographing children in the nude. He contended that the preference was entirely aesthetic . . . but . . . he probably felt more than he dared acknowledge, even to himself . . ." His conclusion, intended, no doubt, to be supportive, pins down the problem: "For posterity . . . there were compensations. If [his] suppressed and diverted sexual energies caused him unspeakable torments . . . they were in all probability the source of those exceptional flashes of genius that gave the world his remarkable creative works" (Cohen 228, 231).

Is this special pleading? Are the "Alice" books the work of an actual or incipient pedophile? Certainly Carroll's case has not been helped by the critics. Although there was never any accusation, during his life, of impropriety—although there were breaths of scandal—his books have been taken as evidence of his guilt. Ironically, the first "psychoanalytic" critic was a satirist, A. M. E. Goldschmidt, in "*Alice in Wonderland* Psycho-Analysed" (1933) but the idea was taken up more seriously by writers such as Florence Becker Lennon, in *Victoria Through the Looking Glass: The Life of Lewis Carroll* (1945), Phyllis Greenacre, in *Swift and Carroll: A Psychoanalytical Study of Two Lives* (1955), and others. They found sexual symbols (sometimes quite extreme) scattered through the texts: Alice falling down a deep hole, changing sizes, fluids, locks and keys, doors and small tunnels, hair grabbing, the unicorn running the king through with his horn, neck length, little houses, certain numbers, the king's pencil, and so on. No matter that more recent critics treat such interpretations rather more skeptically. Donald Thomas regards the psychoanalytical school as having been "piteously hoaxed" (Thomas xi), and Martin Gardner has observed that "books of nonsense fantasy for children are not such fruitful sources of psychoanalytic insight as one might suppose them to be. They are much too rich in symbols. The symbols have too many explanations" (Gardner xv). No matter that a little scholarly investigation shows that attitudes to sexuality, adult–child relationships, the representation of children, or even the age of menarche were very different 150 years ago (see, for example, Higonnet 109–10, 123–25, and Kincaid 196). These books are being put in the hands of children *now*.

The fact, and it is an uncomfortable fact for academics working with children's books, is that the relationship between author, book, and effect is rarely thought through: power is exercised in its rawest form. A recent British example encapsulates this: in May 2004, the author William Mayne, who has been described as having "some claim to be the most important modern English children's writer . . . [whose] influence on British children's literature has been pervasive" (Hunt, "William Mayne" 650, 651), and who had written around one hundred children's books, was, at the age of seventy-six, convicted of assaults on children in the 1960s and 1970s. In an article in the London *Times* in 2005, "Archbishop Backs Books by Paedophile Author," the Archbishop of Canterbury was reported as saying: "Yes, it would colour me if I read [his books] now, knowing what has happened. . . . Yet a writer is not the sum of his activities. We would be in trouble with a lot of authors if their lives were what we judged." One response, from Michele Elliott, director of Kidscape, a child safety group, sums up the opposing view: "I'm shocked anyone would say we should be non-judgmental about the works of a man who has abused children and I am particularly appalled that this is coming from a man of God. . . . I wouldn't touch [Mayne's] books with a barge pole. Books are the sum of you as a

person. To divorce the writings of an author from the author himself is impossible"
(Brooks 2005).

Thus, whatever our second elephant is, it is not an academic issue. It is easy to
argue that, especially in *Through the Looking-Glass*, we are reading a nostalgic love
letter, one of the most touchingly self-deprecating scenes of parting in all literature
as Alice leaves the White Knight to become a Queen. The final poem (the first letters of each line of which spell ALICE PLEASANCE LIDDELL) can be read as the
quintessence of sadness:

> Still she haunts me, phantomwise,
> Alice moving under skies
> Never seen by waking eyes. (245)

And yet, for many readers, Carroll stands condemned. The position of adults as
having power in the literary system that children's literature inhabits has produced
an elephant that academics in the field have to face down.

Which brings us to the third of our elephants. The question, dry as it is, of
whether a book is for children, is nonetheless one that keeps tripping anyone
working in the field. Perry Nodelman, in *The Hidden Adult, Defining Children's
Literature* (133–244), devotes around fifty thousand words to the problem, looking
at divergent views, from those critics who deny that there any distinctions between
children's books and any other kind, to those, at the other extreme, who list
common characteristics. Again, the "Alice" books may be used to demonstrate (at
least) the complexity of this problem.

It seems obvious enough that Carroll at least *began* the books with the aim of
entertaining specific children, and a good deal of the text has an unusually (now as
then) single focalization that marks the book off from its contemporaries and that
accords a unusual respect to its implied readers. But, having said that, we might also
be aware that Carroll was careful to foster this impression. The books are bracketed
by poems beginning

> All in the golden afternoon
> Full leisurely we glide (3)

and

> A boat, beneath a sunny sky
> Lingering onward dreamily (244)

and the legend has it (backed up by a retrospective entry in Carroll's diary and
somewhat inexact testimony from other participants) that he told the story to Alice
and her sisters while rowing on the Thames near Oxford on 4 July 1862. The fact
that it was raining that day has not dented the idyllic myth, possibly because the
idea that books written for a *specific* child are in some way superior to others: if

there is a real relationship involved in the telling, then the problems of power imbalance and violation (as promulgated by Rose) disappear. Storytelling becomes essentially a *caring* act that has a *genuineness* that short-circuits the adult–child divide (hence, perhaps Elspeth Grahame's embroidering of the genesis of *The Wind in the Willows* or the general biographers' insistence on the innocence of the relationship between J. M. Barrie and the Llewelyn Davies boys (see, for example, Wullschläger 125–26; Carpenter 176-78).

As we have seen, how long the book remained, through its composition, *for* the actual Alice is questionable. The opening (and nostalgic) verse of *Alice's Adventures* can easily be read as patronizing—and not only, or even primarily—by experienced readers:

> . . . For both our oars, with little skill,
> By little arms are plied,
> While little hands make vain pretence
> Our wanderings to guide. . . . (3)

This, as with the "frames" of both books—so often read by critics as Carroll's retreat from the dangerous religious nihilism of the books themselves—sentimentalizes childhood, an act only available to the observing adult. As Victor Watson points out, Carroll demonstrated how a children's story could become a celebratory utterance of greeting, farewell, or longing. Since that time, many of the greatest children's books have had about them a touch of the valedictory (Watson 18). More positively, as Barbara Wall has observed, the legacy of this actual, real-life involvement of adult with child survives in the mode of address:

> Narrator-Carroll could share with ten-year-old narratee-Alice [the real Alice]
> delight in the adventures of seven-year-old-character Alice . . . by constantly
> externalising Alice's consciousness into direct speech . . . The narrator . . . while
> he never turns aside from his heroine Alice, and never allows anything outside
> her consciousness to engage the attention of his readers, is always inviting his
> other Alice, his narratee-Alice—indeed, his implied reader—to join him in
> amused appreciation of her directness, earnestness, and poise. (Wall 100, 102)

This mode of address, which erases (or appears to erase) the presence of the controlling adult—controlling in the sense that the reader has to acquiesce to a certain readerly stance in order to access the adult-controlled meaning—is Carroll's legacy to the children's book. He comes very close to evading the "adult" voice and to writing a book *amenable to* his concept of childhood.

But no book is timeless (despite blurb writers' clichés), and it may well be that the "Alice" books are books that *were* for children, a specific generation of children who would have recognized the implied reader role and (more mundanely) would have appreciated the parodies. They might also have responded to the sympathetic portrayal of the repressed female child or empathized with the denial of freedom and power, which is, after all, only a dream. If the books are *still* for children, then it could be argued that that is because (marketing apart) they are ostensibly *about* a child and that the aspects of childhood that Carroll was in touch with are, if not timeless, at least capable of resonating over three centuries.

Because children are part of the critical and philosophical equation, working with children's books requires the kind of complexity, ambiguity, and flexibility that Carroll demonstrated in these densely woven masterpieces. Those elephants in the intellectual living room need to be confronted simply because they take up too much intellectual space that could be put to better use.

And if your response is, like Alice's in *Through the Looking-Glass* is: "I ca'n't believe *that!*" then we should consider the response of the White Queen:

> "Can't you?" the Queen said in a pitying tone. "Try again: draw a long breath, and shut your eyes."
> Alice laughed. "There's no use trying," she said: "one *ca'n't* believe impossible things."
> "I daresay you haven't had much practice," said the Queen. "When I was your age, I always did it for half-an-hour a day. Why, sometimes I've believed as many as six impossible things before breakfast." (Carroll 177)

WORKS CITED

Alderson, Brian. "The Irrelevance of Children to the Children's Book Reviewer." In *Children's Literature: The Development of Criticism*, Peter Hunt, ed. London: Routledge, 1990.

Batey, Mavis. *The World of Alice*. Norwich: Pitkin Guides, 1998.

Broad, Sara. "Beyond Belief: *Harry Potter* in Text and Film." *The Journal of Children's Literature Studies* 5, no.1 (2008): 22–31.

Brooks, Richard. "Archbishop Backs Books by Paedophile Author." *Times Online*, 17 April 2005.

Carpenter, Humphrey. *Secret Gardens: A Study of the Golden Age of Children's Literature*. London: Unwin Hyman, 1987.

Carroll, Lewis. *Alice's Adventures in Wonderland and Through the Looking-Glass*, Peter Hunt, ed. Oxford: Oxford UP, 2009.

Chambers, Aidan. *Booktalk*. London: The Bodley Head, 1985.

Cohen, Morton N. *Lewis Carroll: A Biography*. London: Macmillan, 1995.

Furedi, Frank, and Jennie Bristow. *Licensed to Hug*. London: CIVITAS, 2008.

Gardner, Martin, ed. *The Annotated Alice: The Definitive Edition*. New York: Norton, 2000.

Goldschmidt, A. M. E., 1933, "*Alice in Wonderland* Psycho-Analysed." Robert Phillips, ed. *Aspects of Alice*. Harmondsworth: Penguin, 1974, 329–32.

Graham, Eleanor. "How the Story Was Told." Introduction to Lewis Carroll, *Alice's Adventures in Wonderland* and *Through the Looking-Glass*, Harmondsworth: Puffin (Penguin), 1946.

Grahame, Elspeth, ed. *The First Whisper of* The Wind in the Willows. London: Methuen, 1944.

Higonnet, Anne. *Pictures of Innocence: The History and Crisis of Ideal Childhood*. London: Thames and Hudson, 1998.

Hunt, Peter. *Criticism, Theory and Children's Literature*. Oxford: Blackwell, 1991.

———. "William Mayne." In *Twentieth-Century Children's Writers*, Tracy Chevalier, ed. 649–51. 3rd ed. Chicago: St. James Press. 1989

Kincaid, James. *Child-Loving: The Erotic Child and Victorian Culture*. New York: Routledge, 1992.

Le Guin, Ursula K. "Why Are Americans Afraid of Dragons?" In *The Language of the Night: Essays on Fantasy and Science Fiction*. Rev. ed. New York: HarperCollins, 1989, 34–40.

Lewis, C. S. "On Three Ways of Writing for Children." In *Of Other Worlds*. London: Geoffrey Bles, 1966, 22–34.

Lewis, David. "Children's Literature Studies: The State of the Art?" *Children's Literature in Education* 28, no. 4 (1997): 235–38.

Malvern, Jack, "Harry Potter and the Vatican Enforcer." *Times Online*, 14 July 2005.

Mosley, Leonard. *The Real Walt Disney [Disney's World]*. London: Futura, 1987.

Nodelman, Perry. *The Hidden Adult, Defining Children's Literature*. Baltimore: Johns Hopkins UP, 2008.

Phillips, Robert, ed. *Aspects of Alice*. Harmondsworth: Penguin, 1974.

Rose, Jacqueline. *The Case of Peter Pan, or, The Impossibility of Children's Fiction* London: Macmillan 1984.

Rudd, David. "Theorising and Theories: The Conditions of Possibility of Children's Literature." In *International Companion Encyclopedia of Children's Literature*, Peter Hunt, ed. London: Routledge.

Salinger, J. D. *Raise High the Roof Beam, Carpenters and Seymour—an Introduction*. Harmondsworth: Penguin, 1964.

Thomas, Donald. *Lewis Carroll: A Portrait with Background*. London: John Murray, 1996.

Tucker, Nicholas. "Edward Ardizzone." *Children's Literature in Education* 1, no. 3 (1970): 210–19.

Vallone, Lynne. "Notes." In *Alice's Adventures in Wonderland* and *Through the Looking-Glass*, by Lewis Carroll. New York: The Modern Library/Random House, 2002, 245–62.

Wall, Barbara. *The Narrator's Voice: The Dilemma of Children's Fiction*. Basingstoke: Macmillan, 1991.

Wallace, Richard. *Jack the Ripper, "Light-Hearted Friend."* Melrose, MA: Gemini Press, 1996.

Watson, Victor. "The Possibilities of Children's Fiction." In *After Alice*, Morag Styles, Eve Bearne, and Victor Watson, eds. London: Cassell, 1992.

Wullschläger, Jackie. *Inventing Wonderland: The Lives and Fantasies of Lewis Carroll, Edward Lear, J.M. Barrie, Kenneth Grahame and A.A. Milne*. New York: The Free Press, 1995.

Zipes, Jack. *Sticks and Stones: The Troublesome Success of Children's Literature from Slovenly Peter to Harry Potter*. New York: Routledge, 2001.

FURTHER READING

Brooker, Will. *Alice's Adventures: Lewis Carroll in Popular Culture.* New York: Continuum, 2004.

Carroll, Lewis. *Alice's Adventures under Ground* (facsimile). Introduction by Martin Gardner. New York: Dover, 1965.

———. *The Nursery Alice* (facsimile). Introduction by Martin Gardner. New York: Dover, 1966.

Coats, Karen. *Looking Glasses and Neverlands: Lacan, Desire, and Subjectivity in Children's Literature.* Iowa City: U of Iowa P, 2004.

Dusinberre, Juliet. *Alice to the Lighthouse: Children's Books and Radical Experiments in Art.* London: Macmillan Press, 1987.

Geer, Jennifer. "'All Sorts of Pitfalls and Surprises': Competing Views of Idealized Girlhood in Lewis Carroll's *Alice* Books." *Children's Literature* 31 (2003): 1–24.

Goldthwaite, John. *The Natural History of Make-Believe.* New York: Oxford UP, 1996.

Hollindale, Peter. *Signs of Childness in Children's Books.* South Woodchester: Thimble.

Leach, Karoline. *In the Shadow of the Dreamchild: The Myth and Reality of Lewis Carroll.* 2nd ed. London: Peter Owen, 2008.

McGillis, Roderick. *The Nimble Reader: Literary Theory and Children's Literature.* New York: Twayne, 1996.

Reynolds, Kimberley. *Radical Children's Literature: Future Visions and Aesthetic Transformations in Juvenile Fiction.* Basingstoke: Palgrave Macmillan, 2007.

Sigler, Carolyn, ed. *Alternative Alices: Visions and Revisions of Lewis Carroll's* Alice *Books.* Lexington: UP of Kentucky, 1997.

Talbot, Bryan. *Alice in Sunderland.* London: Cape, 2007.

Wilson, Robin. *Lewis Carroll in Numberland: His Fantastical Mathematical Logical Life.* London: Allen Lane, 2008.

....

CHAPTER 2

RANDALL JARRELL'S *THE BAT-POET*: POETS, CHILDREN, AND READERS IN AN AGE OF PROSE

....

RICHARD FLYNN

THE *most feared and respected poet-critic of his generation, Randall Jarrell didn't begin writing for children until 1962, when then-junior editor Michael di Capua encouraged him to translate tales by the Brothers Grimm and Ludwig Bechstein for a Macmillan series. Before his untimely death in 1965 he wrote four original children's books,* The Gingerbread Rabbit, *illustrated by Garth Williams, and* The Bat-Poet *(1964), New-bery Honor book* The Animal Family *(1965), and the posthumous* Fly By Night *(1976), all illustrated by Maurice Sendak.*

Born in Nashville, Tennessee, on May 6, 1914 he spent much of his early childhood in Long Beach and Los Angeles, California, returning to Nashville in 1927 after his parents' divorce. He attended Vanderbilt University where he met early mentors Robert Penn Warren, Allen Tate, and John Crowe Ransom. After receiving the MA, Jarrell taught at Kenyon College and The University of Texas, where he met and married his first wife, Mackie Langham. Jarrell enlisted in the Army Air Forces in 1942, spending the war stateside after washing out as a pilot. After the war, he taught for a year at Sarah Lawrence while serving as literary editor of The Nation; *and in 1947, he took a teaching position at The Woman's College (now the University of North Carolina at Greensboro), where he remained for the rest of his life. Jarrell's lively, witty, and sometimes cruel book reviews and his poems about World War II collected in* Little Friend, Little Friend *(1945) and* Losses *(1948) secured his early reputation.*

The Seven-League Crutches *(1951) concerned itself with postwar devastation of Europe, with fairy tales, and with the plight of women and children. When Jarrell's Selected* Poems *(1955) appeared, Karl Shapiro remarked that it might be subtitled "Hansel and Gretel in America." Jarrell met Mary von Schrader, who had two daughters, and, after his divorce from Mackie, they were married in 1952. From 1956 to 1958, he served as Consultant in Poetry at The Library of Congress (now called Poet Laureate) where he delivered scathing lectures such as "The Appalling Taste of the Age," which lamented America's declining literacy and the dumbing down of children's books. He won the 1960 National Book Award for Poetry for* The Woman at the Washington Zoo, *and his cultural criticism was collected in* A Sad Heart at the Supermarket *(1962). In addition to poetry and children's books, Jarrell published an academic satire,* Pictures from an Institution, *and translations of Rilke's poetry, Goethe's* Faust, Part I, *and Chekhov's* The Three Sisters.

Robert Lowell, in his memorial tribute, identified Jarrell's major theme as "Above all, childhood! This subject for many a careless and tarnished cliché was for him what it was for his two favorite poets, Rilke and Wordsworth, a governing and transcendent vision." Jarrell's last book of poems, The Lost World *(1965), includes the terza rima title poem about his childhood in "the blue wonderland / Of Hollywood" as well as three poems from* The Bat-Poet. *He was struck by a car and killed while walking on the Chapel Hill bypass on October 14, 1965.*

In his 1951 essay, "The Age of Criticism," Randall Jarrell lampoons the kind of criticism that "might just as well have been written by a syndicate of encyclopedias for an audience of International Business Machines"(Poetry and the Age 72–73). Elsewhere he observes with great bitterness, "the poet is a condemned man for whom the State will not even buy breakfast. . . . The poet lives in a world whose newspapers and magazines and books and motion pictures and radio stations and television stations have destroyed, in a great many people, even the capacity for understanding real poetry, real art of any kind" (Poetry and the Age 18). Throughout the remainder of his career, Jarrell would repeatedly pursue his brief against the antipoetic nature of American culture in such essays as "The Appalling Taste of the Age" and "A Sad Heart at the Supermarket." The twenty-first century is at least as hostile to poetry as the mid-twentieth—we have the Internet, cell phones, and twenty-four-hour cable news, for instance—and while Jarrell is unjustly remembered as a brilliant critic and merely a talented poet, his polemical criticism, his diatribes against mass culture seem dated. Paradoxically, his writing for children, which his contemporaries viewed with a fair amount of condescension, has earned him a secure place in what his collaborator and illustrator Maurice Sendak has dubbed the "Western Canon, Jr."[1]

This essay focuses on *The Bat-Poet* (1964), a work that responds to what Jarrell perceived as antipoetic times with the nuance and emotional depth that is the province not of criticism but of imaginative literature. Combining fiction and poetry, Jarrell's bittersweet animal fable meditates on the plight of the poet in an age of prose. It is a work that I have lived with for a number of years, years in which the teaching of English in universities has undergone transformations that have served to broaden the canon so that students now regularly study children's works in English departments. Nevertheless, during this time, criticism—or critical theory— has gained even greater prestige than it had in the 1950s. I am not about to engage in what Jarrell satirically called "A Fit of Criticism Against Criticism," but my experiences as a reader, student, and teacher who has lived with *The Bat-Poet* for thirty-five years make me sympathetic with Jarrell's injunction that we need "to care more for stories and novels and poems and plays, and less for criticism" (*Poetry and the Age* 94). "Write so as to be of some use to a reader," Jarrell continues (94). Here, I hope to be of use by combining autobiography, biographical criticism, and a pedagogically inflected approach to explore the enduring appeal of Jarrell's children's story.

"Once upon a time . . . a little light brown bat, the color of coffee with cream in it" (1) discovers poetry by listening to the mockingbird, a master poet:

> The bat loved to listen to him. He could imitate all the other birds—he'd even imitate the way the squirrels chattered when they were angry, like two rocks being knocked together; and he could imitate the milk bottles being put down on the porch and the barn door closing, a long rusty squeak. And he made up songs and words all his own, that nobody else had ever said or sung. (3)

When the bat becomes estranged from his fellow bats by virtue of his remaining on the porch at the end of the summer while they sleep in the barn, he wakes up during the daytime and enjoys the "queer feeling" it gives him. He wants to tell the other bats about his daytime experience, but they refuse to listen. He tries to make them listen by attempting to make beautiful sounds like those of the mockingbird. Unable to imitate the melody, the bat recognizes that "if you get the words right, you don't need a tune" (5) so he makes a poem about the daytime. But when he tries to say it to the other bats, they scold him: "when you say things like that we don't know what you mean" (6). The bat is discouraged, but he keeps on making poems, first about an owl, which wins the mockingbird's grudging approval, and then a portrait of the chipmunk, his uncritically appreciative audience. The bat suffers from writer's block when he discovers he can't compose a poem to order about the cardinal; he overcomes this block by making "The Mockingbird," yet he alienates his difficult mentor in doing so. Finally, the bat creates his autobiographical masterpiece, "A bat is born,"[2] only to forget the poem as he begins to hibernate before he can say it to the other bats.

This synopsis of *The Bat-Poet* hardly does justice to the story's enduring intellectual and emotional appeal. Jarrell thought of the book as being "half-for-children, half-for-grown-ups" (*Randall Jarrell's Letters* 491). Both child and adult readers have continued to appreciate it for over forty-five years, so that it is now considered a canonical children's text. I have found *The Bat-Poet* to be especially useful pedagogically, as it both appeals to college students in my children's literature classes and raises a number of important questions that set the tone for our discussions about children's poetry, particularly in terms of expanding my students' tastes beyond the Prelutsky and Silverstein poems they already know and love.

Although I was nine years old when *The Bat-Poet* was first published, I was not fortunate enough to have read it as a child myself. I first encountered Jarrell's fairy tale as an undergraduate college student in the mid-1970s, a time when the tenets of the New Criticism still held sway in college English departments and when most English departments would scoff at the idea of offering courses in children's literature. For me, Jarrell's children's poetry primer was assigned in a course called Practical Criticism, a required course meant to introduce English majors to writing in the discipline. Along with Jane Austen's *Emma*, Jarrell's allegorical poetry primer was a supplement to the main textbook in the course, I. A. Richards's *Practical Criticism* (1929). That students were assigned Jarrell's now classic children's text at all may be attributed to the professor's fondness for it. That professor, Judith Plotz, was later to become my mentor, directing my dissertation on Jarrell and inciting my interest in the field of children's literature.[3] In my undergraduate days, I had yet to appreciate *Emma* as I do now, and I'm afraid I never developed much of a taste for Mr. Richards, but I fell in love immediately with *The Bat-Poet*.

Since Practical Criticism emphasized genre, we were expected to learn a great deal about poetry and were quizzed on tropes and figures and called upon to demonstrate our skill at scansion. Although I was awestruck by my professor's intellect, such activities seemed "mockingbirdish," while I inclined to the intuitive, emotionally based poetics of the Bat-Poet. I cared a great deal about reading and writing poetry. I longed for, and eventually found (unlike the bat), a community of readers and writers who cared about poetry as well.

In his excellent study of *The Bat-Poet*, included in his book *Poetry's Playground* (2007), Joseph Thomas notes how the Bat-Poet's work bridges the divide between the raw and the cooked poetries that Robert Lowell identified in his 1960 National Book Award acceptance speech. While Lowell was at the height of his fame and influence during my college years, many of the members of my poetry community were influenced by New York School, Beat, Projectivist, and Objectivist traditions. My poetry professor, David McAleavey, had written his dissertation on George Oppen, and a number of my poet friends later became associated with the D.C. contingent of language writers. I, however, studied with formalist poet Marilyn Hacker (my senior year), and my graduate professor Henry Taylor also helped me appreciate working within the formal constraints of rhyme and meter. I found myself straddling a divide between competing poetic camps.

When I use Randall Jarrell's *The Bat-Poet* in my children's literature classes to introduce the genre of poetry, I find that my own students also identify with the Bat-Poet. They identify with his difference and his outsider status, and they often praise his intuitive poetics and criticize the mockingbird's territoriality and pedantic concern with such things as meter. At the beginning of his 1942 lecture, "Levels and Opposites: Structure in Poetry," Jarrell announces that he plans to "disregard the musical structure of poetry: metre, stanza form, rhyme, alliteration, quantity, and so on" because "criticism has paid them an altogether disproportionate amount of attention—partly, I suppose, because they are things any child can point at, draw diagrams of and count" (697). Nevertheless, many of my students have limited knowledge of even these musical structures, and I sometimes find myself defending the mockingbird. Like the Bat-Poet, my students want to learn about poetry but are less interested in technical matters than they are in poetry's emotional resonance. Then again, when I was their age, so was I. While I had little patience with mockingbirdish activities in my youth, nowadays I find myself playing the mockingbird perhaps more frequently than I might wish.

I mention this personal literary history not only because *The Bat-Poet* occupies a pivotal position in the history of American children's poetry, as Joseph Thomas has demonstrated, but also because it serves as a harbinger, or perhaps an emblem, of the shift in literary studies that made it possible for children's literature to be studied seriously in university English departments. Children's literature studies emerged as part of the opening up of the canon to writers and works excluded on the basis of ethnicity, gender, or genre. As the hegemony of the New Criticism waned and critics began to pay greater attention to politics, history, and cultural contexts in addition to aesthetic and linguistic concerns, the privileged and iconic status of the (usually classic) "work" was no longer sacrosanct. Paradoxically, the very forces that made the study of children's literature possible also served to depose the study of poetry from the Parnassian heights to which New Critical analysis and canon formation had elevated it.

Jarrell's children's writing stands on the cusp of this shift: in the 1960s when he composed his children's books, Jarrell was a famous poet who had been Consultant in Poetry at the Library of Congress from 1956 to 1958 (today, that position is called Poet Laureate), had won the National Book Award for *Woman at the Washington Zoo* (1960), and had delivered the major address, "Fifty Years of American Poetry" at the Library of Congress's National Poetry Festival in October of 1962 (which coincided with the climax of the Cuban Missile Crisis). Encouraged to write for children by then-junior editor Michael di Capua and energized by his collaboration with Maurice Sendak, which began when Sendak was chosen to illustrate *The Bat-Poet*, Jarrell found writing for children not only rewarding but also central to breaking through his poetry-writing block to produce his last and best book of poems, *The Lost World*.[4] Yet he did so at some risk to his prestige and to the consternation of friends like Robert Lowell, who wrote to Elizabeth Bishop in April of 1964, "I find them [Jarrell's children's books] awfully clean, charming, innocent, and a nice idyllic thing to do, but a little too much in the genre. I wish he would write something much more weird, unacceptable and his own" (Travisano, "Words in Air" 528).

On the contrary, Jarrell's children's books, particularly *The Bat-Poet*, stand as very much his own, and they are also much more weird and unacceptable than they are idyllic. Just as the bat finds a difficult mentor in the mockingbird, Jarrell also owed much to his early mentors, but he stood fundamentally at odds with them. Born in 1914 in Nashville, Tennessee, Jarrell spent most of his childhood in Long Beach and Los Angeles, California. When his parents divorced, he returned to Nashville to live with his mother in 1927. After graduating from Hume-Fogg high school, Jarrell attended Vanderbilt University from 1932 to 1935, where he studied with John Crowe Ransom and Robert Penn Warren and met another early mentor, Allen Tate. Jarrell was trained by these leading lights of the southern

Fugitive/Agrarian wing of the New Criticism (the movement derived its name from Ransom's 1941 book, *The New Criticism*), but he was a young upstart. An apprentice, like the Bat-Poet, Jarrell admired the work of his mentors, especially their poetry, but he took issue with some of their literary judgments and categorically rejected their politics.[5] In her memorial tribute to Jarrell, Hannah Arendt described Jarrell as "a democrat at heart, 'with a scientific education and a radical youth'" (7). Jarrell's abrasive self-confidence, his impatience with his classmates, as well as his Marxist orientation were off-putting to his Agrarian teachers; in fact, John Crowe Ransom, in a 1941 review of Jarrell's book appearance in *Five Young American Poets*, accuses him of aspiring to be a "postmodernist" (Ransom, "Constellation" 378).[6]

Ransom is reacting here primarily to the introduction Jarrell wrote for his first major collection of poems, "The Rage for the Lost Penny," in the 1940 New Directions volume *Five Young American Poets*, "A Note on Poetry," which later appeared in revised and expanded form as "The End of the Line" in the February 21, 1942, issue of *The Nation*. In both versions, Jarrell advanced the then-heretical view that "Modernist poetry... appears to be and is generally considered to be a violent break with romanticism; it is actually . . . an extension of romanticism" (*Kipling* 77) going so far as to proclaim in the *Nation* version"

> It is the end of the line. Poets can go back and repeat the ride; they can settle in attractive, atavistic colonies along the railroad; they can repudiate the whole system, á la Yvor Winters, for some neoclassical donkey caravan of their own. But Modernism As We Knew It—the most successful and influential body of poetry in this century—is dead. (*Kipling* 81)

In his April 30, 1942, Mesures Lecture at Princeton University, Jarrell delineated a dialectical theory of poetry, which alienated Allen Tate, the mentor who had lobbied successfully to get Jarrell the speaking engagement. Lost for many years, the lecture, "Levels and Opposites: Structure in Poetry" was rediscovered and published by Thomas Travisano in 1996. Joseph Thomas grounds his reading of *The Bat-Poet* on the dialectical theory of poetry Jarrell advances in this lecture, recognizing that Jarrell's "views on poetry were radical for his time" (21) and arguing that *The Bat-Poet* is "insightful" because it "resists binaries" (38). Nevertheless, Jarrell's lost lecture points out that the "ironic or ambiguous structures" so favored by "Richards, Cleanth Brooks, and Empson . . . are merely special varieties of dialectical structures" (Jarrell, qtd. in Travisano, *Midcentury* 171). "Jarrell makes clear," writes Travisano, "that dialectic is just one example chosen from a dizzying multiplicity of structural possibilities. For Jarrell [whom he quotes], 'There are *many* different sorts of structure in poetry, *many* possible ways of organizing a poem; and *many* of these are combined in the organization of a single poem'" (171).

But it is not the incipient "postmodernist" who writes *The Bat-Poet*; it is the fully postmodern poet and critic with a "sad heart at the supermarket." For many of my students—and even colleagues—Jarrell is the author of one six-line war poem, "The Death of the Ball-Turret Gunner." *The Bat-Poet*, however, is very much part of Jarrell's postwar aesthetic (what Stephen Burt describes as Jarrell's "interpersonal style") and his postwar subject matter (childhood, fairy tales, aging mortals, especially women, like the suburban housewife speaker of "Next Day" who is "confused with my life, that is commonplace and solitary") (*Complete Poems* 280). The children's books—and Jarrell's focus on childhood—are central to his aesthetic. In a 1963 reading at the 92nd Street Y Poetry Center, Jarrell opens with three poems from *The Bat-Poet*: "The Mockingbird," "The Bird of Night," and "Bats"—without identifying them as children's poems, just as he had not identified them as such when he submitted them to *The New Yorker* (Mary Jarrell, liner notes). Introducing the fourth poem, "Next Day," he says, "I see in all these poems I haven't got any about men. I've got 'em about animals, women, and children. . . . I guess all the men got killed in the poems I wrote about the war and I haven't got any left" (Reading).

As I discuss in "Jarrell's Wicked Fairy," Eisenhower's America was profoundly disturbing to Jarrell. He had firsthand experience with McCarthyism—his appointment as Poetry Consultant was threatened when he was accused of being a "Communist, on the grounds that he had published in such radical publications as *The Nation* and *The New Republic*, and had associated with Marxists while teaching at the University of Texas" (McGuire 195).[7] He was also intensely involved in the ongoing debates about "mass culture" that dominated much intellectual discourse during the 1950s and early 1960s, using the bully pulpit of the Library of Congress to inveigh against popular culture in addresses such as "The Appalling Taste of the Age,"[8] which appeared in the *Saturday Evening Post*. But Jarrell also published articles celebrating sports cars and "Love and Poetry" in *Mademoiselle*. For all of his crankiness about popular culture, Jarrell truly did wish to appeal to ordinary readers, with the "television watchers and readers of *Reader's Digest*" that Arendt mentions in her tribute (7). In *Poets, Critics, and Readers* (1959), he complains that "the public has an unusual relationship to the poet—it doesn't even know that he is there" (*Sad Heart* 90). And yet this complaint isn't simple elitism, especially as the essay recommends reading "at whim" (113) and focuses on a children's book, Kipling's *Kim*, in making this recommendation. Jarrell recounts the story of reading a journal interview with a "professional critic" who has "no time to read at whim":

> I went back over that interview, looking for some bright spot, and I found it, one
> beautiful sentence: for a moment I had left the gray, dutiful world of the
> professional critic, and was back in the sunlight and shadow, the unconsidered
> joys, the unreasoned sorrows, of ordinary readers and writers, amateurishly
> reading and writing "at whim." The critic said that once a year he read *Kim*; and
> he read *Kim*, it was plain, at whim: not to teach, not to criticize, just for love—he
> read it, as Kipling wrote it, just because he liked to, wanted to, couldn't help
> himself. To him it wasn't a means to a lecture or an article, it was an end; he read
> it not for anything he could get out of it, but for itself. And isn't this what the
> work of art demands of us? The work of art, Rilke said, says to us always: *You
> must change your life.* (112–13)

In the same essay, Jarrell lampoons the "Revised Standard Version of *Mother Goose*: without rhyme, meter, or other harmful adulterants. . . . I don't expect the modern *Mother Goose* to be especially popular with little children who have not yet learned not to like poetry; but it is the parents who buy the book" (*Kipling* 392–93). Poetry, Jarrell implies, is both pleasurable, unrequired reading and is fundamental to our humanity. The overworked professor is like the mockingbird: prestige obsessed and pedantic about literature that he no longer loves. When the Bat-Poet emerges into the "sunlight and shadows" of the daytime world, he wishes to use poetry to speak to the "unconsidered joys" and "unreasoned sorrows" of his fellow bats, but they remain wedded to their "gray, dutiful world"—they have neither the time nor the patience for poetry. In many ways, they have lost their capacity for pleasure.

It is fitting, therefore, that the first "professional critic" of children's literature to take *The Bat-Poet* seriously was Perry Nodelman, a critic who is our most eloquent advocate for exploring "the pleasures of children's literature." Writing in the journal *Language Arts* in 1978 in an essay entitled "The Craft or Sullen Art of a Mouse or a Bat," Nodelman distinguishes Leo Lionni's *Frederick* (1967), which he argues plays into the "condescension toward children's minds and abilities in regard to poetry in almost every elementary text I've seen" (467), from *The Bat-Poet*, which he offers as "a challenging answer to the damaging attitudes toward poetry expressed in *Frederick* and accepted without consideration by many teachers" (472).[9] *The Bat-Poet* presents poets not as they are depicted in *Frederick*—"untrustworthy eccentrics" with "a special way of seeing, that offers an escape from reality"; rather "The Bat-Poet presents a much different idea about poets and their work—one that inextricably involves them with the other important concerns of living" (469). Jerome Griswold links Nodelman's essay with Peter Neumeyer's 1984 essay, "Randall Jarrell's *The Bat Poet*: An Introduction to the Craft," saying that both suggest the book is "a kind of primer that can be used to introduce poetry" to students (61). While I have already admitted to using the book this way with my college students, Nodelman's essay offers *The Bat-Poet* as a corrective to superficially romantic notions of the poet and the poem, while Neumeyer's essay, charming though it may be, tends to perpetuate many of those notions. Nodelman identifies the central paradox of the book: the Bat-Poet's "desire to communicate makes communication difficult" (472).

To which I would add: any real communication—at least any communication that springs from deep desire, that involves genuine human exchange—is by definition difficult. And all too often when it comes to poetry, even students majoring in literature either aren't equipped or don't wish to make the effort it takes to read a poem well. In Jarrell's only novel for adults, the academic satire *Pictures from an Institution* (1954), the narrator calls himself (alluding to Henry Adams) "only a poet—that is to say, a maker of stone axes" (94). In his 1951 essay, "The Obscurity of the Poet," Jarrell observes that it is not just modern poetry that readers find difficult, but any poetry, and perhaps even literature itself. Jarrell's choice of children as an audience is based on what he believes to be their greater receptiveness to reading "at whim," and he hopes to protect them from the harmful effects of a culture that doesn't value reading at all:

> One of our universities recently made a survey of the reading habits of the
> American public; it decided that forty-eight percent of all Americans read, during

a year, no book at all. I picture to myself that reader—non-reader, rather; one man out of every two—and I reflect, with shame: "Our poems are too hard for him." But so, too, are *Treasure Island*, *Peter Rabbit*, pornographic novels—any book whatsoever. . . . I call to this imaginary figure, "Why don't you read books?"—and he always answers, after looking at me for a long time: "Huh?" (*Poetry and the Age* 18–19)

The Bat-Poet's poems are, as Nodelman points out, "remarkably subtle" (472), and as Joseph Thomas reminds us, while the bat might be a naive, intuitive poet, rather than a craftsman like the mockingbird, Jarrell (who, after all, writes the poems and sends them to the *New Yorker*) has spent years perfecting his craft (*Poetry's Playground* 30).

In my classes in contemporary and modern poetry (which I teach in addition to my courses on children's and young adult literature) I have taken to giving my students what I jokingly call their "mantra": "Pay attention to the pronouns." In "The Obscurity of the Poet," Jarrell offers the following diagnosis of what ails reluctant readers, as well as a prescription for their ills:

Anyone who has spent much time finding out what people do when they read a poem, what poems actually mean for them, will have discovered that a surprising part of the difficulty they have comes from their almost systematic unreceptiveness, their queer unwillingness to pay attention even to the reference of the pronouns, the meaning of the punctuation, which subject goes with which verb, and so on; "after all," they seem to feel, "I'm not reading *prose*." *You need to read good poetry with an attitude that that is a mixture of sharp intelligence and of willing emotional empathy, at once penetrating and generous* (*Poetry and the Age* 12; my emphasis).

Perry Nodelman praises this prescription for adults, saying that Jarrell "obviously expects as much penetration, and as much generosity, from children" (472). It may be, however, that Jarrell expected even more from children. He knew that only an engagement with imaginative literature at an early age was likely to produce such readers. And there is no doubt that his wish that the United States could become a nation of real readers motivated him to begin writing for children. In an unpublished manuscript in which Jarrell discusses his childhood reading, he comments that writing for children allowed him "the imaginative freedom of an imagined audience." And this same imaginative freedom helped him find his way toward the poems in what Lowell called Jarrell's "last and best book," *The Lost World*. By thinking about children as an audience and revisiting his own imaginative childhood activity, including his childhood reading, Jarrell became what children's literature critics Mitzi Myers and Uli Knoepflmacher have called a "cross-writer." Adult–child "cross-writing," according to these critics, involves "a dialogic mix of older and younger voices [that] occurs in texts too often read as univocal" (vii). Cross-writing implies the "interplay and cross-fertilization rather than a hostile internal cross fire" (vii) that may be found in works intended for both children and adults and is often particularly pronounced in writers who address younger and older audiences with equal care and respect.

If Jarrell's theories of poetic structure at age twenty-eight were dialectical, his theories of children's literature at forty-eight were dialogic.[10] Stephen Burt even goes so far as to conclude that "for Jarrell, *adults can understand literature if and only if they can imagine how children read*" (165). But as I argue in "Jarrell's Wicked Fairy," imagining how children read is only the beginning. For the cross-writer, poetry involves a complex fusion of the child and adult in which the mature artist, in making the poem, renders the child's "capacity for wonder" articulate. In his later adult–child cross-writing, Jarrell seeks a dialogue between his adult-self and remembered child-self. Like Jarrell, the Bat-Poet finds that cross-writing will allow him to communicate with his audience—the indifferent bats with whom he longs to connect.

In holograph notes about his childhood reading held by the Berg Collection in the New York Public Library, Jarrell explicitly recalls his injunction to "read at whim," recognizing that, as a child, he engaged in such reading strategies. As a child, he also read without regard to literature's cultural prestige. His childhood reading included the classics: Andersen, Grimm, Kipling, Carroll, Stevenson, Grahame, and more, but also a lot of what can only be described as trashy series books, such as the work of Ralph Henry Barbour whose advertising copy he quotes: "In these up-to-the-minute, spirited, genuine stories of boy life there is something which will appeal to every boy with the love of manliness, cleanness, and sportsmanship in his heart." He read the series he called "The Boy with the U.S. Something or other–Indian Service was the best"[11] He devoured the Rover Boys, Tom Swift, the Bobbsey Twins, and even Elsie Dinsmore: "Just as stale chocolate poured over rank peanuts and sold at Woolworths tastes better to a child than the finest candy tastes to a grown up," Jarrell writes, "so *Tom Swift* and *The Rover Boys* and *Roy Blakeley*—any mechanical series of cut and dried wish-fantasies were satisfying to me then."[12]

The notes also show Jarrell distinguishing between adult and child reading, insisting on the liberatory function of children's reading. He recalls a "sense of wonder characteristic of so much children's reading," noting that when we are children "our reading changes us from an almost powerless child trapped in some zoo of grown-ups rules dispensations into animal, Indian, hero big and free in a world almost without limits."[13] Reading at whim is thus empowering: escapist reading and pleasure reading aim at the "satisfaction of Freudian wishes–Unconscious." Jarrell observes that, for a child, reading promotes "change far greater than changes of grown-up reading feeling empathy with the other grown-ups." Childhood reading for Jarrell was a paradise where high culture and mass culture need not be distinguished and where reading was "pure joy." "For it was paradise," he writes, "The pile of yellowing pulp magazines that I borrowed from somebody's back porch or attic—Adventure or Thrilling Western Stories—was a pure joy to me, as much of a joy to me as the Jungle Tales or Alice."

In "Well Water," a poem for adults that appears in *The Lost World*, Jarrell sees poetic creation (which for him involved tapping this same source of childlike wonder) as an arduous task that pays off only suddenly and unexpectedly:

> The pump you pump the water from is rusty
> And hard to move and absurd, a squirrel-wheel
> A sick squirrel turns slowly, through the sunny
> Inexorable hours. And yet sometimes
> The wheel turns of its own weight, the rusty
> Pump pumps over your sweating face the clear
> Water, cold, so cold! You cup your hands
> And gulp from them the dailiness of life.
>
> (*Complete Poems* 300)

To a child, Jarrell writes in the "Libraries" manuscript, "Any water in the world is well water, and cold and a child's thirst is absolute."

This difficult act of creation is reflected in the Bat-Poet's last and best poem. Like Jarrell, the Bat-Poet engages with his child-self dialogically in creating his finest poem. The mother bat in the poem "lives by hearing" while the baby bat's thirst is absolute: he "hangs on tight" and "drinks the milk she makes him." The mother bat negotiates the world "in happiness," through echolalia, a poet herself, whose "shining needlepoints of sound / Go out into the night and, echoing back / Tell her what they have touched." While the mother (like all bats) literally navigates by sound, she demonstrates the way that a poet locates herself in the world by making an emotional connection with it and learning how the world responds. Likewise, through dialogic means, child and adult find themselves "Doubling and looping, soaring, somersaulting" in a dance negotiated through each listening to the other. The mother bat hunts and flies all night "in happiness," but it is the Bat-Poet himself who has reconstructed this childhood moment in making his poem. Perhaps idealizing this symbiotic flight of adult and child, this dance of mother and child, the Bat-Poet hasn't reckoned with the fact of his imminent hibernation: "I wish I'd said we sleep all winter." He has conquered infant amnesia only "for a moment, in the moonlight," recapturing, like the mockingbird's song, a convincing imitation of life through a poetic making of a childhood world that is lost.

And found. In "Thinking of the Lost World," the epilogue to Jarrell's terza rima evocation of the year he spent with his grandparents and great grandmother in the "blue Wonderland" of Hollywood when he was twelve, the adult poet, from the perspective of smog-ridden Los Angeles in the 1960s, negotiates between the worlds of child and adult, past and present:

> Moving between the first world and the second,
> I hear a boy call, now that my beard's gray:
> "Santa Claus! Hi, Santa Claus!" It *is* miraculous
> To have the children call you Santa Claus.
> I wave back. When my hand drops to the wheel,
> It is brown and spotted, and its nails are ridged
> Like Mama's. Where's my own hand? My smooth
> White bitten-fingernailed one? I seem to see

A shape in tennis shoes and khaki riding pants
Standing there empty-handed; I reach out to it
Empty-handed, my hand comes back empty,
And yet my emptiness is traded for its emptiness,
I have found that Lost World in the Lost and Found
Columns whose gray illegible advertisements
My soul has memorized world after world:
LOST—NOTHING. STRAYED FROM NOWHERE. NO REWARD.
I hold in my own hands, in happiness,
Nothing: the nothing for which there's no reward.

(Complete Poems 338)

Like the mother bat, whose "Doubling and looping, soaring, somersaulting" with her baby underneath allows her to fly by night in happiness, the doubling of child and adult, both of them lost and found here, echoes back and forth to tell the speaker what *he* has touched. If the adult emptiness is traded for the more positive emptiness of the child (figured not as emptiness but as potential, the capacity for wonder), the adult speaker nevertheless answers his earlier question, "Where's my own hand?" by recognizing that it is indeed "brown and spotted, and its nails are ridged." But, of course, at the end of the poem we have a pair of hands, as if the gulf between the adult hand and the child hand has been bridged, however evanescently.

The conversation between Jarrell's writing for children and his writing for adults, then, is clear evidence that Lowell was wrong about Jarrell's children's writing being "a nice idyllic thing to do." The stakes were high for Jarrell, and the power of *The Bat-Poet* comes from the fundamental center of his creative principles. In the densest pages of notes in the Berg Library's manuscript, along with the childhood reading lists, appear the following phrases, which should be familiar to anyone who knows Jarrell's late poems, especially "The Lost World":

"I believe"
    miserable boredom of Sunday afternoon drives
    illustrations [from a forgotten childhood book] still magical to me, if
reached out and touched would shock like hitting your funnybone
    Pitamakin Salâmbo "Twenty Years After" "35 Years After" Amazing Stories
    TARZAN
    Four books so soon read up—no way to get back to uptown Carnegie except
by walking or catching rides (lunch money soon used up) rides caught in ladies'
electric cars real thirst for books of child who reads a lot whole body yearned
desperately for them as does for water after long tennis match in hottest summer

While it is not immediately clear to my students, the Bat-Poet's search for an audience and his ultimate success in finding his voice and personal subject matter reflect critical values that are hard-won for Jarrell. These are values that today we often take for granted: that we may consider historical and biographical contexts when we interpret a literary text, that the reader's response may be a valid subject for the critic to consider, that poems are subject to multiple interpretations, that discovering the unity of a "verbal icon" is no longer much valued. My students also learn what is not so obvious: that poetry offers us an important way of looking at the world and a way of connecting with it, that reading a poem or poetic looking requires "a mixture of sharp intelligence and of willing emotional empathy." Most of all, the ambiguous ending of *The Bat-Poet* reminds them of how difficult and fleeting such poetic insights may be. The bat makes his poem about bats, which he knows will connect him with the others, but in order to rejoin them, he must forget the poem as he hibernates.[14]

Furthermore, as I noted at the beginning of this essay, our culture is even more hostile to poetry than Jarrell's was, and as my students who plan to be teachers continually remind me, poetry, and indeed literature, has virtually disappeared from elementary curricula. My course in children's literature is an upper-division elective, and it is taken primarily by English majors and MA students in English. Without advocating a return to the New Criticism, I sometimes do need to remind them just what sort of close attention is required for understanding poetry. Sometimes, I may even offer a dose of New Critical precepts in showing them how a poem works. One of those precepts, which Cleanth Brooks inherited from I. A. Richards's *Practical Criticism*, is called "The Heresy of Paraphrase." In *The Well-Wrought Urn*, Brooks says that aesthetic evaluations of poems should not be made "in terms of 'content' or 'subject matter' in the usual sense in which we use these terms, but rather in terms of structure" (193). But Jarrell in his 1942 lecture had already refuted excessive reliance on the kinds of structure that interested Brooks. Furthermore, modernist notions of impersonality seem antithetical to the Bat-Poet's poetic breakthrough, which depends on his discovery of a personal subject matter. Nevertheless, the bat's poem and Jarrell's story do dramatize the inadequacy of paraphrase. The narrator's prose synopsis of the poem's subject matter at the beginning of its composition captures only a fraction of the feeling generated by the work of art itself:

> For some reason, he began to think of the first things he could remember. Till a bat is two weeks old he's never alone: the little naked thing—he hasn't any fur—clings to his mother wherever she goes. After that she leaves him at night; he and the other bats hang there sleeping, till at last their mothers come home to them. Sleepily, almost dreaming, the bat began to make up a poem about a mother and her baby.
>
> It was easier than the other poems, somehow: all he had to do was remember what it had been like and every once in a while put in a rhyme. (34–35)

The poem itself, with its vivid figurative language, its "doubling and looping," its "shining needlepoints of sound," its movement from soaring to sleeping, really can't be paraphrased:

> The mother eats the moths and gnats she catches
> In full flight; in full flight
>   The mother drinks the water of the pond
>   She skims across. Her baby hangs on tight
>   Her baby drinks the milk she makes him

> In moonlight or starlight, in mid-air
> Their single shadow, printed on the moon
> Or fluttering across the stars,
> Whirls on all night. (37)

In *Practical Criticism*, Richards discusses two forms of paraphrase: one a paraphrase of the "sense of a poem . . . [which] requires only an intelligent use of the dictionary, logical acumen, a command of syntax and pertinacity" and one that

> demands qualities of sensitiveness and imagination, the power to use remote
> experience and to create metaphors, gifts which may seem to belong by birthright
> to the poet alone. It may seem strange to suggest that these gifts could be
> developed by school training, but remembering the original endowment of
> average children and comparing it with the obtuseness of the sample adult, the
> proposal (if we can guard against some of the dangers hinted at above), may not
> in the end prove to be so unduly optimistic. (213)

Gifted children's poet Nancy Willard describes the bat's last poem from a poet's perspective: "When at last the bat-poet composes a poem for the other bats, he has learned to build poems out of facts. But these are radiant facts; images, verbs, music, and story have worked on them" (53). While my students may not become poets like the bat and the mockingbird, I hope that they learn from *The Bat-Poet* at least to become chipmunks. Like the chipmunk, they are generally an appreciative audience, and like the chipmunk, they are eager to learn what a poem is and they want to enjoy poetry. How fortunate it would be for us if Jarrell's little book could help them not only appreciate poetry but also discover for themselves and for future generations of children the imaginative gifts usually reserved for the poet alone.

NOTES

1. In the 1995 Home Arts feature "A Western Canon, Jr.," Sendak gives high praise to both *The Animal Family* (1965) and *The Bat-Poet*:

> Some of the stories in *The Juniper Tree* were translated by the late poet Randall Jarrell and
> two of his own books are in my Canon—*The Animal Family* and *The Bat-Poet*. *The Animal
> Family* is all about loneliness, and how do you have a family and how do you pull a family
> together? It's heartbreakingly great. I'll say this, and I don't care who minds: There is no
> twentieth-century writer of fairy tales to stand alongside Randall Jarrell.

2. In Jarrell's poetry collection for adults, *The Lost World* (1965), the bat's final poem is titled "Bats." Of the bat's four complete poems, three of them appear in *The Lost World*. "The Chipmunk's Day" is omitted. It is also the only poem not to appear in a journal for adults: "The Mockingbird" appeared in the *New Yorker*, and "Bats" and "The Bird of Night" (the poem about the owl) appeared in *The Quarterly Review of Literature*.

3. Professor Plotz is now a well-known scholar of children's literature and childhood studies and a past president of the Children's Literature Association. In the 1987–88 academic year (after I successfully defended my dissertation on Randall Jarrell, which she directed), I served as an informal teaching assistant in her course Children's Literature. This was the extent of my formal training in children's literature. It was also the first time the course had ever been offered at George Washington University. In the fall of 1988, I began my first tenure-track job as an assistant professor of English specializing in children's literature at Indiana State University.

4. For an account of the relationship among Jarrell's cultural criticism, children's writing, and late poetry, see my "Jarrell's Wicked Fairy: Childhood, Cultural Criticism, and the 1950s."

5. For the best account of Jarrell's relationship with his Fugitive mentors, see Burt, *Randall Jarrell and His Age*, 4–7. Just after his junior year at Vanderbilt, Jarrell made his professional debut as a poet with five poems in the May 1934 special poetry supplement of *American Review* coedited by Tate and Warren. In the summer and fall after Jarrell graduated (with a degree in psychology and a minor in philosophy), Warren published Jarrell's poems in the first issue of *Southern Review*, and Cleanth Brooks commissioned and published his first professional criticism, an omnibus review of "Ten Books." After beginning a psychology MA, Jarrell switched to English. Another Fugitive, Donald Davidson, refused to allow him to write his thesis on Auden, so Jarrell ultimately wrote his thesis on A. E. Housman. Having followed Mr. Ransom to Kenyon College where he worked as an instructor and roomed with Robert Lowell in Ransom's attic, Jarrell finally finished his thesis in 1939 and took an instructorship at University of Texas, Austin, where he met and married his first wife, Mackie Langham, and he taught there until he enlisted in the Army Air Forces in 1942.

6. For details about Jarrell's relationship with his New Critical mentors in the 1930s, see my unpublished conference paper, "'The End of the Line': Randall Jarrell, the '30s, and Postmodernism," available on my personal website, http://personal.georgiasouthern. edu/~rflynn/JARRELLPM.htm

7. Never a party member, Jarrell was certainly a fellow traveler before he enlisted in the Army, and he knew that his politics carried a certain amount of personal risk. Writing to Edmund Wilson in April 1942, he jokes about the political ramifications of his dialectical theory of poetry:

> I'm calling the lecture "Levels and Opposites," and part of it is to the effect that the "logical" structure of poetry is, very often, roughly dialectical, this with many examples; but don't tell this to my friends, for they would disown me, or to my superiors, for they would discharge me—or would if they knew or cared what *dialectical* meant. I think I'll introduce it as a word Heraclitus and Plato were fond of, and not carry it down to date; perhaps Kant will be safe, and I have a charming quotation from Blake: "In poetry Unity and Morality are secondary considerations." I'm kidding—halfway.
>
> Four economists from the university [of Texas] went to that Dallas anti-labor meeting and tried to speak; they were given no chance to (the rally was, of course, about as spontaneous as a mink coat—many of which were worn), and went home and said so—the papers mentioned them. Immediately a judge wrote to the Board of Regents saying that the Economics department was teaching Communism—he ended by demanding that the four men be fired. (*Letters* 60).

At the same time, Jarrell appears to be taunting his friends. Writing to Allen Tate after he had rejected Tate's advice about the contents and arrangement of his first separate book of poems, *Blood For a Stranger* (1942), Jarrell recommends Marxist economist Maurice Dobb's *Political Economy and Capital* (1937), calling it "one of the best books [on economics] I've ever read" (*Letters* 63).

8. In addition to my own "Jarrell's Wicked Fairy," see Diederik Oostdijk's "Randall Jarrell and the Age of Consumer Culture," where he discusses the ways Jarrell's cultural essays from the 1950s and 60s combine "the most pessimistic marxist theoreticians of the Frankfurt school" with "the sociological and psychological (mostly Freudian) insights of Arendt, [Ernest] van den Haag, and [David] Riesman" (128).

9. *Frederick* (1967) centers on a mouse that ruminates while his fellow mice prepare for the winter. A kind of anti-"Grasshopper and the Ant," *Frederick* turns out to be about a poet whose verses entertain the other mice after the stores are depleted. Nodelman objects to the romanticized depiction of the poet, who is a mere conduit for natural images. Certainly his poetry is hackneyed. Making poetry is depicted as relatively effortless in *Frederick*, a matter of pure inspiration rather than making.

10. Following Myers and Knopflmacher's definition of cross-writing, we may distinguish the dialogical from the dialectical. Cross-writing seeks to "dissolve the binaries and contraries that our culture has rigidified and fixed" (viii). For the twenty-eight-year old Jarrell, "a successful poem starts from one position and ends at a very different one, often a contradictory or opposite one; yet there has been no break in the unity of the poem. This unity is generated by the tension set up between strongly differing forces, by the struggle of opposites" ("Levels and Opposites" 699). The difference is exemplified in the contrast between Jarrell's youthful verse and his mature conversational style—the interpersonal style Burt identifies. In a dialogue the different voices (in this case of child and adult) are not so much synthesized out of opposites, but coexist in conversation.

11. Through the magic of the Internet, I have identified this series as *THE U.S. SERVICE SERIES*, by Francis William Rolt-Weaver (published between 1909 and 1929).

12. Jarrell may be alluding to the candy invented by his rich uncle Howell Campbell, Goo-Goo Clusters—stale chocolate poured over rank peanuts—the main sponsor of the Grand Ole Opry. The wealthy Campbell paid his poor nephew's Vanderbilt tuition.

13. One can't help being reminded here of Jarrell's "The Woman at the Washington Zoo" trapped by her aging and the "bars of [her] own body": "You know what I was, you see what I am: change me, change me!" (*Complete Poems* 216).

14. Stephen Burt accuses me of giving "a willfully optimistic reading" of *The Bat-Poet* in my book *Randall Jarrell and the Lost World of Childhood* (254). While I won't defend that reading here, I obviously dissent from Burt's thoroughly pessimistic view: "Since 'The End of the Line' Jarrell had been wondering how a postmodern poet—and himself in particular—might come closer to other people. *The Bat-Poet* seems to answer that he cannot" (154).

WORKS CITED

Arendt, Hannah. "Randall Jarrell." In *Randall Jarrell: 1914–1965*, edited by Robert Lowell, Peter Taylor, and Robert Penn Warren, 3–9. New York: Farrar, 1967.

Brooks, Cleanth. *The Well-Wrought Urn: Studies in the Structure of Poetry*. New York: Harcourt, 1947.

Burt, Stephen, *Randall Jarrell and His Age*. New York: Columbia UP, 2002.

Flynn, Richard. "'The End of the Line': Randall Jarrell, the '30s, and Postmodernism." Unpublished conference paper presented at "The First Postmodernists Conference," National Poetry Foundation, Orono, ME, June 1993. Available on personal website: http://personal.georgiasouthern.edu/~rflynn/JARRELLPM.htm

———. "Jarrell's Wicked Fairy: Cultural Criticism, Childhood, and the 1950s." In *Jarrell, Bishop, Lowell, & Co.: Middle-Generation Poets in Context*, edited by Suzanne Ferguson, 93–112. Knoxville: U of Tennessee P, 2003.

———. *Randall Jarrell and the Lost World of Childhood.* Athens: U of Georgia P, 1990.

Griswold, Jerome. *The Children's Books of Randall Jarrell.* Athens: U of Georgia P, 1988.

Jarrell, Mary. Liner Notes to *Randall Jarrell's* The Bat-Poet *Read by the Author.* New York: Caedmon Cassette, 1972.

Jarrell, Randall. *The Bat-Poet.* Pictures by Maurice Sendak. New York: Macmillan, 1964.

———. *The Complete Poems.* New York: Farrar, 1969.

———. *Kipling, Auden, & Co.: Essays and Reviews 1935–1964.* New York: Farrar, 1980.

———. "Levels and Opposites: Structure in Poetry." *Georgia Review* 50, no. 4 (1996): 697–713.

———. "Libraries. Holograph Lecture (?), unsigned and undated. 24 p. With holograph notes, and holograph draft of possibly unrelated piece, 18 p. Latter relates more to Jarrell's reading than the function of libraries." Berg Collection. New York Public Library.

———. *The Lost World.* New York: Macmillan, 1965.

———. *Pictures from an Institution.* New York: Knopf, 1954.

———. *Poetry and the Age.* New York: Knopf, 1953.

———. *Randall Jarrell's Letters: An Autobiographical and Literary Selection.* Exp. ed. Edited by Mary Jarrell. Charlottesville: U of Virginia P, 2002.

———. Reading. The 92nd Street Y's Poetry Center. 28 April 1963. *New York Times* Audio Special. (Streaming audio). http://www.nytimes.com/books/99/08/01/specials/jarrell-audio.html.

———. *A Sad Heart at the Supermarket: Essays and Fables.* New York: Atheneum, 1962.

Lionni, Leo. *Frederick.* New York: Knopf, 1967.

McGuire, William. *Poetry's Catbird Seat: The Consultantship in Poetry in the English Language at the Library of Congress, 1837–1987.* Washington, DC: Library of Congress, 1988.

Myers, Mitzi, and U. C. Knoepflmacher. "'Cross-Writing' and the Reconceptualizing of Children's Literary Studies." *Children's Literature* 25 (1997): vii–xvii.

Neumeyer, Peter. "Randall Jarrell's The Bat Poet: An Introduction to the Craft." *Children's Literature Association Quarterly* 9, no. 2 (1984): 51–53, 59.

Nodelman, Perry. "The Craft or Sullen Art of a Mouse or a Bat." *Language Arts* 55 (1978): 467–72.

Oostdijk, Diederik. "Randall Jarrell and Consumer Culture." In *Reading the Middle Generation Anew: Culture Community and Form in Twentieth-Century American Poetry*, edited by Eric Haralson, 113–32. Iowa City: U of Iowa P, 2006.

Ransom, John Crowe. "Constellation of Five Young Poets." *The Kenyon Review* 3 (1941): 377–380.

Richards, I. A. *Practical Criticism: A Study of Literary Judgment.* New York: Harvest/Harcourt, 1929.

Sendak, Maurice. "A Western Canon, Jr." HomeArts feature. Archived at http://web.archive.org/web/97801953797855/www.homearts.com/depts/relat/sendakb4.htm (retrieved 28 May 2009).

Thomas, Joseph T., Jr. *Poetry's Playground: The Culture of Contemporary American Children's Poetry*. Detroit: Wayne State UP, 2007.

Travisano, Thomas. *Midcentury Quartet: Bishop, Lowell, Jarrell, Berryman, and the Making of a Postmodern Aesthetic*. Charlottesville: U of Virginia P, 1999.

———, ed. with Saskia Hamilton. *Words in Air: The Complete Correspondence Between Elizabeth Bishop and Robert Lowell*. New York: Farrar, 2008

Willard, Nancy. "*The Bat-Poet*: Radiant Facts." *Field: Contemporary Poetry and Poetics* 35 (Fall 1986): 50–54.

FURTHER READING

Ferguson, Suzanne. *The Poetry of Randall Jarrell*. Baton Rouge: Louisiana State UP, 1971.

Jarrell, Mary von Schrader. *Remembering Randall: A Memoir of Poet, Critic, and Teacher Randall Jarrell*. New York: HarperCollins, 1999.

Jarrell, Randall. *No Other Book: Selected Essays*. Edited and with an introduction by Brad Leithauser. New York: Michael di Capua Books/HarperCollins, 1999.

Longenbach, James. *Modern Poetry after Modernism*. New York: Oxford UP, 1997.

Lowell, Robert, Peter Taylor, and Robert Penn Warren, eds. *Randall Jarrell 1914–1965*. New York: Farrar, 1967.

Pritchard, William. *Randall Jarrell: A Literary Life*. New York: Michael di Capua Books/ Farrar, 1990.

Williamson, Alan. "Jarrell, the Mother, the Märchen." *Twentieth Century Literature* 40, no. 3 (Autumn 1994): 283–99.

CHAPTER 3

ARNOLD LOBEL'S *FROG AND TOAD TOGETHER* AS A PRIMER FOR CRITICAL LITERACY

TEYA ROSENBERG

BORN *in Los Angeles in 1933, Arnold Lobel grew up in Schenectady, New York, where his grandparents raised him after his parents divorced. In his childhood, illnesses kept him out of school regularly, resulting in a sense of isolation from his classmates (Gmuca par. 2). Lobel recalled in an interview that he "was bookish and sort of isolated as a child" and comments: "I read books, drew pictures, and stayed in my room. It wasn't the healthiest thing to do psychologically but it certainly led to my eventual career" (White 489). He graduated with a BFA from the Pratt Institute of Art in Brooklyn in 1955 and married Anita Kempler, a classmate at Pratt, shortly thereafter. The Lobels made their home in Brooklyn for many years, raising two children, Adrianne and Adam.*

Lobel began illustrating children's books for other authors in the early 1960s, and his first author-illustrator effort was A Zoo for Mr. Muster (1962). That book established his predilection for animal characters: Mr. Muster is a human, but the rest of the characters are the zoo animals who love him. Lobel called himself an "unrepentant anthropomorphist" (McCullough 54), and his cast of characters over the years included not only Frog and Toad but also, among others, an owl, a grasshopper, and assorted mice. His Caldecott-winning book, Fables (1981), stars a variety of animal characters whose adventures or eccentricities set up short and often amusing morals. Frog and Toad, his most famous characters, marked a turning point in his writing, Lobel said, in that they resulted from a realization that he could focus less on the child audience and "start writing more out of my own feelings," creating work that "had resonances in my own life" (Rollin 195). His goal was to entertain both children and adults as well as to express himself.

Lobel spent his last years in Manhattan, was diagnosed with AIDS in 1986, and died in 1987, at age fifty-four, of cardiac arrest (Shannon 18, Stout 61). He considered himself "a trained illustrator and a lucky amateur in terms of writing" (Natov and DeLuca 73), but the numerous awards for and the continuing popularity of his stories demonstrate that they resulted from more than training and luck. As Anita Lobel says in Horn Book, *"Arnold's books . . . surpass surface glitter, and they reach beyond the merely cute or topical or trendy" (684). With a keen sense of human nature and of the absurd, Lobel produced many enduring and entertaining books.*

Since their publication in the 1970s, the Frog and Toad books (*Frog and Toad Are Friends* [1970], *Frog and Toad Together* [1972], *Frog and Toad All Year* [1976], and *Days with Frog and Toad* [1979]) by Arnold Lobel have been favorites for many families as well as for teachers. The foibles of short round Toad, prone to irrational outbursts, and leggy lean Frog, always loyal to his friend, are part of many families' traditions as well as the focus of a variety of elementary school lesson plans that use Frog and Toad stories as the basis for teaching reading, social skills (friendship, letter writing), mathematics, geography, philosophy, and biology.[1] When I introduce the course readings for my children's literature survey course, the Frog and Toad book is often the one text that 90 percent or more of the class knows. Popular, funny, and, as beginning chapter books, an important part of the continuum of children's literature from picture books through novels, the Frog and Toad books are classics well worth including not only in grade school curriculum but also in university-level children's literature surveys. They are primers for many kinds of literacy, including analytical, critical reading from a variety of theoretical perspectives.

Introducing the study of children's literature as an academic subject is often challenging. Most students like the literature (especially the brevity) and enjoy the idea of talking about it but often resist thinking critically about it. Such resistance is, of course, not limited to children's literature classes—often people are resisting readers because they think reading analytically and critically "spoils" the story or ruins its entertainment value. Many undergraduate students who take children's literature courses have not yet discovered that, as Roderick McGillis asserts, "Reading critically is a liberating activity," a way of realizing how literature can influence our thinking, and is also "fun" ("Delights" 204).

Breaking down a general resistance to reading critically is paradoxically both easier and more difficult in children's literature classes. On the one hand, students come into class discussions feeling that they understand the readings, which they may not feel with lengthier or more obviously complex texts for adults. They thus feel more confident in making statements or suggestions about analyzing a text. On the other hand, they also often want to defend texts, particularly those treasured from childhood, against too much scrutiny. The protective impulse emerges either from nostalgia for a presumed simpler past or from fear of realizing things they would rather not about a text, themselves, or the society that produced both. Another challenge is that most critical analysis they have done has been chiefly with longer, more complex texts that offer obvious literary elements to study. For many, the simpler the text, the harder it can be to analyze.

Thus, class members are often puzzled when first asked to comment on a Frog and Toad book. Many respond that the characters are cute or that they remember the two amphibians fondly from childhood. Occasionally, students will note a particular story that seems odd or dark, not meeting their expectations. "A Swim" from *Frog and Toad Are Friends*, in which Toad doesn't want Frog or the other creatures to see him in his bathing suit because they'll laugh at him and then they do, and "The Dream" from *Frog and Toad Together*, which has Toad dreaming of his own dramatic magnificence while Frog slowly shrinks and disappears, are examples of stories that do not fulfill expectations of light and humorous stories. Some students point out that Toad seems to have OCD (obsessive-compulsive disorder). On the whole, however, the dominant opinion during the opening discussion of a Frog and Toad book tends to be that there is nothing to say—the stories are too simple and seem to defy analysis. Asking questions and reading more carefully soon reveals the depths of the Frog and Toad stories, illustrating well Jill Paton Walsh's point that "the children's book presents a technically most difficult, technically most interesting problem—that of making a fully serious adult statement . . . and making it utterly simple and transparent. . . . [T]he need for comprehensibility imposes an emotional obliqueness, and indirectness of approach, which like elision and partial statement in poetry is often itself a source of aesthetic power" (192–93). The Frog and Toad stories do indeed make fully adult statements, but their humor and elision veil their complexities.

More to the point, the Frog and Toad stories, because their poetic brevity masks emotional, generic, and social complexities, respond well to examination from a number of literary critical angles. Despite Margery Fisher's discouragingly anti-intellectual warning that the stories should not be subject to the "dreary academic fate" of being analyzed and that "readers . . . be content to share in the sheer enjoyment behind the stories" (2229–30), scrutiny from formal, structural, and cultural perspectives allows a new understanding of the stories and can, for many students, break down resistance to analysis of literature, culture, and their own reactions to both.

Preliminaries

While all four books of the series work well together as a basis for analysis, I usually teach *Frog and Toad Together*, the second in the series and winner of a Newbery Honor award in 1973. By the time we start studying it, we have discussed folktales, picture books, and at least two novels. Most members of the class have accepted the idea that reading experience is not necessarily age specific and that some children have read more than some adults. We work to avoid generalizations about children that suppress exploration of ideas and approaches to the literature. We have discussed literacy in terms of learning letters and words; of learning common literary patterns and recognizing them in multiple texts; of learning codes such as those in picture-book illustrations; and of noticing portrayals of class, race or ethnicity, and gender. The class is, mostly, prepared to tackle *Frog and Toad Together* on multiple levels.

For many, however, *Frog and Toad Together* does cause some return to their position at the start of the semester; again, the seeming simplicity of the stories is a barrier—the stories don't have the obvious journeys or symbolism of folktales such as the Little Red Riding Hood variants we discuss or of novels such as George MacDonald's *The Princess and the Goblin* (1872) or Louise Fitzhugh's *Harriet the Spy* (1964). Nor do the pictures work in the more complicated ways of Sendak's *Where the Wild Things Are* (1963) or Anthony Browne's *Voices in the Park* (1998). To suggest that the text isn't as simple as it initially seems, I introduce mid-twentieth-century debates about engaging young readers that inspired both the I Can Read books from Harper and Brothers and the Beginner Books from Random House. Both series started in 1957, with Harper introducing *Little Bear* by Else Minarik and Maurice Sendak, and Random House introducing Dr. Seuss's *The Cat in the Hat*. While *The Cat in the Hat*'s origins are more firmly situated in a reaction against controlled vocabulary and "look-say" readers such as the Dick and Jane books from the Scott Foresman company (see Nel), both series can be seen as reacting against texts that, in the words of one reading expert, "deny the students the opportunity of reading anything in their readers that is worth reading" (Trace 105). Showing one or two stories from a Dick and Jane reader[2] establishes that in comparison, the five stories of *Frog and Toad Together* have substance, which helps the class start to consider the literary qualities of the book.

SIMPLE? YES, BUT ...

Following the practice of formalism, and particularly of New Criticism, my starting point for analyzing *Frog and Toad Together* is to look closely at how literary elements convey unity and complexities. Over the past forty or so years, formalism, and especially New Criticism, has lost the prestige it had when it developed in the 1920s and 30s, but the principle of looking closely at the text remains the starting point of most literary studies. When it comes to analyzing children's literature, however, even the most seasoned literary scholars, if they haven't studied it before, tend to forget that basic approach. Distracted by the term "children's," readers focus only on audience response and neglect what the literature does. As Terry Eagleton points out, the New Critics discouraged such response:

> The New Critics broke boldly with the Great Man theory of literature, insisting that the author's intentions in writing, even if they could be recovered, were of no relevance to the interpretation of his or her text. Neither were the emotional responses of particular readers to be confused with the poem's meaning: the poem meant what it meant, regardless of the poet's intentions or the subjective feeling the reader derived from it. (1–42)

Adopting the approach of New Criticism can be a useful starting point for examining children's literature, encouraging readers to put aside generalizations about what children know, like, and/or are capable of understanding. It also forces them, as Perry Nodelman and Mavis Reimer urge, to pay attention to their own responses and observations and in turn to pay attention to and respect the text (16). Ultimately, it improves critical literacy by encouraging a focus on recognizing and understanding literary elements within a text, even one with such basic language as *Frog and Toad Together*.[3]

Since the initial reaction is that *Frog and Toad Together* is "simple," I ask students to list the elements of the stories that are simple. This list usually includes the diction: the words are generally common and of one or two syllables. Along with the simple words, the sentences also tend to be simple, literally so. The majority of the sentences have one main clause only, although in many cases, those sentences will include phrases, so that the sentences, while at times abrupt, are closer to real speech than those of readers such as the Dick and Jane series. There are occasional compound or complex sentences although these are not terribly complicated. Besides the diction and syntax, other literary elements are similarly simple at first glance. The five stories have brief and uncomplicated plot arcs with few characters: Frog and Toad and just a few bit parts played by other small creatures. The characterization of the two main characters occurs mostly through their actions and dialogue, with few adjectives, and the settings are rarely described.

All of this simplicity of plot, character, and setting are located in the words, or verbal text. The books are illustrated, and Lobel considered them picture books. Adding the pictures, or visual text, to the discussion introduces ground that New Critics, with their tight focus on the verbal art of poetry and complex fiction, wouldn't have thought to explore. As McGillis points out about discussions of the illustrated work of William Blake, "only in the wake of the New Criticism has the connection between Blake's two artistic methods been explored" (*Nimble Reader* 41). That is, with the growth during the later twentieth century of more interdisciplinary critical approaches to literature, reading pictures as literary element became possible. Picture books can benefit from formalism's close reading, but as Nodelman notes, reading picture books is an inherently complex act because it requires interpreting two different sorts of text simultaneously (*Words about Pictures* 20–21).

One of the complexities of *Frog and Toad Together* is that nearly all the descriptive details, whether about setting or character, come from the visual text.

The pictures communicate that Frog and Toad live in a rural or suburban area, full of trees, meadows, and flowers in the summer stories and lots of unsullied snow in the winter stories. They live in snug little houses with leaded pane windows, surrounded by flowers, with nice china and comfortable beds. They have access to rivers and woods and hills. The setting contributes to characterization as well: the flowers, grasses, other animals such as birds, turtles, mice, and so on indicate the size of Frog and Toad as mostly to scale with actual frogs and toads. Only occasionally are there departures, usually when trees are included in the pictures. On the page reproduced below, from "The Surprise" in *Frog and Toad All Year*, the first picture suggests either that Frog is human-sized or that the trees are miniature. In the second picture, Toad walks through grass that better represents a realistic scale (*All Year* 45); that is, the grass is human-sized and Toad is toad-sized (fig. 3.1).

In general, though, the pictures communicate that Frog and Toad are an actual frog and toad, in size and other physical attributes, thus contributing to a paradox: are Frog and Toad animals or humans? They are the size we know frogs and toads should be, yet they are also humans. They wear what my students call "old man clothes": belted trousers and tweedy-looking jackets. They walk instead of hop, they live in houses, and they eat cookies, ice cream, and sandwiches rather than insects. The balance between animal and human is a tension that can never be resolved in favor of one or the other; they are always both.

A further paradox is that Frog and Toad are simultaneously adults and children. That is, they live alone in their own homes, they have possessions such as fine china, and, upon occasion, they indulge in a glass of wine (see frontispiece of *Frog and Toad Together*), all elements associated with adult lives. On the other hand, they lack the adult responsibilities of jobs and bills and enjoy activities associated with children: flying kites, eating cookies, or playing leap frog (*Together*), while in other books, they go sledding (*All Year*) and unsuccessfully deal with oversized ice cream cones (*All Year*). While these activities do not belong exclusively to childhood, they are expressions of freedoms and attitudes associated with children.

The paradoxes created through the visuals and resulting characterization add a level of complexity reinforced by the presence of irony in the stories. Paradox and irony are two elements that New Critics particularly admire and look for as an indication of literary artistry (see Eagleton 45 and Richter 707), especially when those paradoxes and ironies unify and are unified by theme. The thematic unity of *Frog and Toad Together* exists in the overall idea of "together" that the title introduces, reinforced by the composition of the frontispiece, in which Frog and Toad sit on either side of a fireplace drinking wine with their hands and feet creating a circle, and by the picture of the two flying a kite, connected to each other by the string they both hold (table of contents). The final picture and words of the last story similarly reinforce the theme as they play leapfrog and have "a fine, long day together" (64). Visually and verbally, the opening and closing of the book establish the thematic unity of the book, which provides a framework for exploring the individual stories and how they refine that larger idea of togetherness.

Frog ran through the woods

so that Toad would not see him.

Toad ran through the high grass

so that Frog would not see him.

Figure 3.1. Copyright © 1976 by Arnold Lobel. Used by permission of HarperCollins Publishers.

The stories constantly challenge and complicate that unifying theme. The first story, "A List," opens with Toad alone writing his list. Although Frog appears in three of the items on the list, Toad's insistence that he can do nothing once the list blows away creates a physical separation between the friends as Frog runs after the list and then a more abstract separation as Toad remains focused on his inability to act. The resolution of the situation occurs only when Frog inadvertently mentions an item on the list, allowing Toad to write "Go to sleep" and cross it out, freeing him from the stasis created by the lost list and uniting them in sleep (16–17). Ironically, Toad endows the physical list with far more significance than the activities it describes.

"A List" establishes a pattern that shows up in the next story, "The Garden," in which Toad initiates an action, Frog supports him even when Toad takes the situation in absurd directions, and a resolution occurs in which Toad clearly has not learned the obvious lesson. Toad initiates a situation, as he did with the creation of the list, by admiring Frog's garden and wanting to create his own. Through his lack of understanding about seeds and his impatience, he becomes frustrated, but Frog's knowledge and advice redirect that frustration: Toad no longer yells at the seeds but instead keeps them company and reads, sings, and plays violin to them. He ultimately despairs because they still don't grow. Of course, eventually the seeds do sprout, but Toad has no conception that they grow despite his actions. In "The Garden," the lesson seems to be that seeds will grow given sun, water, and time— Frog's advice (23)—but Toad's conclusion is that creating a garden is hard work. The fact that he is correct complicates the basic irony of Toad's misunderstanding: creating a garden is hard work, but not for the reasons Toad thinks. In this second story, another level of irony becomes apparent—it is an irony predicated on knowledge of a convention of children's literature in which the experiences within a text are lessons for the characters. In this case, Toad does not learn a lesson about how seeds grow, thus mocking and subverting that convention.

"Cookies," the third story of the collection, demonstrates yet another variation on the pattern of Toad initiating an action that escalates into a problem and on the irony of a lesson not learned. In this case, Toad bakes cookies, and they are so tasty that he and Frog are tempted to overeat. This story most obviously offers a lesson, and Frog is the voice of that lesson: use willpower to counter the problem of overeating. But Toad actively resists and undermines the lesson. After Frog's multiple attempts to put the cookies away and his final solution of giving the cookies to the birds, Toad rejects Frog's willpower—"You may keep it all"—and asserts his desire to eat more sweet food: "I am going home now to bake a cake" (41). Toad shifts from being the butt of ironic undermining of lessons to actively challenging the lesson.

In the first three stories, then, the plots create humorous irony in the absurdity of Toad's views, in the conflict between the two characters, and in the challenge to notions of children's stories as teaching the characters and thus the audience. The final two stories complicate the patterns. The first words of "Dragons and Giants" highlight the unifying concept: "Frog and Toad were reading a book together" (42). Inspired by their reading, they embark on a quest to discover if they are brave. After encountering a snake, an avalanche, and a hawk, they run home and hide, declaring admiration for each other's bravery (50) and "just feeling brave together" (51). This story breaks the pattern of Frog as rational, knowledgeable adult and Toad as irrational, naive child, presenting both characters as vulnerable and lacking understanding. An irony lies in Frog and Toad asserting an understanding of bravery that does not correspond to a common definition—they do not face their fears or overcome foes. Further irony exists with the point that the story could be considered a *Don Quixote* for inexperienced readers. As with Cervantes's classic, it interrogates the conventions of romance and fairy tales in which those who "fight dragons and giants . . . are never afraid" (42). Reality is dangerous, and fairy tales, this story suggests, don't give helpful information for how to deal with that danger. Frog and Toad, however, do show an appropriate response in running away from danger—thus, irony exists also in contradicting the textual authority of fairy tales.[4]

The final story of the book further breaks the patterns of the earlier stories and complicates the theme of togetherness. It departs from the structure of Frog as guide and Toad as unconscious or unwilling student, and it undermines the balance and equality between the two found in "Dragons and Giants." The title of the story, "The Dream," and the opening sentence signal that the story is entering the territory of the psyche: "Toad was asleep, and he was having a dream" (52). In his dream, Toad is on stage and his elaborate Elizabethan costume with its enormous hat emphasizes his highly dramatic personality as does his position in the pictures: in most of them he is in the higher position, occupying a majority of the space while Frog is usually below Toad in the audience. The verbal text establishes the egocentric nature of the dream through both content and typography, with all capital letters stressing the volume of the pronouncements: "PRESENTING THE GREATEST TOAD IN ALL THE WORLD!" (53). The list of Toad's skills—he plays the piano "VERY WELL" (54), walks a high wire without falling (56), and dances wonderfully (58)—and his constant questioning of whether Frog can do as well further the egocentric nature of the dream and Toad's desire to dominate his knowledgeable friend.

The effect on Frog, however, demonstrates the problematic nature of Toad's assertion of superiority. With every accomplishment and query, Frog "looked smaller" (54) until he finally disappears. When Toad realizes that Frog is "so small that he could not be seen or heard" (59), he literally goes into a tailspin (60–61), but he first acknowledges that Frog's diminution is his fault: "'Frog, what have I done?' cried Toad" (59). He rejects the "strange voice from far away" that has been announcing his greatness, screaming at it to "shut up!" (60). Since multiple voices or characters in dreams are usually seen as manifestations of the dreamer's self, Toad rejects a previously unacknowledged egocentric part of himself, the part that estranges him from Frog. The end of the story affirms the rightness of that rejection as Toad, woken by Frog who is his "own right size" (62), notices the sunshine outside and expresses his pleasure that Frog is there. In turn, Frog states his loyalty and the continuity of their friendship:

"Frog," [Toad] said,
"I am so glad
that you came over."
"I always do," said Frog.

"The Dream" is perhaps the darkest and most complex of the stories, not only offering irony in Toad's need to assert himself but also exploring the potential for considering the reality of relationships.[5] Friendship often does include competition, however suppressed it might be, and the story also suggests that Frog's guiding nature sometimes seems condescending or dominating to Toad. Lobel comments, in answering Lucy Rollin's question about why he stopped writing Frog and Toad stories, that "it . . . occurred to me, when I was writing the last [book], that there was a certain cruelty in the relationship, in Frog being the controlling one and Toad being controlled . . . and I perceived something there that I didn't want to continue" (192). Although he says he didn't notice it until the final book (*Days with Frog and Toad*), that pattern of controlling and controlled, and rebellion against it, is already present in "The Dream."

As I have discussed, the five stories resonate with multiple levels of irony, an element New Critics particularly like to find in literature as proof of its sophistication. The question that often arises in discussion of irony in children's literature, however, is whether the intended audience actually perceives it. In response to such a question, a New Critic would say, "Who cares? The irony is there and it helps unify a seemingly disparate group of stories." That question about audience, however, speaks to the larger challenge of resistance to analyzing children's literature. One way of resisting is to assert that the implied audience (children) will not notice the ideas analysis reveals, the implication being that if the implied audience does not notice, neither should other readers. One way to counter such resistance is to bring actual child readers into the discussion. Gareth B. Matthews, in "Children, Irony and Philosophy," deals with exactly this question of perceiving irony. He notes that although *Frog and Toad Together* is directed to children of five or six learning to read on their own, the stories are suitable for reading aloud to younger children, and furthermore, that children do recognize different humorous elements, including irony, quite early. Matthews presents as evidence his discussions about "The Garden" with his four-year-old grandson, Julian, demonstrating in the process that Julian does indeed perceive irony in the story:

> I asked Julian specifically about the last line of the story, that is, Toad's comment, "You were right, Frog, it was very hard work." He said it was funny because what Toad did "wasn't really hard work." It wasn't really hard work, Julian explained because the things Toad did, such as reading the seeds a story, reading them poems, or playing music to them, "didn't really help," that is, didn't help make the seeds grow. (85)

Julian also understood that Toad shouting at the seeds wasn't helpful either and asserted that the seeds themselves would tell Toad that they just need time (85). While anecdotal evidence from one child/adult conversation is not conclusive, acknowledging that at least one four-year-old can perceive and understand irony does thwart many students' dismissal of discussing its presence and validates noticing not only irony but also other potential complexities in and about the stories, such as their place within literary historical genres.

GENRES OF FROG AND TOAD

To identify *Frog and Toad Together* as children's literature, and even more specifically as an early reader, is to classify it. Each label creates certain expectations about the book's content and how it operates. Genre criticism adds author and particularly audience back into critical analysis, for the codes of genres both manipulate and are manipulated by authors and they guide readers (Todorov 18–19). Within the very broad genre of children's literature, *Frog and Toad Together* can be placed in a variety of genres such as primer, picture book, or animal fantasy. Considering the text from the perspective of genre contributes to critical literacy by introducing that elements within a story can have different meanings depending on the genre focus used to examine it. Analyzing *Frog and Toad Together* as animal fantasy, for example, means looking at the ways it fulfills the codes of that genre, the chief of which is the use of anthropomorphized animals.[6] While the New Critical approach encourages focusing on that convention as paradox, the use of animals as representative of humans brings other consideration to the discussion. Lobel discusses using animal characters as a way of avoiding cultural or social specificity:

> By using animals, by pulling it away from everybody, everything, you bring it to
> everybody. I mean, Frog and Toad belong to no one but they belong to everyone,
> every sector: rich children, poor children, white children, black children.
> Everybody can relate to Frog and Toad because they don't exist in this world.
> (Natov and DeLuca 95)

Lobel's assessment corresponds to that of David Rudd, who writes that animals "are frequently used in children's literature as a way [of] eliding problematic issues which . . . include those of ethnicity, sexuality, and childhood as a dependent site" (40). Lobel's additional comments about employing animal characters in his fiction support Rudd's analysis. Lobel says that he finds animal characters useful "because you can give animals the freedom of adults while they still maintain the attitudes of children" (Natov and DeLuca 95), one of the paradoxes of the stories.

The freedom Lobel found in using animal characters he also found in creating the world in which Frog and Toad live:

> I'm very careful in the stories not to make any direct allusions to modern life. . . .
> Frog and Toad don't call each other on the telephone. Toad takes a walk, and he
> visits Frog. He could, I suppose, pick up the telephone and call, but that would be
> too much, the world would be too much with them. (Natov and DeLuca 95)

He goes on to say that leaving out the technology creates "a wider audience" for the stories. In creating a world without technology, he creates a pastoral world, and the connection to the genre of the pastoral reveals and adds depth to some elements of the Frog and Toad stories.

In the context of the pastoral, the brevity of early reader sentences and stories takes on new significance. They reflect the original form of pastoral lyrics, which were similarly succinct, and Lobel's use of dialogue resembles the focus on dialogues or exchanges in that early poetry (Shannon 87–88). Such association pushes brevity from a utilitarian purpose (help beginning readers) into a more artistic realm (association with ancient poetic tradition). In the one book-length scholarly study of Arnold Lobel's work, *Arnold Lobel* (1989), George Shannon draws attention to the ways that the Frog and Toad stories adhere to the pastoral traditions, but he also uses those elements to look closely at the methods by which Lobel creates his characters and their world: the pictures with their muted colors, the interactions between the two characters, and the use of repetition and rhythm in the words. In a sense, Shannon's reading resembles that of a New Critic, but rather than finding a unity of complexities, he discusses Frog and Toad's appeal to readers. He finds that the conventions of the pastoral contribute to the comedy in the stories, the humor that pushes the series from a gentle and sometimes stagnant nostalgia so often the fate of the pastoral to a lively exploration of the dynamics of a relationship.

In the Frog and Toad stories, the humor comes from the dichotomy of the two characters' roles. As Shannon notes, the pastoral has many binaries: city and country, art and nature, past and present, and so on. Frog and Toad, he suggests are "the pastoral personified. Toad is a slug-a-bed, while Frog is forever saying 'Let's go!' . . . Toad is impulse, while Frog is reason" (95). Shannon writes, the "appreciation of coexisting opposites . . . and incongruities that is the base of the pastoral is also the heart of Lobel's comic perception" (98). The binaries that Shannon perceives as pastoral and comic are also at the heart of a theory about tragedy and its origins. In *The Birth of Tragedy* (1871), Friedrich Nietzsche developed the terms "the Apollonian" and "the Dionysian" to describe artistic impulses within a culture that led to the creation of tragic drama, but over time they have also come to mean impulses or characterizations within literary texts. Frog and Toad's interactions resemble the Apollonian drive for order and restraint in tension with the Dionysian drive to the impulsive and hysterical; the tension tipping from balance into conflict creates humorous effects and thus ironic tragedy, also known as comedy.

Often, after discussing Frog and Toad for a while, someone in class will mention similarities to *Grumpy Old Men* (1993), with Walter Matthau and Jack Lemmon, a movie in which the two actors reprise the dynamic they originated in *The Odd Couple* (1968). Once comedy duos enter the discussion, the names of similar teams come fast and furious: Lloyd and Harry of *Dumb and Dumber* (1994), Ernie and Bert from *Sesame Street* (1969–present), Lucy and Ethel from *I Love Lucy* (1951–60), Ralph Kramden and Ed Norton from *The Honeymooners* (1955–56). Some students will go further back in time, mentioning Laurel and Hardy or Abbott and Costello. They are not alone in making those connections; Joseph Stanton, in "Straight Man and Clown in the Picture Books of Arnold Lobel" similarly identifies "Abbott and Costello, Lewis and Martin, Lucille Ball and Desi Arnez, Tom and Dicky Smothers" as teams similar to Frog and Toad (76). While many of Stanton's examples are not well known to students these days, they are nonetheless delighted to make connections to the movie and television culture that they know more thoroughly than the literary traditions we have been discussing up until that point.

In *Comedy* (2005), Andrew Stott suggests that "the theme of comedy as a divided and doubled experience is . . . embodied for us in the double act, a staple of comic performance since the appearance of Dionysus and his servant Xanthias in Aristophanes' *Frogs* (405 BC)" (9). Generally, comedy duos have a straight man and a clown, and one can certainly argue that Frog is the straight man and Toad the clown, as Stanton does, describing Frog as "a calmly reasonable foil" to Toad's "excessively emotional, overreacting clown" (76). A closer look, however, at the comic dynamic between Frog and Toad complicates this description.

The humor of Frog and Toad's interactions comes from the presence of the Apollonian/Dionysian binary in flux. Before and after conflict, the binary elements are held in a tension that is complementary—each contributing to the functioning of their friendship. In "Cookies," Toad bakes tasty cookies and Frog willingly takes part in enjoying them. When both have satiated any hunger they might have, Frog's reaction is to stop eating while Toad wants to continue the pleasure of eating. Conflict arises as Frog urges restraint and Toad pursues excess, but it never becomes tragic, and the triviality is amusing. The conflict also represents a situation familiar to the implied audience: the child's desire to eat more cookies in a struggle with the parental dictum of restraint. In this case, "Cookies" is subversive because although Frog wins the struggle about the cookies, Toad undermines parental authority through his agency: he may be a Dionysian child figure, but he has adult autonomy to return to his own home and bake a cake.

The dynamic between the Apollonian and the Dionysian does not remain the same in every story. Sometimes Frog's Apollonian tendencies simply stand back and let Toad's Dionysian excess or irrationality run its course, as in "A List," when Toad is paralyzed by the loss of his list, or in "The Garden," when Toad's absurd strategies to encourage the seeds' growth must simply play out until Toad "felt very tired, and he fell asleep" (27). Yet another variant is apparent in those stories in which Frog not only goes along with but also succumbs to the Dionysian, as in "Dragons and Giants," when, in their quest out into the natural world to discover whether or not they are brave, both are overcome by panic.[7] The shifting roles Frog plays as foil to Toad both relates to and diverges from the routines of well-known comedy duos. Turning the discussion to those examples draws on students' knowledge of popular film and television but also opens possibilities for exploring further dimensions beyond paradox, irony, and comedy in Frog and Toad's relationship.

TOGETHER INDEED: GENDER AND SEXUALITY

The majority of popular comedy duos are same sex, a point that introduces considerations of gender and sexuality. Such discussion in children's literature classes often produces as much or more resistance than literary analysis itself. The resistance seems mainly a product of discomfort in connecting childhood with supposedly "adult" concerns, although for some people it also comes from reservations about challenging what they consider norms of identity. Considering gender roles produces somewhat less resistance than discussing sexuality, possibly because gender discussions have been occurring publicly longer than those of sexuality and also because gender is less threatening to ideas of childhood innocence than sexual identity. In terms of gaining critical literacy, analyzing the portrayal of gender and sexuality introduces students to New Criticism's almost polar opposite: considering the author's biography often is part of the process as is paying attention to social and cultural ideologies and to individual responses and beliefs.[8]

For discussing gender, we focus on comparing cultural constructions (masculine and feminine) with biological designations (male and female). People seem to be more aware of the differences between the terms than they were ten or more years ago, and, recently, class members have started pointing out that those binaries do not account for the spectrum of gender possibilities. Having definitions develop from class discussion usually helps counter resistance to applying the terms to Frog and Toad because there is less sense that they are being forced to adopt ideas not their own.

Although the definitions may vary slightly from class to class or semester to semester, the basic idea established is that masculine and feminine roles are not essentially male or female and are somewhat arbitrarily connected to certain traits. Rationality, calmness, and dominance are considered masculine while illogic, hysteria, and submission are labeled feminine. If the class hasn't already made the connection between the binaries of comedy and of gender, then I point out that the straight man/clown binary often lends itself to discussion in terms of masculine and feminine. The straight man is often a more masculine role while the clown occupies the more feminine role. Initially, it seems as though Frog occupies the masculine role while Toad's role is feminine, but closer examination shows that they complicate this, as they do the straight man and clown binary but in somewhat different ways: Toad may bake cookies and cakes, but he frequently dominates, determining the activities when they are together. Frog is usually the rational one, but he also nurtures Toad with constant support and encouragement.

The nature of the same-sex comedy duo further complicates the straight man and clown roles. One partner has to assume gender identity not usually associated with his or her biological identity, but also the intensity of the relationship and constant companionship is more usually associated with marriage, which introduces the topic of sexuality. Lawrence J. Epstein, in *Mixed Nuts: America's Love Affair with Comedy Teams* (2004), observes about Laurel and Hardy: "Sometimes [they] seem less a team than a couple. Some observers have suggested that homoerotic elements are present in a few of their films" (90). He describes routines that support those suggestions, ones that have bedroom scenes with the two characters or slapstick involving the loss of clothing. There are no directly sexual elements, a point Douglas Brode makes: "Though there is no overt homosexuality in any Laurel and Hardy film . . . there is, all the same, a clear element of homoeroticism" (287). That homoeroticism is not obvious in Frog and Toad—there is no overt sexuality in any of the stories—so perhaps the better term is "homosocial," indicating a close same-sex friendship that is not sexual. As Eve Kosofsky Sedgwick points out in *Between Men: English Literature and Male Homosocial Desire* (1985), heterosexuality in most Western culture defines itself in opposition to homosexuality. The homosocial, particularly male homosocial, is often marked by homophobia as a way of maintaining an opposition that supports the patriarchy. Sedgwick's argument is, at its heart, a feminist examination of male power, but her sense that the homosocial is never entirely separate from sexuality and homophobia has ramifications for studying comedy duos in general and Frog and Toad in particular. The appropriate term for their partnership may be homosocial, but the suggestion of homosexuality is always a part of that term.[9] *Frog and Toad Together* illustrates Sedgwick's argument with incidents that suggest a gay subtext: In "Dragons and Giants," when they run home after encountering the snake, the avalanche, and the hawk, Toad "jumped into the bed and pulled the covers over his head" while Frog "jumped into the closet and shut the door" (50). They both "stayed there for a long time, just feeling very brave together" (51). When I read this passage aloud, students pick up immediately on Frog "being in the closet," a term for a homosexual who has not publicly announced or acknowledged his or her sexual identity. In "Alone" the last story in *Days with Frog and Toad* (the final Frog and Toad book), the end describes Frog and Toad being "two close friends sitting alone together" (64) and the picture shows them on an island with their arms around each other (fig. 3.2).

Lobel's biography supports the homosexual possibilities suggested by these and other elements of the series. Shannon notes that Lobel was homosexual (11), something he acknowledged late in his life and after many years of marriage. Lobel and his wife, Anita, separated in the early 1980s (8), and Lobel had a male companion for the last years of his life (16). The point here is not to out Lobel; presumably since

Figure 3.2. Copyright © 1976 by Arnold Lobel. Used by permission of HarperCollins Publishers.

Shannon acknowledges the help of Adam and Adrianne, Lobel's children, in writing his study of the author/illustrator, Lobel's sexuality is not a secret.[10] His background, however, supports reading Frog and Toad as not just homosocial, but potentially closeted homosexual.

The reaction to such discussion is the most interesting part of the approach. At this point, students in my classes tend to respond in much the way Kenneth Kidd describes his classes reacting to a reductive queer reading of *Wind in the Willows*, protesting that the story cannot be "about *that*," or convinced that Lobel has, as Kidd says of Grahame, "smuggled a homosexual plot into an otherwise respectable children's book" (115). They are not alone in their reaction. Many of the discussions that acknowledge the homoerotic possibilities of comedy duos' routines protest or dismiss the reading. Brode says, "Ultimately, it matters less whether one buys the homosexual reading of Laurel and Hardy's 'love' than that they are indeed perceived as loving each other. Whether it is homosexual or platonic is none of our business" (287), while Epstein argues that "ultimately the Laurel and Hardy characters are not concerned with eroticism at all. Their characters are boyish, innocent, steeped in Victorian morality and protected by their childlike natures from all the nasty realities that come with adulthood" (91). Epstein's language suggests the fears people have about noting sexuality in children's texts: he presents the child and childhood ("boyish" and "childlike") as unconnected with "nasty" sexuality. Although students hesitate to discuss the basis of their negative reaction, it seems to come from fears of predation and pedophilia as well as the desire to maintain the perception of innocence, purity, and simplicity in childhood—ideas that for many people are incommensurate with any form of sexuality.

Students and critics of comedy are not alone in their fears. Self-identified gay writers have noticed and commented on the homosocial in Frog and Toad stories, and they too resist a more sexual reading. Christopher Bram, writing in *Christopher Street*, a gay arts magazine, lauds the Frog and Toad books for the depiction of friendship, which he does not see portrayed as well in much of children's literature. Toward the end of the article, he addresses the audience:

> By now, you are probably wondering, both because of this review and the nature
> of the magazine you are reading, if Frog and Toad might possibly be, well, gay.
> True, they do not sleep together or even share the same house, but the intensity
> of their attentions and worries certainly point in a homosexual direction. I do not
> want to entertain that possibility. (61)

Bram goes on to argue that the relationship possesses the fervor of childhood friendships when "we are not bound by authority or physical need" (61). He seems to want to maintain the fiction of purity associated with children and childhood.[11] Bram wrote in 1981, a time before same-sex marriage was a topic of public legal and political conversations. In 2007, in a blog titled "Frog and Toad Are Gay," another author is more candid about seeing Frog and Toad as role models for gay couples:

> The "I Can Read" children's four-book series, "Frog and Toad," is a primer for
> same-sex relationships. Whether you and your buddy are "best friends forever"

or a married couple, this series will model the skills needed to have a long-term same sex relationship. The series takes you through the everyday circumstances of Frog and Toad with simplicity and humor, without moralizing, on what characterizes an enduring gay relationship: compassion, affection, gratitude, generosity, creativity, thoughtfulness, laughter, and sharing life together.

This almost naive reading of the relationship between Frog and Toad ignores the more complicated aspects of their friendship, and ironically, the writer says the same things that students say during opening discussions of *Frog and Toad To-gether*, when they see the stories as chiefly teaching the positive elements of platonic friendship. The candor, and sweetness, of the blog entry, with its sense of having escaped homophobia, is undermined by the final comment in the comments section of the blog: "you are fucking gay idiots get a life you ignorant bastards," a reaction that brilliantly illustrates Sedgwick's ideas about the homosocial: homophobia may be challenged, but it is not dead.[12]

In any case, this blog entry about the Frog and Toad series brings the conversation back to my original point: the Frog and Toad books are primers, teaching their audience many things: how to read, how to analyze literature, or how to be partners in a supportive relationship. The resistance to reading the characters as gay connects with the homophobic nature of culture but also with their being in children's books. Just as students, thinking of children's texts only in terms of utilitarian effects on audience and lulled by the seeming simplicity of the stories, initially do not see anything much to talk about in *Frog and Toad Together*, so too a general sense that children, and thus children's stories, have no connection to "adult concerns" such as sexuality leads to reaction against considering the presence of such concerns. This response occurs despite the fact that children live in the adult world and are exposed constantly to adult concerns in their lives.

The ideological constructions of culture and society about children often block deeper critical thought about children's literature. Another example of such blocking is how easily students agree with Lobel's comment that using animals as characters allows them to "belong to everyone, every sector: rich children, poor children, white children, black children. Everybody can relate to Frog and Toad" (Natov and DeLuca 95). Only after I've asked them to look more carefully at the lifestyle Frog and Toad lead and especially to consider what the pictures show about their homes do some people start to mention that not everyone has pretty cottages in the country, nor do all people have fine china or leisure to sit in front of a fire sipping wine. Frog and Toad are very middle class, but that secure, suburban life with its amenities is so thoroughly ingrained as the default North American life, even though many people do not actually possess it, that a number of readers don't even notice the class ramifications of Frog and Toad's lifestyle. My intention is that by the end of discussing *Frog and Toad Together*, students have gained some ideas and approaches to analysis that encourage them to question that which they have previously taken for granted (results may, and do, vary). The three approaches used here, New Criticism, genre studies, and gender studies, are starting places. If one has time, then there is much that could be said using Marxist and psychoanalytic approaches, for example.

In her comment that readers should "share the sheer enjoyment behind the stories," Margery Fisher is right. They should not, however, consider analyzing the Frog and Toad series "a dreary academic fate" (2229). As Nodelman and Reimer suggest in *The Pleasures of Children's Literature*, thinking and pleasure are not binary opposites (22–23). Analyzing literature offers pleasures as well. In the case of Frog and Toad, looking more closely at their stories, considering the conventions of genres to which those stories belong, and noticing the nature of the relationship reveal not only the complexities of the stories, but also the artistry of conveying so much with such brevity, showing that Lobel's famous I Can Read series not only stands up to analysis but also rewards it with multiple levels of meaning that enhance children's literature classes, breaking down resistance and, one hopes, increasing knowledge as well as pleasure.

NOTES

1. For examples of lesson plans, see Scott, Schultz, Epps, Geist and Tarlow, and Wartenberg.

2. I show the first story of *Guess Who* (circa 1951), "Dick," which consists of the following verbal text: "Look, Dick. Look, look. Oh, oh. Look, Dick. Oh, oh. See Dick. Oh, see Dick" (5–8). Without the pictures, there is no plot. In fact, the most interesting thing about *Guess Who* and other Dick and Jane books is that the pictures do much of the narrative work.

3. For a helpful, brief overview of New Criticism, see Richter (703–8). For a more in-depth introductions to New Criticism, see Robert Dale Parker (chap. 2) and Roderick McGillis in *The Nimble Reader* (chap. 2).

4. Frog and Toad running away from predators also connects with the tension between being human and being animal: they read as humans but react as animals.

5. Lobel comments in one interview that the story was based on "a very particular relationship I have with a friend who tends to be an expert in one-upmanship" (Natov and DeLuca 77).

6. Animal fantasy differs from animal realism, in which the animal characters have no human consciousness or none that the readers can access. Examples are *The Black Stallion* (1941) by Walter Farley or *Old Yeller* (1956) by Fred Gipson.

7. The word is particularly suitable in this case, given its Greek origin as a description of the reaction to seeing or experiencing Pan, the Greek god of nature, in all his beauty and danger.

8. Because many students express some discomfort with using sexuality as an approach to analyzing *Frog and Toad Together*, I often point out that seeing the book as depicting a gay relationship is one possible reading among many. While critics and teachers committed to political awareness and change may find such reassurance annoying, I do believe that leaving an escape route for the discomfited is better than having students reject critical analysis and interpretation completely.

9. Over the past couple of semesters, the term "bromance" has started coming up when we discuss the homosocial, and it seems to defuse tension and open up discussion.

Although it has yet to be included in mainstream dictionaries, "bromance" is increasingly used to describe television and film comedies about same-sex friendships that are very intense. It seems that Hollywood has succeeded in assuring mainstream society that such friendships are not threatening to the patriarchal, heterosexual status quo, usually by having at least one of the friends enter a heterosexual marriage. (Setoodeh, "Isn't it Bromantic?")

    10. Lobel and Frog and Toad are memorialized with a block in the AIDS Quilt, not itself an indication of being gay, but demonstrating that his illness was not a secret.

    11. Bram's description of childhood friendship has strong resemblances to the points made by a number of cultural critics about the modern (i.e., post-Enlightenment) view of childhood. See particularly Anne Higonnet, *Pictures of Innocence*.

    12. As of July 2010, the comments section had expanded with an additional homophobic comment from a father citing biblical chapter and verse and a reply, in verse, from the blog author, both of which illustrate well the ideologies surrounding childhood.

WORKS CITED

Bram, Christopher. "Little Green Buddies." *Christopher Street* 5, no. 6 (May 1981): 59–61.

Brode, Douglas. "Stan Laurel and Oliver Hardy: Yin and Yang." In *Fools and Jesters in Literature, Art, and History: A Bio-Bibliographical Sourcebook*, edited by Vicki K. Janik, 281–89. Westport, CT: Greenwood, 1998.

Eagleton, Terry. *Literary Theory: An Introduction*. 2nd ed. Minneapolis: U of Minnesota P, 1996.

Epps, Jonna. "Frog and Toad: A Lost Button." *The Educator's Reference Desk*. Information Institute of Syracuse. May 1994. Web. 2 February 2009.

Epstein, Lawrence J. *Mixed Nuts: America's Love Affair with Comedy Teams*. New York: Public Affairs, 2004.

Fisher, Margery. Review of *Frog and Toad Together*, by Arnold Lobel. *Growing Point* 12 (October 1973): 2229–30.

"Frog and Toad Are Gay." *Guy Dads*. 16 November 2007. Web. 20 January 2009.

Geist, Ellen, and Ellen Tarlow. *Teaching with Favorite Arnold Lobel Books*. New York: Scholastic, 2005.

Gmuca, Jacqueline. "Arnold Lobel." In *Dictionary of Literary Biography*. Vol. 61, *American Writers for Children since 1960: Poets, Illustrators, and Nonfiction Authors*, 165–76. Detroit: Gale, 1987. *Literature Resource Center*. Web. 1 February 2009.

Gray, William S., May Hill Arbuthnot, and A. Sterl Artley. *Guess Who*. Illustrated by Corinne Boyd Dillon. Toronto: Gage, [n.d.].

Higonnet, Anne. *Pictures of Innocence: The History and Crisis of Ideal Childhood*. New York: Thames and Hudson, 1998.

Kidd, Kenneth. "Introduction: Lesbian/Gay Literature for Children and Young Adults." *Children's Literature Association Quarterly* 23, no. 3 (1998): 114–15.

Lobel, Anita. "*Frog and Toad Are Friends*." *Horn Book* 76, no. 6 (2000): 684–85. *Academic Search Complete*. Web. 14 September 2008.

Lobel, Arnold. *Days with Frog and Toad*. New York: Harper and Row, 1979.

——. *Frog and Toad All Year*. New York: Harper and Row, 1976.

——. *Frog and Toad Are Friends*. New York: Harper and Row, 1970.

———. *Frog and Toad Together*. New York: Harper and Row, 1972.

Matthews, Gareth B. "Children, Irony and Philosophy." *Theory and Research in Education* 3, no. 1 (2005): 81–95. *Sage Publications*. Web. 13 September 2008.

McCullough, David. "Arnold Lobel and Friends." *New York Times*, 11 November 1987. *ProQuest Historical Newspapers*. Web. 13 September 2008.

McGillis, Roderick. "The Delights of Impossibility: No Children, No Books, Only Theory." *Children's Literature Association Quarterly* 23, no. 4 (1998–99): 202–8.

———. *The Nimble Reader: Literary Theory and Children's Literature*. New York: Twayne, 1996.

Natov, Roni, and Geraldine DeLuca. "An Interview with Arnold Lobel." *The Lion and the Unicorn* 1, no. 1 (1977): 72–96.

Nel, Philip. *The Annotated Cat: Under the Hats of Seuss and His Cats*. New York: Random, 2007.

Nietzsche, Friedrich. *The Birth of Tragedy*. 1871. Translated by William. A. Haussmann. New York: Russell & Russell, 1964.

Nodelman, Perry. *Words about Pictures: The Narrative Art of Children's Picture Books*. Athens: U of Georgia P, 1988.

Nodelman, Perry, and Mavis Reimer. *The Pleasures of Children's Literature*. 3rd ed. Boston: Allyn and Bacon, 2003.

Parker, Robert Dale. *How to Interpret Literature: Critical Theory for Literary and Cultural Studies*. New York: Oxford UP, 2008.

Richter, David H., ed. *The Critical Tradition: Classic Texts and Contemporary Trends*. 2nd ed. Boston: Bedford, 1998.

Rollin, Lucy. "The Astonished Witness Disclosed: An Interview with Arnold Lobel." *Children's Literature in Education* 15, no. 4 (1984): 191–97.

Rudd, David. "Cultural Studies." In *Teaching Children's Fiction*, edited by Charles Butler, 29-59. Basingstoke: PalgraveMacmillan, 2006.

Schultz, Kirstin. "Friendship." *The Educator's Reference Desk*. Information Institute of Syracuse. 19 September 2001. Web. 2 February 2009.

Scott, Linda. "*Frog and Toad Are Friends* by Arnold Lobel." *Teacher CyberGuide*. San Diego: San Diego County Office of Education, 1997, http://www.sdcoe.k12.ca.us/score/frog/frogtg.html 2 February 2009).

Sedgwick, Eve Kosofsky. *Between Men: English Literature and Male Homosocial Desire*. New York: Columbia UP, 1985.

Setoodeh, Ramin. "Isn't It Bromantic?" *Newsweek*, 8 June 2009. *Academic Search Complete*. Web. 26 June 2009.

Shannon, George. *Arnold Lobel*. Boston: Twayne, 1989.

Stanton, Joseph. "Straight Man and Clown in the Picture Books of Arnold Lobel." *Journal of American Culture* 17, no. 2 (1994): 75–84. *Academic Search Complete*. Web. 13 September 2008.

Stott, Andrew. *Comedy*. London: Routledge, 2005.

Stout, Hilary. "Arnold Lobel, Author-Illustrator." *New York Times*, 6 December 1987. *ProQuest Historical Newspapers*. Web. 14 September 2008

Todorov, Tzvetan. *Genres in Discourse*. Translated by Catherine Porter. Cambridge: Cambridge UP, 1990.

Trace, Arther S., Jr. *Reading without Dick and Jane*. Chicago: Henry Regnery, 1965.

Walsh, Jill Paton. "The Rainbow Surface." In *The Cool Web: The Pattern of Children's Reading*, edited by Margaret Meek, Aidan Warlow, and Griselda Barton, 192–95. London: Bodley Head, 1977.

Wartenberg, Thomas. *Teaching Children Philosophy*. 25 May 2009. Web. 20 July 2009.

White, David E. "Profile: Arnold Lobel." *Language Arts* 65, no. 5 (September 1988): 489–94.

FURTHER READING

Butler, Charles, ed. *Teaching Children's Fiction*. Basingstoke: Palgrave, 2006.

Derrida, Jacques. "The Law of Genre." Translated by Avital Ronell. In *On Narrative*, edited by W. J. T. Mitchell, 51–77. Chicago: U of Chicago P, 1981.

Doonan, Jane. *Looking at Pictures in Picture Books*. Stroud, Gloucester: Thimble, 1993.

Foucault, Michel. *The History of Sexuality*. Vol. 1 *An Introduction*. 1976. Translated by Robert Hurley. New York: Pantheon, 1978.

Higonnet, Anne. *Pictures of Innocence: The History and Crisis of Ideal Childhood*. New York: Thames and Hudson, 1998.

Moebius, William. "Introduction to Picturebook Codes." *Word and Image* 2, no. 2 (1986): 141–58.

Silk, M. S., and J. P. Stern. *Nietzsche on Tragedy*. Cambridge: Cambridge UP, 1981.

BLENDING GENRES AND CROSSING AUDIENCES: *HARRY POTTER* AND THE FUTURE OF LITERARY FICTION

KARIN E. WESTMAN

J. K. Rowling (rhymes with "bowling") was born Joanne Rowling on 31 July 1965 in England. When publishing Philosopher's Stone, *Rowling's publishers asked Rowling to use her initials and surname in order for the book to appeal to boys as well as girls, so she chose her grandmother's name, Kathleen, for a middle name. Rowling earned a degree in French and Classics from the University of Edinburgh, working as a researcher at Amnesty International following graduation and then as a teacher in Portugal. In 1990, on a train from Manchester to London and without a pen at hand, she began imagining the world of Harry Potter. Over the next five years, Rowling made notes for five books and, as a single mother living on public assistance in Edinburgh, drafted the first volume. The subsequent success of the seven-book series has brought Rowling not only great fortune and fame—according to Rowling's website, the books are available in two hundred territories and translated into sixty-seven languages—but also unprecedented opportunities to advocate for literacy and to support charitable causes for social change. The recipient of numerous awards and honors, Rowling lives in Edinburgh with Jessica, the daughter from her first marriage, and with her second husband, Dr. Neil Murray, and their children, David and Mackenzie.*

Through her *Harry Potter* series (1997–2007), J. K. Rowling has left an indelible mark on children's and young adult literature, both its literary landscape and its marketplace. Rowling imagines her series as "one big book" (Anelli and Spartz), reminding us that it offers a seven-volume study of one character's development—a *bildungsroman*, in fact, of Harry's life from age eleven to seventeen. The novel of formation, however, is only one of many genres represented across the pages of the series, and this generic hybridity illustrates the significance of the series in terms of literary form as well as critical and popular response. Drawing upon traditions of psychological realism, mystery, the gothic, the school story, satire, and fantasy, Rowling creates a compelling narrative that prompts both sympathetic engagement and critical reflection. Thus, the formulas of popular genre fictions are present across the series, but they are augmented in turn by attention to individual character and social institutions. Fantasy creates a magical world of wizards, for instance, but psychological realism and satire diminish differences between the wizarding and "Muggle" worlds, revealing similar ideologies of prejudice. Individual genres are invoked, stretched, and transformed, creating new iterations and relations of literary forms that defy easy classification.

Such generic blending not only reflects Rowling's wide range of literary influences and thematic goals but also bends the expected narrative conclusions for literature and literary history, testing our established categories for these individual genres and for the genre of children's literature.[1] The overwhelming popularity of the series with readers of all ages[2] has challenged conventions about child readers, adult readers, children's literacy, children's book publishing, the publishing industry, the role of marketing, and the role of the fan. Eroding any clear distinction between the "popular" and the "canonical," between one genre and another, Rowling's *Harry Potter* series prompts debate about boundaries—their efficacy and their necessity—for our experience, enjoyment, and critical history of children's literature.

This essay takes up three of the many genres converging within Rowling's *Harry Potter* series—the *bildungsroman*, the school story, and fantasy—to demonstrate how Rowling plays with generic forms and boundaries toward a similar theme: the value of moral agency, born from sympathy for others. The essay concludes with the implications such generic hybridity has for a fourth genre: children's literature.

THE *BILDUNGSROMAN*

The *Harry Potter* series offers a seven-volume study of one character's development, a *bildungsroman* (novel of formation) that follows the adventures of Rowling's title character from age eleven, when he first learns that he will attend Hogwarts School for Witchcraft and Wizardry, to age seventeen, when he comes of age in the wizarding world. Harry's orphaned childhood, his vexed relationship with his

close-minded aunt and uncle, his immersion in a hierarchal and often unjust wizarding society, his supplementary self-education with his friends and Dumbledore's
Army, his love for Ginny, and his increasing reliance on a sympathetic and moral
imagination to fight the evils of wizarding society all demonstrate how his story
contains the "principal elements" of the *bildungsroman* (Buckley 18).[3] The *bildung*
that Rowling emphasizes, then, is Harry's moral and emotional development, as
her choice of narrative style places the emphasis upon subjective, internal experience as much as external actions within the world.

Though the novels might seem to take an omniscient view of Harry's experiences, "Harry is the eyes through which you see the world," as Rowling reminded
readers in 2003 during a global webcast from Royal Albert Hall. Rowling's choice of
narrative style reflects this singular perspective: a third-person, limited omniscient
point of view. We rarely see or hear anything that Harry does not see or hear—
though we may, like Hermione, identify some patterns to Harry's experiences that
escape his notice. Rowling's seven-novel sequence is certainly plotted with calculated detail and page-turning suspense, but always in the service of Harry's character. As we (mis)perceive the world through Harry's eyes, Rowling not only emulates
the narrative misdirection of Jane Austen's *Emma* (1816)—"the most skillfully managed mystery I've ever read" (Rowling "Let Me Tell You a Story")—but, like her
favorite author, also places the narrative emphasis upon character. Book by book,
year by year, we gain perspective on Harry and his world. Our ironic distance
emerges gradually from a tension between our previous knowledge of Harry's character alongside his new circumstance or thought, rather than being the result of an
intrusive narrative voice. The result is a narrative that traces the influence of society
upon the individual in order to mark the limitations of private vision while also
evoking the power of sympathy for others.

Like Austen, Rowling favors a narrative style that relies upon limited omniscient point of view to restrict the reader's experience of the story to one character's
view of the world—what Wayne Booth describes in *The Rhetoric of Fiction* (1961) as
"Sympathy through Control of Inside Views" in his influential discussion "Distance
in *Emma*."[4] As readers, we only gradually realize the degree to which our perspective on the wizarding world is primarily shaped by Harry's perspective, just as
Emma's limitations prevent our knowledge of Frank Churchill and Jane Fairfax's
engagement in Austen's novel. We are nearly always aligned with Harry's perspective, receiving very little third-person description of setting or character that is not
first processed through Harry. "Real world" details of the Muggle and wizarding
worlds only enter his consciousness and therefore the series' narrative as he experiences them and not before. While Harry's friends Hermione and Ron may have
known about other wizarding academies like Beaux Batons and Durmstrang since
Philosopher's Stone (1997), readers did not know that there were other schools in the
wizarding world until Harry learns of their existence at the Quidditch World Cup
in *Goblet of Fire* (2000).

Rowling had been criticized, until *Goblet*, for creating a world disconnected
from the realities of contemporary culture, but her choice of an Austen-like

narrative style accounts for this charge. Like Austen, Rowling introduces social, political, and economic realities as they affect her main character's life, focalizing them through his experience of these external forces rather than an omniscient narrative voice.[5] In *Emma*, our heroine takes note of the poor when they can serve as a moral lesson for herself and her friend Harriet (79); in *Harry Potter*, our hero becomes attuned to systemic wizarding prejudice when Draco Malfoy calls Hermione "You filthy little Mudblood" (*Chamber* 86). Harry sees and comprehends much more about his world as he grows older, and so with each year (and book) *we* know more. Rowling's limited omniscient view, focalized through Harry, therefore also explains the varying tones and emphases of each book—why *Philosopher's Stone* seems so filled with joy relative to later novels, why the Hogwarts girls are often described as "giggly" (*Azkaban* 56) and silly in *Azkaban* (1999) and *Goblet* by a confused preteen boy, why the relative simplicity of *Philosopher's Stone* (derided by some readers and reviewers) disappears into the complexity and confusion of subsequent volumes.[6] Our frame of reference for each book is dynamic, expanding to account for Harry's new knowledge of his world rather than fixed from the start of the series.

Rowling's narrative style for this seven-part *bildungsroman* thus privileges psychological realism, reminding us that the series is concerned with character more than with external details, interior emotions as much as exterior actions. A limited omniscient narrative style emphasizes the development of Harry's character, and this persistent proximity to his character forges our connection to him. Harry's errors in judgment—from mistaking Snape for the prime adversary in *Philosopher's Stone* to leading five friends to probable death at the Ministry of Magic in *Order of the Phoenix* (2003)—evoke our sympathy because we generally err with him, having followed his train of thought and endorsed his course of action, knowing no more than he does. We are often at the mercy of his gaze, his limited perspective, and his degree of emotional maturity. We do gain a more ironic relationship to Harry's character, but it evolves gradually over the course of the series, and this irony results from a tension between our previous knowledge of Harry's character alongside his new circumstance or thought, rather than being the result of an intrusive narrative voice. Ironic moments may occur inside a given novel—perhaps we realize, before Harry, why his stomach gives a lurch when he sees Cho Chang in *Azkaban*—but such ironic perspective is mostly noticeable between volumes. Often, Hermione fulfills the role otherwise assigned to Austen's narrative voice when she reminds Harry and Ron of forgotten or overlooked information that provides analytical distance on Harry's seemingly unassailable position. Eager to rescue Sirius from apparent captivity and torture at the Ministry's Department of Mysteries, Harry chafes as Hermione offers her reasoned observations: "[I]t's five o'clock in the afternoon . . . the Ministry of Magic must be full of workers . . . how would Voldemort and Sirius have got in without being seen?" (*Phoenix* 645). So immersed in the emotionally real world of his visions, Harry can lose the larger context of the world around him. Through such comments by Hermione, we are reminded of our tightly focalized view of the novel's world and the limitations of our hero's perceptions of it, even as we sympathize with Harry's conclusions.

By combining a narrative style that emphasizes sympathetic engagement with Harry's character and the genre of the *bildungsroman*, Rowling encourages readers to view the adult world with skepticism as well as sympathy. We are prompted, along with Harry, to wonder at the values of adult society. From their position as children navigating an adult world, Harry and his friends note fault lines in its ideologies, thanks to their alternate point of view. Harry "wishe[s] he had about eight more eyes" as he observes Diagon Alley and the wizarding world for the first time in *Philosopher's Stone* (56), but even his two eyes tell him (and by extension us) quite a lot about the realities of this society. The mutual curiosity Harry and Ron have of each other on the train—"'Are all of your family wizards?' asked Harry, who found Ron just as interesting as Ron found him" (*Philosopher's* 74)—prompts an easy exchange about social class because Harry holds no prejudice against poverty, having been poor himself (*Philosopher's* 75). What Harry observes during lunch on that first train ride and during his first visit to Ron's home in *Chamber of Secrets* is the degree of anxiety and embarrassment poverty brings in the wizarding world, as it does in his own. Harry's new position of wizarding wealth therefore provides a dual perspective on the values of both societies. The eleven-year-old Draco Malfoy, as prejudiced as his wealthy parents, reminds us that children are not necessarily able, by nature, to imagine alternatives to prevailing social norms. However, those children who can recognize or imagine alternatives are able to offer new ways of seeing. Having been both poor and rich, Harry's double perspective, along with his child's point of view, reveals the construction and persistence of class prejudice as well as ways to mitigate its debilitating consequences through shared confidence, humility, and sympathy.

THE SCHOOL STORY

Rowling's choice of setting—a coeducational boarding school—locates the *Harry Potter* series within a well-established and popular tradition of British literary history: the school story.[7] However, in considering Rowling's place within this genre, we need to move beyond what has been a fairly limited definition and history, usually represented by Thomas Hughes's *Tom Brown's Schooldays* (1857) and Enid Blyton's school series such as *Malory Towers* (1945–51). In contrast to the physical and spiritual knowledge of *Tom Brown's Schooldays*, the educational world of *Harry Potter* emphasizes the value of academic inquiry for intellectual growth, usually achieved through a pedagogy of collaborative exchange. In contrast to the moral certitude of Blyton's school stories, Rowling's school story recognizes and even rewards ambiguity as part of the educational endeavor.[8] With this wider critical lens of "school story" in hand we can see Rowling's series as a contribution to an evolving cultural narrative about the intersection of education and politics and recognize her complex representations of teaching and learning for individual moral growth.

In both purpose and method, the education Harry receives stands in sharp contrast to the education of the archetypal schoolboy of literary history, Hughes's hero, Tom Brown. In *Tom Brown's Schooldays*, Tom learns to embody a masculine identity that rests upon physical and spiritual prowess; this education emerges in equal measure from interactions with other students and the preaching of Rugby's headmaster Doctor Arnold, rather than from the intellectual inquiry, critical thinking, and collaborative practices that characterize the educational experiences of Hogwarts under Albus Dumbledore. At Hogwarts, intellectual endeavor takes center stage, as Harry and his friends learn about the process of critical thinking, as well as the practice of magic, through formal classroom instruction[9] and informal self-directed learning. As Charles Elster rightly remarks of the series, "learning is depicted as an active search for answers." However, Elster is mistaken in his next claim: that this search is "only tangentially related to classroom learning tasks" (204). As the series progresses, Harry, Ron, and Hermione take the strategies and skills of formal learning and apply them to their extramural studies. Authority derives from knowledge—historical, theoretical, and applied—and from the ability to engage in collaborative, practical pedagogies to acquire it.

At Hogwarts, the development of the mind takes precedence over the development of the body, and authority is earned through knowledge rather than conferred by rank or age. The school library, rather than the school pitch, is the favored location for this educational development. Ron's offhand remark—"When in doubt, go to the library" (*Chamber* 189)—offers a neat summation of the series' insistence that past endeavors can be crucial to future success, such as how to evade death by a Basilisk in *Chamber* or the identity of a half-blood Prince in *Half-Blood Prince* (2005). In emphasizing this archival resource, Rowling has her characters value the history and research of ideas alongside their integration and practical application. As Harry, Ron, and Hermione formulate research questions, identify likely sources, and assess the results, they engage in a process of critical thinking based on inquiry and informed speculation. In solving mysteries, they acquire skills in logic and creative problem-solving designed to make them independent thinkers. As a result, educational authority emerges foremost from knowledge and its ethical use rather than from physical strength or spiritual belief, as it does in *Tom Brown's Schooldays*.

This mutual respect for knowledge extends to the dynamic between student and teacher, as a collaborative pedagogy allows students and teachers to share ideas and even exchange roles. In advocating this dynamic, Rowling's Hogwarts is far from the hierarchies that inform the educational world of the traditional school story. Instead, we are immersed within a system that rewards intellectual merit and acknowledges lifelong learning. During the first three books of Rowling's series, we spend time with Harry in his classes on subjects such as Transfiguration and Herbology, in which he and his fellow students usually work in pairs or small groups to put into practice the abstract principle of a spell, charm, or informative detail about the world around them.[10] The collaborative approach toward learning in Harry's other classes emphasizes the possibility that someone with knowledge—whether young or old—can instruct another. This shared instructional prerogative appears early in the series and continues throughout: as Harry, Ron, and Hermione pool their resources to discover the identity of Flamel and the location of the stone, for instance, but also in Hermione's oft-repeated lessons to Harry and Ron from *Hogwarts: A History* or her reminders of classroom teachings that are crucial to their success outside its walls, from the properties of Devil's Snare in *Philosopher's Stone* to the red cross of the *Flagrate* spell on the doors at the Department of Mysteries in *Order of the Phoenix*. Learning is a collaborative endeavor in which someone who has knowledge helps another person acquire it. This fairly informal exchange of roles becomes more formal as the series proceeds, as students like Harry and Hermione become teachers according to need and ability and vice versa. The result is a fluid educational dynamic that resists traditional hierarchies of age and experience but values situational knowledge and talent. In this aim, Rowling's series stands in contrast to the world of *Tom Brown's Schooldays* and its world of sport, spiritual faith, and traditional hierarchies of power between men and women, between teachers and students.

Rowling revises another expected school story narrative, often evinced in the works of such authors as Enid Blyton, and does so by introducing the moral ambiguity of psychological realism. In *Harry Potter*, Harry and his fellow students often struggle to determine what is good and what is bad, grappling with ambiguities of character and action. Whereas Blyton's characters successfully resolve uncertainty whenever it appears, Rowling's characters must learn to live with ambiguity and to develop strategies for action within an uncertain world. As we follow Darrell Rivers from her *First Term at Malory Towers* (1946) to her *Last Term at Malory Towers* (1951), the complications that Darrell experiences are generally within her control and are resolved by her realizing the fault and changing her behavior. When Darrell loses her temper during *First Term*, for instance, shaking the annoying Gwendolyn Mary and shouting at her, it takes only a few minutes of reflection—and a few pages of the book—for Darrell to realize and admit her error to herself (52) and subsequently to apologize first to Gwendolyn Mary (53) and then to the other girls of her form (56). Like other girls who experience a change of perspective, Darrell's transformation happens quickly, even "magically" (*Second Form* 154) in its rapidity and results. There is little or no angst; instead, our attention goes toward the result rather than the process, toward a norm of behavior rather than contextual assessment and response. Throughout *Malory Towers*, certain actions (like stealing, cheating, and lying) are categorically wrong, while other actions (like being someone's friend and saving someone's life) are categorically right. Within these fixed parameters, the lives of Darrell and her schoolmates reinforce clear categories of behavior.

While Blyton's *Malory Towers* presents moral certitude and stable identity, Rowling's school series presents ambiguity as a condition of being that must be negotiated with sympathy. Across the series, Harry and those around him must make decisions that require them to choose between competing moral and ethical rights. Unlike the world of *Malory Towers*, the world of *Harry Potter* teaches that certain actions—like stealing, cheating, and lying—are not categorically wrong;

instead, the context for these actions must determine whether one should steal, cheat, and lie or even kill. Indeed, Rowling has appropriately remarked that Harry is "not good in the Enid Blyton sense," particularly as he "breaks a lot of rules" (Renton). *Chamber of Secrets*, for instance, finds Harry, Ron, and Hermione lying and stealing in order to concoct the Polyjuice Potion required for their reconnaissance missions, so they can learn more about the Heir of Slytherin and in turn protect others. In *Goblet of Fire*, during the Triwizard Tournament, Harry discovers that cheating—finding out the details of a task in advance or receiving assistance toward completing it—is acceptable and that he must engage in this practice, too, in order to survive. In the midst of tackling other research tasks associated with their challenge to the evil Voldemort, Harry and Ron frequently copy Hermione's work in order to complete their own assignments for class; Hermione only stops them when they take her help for granted, resuming her assistance when they are more conscious of what they receive. In these and many similar situations, Harry, Ron, and Hermione balance one form of "good" behavior against another, looking toward how the "good" ends justify the suspect means. Some choices seem fairly easy, however, in comparison to other, more ambiguous ones. Frequently, the power of life and death rests in Harry's hands. Even early on in the series, Harry must decide whether to take the life of Sirius Black, the one presumed responsible for the murder of his parents, and whether he should allow Sirius and Lupin to kill Peter Pettigrew for his betrayal of trust (*Azkaban* 251, 275). In Blyton's *Malory Towers*, Darrell Rivers's education depends upon absolutes and certainties for its success. Throughout his school years at Hogwarts, all that Harry can be certain of is uncertainty, as he struggles to make the best decision within a complex and competing array of choices.

FANTASY

Rowling has readily acknowledged that fantasy is not her preferred genre (Johnstone 15), so perhaps it comes as no surprise that her series emphasizes the realistic impulses within the fantasy genre. Indeed, it is probably best not to read the *Harry Potter* series alongside the high fantasy tradition of J. R. R. Tolkien, C. S. Lewis, Ursula Le Guin, or Susan Cooper, or even the myth-based fantasy of Alan Garner, Diana Wynne Jones, or Terry Pratchett; the result, for many readers, is to find Rowling's series flawed, as failing to live up to certain expectations of the fantasy genre. Rowling is much more interested in how fantasy provides perspective on everyday experience and the individual's place in society. Her inclusion of certain genres—like the *bildungsroman* and the school story—align her primarily with the domestic (or low) fantasy of authors such as E. Nesbit, Elizabeth Goudge, and Paul Gallico (all three acknowledged favorites of Rowling) as well as authors like Philip Pullman and Jonathan Stroud, who are also interested in the intersection of the personal and the political within quotidian experiences. The result of Rowling's strategy is a hybrid fantasy[11] with a particular social message. Through a parallel world suggestive of contemporary British society in which magical and nonmagical people negotiate survival, Rowling's series critiques a politics of absolute power based on self-interest, secrecy, and difference and values instead a democratic power structure based on trust, altruism, and shared knowledge.

In *Harry Potter*, the wizarding world struggles to negotiate a very contemporary problem in Britain: the legacy of a racial and class caste system that, though not entirely stable, is still looked upon by a minority of powerful individuals as the means to continued power and control. Rowling's detailed portrait of a late capitalist, global consumer culture marks the wizarding community as an echo of and commentary on both the Muggle world of the novels and the contemporary world of post-Thatcher England—a connection Rowling herself acknowledged as early as 2001 in a Canadian Broadcasting Corporation interview (Solomon). In Rowling's series, we are asked to question the Ministries of Cornelius Fudge and Rufus Scrimgeour, along with the fascist insurgency of Lord Voldemort, because all three attain their authority by privileging the rights of wizards over the rights of other magical species (house elves, goblins, giants) and over the rights of Muggles, nonmagical people; further, they attain their authority through a politics of difference, self-interest, and secrecy. We learn about this politics of difference first through Hogwarts, where the fear of miscegenation finds expression through Slytherin's split with the other three founders of the school many years before (*Chamber* 114) and where current students like Draco Malfoy sling taunts of "Mudblood" (*Chamber* 86) to segregate Muggle-born witches and wizards such as Hermione from "pure bloods" like himself. Draco's opinion may be a minority one, but we soon learn, along with Harry, that it is powerful and long-standing. For those like the Malfoys, the legacy of a wizard's blood trumps other categories of identity—even though, as Ron explains to Harry, "[i]t's mad" to make a distinction between "dirty blood" or "[c]ommon blood" and "pure blood": "Most wizards these days are half-blood anyway. If we hadn't married Muggles we'd've died out" (*Chamber* 89). The choice of the adjective "common" indicates the role class plays within this ideology of "purity": since claims of "pure blood" are illusory in a wizarding culture that has married Muggles to survive, such difference stands in for a set of ideological beliefs based on differences in social class and its concomitant power.

These ideologies of difference, compounded by self-interest, condemn the institutional authorities who advocate them, and readers are asked to question their treatment of Muggle-born people and other magical species. Harry is disgusted to discover in *Goblet of Fire* that Cornelius Fudge values the continuity of his Ministry above pursuit of a newly reborn Voldemort, as Fudge "refus[es], point blank, to accept the prospect of disruption in his comfortable and ordered world" (*Goblet* 613) and complains to the Headmaster that Dumbledore and his followers "are all determined to start a panic that will destabilise everything we have worked for these last thirteen years!" (*Goblet* 613). The Ministry of Rufus Scrimgeour, if more proactive in the fight against Voldemort, expresses similar self-interest in its concern about civic appearances at the expense of civil rights. The Scrimgeour Ministry is not above following the footsteps of an earlier Ministry official, Barty Crouch Senior, and arresting the innocent Stan Shunpike, since, as Hermione explains, "[t]hey probably want to look as though they're doing something" (*Prince* 209). This concern about self-image extends to Scrimgeour's repeated request for Harry to be seen "popping in and out of the Ministry from time to time" to offer "the right impression"—that impression being, as Harry intuits, that he is "working for the Ministry" and "approve[s] of what the Ministry was up to" (*Prince* 324). Such hypocrisy galvanizes Harry and asks readers to question the pursuit of power at the expense of individual rights, placing the Ministry on a continuum with the fascist zeal of Voldemort. The puppet Ministry of the Imperius-ed Pious Thicknesse, with Dolores Umbridge serving as Head of the new Muggle-born Registration Commission (*Hallows* 206), occupies the space between, producing propaganda reminiscent of Hitler's Third Reich: "*Mudbloods and the Dangers They Pose to a Peaceful Pure-Blood Society*," reads one of Umbridge's pamphlets (*Hallows* 205)—and acting on those ideas, as "Muggle slaughter [becomes] little more than a recreational sport under the new regime" (*Hallows* 356). No longer even tolerated for their difference, Muggles and any mixed beings are killed for it.

The wizards of Rowling's Ministries are undone by their leaders' desires to restrict power and knowledge to a select few who disregard the rights of others. A democratic power structure based on trust, altruism, and shared knowledge emerges as a viable, preferable alternative to isolation, hypocrisy, and ideologies of difference. Success depends first upon individuals—Harry, Ron, and Hermione—who share their knowledge and trust others and then depends upon the community that follows their lead. Rowling's narrative suggests that when a select few have control, and those few advocate a power dynamic that threatens individual rights within the wider community, those within the community with any power must rebel. Harry embodies this ethic. When talking back in Umbridge's class in response to her claim that no one seeks to attack them—"'Hhmm, let's think . . .' said Harry in a mock thoughtful voice. 'Maybe . . . Lord Voldemort?'" (*Phoenix* 220)—or when announcing to the class that Cedric's death was "murder" (*Phoenix* 221), Harry certainly assuages his adolescent temper, but he also makes visible the network of lies propagated by suspect Ministry officials. As Neville reminds Harry two years later in *Deathly Hallows* (2007), . . . it helps when people stand up to them, it gives everyone hope. "I used to notice that when you did it, Harry":"it helps when people stand up to them, it gives everyone hope" (*Hallows* 462). Indeed, in *Deathly Hallows*, readers learn that Neville follows Harry's lead, challenging the teachings of the Death Eater Alecto Carrow that "Muggles are like animals, stupid and dirty, and how they drove wizards into hiding by being vicious to them, and how the natural order is being reestablished" (*Hallows* 462). By speaking out in public against a self-interested politics of difference, Harry and the rest of Dumbledore's Army question the hegemony of these beliefs and suggest another way to live in the world. Harry realizes that he should not be "keeping his secrets clutched tightly to his chest, afraid to trust" (*Hallows* 469). Instead, he agrees with Ron and Hermione that they must forego those strategies of the past favored by Voldemort, various Ministries, and often Dumbledore himself, in favor of a public, shared knowledge, trusting to empathetic and sympathetic responses rather than retreating into isolation and fear.

Rowling's series ends with individual change in terms of Harry's character and a change in Ministry leadership; however, there is institutional continuity, tempering the range of alternatives available through Rowling's fantasy. Nineteen years later, the Ministry and Hogwarts continue as before, it would seem, and wizards continue to shape and intervene in Muggle experience, given that Ron has recently "Confund[ed]" the Muggle examiner when taking his Muggle driving test (*Hallows* 604). This last detail of wizard-Muggle relations is of a piece with the series as a whole. Wizarding self-interest, both at the individual and institutional level, has been the norm since the International Statue of Wizarding Secrecy in 1692 (*Whisp* 16); in turn, wizards are always ready to point their wands at Muggles—and, as needed, at other wizards and magical creatures—and alter their experience of the world. Rowling's series is quick to indict wizards who perform such spells on Muggles, other magical species, and one another when they do so for personal gain rather than public good. We are certainly asked to admire, for instance, the reports of "wizards and witches risking their own safety to protect Muggle friends and neighbours [against attacks by Death Eaters], often without Muggle knowledge" (*Hallows* 357). However, wizards remain, in the words of Griphook the Goblin in *Deathly Hallows*, the ones in power, the ones who, by "refus[ing] to share the secrets of wandlore with other magical beings, . . . deny us the possibility of extending our powers!" (*Hallows* 395). A wizard's own integrity of self, it seems, is more valuable than that of a Muggle or another magical creature, an exercise in institutional privilege that Rowling's series demonstrates but does not fully explore[12] alongside Harry's sacrifice of self—a limitation, perhaps, born of Rowling's intergeneric fusion of fantasy with the *bildungsroman* and the school story, among other genres, which consequently restricts readers to the growth of Harry's character rather than the growth of a society.

CHILDREN'S LITERATURE

Popular among adult readers and accorded "adult" literary antecedents by its author and others, the *Harry Potter* series has tested the boundary of another genre: children's literature. Rowling herself has never specified children as her intended audience—"I wrote primarily for myself," she has remarked ("Comic Relief")—and in an early interview from 1998, she acknowledges the lower status of children's literature in contemporary culture in order to challenge this view and expand its readership. "There is a perception on the part of some people that children's books are worth less than adult books," Rowling explains. "I'm very frequently asked: 'When are you going to write your adult book?' If a book appeals," she concludes, "it's going to appeal to everyone" (qtd. in Blakeney). "Appeal[ing] to everyone" defies the boundaries of genre, however, especially for publishers and for those readers and critics who see popular or children's literature as suspect in its appeal. Refusing to stay within the bounds of children's literature, Rowling's series represents the function of cross-over fiction at the present time.

Rowling's challenge to accepted generic categories is hardly new, but the extreme response to her work reveals the persistent connection between genre classification and ideology. As James Thomas remarks, the *Harry Potter* books "are easy to underestimate because of what I call the three Deathly Hallows for academics": "They couldn't possibly be good because they're too recent, they're too popular, and they're too juvenile" (qtd. in Gibbs). History may show us, as Anne Lundin reminds us in her study *Constructing the Canon of Children's Literature* (2004), that during the nineteenth century in Britain and the United States, "the lines were blurred without demarcation between adult and children's literature" (60), a cultural process mapped, too, by Beverly Lyon Clark in *Kiddie Lit* (2003). However, subsequent history shows us how scholars and librarians of the twentieth century sought to establish that line between adult literature and children's literature. Once the line was drawn, parties on both sides wished to see value in their portion, and we can trace cultural practices that tried to value of what fell on the "child" side of the line, such as a name change from the more general phrase of "children's books" to the more elevated one of "children's literature" (Lundin 142–43). There remained, however, two distinct audiences for two types of literature—children and adults—even if in practice the line was still crossed.

Further, those championing children's literature have found themselves engaged in a repeated "fight against the academic hegemony of 'Eng. Lit.' to gain any recognition" for children's literature, as Hunt concludes in an earlier essay from 1991 ("Children's Literature" 82). In another essay from 1995, Hunt traces the distinct hierarchy of children's literature that evolved during the twentieth century, proffering the following taxonomy: first, "a body of texts that have no respectability," followed by "a canon—a few books (Kipling, Carroll, MacDonald) that haunt the lower slopes of the 'grown-up' canon—and then [third] a far larger group whose members look very much like adult books" ("Poetics" 44). Thus, even though a defining criterion of value would seem to be the cross-readerly appeal of a children's book—its ability to meet the aesthetic requirements for "good" adult art—only a few children's books meet this criterion and are allowed to enter the hallowed gates of literature; others are left, in Hunt's words, to "haunt the lower slopes" ("Poetics" 44) leading to those gates, or, even worse, prohibited from even beginning the ascent. In sum, as Andrew Blake of King Alfred College in Winchester remarks, "academic snobbery means that you don't look at kids stuff or fantasy" (qtd. in Mcveigh).

Financial success certainly buys some degree of legitimacy for children's literature[13] – from the publishing world, if not from academics or other cultural arbiters – but cultural and scholarly acceptance remains elusive, as responses to Rowling's series show. Reviewers and critics do not hesitate to cordon off the *Harry Potter* series as child fare, worthwhile only for the child reader or the less intellectual adult reader. In her editorial for the *New York Times* on 7 July 2003, "Harry Potter and the Childish Adult," A. S. Byatt performs this role of literary gatekeeper, denying the *Harry Potter* series entrance to the world of Literature. Her diatribe against Rowling's best-selling, prize-winning series prompted Charles Taylor's response in *Salon.com*, titled "A.S. Byatt and the Goblet of Bile." As Taylor and others have observed, Byatt is hardly alone in her criticism: she joins the ranks of other arbiters of literary fiction who have decried the series' popularity, claiming that its success illustrates only the regressive reading pleasures of its "childish" or "rejuvenile" audience. Philip Hensher expressed similar concerns when Philip Pullman appeared next to Seamus Heaney on the short list for Britain's Whitbread award, while others lamented Pullman's appearance on the long list for the Booker Prize. Children's literature is thus seen to partake in a cultural trend of regressive nostalgia for "genre" fiction; adults who read it are looking for "comfort," as Byatt remarks, rather than the challenge and thrill of art. That such children's books are also bestsellers only confirms their lowly status in the eyes of these critics, the books' artistic worth further compromised by their popular appeal.[14]

A common theme emerges from these same critics: that the children's books in question fail an aesthetic test for narrative art by valuing story, including the stories of earlier literary works. According to Robert McCrum of the *Observer*, "J. K. Rowling has mastered the first (perhaps the only) three lessons of bestsellerism": "plot, plot, and more plot." Philip Hensher, in an early review of the Harry Potter books, warms to this theme:

> They are written in a way which is designed to be seductively readable; they never give way to reflection or those momentary flashbacks of recall that prove so confusing to young readers, but exist in a sort of "And then, and then, and then" which children find irresistible. But the world of these books is thin and unsatisfactory, their imagery is derivative, their characterisation automatic, and their structure deeply flawed. ("Give Me a Break")

Hensher's aesthetic evaluation of Rowling's series locates her novels within the category of genre fiction, a rhetorical move echoed by others who wish to cast doubt on the aesthetic value of her efforts and the quality of her readership. Phrases like "terrific page-turners," or claims that "Rowling is as swish and savvy as Le Carre or Christie" (Craven), mark the series as enjoyable but facile, formulaic rather than original, accessible to developing readers of all ages but not worthy of developed ones. Byatt contributed to this well-established vein of criticism when she insisted that Rowling's series is simply "derivative," suggesting (to employ Rowling's imaginative universe as a metaphor) that Rowling's narrative is a mere magpie's collection of shiny literary trifles easily dismantled by one industrious niffler. Hensher developed this argument in a later review as well: "[Rowling's] indebtedness to other writers; the unthinking conventionality of the world; the disorganized and vague nature of the fantasy element; she isn't a bold writer, or a really authoritative one. You always have the feeling that you've read this somewhere before." "In short," Hensher concludes, "it is difficult to make a case for J. K. Rowling on literary grounds" ("Art of Making Money"). For Hensher, Byatt, and others, "plot" and literary echoes become the sign of the popular, the best seller, the child—three terms that have a suspect history in British culture, as we have seen, when paired with "literature."

But what of those millions who choose to read *Harry Potter* as literature, a reading audience comprised of children and adults, both of whom frequently *are* well read? Some literary gatekeepers welcome children's books into the literary fold, throwing open those same gates that Byatt and Hensher would bar—including the committee that awarded Pullman with the Whitbread. These readers point to well-established literary figures like W. H. Auden ("There are no great children's books which are only children's books" [qtd. in Wullschlager]) and C. S. Lewis ("the neat sorting-out of books into age-groups, so dear to publishers, has only a very sketchy relation with the habits of any real readers" ["On Three Ways" 28]— for their comments on the audience for children's literature. Further, for many of the cultural arbiters who defend a varied audience for children's literature, the very emphasis that consigns children's authors like Rowling to life outside the canonical gates recommends them for admission: a well-plotted, allusive story. Marina Warner for *The Observer* locates Rowling's series within "an alternative genealogy of Eng Lit," a "lineage [that] would run from Spenser through Shakespeare's late plays to Christina Rossetti's 'Goblin Market.'. . . This family of stories," she continues, "isn't only whimsical and fey, but can be shrewd, tough and satirical, too." In *Children's Literature* (2001), Peter Hunt chooses not read the *Harry Potter* series as derivative, believing that "it would be insulting the obvious intelligence of Rowling to suggest [her attention to the literary past] is accidental" (123); Hunt claims instead that Rowling is "tracing echoes" (122) and that the series offers "an eccentric blend of the comfortably predictable and the unsettlingly unexpected" (123). Young adult author Jennifer Donnelly uses the appeal of Harry's story as reason enough to remove this particular distinction between children's literature and adult literature: "Just because we choose to take Harry Potter along on the morning commute," she explains, "it doesn't mean we're regressing." "It simply means," she continues, "we like Harry. His world and his struggle to find his place in it interest us. Should we deny ourselves the pleasure of his company simply because he's 14 and we're not?"

Philip Pullman would agree with Donnelly's argument, having himself spoken on the appeal of story for all readers, most publically in his acceptance speech for the Carnegie Medal in 1996. In this widely disseminated speech—it appears on the Random House website for *His Dark Materials*—Pullman reverses the established hierarchy to value children's books over contemporary adult offerings for this very element of fiction. His comments are worth quoting at length:

> There are some themes, some subjects, too large for adult fiction; they can only be
> dealt with adequately in a children's book. The reason for that is that in adult
> literary fiction, stories are there on sufferance. Other things are felt to be more
> important: technique, style, literary knowingness. Adult writers who deal in
> straightforward stories find themselves sidelined into a genre such as crime or

science fiction, where no one expects literary craftsmanship. But stories are vital. . . . And by story I mean not only Little Red Riding Hood and Cinderella and Jack and the Beanstalk but also the great novels of the nineteenth century, *Jane Eyre, Middlemarch, Bleak House* and many others: novels where the story is at the center of the writer's attention, where the plot actually matters. ("Carnegie")

The vitality of story to literary endeavor and to art emerges from Pullman's speech—along with a not-so-implicit critique of the current state of literary fiction, as the speech proceeds: "The present-day would-be George Eliots," Pullman says, "take up their stories as if with a pair of tongs. They're embarrassed by them. If they could write novels without stories in them, they would. Sometimes they do," he concludes ("Carnegie").[15] For Pullman, as for others who value story, "big themes" are "embodied best in story" ("Re: A. S. Byatt"), making story the location for literary value, for literary art. Rowling's adept blend of generic forms results not in a literary patchwork, then, which carelessly shows its seams (as Byatt would say). Rather, Rowling's narrative reveals different colors in various lights and tests our current generic vocabulary.

Such narrative "flexibility" (Craven) and diverse literary genealogy become the location of both the criticism leveled against children's books like Rowling's series and the source of their literary value. It's also this very quality—flexibility—that may well make Rowling's fiction desirable to contemporary readers; it also marks the series' ability to cross the lines imposed by critics, as well as publishers.[16] Flexible in their narratives, frequently embraced by a "more complex, hybrid and mobile readership" (Connor 27), works of children's literature like Rowling's *Harry Potter* present a multiplicity that threatens the boundaries of literary fiction for some and energizes its future for others. As Jackie Wullschlager notes, Rowling, like other authors before her, "has grasped the possibilities of a double articulation" and created a series which "stimulat[es] the imagination of different readers at different levels." At issue is the cultural status and value of "story" in the hands of a diverse readership, coupled with a long-standing tradition of excluding the popular and the best-selling, even when that literature is also prize-winning.

Along with Philip Pullman, Mark Haddon, and other best-selling and prize-winning authors writing for children and adults, then, Rowling reveals the dual role children's literature currently serves in contemporary culture, particularly contemporary British culture. On the one hand, children's literature is seen to partake in a cultural trend of regressive nostalgia for "genre" fiction; adults who read it are looking for "comfort," as Byatt remarks, rather than the challenge and thrill of art. That such children's books are also best sellers only confirms their lowly status in the eyes of these critics, the books' artistic worth further compromised by their popular appeal. On the other hand, children's literature is heralded as the savior of literary fiction and the equal of "adult" fare. The works of Rowling and Pullman, as Natasha Walter argues for *The Independent*, offer "imagination" and a "flaring new energy," which can "lead us out of the well-trodden paths" of contemporary adult reading. If best-selling, popular, cross-over children's literature has indeed become the flash point for the future of literary fiction in Britain, Rowling's series is a standard-bearer for future definitions of the genre of "children's literature."

NOTES

1. As Peter Hunt (2001) remarks, "One of the delights of children's literature is that it does not fit easily into any cultural or academic category" (1). However, Hunt's working definition—"texts for children" (3)—indicates that certain expectations about purpose and audience create a genre of children's literature, even if, as Hunt and others demonstrate, this literature lacks "generic 'purity'" (3).

2. There have, of course, been detractors, including Harold Bloom (2000), Philip Hensher (2000), Jack Zipes (2001), and A. S. Byatt (2003). For these critics, Rowling's formulaic novels fail an aesthetic test for narrative art: "the world of these books is thin and unsatisfactory, their imagery is derivative, their characterisation automatic, and their structure deeply flawed" (Hensher 2000). Their critiques also decry the series' popularity, claiming that its success illustrates only the regressive reading pleasures of its child and childish adult audiences.

3. Jerome Buckley offers a useful summary of the *bildungroman*'s "principal elements" in *Season of Youth: The Bildungsroman from Dickens to Golding* (1974): "childhood, the conflict of generations, provinciality, the larger society, self-education, alienation, ordeal by love, the search for a vocation and a working philosophy" (18). Within this narrative framework, protagonists "are subjective and self-conscious to a high degree"; while reaching maturity, they "will feel [their] bondage, the multiple constraints of living," "bringing [their] own inner resources of sensitivity to confront a hostile and insensitive environment" (280–22). By the end of the story, it is their "quickened imagination, moral or aesthetic, that animates and eventually outlives the troubled season of youth" (282).

4. In connecting Rowling and Austen through their narrative form, my argument stands in contrast to Maria Nikolajeva's claim that "Rowling does not use any of the more sophisticated narrative techniques for conveying psychological states" and that the "*Harry Potter* novels are clearly action-oriented rather than character-oriented" (134). For an extended discussion of Austen's influence on Rowling, see Westman, "Perspective, Memory, and Moral Authority: The Legacy of Jane Austen in J. K. Rowling's *Harry Potter*" (2007).

5. See, for example, Westman, "Spectres of Thatcherism: Contemporary British Culture in J. K. Rowling's *Harry Potter* Series" (2002), Anatol, "The Fallen Empire: Exploring Ethnic Otherness in the World of Harry Potter" (2003), Chevalier, "The Liberty Tree and the Whomping Willow: Political Justice, Magical Science, and Harry Potter" (2005), and Horne, "Harry and the Other: Answering the Race Question in J. K. Rowling's *Harry Potter*" (2010).

6. In *Re-Reading Harry Potter* (2003), Suman Gupta attempts to explain the changes between books through theories of "progression" and "elaboration" (94–96), without addressing this formal element of Rowling's prose fiction.

7. For a succinct yet comprehensive overview of the school story, see Jeffrey Richards, "The School Story" (1992). Peter Hunt offers a lively and even more concise overview in the entry "School Stories" for his *Children's Literature* (2001). See also the

discussions of the school story in chapters 6–10 of *Children's Literature, An Illustrated History* (1995), edited by Peter Hunt.

8. One of Rowling's favorite books as a child—Noel Streatfeild's *Ballet Shoes* (1936)—reminds us that the school story can also be a story of vocation and career. We should also acknowledge the transformation of the school story across the cultural landscape of the twentieth century: for many of Rowling's generation, the words "school story" do not raise images of Hughes's Tom Brown, Blyton's Darrell Rivers, or Streatfeild's Fossils, but the rebellious trio of Lindsay Anderson's cult film *If...* (1968). This trio's anarchic impulse to destroy the stifling intersection of school and state finds voice through Rowling's trio, too, as Harry, Ron, and Hermione turn to rebellion as a final solution for educational reform when all other means fail.

9. For further discussion of formal classroom instruction at Hogwarts, see Elisabeth Gruner's "Teach the Children: Education and Knowledge in Recent Children's Fantasy" (2009).

10. History of Magic, with its lectures by the ghost, Professor Binns, appears to be the exception to this pedagogical rule—Rowling's humorous commentary, perhaps, on the traditional view of history as impersonal and absolute as well as Binns's faulty belief that teaching, like the writing of history, is a singular, nonparticipatory event.

11. Rowling's series seems to defy easy categorization for a number of critics, including Farah Mendlesohn, who notes the hybrid quality of Rowling's fantasy and locates the series in two of her categories of fantasy: intrusion fantasy and portal-quest fantasy (246–47).

12. See Horne for further discussion of these limitations in Rowling's series.

13. Queried by fans about his comment in 2000 in *The Writer's Handbook* that "children's fiction was patronised by general publishing," Philip Pullman, author of *His Dark Materials*, replies in 2003 that "the scene has changed—more, I suspect, because some children's books have made large amounts of money than because literary editors have suddenly become aware of quality they were unable to see before" ("About the Writing").

14. For a comprehensive overview and analysis of Harry Potter detractors, see Nel, "Is There a Text in This Advertising Campaign? Literature, Marketing, and Harry Potter" (2005).

15. Pullman revealed on the ChildLit listserv in 2003 that he was thinking of A. S. Byatt as he describes those "present-day would-be George Eliots" who self-consciously "take up their stories as if with a pair of tongs" ("Re: A. S. Byatt").

16. As Steven Connor remarks in *The English Novel in History, 1950–1995* (1996), "Despite the survival of very strong forms of stratification, both the reading and readerships of fiction have become more complex, hybrid and mobile in the postwar period than previously" (27). Although Connor speaks to the contemporary readership of Britain, his observations may hold true for readers from other nations, given the global success of Rowling's series and other literature for children. According to Connor, readers have "multiple affiliations and participate in multiple readerships and forms of reading" (23), and I would claim that many look to contemporary children's literature to fulfill those readerly desires.

WORKS CITED

Anatol, Giselle Liza. "The Fallen Empire: Exploring Ethnic Otherness in the World of Harry Potter." In *Reading Harry Potter: Critical Essays*, edited by Giselle Liza Anatol, 163–78. Westport, CT: Praeger, 2003.

Anelli, Melissa, and Emerson Spartz. "The Leaky Cauldron and Mugglenet Interview with
    Joanne Kathleen Rowling." *The Leaky Cauldron*. 16 July 2005; http://www.the-
    leaky-cauldron.org.
Austen, Jane. *Emma*. 1816. New York: Oxford UP, 1990.
Blakeney, Sally. "The Golden Fairytale." *The Weekend Australian*, 7 November 1998, R10.
    Lexis-Nexis Academic. Accessed 1 June 2006. http://web.lexis_nexis.com/universe.
Bloom, Harold. "Can 25 Million Book Buyers Be Wrong? Yes." *The Wall Street Journal*,
    11 July 2000.
Blyton, Enid. *First Term at Malory Towers*. 1946. London: Egmont Books Limited, 2000.
———. *In the Fifth at Malory Towers*.1950. London: Dean, 1998.
———. *Last Term at Malory Towers*. 1951. London: Dean, 1994.
———. *Second Form at Malory Towers*. 1947. London: Granada, 1967.
———. *Third Year at Malory Towers*. 1948. London: Granada, 1967.
———. *Upper Fourth at Malory Towers*. 1949. London: Egmont UK Limited, 2006.
Booth, Wayne C. *The Rhetoric of Fiction*. Chicago: U of Chicago P, 1961.
Buckley, Jerome Hamilton. *Season of Youth: The Bildungsroman from Dickens to Golding*.
    Cambridge: Harvard UP, 1974.
Byatt, A. S. "Harry Potter and the Childish Adult." *New York Times*, 7 July 2003.
Chevalier, Noel. "The Liberty Tree and the Whomping Willow: Political Justice, Magical
    Science, and Harry Potter." *The Lion and the Unicorn* 29 (2005): 397–415.
Clark, Beverly Lyon. *Kiddie Lit: The Cultural Construction of Children's Literature in
    America*. Baltimore: Johns Hopkins UP, 2003.
"Comic Relief Live Chat Transcript." March 2001. *Quick Quotes Quill*. 1 June 2006. http://
    www.quick-quote-quill.org.
Connor, Steven. *The English Novel in History, 1950–1995*. New York: Routledge, 1996.
Craven, Peter. "Hooray for Harry." *The Australian*, 16 July 2005, 1. *Lexis-Nexis Academic*.
    6 June 2006. <http://web.lexis_nexis.com/universe>.
Donnelly, Jennifer. "Paperback Writer." *The Guardian*, 10 July 2004. 13 July 2004. http://
    books.guardian.co.uk/departments/childrenandteens/story/0,6000,1257803,00.html.
Elster, Charles. "The Seeker of Secrets: Images of Leaning, Knowing, and Schooling."
    In *Harry Potter's World: Multidisciplinary Critical Perspectives*, edited by
    Elizabeth E. Heilman, 203–20. New York: RoutledgeFalmer, 2003.
Gibbs, Nancy. "J. K. Rowling." *Time* 17 December 2007. Accessed 19 December 2007.
    http://www.time.com.
Gruner, Elisabeth Rose. "Teach the Children: Education and Knowledge in Recent
    Children's Fantasy." *Children's Literature* 37 (2009): 216–35.
Gupta, Suma. *Re-Reading Harry Potter*. London: Palgrave, 2003.
Hensher, Philip. "Harry Potter and the Art of Making Money." *The Independent*, 19 June
    2003, 15. *Lexis-Nexis Academic*. 18 June 2006. http://web.lexis_nexis.com/universe.
———. "Harry Potter, Give Me a Break." *The Independent*, 25 January 2000, 1.
Horne, Jackie C. "Harry and the Other: Answering the Race Question in J.K. Rowling's
    Harry Potter." *The Lion and the Unicorn* 34 (2010): 76–104.
Hughes, Thomas. *Tom Brown's Schooldays*. 1857. New York: Oxford, 1999.
Hunt, Peter. *Children's Literature*. London: Blackwell, 2001.
———. "Children's Literature and the Academy: Problems of a 'New' Literature." *New
    Literature Review* 21 (1991): 82–89.
———, ed. *Children's Literature, An Illustrated History*. Oxford: Oxford UP, 1995.
———. "Poetics and Practicality: Children's Literature and Theory in Britain." *Lion and
    the Unicorn* 19 (1995): 41–49.

If . . . Directed by Lindsay Anderson. Performed by Malcolm McDowell, David Wood, Richard Warwick, Christine Noonan, and Rupert Webster. 1968. Paramount. DVD. The Critereon Collection, 2007.

Johnstone, Anne. "Happy Ending, and That's for Beginners." *The Herald* (Glasgow), 24 June 1997, 15.

Lewis, C. S. "On Three Ways of Writing for Children." 1952. In *Of Other Worlds: Essays and Stories,* edited by Walter Hooper, 22–34. London: Geoffrey Bles, 1966.

Lundin, Anne. *Constructing the Canon of Children's Literature: Beyond Library Walls and Ivory Towers.* New York: Routledge, 2004.

McCrum, Robert. "Underwhelmed." *The Observer,* 24 December 2000. Accessed 25 April 2001. http://guardian.co.uk/Archive/Article/0,4273,4109617,00.html.

Mcveigh, Karen. "At a University Near You—Harry Potter and the Philosopher's Work." *The Scotsman,* 31 July 2003, 10. *Lexis-Nexis Academic.* 18 June 2006. http://web. lexis_nexis.com/universe.

Mendlesohn, Farah. *Rhetorics of Fantasy.* Middletown, CT: Wesleyan UP, 2008.

Nel, Philip. "Is There a Text in This Advertising Campaign? Literature, Marketing, and Harry Potter." *Lion and the Unicorn* 29 (2005): 236–67.

Nikolajeva, Maria. "Harry Potter—A Return to the Romantic Hero." In *Harry Potter's World: Multidisciplinary Critical Perspectives,* edited by Elizabeth E. Heilman, 125–40. New York: RoutledgeFalmer, 2003.

Pullman, Philip. "About the Writing." *Philip-Pullman.com.* 20 May 2004. http://www. philip-pullman.com/about_the_writing.asp.

———. "His Dark Materials—Philip Pullman—Carnegie Medal Acceptance Speech." 1996. Random House. 2 June 2004. http://www.randomhouse.com/features/pullman/ philippullman/speech.html.

———. "Re: A.S. Byatt on 'Harry Potter and the Childish Adult.'" Online posting. 8 July 2003. Childlit Discussion List. 9 July 2003.

Renton, Jennie. "The Story Behind the Potter Legend." *Sydney Morning Herald.* 28 October 2001. *Quick Quotes Quill.* 1 June 2006. http://www.quick-quote-quill.org.

———. "The School Story." In *Stories and Society: Children's Literature in its Social Context,* edited by Dennis Butts, 1–21. New York: St. Martin's Press, 1992.

Rowling, J. K. *Harry Potter and the Chamber of Secrets.* London: Bloomsbury, 1998.

———. *Harry Potter and the Deathly Hallows.* London: Bloomsbury, 2007.

———. *Harry Potter and the Goblet of Fire.* London: Bloomsbury, 2000.

———. *Harry Potter and the Half-Blood Prince.* London: Bloomsbury, 2005.

———. *Harry Potter and the Order of the Phoenix.* London: Bloomsbury, 2003.

———. *Harry Potter and the Philosopher's Stone.* London: Bloomsbury, 1997.

———. *Harry Potter and the Prisoner of Azkaban.* London: Bloomsbury, 1999.

———. *J. K. Rowling Official Site.* 2006. http://www.jkrowling.com.

———. "Let Me Tell You a Story." *Sunday Times,* 21 May 2000: 8.

"Royal Albert Hall Webcast." 2003. http://www.accio_quote.org/.

Solomon, Evan. "J. K. Rowling Interview." *Hot Type.* CBC. July 2000. http://cbc.ca/ programs/sites/hottype_rowlingcomplete.html.

Streatfeild, Noel. *Ballet Shoes.* 1936. New York: Dell, 1979.

Taylor, Charles. "A. S. Byatt and the Goblet of Bile." *Salon.com,* 8 July 2003. http//www. salon.com/books/feature/2003/07/08/byatt_rowling/.

Walter, Natasha. "Why Shouldn't the Booker Prize Go to a Children's Book?" *The Independent,* 24 August 2001, 5. *Lexis-Nexis Academic.* Accessed 7 December 2001. http://web.lexis-nexis.com.

Warner, Marina. "Did Harry Have to Grow Up?" *The Observer*, 29 June 2003. Accessed 19
     June 2004. http://books.guardian.co.uk/departments/childrenandteens/
     story/0,6000,986970,00.html.

Westman, Karin E. "Perspective, Memory, and Moral Authority: The Legacy of Jane
     Austen in J. K. Rowing's *Harry Potter*." *Children's Literature* 35 (2007): 145–65.

———. "Spectres of Thatcherism: Contemporary British Culture in J. K. Rowling's Harry
     Potter Series." In *The Ivory Tower and Harry Potter: Perspectives on a Literary Phenom-
     enon*, edited by Lana Whited, 305–28. Columbia: U of Missouri P, 2002.

Whisp, Kennilworthy [J. K. Rowling.] *Quidditch Through the Ages*. London: Bloomsbury,
     2001.

Wullschalger, Jackie. *The Financial Times*, 20 November 1999, 4. *Lexis-Nexis Academic*. 6
     June 2006. http://web.lexis_nexis.com/universe.

Zipes, Jack. *Stick and Stones: The Troublesome Success of Children's Literature from Slovenly
     Peter to Harry Potter*. New York: Routledge, 2001.

FURTHER READING

Anatol, Giselle, ed. *Reading Harry Potter: Critical Essays*. Westport, CT: Praeger, 2003.

Beckett, Sandra L. *Crossover Fiction: Global and Historical Perspectives*. New York: Rout-
     ledge, 2009.

Blake, Andrew. *The Irresistible Rise of Harry Potter: Kid-Lit in a Globalised World*. London:
     Verso, 2002.

Clark, Beverly Lyon. *Kiddie Lit: The Cultural Construction of Children's Literature in
     America*. Baltimore: Johns Hopkins UP, 2003.

English, James F. *A Concise Companion to Contemporary British Fiction*. London: Black-
     well, 2006.

Falconer, Rachel. *The Crossover Novel: Contemporary Children's Fiction and Its Adult
     Readership*. New York: Routledge, 2009.

Fry, Stephen. "Launch Day Interview Aboard the Hogwarts Express." *Bloomsbury Press*. 8
     July 2000. *Accio Quote*. 31 May 2007. <http://www.acio-quote.org/articles/2000/0700-
     bloomsbury-fry.html>.

———. "Living with Harry Potter." *BBC Radio 4*. 10 December 2005. *Accio Quote*. 31
     August 2007. <http://www.accio_quote.org/articles/2005/1205_bbc_fry.html>.

Heilman, Elizabeth. *Critical Perspectives on Harry Potter*. 2nd ed. New York: Routledge,
     2008.

Richards, Jeffrey. *Happiest Days: The Public Schools in English Fiction*. Manchester:
     Manchester UP, 1988.

Squires, Claire. *Marketing Literature: The Making of Contemporary Writing in Britain*.
     London: Palgrave, 2007.

Whited, Lana, ed. *The Ivory Tower and Harry Potter: Perspectives on a Literary Phenom-
     enon*. Columbia: University of Missouri Press, 2002.

PART II

PICTURES AND POETICS

CHAPTER 5

WANDA'S WONDERLAND: WANDA GÁG AND HER *MILLIONS OF CATS*

NATHALIE OP DE BEECK

BORN and raised in New Ulm, Minnesota, picture-book innovator Wanda Gág (1893–1946) presented herself as a blend of down-to-earth provincial and twentieth-century New Woman. She grew up in a German-speaking household and, after moving away from her rural enclave, she liked to speak fondly of her "peasant" roots. Her lifelong nostalgia for Old World folktales and traditions resulted in her translating and illustrating several of the Grimms' fairy tales and contributed to the structures underlying her influential picture books.[1]

Gág idealized her childhood and heritage, but her youth was a time of incredible responsibility and an independence born of necessity. She demonstrated an entrepreneurial streak as a teenager, when her father's death threatened to split her family and her earnings from freelance writing and illustration went to supporting her ill mother and six younger siblings. Her mother's death, while she was in art school, cemented her role as household breadwinner, and she struggled to reconcile her ambitions and her familial duty.

After making a permanent move to the metropolitan East Coast, Gág developed a respectable New York gallery following for her prints and drawings. She longed to devote all her time to fine art, yet she depended upon commercial art to pay the bills; with profits in mind, she amassed a portfolio of children's stories. Her picture-book debut, Millions of Cats (1928), was a hit, and several more picture books followed. Gág considered children's literature an extension of her commercial work, but as her reputation as an author-illustrator grew, she embraced her role as a proponent of mischievous fairy tales and oral storytelling.

While attending the Minneapolis School of Art in 1914, twenty-two-year-old Wanda Gág preferred what she called "graphic simplicity of line and color" to elaborated drawings. She complained in her journal about teachers who "warned me that unless I 'blocked in' the entire figure first (using about 4 or 5 lines) I would not be able to get the correct proportions and the action." She begged to differ and took a direct approach, "just drawing carefully in charcoal, starting at the head and going downward. . . . I have each of my lines meaning something very definite as I put them down one after the other" (Gág, *Growing Pains*, 420). She also expressed interest in reproducibility and printmaking, anathema to believers in singular, auratic art works (381). Resisting traditionalism and one-of-a-kind masterpieces, Gág aligned herself with popular culture, including comics, animation, and advertising. This preference might have maddened her drawing professors, but it led to the modernism of her mature work, including contemporary folktales for a new generation of visually literate young readers.

Gág, who admired nineteenth-century American painter James Abbott McNeill Whistler and his stubborn experimentalism, took an up-and-comer's stance against academicians. In her journals, she defended her composition methods against what she perceived as unnecessary guidelines. Like Whistler, Gág advocated less-is-more, line-based sketching, which she eventually would practice in her groundbreaking children's literature. This fresh style of illustration put Gág in line with modern art and the most innovative cartooning of her era, which itself redirected children's literature from the illustrated, or merely decorated, written text toward the text with a balance of interdependent words and pictures.

In 1917, Gág left her home state of Minnesota for a one-year scholarship at the Art Students League. In late 1910s and early 1920s New York, Gág found commercial opportunities and a gallery scene amenable to her fashionable yet pragmatic sensibility.[2] The youthful confidence of her earlier work in Minneapolis and New Ulm led to an energetic artistic career. She created graphic illustrations and prints, editorial cartoons for the leftist journal *The Liberator* (which became *New Masses*), and eventually picture books including *Millions of Cats* (1928), *The Funny Thing* (1929), *Snippy and Snappy* (1931), and *The ABC Bunny* (1933). Gág found that picture books, with their double-page spreads and multiple openings, were a promising medium for playing with the line and layout she had enjoyed since her student days. Picture books also had the potential to please a wide readership, whereas fine art and editorial cartooning were not always such lucrative or dependable pursuits. A passionate artist as well as a canny businessperson, Gág produced *Millions of Cats* and her other children's books with an interest in traditional storytelling, a desire for modernist respectability, and an eye on the bottom line.

Gág was a quintessential modernist, complicit in and yet critical of twenties cosmopolitanism and capitalism. She presented herself as a tough small-town girl making it in the big city, and her work for young readers reflects ambition tempered by practicality. Nostalgic for country living in Minnesota and on old farms not far from New York, but worldly in her artistic influences and her knowledge of the business world, Gág created humorous books that conveyed the anxieties of accelerated twentieth-century life; she effectively preserved the past by making brand-new commodities. Her paradoxical approach thus borrows from both the oral tradition and contemporary modes of production. Thus, *Millions of Cats*, a mass-produced book about having too much of a good thing, was a fitting break-through effort for Gág as a popular artist and visual-verbal storyteller. *Millions of Cats* is a modernist folktale and a text that formally and thematically influenced the twentieth-century picture books that followed.

Growing up, Gág had told stories to children; had written and illustrated for the *Minneapolis Journal*'s "juvenile supplement," the *Journal Junior*; and had developed a portfolio aimed at young readers (Gág, *Growing Pains*, xxxii).[3] Living in Manhattan, she designed folding story boxes for the short-lived Happiwork toy company while she made a living by her graphic art (Hoyle xv).[4] But children's books in general and original folktales like *Millions of Cats* in particular were not her primary ambition. She had little success with her portfolios of children's stories, or as a fine artist, until she "fled to the country"—rental properties in rural Connecticut and New Jersey—in 1923, when she was thirty years old. "I was weary of expressing other people's ideas when my own were clamoring for expression," she wrote. At home outside the city, "I drew only what I wanted. . . . This 'selfishness' resulted in my being accepted by the Weyhe Galleries—this eventually creating interest in my rejected juveniles [i.e., children's books]" (Mahony and Whitney, *Contemporary Illustrators*, 32).

Gág's March 1928 exhibition at the Weyhe Gallery in New York came to the attention of Coward-McCann editor Ernestine Evans, who asked to see Gág's material for children. *Millions of Cats*, an original narrative with the structure of a classic folktale, had developed from a story Gág made up for the children of friends in Connecticut (Winnan 36), and this was to be Gág's literary debut.[5] On 10 April 1928, the artist wrote in her diary: "Last week I signed a contract for a children's book—my *Millions of Cats* with about 30 illustrations. . . . It's pretty much of a rush job, and how I will ever have the energy to do that and slide in a few spring landscapes besides, I don't know" (Winnan 256).

Yet she managed to do it. Coward-McCann published the book in September 1928, just five months after Evans met Gág—a whiplash-inducing turnaround time. The speedy production attests to the thriving children's publishing industry of the 1920s and the publisher's confidence that *Millions of Cats* would impress holiday shoppers.[6] Books for young readers typically nodded to preindustrial lore and cozy scenes of rural life, notwithstanding the fact that the 1920s children's book industry was an intensive business. As Gág's experiences suggest, modern children's writers and editors gave hands-on attention to marketing as well as technical details of production. Like any professional artists, they were expected to be both visionaries and salespeople.[7] And although Gág was new to the children's book industry, she was savvy after more than a decade in the art marketplace. If *Millions of Cats* was a "rush job," it was preceded by years of practical experience and storytelling. Gág knew who she was as an artist and how best to promote her work. *Millions of Cats* is an elegant commercial product that closely resembles a homemade toy book; it features economical, lively prose, a catchy rhyming refrain, hand-lettering by Wanda's brother, Howard, and Wanda Gág's deceptively simple black-and-white compositions.[8]

For all its originality, *Millions of Cats* opens in a predictable fashion, initially promising few departures from fairy-tale formula: "Once upon a time there was a very old man and a very old woman." Gág's pictures depict a tiny cottage, a bearded man smiling as he smokes his pipe, and a round, mischievous-looking woman with arms akimbo, wearing a long country dress and apron. They appear cheerful, even though the text informs readers "they couldn't be happy because they were so very lonely" (unpaged). For all Gág's skill as a designer, the layout of this introductory page seems clumsy and merits closer consideration. The initial words appear in the upper right corner and the conclusion of the statement in the lower left, directing a viewer in a diagonal direction contrary to the natural flow of reading. The pictures bracket the words, arresting the narrative's progress and slowing the reader down. This curious effect could be said to suspend the vision in time, along with this fairy-tale setting, before the action (and irrevocable change) commences. With a turn of the page, the visuals unspool and the story is off, with the very old man setting out across a hilly landscape in search of "a sweet little fluffy cat" to become their companion. What he finds in the third spread are "Hundreds of cats, / Thousands of cats, / Millions and billions and trillions of cats" —and they bring near-disaster on his bucolic idyll.

Millions of Cats's rustic setting—the cottage of the generic "very old" couple, a verdant summer landscape of leafy trees and cumulus clouds, and not a skyscraper or machine in sight—nods to Old World landscapes and fairy tales familiar to many transatlantic immigrants. Gág credited the book's setting and style to the German and Eastern European tales she heard from her family when growing up. Like Gág, children's writer-illustrators of the twenties and thirties often highlighted their international origins and constructed provincial fantasies for comparatively urbane audiences. Hungarian-born Miska Petersham and his wife, Maud, who coillustrated the chapter book *Poppy Seed Cakes* (1924) and collaborated on the large-format picture book *Miki: The Book of Maud and Miska Petersham* (1929) and its sequels, exuberantly celebrated ethnicity. In *Miki*, an American boy, modeled after the Petershams' son, travels "on a boat, and on a train and another train" to the quaint Hungary of his paternal family. There, he stays with "a nice kind old man and a very fat smiling old woman," meets friendly villagers, visits Budapest, and learns traditional Hungarian stories, customs, and dances. The Petershams, like Gág, presented generic peasant types for the entertainment and education of an American readership. Their work influenced other world-traveling writer-illustrators like Ingri and Edgar Parin d'Aulaire, whose story of a boy in Norway, *Ola* (1932), echoes *Miki* and likewise led to sequels. In the 1910s and 1920s, illustrated folktale collections were popular, and—like Charles Finger's *South and Central American Tales from Silver Lands*, which won the Newbery Medal in 1925—many Newbery titles of the twenties covered international subject matter (albeit filtered through Anglo-American or Western European ideologies, like Hugh Lofting's 1923 Medalist,

The Voyages of Doctor Dolittle, or Arthur Bowie Chrisman's 1926 Medalist, *Shen of the Sea*). *Millions of Cats* was a 1929 Newbery Honoree, or runner-up, competing with John Bennett's Asian-themed, comical folktale collection, *The Pigtail of Ah Lee Ben Loo*, and that year's winner, Eric P. Kelly's *The Trumpeter of Krakow*, a historical novel set in fifteenth-century Poland. In addition, the New York Public Library collected international children's titles in many languages, to entertain and educate readers with an interest in travel and heritage. Gág's self-consciously folksy picture books and, later, her Grimm fairy-tale retellings characterized this popular direction in children's literature.

Gág's ethnicity and regional American roots, which still help her maintain an audience in her home state of Minnesota, charmed the first- and second-generation American adults who were the likely buyers of children's books. Further, Gág's own childhood hardships contributed to a human interest story that boosted her reputation as a fine artist and as a children's creator. Her father and later her mother died when she was still an adolescent, leaving her to raise six younger siblings; her early sketches and prints include fond likenesses of her brother and five sisters. Her precocious entrepreneurialism was a response to her mother's and then her siblings' financial and emotional needs. Barbara Bader has called Gág "ready-made for the role of nursery celebrity," and Gág gladly played the part with frequent allusions to her Bohemian heritage and immediate family (Bader 32). In a profile for a reference volume on children's illustrators, Gág wrote, "although my ancestry (of which I am very proud) is one hundred per cent peasant, it is a curiously articulate peasantry—and each Gág born into this hopelessly artistic family accepted pencil and paper along with the rest of life's inevitabilities" (Mahony and Whitney 1930, 31). A month before *Millions of Cats*'s publication, *Century* printed a treacly, dramatic profile that mimed Gág's self-description and described her as a fairy-tale figure herself: "This Gág comes from peasant stock, some valiant wood-carvers among them, and she knows her Thoreau. Solitude is precious to her" (Herendeen 429).

Gág's pastoralism and concern for socioeconomic class did not emerge only from her family's hardships or her basic love of fairy tales, however—although these factors were important. Gág's creative work developed in a period when urban dwellers witnessed the erasure of agrarian ways of life, immigrants and tourists enjoyed global mobility, and families expressed concern for children's well-being in the modern metropolis. "Curiously," according to *Century*'s adoring correspondent, "while Wanda Gág is entirely 'post-war,' modern, unshackled and all the rest of it, her work . . . antagonized no one. . . . Here to my mind is a real American. All the more American for being, as they say, 'second generation' American" (Herendeen 430–31). The writer suggests the broad appeal of Gág's artwork, as well as the artist's colorful persona.[9] *Millions of Cats* responded to the 1920s as surely as it structurally mimicked stories told at the hearth.

Millions of Cats could be described as an endorsement of the simple life in a complicated, information-heavy decade. The elderly couple is tempted to take more than they need and then deals with the unpleasant consequences; they temporarily forget that all they really need is one cat and their country cottage. Rural self-sufficiency is a common theme in Gág's single-panel art as well: a later source praised Gág's images of dilapidated household items and farm equipment, locating "the source of their inspiration in poverty—*The Tired Bed, Kitchen Shelf, The Franklin Stove, Spinning Wheel, Stone Crusher*" (Mahony and Whitney 1936, 19). By their titles alone, Gág's fine-art prints signal the utilitarian functions of domestic objects, although "poverty" is less the issue than an admirable work ethic, which Gág implies is fading in the new culture of convenience. Humble items like beds and stoves also acknowledge Gág's studies of impressionist and postimpressionist painters like Vincent van Gogh, another quintessential modernist who depicted quotidian objects and common people.[10]

Like Van Gogh—and like the atmospheric paintings and cinematic visions of the German Expressionists—Gág's work gives evidence of her fascination with "the atmosphere around objects," beyond the objects themselves (Winnan 252). She wanted to create a "[v]isualization of a flowing energy" and a "visible aura" around the inanimate and animate things she depicted (32). This interest resonates in the illustrations of malevolent clouds in *Millions of Cats*, which starts under an ink-stippled, open sky. When the very old man leaves the cottage and proceeds left to right across the wide double spread, he passes through farmland and over rolling hills. When a turn of the page reveals a bizarre herd of "Cats here, cats there, / Cats and kittens everywhere," the man recoils in a gesture of astonishment, leaning back and raising both hands. The dancing cats act playful and attentive, raising their pointed ears at the visitor. But the darkening skies lend an ominous note to the humorous scene.

The man is bewildered by so many delightful specimens, "and before he knew it, he had chosen them all" as pets. His shock at the profusion of desirable objects, and his excessive desire, can be read as symptoms of—and Gág's comment on—modern experience. (Critic Mary Kissell compares him to "a child in a candy store" and "a sort of naïve pied piper" who leads the cats home [58].) As he invites the cats back to his too-tiny cottage, a blank disc of sun ducks behind a doughy cloud and the thickly inked skies practically vibrate with tension. The man maintains a blithe facial expression, but the visual ambience lets readers know all is not well. Gág's pictures are cartoonish and comical, yet they are not entirely gentle or lacking in suspense. The imagery amplifies the uncanny threat posed by the cats, who in folktale fashion drink an entire pond and defoliate the hills, destroying the landscape they cross (not unlike a herd of cattle in the transformed American West of the early twentieth century).

The stormy skies accompany the old man all the way home, to the place where the story culminates in a cat-eat-cat battle. When the old woman protests, "They will eat us out of house and home," the man proposes, "We will let the cats decide which one we should keep." He asks the cats (which, being folktale cats, understand him perfectly),

> "Which one of you is the prettiest?" . . .
> "I am! I am! I am!" cried hundreds and thousands and millions and billions and trillions of voices, for each cat thought itself the prettiest.
> And they began to quarrel.

Gág pictures the man and woman racing for their cottage under a dark line of clouds. She then takes readers inside the cottage for a view of the duo's backs as they peer out a window, the outdoors hidden from view. A third illustration shows them hurrying outside again, to find a nearly empty hillside: "They could not see a single cat! / 'I think they must have eaten each other all up,' said the very old woman. 'It's too bad!'" Expertly, Gág spares her gentle readers an atrocious scene of cat carnage (visible to the couple from the window), then moves toward a happy resolution as the couple finds a "thin and scraggly" kitten hiding in the grass. "Oh, I'm just a very homely little cat," says the kitten when asked how it escaped being eaten. "So when you asked who was the prettiest, I didn't say anything." The couple has gotten their wish for a pet, and a ten-stage sequence shows the kitten drinking from a saucer of milk to become "nice and plump." The tale ends with the contented couple in their rocking chairs, the cat playing with a ball of yarn between them; the wordless final page pictures the surviving kitten curled beneath a flowery shrub.

The cat battle has been read as a comment on violence, and critiques of war and mass media are implicit in Gág's literature and art. These critiques also are explicit in her statement that "old fairy tales constitute an ideal medium for getting across (without pointing morals) such things as resourcefulness of poor people, the frequent fall of vanity [as in the cat battle], the importance of being kind to animals and wayfarers, the value of a sense of humor and of common sense, and of respect for the intelligence of quiet, modest people" (Gág 1939, 79). By 1939, on the eve of World War II, Gág likely had developed a more nuanced view of fairy tales and conflict than she had when inventing *Millions of Cats*. Yet whether or not a text like *Millions of Cats* in fact promotes lofty values, Gág's comments indicate the time-sensitive nature of every ostensibly timeless picture book. "It is possible to go too far in assuming that Gág consciously used current issues in her work, as Richard Cox does when he asserts that Gág's folktales 'were partly allegories of modern problems' and that 'the cat battle . . . may reflect her revulsion against . . . World War I,'" writes Kissell. "The violence of folktales, when they contain violence, is archetypal conflict; likewise, their themes are archetypal themes" (61).[11] Yet Gág advocated the fairy tale over other modes of storytelling for its ability to inform her era's jaded children and distract them from less wholesome entertainment. Although this philosophy was only nascent in *Millions of Cats*, the book's success gave Gág a public platform; she used her popularity to articulate her concern for modern children's welfare and to recommend a salutary dose of fairy tales. Although *Millions of Cats* is still enjoyable today, it is not timeless (if that term is understood to mean apolitical, atemporal, or ideal for children of any era). Its archetypes indirectly address the related issues that worried Gág in 1928, including a declining oral tradition, a delight in sensational mass entertainment, and a failure to value—or even to remember—the flavor of storytelling shared across nations and generations.

In its day, *Millions of Cats* impressed children's critics and booksellers. "Four and five-year-olds are very contemporary-minded. Recognizing this, many of our 'young' booklists might well be taken out of camphor and thoroughly renovated," wrote Alice Dalgliesh in the *Horn Book Magazine*, in an article illustrated exclusively with images from Gág's *Cats* and *ABC Bunny* (Dalgliesh 158). Librarian Anne Carroll Moore, who wielded enormous book industry power as a newspaper critic and as the director of the New York Public Library's Central Children's Room, wrote, "Wanda Gág sees everything as a child sees and she draws with a strength and beauty far removed from the commercialized art which is flooding the market with flashy picture books in crude color" (Moore 111). Moore, a proponent of storytelling and vehement foe of comics, praised the "living folk-tale quality of the text. . . . One marvels at the vigorous technique and the fertility and variety of an imagination which could give birth to such an old world picture story-book in present-day New York" (110–13). Editor May Massee wrote, "*Millions of Cats* is a perfect nonsense book and has been so adopted by the children" (Massee 244). Defenders of oral storytelling, who lamented the demise of village community in the industrialized twentieth century, welcomed *Millions of Cats* as a modern fairy tale. In doing so, they tactfully overlooked Gág's—and their own—participation in the East Coast publishing industry, a far cry from the spinning wheels and stone hearths of Old World fairyland.

Gág came to be viewed as a spokesperson for folktales and fairy tales. In a 1939 article, "I Like Fairy Tales," Gág saluted fairy tales' productive use of ambiguity. She was troubled that children saw and heard news of "the latest trunk-murder or love-nest scandal." She held forth against "goriness" in cinema, "blood-curdling Bang! Bang! adult program[s]" on the radio, "the lurid 'funnies,'" tabloid newspapers, and child-specific "toy automatics, sawed-off shotguns, and machine guns with shooting sparks" (Gág 1939, 76). Her concerns explain her choice to convey suspense and danger through atmospheric details like jagged, blustery skies and through the offstage brawl in *Cats*. "I think a great deal depends upon how such incidents are presented—that is, they should be handled in a playful or offhand manner, and not too realistically," she wrote (77). She recommended implying violence, if necessary, without resorting to graphic imagery. One might argue that the child's imagination will fill in the hideous gaps, yet Gág takes the position that old-fashioned forms of storytelling might produce a less-traumatized modern subject.

Gág's vision for a new breed of fairy tales, her lifelong resistance to convention, and her feel for popular culture enabled her to create a watershed American picture book. While the writing style won favor for its folk quality, the real innovation took place in the handspun art and the balance of words and pictures. Instead of having one stand-alone picture per page, with pictures subordinate to written narrative, Gág designed each double-page spread as a harmonious composition. She repeats layout patterns throughout the text, creating visual coherence, without duplicating layouts in consecutive spreads (e.g., a double spread with a long-distance shot of a complete landscape of "millions of cats" is followed by a spread that pairs blocks of text with middle-distance, portrait-style images of the man cuddling individual cats).

"Gág pioneered the format of composing each opening of the book (two facing pages) as one unique design, integrating the illustrations and the text," writes Winnan (37). Illustrated books of the era already included design features like decorative page borders to unify double-page spreads; for example, author Cornelia Meigs's railway fantasy, *The Wonderful Locomotive* (1928), exemplifies sophisticated page design with occasional framed, full-page images by Berta and Elmer Hader. But to 1928 audiences, Gág's black-and-white illustrations were a revelation, since *Millions of Cats* featured the familiarity of a fairy tale and the originality of visual sequence, variegated page compositions balancing words and pictures, and an overall cohesive design in which hand-lettered text functioned as an integral part of each visual.

In the years immediately following *Cats*, other children's writer-illustrators imitated Gág's homespun style. Double spreads in imitation of Gág, including a cross-country scene in Virginia Lee Burton's *Mike Mulligan and His Steam Shovel* (1939) that visually quotes the journey of the very old man in *Cats*, quickly became picture-book conventions. From the late twenties through the thirties, full-color double spreads—including memorable wordless spreads in Maud and Miska Petersham's *Miki* (1929), Elizabeth Mackinstry's *Aladdin and the Wonderful Lamp* (1935), and Lucy Herndon Crockett's *Lucio and His Nuong* (1939)—were an attractive addition to many pictorial sequences.

Truly sequential picture books and comics had of course existed before Gág experimented with their formats, notably in the mid-nineteenth-century European mode of Swiss lithographer Rodolphe Töpffer and in German comics artist Wilhelm Busch's "Max and Moritz" strips. As a printmaker, Gág likely knew the wordless, woodcut novels of the Belgian artist Frans Masereel, whose *Passionate Journey* (1919) and *The City* (1925) influenced the melodramatic wordless novels of American graphic artist Lynd Ward, starting with *God's Man* (1929), and the likewise wordless *He Done Her Wrong* (1930) by slapstick comics creator Milt Gross.[12] Masereel (although he personally rejected categorization) favored a German Expressionist style, which "focused on the social ills of a technological culture," writes David Beronä (11). Gág's picture books share the charcoaly, high-impact graphics and cautionary, counterindustrial bias of the Expressionists. In New York, she undoubtedly encountered the cinema of F. W. Murnau and Fritz Lang, aptly borrowing from their brooding, shadowy visuals for *Millions of Cats* and her later illustrated folktale translations. In child-specific picture books and comics, Gág had precursors in the British tradition of publisher Edmund Evans's group, and playful imagery in the American style of W. W. Denslow and comic-strip whiz Peter Newell.

Prior to the 1920s, illustrations in newspapers and books generally supplemented informational captions or two-liner he-said/she-said jokes. In these comics, illustrations were incidental to verbal punch lines. In the twenties, readers began encountering a combination of word and picture in the so-called gag cartoon (and the "Gág cartoon," punsters). According to Robert C. Harvey, *New Yorker* editor Harold Ross and cartoonist Peter Arno popularized, but did not invent, the form. In gag cartoons, the picture is not decorative. Instead, it is essential to understanding the written remarks: "The picture sidles into a reader's consciousness as a kind of visual puzzle, meaningless until reading the caption 'explains' it. The picture likewise 'explains' the caption," Harvey writes, and humor arises from the "surprise" of that juxtaposition (81).

Harvey's comments on cartoons resonate with Maurice Sendak's memorable formula for ideal picture-book storytelling, as practiced by British caricaturist Randolph Caldecott: "Words are left out—but the picture says it. Pictures are left out—but the word says it" (21). In modern times, an increasingly visually literate population decoded both words and pictures to make meaning. In the same decade that pictorial humor for adults was developed in single-panel cartoons, American picture-book creators and editors began counting on children to decode sequential word-and-picture progressions. Gág took this practice in the direction of visual-verbal literature for children. *Millions of Cats* was among the earliest American picture books to give pictures and words close to equal weight in the book design. Although *Cats* is still very much part of print culture and its written story makes sense without the pictures, such an interdependent word-and-picture sequence was unusual for a U.S. children's market where illustrated books (which included decorative but usually not diegetic pictures) were the norm.

In a 1947 retrospective on children's literature, Hellmut Lehmann-Haupt singled out *Millions of Cats* as a noteworthy example of "genuine animated drawing," akin to comics. He wrote that in early to mid-twentieth-century America, comics and sequential picture books exist in "the limbo of 'illegitimacy'" because of an association with crude, easy humor, and this kept sequential illustration from developing in the United States as it did in Europe. His concerns were borne out in 1954 by Fredric Wertham, whose fearmongering *Seduction of the Innocent* warned that crime and horror comics could harm impressionable young minds and lead to juvenile delinquency. "It is not the instrument which is at fault, but the tune that is played on it," Lehmann-Haupt cautioned; Gág "knew how to play the instrument" of comics, with an artful and wholesome balance of words and pictures that did not endanger tender minds (212). He compared Gág to British and European artists Kate Greenaway, Randolph Caldecott, Edward Ardizzone, and Jean de Brunhoff. British painter and poster artist William Nicholson, whose high-energy *Clever Bill* (1926) and lesser-known *The Pirate Twins* (1929) impressed U.S. audiences and influenced children's publishing, likewise was a Gág contemporary. Through her publishing contacts and venues like the *Horn Book Magazine*, Gág was aware of picture books by fellow artists, although she took a resolutely independent-minded approach to her own art for children.

On the reputation of *Cats* and the picture books that followed, Gág found herself in great demand and had to turn down invitations to illustrate other people's work. "*Millions of Cats* brought Gág financial security for the first time in her life, but to her it was only a means to an end," writes Audur Winnan (39). During the Depression, Gág took on these assignments to stay solvent, but in a sense this wonderfully playful, innovative creator was a reluctant children's author whose primary interests lay in printmaking and sketching. Based on her comments, she did not consider *Millions of Cats* the aesthetic equivalent of her gallery work. Regardless, the book is an extension of her printmaking and sketching, and in hindsight it shares key formal and political concerns of modernism.

For children's literature scholars today, *Millions of Cats* stands somewhere between a domestic craft and a modernist experiment in word-and-picture art. And for all its experimentalism, *Millions of Cats* has become a canonical text of children's literature. Sequential pictorial narratives strike readers today as commonplace fare, and Gág's black-and-white style lacks the multiple colors that can charge the most pedestrian book with excitement. Yet this now-prosaic-seeming text can be read as a landmark intersection of modernism and children's literature. On the one hand, Gág's idealism and conservative subject matter suggest longing for a folk past rather than modern spontaneity. *Millions of Cats* imitates an often-retold folktale of an earlier century, even though it is of twentieth-century vintage. On the other hand, Gág's cosmopolitan career and success as an independent woman belie her stylish focus on quaint rural scenery and obsolete artifacts. Her mass-reproducible picture book is a contemporary commodity, even if it venerates the oral tradition and handicraft. Gág combined nostalgia and novelty alike, and this placed her in tune with changing times in the late 1920s United States. *Millions of Cats* reconnects today's readers with that generative era.

NOTES

1. Some details and opinions in this essay appear in Nathalie op de Beeck's *Suspended Animation: Children's Picture Books and the Fairy Tale of Modernity* (Minneapolis: University of Minnesota Press, 2010).

2. In 1918, at the Art Students League, Gág began making etchings and drypoints, and in later years she experimented with charcoal drawing, lithography crayon drawing, and printing on unusual surfaces, notably sandpaper, for added textural dimension.

3. "I drew postcards and place cards, and instead of writing and illustrating stories and poems for pleasure, I now did so with the purpose of turning them into cash," Gág wrote of her youthful pursuits (*Growing Pains* xxxii). While keeping a ledger of this income, starting when she was fifteen years old (1908), Gág also began writing the diaries published in 1940 as *Growing Pains*.

4. "The boxes came flat, to be folded by the child, then stacked or nested; the story [e.g., The House That Jack Built] proceeded in continuous pictures and running text around each box and from the smallest to the largest" (Bader 33). Bader includes a photograph of one of these ingenious boxes (35).

5. The text's "earliest form may have existed by 1920, certainly by 1922; before it reached the public in 1928, it had a number of years to attain its astonishing economy, first in oral and then in written versions" (Kissell 57).

6. In her diary, Gág notes her busy winter schedule, due to seasonal promotion of the book in New York and in Washington, DC. A year later, in October 1929 and on the brink of the Depression, Gág oversaw the reprinting of the very popular *Cats* along with the first edition of her second picture book, *The Funny Thing*, which imitates the homemade, folksy qualities of *Cats* without the original's edginess. "Heaven knows what would have happened to the books if I hadn't been there to avert several calamities," she wrote, giving evidence for her reputation as a perfectionist (Winnan 257). On Gág's attention to detail, see Alma Scott.

7. Authors participated in the annual November marketing bonanza of Children's Book Week along with promotional activities like in-store appearances. In 1929, Gág read *The Funny Thing* for radio broadcast (Winnan 40).

8. Kissell likewise points out *Millions of Cats*'s "rhythmic language and cadenced rhyme" and "the standard home-journey-home plot structure of fairy tales" (57).

9. While she had strong opinions against disturbing content in children's literature, Gág did not lead the life of a schoolmarm. Her flirtatious personality undoubtedly contributed to her popularity. "She often said that she had three passions: art, sex, and growing things [i.e., gardening]," writes Winnan (42).

10. See Winnan, 30. Gág admired Van Gogh to the extent that she made a brush and ink drawing, *Old Shoes—Earle's* (1927), quoting Van Gogh's iconic 1880s paintings of peasant boots. Gág's twenties homage belongs on a modern-to-postmodern timeline from Van Gogh's painting to Walker Evans's photo to Andy Warhol's silkscreen *Diamond Dust Shoes*, à la Fredric Jameson's critical analysis in *Postmodernism: Or, The Cultural Logic of Late Capitalism*, 6–16.

11. Kissell, 61. For a contrary opinion, see Richard W. Cox.

12. Milt Gross's wordless comic book *He Done Her Wrong* (1930), which Gross glibly subtitled *The Great American Novel*, appears in a recent, unexpurgated reprint edition.

WORKS CITED

Bader, Barbara. *American Picture Books from Noah's Ark to The Beast Within*. New York: Macmillan, 1976.

Beronä, David A. *Wordless Books: The Original Graphic Novels*. New York: Abrams, 2008.

Cox, Richard W. "Wanda Gág: The Bite of the Picture Book." *Minnesota History* 44 (Fall 1975): 238–54.

Dalgliesh, Alice. "Small Children and Books." *Horn Book Magazine* 9, no. 3 (August 1933): 158–63.

Gág, Wanda. *Growing Pains: Diaries and Drawings for the Years 1908–1917*. St. Paul: Minnesota Historical Society Press, 1984.

———. "I Like Fairy Tales." *Horn Book Magazine* 15, no. 2 (March–April 1939): 74–80.

———. *Millions of Cats*. New York: Coward-McCann, 1928. Unpaged.

Gross, Milt. *He Done Her Wrong*, edited by Gary Groth. Seattle: Fantagraphics, 2005.

Harvey, Robert C. "Comedy at the Juncture of Word and Image." In *The Language of Comics: Word and Image*, edited by Robin Varnum and Christina T. Gibbons, 75–96. Jackson: UP of Mississippi, 2001.

Herendeen, Anne. "Wanda Gág: The True Story of a Dynamic Young Artist Who Won't Be Organized." *Century* (August 1928): 427–32.

Hoyle, Karen Nelson. "Introduction to the Reprint Edition." In *Growing Pains: Diaries and Drawings for the Years 1908–1917*, xiii–xxiii. St. Paul: Minnesota Historical Society Press, 1984.

Jameson, Fredric. *Postmodernism: Or, The Cultural Logic of Late Capitalism*. Durham, NC: Duke UP, 1991.

Kissell, Mary. "Wanda Gág's Millions of Cats: Unity Through Repetition." In *Touchstones: Reflections on the Best in Children's Literature*. Vol. 3, *Picture Books*, edited by Perry Nodelman, 54–62. West Lafayette, IN: ChLA Publishers, 1989.

Lehmann-Haupt, Hellmut. "Animated Drawing." In *Illustrators of Children's Books, 1744–1945*, edited by Mahony, Latimer, and Folmsbee, 197–214. Boston: Horn Book Inc., 1947.

Mahony, Bertha E., Louise Payson Latimer, and Beulah Folmsbee, eds. *Illustrators of Children's Books, 1744–1945*. Boston: Horn Book Inc., 1947.

Mahony, Bertha E., and Elinor Whitney, eds. *Contemporary Illustrators of Children's Literature*. Boston: Bookshop for Boys and Girls/Women's Educational and Industrial Union, 1930.

———, eds. Five Years of Children's Books. Garden City, NY: Doubleday, Doran, 1936.

Massee, May. "Developments of the Twentieth Century." In *Illustrators of Children's Books, 1744–1945*, edited by Mahony, Latimer, and Folmsbee, 221–46. Boston: Horn Book Inc., 1947.

Moore, Anne Carroll. "Millions of Cats." In *The Three Owls: Third Book: Contemporary Criticism of Children's Books, 1927–1930*, 110-13. New York: Coward-McCann, 1931.

Petersham, Maud, and Miska Petersham. *Miki: The Book of Maud and Miska Petersham*. Garden City, NY: Doubleday, Doran, 1929.

Scott, Alma. *Wanda Gág: The Story of an Artist*. Minneapolis: U of Minnesota P, 1949.

Sendak, Maurice. *Caldecott and Co.: Notes on Books and Pictures*. New York: Farrar, Straus and Giroux, 1988.

Winnan, Audur H. *Wanda Gág: A Catalogue Raisonné of the Prints*. Washington, DC: Smithsonian Institution Press, 1993.

FURTHER READING

Cartwright, Lisa and Marita Sturken, *Practices of Looking: An Introduction to Visual Culture*. New York: Oxford UP 2001.

Gág, Wanda. "A Hotbed of Feminists" (from *The Nation*, 22 June 1927). In *These Modern Women: Autobiographical Essays from the Twenties*, 126–34. Edited by Elaine Showalter. New York: Feminist Press, 1989.

Hoyle, Karen Nelson. *Wanda Gág: A Life of Art and Stories*. Minneapolis: U of Minnesota P, 2009.

Elkins, James. *Visual Studies: a Skeptical Introduction*. NY: Routledge, 2003.

L'Enfant, Julie. *The Gág Family: German-Bohemian Artists in America*. Afton, MN: Afton Historical Society, 2002.

Liddell, Mary. *Little Machinery: A Critical Facsimile Edition*, edited by Nathalie op de Beeck. Detroit: Wayne State UP, 2009.

Mickenberg, Julia. *Learning from the Left: Children's Literature, the Cold War, and Radical Politics in the United States*. New York: Oxford UP, 2005.

Mitchell, WJT. *What Do Pictures Want? The Lives and Loves of Images*. Chicago: U Chicago P, 2005.

CHAPTER 6

A CROSS-WRITTEN HARLEM RENAISSANCE: LANGSTON HUGHES'S *THE DREAM KEEPER*

KATHARINE CAPSHAW SMITH

As the most accomplished and wide-ranging African American writer of the twentieth century, Langston Hughes (1902–67) sought connection with all constituencies of the black community, producing poetry, plays, novels, short stories, essays, political writing, newspaper columns, and children's books. Not only did he engage audiences invested in particular genres, but also his art attempted to break down barriers between readerships: for example, he published exuberant blues and jazz poetry within the NAACP's Crisis *magazine, a journal invested in social progress and political change, and issued a weekly column in the* Chicago Defender *in which the fictional everyman "Jesse B. Semple" offered humorous reflections on lived urban experience. Such publications demonstrated Hughes's commitment to sharing literary art with all and to erasing boundaries between readerships and factions within the black community. His lifelong commitment to children's literature extended from his first publications, poems and essays in W. E. B. Du Bois's and Jessie Fauset's* The Brownies' Book *magazine (1920– 21), to his last composition, a picture book,* Black Misery *(1969). In between, he coauthored leftist children's fiction in the 1930s with Arna Bontemps and wrote many nonfiction books for young readers in the 1950s and 1960s. Hughes believed deeply in the beauty and integrity of African American life and used children's literature as a means to connect the young with black history, psychology, and culture.*

Langston Hughes's poetry collection, *The Dream Keeper* (1932), is a landmark publication within the field of American children's literature. The volume collects the
masterpieces that established Hughes as the "Negro poet laureate" of the 1920s,
including "I, Too," "The Negro Speaks of Rivers," "Mother to Son," and many
more. Published originally in periodicals like the *Crisis* and *The Brownies' Book* and
in poetry volumes like *The Weary Blues* (1926) and *Fine Clothes to the Jew* (1927),
the texts in *The Dream Keeper* originally attracted attention from the young as well
as from adults. Because many of the texts were either cross-written for both adults
and children or addressed originally to adults, *The Dream Keeper* demonstrates the
fluid boundaries between audiences in the 1920s and 1930s. Considering the significance of the poems in *The Dream Keeper*, it is a wonder that Hughes is not considered a luminary within children's literature. If he is remembered for his work for
young people, critics typically focus on his collaborations in fiction with Arna Bontemps in the 1930s. However, *The Dream Keeper* is a monumental contribution to
the field of children's poetry, one that reveals the aesthetic and political concerns of
the Harlem Renaissance and that demonstrates the centrality of childhood to social
change.

As readers of Hughes, we can discover much about the child's place within the
Harlem Renaissance and about the dynamics of literary production by attending to
The Dream Keeper. In the nineteenth and early twentieth centuries, many children's
"classics" appeared as novels when published, a situation that reflects established
publishing and authorship structures within white-authored children's literature.
African American children's literature, however, infrequently attracted the support
of mainstream children's publishers and rather found expression in more local and
ephemeral forms, like plays and pageants (many of which remain unpublished),
newspaper writing, and magazine publication. Of course there were popular white-
authored children's magazines in the 1920s and 1930s as well, but African American
authors rarely secured publishing contracts for children's novels, books of poetry,
or short-story collections. Within such a context, *The Dream Keeper* testifies to
Hughes's popularity among young readers. One can imagine young people
becoming familiar with major Hughes poems first in early 1920s newspaper publications and then perhaps through family and community recitation and again in
Hughes's collections for adults (which parents may have shared with children). By
the time white librarian Effie L. Power of Cleveland, Ohio, wrote to Hughes in 1931
to ask for a children's poetry collection, he was already popular among young African American readers, as well as among white and black adults, and in black oral
settings.

Three salient points surface with this perspective in mind: first, while the volume was published in 1932, its poems were originally published largely in the early
and mid-1920s, and as such retain the spirit of the cultural renaissance rather than
that of the Great Depression; second, the original publication in periodicals contributed to the cross-written dynamics of many of the poems, since they often
address concerns of both adults and children; and, third, although Hughes had
achieved popularity among black child audiences, *The Dream Keeper* was published

by Knopf, a mainstream house, and implicitly had an interracial and intergenerational audience in mind, a fact that contributes to the deliberate structuring of the text's sections. *The Dream Keeper* contains poems that remain frequently anthologized and reflects the genius of the artist and the range of his attention and productivity during the 1920s.

Hughes was one of the major writers of the Harlem Renaissance, a period loosely bracketed by the "red summer" of race riots in 1919 and the publication of Zora Neale Hurston's *Their Eyes Were Watching God* in 1937. The Harlem Renaissance, or "New Negro" Renaissance, was propelled by large-scale migration of African Americans from the rural South to the urban North after World War I. In cities like New York and Washington D.C., African Americans sought new opportunities for economic and political agency and new definitions of black identity. Through a variety of artistic expressions—including literature, dance, visual arts, and music—African Americans interacted with historical perspectives on blackness in America, engaging with the legacy of southern racism and violence, and erected new versions of black identity as progressive and urbane. These new definitions sometimes revalued connection to Africa, an impulse that dovetailed both with white modernist interest in the supposed essential "truth" of African passions and with white popular interest in the exotic and sexualized African subject. Thus, Harlem was "in vogue" for white Americans as well as for black but for quite different reasons. As the center of the cultural renaissance, both in practice and in the popular imagination, Harlem became the place where writers and political groups, like the NAACP, galvanized their efforts. Offering new versions of black childhood became another means by which writers seized control of representation and aimed to develop an innovative cultural identity. *The Dream Keeper* enables us to understand the significance of childhood to black cultural reinvention in the 1920s and 1930s. Importantly, Hughes was not alone in his commitment to children's literature, as major writers like W. E. B. Du Bois, Countee Cullen, Georgia Douglas Johnson, Jessie Fauset and many others, involved young people in efforts to recast and reclaim history and black identity.

It should be noted that the most recent edition of *The Dream Keeper* (Knopf 1994) retains the sections and section headings of the original but that the poems within each section do not appear in the original order. Presumably the contemporary editors wished to issue more poems per page and rearranged the poems within each section in order to utilize space most efficiently. (When citing poems, I use page numbers from the 1994 edition.) Also important to note is the fact that the 1994 edition does not retain the original drawings by Anna Sewell, most famous for her illustrations of Laura Ingalls Wilder's *Little House* series. Hughes had written to Sewell to suggest that she avoid "kinky headed caricatures" in the illustrations, explaining, "I hope that they can be beautiful people that Negro children can look at and not be ashamed to feel that they represent themselves" (qtd. in Rampersad 235). Indeed, Sewell's tender illustrations avoid caricature. The 1994 edition contains lovely scratchboard illustrations by African American artist Brian Pinkney and, as mentioned, retains the section groupings that organize the poems.

In general, African American children's texts of the 1920s reveal a deep interest in the natural world and in fantasy, as is apparent in poetry, illustrations, and fiction within Du Bois's and Fauset's children's magazine, *The Brownies' Book* (1920–21). This attention to nature and to staples of children's fantasy literature, like fairyland, suggests much about the desire of black writers to offer children a space insulated from racial strife. However, like poet Effie Lee Newsome's important children's page in *Crisis* magazine (1925–30), nature poetry often discloses an awareness of the black child's political position and vacillates between offering refuge from racism through nature and fantasy and using the landscape as a means to bolster the child's sense of racial pride in anticipation of social conflict. Similarly, the early sections of *The Dream Keeper* do not seem at first glance particularly race conscious but do involve a fusion of the political with subjects from fantasy or nature. The collection's first section contains several poems that Hughes originally published as a teenager in *The Brownies Book*, including "Fairies," "Winter Sweetness," "April Rain Song," and "Autumn Thought." These gentle verses bring a reader into conventional settings for children's texts. One could suggest that the original Knopf audience, then, would not be confronted immediately with the more socially challenging poems that conclude the volume and instead would ease into the book with texts that sound comforting and claim a kind of universal experience of the pleasures of romanticized childhood. However, even in this first section, glimmers of the particular position of African American childhood surface: the title poem, which is the first in the volume, contains a seed of fear, since the speaker wishes to protect the child's dreams "from the too-rough fingers / Of the world" (2). While one could see "The Dream Keeper" as rejecting sadness and embracing ambition and optimism, the initial poem also reveals imminent sorrow. The speaker desires to shelter the dreams of the reader and also acknowledges the presence of the "too-rough fingers" that destroy hope and vision. In fact, Hughes in this poem reflects a typical sentiment among black children's writers of the 1920s. In the pages of the *Crisis* and *The Brownies' Book*, fanciful stories of fairyland sit side-by-side with images of protest parades against lynching; poems impel children to retreat into nature even as editorials push black children to become race leaders through social action. Writers of African American children's literature of the 1920s were torn between the desire to protect children and recognition of the impossibility of sequestering black childhood from political realities. Hughes's first poem, the title of the collection, reflects this cultural ambivalence. In an era marked by Ku Klux Klan activity, race riots, and lynching, the idea of a childhood sheltered from political realities was, in practice, impossible.

With the Harlem Renaissance in mind, even a short poem like "Winter Sweetness" might take on race implications. It describes "a maple-sugar child" (4) looking out of the window of a house made of sugar. Recognizing that a central goal of *The Brownies' Book* was, in its own words, "to make colored children realize that being 'colored' is a normal, beautiful thing" (Du Bois, "The True Brownies" 286), Hughes's poem values the brown child looking from the window as being equally sweet as the landscape. Hughes might also be riffing on the edible child motif from racist popular culture, which envisioned black children as prey to alligators or as brown sugar candies (sometimes marketed as "Nigger Babies"); the "maple-sugar child" is not composed from plantation molasses, but rather from the forests of fairy tale. Even a poem like "Winter Sweetness," placed early in the volume perhaps in order to disarm a white audience ready to take issue with confrontational texts, has particular cultural meaning and reflects the fusion of the fantastic and political in 1920s black children's literature.

The second section of *The Dream Keeper*, entitled "Sea Charm," maintains the ostensibly race-neutral tone of the first but contains poems influenced by Hughes's world travels. In the early 1920s, as a seaman, he visited the west coast of Africa, France, and Italy, and he visited his father in Mexico in 1919 and 1920. In addition to several poems on sailors and sea travel, the section includes texts reflecting an awareness of global poverty, including "Mexican Market Woman" and "Parisian Beggar Woman." But perhaps the most striking poem in the section is "Beggar Boy," in which the speaker marvels at a brown child's resilience. Describing the child as "ugly," the speaker puzzles over the fact that "he plays upon his flute a wild free tune / As if Fate had not bled him with her knife!" (21). Important to note is the speaker's position as an outsider to the subject: the brown "beggar boy" is not identified through a specific ethnicity or nationality, and the speaker's assessment of the child is decidedly negative. What a surprise that the underestimated dark child can create art, "a wild free tune," one that is "free" of the speaker's judgment and free of the final line's comment on his life's possibilities! With this poem, Hughes indicates that the world miscalculates the resilience of ethnic childhood. The poem also alludes to the African American cultural trope of creativity in response to oppression, as in the mode of Paul Laurence Dunbar's famous "Sympathy," whose speaker asserts, "I know why the caged bird sings." In Hughes's poem, music liberates the spirit of the child, allowing him to resist the "Fate" that supposedly limits his future. And the adult can only marvel at the child's courage. The disjunction between the optimistic dreaming child and the world that surrounds him structures much of the poetic attention in *The Dream Keeper*. One final element to note in the "Sea Charm" section is its attention to death. Many poems either describe death directly, like "Irish Wake" and "Death of an Old Seaman," or allude to its inevitability, as at the end of "Parisian Beggar Woman": "Nobody but death / Will kiss you again" (22). Similarly, the section associates the sea with ambiguity. It could bring promise and change or the nothingness of "A wide, deep death" (14), as in "Sea Charm" that concludes the section in the original edition. These early sections, then, promise (at first glance) innocent children's poetry on nature, fairies, and the sea to an interracial audience. What becomes prominent, however, is Hughes's repeated attention to the tension between the hopes of childhood and children's harsh experiences in the world.

"Beggar Boy" becomes an apt preface to the third section of the text, "Dressed Up," since the earlier poem highlighted creativity as a response to an unkind world. In "Dressed Up," Hughes focuses on blues poetry and offers a preface that explains the difference between spirituals and blues music, stressing that, "the mood of the

Blues is almost always despondency, but when they are sung people laugh" (26). Like "Beggar Boy" whose "wild free" music enables the child to overcome hardship, in the "Dressed Up" section, Hughes presents blues music as a form of transcendence, one that acknowledges pain but allows for creation and catharsis through art. What distinguishes Hughes's collection from other African American children's literature of the Harlem Renaissance is its sensitivity to the child's emotional complexity. While other texts of the day might discuss prejudice or depict the wrongs of racism, few would state outright that black children have a right to sing the blues.

In order to understand the significance of Hughes's emotional sophistication, one must place *The Dream Keeper* within the larger cultural picture. Much African American children's literature emerged from the "uplift" movement of the 1910s, which strived to create a new version of black identity through social progress and modernity and advocated cultivating a "talented tenth," to use W. E. B. Du Bois's term, of progressive individuals who would lead the masses through admirable example. According to Kevin K. Gaines, the "uplift" movement combined both "collective social aspiration, advancement, and struggle" with ideals based on "class stratification as race progress" (xv) advanced by the black elite. Even in literature of the "New Negro" movement for adults, the emphasis on transformation and social improvement often dominated. As David Krasner explains, "Black art served in the capacity of guidance, defining the moral and ethical order and boundaries for a society fragmented, dislocated, and detached from the mainstream" (13). Children's literature emerging from the "uplift" movement, such as some material within *The Brownies' Book* and *Crisis* publications under Du Bois, acknowledged racism and impelled children to become socially active, only hinting at the actual psychological experience of black youth. As Dianne Johnson notes, letters to Du Bois's children's magazine revealed subtle responses to racist social structures, like schools. Alice Martin, a young person from Philadelphia, wrote *The Brownies' Book* in June 1920, "Sometimes in school I feel so badly. In the geography lesson, when we read about the different people who live in the world, all the pictures are pretty, nice-looking men and women, except the Africans. They always look so ugly" (Martin 178). But such expressions of sorrow are not the norm in the "uplift" approach dominating black children's literature; even early twentieth-century African American adult autobiographies that discuss childhood do not dwell in suffering. As Jennifer Lynn Ritterhouse argues, "these stories minimize certain aspects of the childhood experience—such as the child's natural desire for acceptance from other human beings and the depth of the pain, fear, and confusion that accompany rejection and ill use—in favor of a reasoned commentary on the pathological nature of whiteness" (112). Hughes's collection becomes that much more innovative within the context of representations of black youth, for no other writer of the 1920s would imagine blues poetry as suited to "New Negro" childhood.

To be sure, Hughes infuriated the literary elite when publishing poetry of the "low down" sort, even for adults. To offer a broad generalization, the aesthetic energies of the Harlem Renaissance were split between those who advocated cultural reinvention through art that engaged with the western tradition (sometimes amending and intervening in the tradition), like Countee Cullen, Du Bois, and Alain Locke, and writers who turned to folk forms in order to reinvent and revalue identity, like Hughes, Sterling Brown, and Zora Neale Hurston. Such a division was not always rigid, as some early Hughes poetry pulls together threads of the "uplift" tradition with folk reinvention. Certainly Du Bois and Locke were interested in folk music, but they preferred the spirituals as a model of artistic distinctiveness, as Du Bois outlines in *The Souls of Black Folk* (1903) and Locke in *The New Negro* (1925). But for the purposes of addressing Hughes's blues poetry, his triumphant essay "The Negro Artist and the Racial Mountain" (1926) enables us to understand the significance of the form as a mode of rebellion against middle-class literary expectations. He explains, "Let the blare of Negro jazz bands and the bellowing voice of Bessie Smith singing Blues penetrate the closed ears of the colored near-intellectuals until they listen and perhaps understand. . . . We younger Negro artists who create now intend to express our individual dark-skinned selves without fear or shame" ("The Negro Artist" 95). By offering blues poetry to young people, often imagined as the newest of "New Negroes" on the path to social progress, Hughes displayed great audacity and courage, as well as a fundamental respect for the lived experience of children. Indeed, we find that Hughes's blues poetry for children offers another dimension of an important pattern in early black children's literature. Many middle class intellectuals, like Du Bois in particular, did not imagine childhood as segregated from adult political concerns; he published accounts and images of lynching in the *Crisis* across from the Children's Page in order to impel social action. The *Crisis* also intersperses images of middle class black children within discussions of politics and race relations. We find that Hughes's blues poetry, then, also refuses to segregate childhood from larger social issues. Despite the first section's emphasis on nature, Hughes will not pretend that children are insulated from adult concerns, and in this way he resembles writers from the "uplift" school of black children's literature, which engaged child readers in civil rights efforts. But while "uplift" writers often emphasize children's investment in adult political life, Hughes allows children expressions of emotional honesty, disappointment, and pleasure through blues poetry.

One of Hughes's most famous poems, "The Weary Blues," appears in this section. Published in the May 1925 issue of *Opportunity* magazine and the first-prize winner of its annual poetry contest, "The Weary Blues" was tellingly inspired by Hughes's childhood experience with blues music. He explains in *The Big Sea*, "It was a poem about a working man who sang the blues all night and then went to bed and slept like a rock. That was all. And it included the first blues verse I'd ever heard way back in Lawrence, Kansas, when I was a kid" (215). Attached in Hughes's memory to youth, the poem depicts a spectator watching a blues singer "Down on Lenox Avenue" (30) in Harlem. Unlike other blues poems in this section, such as "Dressed Up" or "Homesick Blues," which are written entirely in dialect, this poem includes both the dialect of the blues singer and the conventional English of the speaker. By writing the poem in this way, Hughes unsettles any assumption that Hughes's natural, unschooled poetic voice as an African American would be dialect.

In addition, by including the perspective of the outsider, there is a distance from the blues singer that enables a reader to see the blues as art, and art in performance. The reader is with the speaker in the Harlem club—a setting that might not seem appropriate for a child audience—watching and listening to the bluesman perform. The speaker becomes more than a documentarian of the scene. Lines between the speaker and the blues performer start to break down, for as the speaker listens to the performer, the sound of music enters into the language of the speaker, enacting a call and response dynamic. "O Blues!" (30), the speaker cries when listening to the piano, joining in with the performance. The bluesman then responds with his own voice, "Ain't got nobody in all this world, / Ain't got nobody but my self," and the speaker becomes a rhythm section in describing the bluesman: "Thump, thump, thump, went his foot on the floor" (30). The poem initially establishes a separation between the speaker and the bluesman through different linguistic modes, a gesture that affirms both that dialect is not the innate voice of the black poet and that blues singers are artists. But once this linguistic separation is established, the poem blends the voices, allowing the blues to come through the educated voice of the speaker.

While blues songs might be sung alone, the blues performance actually creates community through audience response and understanding. By offering blues poems to a child audience, Hughes aims to build a similar sense of connection, a form of empathy regarding the difficulties of being young and black. The topics of other blues poems in this section invest children in the larger social context, as "Bound No'th Blues" refers to the "Great Migration" of African Americans from the Deep South to the urban North in the 1920s and acknowledges the isolation that comes with migration: "Hates to be lonely, / Lawd, I hates to be sad" (28). While one might imagine the Great Migration as a wholly hopeful moment for African Americans, many of whom were fleeing the terrors of the South for opportunity in the "Mecca of the New Negro" (as Alain Locke subtitled the "Harlem number" of *Survey Graphic* that he edited), Hughes's poems on migration allow for the expression of longing and loss. The melancholy speaker of "Po' Boy Blues" asserts, "Since I come up North de / Whole wide world's turned cold" (37). In "Homesick Blues," the speaker wishes to leave the north; he proclaims, "Lookin' for a box car / To roll me to de South" (43). As in the discussion of "The Weary Blues," it is important to note that the dialect blues poems in *The Dream Keeper* are versions of the black folk voice and are not the voice of Hughes himself. According to Steven C. Tracy, "Hughes attempted to present a variety of the subjects dealt with in the blues, and in order to do that it was necessary to speak in voices other than his own. Hughes told Nat Hentoff that much of his poetry 'is in the form of a kind of dramatic monologue,' indicating that there are speakers other than Hughes who are expressing themselves and characterizing themselves as they speak, not only through their language but by their choice of the blues as the vehicle of expression" (Tracy, *Langston Hughes and the Blues* 183). Even in the blues poems that appear as monologues, the intention is to enact a call-and-response dynamic, building connection and exchange with the reader. By including a range of blues poems in his children's collection, Hughes acknowledges the depth of his audience's emotional response to poverty and migration. Few other children's writers of the moment would permit a child reader to engage with her own negative and troubling feelings.

The "Dressed Up" section also contains "When Sue Wears Red," a poem that, like "The Weary Blues," was inspired by an experience from Hughes's youth. He explains in *The Big Sea* that as a high school student in Cleveland he "went calling on a little brownskin girl": "I met her at a dance at the Longwood Gym. She had big eyes and skin like rich chocolate. Sometimes she wore a red dress that was very becoming to her, so I wrote a poem" (52). First published in the *Crisis* in 1923, "When Sue Wears Red" alternates between lovely descriptions of the young wom-an's beauty and the speaker's exuberant joy at seeing her, exclaiming, "Come with a blast of trumpets, / Jesus!" (38). The repeated religious language in the poem cuts two ways. On the one hand, it grants Susanna value, for not only is she equal to an Egyptian queen, but also she is worthy of religious praise. On the other hand, the repeated "Jesus!" suggests something akin to cursing, especially if we recall the per-spective of a teenage boy gazing at a beautiful girl. This poem provides a bridge to the next section of *The Dream Keeper*, "Feet O' Jesus," which also combines the sacred and the secular. Steven C. Tracy describes Hughes's musical interests: "The fact that Hughes could throw one arm around spiritual and gospel music and the other arm around the blues simultaneously would seem remarkable, even blasphe-mous, in some circles" ("Langston Hughes and Afro-American Vernacular Music" 103). Hughes saw a correspondence between the creative energies of the blues and the expressiveness of the black religious experience. Many of the poems in "Feet O' Jesus" take the dramatic monologue approach of the blues poems, and many con-tain exclamations of praise that recall responses to the piano player in "The Weary Blues" or to Sue in "When Sue Wears Red." In "Prayer Meeting," a speaker repeats the first lines (as in the blues pattern), and in "Ma Lord," the speaker seems to walk with Jesus through a blues song: "Ma Lord's life was trouble, too, / Trouble every day" (48). Although focusing on the religious, poems in "Feet O' Jesus" correspond in tone, voice, and form to the blues poetry that preface them, another instance of Hughes's syncretic artistic vision.

The final section of *The Dream Keeper*, "Walkers with the Dawn," is the book's most powerful and provocative. It contains Hughes's best-known poetry, including "Aunt Sue's Stories," "The Negro Speaks of Rivers," "Mother to Son," and "I, Too," among others. If we assume an interracial child audience for the collection, then the placement of these poems seems deliberate and suggestive. The reader has been eased into the text with supposedly race-neutral poems and then passed through folk expressions of black identity, to conclude with poems that emphasize race pride and distinction. These poems also help us understand the position of Hughes as a children's writer and the particular character of Harlem Renaissance children's literature. While he was probably the only writer of the period to offer blues poetry to children, Hughes was not entirely severed from the "uplift" school of children's literature. The poems in "Walkers with the Dawn" combine the energies of Hughes's folk aesthetic with the imperative of the "uplift" movement for young readers to make black children race leaders and to embrace education and social progress.

Tracy notes Hughes's attachment to the "Old Guard" of Harlem Renaissance figures, like Du Bois, Locke, and James Weldon Johnson, explaining that "he inherited
a legacy of higher education and scholarship, a sense of racial pride and mission, an
interest in both journal and book publication as a means of galvanizing his audience, and a belief in the importance of the African and African-American past in
establishing the identity that the New Negroes were trying so hard to find" (*Langston Hughes and the Blues* 39). Certainly the poems in the last section of *The Dream
Keeper* embody these values, but Hughes also infuses into the texts his affection for
the folk. In fact, it is the juncture between the "Old Guard" values and the folk aesthetic that distinguishes the approach of the poems from others that might also
argue for "uplift," racial pride, and social progress. And in this juncture, we find the
child subject who is also torn between the middle-class insistence on literacy and
her own love of folk culture.

Hughes's poems in "Walkers with the Dawn" reflect the particular cultural
position of black children in the 1920s and early 1930s, as schooling and literacy rates
increased dramatically, particularly in the South. According to Anderson and Ross,
"Between 1900 and 1930, black literacy jumped from 50 percent to 80 percent, the
proportion of black children in school reached nearly 90 percent, and, for the first
time, black public high schools became common" (11). Within the context of the
southern classroom, however, severe inequities remained, and teachers found themselves leading classes either without materials or with biased history books. Increases
in school attendance encouraged children to value "authoritative" textual histories
that excluded or deformed the black experience. Many schoolteacher writers of the
1920s wrote against the erasures and manipulations of black history in schools,
offering plays, short stories, and poems that celebrated heroes who emerged from
enslavement, like Frederick Douglass, Phillis Wheatley, Ellen and William Craft, and
Harriet Tubman. Offering such history in print, or staging plays in school venues,
became potent efforts at intervention and inclusion. While *The Dream Keeper* does
not include poems dedicated to black heroes or heroines, Hughes's poems were
issued during this moment in which children were pressured to value schooling
(which was often racist) and when adults attempted to reshape its curriculum. A
poem like "Aunt Sue's Stories" becomes an especially apt commentary on childhood, textuality, and cultural value. It begins by describing Aunt Sue sharing stories
of her history with a small child. This tender rendering of the oral tradition places the
child at the center, of course, as the recipient of the cultural legacy carried by the folk.

Hughes resolutely embraces the oral tradition and folk culture as the most significant cultural inheritance, for the speaker explains that the child values the truth
of Aunt Sue's stories: "He knows that Aunt Sue / Never got her stories out of any
book at all, / But that they came / Right out of her own life" (68). From one perspective, then, we can consider "Aunt Sue's Stories" as Hughes's own form of pedagogical intervention. While schoolteachers were writing hero stories in order to combat
biased textbooks, Hughes offers here his own contribution to educational revision.
African Americans do not have to look only to the most exemplary and singular lives
under enslavement, he suggests. A child's aunt or mother or father holds a wealth of

history and experience in memory. The casual phrasing, "Never got her stories out of any book at all" (68), dismisses the inauthentic in favor of the living folk voice.

Of course, the poem itself is not an oral text. It first appeared in print in July 1921 in the "Education Number" of the *Crisis* magazine, a fact that points to Hughes's awareness during the Harlem Renaissance of publication as a site of power. Invested in schooling as a mode of authority, the literate African American child would want to see stories in print. As one child in *The Brownies' Book* in 1920 commented on her mother's versions of black history, "Well, that's just stories. Didn't they ever do anything in a book?" (Seymour 45). Hughes was aware that textuality conferred weight. In general, the Harlem Renaissance as a movement was devoted to bringing the black perspective into print. Not only were writers for adults using contacts with white patrons and benefactors, as well as starting their own literary magazines, in order to gain the authority of print for their artistic visions, but also children's writers were resisting the white textual versions of history forced on children in public schools. Poems like "Aunt Sue's Stories" valued the oral, but did so in the form of print publication. For Harlem Renaissance writers who hoped to refigure the identity of the black community for a national audience, it was not enough to keep Aunt Sue's stories "on the front porch," to quote Hughes. They had to have life in print as well.

What are these "stories" that contain the most important cultural history, now given permanency through publication? The poem describes slavery, mentioning both the work enslaved people performed as well as the art they created through music. Typically children's texts of the period refuse to mention slavery, preferring instead to spotlight antebellum social and artistic achievements. The exploitation and degradation of enslavement become nearly unspeakable in black children's literature of the era. In some ways, then, Hughes's poem is quite daring for even describing African Americans as slaves and naming the labor they endured. The poem's reference to "Sorrow songs" as the art emerging from enslavement fits into the mode established by "Beggar Boy" and in the "Dressed Up" and "Feet o' Jesus" sections, in which music and creativity enable transcendence. The poem's recovery of spirituals also links Hughes with writers for adults, such as Alain Locke in *The New Negro*, who posited that the revitalization of folk music would prove to be the highest artistic accomplishment of modern black America. By realizing that "Aunt Sue's Stories" is not typical of the attitude toward slavery among black children's writers in the 1920s and 1930s, we can recognize *The Dream Keeper*'s innovation and courage.

One must also understand that a poem like "Aunt Sue's Stories" not only tapped into the educational pressures on young African Americans but also participated in a major ideological current of the Harlem Renaissance: the desire to authenticate and record African and African American history and to draw connections between the modern African American and Africa. As Arthur A. Schomburg's essay in *The New Negro*, "The Negro Digs Up His Past" (1925), makes clear, "There is the definite desire and determination to have a history, well documented, widely known at least within race circles, and administered as a stimulating and inspiring tradition for the coming generations" (231). For many popular figures of the

New Negro Renaissance, both black and white, emphasis fell on Africa rather than on enslavement. Popular culture in the 1920s frequently played with the possibilities of an African connection; sometimes the attachment to Africa became exoticized, as in the case of performer Josephine Baker, or eroticized, as in the "tom tom" beats of jazz, or problematized, as in Countee Cullen's poem "Heritage," which asks "What is Africa to me?" For white modernist writers, African Americans became associated with the "primitive" energies of Africa, offering a sense of the substantial and essential in the face of a superficial and empty postwar society. Attention to Africa became the serious academic pursuit of Carter G. Woodson, founder of the Association for the Study of Negro Life and History in 1915 and creator of Negro History Week in 1926. Du Bois, in *Dusk of Dawn*, said of the Harlem Renaissance, "Perhaps its greatest single accomplishment is Carter Woodson's Negro History Week" (203). Among Woodson's circle, drawing connections between Africa and the American experience was serious business, an occasion to describe and document the diversity of African history and to bring to light the suppressed history of enslavement. While purveyors of the "jazz age" might have been more interested in pleasurable African rhythms, for many black intellectuals and teachers, the history of Africa enabled a richer awareness of the history of antebellum America. We see that Hughes's "The Negro Speaks of Rivers" and "The Negro" emerges from a confluence of popular, literary, and intellectual attention to Africa and African American history.

Richly allusive, both poems pull together strands of history in order to argue for the continuity of Africa and African American experience. In "The Negro," four stanzas name particular roles embodied by African Americans (slave, worker, singer, and victim), and each is connected to an event in Africa. The third stanza links the construction of the Egyptian pyramids to that of the Woolworth Building, one of the oldest New York City skyscrapers. Similarly, the poem credits Africa for African American music, connecting spirituals to ragtime. In describing "I've been a victim" (59), the poem makes oppression in Africa immediate and manifest in the American South. Referring to violence linked to labor taxes imposed by Belgian powers, the poem allows the reader to draw parallels between the oppressive colonial system in the Congo and the brutalities of the Jim Crow South. Like many poems in the final section of *The Dream Keeper*, "The Negro" uses a collective "I" as its speaker, allowing the speaker's individual assertion of racial pride to speak for the community. "I am a Negro: / Black as the night is black. / Black like the depths of my Africa" (59), the poem concludes, allowing any African American reader to claim "my" Africa as a site of historical continuity with the American experience.

"The Negro Speaks of Rivers," one of Hughes's most frequently anthologized poems, follows a pattern similar to that of "The Negro." Again the voice is representative of the experience of African Americans, as the speaker uses descriptions of rivers in Africa and in the United States in order to reveal continuities between the two sites and their histories. Like other texts in *The Dream Keeper*, this poem was also associated with Hughes's youth, since he composed it as a troubled eighteen-year-old reluctantly headed to Mexico to reunite with his father. He describes crossing the Mississippi in *The Big Sea*: "I began to think what that river, the old Mississippi, had meant to Negroes in the past—how to be sold down the river was the worst fate that could overtake a slave in times of bondage. . . . Then I began to think about other rivers in our past—the Congo, and the Niger, and the Nile in Africa" (55). One of the pleasures of reading Hughes's poetry is the awareness of its emotional layering. Under the apparent simplicity and directness of a line like, "My soul has grown deep like the rivers" (*Dream Keeper* 62), comes the contextual knowledge evoked by allusions to the Congo, the Nile, and to the slave trade on the Mississippi. The speaker's voice contains multitudes, to refer to Walt Whitman, a favorite poet of Hughes. Interestingly, Hughes dedicated this poem to W. E. B. Du Bois when he published it in *The Weary Blues*, a fact that should be remembered when considering Hughes's liminal position between the younger generation's interest in the folk and the more traditional "Old Guard" of the Harlem Renaissance. Hughes believed in many of the ideals of the older generation, including the desire to document and venerate African American history. Hughes many not have seen textbook histories as the primary site of cultural value, as did many schoolteacher writers of the "uplift' camp, but he made sure that oral legacies had a life in print.

A final way in which the poems in "Walkers with the Dawn" reflect the particular cultural position of black childhood is in the section's emphasis on youth leadership. Since the book presents itself as the repository for children's dreams, by the end of the text we discover that it is only in youth social action that dreams will be accomplished. The popular poem "Mother to Son," first published in the *Crisis* in 1922, insists that children take up the mantle carried by parents. A frequent image in social progress and "uplift" literature of the 1910s and 1920s, the "upward climb" to progress had become a commonplace metaphor, appearing in the visual arts in the paintings of Aaron Douglas and Lois Mailou Jones, and in children's literature in Sara Estelle Haskin's *The Upward Climb: A Course in Negro Achievement* (1927) and within Arthur Huff Fauset's *For Freedom* (1928). In "Mother to Son," Hughes describes the challenges of social progress by materializing the metaphor of the "upward climb." The speaker begins conversationally, "Well, son, I'll tell you: / Life for me ain't been no crystal stair" (64). The speaker turns to her child, insisting that he continue her efforts, since the child has a responsibility to achieve the ambitions of the older generation, to carry the elders' dreams forward. While this idea might seem a kind of truism across cultures and eras, within the context of the Harlem Renaissance, "Mother to Son" takes on particular weight as a text that places children at the forefront of social change. The process of cultural reinvention during the New Negro movement relied in part on the reinvention of black childhood, as writers and critics erected versions of youths' modernity and capability in order to combat disparaging "pickaninny" images in racist popular culture and the infantilization of African Americans as "boys." By virtue of their investment in educational structures, and their distance from enslavement and Reconstruction, children were frequently imagined as inhabiting a more powerful cultural position than adults, becoming the "New Negro" to the adult "Old Negro," and were expected to spearhead social change. Certainly Du Bois at the *Crisis* helped recreate the image of black childhood, imagining children as "embryonic men and women rather than as babes or imbeciles"

("Discipline" 270). In this light, "Mother to Son" becomes a particularly potent statement of the pressures placed on New Negro children but also represents Hughes's
belief in the continuity between the generations. The older person is not set in opposition to the progressive youth; instead, the child is set up as being able to achieve the
dreams of the mother. They have both been working toward social progress.

The poem "I, Too" could be read in light of the era's assertion of youth leadership. Many have noted the allusion to Walt Whitman's "I Hear America Singing"
(1867) in the first and last lines and the resonance of the poem's domestic metaphor
for a community that often worked in domestic spaces they did not inhabit. In terms
of the significance of the poem for a child audience, the poem turns on the word
"Tomorrow" (63). Change is at hand, the poem asserts, not sometime in the future,
but just hours away, and will be led by the youth who will take their place at the
table. One might consider whether this poem and others in the section that refer to
youth leadership are intended to speak to both young readers and adults reading
over their shoulder. This phenomenon, called "cross-writing" in the study of children's
literature, typically involves attention to the "dialogic mix of older and younger
voices . . . in texts too often read as univocal" (Knoepflmacher and Myers vii). Unlike in some white-authored children's texts, which cater to an adult sense of superiority, the power dynamic shifts in New Negro texts: here, children are authorities,
and adults (by virtue of their distance from schooling) are those who require youth
direction. Cross-written poems enact this relationship, speaking at once to children
who will become race leaders and to adults whose cultural memory becomes the
inspiration for the young, as in the examples of "Mother to Son" and "Aunt Sue's
Stories."

The poem "Youth" concludes the original arrangement of *The Dream Keeper*
and offers a compelling example of Hughes's attention to audience and desire to
cultivate child leadership. Originally published in the August 1924 issue of the *Crisis*
and later in *The Weary Blues* (1926), the poem encourages its audience to embrace
futurity and possibility:

> We have tomorrow
> Bright before us
> Like a flame.
>
> Yesterday
> A night-gone thing,
> A sun-down name.
>
> And dawn-today
> Broad arch above the road we came.
>
> We march! (65)

In the last line, Hughes emphasizes community and solidarity, exhorting his young
audience to pull together, almost militaristically, to move toward a new tomorrow.

When Hughes published this poem in his 1926 collection for adults, he did not title it "Youth," but rather "Poem," and omitted the last line. When he issued it with child readers in mind, both in the *Crisis* (which had an audience of children and adults) and in *The Dream Keeper*, Hughes kept the exclamatory final phrase. The reinsertion of "We march!" in the children's volume also might suggest Hughes's increasingly radical leanings during the 1930s, when Hughes would become close to the Communist Party. Children, presumably, needed to know that the poem concerned their obligation as race leaders. They needed to know it was their responsibility to march forward and that the rainbow of a new day rose over them. When cross-written poems appear during the Harlem Renaissance, they place the child in a position of leadership and figure the adult as witness, supporter, and follower. And when acknowledging a cross-written audience, Hughes makes transparent the child reader's identification with race leadership by retitling the poem "Youth." In issuing cross-written texts, children's writers like Hughes attempted to bring children to the fore of cultural change. Like Du Bois, Kelly Miller, James Weldon Johnson, and other established and more traditional African American intellectuals, Hughes believed in the idea of youth leadership and progress through social action. Although he does not specify the targets of such efforts—an antilynching campaign or educational parity or artistic equity—he concludes the volume with the exhortation to action.

Langston Hughes's *The Dream Keeper* conveys the spirit of the Harlem Renaissance and speaks to the particular position of children within that movement. But, importantly, his poetry seeks to bridge divides between the old and the young, between the folk and the progressive. Commenting on Hughes's career as a children's writer, Steven C. Tracy notes that the work addresses "people in words that bring them together, that reach out to and embrace rather than lashing out and fragmenting" ("Dream Keeper" 93). Writing within a cultural moment that sometimes used oppositions in order to create new versions of cultural identity, Hughes refused to sever the generations from one another. His children's book demonstrates his love of the folk and reverence for the past, even as it forges connections with Africa and a vision of child leadership.

WORKS CITED

Anderson, Eric, and Alfred A. Moss, Jr. *Dangerous Donations: Northern Philanthropy and Southern Black Education, 1902–1930*. Columbia: U of Missouri P, 1999.

Du Bois, W. E. B. "Discipline." *Crisis* 12, no. 6 (1916): 269–70.

———. *Dusk of Dawn: An Essay Toward an Autobiography of a Race Concept*. 1940. New Jersey: Transaction P, 1984.

———. *The Souls of Black Folk*. 1903. New York: Bantam, 1989.

———. "The True Brownies." *Crisis* 18, no. 6 (October 1918): 285–86.

Fauset, Arthur Huff. *For Freedom*. Philadelphia: Franklin, 1928.

Gaines, Kevin K. *Uplifting the Race: Black Leadership, Politics, and Culture in the Twentieth Century*. Chapel Hill: U of North Carolina P, 1996.

Haskin, Sara Estelle. *The Upward Climb: A Course in Negro Achievement*. New York: Council of Women for Home Missions, 1927.

Hughes, Langston. *The Big Sea*. 1940. New York: Hill and Wang, 1997.

———. *The Dream Keeper*. New York: Knopf, 1932.

———. *Fine Clothes to the Jew*. New York: Knopf, 1927.

———. *I Wonder as I Wander*. 1956. New York: Hill and Wang, 1993.

———. "The Negro Artist and the Racial Mountain." 1926. In *The Portable Harlem Renaissance Reader*, edited by David Levering Lewis, 91–95. New York: Penguin, 1994.

———. *The Weary Blues*. New York: Knopf, 1926.

Knoepflmacher, U. C., and Mitzi Myers. "Cross-Writing and the Reconceptualizing of Children's Literary Studies." *Children's Literature* 25 (1997): vii–xvii.

Krasner, David. *A Beautiful Pageant: African American Theatre, Drama, and Performance in the Harlem Renaissance, 1910–1927*. New York: Palgrave, 2002.

Locke, Alain, ed. *Harlem: Mecca of the New Negro*. Special edition, *Survey Graphic Magazine* 6, no. 6 (March 1925).

———. *The New Negro*. 1925. New York: Simon & Schuster, 1992.

Martin, Alice. "Letter to the Jury." *The Brownies' Book* 1, no. 6 (June 1920): 178.

Rampersad, Arnold. *The Life of Langston Hughes*. Vol. 1, *1902–1941, I, Too, Sing America*. New York: Oxford UP, 1986.

Ritterhouse, Jennifer Lynn. *Growing Up Jim Crow: How Black and White Southern Children Learned Race*. Chapel Hill: U of North Carolina P, 2006.

Schomburg, Arthur A. "The Negro Digs Up His Past." *The New Negro*, edited by Alain Locke, 231–37. New York: Simon & Schuster, 1992.

Seymour, Bella. "Letter to the Grown-Ups' Corner." *The Brownies' Book* 1, no. 2 (February 1920): 45.

Tracy, Steven C. "The Dream Keeper: Langston Hughes's Poetry, Fiction, and Non-Biographical Books for Children and Young Adults." *The Langston Hughes Review* 17 (Fall/Spring 2002): 78–94.

———. "Langston Hughes and Afro-American Vernacular Music." In *A Historical Guide to Langston Hughes*, edited by Steven C. Tracy, 85–118. New York: Oxford UP, 2004.

———. *Langston Hughes and the Blues*. Urbana: U of Illinois P, 1988.

FURTHER READING

Johnson, Dianne. *Telling Tales: The Pedagogy and Promise of African American Youth*. New York: Greenwood P, 1990.

Martin, Michelle. *Brown Gold: Milestones of African-American Children's Picture Books, 1845–2002*. New York: Routledge, 2004.

Mickenberg, Julia L. *Learning from the Left: Children's Literature, the Cold War, and Radical Politics in the United States*. New York: Oxford UP, 2006.

Smith, Katharine Capshaw. *Children's Literature of the Harlem Renaissance*. Bloomington, IN: Indiana UP, 2004.

Stewart, Michelle Pagni, and Yvonne Atkinson, eds. *Ethnic Literary Traditions in American Children's Literature*. New York: Palgrave Macmillan, 2009.

Thomas, Joseph. *Poetry's Playground: The Culture of Contemporary American Children's Poetry*. Detroit: Wayne State UP, 2009.

CHAPTER 7

....

DUMBO, DISNEY, AND DIFFERENCE: WALT DISNEY PRODUCTIONS AND FILM AS CHILDREN'S LITERATURE

....

NICHOLAS SAMMOND

WALTER *Elias Disney (1901–66) was born in Chicago and grew up in Marceline, Missouri, Chicago, and Kansas City. Returning to Kansas City after World War I, by 1921, Disney had established himself in animation and had begun a working relationship with the animator Ub Iwerks (among others). Iwerks in particular played an important role in developing many of the early Disney characters and a good deal of its signature visual style. By the early 1930s, when Walt Disney Productions had become a dominant force in the animation industry, Walt Disney was no longer an animator. Still, the company depicted its products as fully informed by his sensibilities and— because of Disney's purportedly childlike, all-American character—as inevitably good for children. It is for this reason that Disney is often mistaken for the author of his company's films. Although in the early years he did keep close tabs on his creative talent, by the time the company was producing* Dumbo *(1941), the focus of this essay, Walt Disney had adopted a much more hands-off approach. This situation was intensified by an animators' strike during the film's production, and by Disney's travels in South America, which were meant to keep him far from contract negotiations. (As a result, it would be more accurate to attribute* Dumbo's *authorship to supervising director Ben Sharpsteen and lead animators Dick Huemer and Joe Grant.) This short essay will build upon a close reading of* Dumbo *to locate children's films in the field of children's literature. More specifically, the film will serve as an example of how movies aimed at a children's/family market may refract contemporary concerns about the proper upbringing of children and about regulating social and cultural relations.*[1]

Is the movie *Dumbo* a part of children's literature? There are at least two reasons to think that it is, and to think about film in general (and the work of Walt Disney Productions in particular) in relation to that field.[2] First, since their inception the movies have been seen by a concerned middle class as a potential competitor to print literature in the proper education and upbringing of their children. Second, in response to that anxiety, Hollywood has long made a point of associating films for children with, if not literature, an idea of the literary.[3] By the time that Disney began producing feature-length cartoons in the late 1930s, it carefully placed those films within a lineage of children's moral literature that included not only lesser lights like Collodi but also the "classic" eighteenth- and nineteenth-century work of Perrault and the Grimms.[4] Yet even when a film was connected only tangentially to the history of children's literature, as was the case with *Dumbo*, Disney's narrative and visual strategies gestured toward an intimate association with that literature, crafting a message that fused American ideals of individualism and self-making with the bourgeois morality of the earlier tales. By creating a message that placed parents' desires for the success of their children in a democratic capitalist society within an historical continuum that seemed to stretch back for centuries, Disney made a name for itself as producing films (and books, clothing, and toys, etc.) that were good for children. At the same time it reaffirmed a politics of the one over the many (or a politics of the many led by the one) as anything but political or ideological, as a timeless human asset meant to be developed in each of us. Disney also gave this strategy of self-positioning greater emotional heft by incorporating storylines into its plots that made reference to contemporary anxieties about threats to children's well-being, which also made those fears appear timeless. In the case of *Dumbo*, those anxieties centered around attenuating American individualism to meet the demands of the day—namely the Great Depression, the rise of authoritarianism, and an impending world war. And the film deepened that affective charge by tapping into popular fantasies of racial difference, using them to add nuance to conflicting ideas of inclusion and exclusion, individualism and belonging, all toward the end of promulgating the fantasy of marginal differentiation that is at the core of the Disney ethos.

Before delving into *Dumbo*, though, a bit of backstory is in order. Since the opening of the modern movie industry in the late nineteenth century, fears about the effects of film on the child's developing mind have been center stage in arguments for the censorship and regulation of the medium.[5] The earliest arguments for state supervision of the nascent movie industry were split between warnings about the physical dangers of movie going—diseases lurking in the miasmatic confines of unventilated theaters, inappropriate sexual behavior by adult patrons, and the occasional nitrate-film-induced fire—and the content of the movies, which offered up a melange of slapstick comedy, melodrama, crime, westerns, and romance that could easily, it was argued, make a child "prematurely sophisticated." By the late 'teens and early twenties, the movies had become the primary mass entertainment in North America (if not worldwide), most exhibition venues had substantially cleaned up, and calls for the regulation of the industry centered much more on what appeared on the screen. By the time that the industry had established itself in Hollywood in the 'teens, there had been a variety of efforts to make movies that were as good for children as a good book would be. By 1911, Jane Addams had argued for a program of socially responsible cinema at her Hull House settlement to counter crime and sex dramas of the early silent era. Perhaps most famously, in 1916 Hugo Munsterberg published *The Photoplay: A Psychological Study*, in which he argued for the potential benefits of good movies. And around the same time, Yale's Historical Film group attempted to produce films for the classroom.[6] Meanwhile, expressions of concern in the popular press, and particularly in women's magazines, about the dangers of popular movies on a growing middle-class child audience fueled calls for state and federal censorship. By 1922, such arguments for the regulation of content and for a better sort of movie, and the limited success of Hollywood's attempts to address them by promising "quality" fare, led movie producers to establish the Hays Office, an instrument through which the industry would appear to self-regulate and thus avoid external censorship.

What emerged from this back-and-forth (and from arguments as to whether film was an art at all) was a largely dichotomous view of films: they could be either good or bad for children. This belief was encouraged by social reformers anxious that unregulated moviemaking was undermining the moral fabric of the nation via its children.[7] And perhaps nothing had a greater influence on this discourse than the Payne Fund Studies, a set of twelve psychological and sociological experiments and surveys conducted between 1928 and 1935 that attempted to determine scientifically (or scientistically) exactly what effects movies had on children. While in large part these studies were inconclusive (as media-effects studies tend to be), a popular summary of the studies by journalist Henry James Forman, and the publicity generated, rallied popular opinion against excesses of sex, violence, horror, and crime in Hollywood films (Forman 1932a, 1932b, 1932c, 1934).[8] This led the Hays Office to promulgate (in 1930) and then to vigorously enforce (in 1934) the Production Code—a set of guidelines governing the depiction of sexuality, crime, morality, political speech and action, and racial integration—in the hopes of convincing middle-class pressure groups such as the National Board of Review or the Legion of Decency that the industry was committed to the edification of the public in general, and of children in particular (Jowett, Jarvie, and Fuller). In the world of cartoons, this would effectively tame the popular animated flapper Betty Boop and would even limit the barnyard humor of up-and-coming star Mickey Mouse.[9] Writing in *Look* magazine in 1939, Leon Schlesinger, the executive producer of Warner Brothers' Looney Tunes and Merrie Melodies, solemnly intoned that

> we cannot forget that while the cartoon today is excellent entertainment for young and old, it is primarily the favorite motion-picture fare for children. Hence we always must keep their best interest at heart by making our product proper for their impressionable minds. (Schlesinger, qtd. in Sampson 4)

Schlesinger was being a tad disingenuous. Responsible for some of the most violent, racist, sexually charged cartoons in circulation at the time, he was less interested in producing films deemed good for children than in *appearing* to do so. In adopting that stance, he was making the appropriate gesture of concern to an institutional and discursive matrix that positioned the children of the time as vulnerable to the images and messages they consumed in mass entertainments, especially in the movies.

Walt Disney Productions would do Warner Brothers and the other major cartoon studios one better by indirectly suggesting that its films were actually good for children. The company carefully crafted a hagiography of Walt Disney as a Horatio Alger figure whose rise from humble beginnings to superstardom inspired each of his workers and was infused into each of his products, offering a veritable antidote to the tawdry, immigrant-produced mass products of his competitors.[10] Moving toward a form of animation in the 1930s that was rounder, softer, cuter, and more pastoral than that of its competitors, Disney favored a style that made characters such as Mickey appear childlike.[11]

Yet it was through its feature films that Disney fully established its relationship as an adjunct to children's literature. Between 1937 and 1960, the company produced film versions of *Snow White* (1937), *Pinocchio* (1940), *Dumbo* (1941), *Bambi* (1942), *Song of the South* (1946), *Wind in the Willows* (*Ichabod and Mr. Toad* [1949]), *Cinderella* (1950), *Alice in Wonderland* (1951), *Peter Pan* (1953), and *Sleeping Beauty* (1959). Although the company made other feature films, it was around these that Disney formed the center of its brand and its reputation. With a few exceptions, each film opened on the image of a large, leather-bound volume, presenting the story visually as a "classic tale" and leading the reader into the narrative through the mechanism of a zoom into the first page of the slowly opening book. Here, through a dissolve, the ornate script of a seemingly ancient book and the beginning of an explicitly written narrative shifted to a purely cinematic story. But the frame remained: we were in a fairy tale, and we were in classic children's literature.[12]

Like Schlesinger, Walt Disney could also be disingenuous. Asked why he made children's movies, Disney was known to answer that he didn't; he only made "family entertainment." Technically, this was true. Like other cartoons of the era, Disney's animated features had jokes and references for the adults and a simple story for the children. But at the level of structure, the films played upon separation anxiety in both parent and child. The standard narrative schema for a Disney film had its youthful protagonist separated from her/his parent or parents, made to face perils and challenges with the help of friends (though largely on her/his own), and then, having grown older and wiser, reunited with his/her family and community as a more independent and self-sufficient individual. Resonating with parents' anxiety about the entry of their children into public life, and children's apprehensions about separation from their parents (particularly their mothers), the company charged its stories with enough angst for every member of the family. And although the anxieties evoked in the plots of Disney stories were very culturally and socially specific to the United States of the mid-twentieth century, their expression through the medium of the seemingly "timeless" fairy tale made them seem as if they were primal. Even in the case of a story like *Dumbo*, which was not a "classic," this was true, and in both its deviation from and adherence to that design the film becomes a good lens through which to examine Disney's evolving mode of address to those anxious families.

DUMBO AND INDIVIDUALISM AS
SELF-GOVERNMENT

The short feature *Dumbo* (1941) is often lost between the two Disney "timeless classics" that preceded and followed it, *Pinocchio* (1940) and *Bambi* (1942). In comparison it seems at first glance a forgettable and odd confection. Yet the film is noteworthy, not only because it succeeded financially where the other two initially faltered, but also because if *Pinocchio* is about the guidance a child needs to become fully human and *Bambi* offers the assurance that the origins of the middle-class family are in nature itself, *Dumbo* suggests that even a damaged social order can be mended through the development and celebration of every child's individual talents.[13] More than simply celebrating individualism, though, the film places the skills of the individual at the service of the social order, which in turn is able to celebrate his now contained and legible difference. For a United States on the verge of entering World War II, and poised between two opposing ideals of child care—behaviorism and neo-Freudian "permissiveness"—the circus world in which Dumbo was to find his place alloyed the discipline of domestication with the adventure of self-discovery.

Based on Helen Aberson and Harold Perl's 1939 book of the same name, *Dumbo* was published first as a "Roll A Book" (a picture book done as scroll painting), a format that apparently was local to the Syracuse publisher who released it. It remains unclear whether the book ever received widespread distribution; it was one of a number of titles that Disney bought the rights to following the success of its 1937 *Snow White* (Barrier 176). The film's plot is fairly straightforward. It opens with a seeming nod to the impending war: a squadron of storks flying in formation delivers babies to the various animal workers of a circus wintering in Florida (fig. 7.1). (Although *New York Times* critic Bosley Crowther would wonder whether parents were hard put explaining this phenomenon of mass parturition to their children, Disney would repeat the fantasy of simultaneous "childbirth" across many species in *Bambi* [1942] and in subsequent nature documentaries.)[14] For reasons unspecified, Dumbo arrives late, after the circus has decamped on tour. Once his freakishly large ears are discovered, he and his mother are shunned by the other elephants. This situation worsens when Dumbo causes the ringmaster's new trick of an elephant pyramid to go wrong, and he is symbolically orphaned when his mother,

Figure 7.1   Military motifs in *Dumbo* link child-rearing with the looming war.

angrily defending him from the taunts of children, is imprisoned as a "mad elephant." Finally, he is forced to don makeup and perform with the clowns rather
than with the elephants, doing a high dive from a burning building into a bucket of
white glop as the climax of their act. (This act is a hit and the clowns—caricatures
of Disney animators then on strike—take credit for Dumbo's success and use it to
demand a raise.)[15] Soon after this low point, Dumbo discovers that he can fly.
Though he first believes that this is because of a "magic feather" given to him by a
flock of crows, at a crucial moment (losing the feather as he plummets toward his
death in the high-dive act), Dumbo learns that it is actually his gigantic ears that let
him take flight. Having accepted that what makes him different is his greatest asset,
he gains fame for himself and freedom and ease for his mother.

As much as this plot conforms to the Disney template, the film contains a beautiful, graceful, and strange moment in which it seems to escape the bounds of that
constraining narrative. Walking back from a visit to his imprisoned mother, Dumbo
and his sidekick, a mouse named Timothy who is decked out as a ringmaster, drink
from a bucket of water that (unbeknownst to them) is mixed with champagne.
Drunk, they hallucinate, and through their gaze we enter the musical number "Pink
Elephants on Parade" (fig. 7.2). This sequence begins when Timothy watches a
drunken Dumbo blow a series of increasingly elaborate bubbles with his trunk.
Egging him on, the mouse suggests to Dumbo that he blow a square one, then a
gigantic one. He does, and both he and Timothy stare, aghast, as the giant bubble
morphs into an enormous pink elephant floating in a velvety black background.
The translucent pachyderm blows another elephant out of its trunk, which blows
another elephant out of its trunk . . . and so on until there is eventually a throng.
The pink elephants play their trunks as if they were horns in a brass band, and the
tune they belt out is at turns whimsical and ominous. The creatures continuously
morph into multiples of themselves and combine or divide to form a variety of
other shapes, including a pyramid, a cobra, and a marching figure whose body is
made up of nothing but differently colored elephant heads. Set almost entirely
against this inky black background, in both its words and its images, the song tee-
ters between dream and nightmare, whimsy and paranoid terror. When it ends, the
metamorphic elephants slowly and gently resolve into the fluffy pink morning
clouds of Disney's trademark gentle cinematic realism, floating above a tall tree in
which a flock of minstrel crows (led by Jim Crow) find Dumbo and Timothy
sleeping on a branch (fig. 7.3).

Figure 7.2   The musical number "Pink Elephants on Parade" demonstrates what film theorist Sergei Eisenstein celebrated as animation's "plasmatic" quality, it's ability to represent the revolutionary potential in even everyday objects.

Two things are important here. First, the pink elephants are a perfect example of a quality that Soviet filmmaker and theorist Sergei Eisenstein found most revolutionary about animation in general and Disney's animation in particular: the animate stuff of the elephants—the outlines and weighted shapes that morph without apparent regard for narrative logic and that could at any moment transform into anything else—demonstrated its "plasmaticness," its ability to express the (r)evolutionary potential of a primal matter that predated capitalist commodity fetishism, that could convey any idea, however outlandish (Eisenstein 8–24 and 41–62). Second, the hallucination is shared by Timothy and Dumbo (hence, by the audience); it is not the solitary delusion of either the mouse or the elephant. Dark, and yet very compelling, the dance of the pink elephants is a collective vision of radical change—the possibility that the stuff of life could be made into anything at all. The chorus of the song that accompanies all of this dynamically potentiated transformation is at turns upbeat and ominous, warning the viewer to "Look out! Look Out!" Yet by the end of the number this plasmatic primal force is tamed in the service of Disney's narrative, its radically transformative creatures resolving into mere background elements in the tale of Dumbo's awakening to his special talent— a tale in which he will be appreciated for being unique precisely because his talent can be harnessed in service of a less than unique spectacle.

This segment is both apart from and a part of the narrative. Induced by drinking, it arises out of the fantastic bubbles that Dumbo blows with his trunk. At the same time, although both mouse and elephant first witness the apparitions on the circus grounds, the sequence takes place in a largely undifferentiated black void with no direct connection to the narrative space of the plot. It unfolds in a spare and unrealistic style very different from that of the rest of the film, and at one point even plays with and acknowledges the screen and film frame. The rest of the film hews very much to the Disney logic of what Norman Klein has described as "full animation"— in which the animate space is meant to imitate that of realistic live films, and characters are meant to have weight and substance, and never to transform into something entirely other than themselves (Klein, 110–46). In the pink elephant sequence, though, the Disney animators suddenly and dramatically acknowledge the play of line and form, the ultimate plasticity (Eisenstein's "plasmatic quality") of the animate form.[16]

Like Dumbo's talent, this flight of fancy is ultimately contained, constrained, and put in the service of a much more traditional narrative. The sequence doesn't just happen: it happens because Dumbo gets drunk. The pink elephants, fancy-free in their uniform and multifarious difference, ultimately have a definite purpose: they merely describe Dumbo's drunkenness. Likewise, Dumbo's fabulous ability to fly, which also renders him a fantastic creature outside of the bounds of the normal, is in the end yoked in the service of a simultaneously lesser and greater good, the success of the circus. This contribution is framed as his rise to media stardom, rather than as his contribution to, say, the collective betterment of all the circus workers. He and his mother benefit from his skills, but not the elephants who shunned him or the rabble-rousing, unionizing clowns. Like children, who are often understood to be the raw material of future societies, the plasmatic pink elephants, in their ability to take any form—either that of hopes or of fears—are finally contained and converted into something that resembles a nursery ceiling, a sky under which Dumbo will awake to his new potential, which will itself be contained (fig. 7.3).

So, just as the pink elephants resolve into the fluffy pink clouds of the morning after, Dumbo's seemingly grotesque deformity develops into his (and his community's) greatest asset. Dumbo awakes to the evidence of his ability to fly (his perch in the tree) and, falling to the ground, immediately denies it. What convinces him is not his conscience/sidekick, Timothy, but a flock of crows led by Jim Crow

Figure 7.3   At the end of "Pink Elephants on Parade," the elephants transform into pink clouds in a pale blue dawn sky.

(voiced by Cliff Edwards, a white man doing an imitation of then-popular black minstrel Flournoy Miller, and sounding a little reminiscent of popular white black-face minstrels Moran and Mack, who were known as the Two Black Crows).[17] After waking him in the tree, the crows are incredulous that he could have flown there and sing the mocking "When I See an Elephant Fly," in which they make wordplay similar to the dozens, scat sing, and imitate the Mills Brothers. In the song, the crows pun on all of the impossible things that they've seen or heard, such as a house fly (housefly and flying house) a rubber band (elastic or ensemble), or a diamond ring (the thing and the sound), the punch line being that they *really* will have seen everything when they see an elephant (actually) fly.

Timothy is so enraged by this song that he lectures the crows on their cruelty, telling them that while still young, Dumbo was torn away (slave-like) from his mother (who still languishes in chains), and that although an elephant he has been forced to perform as a lowly clown. Chastened, the crows conspire to trick Dumbo into accepting his special ability by giving him one of their feathers and telling him it is magical. Dumbo departs, believing that the feather has imbued him with the power to fly. Only later, when the feather slips from his grasp in midair and he and Timothy plummet toward their deaths, does Timothy convince him that his own seeming deformity, not the gift given him by the minstrel crows, is what allows him to fly. Having embraced his difference, Dumbo becomes a hit, and through his celebrity gains the power to free his mother and make the circus a huge success (fig. 7.4).

At first glance, this plot seems an outright celebration of individualism, a paean to the very Alger-like qualities epitomized in the biography of Walt Disney himself. But a closer look suggests a slightly different message. Yes, Dumbo triumphs once he accepts his uniqueness (which is a very different thing than accepting a common difference that one shares with some, such as with elephants or crows, but not with others). But rather than entrepreneurially striking out on his own (as had Disney), Dumbo offers his talents in service of the same circus that had treated him and his mother so very cruelly. Like the pink elephants, his incredible potential exists only to serve a rather mundane master: the narrative. And that narrative is not about individual success, nor is it about the collective success of workers such as the unionizing clowns. Rather, it is a victory in which one's own personal gain is realized by finding one's proper place in society, and by serving a very hierarchical

Figure 7.4 The crows in *Dumbo*, based on minstrel stereotypes, are left behind as Dumbo disappears into his brave, new future.

greater good like that of the circus. In this balancing of conformity and individualism, *Dumbo* fit well with contemporary concerns about children consuming media that would yield valuable life lessons. It also dovetailed with discourses about children's development inflected by the Great Depression and the looming possibility of war. These discussions struggled to balance the recognition of a child's unique abilities and her/his rights as an individual against concerns about the role of children in ensuring future social cohesion.

Dumbo was released a little more than a month before the Japanese attack on Pearl Harbor, and the cultural field into which the film entered, at least in terms of understandings about children and child-rearing, was in transition. The management-oriented, behaviorist mode of child-rearing, which had dominated since the late teens and early twenties, and which was typified by John B. Watson's popular *Psychological Care of Infant and Child* (1928), was falling into disrepute. The rise to power of the Nazi party in Germany in the 1930s—with its emphasis on one people and one culture as a fundamental organizing principle for the state, and with the burgeoning popularity of its Hitler Youth movement—called seemingly similar rationalized modes of child-rearing into question in the United States. (Disney would formalize this distaste in 1943 with its propaganda cartoon *Education for Death*, which parodied the German educational system and the Hitler Youth as a systematic and soul-destroying erasure of individuality in service of the state.)

Even before the war, though, the vicissitudes of the Great Depression had begun to undermine faith in the discourses of efficiency, discipline, and control that had buttressed management-oriented approaches to child-rearing, and that appeared to be failing the children of the American middle class. There was a growing anxiety that behaviorist modes of child-rearing, which ideally were supposed to train children to be self-managing, were instead undermining their free will, making them overly obedient and submissive and, like the Hitler Jugend, unable to act independently or entrepreneurially. For example, in *Babies Are Human Beings* (1938), C. Anderson Aldrich and Mary Aldrich argued that children forced to adhere to the strict regimes of management-oriented child-rearing were likely to grow into adults who were unspontaneous, efficient, and cold: "Anyone who has watched a mechanical robot perform his incredible acts of skill, has probably been conscious not only of wonder but also of a certain obscure impression of fear. The spectacle of someone acting correctly without feeling anything is so inhuman that it is vaguely unpleasant" (23).

So, even as the exigencies of war gave this rising counterdiscourse an increased sense of urgency, there was a chorus of voices in favor of regimes that balanced the development of a resilient and adaptable child imbued with a vital national character against the perceived need for an orderly and obedient society. During the early twentieth century, behaviorism and similar management-oriented child-rearing regimes had been embraced as a corrective response to the purportedly excessive indulgence of middle-class child-rearing in an emerging consumer culture. The rise at mid-century of discourses concerned with fostering the emotional self-awareness and self-satisfaction of the child was meant to dial back that overcorrection, to find

a balance between excessive indulgence and the sort of rigid behaviorist programming that could lead to the authoritarian excesses of fascism.

By 1940 and the production of *Dumbo*, then, discourse around children and
child-rearing (to which Walt Disney Productions had become increasingly attuned
during the 1930s) was shifting away from management-based models and toward
what would come to be known as a "child-centered" or "permissive" model of
childhood that imagined the properly raised child as one who was allowed to find
her/his own inner talents and strengths without undue interference from parents or
other adult authority figures.[18] Although his best-selling *The Commonsense Book
of Baby and Child Care* (1946) would not appear until later in the decade, by 1941
Benjamin Spock was espousing its basic principles in *Parents' Magazine*.[19] And even
before this child-centered model became a national craze, Spock's friend and col-
league, the renowned anthropologist Margaret Mead, was rallying parents, teachers,
and child-rearing experts to the cause of anti-authoritarianism in *And Keep Your
Powder Dry* (1942), in which she puzzled through the fine line between marshalling
a nation to war and instilling individualism in children:

> Winning the war is a job of social engineering, we have said.... [But how]...
> does such a course differ from fascism and its ruthless control of human beings?
> Dr. Goebbels' methods of manipulating humanity are based upon what he
> believes to be an accurate analysis of what human beings are like.... Nazi
> propaganda is based on very careful calculations—on just how much hate and
> hostility is available in human beings. Wherein lies the difference between the
> streamlined Nazi state and a state in which we, as Americans, analyze and use the
> strengths and weaknesses of the American character? (176–77)

For Mead, the answer to that question lay in the ability of parents (mothers, really)
to understand the essential balance of cooperation and individuality that defined a
singular American culture, and to model that culture for their children in their day-
to-day behavior. Rather than succumbing to indoctrination or behaviorist programming, the child would come to be patriotic and supportive of the war effort by
discovering her or his place in an evolving national culture, retaining her or his
inherent individuality and then freely offering it up to the greater good. The child
could and should want to triumph over the enemy, but not at the expense of her or
his humanity and uniqueness. This was a delicate balance to achieve, and there was
a danger that a child raised in such a climate would see the conflict and scarcity of
war as the natural order of things, not an exceptional situation.

So, as the United States entered the war, its professional class engaged in a
detailed discussion of child-rearing that explicitly countered Nazi methodologies
and implicitly tarred the rigors and discipline of earlier management-oriented
child-rearing philosophies with the same brush. Also writing in 1942, Dorothy
Baruch warned that while children needed to practice thrift (as in rationing), they
also needed to know that life was ultimately abundant:

> Too many hardships and deprivations, too many blockings and frustrations,
> create defeatism. In face of them, it becomes difficult to believe that life holds

anything worth while [sic]. A child must learn first and early that life can be
good. He then continues to search for the good. . . . Once having found this
conviction, he can hold to it when hardships do come. He can see his way to
better things. On the other hand, if he has never had proof of anything better, he
will hardly have gained impetus to struggle ahead (76).

These are the very sorts of obstacles that young Dumbo faces. Expected to fit
into the highly regimented society of the circus, to follow orders, and to perform a
specific role in that microsocial order, he is marginalized for his difference. Convinced that his failure to meet those expectations is an indictment of his fundamental
character—of which his physical difference is an outward manifestation—by the
middle of the film Dumbo has grown sure that his lot in life is to suffer. Only when
he is faced with evidence that his difference is actually valuable to those around him
do his spirits soar, as then can his body.

Yet his reward is more than just pride in a job well done or the simple pleasure
of finding acceptance: he actually becomes a star, with all the perquisites that flow
from celebrity. After Dumbo learns that he doesn't need the magic feather given him
by the crows, he steals the show. Dive-bombing the labor-activist clowns, he drives
them into the set of the burning building from which he has just leapt, sending them
scattering with their pants afire (i.e., as liars). Filling his trunk with peanuts, he strafes
the herd of female elephants who had belittled him and ostracized his mother. The
crowd goes wild. The newspaper montage that follows, in the style of a 1930s back-
stage drama, announces his rise to fame: he is insured for a million dollars, sets an
altitude flying record, appears on the cover of *Time Magazine*, and has a line of military bombers designed after him.[20] Finally, the montage gives way to the circus train
on its way to its next engagement. The herd of elephants is now singing a whitened
version of "When I See an Elephant Fly" in their car, emptying the song of its minstrel dialect, and as we pan along the length of the rickety, old, wooden circus train,
we see a sleek, ultramodern car has been added to it. Exclusively for Dumbo, it ends
in an open veranda, on which sits, his mother, Mrs. Jumbo, who gazes adoringly up
at Dumbo flying at the lead of the flock of the crows, a set of aviator's goggles on his
forehead. As the scene slowly irises to black on the receding circus train, the crows
settle on telegraph lines by the train tracks and pick up the chorus of their song from
the elephants, celebrating that they *have* seen an elephant fly, asking each other
whether any of them got his autograph, and crowing "Well, so long glamour-boy!"

So, even though they have provided the psychological cure that allowed Dumbo
to overcome his resistance to his own special talent (his fear of flying), in the end
the crows are reduced to nothing more than adoring fans. They move from being
the *deus ex machina* of the story (Magical Negroes—African Americans who offer
wisdom gained through their oppression to white protagonists—in animal form)
to just a part of the scenery, nothing more than backdrop, like the pink elephants
reduced to clouds.[21] Like the Tuskegee Airmen—African American pilots who
fought in World War II but were denied the rights and privileges of their rank, and
who were instrumental in forcing the integration of the U.S. armed forces in 1948—
an equal place in the American Dream is yet a few years off for them.

Beyond their utility as a plot device, the crows are important for understanding why Dumbo's seeming disability, his difference, doesn't lead him into disaffection, depression, or rebellion. Besides providing the physical object of the magic feather—a material token of their blackness—the crows also find Dumbo credible: they are willing to consider the possibility that he can fly, and that, if he can, it is a good thing, not a violation of the natural order. The crows see him *in* his difference, rather than *in spite of* his difference. Speaking from the vantage of (quasi-racial) outsiders, the crows can express good-natured disbelief at the possibility of an elephant flying in "When I See an Elephant Fly," but the lyrics of the song suggest that because they too have been marginalized for being different—the jive and wordplay of the song indicating that they no longer take signifiers at face value—they can consider the possibility of a flying elephant alongside other things that exist only as puns (such as a housefly being a bug or a flying house). A debased parody of double consciousness as racist caricature, the crows can from their own experience admit that what the majority sees is not all there is to see. In that they are operating in the tradition of black-face minstrelsy, and in that they themselves do not benefit from their knowledge, the crows exist only to enlighten and enable the film's ostensibly white protagonist. This they do well: Dumbo, witnessing their difference, and their belief in his, is heartened. As Madeleine Dixon put it in a popular child-rearing manual published in 1942:

> Every first time he sees people who are different from those he knows he will be a bit afraid. When he knows them better he will not be afraid. He will learn to his amazing joy that for every difference that disturbed him there will be one that delights him. The little almond cake that his neighbor has at the Passover, or the small beautiful hut that he builds in the yard or on the roof to eat in at another festival time, the celebration of a special Christmas of the gypsies from South America . . . the song and rhythm of these Negro children on the street around the corner. . . . (31)

Yet this awareness doesn't lead the young elephant to embrace those margins, or to assume that he is permanently condemned to them. Since this is Disney, the acceptance Dumbo experiences encourages him instead to embrace his role in the circus (as a clown/elephant that leaps from the set of a burning building into a vat of white goo)—but to do so in a way that foregrounds his unique talent as that which marginally differentiates him from either the other clowns or the other elephants. And so he becomes a unique commodity, valuing himself and becoming valuable to others. Instead of creeping away in shame, Dumbo flies into the sunset, while the crows stay behind, longing for his autograph. He hasn't given in to the crushing expectations of mindless conformity that the other elephants demanded of him, nor to blind obedience to the (unionized) collective of inferiors, the clowns, to whom he had been consigned. He does not conform; rather, he appears to remain true to himself. In this he anticipates the postwar moment in which fear of the blind obedience of the fascists was converted into anxiety about Soviet conformity, and in which understanding and engendering individualism in the face of a burgeoning postwar mass culture came to seem even more crucial. As Robert Lindner put it in *Must We Conform?* (1956):

Mass Man, the universal psychopath, is born when the individual ego is weakened to the point at which it loses separate identity and is forced, for security, to merge with that mass. . . . There is that within us that cannot be denied without destroying the essence of humanity. It is a drive to master, to overcome, to express positive protest against whatever stands in the way of the far-off and unknown goals of evolution. When this in-built urge is impeded or suppressed . . . in place of a man stands a goose-stepping automaton driven by animal lusts. . . . The betrayal of the instinct that has enabled man to rise up from the primeval swamp is accomplished by the spread of a myth that . . . urges us ever closer to the edge of an abyss in which lie the wrecks of former civilizations that have succumbed to it . . . the myth of *conformity*, the big lie of *adjustment*. (27, emphasis in original)

Read in this light, *Dumbo* becomes a warning to children who are popular against marginalizing those who are less so, and to social leaders (and parents) to valorize and celebrate difference in all children. A decade after the end of the war, Lindner's vitriolic rejection of conformity represented, if not the norm in child-rearing, then at least an acceptable defense of a common (and paradoxical) call for greater non-conformity.

By the end of the 1950s, it would become harder (though by no means impossible) for the white majority to exclude African Americans from this logic of embracing diversity. With its rulings in *Brown vs. the Board of Education of Topeka, Kansas* in 1954 and 1958, the U.S. Supreme Court firmly upheld that the *de jure* concept of "separate but equal"—which underpinned the *de facto* condition of marginalization that informed the crows' symbolically unique perspective—was abhorrent to concepts of equality enumerated in the United States Constitution.[22] A key support in the success of *Brown* had been studies by the social psychologists Kenneth and Mamie Clark, who had demonstrated that segregation and derogatory images of black culture inevitably led children of color to view themselves as inferior to their white peers (Clark and Clark). For these children, the difference that Disney's crows represented was not a magical avenue to inclusion, but a reaffirmation of their exclusion. Even though the years following the *Brown* decisions would see a more robust, public, and mainstream civil rights movement that called even indirect representations of African American life and culture such as the crows into question, that time was a ways off: when the film was made, and even when it appeared on television more than a decade later, no one would question the crows' central role in the film and its seemingly progressive message. The dominant racial logic at the time of the film's making required that the crows be left by the side of the tracks as the circus train receded into the sunset of the future: their difference was instructive for a white protagonist and an imagined white audience, but only through the paradoxical reaffirmation of their exclusion.

In fact, when veteran Disney animator Dick Huemer was confronted years later, in 1978, with the suggestion that the crows were racist, he bridled, suggesting that the "colored" choir who had sung "When I See an Elephant Fly" and voiced some of the crows' voices had

> liked it very much and enjoyed doing it hugely. They even offered suggestions, and we used some of their ideas, lines of dialogue or words, little touches. . . . I don't think the crow sequence is derogatory. In fact, when someone mentioned the possibility to me, I was quite taken aback. I never gave that angle a through [sic] and I still don't. (qtd. in Adamson 45)

There is nothing disingenuous in this reply. For Huemer, the inclusion of people of color as voice talent, and their willing assent and contribution to the crows' characterization, is proof of the filmmakers' good intentions and therefore of the beneficial outcome of the process. But hindsight is 20/20, and ultimately the issue is not the racism of the depiction but its relation to the fantasy of inclusion and difference—the repetitive narrative of separation, self-discovery, and social reincorporation—that is the Disney staple. Dumbo never looks back as he and his circus train follow the setting sun, leaving the crows behind. Having learned from the crows to look inward, he leaves behind a model of child-rearing that imagined the child as a solitary unit programmed for optimal performance, whose social role was defined by that programming, and who was almost always imagined as white. In its place, the new child would be more relational, both to itself and to those around it . . . yet still implicitly white. In the United States of the 1930s, child-rearing experts worked to articulate the tools that the developing child needed to compete in the social and material world of the Great Depression, and the producers of popular media worked to frame their products as providing those tools. While World War II lifted the United States out of its economic depression, it did not inspire an immediate and concomitantly rapid shift in child-rearing discourse. Instead, the war contributed urgency to the gradual move away from management-oriented and rigid models of child-rearing, shifting them toward a model of "character" that balanced an idealized individualism against the conformity thought necessary for functioning in a rationalized society. Dumbo still had to find his proper place in society, but he had to arrive at it through his own self-discovery rather than through programming. This involved learning from others and seeing one's self in them. As Dorothy Baruch suggested in 1942,

> the child should have a chance to know that individual liberty can be yielded for the good of the many. . . . He must acquire also deep social awareness. He must come to respect . . . the capabilities of others and what contributions they can make to society. He must also come to the place where he can identify himself with them. He must have concern for their welfare. (107)

While on the whole this shift seems generally progressive, with some notable exceptions, it was one that preserved the *status quo ante* of segregation even as it argued for cross-racial identification. Indeed, in its ostensibly tolerant discourse about locating one's own difference by recognizing that of others, it had the potential to reify that difference as exemplary. Thus, Dixon's African American children became models of "song and rhythm" who dwelt on that street around the corner, who could show the unmarked white object of child-rearing discourse how difference (at a distance) could be instructive. It was possible to have an orderly society that still celebrated diversity without actually integrating those who provided the fundamental baseline for recognizing difference. That was the world of *Dumbo*, which counterposed the overweening social policing of the conformist elephants against the blind self-interest of the union-organizing clowns, and which marked a humble, talented, and unique Dumbo as the happy medium. Yet unlike the altruistic versions of child-rearing offered by Dixon, Baruch, or Mead, Disney's depiction of this attenuated individualism was one in which unfettered competition and marginal differentiation were key. In Disney's cosmos, one received help from others in order to discover one's own unique talents, and to grasp how their pursuit would naturally enrich one's own life, benefiting the community as a result. Others did not exist as equals, but as the facilitators of the protagonist's growth who necessarily were left behind once that growth was achieved. This has been Disney's narrative for generations. Although constantly adjusted for the exigencies of a given historical moment, it is one that resonates with a model of the developing subject (aka the child) as always operating in a free-market economy. It is one that favors neither an abstract and absolute individualism nor a collective identity—whether that identity is marked by race, by gender, or by class. Instead, it promulgates an idealized, interiorized, and invisible difference in its protagonists that valorizes the marginal differentiation, self-commodification, and uniform individualism that mark capitalist democracy.[23] In all of this back-and-forth, Disney continues to position itself, and to be positioned as, children's literature on screen, a place where children gain the tools of self making that they use to fashion themselves into the best future adults possible.

NOTES

1. Research support for this essay was provided by the Connaught Fund at the University of Toronto, the Jackman Humanities Institute, and the Social Science and Humanities Research Council of Canada. Thanks to Aubrey Anable for her critical reading of early drafts. The author also thanks the editors for their patient and very constructive criticism in the redrafting process.

2. The name "Walt Disney Productions" is one of many that refer to the company, from its early incarnation as the Disney Brothers Studios in the 1920s, to the spinoff Retlaw ("Walter" spelled backwards) in the 1950s, and beyond. It is meant to refer to the parent company usually referred to simply as "Disney" and to its overall marketing to families and children.

3. For an overview of children and the movies, see Wojcik-Andrews. For a critique of Disney's place in children's culture, see Giroux. For a local history of the emergence of children's film in the Great Britain, see Staples. For a discussion of the emergence of the teen movie market in the 1950s, see Doherty.

4. For a discussion of the place of the fairy tale in mass culture, see Zipes. For a discussion of Disney's marketing to children, see deCordova 1983 and 1994.

5. See, for instance, Couvares, Grieveson, or Wittern-Keller.

6. For a detailed discussion of these efforts, see Jowett, Jarvie, and Fuller.

7. See, for instance, Lindsay or Arnheim.

8. For perceptive analyses of the programmatic, logical, and theoretical shortcomings of media-effects theory, see Freedman; Gauntlett; or McLeod, Kosicki and Pan.

9. See, for instance, Sklar or Barrier.

10. See Sklar, Smoodin, or Sammond.

11. Evolutionary biologist Stephen Jay Gould has described the mouse's devolution as "neotyny."

12. Disney reinforced this association by releasing many of its cinema and television products in book form under the Little Golden Book imprint of Western Publishers.

13. For discussions of Disney's use of nature, see, Mitman, Sammond, or Chris.

14. The term "childbirth" is used intentionally here. Although animals were depicted being born, Disney's approach to those births was decidedly and intentionally anthropomorphic.

15. See Sito, 129.

16. The sequence was animated by Hicks Lokey and Howard Swift and directed by Norm Ferguson. Mark Langer has argued that this segment is rendered in the "East Coast" style of the Fleischer Brothers or the Van Beuren studio, in opposition to Disney's standard "West Coast" style (Langer 305–21). For Langer, this indicates Walt Disney's distance from the project (as opposed to his usual micromanagement) and explains why the film temporarily abandons what Klein has described as Disney's naturalistic "full animation." This analysis does not contradict the reading here of the scene as expressing a containment of the radical expressivity of animation. Indeed, it becomes a demonstration of that submission to Disney's larger narrative performance of difference and its containment.

17. Edwards also supplied the voice of Jiminy Cricket in *Pinocchio* (1940).

18. For a more detailed discussion of Disney's relationship to child-rearing during this period, see Sammond, chaps. 1–3.

19. See "Benjamin Spock, M.D. In Our June 1941 Issue" in *Parents' Magazine* 30, no. 10 (October 1956). This retrospective look in the magazine's thirtieth-anniversary issue reprints Spock's more permissive take on child-rearing at the beginning of World War II, five years before his popular child-rearing manual first appeared. For a broader discussion of progressive, antifascist child-rearing during the period, see Mickenberg.

20. This montage also recalls the rise to fame of the notoriously anti-Semitic Nazi sympathizer Charles Lindbergh roughly a decade earlier. As such, it has formed part of the fabric of arguments that Walt Disney was himself an anti-Semite, which are on the whole of limited value.

21. For a discussion of the Magical Negro, see, for instance, Gabbard.

22. In the 1954 ruling, the Court called the "separate but equal" doctrine outlined in *Plessy v. Ferguson* (1896) inherently unequal but failed to adequately outline a process for corrective integration. In *Brown* II, the court required that desegregation be achieved "with all deliberate speed," a term whose vagueness would trouble the process of desegregation for generations to come.

23. This is a narrative that continues today and that we can witness being played out in online discussions about Disney's first African American princess in a feature film, Princess Tiana in *The Princess and the Frog* (December 2009). Anonymous online posters have questioned whether it is right, given animation's negotiation of the fine line between caricature and representation, for Disney to craft explicitly African American characters at all, whether its depiction of African American life and history will be accurate and positive,

and whether the hipness of the character is yet another of Disney's seductions of little girls into the unreal and gender-constraining discourse of the princess.

WORKS CITED

Aberson, Helen, and Harold Pearl. *Dumbo the Flying Elephant*. Racine, WI: Whitman, 1941.

Adamson, Joe. "With Disney on Olympus: An Interview with Dick Huemer." *Funnyworld* 17 (1978): 37–45.

Aldrich, C. Anderson, and Mary M. Aldrich. *Babies Are Human Beings: An Interpretation of Growth*. New York: Macmillan, 1938.

Arnheim, Rudolph. *Film as Art*. Berkeley: U of California P, 1957 [1933].

Barrier, Michael. *The Animated Man: The Life of Walt Disney*. Berkeley: U of California P, 2007.

Baruch, Dorothy. *You, Your Children, and War*. New York: D. Appleton-Century, 1942.

"Benjamin Spock, M.D. In Our June 1941 Issue" *Parents' Magazine* 30, no. 10 (October 1956): 108.

Chris, Cynthia. *Watching Wildlife*. Minneapolis: U of Minnesota P, 2006.

Clark, Kenneth B., and Mamie P. Clark. "Emotional Factors in Racial Identification and Preference in Negro Children." *The Journal of Negro Education* 19, no. 3 (Summer 1950): 341–50.

Couvares, Francis G., ed. *Movie Censorship and American Culture*. Washington: Smithsonian Institution Press, 1996.

Crowther, Bosley. "Walt Disney's Cartoon, 'Dumbo,' a Fanciful Delight, Opens at the Broadway." *New York Times*, 24 October 1941, 27.

deCordova, Richard. "Ethnography and Exhibition: The Child Audience, the Hays Office and Saturday Matinees." Edited by Lynn Spigel. *Camera Obscura* 23 (Winter 1983), 91–107.

———. "The Mickey in Macy's Window: Childhood, Consumerism, and Disney Animation." In *Disney Discourse*, edited by Eric Smoodin. New York: Routledge, 1994: 203–13.

Dixon, C. Madeleine. *Keep Them Human: The Young Child at Home*. New York: John Day, 1942.

Doherty, Thomas: *Teenagers and Teenpics: The Juvenilization of American Movies in the 1950s*. Philadelphia: Temple U P, 2002.

Eisenstein, Sergei. *Eisenstein on Disney*. Translated by Jay Leyda. Calcutta: Seagull Books, 1986.

Freedman, Jonathan L. *Media Violence and Its Affect on Aggression: Assessing the Scientific Evidence*. Toronto: U of Toronto P, 2002.

Forman, Henry James. "Molded by the Movies." *McCall's Magazine* 60, no. 2 (November 1932): 17: 54–56, 62.

———. "Movie Madness." *McCall's Magazine* 60, no. 1 (October 1932): 14–15, 28–30.

———. *Our Movie Made Children*. New York: MacMillan, 1934.

———. "To the Movies—But Not to Sleep!" *McCall's Magazine* 59, no. 12 (September 1932): 12–13, 58–59.

Gabbard, Krin. *Black Magic: White Hollywood and African American Culture*. New Brunswick: Rutgers UP, 2004.

Gauntlett, David. "Ten Things Wrong with the 'Effects Model.'" In *Approaches to Audiences—A Reader*, edited by Roger Dickinson, Ramaswani Harindranath, and Olga Linné. London: Arnold, 1998. Accessed online at http://www.theory.org.uk/david/effects.htm on 4 August 2010.

Giroux, Henry. *The Mouse That Roared: Disney and the End of Innocence*. London: Rowman Littlefield, 2001.

Gould, Stephen Jay. *The Panda's Thumb: More Reflections in Natural History*. New York: Norton, 1980.

Grieveson, Lee. *Policing Cinema: Movies and Censorhip in Early Twentieth-Century America*. Berkeley: U of California P, 2004.

Jowett, Garth, Ian Jarvie, and Kathryn Fuller. *Children and the Movies: Media Influence and the Payne Fund Controversy*. New York: Cambridge UP, 1996.

Klein, Norman. *Seven Minutes: The Life and Death of the American Animated Cartoon*. New York: Verso, 1993.

Langer, Mark. "Regionalism in Disney Animation: Pink Elephants and Dumbo." *Film History* 4, no. 4 (1990): 305–21.

Lindner, Robert. *Must You Conform?* New York: Rinehart and Co., 1956.

Lindsay, Vachel. *The Art of the Moving Picture*. New York: Modern Library, 2000 [1915].

McLeod, Jack M., Gerald M. Kosicki, and Zhongdang Pan. "On Understanding and Misunderstanding Media Effects." In *Mass Media and Society*, edited by James Curran and Michael Gurevitch. London: Edward Arnold, 1991, 235–66.

Mead, Margaret. *And Keep Your Powder Dry*. New York: Morrow, 1942.

Mickenberg, Julia. "The Pedagogy of the Popular Front: 'Progressive Parenting' for a New Generation, 1918–1945." In *The American Child: A Cultural Studies Reader*, edited by Caroline Levander and Carol Singley, 226–45. New Brunswick: Rutgers UP, 2003.

Mitman, Gregg. *Reel Nature: America's Romance with Wildlife on Film*. Cambridge, MA: Harvard UP, 1993.

Munsterberg, Hugo. *The Photoplay: A Psychological Study*. New York: Routledge, 2002 [1916].

Sammond, Nicholas. *Babes in Tomorrowland: Walt Disney and the Making of the American Child, 1930–1960*. Durham: Duke UP, 2005.

Sampson, Henry. *That's Enough, Folks: Cartoon Images in Animated Cartoons, 1900–1960*. London: Scarecrow Press, 1998.

Sito, Tom. *Drawing the Line: The Untold Story of the Animation Unions, from Bosko to Bart Simpson*. Lexington: U of Kentucky P, 2006.

Sklar, Robert. "The Making of Cultural Myths—Walt Disney." In *The American Animated Cartoon: A Critical Anthology*, edited by Gerald Peary and Danny Peary. New York: E.P. Dutton, 1980, 58-65.

Smoodin, Eric. *Animating Culture: Hollywood Cartoons from the Sound Era*. New Brunswick, NJ: Rutgers UP, 1993.

Spock, Benjamin. *The Common Sense Book of Baby and Child Care*. 3rd ed. New York: Duell, Sloan, and Pearce, 1957 [1946].

Staples, Terry. *All Pals Together: The Story of Children's Cinema*. Edinburgh: Edinburgh UP, 1997

Watson, John B. *Psychological Care of Infant and Child*. London: Allen and Unwin, 1928.

Wittern-Keller, Laura. *Freedom of the Screen: Legal Challenges to State Film Censorship, 1915–1981*. Lexington: U of Kentucky P, 2008.

Wojcik-Andrews, Ian. *Children's Films: History, Ideology, Pedagogy, Theory*. New York: Routledge, 2000.

Zipes, Jack. *Relentless Progress: The Reconfiguration of Children's Literature, Fairy Tales, and Storytelling*. New York: Routledge, 2008.

FURTHER READING

Bell, Elizabeth, Lynda Haas, Laura Sells, eds. *From Mouse to Mermaid: The Politics of Film, Gender, and Culture*. Bloomington: Indiana UP, 1995.

"Bringing Up Baby on Books . . . Revolution and Counterrevolution in Child Care." *Newsweek* 45, no. 20 (16 May 1956)

Cook, Daniel T. "The Rise of 'The Toddler' as Subject and as Merchandising Category in the 1930s." In *New Forms of Consumption: Consumers, Culture, and Commodification*, edited by Mark Gottdiener. Lanham, MD: Rowman & Littlefield Publishers, 2000, 111–30.

Leslie, Esther. "Sigfried Kracauer, Dumbo and Class Struggle." In *Hollywood Flatlands* New York: Verso, 2002, 200–18.

Nasaw, David. "Children and Commercial Culture: Moving Pictures in the Early Twentieth Century." In *Small Worlds: Children & Adolescents in America, 1850–1950*, edited by Elliot West and Paula Petrik. Lawrence: University Press of Kansas, 1992, 14–25.

Tuttle, William J. "The Homefront Children's Popular Culture: Radio, Movies, Comics—Adventure, Patriotism, and Sex-typing." In *Small Worlds: Children & Adolescents in America, 1850–1950*, edited by Elliot West and Paula Petrik. Lawrence: University Press of Kansas, 1992, 143–64.

CHAPTER 8

REDRAWING THE COMIC-STRIP CHILD: CHARLES M. SCHULZ'S *PEANUTS* AS CROSS-WRITING

CHARLES HATFIELD

CHARLES M. Schulz (1922–2000) is indelibly linked to his strip Peanuts, *which was launched in 1950 and syndicated by United Feature Syndicate.* Peanuts' *reach expanded from seven newspapers at its start to about 2600 at the time of Schulz's retirement in 2000; by then* Peanuts *reached hundreds of millions of readers in scores of countries. The licensing of* Peanuts *has likewise been a commercial juggernaut, growing so vast that in 1971 Schulz established a company (now known as Charles M. Schulz Creative Associates) to control the licenses. Spinoffs in other media are legion, including books (since 1952), comic books, greeting cards, a stage musical, and countless others. Most famously, animated versions of* Peanuts *have appeared on television (commercials first, then longer programs starting with* A Charlie Brown Christmas *in 1965) and in features. Schulz, famous for his untiring work ethic, insisted that the original strip was the core of it all and that it would never be compromised by commercialism. A devotee of comics, Schulz set out from childhood to be a cartoonist and lived out that ambition all his life; he died immediately upon retirement. Other cartoonists were and continue to be lavish in their praise of Schulz, who is regarded a master of the form. The strip's history is readily available: since 2004 Fantagraphics has published the biannual* Complete Peanuts, *each volume containing two years of the strip (thirteen have been released as of this writing, spanning to 1976). Given its influence,* Peanuts *constitutes a significant popular representation of childhood.*

The critical study of comics for and about children has been relatively neglected. This is so despite the recent upsurge in comics studies and despite the general understanding that studying children's culture entails studying the myriad ways children are addressed and depicted: not only in sanctioned literature but also in popular artifacts both verbal and visual; not only in texts obviously aimed at young readers but also in those aimed at adults. This understanding calls for increased study of children's comics, yet thus far the genre has been underserved, a lapse that has impoverished children's literature scholarship. Conversely, the lack of a critically informed perspective on childhood detracts from the emergent field of comics studies (Hatfield). Thus far the new comics studies has mostly rejected or underplayed the putative link between comics and childhood, as if to boost the art form to a higher seriousness. This is a mistake, since the linkage of comics and children's culture is not only long lived and complex but also frankly crucial to understanding comics history. Just as any overview of children's literature is incomplete without acknowledging influential comics for children (consider that cartoonists Hergé, Carl Barks, and Osamu Tezuka, to name but three obvious examples, are among the most popular children's storytellers of the past century), so too any history of comics that does not acknowledge such beloved works is bankrupt. In short, comics studies and children's literature studies are overdue for a summit. Studying depictions of children in comic strips is a particularly urgent task because strips constitute an ever-present but underexamined part of the larger cultural scripting of childhood. Charles Schulz's achievement, in his ubiquitous, nearly fifty-year-long strip *Peanuts*, offers an opportune way of undertaking that larger task.

By now *Peanuts* is so familiar that it has about it the air of something inevitable and simply given, rather than an achievement arrived at through artistry, hard work, and historical contingency. Schulz's mixing of the daily comic-strip genre with sharp, personality-based humor, a repertory company of children, and a streamlined cartoon modernism has been so influential that it has camouflaged its own originality and is now regarded as a natural and expected vein for cartoonists to work in. Its seeming inevitability is the very measure of its success. Because *Peanuts* did so much to define what is considered natural in present-day strips, recognizing what made it innovative at the moment of its emergence requires thinking backward. In particular, understanding *Peanuts* requires that we reexamine the comic-strip child as trope, convention, and vehicle for social commentary. As postwar America's preeminent comic strip, *Peanuts* wrought great changes to comics' depiction of children and thus played a key part in the postwar construction of childhood.

Comics, as is now well known, have never been confined to the realm of childhood. The very origins of the form are "adult," and it was only in the late nineteenth to early twentieth century that the American comic strip began to focus especially on children. Even then, in the ranks of the mischievous, sometimes anarchic "kids" of the early newspaper comics page, the implied audience included adults as well as young readers. Because the newspaper itself was an adult medium, the comics page was a zone of ambiguity, offering social and political satire as well as knockabout slapstick humor, graphic fantasy, and marketable (child and adult) characters. Often comic strips subverted traditional mores and canons of value through the pointedly satirical and carnivalesque use of children, practicing a popular, nose-thumbing kind of *cross-writing*.

As defined by Mitzi Myers and U. C. Knoepflmacher, cross-writing entails "a dialogic mix of older and younger voices [that] occurs in texts too often read as univocal." The term denotes an "interplay" between adult and child perspectives, one that implies a mixed readership and an author who respects adult and child readers equally (vii). Cross-writing, Myers and Knoepflmacher explain, serves as a means of "dissolving the binaries and contraries" between adult and child, binaries that our culture has reified and continues to reinforce (viii). The newspaper comics page became a space that practically encouraged such cross-writing, a space claimed by children and adults alike.

Child characters presided over the emergence of comic strips as a market genre. Richard Outcault's seminal *Hogan's Alley* and *McFadden's Row of Flats* strips (1895–98), often credited with launching or at least legitimizing the genre, depicted an ever-changing mob of ragged, energetic street children, most notably the Irish American slum urchin the Yellow Kid, in weekly installments dense with streetwise language, cruel slapstick, and allusive sloganeering about the political events of the day (see Outcault). These cartoon kids were a calculated affront to polite society. Outcault's later *Buster Brown* (1902–21) had a superficial varnish of middle-class respectability (Buster being a well-scrubbed pageboy) but still used kids to twit bourgeois mores and manners; Buster's penitent moralizing served to veil yet more winking, tongue-thrusting satire. Rudolph Dirks's *The Katzenjammer Kids* (from 1897) was an undisguised riff on Wilhelm Busch's *Max und Moritz* of nineteenth-century *bildergeschichten* fame and rehearsed anarchic child antics and punitive adult reprisals alike with a joyous bloodthirstiness. The Katzenjammers were all about power and repression. As if in a middle-class rejoinder to the working-class rowdiness of such strips, the superb draftsman and designer Winsor McCay curbed the more nightmarish aspects of his compulsive dream strips and produced the storybook-like classic *Little Nemo in Slumberland* (1905–14, 1924–27), whose titular hero was pitched each week into bouts of Surrealism *avant la lettre* and gorgeous Art Nouveau worldscapes that served as stylized versions of a child's dreams. Though inimitable, *Nemo* inspired a number of frank imitations, such as George McManus's *Nibsy the Newsboy in Funny Fairyland* (1906) and Frank King's *Bobby Make-Believe* (1915–18). Lyonel Feininger, later a renowned Bauhaus artist, produced his own short-lived but noteworthy dreamlike strips, the absurd picaresque *The Kinder-Kids* and the more sedate *Wee Willie Winkie's World* (both 1906). In a more down-to-earth mode, James Swinnerton, among the earliest strip cartoonists and also one of the first to focus on children (see the proto-strip *Little Bears* or *Little Bears and Tykes*, c. 1892–96), brought together innocence and rowdiness in *Little Jimmy* (1904–58), about a distractible youngster continually drawn into the misadventures of rascally boys and other troublemakers. All of these features, and the many other strips focusing on child characters, aimed for audiences of both children and adults; all of them attempted a kind of multiple address, in hopes of capturing both adult newspaper buyers and their children. In short, the early American strips were a fertile field for cross-writing. Appealing to a radically mixed audience, their satirical use of children was protean and adaptable to various situations, whether rollicking through the slums with the Yellow Kid and his fellow urchins or upsetting the staid rhythms of middle-class households à la Buster Brown. What comics historians Bill Blackbeard and Martin Williams have called the *"demon child"* (19) became a leitmotif in the early days of the medium, providing a socially marginal, ambiguously positioned type of character who could reach young and old readers alike. The father of the demon child (if we may speak of a single father) was Germany's Busch, whose late nineteenth-century picture stories, inheritors of both satirical and children's book traditions, inspired a rash of feisty, antiauthoritarian comics kids. The American-born Outcault and German-born Dirks and their successors came not long after. A torrent of comic-strip children would follow, some considerably less demonic than their forebears, as the majestic *Little Nemo* and its followers signaled the gentrification of this once-disreputable genre. Nemo excepted, the best known of the very early strip kids were active rather than passive, and mischievous if not downright demonic. Causing trouble, or getting into trouble, was their *raison d'être*. Along with a raft of equally stylized and marginalized ethnic types, such as Fred Opper's Irish simpleton Happy Hooligan, such children comprised the repertory company of the United States' earliest serial comics. This was the tradition Charles Schulz grew up with and that he longed to join from an early age.

Children read the early comics in droves, but newspaper comics were not made "for" them or assigned to them in any exclusive sense. As an extension of popular journalism, the newspaper comics page reached a diverse, multigenerational audience; unlike the later comic books, they were not ghettoized as juvenilia. However, children were present at the feast and often served as models for the entertainment. This occasioned controversy: children's comic reading stoked a minor media panic among social reformers and the genteel middle class, a panic attested to by a spate of articles appearing in popular and literary journals (*Atlantic Monthly, Ladies' Home Journal, Bookman,* etc.) circa 1906 to 1912. Said articles typically objected to the comics' vulgarity and crudeness, and, implicitly, their status as symptoms of an emerging mass culture that threatened existing social hierarchies (Gordon 41–42). Educator Percival Chubb epitomized the progressive critique of comic strips, arguing that parents, for the sake of cultivating elevated tastes in their children, should bar comics from the home; that such productions of the "unhealthy and unlovely" culture outside the home encouraged irreverence and disrespect, and so should be banned from the domestic sphere (Nyberg 32). In hindsight, such panic is perfectly understandable, given the mushrooming popularity of strips during this period and the fact that the strips' antiauthoritarian demon-children so often upended or poked fun at the idea of childhood innocence.

Despite this controversy, American comics—in the popular sense of the recurrent, marketable, and character-based strip—coalesced around images of kids.

Since then the comic-strip child has been a mainstay of the medium and a remark-ably pliant vehicle of humor and satire, a tradition extended in *Peanuts* and since carried on with varying degrees of bite in recent and contemporary strips such as *Bloom County, Foxtrot, The Boondocks,* and *Cul de Sac.* In other words, the strip genre has continued to be a major source, reenforcer, and satiric funhouse mirror for popular ideas about childhood. This is why, leaving aside the sheer aesthetic wonder of the best examples, the study of comics should be an integral part of the study of children's literature and culture. The comics tradition of depicting chil-dren is rich and varied and constitutes a vast archive of childhood images spanning a range of attitudes, styles, and subgenres: consider the everyday, often pensive humor of Percy Crosby's *Skippy,* one of Schulz's major influences (1923–45); the Dickensian melodrama and astringent conservative politics of Harold Gray's *Little Orphan Annie* (from 1924); the delicate, feather-light irony and graphic cool of Crockett Johnson's *Barnaby* (1942–52); the boyish-sentimental yet briskly modern-istic gag panels of Hank Ketcham's *Dennis the Menace* (from 1951); the never-ending domestic idyll of Bil [sic] Keane's *Family Circus* (from 1960); the more subtly shaded realism of Lynn Johnston's growing children in *For Better or for Worse* (Canadian in origin but handled by a U.S. syndicate, from 1979); the extraordinary synthesis of moods, themes, and graphic experiments in Bill Watterson's *Calvin and Hobbes* (1985–95); and many, many others.

To this day, the strip kid remains a reassuringly familiar but endlessly plastic device, not so much a "real" child as a graphic invocation of childhood: a graphic *character* in the sense of sign or symbol. As Thierry Smolderen has argued, the growth of comics hinged on the development of such characters, "graphic synthe-sized entit[ies] that only [exist] in the visible world of the drawings." For such a character, "the drawing [and only the drawing] is its reality" (as discussed in Diereck and Lefèvre 21). In other words, the children who crowded the early newspaper comics page were not children in any straightforwardly mimetic way but rather were vehicles for satire, romping, carnivalesque humor, and, inevitably, adult nos-talgia. For this reason, we need to reexamine continually the presumed link between comics and children. In ironic testimony to their adult origins, comic strips give us heightened, often fanciful images of children's lives; while they have shaped, and keep on shaping and tweaking, popular conceptions of childhood, they speak implicitly to adult concerns. Even though comics continue to be assigned in American cultural mythology to some protected (albeit besieged) state of childlike innocence, their continuing adult appeal belies their putative childishness. Nowhere is this duality more evident than in Schulz's depiction of children in the microcos-mic world—the stereotypic "neighborhood"—of *Peanuts,* by common consent the most important late twentieth-century comic about kids.

Exactly what does it mean to say that *Peanuts* is a strip "about" children or a children's strip? The answer is not obvious. At the end of the first week of *Peanuts*—that is, in a strip first published on Saturday, October 7, 1950—Schulz himself asks this question or, rather, has Charlie Brown ask it (fig. 8.1). Standing beneath a street sign that reads, "Watch out for children," Charlie Brown and his playmate Shermy

Figure 8.1 Charles Schulz, *Peanuts,* 7 Oct., 1950. Reprinted in *The Complete Peanuts: 1950–1952.* Ed. Gary Groth. Seattle: Fantagraphics, 2004, page 2. Reproduced courtesy of United Media.

gaze out in opposite directions, as if scanning the horizon. After three panels' wait time, the two boys walk away, Charlie Brown saying, "Let's leave . . . I don't think any are coming!" (Schulz, *Complete 1950*, 2). The joke depends on a kind of misrecognition: the two boys cannot recognize that the sign aims not at children seeking other children but at adults who are supposed to be mindful of children's safety. That is, the boys cannot recognize that the sign is not meant *for them.* By singling out children as objects, the sign categorically excludes them as subjects: children are not to do the "watching out" but rather are to be watched out for. Either Charlie Brown and Shermy cannot see this, or they do not recognize themselves in the word *children.*

This simple gag comments on a defining feature of our culture, including much children's literature: the denial of children's agency and the envisioning of children as objects of adult solicitude (regarding which, see, e.g., Nodelman and Stallcup). The gag resonates with many others in the early months of *Peanuts,* as Charlie Brown, Shermy and Patty (the strip's original gang) refer, sometimes directly, sometimes obliquely, to matters of age and aging. Charlie Brown worries about his squeaking "joints" and advancing age (11/24/50); Shermy declares that he will be "older and wiser" six weeks from now (12/12/50); Charlie Brown anticipates shaving (1/06/50; 2/23/50); Patty rejects Shermy's proposal of marriage because she hasn't "known [him] long enough," to which Shermy replies that he's "only been alive for a few years" (12/27/50); Charlie Brown worries about getting drafted (5/21/50); and, in an acrid Valentine's Day strip, Charlie Brown tells Patty that she's "getting on in years" (*Complete 1950*, 16–67). The kids' degree of knowingness varies from strip to strip, but the formula is clear: Schulz draws humor from the incongruous matching of small, cute children and their archly precocious dialogue. The formula intensifies with the introduction of new characters, especially Schroeder, a baby at first, whose arrival prompts Charlie Brown to remark, "I always feel so uncomfortable near children!" (67–69). Schroeder serves as a foil to Charlie Brown's attempts to act as a parent, sometimes with the effect of reconfirming Charlie Brown's own childishness—as when Charlie Brown tries to dissuade Schroeder from thumb-sucking, only to take it up himself, an anticipation of later gags about Linus with his thumb and blanket (84).

The early *Peanuts* exhibits a blatant self-consciousness about matters of age, height, and scale, all markers of the precincts of childhood (reminding us that Schulz's original and preferred title for the strip was *Li'l Folks*). Some *Peanuts* gags revolve around the disparity between the kids' smallness and the overwhelming size of their surroundings—as when Charlie Brown sits baby Schroeder, the budding pianist, down at a "real" piano as opposed to a toy one, a dislocation that starts Schroeder bawling (10/02/51, fig. 8.2). Schulz, as he begins to find his way creatively, runs through a series of infant characters who serve as comic contrasts to Charlie Brown until they grow beyond babyhood, only to be replaced by new infants. This pattern perhaps stemmed from Schulz's real-life interactions with very young children; after all, he would have been a new father circa 1951–54. Though Schulz claimed to have no abiding interest in children and disclaimed his own children as influences (see, for example, Inge 138–39), autobiographical inferences remain tempting. In any case, the changes in the strip's baby characters testify to his search for a larger and more promising repertory company: each infant in turn becomes a distinct individual whose comic potential is based on more than mere age difference with Charlie Brown. One sees Schulz repeatedly sloughing off formulaic humor based merely on age or size and discovering instead the core attributes of his characters.

Schroeder is the first to undergo Schulz's peculiar version of growing up, that is, growing just enough to become a peer for the still-childlike Charlie Brown but no further. He comes into his own as a pianist and worshiper of Beethoven in the fall of 1951. The pattern repeats with Lucy, then Linus: early gags emphasize their smallness and vulnerability vis-à-vis Charlie Brown, as when Lucy gets a piggyback ride from him (4/16/52); but over time, age differences cease to matter or even to be acknowledged. Most of the characters come to inhabit that same generic, ambiguously defined state of "childhood" as Charlie Brown and to display the same disarming mix of naiveté and precocious worldliness. They do not cease to be children, any more than Charlie Brown does, but the stereotypic hallmarks of infancy—exaggerated smallness, diminutive language, and, in Lucy's case, a craftily exploited cuteness—are mostly pushed aside. Indeed Charlie Brown's own childishness becomes subtler.

Early *Peanuts* strips undergo a tug-of-war over popular ideas of childhood, with some relying uncritically on cuteness and diminutive humor but others pushing hard against childhood clichés. For instance, in the second *Peanuts* strip ever (from October 3, 1950), Patty strolls down the street reciting the familiar rhyme, "Little girls are made of sugar and spice," then, without provocation, socks Charlie Brown in the eye. Such strips, as historian Ben Schwartz has said, commit a kind of "emotional mugging" that belies the bland security of Schulz's new-mown suburban world (11).

Figure 8.2 Charles Schulz, *Peanuts*, 2 Oct., 1951. Reprinted in *The Complete Peanuts: 1950–1952*. Ed. Gary Groth. Seattle: Fantagraphics, 2004, page 5.
Reproduced courtesy of United Media.

In fact Schulz repeatedly undermines adult beliefs about childhood as a carefree, idyllic state of grace; insistently, he pokes at the dream of childhood innocence, as if to undercut our utopian hopes. His version of childhood is rarely sentimental and often piercingly frank; as one reviewer has put it, the children of *Peanuts* live lives of "quiet malevolence" (Resnick 12). Despite the strip's surface cuteness, cruelty among children is one of its earliest and most obvious themes, as biographer David Michaelis notes ("Life" 292). Schulz himself recognized that his cartoon kids were ruthless egotists and that *Peanuts* may have been "the cruelest strip going" (Michaelis, *Schulz* 272), though he would later seek to disavow or distance himself from this quality (Inge 152). Famously, one *Peanuts* Sunday (2/23/58, fig. 8.3) has Charlie Brown raging against a radio announcer's invocation of "the gay wonderful laughter of little children"; having been teased and humiliated by the whole neighborhood gang, Charlie Brown kicks the radio across the room (Schulz, *Complete, 1957,* 180). Early on, *Peanuts* seems to push against and work its way past such clichés, as Schulz grows into his little world and tries out, then discards, various stereotypes of childhood.

Schulz's fictive kids—those graphic synthesized entities—were of course meant to cast a critical eye on adults, as indeed children's literature often serves as a mockery of adult presumptions and a critique of adult institutions (regarding which, see, e.g., Lurie). Like many of his forebears from Outcault onward, Schulz used children as satiric mouthpieces, needling himself and other grown-ups through a succession of childlike alter egos. In fact he intensified this time-honored technique, pushing past what his predecessors had done. Many commentators have

Figure 8.3   Charles Schulz, *Peanuts,* 23 Feb., 1958. *The Complete Peanuts: 1957–1958.*
Ed. Gary Groth. Seattle: Fantagraphics, 2005, page 180. Reproduced courtesy
of United Media.

observed how Schulz derived humor by ironically mixing child characters with adult hang-ups, adult language—especially psychobabble and small talk—and, most acidly, adult dissimulation and hypocrisy (see for example Harvey 215–16). Schulz's li'l folks often mouth adult commonplaces: for example, in one early strip (12/18/50), Shermy and Charlie Brown cheerily trade a series of meaningless clichés:

> Charlie Brown: Looks like it may get a little colder . . .
> Shermy: Yes, it looks that way . . .
> Charlie Brown: Well, don't take any wooden nickels!
> Shermy: Don't do anything I wouldn't do!

In the strip's last panel, Charlie Brown walks away, smile gone, and quips, "Now there was a real adult conversation!" (*Complete 1950*, 23). Similarly, spoofs of male/female courtship, as when Shermy and Charlie Brown compete for Patty's affection, or Lucy for Schroeder's affection, often serve to underline adult clichés. Most notable, though, is the invocation of psychobabble, as when (1/19/51) Patty and Shermy debate the reasons for Charlie Brown's incessant crying:

> Patty: Maybe he's maladjusted
> Shermy: Do you think it could be his environment?
> Patty: Maybe he's frustrated or inhibited . . .

As it turns out, Charlie Brown's shoes are simply too tight (*Complete 1950*, 32). Such parrotings of psychiatric language are common in early to mid-period *Peanuts*: Schulz's strip children were prone to use words like "depressed," "inhibited," and "neurotic," a tendency perfected in the repeated shtick of Lucy as amateur psychiatrist (begun in March 1959). This clinical babble cuts in two directions at once, on the one hand satirizing the fatuousness of pop psychology as it mushroomed in mid-century America, on the other hand speaking, with real candor, to the problems of depression and alienation experienced by Schulz and many of his readers. Schulz milked these very feelings, reportedly believing that his own melancholy and anxiety were important sources of his comic talent: "Unhappiness is very funny. Happiness is not funny at all" (Michaelis, *Schulz* 436).

Schulz maintained that children do in fact learn to talk the way his characters talked and that he was simply showing a too-little-acknowledged aspect of children (Inge 113). If so, he nonetheless departed from the prevailing conventions of his day by pushing the visual/verbal ironies of his strip to an extreme. If the comic-strip child had played a crucial role in establishing the medium, Schulz reinvigorated the trope, representing and reinterpreting childhood to children and adult readers alike, in effect cross-writing more frankly than any strip cartoonist had done before. He brought lasting angst to the comic-strip child. Through Charlie Brown and company, he addressed feelings barely admissible in consensus culture, feelings from which children are presumed to need protection: frustration, deep loneliness, and a haunting sense of failure and absurdity. In fact Schulz—ironically, given his own commercial triumphs—stuck pins in the American ideology of success; his characters failed more often than they succeeded. Charlie Brown in particular, though starting off as a freewheeling jokester, came to epitomize Schulz's understanding of loneliness and failed promise, an understanding in tune with the darkening undertones of postwar American life. Charlie Brown's plight spoke to a sense of hollowness, fatigue, and bewilderment at the heart of American culture; as Michaelis notes, the character embodied the mood of readers "who felt guilty at being discontented in an epoch of unprecedented prosperity" (*Schulz* 324). All of this, though, occurred within the comforting, ritualistic genre of the daily strip, offering, by dint of sheer repetition, a vision of struggle and endurance through which child characters could speak plainly but gently to both child and adult readers.

Schulz's work, then, once past its early, embryonic phase, seldom talked down to children. The *Peanuts* kids developed conflicted and believably complex personalities. Their concerns were genuine and relatable. Like much great children's literature, *Peanuts* combined minimalism of execution with complexity of tone. In it, Schulz countered the roistering humor of early comic-strip kids with a restiveness or sense of unease, as the familiar, reassuring qualities of the daily strip genre collided with an instinctive, almost despairing sense of irony. Of all Schulz's predecessors, only his revered Percy Crosby, the tragically ill-fated author of *Skippy* (1923–45), had gotten close to this mix of melancholy, astringency, tenderness, and the sheer irrepressible joy of doodling (see Gardner; Robinson). About *Peanuts* there was a delicacy, a knife's-edge balancing of fragility and poise, the result of Schulz's graphic humor being put under the enormous pressure of his psychological insight.

Some have questioned whether, under such pressure, Schulz's children can remain inviting and convincing evocations of childhood. Noting the seemingly ironic distance between child characters and adult diction, Umberto Eco famously remarked that Schulz's characters are "monstrous, infantile reductions of all the neuroses of a modern citizen of the industrial civilization" (qtd. in Inge 135). They are monsters, suggests Eco, because they distill the neurotic self-regard of mid-twentieth-century adults. As cartoonist Howard Cruse has observed, if in the 1950s "Vance Packard and Jules Feiffer mined the adult world for lost souls," then "*Peanuts* covered the playground" to similar effect ("Dear Sparky" 55). Indeed Schulz's neurotic suburban children seemed to live just next door to the psychologically tortured urbanites of Feiffer, with their dizzying verbal contortions and deadpan hostility. Feiffer himself recognized the kinship (Michaelis, "Life" 293).

If Schulz's treatment of his child characters was ironic and empathetic adults were among his most ardent readers, does it therefore follow that *Peanuts* was out of the reach of real children or fundamentally misleading about childhood? Consider that the irony in *Peanuts* simply spikes an irony always already implicit in comics: the incommensurability of, or tension between, image and word. Schulz's combination of child personas and adult chatter underscores comics' lack of a perfect fit between the visual and verbal, a lack or gap that, we might say, compels us readers to reconcile these disparate elements. In a sense, though, word and image are never to be fully reconciled but always held a little apart, in suspension, the incompleteness of each never quite made complete by the other. This gives strips like *Peanuts* an edge: at some level we have to suspend judgment rather than resolve the disparate meanings of image and word into an easy, homogeneous whole. While authors and readers alike presumably aim to join picture and word into a wholly convincing world—we want to *believe* in it, after all, at least for the duration of the reading—the constant shuttling between different kinds of messages calls attention to, as Robert P. Fletcher argues, that world's very fictiveness (383). In this regard, Ole Frahm claims that comic art by its very nature mocks efforts to achieve a stable unity of text and image: no matter how apparently simple and transparent the comic in question, the form never disappears into the content but, rather, keeps us constantly aware of our own role as readers ("Weird Signs"). An aesthetics of comics, Frahm says, must therefore be an aesthetics of parody, spoofing and frustrating our desires for wholeness. In making this more obvious, *Peanuts* may have been, as Garry Trudeau remarks, the first "postmodern" comic strip (A38).

Perhaps *Peanuts* does mock our desires for wholeness. Schulz's strip kids, in hindsight, clearly served him as mouthpieces, as his doubles, shadow-selves, and antagonists. Inhabiting an impossible, two-dimensional world, they gave vent to different aspects of his personality. With this in mind, it would be easy enough to argue that Schulz's children aren't "really" children or that the strip is manifestly meant for adults. One early interviewer even called the strip a "libel" on childhood (Inge 3). Or, if one prizes this quality in Schulz, it would be just as easy to claim that he eventually surrendered it: that *Peanuts*, though originally in sync with adult concerns, unfortunately sold out, toning down its dark, sophisticated humor to a more coddling, less challenging version, a multimedia version in which merchandising and licensing became paramount. In later years, Schulz did reject the bitter knowingness of his early work: as *Peanuts* became more popular, he came to feel that his formative strips were too harsh. The later *Peanuts* would be softer, more anodyne, less piercing. By this light, the strip could be said to have become just another example of calculated children's entertainment: a strip begun as an adult mockery of children, or a mockery of adults *through* children, but then overmarketed in an aggressive, saturating way that proved inimical to its original tone and fatal to its special humor. It would be easy to see an accommodating cynicism behind this. As Schulz and company sold the *Peanuts* characters to an ever-growing mob of licensees and merchandisers, the strip, it could be argued, slipped from its original emotive foundation and became, in the worst sense, "childish" pabulum. Indeed complaints like these began to surface less than halfway through the life of the strip (Michaelis, *Schulz* 386–87).

This argument, however, is reductive, ignoring both the ways that *Peanuts* appealed to children from the first and the fact that it continued to incorporate veiled autobiography and outright poignancy all the way to its end. We would be mistaken to assume either that a "proper" representation of children should be free of the bleakness and doubt so often revealed in *Peanuts* or that, conversely, only the bleakness in *Peanuts* gives it integrity. The first of these assumptions would be sentimentalist, the second shaped by knee-jerk antisentimentalism: the self-consciously oppositional ethos of underground and alternative culture. Both views are guilty of oversimplification. *Peanuts* could be dark yet still friendly and accessible to child readers; Schulz's cross-writing reached across boundary lines. If I may divert momentarily to my own memories, my childhood included much happy reading of *Peanuts*, if not in the newspapers then in the ever-present Fawcett Crest paperbacks of the sixties and after; indeed, those were compulsively readable books, their very simplicity and minimalism making them endlessly beguiling. *Peanuts* was such a trustworthy companion that I never thought to question its place within my childhood. As a boy I not only watched the animated *Peanuts* specials on television but also read books of early, pre-television *Peanuts* alongside those of later periods; though I could recognize changes in the strip's style, I never saw a disconnect between early and later versions. Nor did I doubt that Charlie Brown represented childhood in a way that I could understand, empathize with, and make a part of my own life. Countless tributes to Schulz from readers who grew up with *Peanuts* suggest that my experience was not untypical: interested child readers seem to have little difficulty in recognizing the *Peanuts* characters—from any period—as their own. This is not to say that Schulz's depiction of (a narrowly suburban, middle-class, and almost entirely white) American childhood was wholly accurate or true, but merely that it was persuasive, meaning that its cross-writing contained observations and feelings that both adults and children could recognize as truthful, urgent, endearing, and funny.

The influence of that cross-writing has been profound, particularly in the field of comics. Just as children's literature has influenced "adult" literary production in varied and unpredictable ways—the axial idea in Juliet Dusinberre's *Alice to the Lighthouse* (1987)—Schulz has left a deep handprint on his native form. Alternative or art comics creators have been anxious to acknowledge his influence while disavowing his more commercial leanings. If, as Jeet Heer has suggested, recent art comics constitute "a reclamation project," an effort to "redeem" and recontextualize the comics of the past and liberate them from their commercial settings (121), then *Peanuts* has been reclaimed with a vengeance, inspiring homages and parodies from a great many alternative comics artists ostensibly working for adults. This may seem surprising, given the frequent promotion of Schulz (especially at the time of his death in 2000) as the saintly epitome of a kinder, gentler sort of cartooning, but his work has very deeply affected many authors working in the tradition of underground and alternative comics. Though today's alternative comics artists, rooted as they area in the comic book subculture, are in some senses a world away from the refrigerator-ready newspaper strips epitomized by *Peanuts*, many such artists claim Schulz as a crucial influence. Indeed, for some, Schulz has been a more important influence than even the radical underground "comix" creators of the sixties and seventies. The debt that today's art comics owe to Schulz is enormous—evidence for the point that children's culture can never be cordoned off wholly from the larger field of cultural production.

That debt is encapsulated by, for example, the reflective comments of the acclaimed Canadian cartoonist known as Seth. Designer of the *Complete Peanuts* reprint series (since 2004), Seth has worked extensively with Schulz's images; he is also on the front rank of alternative comic book and graphic novel artists. In an issue of *The Comics Journal* devoted partly to Schulz (December 1997), Seth writes:

> [Schulz] took what was essentially a gag-a-day format and bent it into something very personal, very affecting. Having read and re-read those classic strips thousands of times I can say pretty safely that his work has had a lasting, subtle effect on my own viewpoint of the world. [. . .] Somehow, [his] lonely, unpleasant view of human affairs always rang very true to me. ("Dear Sparky" 68)

Schulz's lasting effect on the artist can be seen in a one-page comic created by Seth in 1994 titled "Good Grief!": a mini-essay, verbal and visual, on the topic of loneliness, which, in Schulzian fashion, is a recurrent theme in Seth's work (fig. 8.4). Here Seth weaves together Schulz's words, culled from the book *You Don't Look 35, Charlie Brown!* (1985), with Seth's own haunting, man-on-the-street portraits of blank, unreadable faces. At the top, serving as a kind of epigraph, is a classically four-panel *Peanuts* strip by Seth that reverses the technique of the rest of the page: in this case Schulz's visual style is carefully mimicked but combined with words attributed (perhaps falsely) to the seventeenth-century *haiku* poet "Basho" [sic]:

> The god is absent;
> His leaves are piling . . .
> And all is deserted.

That this combination does not seem strange is itself a telling commentary on the darkness underlying Schulz's friendly cartoon world. By blending styles and sources, Seth pays tribute both to Schulz's graphic panache and to his disconcerting acuity. The result underscores the way that *Peanuts*, though a mainstream newspaper strip, informs Seth's work in the genres of the alternative comic book and graphic novel. Though Seth's work does not often engage childhood directly, he cites *Peanuts* very frequently, and his stories are punctuated with moments of visual poetry reminiscent of Schulz at his most lyrical (see for example Seth's novel *It's a Good Life, If You Don't Weaken* [1999]). Most obviously, Seth's (grown-up) characters battle depression in monologues and conversations that echo Charlie Brown's melancholy.

This antiheroic ethos blankets the autobiographical and semiautobiographical alternative comics that have flourished over the past twenty-five years, many of which seek to reunderstand childhood from subversive and critical perspectives and therefore draw upon the imagery of children's comics and/or adopt naive styles modeled on children's art (e.g., R. Crumb, Lynda Barry, Phoebe Gloeckner, Marjane Satrapi). Some blatantly acknowledge a debt to Schulz. For example, Chris Ware, another alternative cartoonist who has contributed to the recent rediscovery and reclamation of past strips, blatantly echoes Schulz in his moving yet pitilessly

Figure 8.4. Seth, "Good Grief!" *An Anthology of Graphic Fiction, Cartoons, and True Stories.* Ed. Ivan Brunetti. New Haven: Yale UP, 2006, page 36. Reproduced courtesy of the artist and with thanks to *Drawn and Quarterly.*

bleak graphic novel *Jimmy Corrigan: The Smartest Kid on Earth* (2000), the protagonist of which, a balding, recessive schlemiel whose life is almost unbearably lonely, could be a dead ringer for a grown-up Charlie Brown at his most abject. Ware, like

Seth, openly declares his indebtedness to Schulz, whose characters he has described as "the first real sympathetic cartoon characters" and whose cartooning he has praised for "show[ing] where the real art and dignity in the comic strip resides" ("Preliminary Drawings" 68–70). For Ware, Schulz is a master and his characters are a focus of intense identification, and so Ware too has done stylistic homage to *Peanuts* (see for example "Charlie Brown"). Tellingly, among Ware's most poignant and devastating comics are those about children and hapless, infantilized adults.

Recent art comic anthologies, such as the Ware-edited *McSweeney's Quarterly Concern* Issue Number 13 (2004) and the Ivan Brunetti–edited *An Anthology of Graphic Fiction, Cartoons, & True Stories* (2006), have continued to lionize Schulz and his influence, confirming the reach of his cross-writing and extending his ambiguous treatment of childhood. Such tributes implicitly invoke Art Spiegelman's well-regarded comic strip "Abstract Thought is a Warm Puppy," first published in *The New Yorker* in February 2000 on the eve of Schulz's retirement, in fact just days before his death, and since reprinted several times (for example in the above-mentioned Brunetti volume, which also includes our Seth example). Spiegelman—whose own cartooning career to 2000 differed sharply from Schulz's in terms of aesthetics, ideology, and audience—unexpectedly yet decisively validated the art-comics appreciation of *Peanuts*. "Abstract Thought" is ambivalent but full of praise, valorizing Schulz's art while resisting its obvious commerciality and influence. Spiegelman couches all this in a pastiche of Schulz's own style, echoing the daily and Sunday strip layouts of *Peanuts* itself. The question he finally poses, and he asks it in a spirit of genuine awe, has to do with *Peanuts*' radical instability and richness as an exemplary piece of cross-writing: "How did 'Peanuts' consistently depict genuine pain and loss and still keep everything so warm and fuzzy?!" At the heart of this questioning is Spiegelman's bemused recognition that somehow *Peanuts* was both a shamelessly commercial element of children's culture and at the same time deeply "personal," "authentic," and artistically excellent. This almost-grudging tribute became a watershed in the critical reconsideration of Schulz, celebrating his artistry while resisting his self-deprecating populism and his willing confinement to a steady formula (for less forgiving criticism of Schulz, see, for example, Pekar).

Homages like these, as Gene Kannenberg points out, testify to Schulz's continuing relevance, calling attention to both his story-telling devices and the social, psychological, and philosophical undercurrents of his work (101). By now *Peanuts*, despite its pigeonholing as a children's strip, practically constitutes a template, in Kannenberg's terms an interpretive system, through which other cartoonists can address their artistic and personal concerns in a variety of comics for both children and adults. Today Schulz's influence shapes the work of both mainstream and avant-garde cartoonists, corroborating Dusinberre's point that beloved elements of children's literature and culture may inspire experimental, anti-mainstream art and demonstrating, once again, that the dialogue with children's culture goes on at myriad levels of cultural production.

Of course, much of what Schulz accomplished for comics he accomplished under cover. His legacy to art comics is mixed, in that he often publicly deprecated his own work and maintained that he lacked, or had sacrificed, the "total freedom" of the so-called pure artist (Inge 202). In fact denials of comics' status as Art constitute a leitmotif in his published interviews. As if in keeping with dismissive attitudes toward children's culture, he often adopted a diminutive rhetoric when discussing his work (though he was in fact stubbornly proud of it at the same time). If on the one hand Schulz represents the opening-out of comics to deeper, more personal, and, in some cases, more anguished work, on the other hand he epitomizes—and he knew this—the impulse to compromise one's work in order to secure a larger audience. In this sense his use of child characters was knowing if not ingratiating. We may lament this compromise, or we may embrace it, recognizing that what we value in *Peanuts* is precisely this complexity: the way Schulz combined the bitter with the sweet, thus not only extending but also complicating the tradition of the comic-strip child. Working in the comforting genre of the daily strip, Schulz could sneak past the defenses of readers old and young, writing to himself and cross-writing to millions with both disarming immediacy and an underappreciated power.

In answer to Spiegelman's question—just how did *Peanuts* manage to depict pain and loss and yet stay warm and fuzzy?—Schulz well understood the daily strip genre's repetitive, ritualistic nature. The daily strip requires the creator's and readers' constant return, a fact that, like Schulz's use of children, effectively softened his edge: the sheer stability of the genre mitigated his bitter, melancholy humor, reassuring readers that everything would be all right. Privately, Schulz seemed to have needed such a reassurance himself, for he craved repetition, the steady, regular routine of his work, as if said routine could be his last line of defense against the very issues raised in the work itself (Michaelis, *Schulz* 371–72). This attitude is rather like that of many art comics creators, for whom the sheer labor-intensive formalism and craft of their work imply a way of containing and handling the near-hopelessness or terror evoked in that work. It is as if the artist, teetering on some precipice of existential doubt, defers to the very workaholic intensity of cartooning as a means of stability and hope. In like fashion, Schulz relied on the quotidian ritual of crafting *Peanuts* to overbalance the darkness revealed within the strip itself. The ritual return of Charlie Brown and Co., day after day, palliated Schulz's harshest insights, allowing him (and his readers) to go on enjoying what was, after all, often a tart commentary on failure and loneliness. In this way, the strip genre is optimistic, anodyne, and unfettered by the accretion of too many memories (or prone to remembering only selectively). This quality, arguably, served Schulz as a bulwark against complete collapse. Yet to the alert reader his humor goes hand in hand with a despondent wisdom, a sad knowingness about life's constant way of disappointing us. *Peanuts* balances this sadness with the hopefulness that the idea of childhood tends to evoke in our culture; on some level, Schulz used that sense of hope to reassure his readers in spite of his biting humor. Charlie Brown himself was evocative of endless hope in spite of endless disappointment: fly that kite, pitch that baseball, try, try, to kick that football, over and over. Hopefulness and loss are forever twinned in Schulz's vision of childhood.

This vision isn't simply sad. There is also hope and wish fulfillment and fantasy in *Peanuts* (often via the untamed character of Snoopy). There is funny drawing, too. Above all, there is Schulz's honest and minute attention to day-to-day life: a child's-eye view of life near ground level. Schulz's view of childhood went hand in hand with a studied minimalism: a simple-looking, pared-down style that became the blueprint for late twentieth-century strips. This was a kind of cartoon modernism, informed by the streamlined, modernist school of postwar magazine cartoons (think, for example, of Virgil Partch or Hank Ketcham) but imbued with soulfulness and emotional complexity. Notably, *Peanuts* arrived the same year (1950) as William Steig's *The Agony in the Kindergarten*, an unsettling book of modernist cartoons depicting children, and Schulz applied a comparable graphic shorthand, albeit with a sleeker, more commercial line and a continuing cast of characters. Echoing Steig's cartoon idiom, Schulz began by exploiting the visual/verbal incongruities on which magazine cartoonists thrived (see Bang), at times approaching Steig's power to shock; yet he soon became a master of understatement and gentle characterization. His minimalism had two prongs: not simply a graphic minimalism in his rendering, but also the deliberate minuteness and precision of his humor. He could wring jokes from fine nuances and slight situations—too-tight shoelaces, for example, or watching a leaf fall to the ground.

In this way, Schulz, again like Steig, dovetailed aesthetically with the exploration of everyday life experience extolled by much mid-century children's literature: think of the influence of the Bank Street/Here and Now school, which espoused evocative depictions of small, moment-to-moment impressions and pleasures (as in, famously, Margaret Wise Brown's *The Noisy Book, Goodnight Moon*, etc.). Think, too, of the concomitant streamlining and increasing graphic sophistication of picture-book art in this era, influenced by the infusion of modernist aesthetics (notable in many of Brown's collaborators). Like his predecessor Crockett Johnson, who effectively straddled the worlds of comic strips and children's books, Schulz developed an extremely simplified, almost schematic, and unadorned style (see Nel), though his would become looser as the years passed. While Schulz was far from sharing the progressive political commitments embraced by many Bank Street creators (see Mickenberg 40–42) and the cultural interests of the modernist avant-garde, his work was finely observed and dedicated to the exploration of nuance, in a manner like that of the great mid-century picture-book pioneers. In short, *Peanuts* whittled the comic strip down to the deliciously small and precise, capturing the particulars of day-to-day life from the unhurried perspective of a child. By the sharpness of his observations, Schulz redefined what it is that could stand for a gag in comics, finding humor in very slight changes, or even in stasis, using the panel-to-panel transitioning of the comics form to spotlight minute touches. He took such miniature grace notes of observation and turned them from incidental details of style into the very heart of his gags. Schulz could make a strip seemingly about nothing and imbue that "nothing" with hypnotic charm (one of his biggest lessons for today's alternative comics).

Above all, what made *Peanuts* groundbreaking was its knowing, sometimes surprising revision of the comic-strip child, the fact that Schulz's "li'l folks" spoke for children and adults alike. Though a kid, Charlie Brown perfectly represented middle-class American anomie; though children, the *Peanuts* gang spoke with an astringent truthfulness. Visually they remained cute, but thematically their world was rich and sometimes difficult. In this way *Peanuts* inadvertently prophesied underground and alternative comics, for it helped redefine the relationship between thematic content and graphic form. Schulz's intensely personal approach inspired many less obviously commercial and less convention-bound cartoonists who came after. His successors in art comics have perhaps sacrificed *Peanuts'* utopian quality, its status as a microcosmic retreat for young and old readers alike, but they have tried to hold on to its trademark irony and minimalism, its visual poetry, dedication to nuance, and melancholy truthfulness. Schulz's complex, troubled view of childhood likewise persists: as noted, the subversive reexamination of childhood is a major source of art comics, as if in reaction to the continuing characterization of comics and graphic novels as juvenilia. If the position of comics within hierarchies of literary production, like the position of children's literature, is based on assumptions of immaturity or childishness, then many of the best comics authors have taken up their childhoods and tried to understand them better. Rather than disavowing the association between comics and childlikeness—one of the "symbolic handicaps" that, as Thierry Groensteen has argued (40), continues to obstruct comics criticism—many great comics have embraced it.

Peanuts continues to inform this interrogation of childhood. In fact it casts a long shadow. Despite, or perhaps because of, its trafficking in irony, its sly counterposing of image and text, and its subversion of our expectations of children, the strip has been a persuasive part of the landscape of American childhood for well over half a century: not simply adult constructions of childhood, as Other, as site of memory, or as object of nostalgic pining, but children's visions of childhood as well. If *Peanuts* displays a skepticism toward or mockery of idealized childhood, perhaps this is not a bad thing for young readers to be introduced to. Schulz insisted all along that his strip was never simply "for" children in some exclusive, sealed-off, and patronizing way, but rather sought to treat young readers with trust and respect; in other words, he would not be hemmed in by what had passed for childhood in previous comics (Interview 324; Inge 230–31). Despite this—despite its satirical license and despite all Schulz's disclaimers—*Peanuts* was more genuinely interested in childhood than had been the pioneering strips of Outcault or Dirks. That interest never had to do with condescending to children; it had to do with emotional honesty. If the strip's humor was ironic, that irony was not always corrosive, nor was the strip all about darkness. Indeed some have argued, especially in the wake of Michaelis's controversial biography (2007), that too exclusive an emphasis on Schulz's melancholy does the artist a disservice by clouding over his gifts for lightness, charm, fantasy, and, above all, humor (see "Schulz and Peanuts Roundtable"; Berlatsky). Yes, his vision of childhood was sometimes bleak, but it was also unpredictable, generous, and generative. A seminal example of cross-writing, *Peanuts* reached grown-ups through its recollections of childhood and reached children by recognizing the seriousness of their social and emotional lives. This is why, despite his status as the epitome of commercialism, Schulz still deeply touches readers both old and young.

WORKS CITED

Bang, Derrick, ed. *Charles M. Schulz: Li'l Beginnings*. Santa Rosa, CA: Charles M. Schulz Museum, 2004.

Berlatsky, Noah. "Happiness Is an Unhappy Hipster." *The Comics Journal* 265 (January/February 2005): 172–74.

Blackbeard, Bill, and Martin Williams, eds. *The Smithsonian Collection of Newspaper Comics*. Washington, DC: Smithsonian Institution Press; New York: Harry N. Abrams, Inc., 1977.

Brunetti, Ivan, ed. *An Anthology of Graphic Fiction, Cartoons, & True Stories*. New Haven, CT: Yale UP, 2006.

"'Dear Sparky. . .': Comics Artists from Across the Medium on the Legendary Cartoonist and Creator of *Peanuts*." *The Comics Journal* 200 (December 1997): 49–68.

Diereck, Charles, and Pascal Lefèvre, eds. *Forging a New Medium: The Comic Strip in the Nineteenth Century*. Leuven, Belgium: VUB UP, 1998.

Dusinberre, Juliet. *Alice to the Lighthouse: Children's Books and Radical Experiments in Art*. 1987. Rev. ed. New York: St. Martin's, 1999.

Fletcher, Robert P. "Visual Thinking and the Picture Story in *The History of Henry Esmond*." *PMLA* 113, no. 3 (May 1998): 379–94.

Frahm, Ole. "Weird Signs: Comics as Means of Parody." In Magnussen and Christiansen, *Comics and Culture*, 177–92.

Gardner, Jared. "Percy Crosby and *Skippy*." *The Comics Journal* 298 (May 2009): 144–52.

Gordon, Ian. *Comic Strips and Consumer Culture, 1890–1945*. Washington: Smithsonian Institution Press, 1998.

Groensteen, Thierry. "Why Are Comics Still in Search of Cultural Legitimization?" In Magnussen and Christiansen, *Comics and Culture*, 29–41.

Harvey, Robert C. *The Art of the Funnies: An Aesthetic History*. Jackson: UP of Mississippi, 1994.

Hatfield, Charles. "Comic Art, Children's Literature, and the New Comic Studies." *The Lion and the Unicorn* 30, no. 3 (September 2006): 360–82.

Heer, Jeet. "Little Nemo in Comicsland." *Virginia Quarterly Review* 82, no. 2 (Spring 2006): 104–21.

Inge, M. Thomas, ed. *Charles M. Schulz: Conversations*. Jackson: UP of Mississippi, 2000.

Kannenberg, Gene, Jr. "Chips Off the Ol' Blockhead: Evidence of Influence in Peanuts Parodies." *Studies in American Humor* 3, no. 14 (2006): 91–103.

Lurie, Alison. *Don't Tell the Grown-Ups: Subversive Children's Literature*. Boston: Little, Brown, 1990.

Magnussen, Anne, and Hans-Christian Christiansen, eds. *Comics and Culture: Analytical and Theoretical Approaches to Comics.* Copenhagen: Museum Tusculanum/U of Copenhagen, 2000.

Michaelis, David. "The Life and Times of Charles M. Schulz." In Schulz, *Complete Peanuts: 1950 to 1952,* 291–303.

———. *Schulz and Peanuts.* New York: Harper, 2007.

Mickenberg, Julia L. *Learning from the Left: Children's Literature, the Cold War, and Radical Politics in the United States.* Oxford: Oxford UP, 2006.

Myers, Mitzi, and U. C. Knoepflmacher. "'Cross-Writing' and the Reconceptualizing of Children's Literary Studies." *Children's Literature* 25 (1997): vii–xvii.

Nel, Philip. "Crockett Johnson and the Purple Crayon: A Life in Art." *Comic Art* 5 (Winter 2004): 2–18.

Nodelman, Perry. "The Other: Orientalism, Colonialism, and Children's Literature." *Children's Literature Association Quarterly* 17 (Spring 1992): 29–35.

Nyberg, Amy Kiste. "Percival Chubb and the League for the Improvement of the Children's Comic Supplement." *Inks: Cartoon and Comic Art Studies* 3, no. 3 (November 1996): 31–34.

Outcault, R. F. *The Yellow Kid: A Centennial Celebration of the Kid Who Started the Comics.* Edited by Bill Blackbeard. Northampton, MA: Kitchen Sink Press, 1995.

Pekar, Harvey. "The Potential of Comics." *The Comics Journal* 123 (July 1988): 81–88.

Resnick, Adam. "Long Before 'South Park.'" Review of *Peanuts: The Art of Charles M. Schulz,* by Charles M. Schulz. *Los Angeles Times Book Review,* 3 February 2002, 12.

Robinson, Jerry. *Skippy and Percy Crosby.* New York: Holt, Rinehart, and Winston, 1978.

Schulz, Charles M. *The Complete Peanuts: 1950 to 1952.* Ed. Gary Groth. Seattle: Fantagraphics Books, 2004.

———. *The Complete Peanuts: 1957 to 1958.* Ed. Gary Groth. Seattle: Fantagraphics Books, 2005.

———. Interview by Rick Marschall and Gary Groth. In Schulz, *Complete Peanuts: 1950 to 1952,* 304–37.

———. *You Don't Look 35, Charlie Brown!* New York: Holt, Rinehart, and Winston, 1985.

"The Schulz and Peanuts Roundtable." *The Comics Journal* 290 (May 2008): 26–111.

Schwartz, Ben. "I Hold a Grudge, Boy: Charles Schulz in Postwar America, 1946–1950." *Comic Art* 4 (Fall 2003): 4–13.

Seth [pseud.]. "Good Grief!" 1994. In Brunetti, *An Anthology of Graphic Fiction, Cartoons, & True Stories,* 36.

———. *It's a Good Life, If You Don't Weaken.* 1999. 2nd ed. Montreal: Drawn and Quarterly, 2003.

Spiegelman, Art. "Abstract Thought Is a Warm Puppy." In Brunetti, *An Anthology of Graphic Fiction, Cartoons, & True Stories,* 32–34.

Stallcup, Jackie E. "Power, Fear, and Children's Picture Books." *Children's Literature* 30 (2002): 125–58.

Trudeau, Garry. "'I Hate Charlie Brown': An Appreciation." *Washington Post,* 16 December 1999, A38.

Ware, Chris. "Charles Schulz's Preliminary Drawings." In Ware, *McSweeney's,* 66–71.

———. "Charlie Brown, Snoopy, Linus, Lucy . . . How Can I Ever Forget Them?" In Brunetti, *An Anthology of Graphic Fiction, Cartoons, & True Stories,* 35.

———. *Jimmy Corrigan: The Smartest Kid on Earth.* New York: Pantheon, 2000.

———, ed. *McSweeney's Quarterly Concern,* Issue Number 13. San Francisco, McSweeney's, 2004.

FURTHER READING

Carlin, John, Paul Karasik, and Brian Walker, eds. *Masters of American Comics*. New Haven: Yale UP, 2005.

——. *Comics as Culture*. Jackson: UP of Mississippi, 1990.

Johnson, Rheta Grimsley. *Good Grief: The Story of Charles M. Schulz*. New York: Pharos, 1989.

Kidd, Chip, ed. and compiler. *Peanuts: The Art of Charles M. Schulz*. New York: Pantheon, 2001.

Schulz, Charles M. *Celebrating Peanuts: 60 Years*. Kansas City, MO: Andrews McMeel, 2009.

——. *The Complete Peanuts* [series]. Seattle: Fantagraphics, 2004–.

Walker, Brian. *The Comics: Since 1945*. New York: Abrams, 2002.

CHAPTER 9

THE CAT IN THE HIPPIE: DR. SEUSS, NONSENSE, THE CARNIVALESQUE, AND THE SIXTIES REBEL

KEVIN SHORTSLEEVE

Dr. Seuss (Theodore Seuss Geisel) was born in Springfield, Massachusetts, in 1904. He graduated from Dartmouth College and attended Oxford University before dropping out to pursue a career in advertising. He was famous first for his Quick Henry, the Flit! *advertising cartoons, published in U.S. magazines between 1927 and 1944. Before and during World War II Geisel also produced numerous political cartoons that ridiculed isolationists and totalitarian tyrants.*

His first children's book, And to Think That I Saw It on Mulberry Street, *was published in 1937. Among his many popular titles are* Horton Hears a Who! *(1954),* How the Grinch Stole Christmas *(1957),* Green Eggs and Ham *(1960), and* The Lorax *(1971). In 1957, he published* The Cat in the Hat *and simultaneously cofounded the imprint Beginner Books, inciting a revolution in early readers. His fame and cultural importance in the United States cannot be overstated.* Green Eggs and Ham *was, by the 1980s, the third best-selling book in the English language. Geisel's fiftieth and final book,* Oh, the Places You'll Go! *was published in 1990. He died in 1991.*

Although he produced a few texts in prose, Geisel was best known for his bouncy anapestic tetrameter. His musical and original vocabulary was rendered playfully in dependable rhyme. Geisel married his verses to a wildly exotic illustration style that appeared childlike and approachable, like cartoon art, yet simultaneously reflected the influence of the dream-like landscapes and unpredictable structures of the surrealists.

In 1977, Theodore Seuss Geisel received an honorary doctorate from Lake Forest College in Illinois. His commencement address was a rhyming verse poem that advised caution toward authority. The poem concludes:

> . . . as you partake of the world's bill of fare,
> That's darned good advice to follow.
> Do a lot of spitting out the hot air.
> And be careful what you swallow.
>   (qtd. in Morgan and Morgan 234–35)

Seuss biographers Judith and Neil Morgan relate:

> As Geisel sat down, there was bedlam. Students shouted, cheered and flung their caps into the air. He was startled, for it was his first experience with the fervor with which many young Americans had begun to canonize Dr. Seuss. These graduates were of the generation most critical of the Vietnam War, and from their earliest memories of Dr. Seuss books they had assumed that he too must be skeptical of the establishment. Now they'd heard evidence from the master's lips. (235)

I cite the above passage for two reasons. First, it asserts that the children who read Seuss's books had always understood them to be subversive, a claim that is interesting in its own right. This essay explores how Seuss's texts might have left this impression, not at the surface level of the narrative itself (the politics of which have already been explored by a number of critics), but at a deeper level—in the subtle charm of the carnivalesque atmosphere of his texts and in the symbolic meaning and functions of his nonsense. Second, it makes particular mention of "the generation most critical of the Vietnam War." This claim quietly posits that children who were learning to read with Seuss books in the late fifties and sixties were doing more than just becoming literate; they were activists-in-training. This essay seeks, in several ways, to unpack this encounter of the child-as-future-activist with Seuss books and the turbulent decade of the 1960s. Seuss's texts will be examined via Mikhail Bakhtin's theory of the carnivalesque as outlined in his study, *Rabelais and His World* (1968). Bakhtin posits that a carnivalesque mood is fundamental if one is to envision the downfall of "all that oppresses and restricts" (92). Closely related to the carnivalesque are the offices of nonsense literature, from which Seuss assiduously cribbed. This essay will therefore also explore the intuition Marilyn Apseloff and Celia Anderson propose in *Nonsense Literature for Children: Aesop to Seuss*, "that nonsense literature contributes to the civilizing process" (108). Like many other creators of literary nonsense, Seuss made use of narrative voids, existential dilemmas, and vague endings that ultimately inspire in the reader a personal responsibility for meaning. This inclusive strategy of Seuss's texts can be fruitfully linked to the sixties-era insistence on the concept of "participatory democracy," as promoted, for example, by the radical group Students for a Democratic Society (SDS), which stressed the importance of individual responsibility. This essay will ultimately suggest that Seuss earned his enduring iconic status, not merely because he was a talented writer and artist who occasioned a revolution in early-reader books, but also because, politically and aesthetically, he was ideally poised to produce texts that subtly resonated with the emerging discontent that came to represent sixties youth and sixties activism. While this essay will mention many other Seuss titles, it will focus ultimately on *The Cat in the Hat* (1957) (hereafter *TCITH*), one of Seuss's bestsellers and the flagship of his Beginner Books empire.

While the Seuss phenomenon has not previously been discussed through the lens of the 1960s cultural revolution, this essay is indebted to critics who have, for some time, acknowledged the general orientation of Seuss's political and subversive edge; among them are Rita Roth, Ruth MacDonald, Richard Minear, Henry Jenkins, and Philip Nel. Jenkins is particularly helpful in defining Seuss's basic ideology. In "No Matter How Small: The Democratic Imagination of Doctor Seuss," Jenkins argues that Seuss was interested in spreading a fairer and more liberal democracy in America. Seuss taught children "to trust their own internal responses to an unjust world" (188). He believed that children were born with an innate sense of fairness, justice, and "the virtues of a democratic citizen" (188). Seuss worked toward the education of a postwar American child, "born free of prejudice, repression, and authoritarianism" (189), and, therefore, routinely "subverted adult authority" in his texts, as in *TCITH* (188–89). Specifically, Jenkins argues, Seuss texts "contained criticisms of the existing order, recognizing America's failures to fulfill its own ideals" (195).

According to Jenkins and other critics, *The 500 Hats of Bartholomew Cubbins*, *The King's Stilts* (1939), and *Bartholomew and the Oobleck* (1949) are stories that explore a misuse of power (Roth 147, Jenkins 198–99); *Horton Hears a Who* (1954), *Yertle the Turtle* (1958), *The Sneeches* (1961), and *One Fish Two Fish Red Fish Blue Fish* (1960) strike a serendipitous chord with the civil rights movement or with issues of diversity (Kahn 26, Nel, *Icon* 58, 171–72); *Horton Hears a Who* and *The Cat in Hat Comes Back* (1958) can function as commentaries on nuclear war (MacDonald 75, Menand 59); and *How the Grinch Stole Christmas* and *The Lorax* are critiques on consumerism and, by extension, capitalism.

The studies mentioned above focus on Seuss's narratives. As I noted earlier, I wish to focus on Seuss's aesthetic principles, the carnivalesque atmosphere of his texts, and the symbolic meaning of his nonsense. A few words on what I mean by "nonsense" are required. I am not referring to nonsense as a literary genre, but rather as words, phrases, or texts that function in particular ways in any genre. I write here of nonsense as a set of writerly tools—words, phrases, or texts that revel in inversion fantasies and manifest a topsy-turvyness that typically rejects authoritarian order. What is specifically rejected by these inversions may be natural or hierarchical laws of order and place. Nonsense often rejects commonly endorsed systems, such as linguistic and grammatical systems; neologisms and portmanteau words are thus typical of nonsense. Nonsense is frequently typified by randomness, the seemingly disparate, chimerical construction of a piece of nonsense suggesting a willful disregard for narrative convention and order. And nonsense often celebrates the impossible, positing temporal, spatial, and existential confusion. Nonsense typically ennobles anomaly while simultaneously rejecting the expected, the orderly, and the everyday. Seuss's texts, while usually working as complete stories, nevertheless make liberal use of all the textual elements described above.

The connection between these features of nonsense and those that Bakhtin examines in his study of the carnivalesque is striking. Among the material Bakhtin explores, for example, are various forms of carnival speech and carnival literatures he describes in the following terms:

> ... a genre of intentionally absurd verbal compositions ... that ignores all norms,
> even those of elementary logic ... [In this genre there are] words linked by
> assonance or rhyme but with no meaning and no single theme ... [422–23]. [In
> carnival speech ideas] follow each other without any logical sequence ... [and]
> expressions are turned inside out ... [424]. [This is a genre of] ... exceptional
> linguistic freedom. Even formal grammatical construction [becomes] extremely
> plastic. [471]

The connections between nonsense and carnival go beyond these similarities. Bakhtin, for example, cites examples of carnivalesque speech that are populated by made-up words (203–4, 206, 263), double entendres (225), and riddles (233, 238) and that exhibit a peculiar obsession with large, precise numbers (150, 190, 221). According to Bakhtin, carnivalesque speech is recognizable by its strong element of play (7, 231–35), its seeming ambivalence (11–12, 16, 101, 260), its use of exaggeration (19), and that the carnivalesque was a genre that reveled in the idea of madness (260–61). This vision of the carnivalesque also precisely describes the qualities of literary nonsense, as written by Lewis Carroll and Edward Lear, and as found in sections of nearly every book written by Dr. Seuss.[1]

Bakhtin theorizes that carnival humor "means the defeat of power, [the defeat] of ... kings, of ... upper classes, [and] of all that oppresses and restricts" (92), and that "... these festive comic images ... express their criticism, their deep distrust of official truth, and [the] highest hopes and aspirations" of the population (269). Many critics, Rita Roth among them, summarize the political bent of much of Seuss's work using similar language:

> Geisel deserves serious attention because his work is replete with social
> commentary and critique. "A smasher of conventional boundaries"[2] he explores
> oppression in many forms. (Roth 142)

Bakhtin suggests that a characteristic historical situation is required before a flourishing of carnivalesque imagery occurs. He describes these historical situations as "moments of crisis, of breaking points in ... the life of society and man" (9) and cites as examples the convergence of the Greek, Oscan, and Latin cultures of late antiquity (31, 472), the cultural upheavals of both Ivan the Terrible's and Peter the Great's Russia (218, 270–71), the Renaissance generally, and the French Revolution (119). A similar cultural upheaval, the "Long 1960s," occasioned Seuss's rise to iconic status.

The present study is in line with conventions established in other studies on sixties culture (see, e.g., DeKoven 3) by describing the period of cultural production spanning from 1954 to 1974 as the "Long 1960s," which is equivalent to the era of social unrest that included the civil rights movement, the reaction against McCarthyism, the Cuban Missile Crisis, the sexual revolution, the popularization of the feminist movement, the age of Vietnam War protests, the Spring of Prague, and the Watergate scandal. This period also coincides with the major innovations in music for youth, from the birth of rock and roll (1954) to the height of the Greenwich Village folk scene (1962), to the British Invasion (1964), from swinging London and the Los Angeles and San Francisco sounds of the late sixties, and into the era of the singer-songwriters of the early 1970s.

Like these other youth-oriented movements, Dr. Seuss books were at the height of their cultural importance during this same period. Though Seuss's publishing career stretches over fifty years, I am in agreement with Philip Nel that there is a crucial period to his output (*Icon* 5, 85). Until 1953, Seuss was juggling three careers. He was a children's book author, a filmmaker, and an advertising executive. Seuss dropped his other two commitments in 1953 (Morgan and Morgan 140) and the result was a significant improvement in his work. Prior to 1954 and after 1974, Seuss's works are, with few exceptions, less effective than in this middle period. Within this crucial era Seuss released his best-remembered titles, including *Horton Hears a Who!* (1954) *TCITH* (1957), *How the Grinch Stole Christmas* (1957), *Yertle the Turtle* (1958), *The Cat in the Hat Comes Back* (1958), *Green Eggs and Ham* (1960), *One Fish Two Fish Red Fish Blue Fish* (1960), *The Sneeches* (1961), *Dr. Seuss's ABC* (1962), *Hop on Pop* (1962), *Fox in Socks* (1965), *The Lorax*, (1971), *Did I Ever Tell You How Lucky You Are?* (1973), and *There's a Wocket in My Pocket!* (1974). With the possible exceptions of his first and final books, *And to Think That I Saw it On Mulberry Street* (1937) and *Oh, the Places You'll Go* (1990), none among Seuss's other twenty-three titles for children competes with the popularity and critical appraisal of the books listed above. *The Butter Battle Book* (1984) is more notorious than popular, eliciting mixed reviews. The majority of Seuss's enduring works, then, are produced in a period that corresponds exactly with the period of social and cultural upheaval described as the "Long 1960s."

According to Bakhtin, a carnivalesque setting is a locus of social formation that fosters an atmosphere within which controversial topics and utopian desires may be confronted. Bakhtin describes the building blocks of this libratory atmosphere. A basic element of carnivalesque settings is topsy-turvy reversals. In Seuss's nonsense alphabet, *On Beyond Zebra* (1955), we meet a creature called The Quan and are asked to consider, "Is his top-side his bottom? Or bottom-side top?" In *Hop on Pop* we learn that "Mr. Brown" is "upside-down," and we see that that the fish are in the trees (43, 20). In *Dr. Seuss's ABC* we are witness to turtles, instead of fish, nesting in the trees (47), and we see a camel walking across the ceiling (11). The reversals celebrated in a medieval carnival included several traditions, such as Boy Bishops, in which children would take the place of adults and usurp their authority. Adults are frequently depicted as corrupt or ridiculous in comparison to young people in carnivalesque traditions (Bakhtin, *Rabelais* 57, 241, 251). Seuss's most popular book, *Green Eggs and Ham,* is devised entirely on just such an inversion: the adult will not try the new food that the child struggles to get him to taste, and reversal of order is further emphasized in this text by the character saying, "Sam I am" instead of "I am Sam," and instead of ham and eggs, the menu consists of eggs and ham. The main action in *TCITH* is based on a similar reversal, as the character of the mother (the authority figure) is replaced for the afternoon by a rule-breaking nonsensical cat creature.

Further establishing the carnivalesque setting, Seuss's illustrations are often populated by carnivalesque images. Books such as *If I Ran the Circus* (1956), *If I Ran the Zoo* (1950), and Seuss's bestiaries in other books feature exotic beasts with exaggerated appendages, wild assortments of horns, fantastic hair, feathers, or tails. Seuss often revels in festive settings: In *If I Ran the Circus* the narrator claims:

> I'll bring in my acrobats, jugglers and clowns
> From a thousand and thirty-three faraway towns

Objects and vehicles can resemble circus trains, such as the Zumble Zay in *Marvin K. Mooney* (1972), which features an elephant festooned with colorful banners pulling an ornate carriage topped by striped umbrellas. And Seuss's colorful cities and towns, held aloft by flimsy bending poles, often resemble the temporary constructions associated with circus tents. Seuss's most popular character—and the trademark image Seuss chose for his company—the Cat in the Hat, acts very much like a traditional clown and performs as an acrobat/juggler (15). He also controls two wild "Things" who, like circus animals, are crated in and let loose to perform their tricks.

Bakhtin also claims that carnivalesque imagery rely to a certain extent on images of revelry, appetite, festivity, and drinking (see *Rabelais* 62, 279–82, 298). With Seuss, celebration and feasting are never far off. Books such as *Happy Birthday to You* (1959) and *Mulberry Street* revel in the festive spirit. Exotic food appears in numerous texts, from *Green Eggs and Ham* to the Gooey Gluey Blue Goo that the Goo-Goose is chewing in *Fox in Socks*. And we must remember what it is that the Whos down in Whoville do at Christmas:

> Then the Whos, young and old, would sit down to feast.
> And they'd feast! And they'd feast!
> And they'd FEAST!
>   FEAST!
>   FEAST!
>   FEAST!

. . . on "Who-pudding and rare Who-roast-beast." In *The Cat in the Hat Comes Back*, the Cat eats a cake in the bathtub (11), while in *TCITH* he juggles a lit birthday cake and an open bottle of milk (13–20).

Carnivalesque traditions often feature vulgarity and perhaps do so because it is precisely the vulgarity of the body that authoritarian manners deny (see Bakhtin

147–48, 175–76). Delighting in sexual, scatological, and off-color material, the carnivalesque mood is deeply irreverent of any such repression. In *Yertle the Turtle*, Seuss makes just such use of an off-color joke, and the effect it has on an arrogant king is significant:

> Mack decided he'd had enough and he had
> That plain little turtle got a little bit mad
> And that plain little Mack did a plain little thing.
> He burped!
> And his burp shook the throne of the King!

Mack's burp sets off a chain reaction, and Yertle's kingdom is literally toppled. In the Long 1960s, contemporary adult perceptions of the need for propriety in books for children prevented Seuss from making overt references to more extreme forms of off-color material. Yet there remains in Seuss's artwork a subversive sensual aesthetic that both children and critics have identified. Seuss had, in the past, overtly indulged in ribald material. In 1939 he published *The Seven Lady Godivas*, a tale intended for adults that included not only the nude heroine but also the characters of the seven "Peeping" brothers (including Tom). But even in Seuss's books intended for children, the ubiquitous curves and mounds in Seuss's art are, for Maurice Sendak, "sensuous" and "exotic" (qtd. in Nel *Icon* 89, 94). For Sendak, the "sensuality" in Seuss's art is more than simply sexual, however. In a 2002 interview, Sendak explained to me that he believed one of the ways Seuss's art garnered its popularity among children was via its likeness to bowel movements. What is for some critics a smooth, sensually curvaceous line is for Sendak a subconscious excremental rebellion against all adult authority—toilet training included. Sendak explains in no uncertain terms:

> [I told Seuss that his] books are all about anarchy—and the child—and you have
> the child shoving everything off, saying "Fuck you" and even from the point of
> drawings looking like stool . . . I think the *Cat in the Hat* was incredibly
> important because then—under the guise of being a proper book I am telling you
> can revolutionize your house. You can cover it with shit. Literally. His drawings
> all look like bowel movements . . . in the literal sense [Seuss's artwork] is shitty
> . . . that book is all about getting rid of the tyranny of parents—Cleaning up the
> house. Forget toilet training. Forget everything kids. Laugh it up at will. . . .
>
> (Sendak)

Sendak's reading of the secret of Seuss's success may challenge those who doubt the power and/or direction of the subconscious mind, yet as a child I distinctly recall discussion of this quality of Seuss artwork among my friends at school. The controversy concerned Seuss's book, *Bartholomew and the Oobleck*. In this story a magic wish gone awry turns rain into "oobleck," a gooey mud-like green substance. My classmates eagerly explained to me that oobleck was, in fact, supposed to be poo. The urban legend went that Seuss's original colour for oobleck was brown but that the publishers had turned it green to avoid the direct reference to feces. Seuss's appeal, then, rests, in part at least, on his ability to conjure an off-color and ribald interpretation. This is a distinctly carnivalesque function, the fecal quality implying not simply anarchy, but abject waste—the key element upon which all new growth is based—life and youth out of death and waste (Bakhtin 147–48, 175–76).

Also carnivalesque are the various forms of travesty: political travesty, travesty of the aged, and travesty of superstitious and religious beliefs. As in many nursery rhymes, silly kings populate Seuss's verse, such as the childish monarch in *The King's Stilts* who shuts his eyes to all concerns, preferring to play on his stilts all day. In his early readers, Seuss routinely places figures of authority in silly circumstances, bringing them down to earth by juxtaposing them against something insignificant or ridiculous. In his ABC book he describes, for example, a "King's kerchoo," "The quick Queen of Quincy and her quacking quacker-oo," and a "Policeman in a pail." As Selma Lanes suggests, "The anxiety in Seuss books always arises from the flouting of authority, parental or societal" (81).

The civil unrest of the 1960s was largely defined by an emerging, and extreme, generation gap. The vast chasm that had opened up between young and old was succinctly expressed in the 1968 catchphrase, "Never trust anyone over thirty." Despite the fact that they all wrote for children both before and after reaching thirty, Lear, Carroll, and most authors of nonsense literature, including Seuss, often paint adults in unflattering terms. The mother in *Horton Hatches the Egg* (1940) is irresponsible and selfish, abandoning her child, and many critics have commented on the seemingly neglectful mother in *The Cat in the Hat* who leaves her young children alone at home. In *Hop on Pop*, the father is depicted as a glum, uncomprehending oaf, alternately portrayed on his back looking surprised as the children trample him (40), or slouching with a sour expression, his belly sagging, with the text "Dad is sad . . . He had a bad day" running beside him (32–33). And, as noted earlier, it is the youth who must enlighten the adult in *Green Eggs and Ham*. Similarly, in *Fox in Socks*, it is the older gentleman, Mr. Knox, who has trouble pronouncing difficult passages and finds himself sewn into a box while the youthful character, Mr. Fox, is able to manipulate language with skill. In *I Had Trouble in Getting to Solla Sollew* adults are routinely depicted as people who will misdirect you and waste your time:

> He sat and he worked with his brain and his tongue,
> And he bossed me around just because I was young.

As Elizabeth Sewell claims in *Field of Nonsense*, nonsense is frequently intolerant of magic, superstition, and religious beliefs (171–72). Bakhtin claims the same for carnivalesque traditions and adds that parodies of Christmas carols were consistent with a carnivalesque mood (*Rabelais* 15). While writing *How the Grinch Stole Christmas* in 1957, "[Seuss] agonized for months about how to keep the ending from seeming trite or religious" (Morgan and Morgan 191). Once it came to making the animated television special (1966), this problem returned. Children's holiday specials, such as *A Charlie Brown Christmas* (1965), which featured quotes from the New Testament, and other popular children's Christmas specials, such as *The Night* the Animals Talked (1970) and The Little Drummer Boy (1968), were inspired directly from scenes of the nativity. But when confronted with animation director Chuck Jones' storyboards Seuss announced that he would not allow a star to come beaming down from the heavens at the end of the filmed story. Seuss opted not to let the religious iconography be created from on high, shining down on to the lowly; instead he directed that the star be created by the communal love of the Whos. He created a scene in which the Whos stand together in a circle and chant a nonsense song, "Fah who for-aze / Dah who dor-aze," and a star originates from inside this circle, a product of their love for one another. In a reversal of the biblical story, the star then ascends from the people to the sky, eventually settling in the heavens where it represents community rather than god (ibid.). Ultimately, the inverted origin of the star amounted to an ennobling of the commoner—the Whos—and a disenfranchising of the almighty. The Morgans note that in the final edit, "the filmed Grinch emerged as a rare Christmas special without religiosity" (ibid.). In the topsy-turvy inversion of the star, The Grinch was subtle, subversive, and amounted to an ideological reversal of the Christian adoption of ancient Saturnalian traditions.

Seuss books, then, were not merely subversive in their narratives, as many critics have noted; they were also subversive in their total aesthetic—in their carnivalesque orientation, celebrating the topsy-turvy, the grotesque, festivity, and the travesty of authority. Once a carnivalesque atmosphere is established, that is to say, once the reader is "drunk" with inversion, feasting, mocking, and travesty, the stage is set for the possibility of transformative thinking. And it is in this susceptible and agreeable position that Seuss's readers encountered his political ideology. Like popular music and protest culture, Seuss's success in this period should be understood as a movement. Seuss books were purchased and collected in droves in this period. The New York Times Book Review reported that Seuss titles accounted for four of the top sixteen best sellers for 1958, selling in numbers that sound like Elvis Presley record sales (Nel, Icon 5). In this period book tours for Seuss were conducted by helicopter (Nel, Annotated 11). Seuss commented on his fame with children at this time: "It was as if I were Santa Claus" (qtd. in Nel, Annotated 11). An average American child might expect to receive one or two Seuss titles for Christmas and another one or two on his or her birthday. The books were stacked en masse on shelves in children's bedrooms (Brezzo 12).

Into this bookshelf of politically charged carnivalesque texts, slide a copy of the 1957 release of TCITH. This text introduces Seuss's most widely recognized character, and while it is generally not understood as one of Seuss overtly political "message" books, TCITH is a text that resonates subtly with the emerging discontent that will come to represent sixties youth. It features two children who allow a bizarre cat creature into their home. The children are alone and, the text explains, their mother is away for the day. In Mother's absence this cat proceeds to turn the house upside down. In the first extended sequence the Cat attempts an outlandish balancing/juggling act; while standing on a ball and balancing a fish bowl on the end of an umbrella, the Cat increases the difficulty of his juggling, adding dangerous or fragile household objects, such as a cake with lit candles and a cup and saucer, until all falls in a resounding crash (13–20). In each successive page of this sequence Seuss's image of the Cat grows larger and fills a greater portion of the frame, high-lighting the mounting spectacle and its outlandish details. To emphasize the sur-prising and unusual nature of this event Seuss shakes the very foundation of the house the Cat is visiting; the floor line, colored in blue, appears to go off kilter as the act progresses. Early in the sequence the foundation is turned at a jagged angle (12–15), and later it appears to swim in topsy-turvy waves (16–21).

Disregarding the Fish's plea that he please leave, the Cat then introduces Thing One and Thing Two, allowing them to escape from a locked crate (33). A vicarious thrill is offered to the child reader of *TCITH* when these "Things" proceed to break the rules normally imposed on children, engaging in activities such as flying kites indoors (38–51). While the fish maintains a vocal opposition to the Cat's and the Things' antics, the faces of the two children often register delight and fascination (8, 27–37, 49, 57–60).

As MacDonald (105–6), Nel (*Annotated* 28, 30), and others have noted, and Seuss has confirmed, the adventure featured in *TCITH* can be understood as a reaction against the predictable, boring, yet well-known reading series featuring Dick and Jane. Yet rather than reading *TCITH* as an attack on a specific reading series, the anomaly, disruption, and carnivalesque absurdity of the Cat's incursion might be understood more subversively as an attack on the complacency of Dick and Jane's "Leave-it-to-Beaver" suburbia. Consider, for example, one of the more successful sixties-era protest groups—The Yippies—headed by comic-anarchists Jerry Rubin and Abbie Hoffman. The Yippies specialized in performing nonsensical acts in inappropriate spaces. Jerry Rubin, for example, attended a House Un-Americans Activities Committee meeting dressed in a Santa Claus costume (Leaf and Scheinfeld 00:53:03). Among their other activities were the hosting of "snake dancing lessons" and games such as "Pin the Rubber on the Pope" at the 1968 Democratic National Convention (Kurlansky 274). It was the Yippies' resolute and well-founded belief that it would only be through absurdity, outlandishness, and inappropriate behav-ior that they would (a) get themselves on television news and (b) endear themselves politically to the youth of America. Like Seuss's Cat, who came into the living room with a "Bump!" (4–5), the Yippies similarly burst into the living rooms of America through television news programs, shocking the adults and delighting the youth who were fascinated and amused by their inexplicable antics. *TCITH* prefigures the Yippies but functions similarly, as a way to disrupt the vision of conformist, status-symbol-loving, humdrum suburbia. The heaped pile of household possessions, which includes a fancy dress, a perfume bottle, a decorative lamp, and a frilled um-brella, (55) and the Cat's reckless juggling act of similar objects, (20) suggests that this cat has no respect for material possessions. If nothing else, the child reader of *TCITH* is being tempted to experiment with antiestablishment ways—being shown that new *ways* are easy, close, and desirable. In this regard it is interesting that in the late sixties Seuss's Cat was twice interpreted as an enemy of middle-American values. In Robert Coover's political satire, *The Cat in the Hat for President* (1968),

Seuss's Cat is depicted as a subversive pied piper of youth and change; "The Cat was entertaining maybe, exciting, liberating . . . but he was also, obscurely, a threat. Dangerous, yes he was" (qtd. in Nel, *Annotated* 48). Seuss himself makes a similar allusion. In the animated version of *TCITH* (1971), the Fish picks up the phone and urgently reports, "Hello FBI? I want to report a cat in the hat!" The topsy-turvy invasion of the Cat is also symbolically predictive of other sixties-era protests, such as when students took over the administration buildings at Berkley in 1964 and Columbia in 1968. As Jenkins comments on Seuss's texts: "His stories depicted worlds where children gain control over basic institutions and remake them according to their own innovative ideas" (203).

The conclusion of *TCITH* has generally been understood as subversive. Yet critical discussion of the book's conclusion has not explained its resonances with traditions in nonsense and the practices of the typical sixties rebel. Just before Mother arrives home the house is miraculously put back in order and the Cat and his two Things escape without detection. The fact that order is restored has led some critics, and Seuss himself, to note that this text does not, in fact, subvert all authority; outright anarchy is avoided (Nel, *Annotated* 88; Cott 28). But while this is true it should be pointed out that the clean-up sequence is *not* the conclusion to *The Cat in the Hat*, and if there is a "message" to this book, it comes in the final pages, after the clean up. As many critics have pointed out, Seuss appears to suggest that there are certain things a child may not want to tell his or her parents. Concerning whether or not the children should confess the adventure to their mother, the text asks the reader, "What would you do if your mother asked you?" (61) There is no answer offered in the text, and the question is left ambiguous. Critics tend to agree, however, and, as MacDonald points out, the knowing glance of the fish in the bowl promises that Mother will never be told of what has transpired (109). This scene *is* the conclusion of *TCITH*. The Cat and its cohorts are never discovered by the mother, and no one pays for the multiple infractions against custom and authority. The mother's dominance over her children has not been respected.

What this ending might suggest to a child reader is that her parents may not understand if she tries to tell them what she's been up to—particularly, when she's been up to nonsense. MacDonald points out that Seuss has gone to lengths to juxtapose the mother's "no nonsense" attitude with that of the Cat and the duo of Things. According to MacDonald the mother's straight lines and neatly tied shoe suggest she is a "literalist." While the fantasy characters in the book (and in most cases the children) are depicted with a cartoonish three fingers on each hand, mother has the proper amount, five. As MacDonald notes, it is implied that this mother *could not* believe the story and therefore she will be spared the details (109–10).

Such a reading on the part of a child encourages a generation gap in which it is asserted that authority figures simply won't understand certain experiences of youth. The polemic that Seuss has tapped into here—that of the great gulf between the nonsense of youth and an uncomprehending authority figure—is the same polemic that is later employed by 1960s-era rebels. Consider Bob Dylan's very nonsensical song, "Ballad of a Thin Man" (1965), and the political consequences it engendered. Written in the surreal style typical of Dylan's output in the mid-sixties, "Ballad of a Thin Man" depicts a series of increasingly absurd scenes. Like *TCITH*, it begins with a character walking into a room and being surprised by someone who is not supposed to be there (a nude man) (*Lyrics* 174). Like the Cat, who is a juggler, and the Things, who are like circus performers, "Ballad of a Thin Man" revels in a carnivalesque atmosphere as circus characters are introduced; a "sideshow geek," a "sword swallower . . ."

> Now you see this one-eyed midget
> Shouting the word "NOW"
> And you say, "For what reason?"
> And he says, "How?"
> And you say, "What does this all mean?"
> And he screams back, "You're a cow
> Give me some milk"
>
> (*Lyrics* 175)

The images in "Ballad of a Thin Man" are as purposeless as the Cat's antics. And, much as Seuss worked so carefully to build the tension throughout the balancing sequence, each of Dylan's successive verses is more outlandish than its predecessor. Most interestingly, each of Dylan's verses is bracketed by the chorus, "Something is happening here and you don't know what it is, do you Mr. Jones?" The verses of this song are so surreal that, of course, Mr. Jones (the implied authority figure) could never hope to understand them. And that is the point. Concerning "Ballad of a Thin Man" critic Mike Marqusee writes:

> The wall of incomprehension between the conscious vanguard and mainstream society has become impenetrable . . . here a demarcation was being celebrated, part generational, part political, part cultural . . . the refrain epitomized the hip exclusivity that came naturally to those young people who saw themselves as having possession of a deeper insight than those around them . . . [and although the message was delivered in nonsensical terms], to young people in the end, the message was clear enough. (3–4)

The children featured in *TCITH*, and the implied child readers of that book, partake in the same special knowledge that Marqusee describes: "the hip exclusivity that came naturally to those young people who saw themselves as having possession of a deeper insight than those around them . . ." In both *TCITH* and "Ballad of Thin Man," authority figures are kept at bay, unable, it is assumed in both texts, to comprehend the nonsensical culture of youth. And as Marqusee smartly adds, "to young people in the end, the message was clear enough." The "message" to which Marqusee alludes is the subversive "message" so often garnered by those who engage with a text that leaves out important narrative connections. For what is left unsaid in a text, more often than not—as in Freudian dream analysis—is met with a "reading" that expresses a repressed or subversive desire, one that conflicts in some way with authority. And it is for this reason that numerous Dylan songs featuring similar narrative voids inspired the consideration of subversive political thought. In his book, *Seize the Time* (1970), Bobby Seale, cofounder of the radical, militant Black Panthers, notes that it was while listening to the lyrics of "Ballad of a Thin Man" that he and Huey Newton came to believe that Dylan was predicting an uprising in which the poor African American population would defeat their white oppressors. And it was this "secret message" that provided them with the impetus to organize their platform (Marqusee 208). Dylan intended no such reading, but authorial intent is not required for nonsense to produce an inspirational effect. While no paramilitary units are known to have been inspired by *TCITH*, the text nevertheless shares, in its use of nonsense and its celebration of the generation gap, a subversive technique that Dylan used also and that in Dylan's case inspired a political reaction that went quite beyond anything Dylan would have imagined.

TCITH, like other Seuss texts, also awakens in its readers the possibility of seeing themselves in a profoundly new way, and this is achieved through exposure to existential dilemmas and enigmas typical of nonsense. When such an enigma is encountered, it becomes possible, or necessary even, for the reader to reimagine the world—to remap the boundaries and beliefs by which society and the self are governed—if only for a moment. Edward Lear biographer, Angus Davidson, posits that the mind's imaginative entry into a nonsense world "demands an act of faith such as that made by Alice when she tried to go and meet the Red Queen—of starting in the opposite direction" (qtd. in Sewell 184). Like Bakhtin, who wrote that carnival and its attendant texts "liberate human consciousness and permit a new outlook . . ." (*Rabelais* 274), nonsense performs a similar function.

In "The Big Brag" (1958), a worm with unusually strong eyesight looks around the world and sees the back of its own head. In *Did I Ever Tell You How Lucky You Are* (1973), we meet Poor Harry Hadow who hasn't any shadow. And in *On Beyond Zebra*, we meet two creatures, a big one and a small one. Seuss explains that "the big one, you see, has the smaller one's shadow" and vice versa. These characters have all lost track of an essential part of their being, or they are seeing themselves in profoundly new and unusual ways. The fate of the Sneeches sums up the results of exposure to the existential dilemmas of nonsense:

> . . . neither the Plain nor the Star-bellies knew
> Whether this one was that one . . . or that one was this one
> Or which one was what one . . . or what one was who. (21)

And here we find Seuss's characters, in their struggle to become something other, losing track of an old image of the self and developing a new one. Similarly, in sixties-era political thought it was posited that real social change might only be attained if a new image of the self could be envisioned. Existential dilemmas were *de rigueur* for the quintessential sixties experience. They were, for example, an integral facet of psychedelic drug culture. In fact, having an existential dilemma was almost *the* point of a sixties drug experience—to get out of yourself and be able to see yourself

Figure 9.1. Near & Far: equidistant. From *One Fish Two Fish Red Fish Blue Fish* by Dr. Seuss, registered ® & copyright © by Dr. Seuss Enterprises, L.P. 1960, renewed 1988. Used by permission of Random House Children's Books, a division of Random House, Inc.

Figure 9.2. There & Here: equidistant. From *One Fish Two Fish Red Fish Blue Fish* by Dr. Seuss, registered ® & copyright © by Dr. Seuss Enterprises, L.P. 1960, renewed 1988. Used by permission of Random House Children's Books, a division of Random House, Inc.

and your world from a new perspective. In the psychedelic film, *The Trip* (1967), Peter Fonda plays a character who takes LSD. Fonda's character forgets his name while he is under the influence of the drug. He also is confronted with a series of iconic images and fails to recognize them, including images of President Johnson, Jesus on the cross, and The American Flag (Corman 00:35:00–36:40). This contemporary insistence on the importance of stepping outside of one's self explains why R. D. Laing's study of schizophrenia, *The Divided Self* (1960), was so popular at the time and was, as DeKoven describes it, a "key sixties text" (205). Laing's study is a "key sixties text" because it is founded on existential analysis, on fantasies of transcendence, and is concerned with the topic of considering one's "false self." The surreal landscapes featured in Seuss's illustrations, and his tendency to exploit existential confusion, are suggestive of, and prefigure, the aesthetic of 1960s psychedelic art. In Seuss's *One Fish Two Fish Red Fish Blue Fish* (1960) we find the image of a signpost with two signs pointing in opposite directions. One sign reads, "Near," the other, "Far" (33). In this image Near and Far appear to be equally distant, or equally close. Nonsense often attempts to achieve this leveling—this bringing of the "Far" onto equal footing with the "Near." What was once thought of as too far, and unfamiliar, is now as readily reachable as what is near and familiar (figs. 9.1 and 9.2).

In *TCITH* an existential dilemma (along with a confusion of what is "near" and what is "far") unfolds in the blurring that occurs among the two child characters, the two Thing creatures, and the reader. The result of this blurring is that the reader is potentially left with a subconscious desire for change and for a reordering of authoritarian structures. At the surface level there are the two child characters, the brother and his sister, Sally, who throughout the book are alternately concerned about and fascinated by this weird Cat. Nel points out that the illustrations of Sally's hair bow and the Cat's bow tie link the two characters visually, their bows being the same shape and both colored in red. Nel also points out that the bows reflect the particular character's emotional state at particular moments (*Annotated* 82). The bows then—as when Sally's is perky and the Cat's is droopy (52–53)—tell us how the characters feel, but because they are visually linked, they also suggest that their bearers are reverse mirror images of one another. The Cat then, in psychoanalytic terms, might be understood as Sally's id, a representation of her repressed desires, or at least her struggle to contain them. Note that Sally, the Cat and the two Things are all visually linked by the color red, while the boy character has no red, as he is drawn in black and white. While considering this visual connection between Sally, the Cat and the Things note also that Sally does not rebel against the Cat's antics; only the boy does. And Sally has a name while the boy does not. A question to ask then is whether this text is *about* Sally and her desires. The color red, as in Little Red's riding hood or Dorothy's ruby slippers, is often understood as a color that represents coming of age in the young female heroine. Rather than reading this text as patriarchal, as many have—because the boy takes action and the girl does not—it might be better to understand Sally's *laissez-faire*/indulgent attitude as a foreshadowing of the experimental young woman of the sixties, the Beatlemaniac empowered by the very act of witnessing, or the liberated, laid-back female voice in the 1963 hit song "Walk Right In," who encourages her guests to "let [their] hair hang down" and beckons, "Do you want to lose your mind?"[3]

In the least we may conclude that one or both of these child characters are clearly relating on some level with the Cat. Moving to the next level there are the surrogate "children," Thing One and Thing Two, who act out childish fantasies, such as roughhousing in the parents' bedroom, with reckless abandon and do so without any fear of reprisal. In the illustration below the two children are balanced against the image of the two Things: (fig. 9.3)

Figure 9.3. The children and their alter egos. From *The Cat in the Hat* by Dr. Seuss, trademark TM and copyright © by Dr. Seuss Enterprises, L. P. 1957, renewed 1985. Used by permission of Random House Children's Books, a division of Random House, Inc.

Note also that the Things are held captive in a box (30) before they are set free, much as the children felt captive in the house on a rainy day, captive in their bland, conformist, box home of suburbia.

While Sally is visually linked to the Cat and the Things, and the Things act as surrogates of the children's desires, there is yet one more level that underlies the existential dilemma implicit in the text. At this final level there is the child reader who is asked what he or she would do if faced with this situation: "What would you do if your mother asked you?" (61) Roth (146), MacDonald (109), and Nel (*Annotated* 90) have all noted the significance of the fact that this question redirects the narrative toward the child reader. But while MacDonald asserts that the child reader enjoys this subterfuge "without becoming a guilty participant" (109), I would suggest, rather, that the child reader is here forced into the uncomfortable position of realizing that he or she secretly values the freedom represented by Thing One, Thing Two, and the Cat. The fish now stares directly at the reader (60) and confirms that the child reader is implicitly included in the narrative. What had seemed "far," Thing One and Thing Two, suddenly feels uncomfortably "near." The reader is thus forced to consider the Cat's "new tricks" and ask if these new tricks were really as undesirable as the Fish suggested they were. What was at first strange, exotic, and uncomfortable has suddenly become personal and desirable.

One might look similarly at another Seuss text from this same period, "What Was I Scared Of?" (1961), the strange story of a pair of disembodied pale green pants that persists in crossing paths with a young man who is spooked by them. The title suggests that Seuss's text might be oriented around the idea of teaching children to deal with and resolve unfounded fears. Yet there is a second level of meaning in this text. If the point were merely to suggest that the odd pants should not be feared, one might imagine that the "magic" in them would have been disabled—the text would have proven that the pants were not as they seemed. But this is not what happens. Instead, the nonsensical, inexplicable empty pants are simply accepted, and the child moves into a new paradigm in which empty pants that walk by themselves are normal:

> And, now, we meet quite often,
> Those empty pants and I,
> And we never shake or tremble.
> We both smile
> And we say
> "Hi!" (64)

Likewise this odd Cat and his new tricks are vicariously embraced—and thus the specter of all that is new, or strange, shifts from the realm of the impossible to the realm of the conscious or unconscious desire.

When thinking about Seuss politically it is also important to consider the narrative voids so frequent in his texts and how those narrative voids imply that the reader should take over the responsibility for the narrative. In the final sequence of *On Beyond Zebra*, the reader is presented with a wild swirl of looping and zagging lines, representing some, no doubt, unpronounceable letter. Rather than explain what the letter represents, Seuss asks, "What do you think we should call this one, anyhow?" and thus the "story" ends. The endings of *TCITH*, *The Lorax*, and *The Butter Battle Book* are all similarly ambiguous. The Lorax brings his presence in the narrative to a close by leaving behind a single word, "Unless." Seuss adds, "Whatever that meant, well I just couldn't guess" (unpaged).

The strategy in using these narrative voids is one of inclusion. That is, the reader is incited to reach beyond the normally passive act of reading (or listening) and is incited to interact creatively with the text. Ultimately Seuss's narrative voids and vague endings inspire personal responsibility on the part of the reader for making meaning. This practice can readily be compared to the sixties-era insistence on the concept of "participatory democracy." Participatory democracy is the primary informing concept of the profoundly influential 1962 document, *The Port Huron Statement*, written by Students for a Democratic Society (SDS). Similarly, when John Kennedy says in 1960, "Ask not what your country can do for you. Ask what you can do for your country," he is emphasizing the superiority of the active over the passive citizen. Kennedy is envisioning a citizen who wants to be involved in determining what his country "means." Likewise, with many Seuss texts, full meaning is achieved only via active participation on the part of each individual reader.

As MacDonald and other critics have noted, the child characters in Seuss books are often invited to take action. An obvious example is the passive child in *The Lorax* who, at first, is content just to listen to the story of an environmental disaster. At the end of the book, however, this child is handed the last Truffula seed, and we know that no other authority can help here. Even the narrator has thrown up his hands, "Whatever that meant, well I just couldn't guess." As MacDonald remarks, "his charge for the care of the Truffula seed arouses him to action . . . It is a child who will save this world" (153). To extend the importance of this idea, note

Jenkins's conclusion of his study on Seuss's early work: "the democratic imagination" found in Seuss books "can become powerful tools for political transformation" (204). Mary Lystad looks specifically at the "conclusion" of *TCITH* and explains the message in a way that resonates with the spirit of sixties activism; "the message is clear . . ." she writes, "if the world is bleak, change it, create a new world" (qtd. in MacDonald 111). As the sixties unfolded, youth culture did just that. And their new world, although temporary in some ways—like carnival itself—was manifested in ways a Seuss text might embrace, by festive colors, a carnivalesque atmosphere, youthful nonsense, rhymes and songs about equality, and confrontations with authority.

In *Nonsense Literature for Children: Aesop to Seuss*, Marilyn Apseloff and Celia Anderson propose "that nonsense literature contributes to the civilizing process" (108). Apseloff and Anderson see the verbal "arguments" of sense and nonsense that occur in nonsense rhymes as an ideal training ground for the development of logical thought, and, importantly, they suggest that such texts encourage the child to favor verbal over physical responses to oppression. However, Apseloff and Anderson promise that nonsense is merely a benign critic of society, that it does not serve as an invitation to children to be defiant or disrespectful, and that, ultimately, nonsense will not turn the world upside down (108–9). I would argue that the case with Seuss is not so clear in this regard. Through the inclusive responses that Seuss's nonsense demands, and through a palpable carnivalesque atmosphere that promotes social critique and fosters utopian desires, there is, in Seuss's texts, an unusual agency bestowed on the child reader. In particular, Seuss's texts arguably bestowed political agency on that generation "most critical of the Vietnam War," whose perhaps unwitting parents supplied them with Seuss texts in piles throughout their formative years.

NOTES

1. For an extended argument on Seuss's relationship to literary nonsense, see Nel, *Icon*, 15–38.
2. Here Roth is quoting from Mensch and Freeman.
3. The gender politics of Beatlemania are discussed in Ehrenreich, Hess, and Jacobs. Quotation from the lyrics "Walk Right In," a 1927 song by Gus Cannon's Jug Stompers rerecorded and popularized in 1963 by the Rooftop Singers.

WORKS CITED

Apseloff, Marilyn, and Celia Anderson. *Nonsense Literature for Children: Aesop to Seuss.*
    Hamden, CT: Library Professional Publications, 1997.

Bakhtin, Mikhail. *Rabelais and His World.* Translated by Helene Iswolsky. 1968. Bloomington: Indiana UP, 1984.

Brezzo, Steven. "Introduction" to *Dr. Seuss from Then to Now.* New York: Random House, 1986.

Carroll, Lewis. *The Complete Works of Lewis Carroll.* London: Penguin, 1988.

Coover, Robert. "The Cat in the Hat for President." *New American Review.* no. 4. 1968. 7–45.

Corman, Roger, director. *The Trip.* DVD. Los Angeles: MGM, 2003.

Cott, Jonathan. *Pipers at the Gates of Dawn: The Wisdom of Children's Literature.* New York: Random House, 1983.

DeKoven, Marianne. *Utopia Limited: The Sixties and the Emergence of the Postmodern.* Durham, NC: Duke UP, 2004.

Dylan, Bob. *Lyrics: 1962–2001.* New York: Simon and Schuster, 2004.

Ehrenreich, Barbara, Elizabeth Hess, and Gloria Jacobs. "Beatlemania: Girls Just Want to Have Fun." In *The Adoring Audience: Fan Culture and Popular Media,* edited by Lisa A. Lewis, 84–106. New York: Routledge, 1992.

Jenkins, Henry. "No Matter How Small: The Democratic Imagination of Doctor Seuss." In *Hop on Pop: The Politics and Pleasures of Popular Culture,* edited by Henry Jenkins, Tara McPherson, and Jane Shattuc, 187–208. Durham, NC: Duke UP, 2002.

Kahn, E. J. "Children's Friend." In *Of Sneetches and Whos and the Good Dr. Seuss: Essays on the Writings and Life of Theodore Geisel,* edited by Thomas Fensch, 15–35. Jefferson, NC: McFarland & Co, 1997.

Kurlansky, Mark. *1968: The Year That Rocked the World.* New York: Random House, 2005.

Laing, R. D. *The Divided Self: A Study in Sanity and Madness.* London: Tavistock Publications, 1960.

Lanes, Selma. *Down the Rabbit Hole: Adventures and Misadventures in Children's Literature.* New York: Atheneum, 1971.

Leaf, David, and John Scheinfeld, directors. *The U.S. vs. John Lennon: Artist, Humanitarian, National Threat.* DVD. Santa Monica, CA: Lions Gate Entertainment, 2006.

MacDonald, Ruth. *Dr. Seuss.* Boston: Twayne, 1988.

Marqusee, Mike. *Chimes of Freedom: The Politics of Bob Dylan's Art.* New York: New Press, 2003.

Menand, Louis. "Cat People: What Dr. Seuss Really Taught Us." *The New Yorker* (December 23, 2002): 148–54.

Mensch, Betty, and Alan Freeman. "Getting to Solla Sollew: The Existentialist Politics of Dr. Seuss." *Tikkun* 2, no. 2 (1987): 30–34.

Minear, Richard. *Dr. Seuss Goes to War.* New York: The New Press, 1999.

Morgan, Judith, and Neil Morgan. *Dr. Seuss and Mr. Geisel.* New York: De Capo Press, 1996.

Nel, Philip. *The Annotated Cat: Under the Hats of Seuss and His Cats.* New York: Random House, 2007.

———. *Dr. Seuss: American Icon.* New York: Continuum, 2004.

The Rooftop Singers. "Walk Right In." Vanguard, 1963. Orig. composition by Gus Cannon's Jug Stompers, 1927.

Roth, Rita. "On Beyond Zebra with Dr. Seuss." In *Of Sneeches and Whos and the Good Dr. Seuss: Essays on the Writings and Life of Theodore Geisel,* edited by Thams Fensch, 141–53. Jefferson, NC: McFarland, 1997.

Seale, Bobby. *Seize the Time: the Story of the Black Panther Party and Huey P. Newton.* New York: Random House, 1970.

Sendak, Maurice. Interview with the author, 11, Feb. 2002.

Seuss, Dr. *Batholomew and the Oobleck.* New York: Random House, 1949.

———. *The 500 Hats of Bartholomew Cubbins.* New York: Random House, 1938.

———. *And to Think That I Saw it on Mulberry Street.* New York: Random House, 1937.

———. "The Big Brag," *Yertle the Turtle and Other Stories.* New York: Random House, 1958.

———. *The Butter Battle Book.* New York: Random House, 1984.

———. *The Cat in the Hat.* New York: Random House, 1957.

———. *The Cat in the Hat Comes Back.* New York: Random House, 1958.

———. *Did I Ever Tell You How Lucky You Are?* New York: Random House, 1973.

———. *Dr. Seuss's ABC.* New York: Random House, 1962.

———. *Fox in Socks.* New York: Random House, 1965.

———. *Green Eggs and Ham.* New York: Random House, 1960.

———. *I Had Trouble in Getting to Solla Sollew.* New York: Random House, 1965.

———. *If I Ran the Circus.* New York: Random House, 1956.

———. *If I Ran the Zoo.* New York: Random House, 1950.

———. *Happy Birthday to You.* New York: Random House, 1959.

———. *Hop on Pop.* New York: Random House, 1962.

———. *Horton Hatches the Egg.* New York: Random House, 1940.

———. *Horton Hears a Who!* New York: Random House, 1954.

———. *How the Grinch Stole Christmas.* New York: Random House, 1957.

———. *The King's Stilts.* New York: Random House, 1939.

———. *The Lorax.* New York: Random House, 1971.

———. *Marvin K. Mooney Will You Please Go Now!* New York: Random House, 1972.

———. *Oh, the Places You'll Go!* New York: Random House, 1990.

———. *On Beyond Zebra.* New York: Random House, 1955.

———. *One Fish Two Fish Red Fish Blue Fish.* New York: Random House, 1960.

———. *The Seven Lady Godivas.* New York: Random House, 1939.

———. "The Sneeches." *The Sneeches and Other Stories,* 2–25. New York: Random House, 1961.

———. *There's a Wocket in My Pocket!* New York: Random House, 1974.

———. "What Was I Scared Of?" *The Sneeches and Other Stories,* 42–65. New York: Random House, 1961.

———. *Yertle the Turtle and Other Stories.* New York: Random House, 1958.

Sewell, Elizabeth. *The Field of Nonsense.* London: Chatto and Windus, 1952.

FURTHER READING

Grey, William, Marion Monroe, A. Sterl Artley, and May Hill Arbuthnot. *The New Fun with Dick and Jane.* Illus. Keith Ward and Eleanor Campbell. Glenview, IL: Scott, Foresman and Co, 1956.

Proulx, Travis, and Steven J. Heine. "Connections from Kafka: Exposure to Meaning
     Threats Improves Implicit Learning of an Artificial Grammar." *Psychological Science*
     20, no. 9 (September 2009): 1125–31.
Shortsleeve, Kevin. "The Politics of Nonsense: Civil Unrest, Otherness and National
     Mythology in Nonsense Literature." Ph.D. thesis, University of Oxford, 2007.
Stewart, Susan. *Nonsense: Aspects of Intertextuality in Folklore and Literature*. Baltimore:
     Johns Hopkins UP, 1979.

CHAPTER 10

WILD THINGS AND WOLF DREAMS: MAURICE SENDAK, PICTURE-BOOK PSYCHOLOGIST

KENNETH KIDD

MAURICE Sendak (1928–) was born and raised in Brooklyn, New York, to Polish-Jewish immigrant parents. A perpetually sick child—he endured measles, pneumonia, and scarlet fever by age four—Sendak spent long hours in bed reading, dreaming, and drawing. Seeing the Disney film Fantasia at the age of twelve, Sendak decided to become a cartoonist and was working as an illustrator by the time he was in high school. He illustrated his high school biology teacher's textbook, Atomics for the Millions (1947), and in 1952 paired up with children's author Ruth Krauss, illustrating her groundbreaking A Hole Is to Dig. Encouraged by Krauss and her partner, Crockett Johnson, Sendak tried his hand at writing as well as illustrating, and in 1963, he made his reputation with Where the Wild Things Are, winning the American Library Association's Caldecott Medal the following year. Since that time, he has written and/or illustrated nearly seventy children's books. He has also illustrated adult classics and designed opera and ballet sets for stage and television. Other important children's titles include The Nutshell Library (1962), In the Night Kitchen (1970), Outside Over There (1981), and Brundibar (2003), the latter a collaboration with dramatist Tony Kushner. For his contributions to children's literature, Sendak has been awarded the Hans Christian Andersen Award (1970), the National Medal of Arts (1997), and the Astrid Lindgren Memorial Award (2003). In 2007, Sendak lost his life partner, Dr. Eugene Glynn, and in 2008 acknowledged this loss and his sexuality in The New York Times.

Maurice Sendak's *Where the Wild Things Are* (1963) has never been out of print and as of February 2008 has sold over nineteen million copies (Thornton). Winner of the 1964 Caldecott Medal, it is one of the most successful picture books of all time. *Where the Wild Things Are* (hereafter *Wild Things*) has been performed as an opera and by the time of this book's publication will have been released as a feature-length film, the brainchild of Dave Eggers and Spike Jonze. Thanks to the book's fame and to a five-decades-long career filled with other accomplished work, Sendak is a household name. Underscoring the richness of Sendak's oeuvre, John Cech calls him "one of the principal mythologists of childhood" (7). Indeed, Sendak has become a sort of spokesman for the joys and terrors of childhood and the human condition more generally. Friend and collaborator Tony Kushner, in a brilliant monograph on Sendak, likens his child characters to "the kids described in the best, richest developmental literature, the kids in Piaget and Winnicott, doing the tough work of holding themselves and their world together" (10).

Kushner is right to put Sendak in the company of Piaget and Winnicott, for Sendak is among our best child psychologists. In my book *Making American Boys: Boyology and the Feral Tale*, I argued that from the late nineteenth century forward, authors for boys might be understood as "boy workers" or "boyologists," forerunners as well as companions to the leaders of the Boy Scouts and the YMCA. I showed also how boyology both drew from and helped perpetuate the feral tale, a story of animal-human or cross-cultural encounter, which increasingly became a story about (hetero)normative white male masculinity rather than about liminality or alterity. Remus and Romulus yielded to Mowgli and Tarzan, who in turn made way for Bomba the Jungle Boy, "Teen Wolf," and other heroic, increasingly normative wild boys. I mentioned in passing Sendak's *Wild Things* as yet another refashioning of the feral tale. In this essay I complicate that perspective, suggesting how Sendak self-fashioned as a child expert in and around the success of his famous picture book and its "wild thing" protagonist. The context for my discussion includes 1960s psychological culture but also what I call "picture-book psychology," an ongoing amalgam of ideas about the psychological texture and value of the picture book— and about the psychological wisdom of its best practitioners. Sendak's achievement in *Wild Things* comes not only from personal genius but also from his complex engagement with psychological discourse.

I take cue from Barbara Bader and Leonard S. Marcus, who position Sendak as both legatee and torchbearer of creatively applied child psychology. Bader makes a number of connections between child psychology and picture books in her magisterial history of the genre and, in her chapter on Sendak, cites Anna Freud's remark that psychoanalysis needs "people who could make others *see*" (511). In an interview with David Serlin and Brian Selznick, Marcus remarks "it was during the 1960s and 1970s that psychology for the first time became a popular course of study at the undergraduate level . . . It was against this background that the insights of psychology and psychoanalysis began to find their way into children's books" (Serlin and Selznick, n.p.). When asked to name a children's book directly influenced by psychoanalysis, Marcus replies, "Well, *Where the Wild Things Are* by Maurice

Sendak" (Serlin and Selznick, no page.). While agreeing that *Wild Things* represents a watershed in picture-book psychology, Bader dates the psychologization of the picture book to the 1930s, calling Helen Sewell's *Ming and Mehitable* (1936) "the first picturebook . . . to turn on the turns of a child's mind" (84). She also points out that Marie Ets, a contemporary of Sewell, studied child psychology and designed her picture books as psychological experiments. Even without such direct or conscious psychological fashioning, the picture book might be understood as a site of psychosocial engagement between parent and child, and between child and adult-author—engagement that is at once play and serious business. Picture-book psychology predates Sendak and has helped make possible his work; his work, in turn, has maintained the association of picture books and the psychological.

Writing about American child-rearing rather than children's books, Ann Hulbert nonetheless draws a comparison between Dr. Spock and Dr. Seuss, remarking that children "born in the middle of the baby boom might be forgiven for getting Dr. Spock and Dr. Seuss mixed up" and calling the men "models of a new kind of grown-up authority—they were wonderfully friendly instead of cool or harsh" (227). Like Hulbert, who calls Dr. Spock "America's first truly pop-Freudian" (226), Steven Mintz notes Spock's ability to translate "Freud's ideas about children's psychic development into nonthreatening language that any parent could understand" (279).[1] The pairing of Dr. Seuss with Dr. Spock suggests that other picture-book author-illustrators might likewise translate Freudian ideas into common-sense and everyday scenarios, thus bringing Freud to children and parents alike. Sendak, for all his genius, follows in the footsteps of these various "translators" of Freud, offering a vision of childhood derived from Freud but also inflected by picture-book psychology and by the psychosocial currents of the 1950s and 1960s.

Sendak's work can be understood as rewriting classical Freudian analysis, retaining some of its rigor and edge while making it more palatably American. *Wild Things* has been embraced as a psychological primer, a story about anger and its management through fantasy; it is also a text in which echoes of Freud are audible. I read it as a bedtime story version of Freud's Wolf Man case history of 1918, an updated and upbeat dream of the wolf boy. I am not the first to notice echoes of the Wolf Man in Sendak. In his chapter on psychoanalytic criticism in *The Nimble Reader*, Roderick McGillis remarks insightfully on the continuities as well as differences between these two narratives. McGillis even observes that several illustrations in *Wild Things* are reminiscent of dream-scenes from the Wolf Man case, implying that Freud might be a source or inspiration for Sendak (82). McGillis, however, focuses on the use-value of psychoanalytic interpretation, concluding that "Freud, then, can provide a model for our understanding of *Where the Wild Things Are*" (82). I think McGillis is right to imply that Sendak takes cue from Freud, and I want to pursue that line of inquiry.

Wild Things, I suggest, is a highly successful experiment in picture-book psychology. Knowledgeable about Freud and having undergone therapy for depression, Sendak styled his first picture book, *Kenny's Window* (1956), after a best-selling psychological casebook by Dorothy Baruch about a young boy named Kenneth.

Sendak's text is fascinating but clunky; it features a dream, but dream logic does not govern it or give it shape. In *Wild Things*, Sendak more successfully brings the dreamwork to the picture book. The Wolf Man's dream helped make Freud famous and came to signify his expertise, and so too with Sendak's dream of the wolf boy. In the transition from *Kenny's Window* to *Wild Things* we can see Sendak refining his own brand of picture-book psychology—one insistently (if not always affirmatively) queer. And while Freud's text is very different from that of Sendak, there are pictures within and behind it, including drawings of the Wolf Man's dream made by the Wolf Man himself. Dreaming and drawing link these narratives and are central to picture-book psychology.

DRAWING (FOR) THE CHILD

Before turning to Freud, I want to acknowledge other strains of picture-book psychology that had an influence on Sendak. By the 1920s, in the context of both Freudian-derived child analysis and American programs of child study, the practice of child observation had become linked to both progressive education and to creative work undertaken for children. At Lucy Sprague Mitchell's Bank Street School in New York City—at once a school and a think tank for progressive educators—a key program was the Writer's Laboratory; teachers in training were required to try their hand at transforming new knowledge about childhood into literature for children (see especially Marcus, *Margaret Wise Brown*). Although Mitchell was not herself concerned with picture books, her protégé, Margaret Wise Brown, and others moved the picture book toward a more experimental and experiential style, often focusing on questions of "use" as well as the nonsense of everyday life.[2] A number of innovative writers and artists were trained at Bank Street, among them Ruth Krauss, Sendak's mentor and early collaborator.

Meanwhile, child analysts focused their attention on the drawings and creative play of their young patients, such that the study of children's drawing became central to child analysis. Melanie Klein was a pivotal figure in this regard. Winnicott, who was influenced by Klein, even drew *with* his child subjects. He would draw a "squiggle," have the child draw a squiggle in turn, and keep alternating until a picture emerged, reflecting the collaborative effort of analysis. Psychologist Howard Gardner continues this practice today, pseudonymously reporting on the artistic activities of his own children: "It is as if the young child, hardly out of the crib himself, has begun to create his own offspring—a wholly separate world, a world stocked with marks, forms, objects, scenes, and fledgling artistic works" (11). For child analysts especially, to watch the child draw or play is to see the unconscious at work. While child analysis and the practice of drawing (and writing) *for* the child are distinct practices, they do overlap, such that the successful picture-book writer/illustrator, who draws for and "with" the child, seems nearly a lay child analyst and perhaps also a perpetual child.

This helps explain why pictures of children drawing have become something of a staple in picture books (even as the study of children's drawing is no longer so central to child psychology). Joan Menefee has identified over seventy-five such picture books, beginning with Du Bose Heyward's *The Country Bunny and the Little Gold Shoes* (1939) and continuing well into the present day. Crockett Johnson's *Harold and the Purple Crayon* (1955) is perhaps the most famous such text, but another from the same period is *A Very Special House* (1953) written by Krauss and illustrated by Sendak. In both texts, a child literally draws his world into existence, Harold's adventures being outward-bound while the unnamed protagonist of Krauss and Sendak draws a house of imagination. In both, the drawing spins nearly out of control. As Menefee observes, the incorporation of the artistic child within the picture book (think Max's self-portrait in *Wild Things*) points to the confluence of artistic practice, child psychology, and picture-book production. The author-illustrator often invokes an imago of the creative child to represent both him/herself and the child reader.

"I have been doodling with ink and watercolor on paper all my life," Sendak notes. "It's my way of stirring up my imagination to see what I find hidden in my head. I call the results dream pictures, fantasy sketches, and even brain-sharpening exercises" (qtd. in Cummins 26). It's important to note, however, that those "dream pictures" derived in part from sketches he made of Brooklyn street kids playing outside his window in the late 1940s, while he was broke and living with his parents. Sendak, that is, was an informal child observer who came up with his own program of picture-book production based on what he saw and heard. "I became absorbed in the lives of the children across the street," he reports. "These early, unprecise, wavery sketches are filled with a happy vitality that was nowhere else in my life at the time. They add up to the rough delineation of the child all my future characters would be modeled on. I loved Rosie. She knew how to get through a day" ("Really Rosie" 180). Rosie made her debut in Sendak's third book, *The Sign on Rosie's Door* (1960). For Sendak, the exuberant Rosie, who casts herself and her friends in street theatricals, becomes a prototype for the creative self, if only to be later eclipsed by Max. Sendak is clear about Rosie's importance, describing himself as a lay rather than professional observer of childhood and as an artist in the making. "There is Rosie, the living thread, the connecting link between me in my window and the outside over there. I did, finally, get outside over there. In 1956, after illustrating some dozen books by various writers, I did a Rosie and wrote my own. It's called *Kenny's Window* and in it I paid homage to Rosie's street and house" ("Really Rosie" 180–81).

While Sendak was not formally trained by the likes of Mitchell, he was mentored by two important women in children's literature, namely, Krauss, an innovative picture-book psychologist in her own right, and also Ursula Nordstrom, Harper's legendary children's book editor. Nordstrom worked tirelessly on behalf of writers and artists, serving variously as midwife, muse, and analyst. As Leonard S. Marcus reports in *Dear Genius*, Nordstrom would do "sessions" with mentees that took on "thrilling overtones of an impromptu experiment in self-revelation, a stripping down to one's own raw center as a means toward discovering the core material from which a deeply felt book might emerge" (xxvii). These "sessions" likely mirrored the psychoanalytic encounters Sendak underwent. Nordstrom also often joked about picture books as having psychotherapeutic power (see Marcus, *Dear Genius*, 69).

Another crucial component of Sendak's education as a picture-book psychologist was an ongoing debate about the place of fantasy in a child's reading life. The value of fairy tales had long been a subject of debate, and in the early twentieth century the so-called fairy tale wars erupted between Mitchell's camp, which attacked fairy tales as distracting nonsense, and more traditional children's librarians such as Anne Carroll Moore, who defended fairy tales, myths, and legends against the encroachments of the modern realist (usually urban) tale. As Jacalyn Eddy reports, many child experts at first inveighed against fantasy, but gradually the tables turned, with the experts often championing fantasy along psychological lines (110–17). By mid-century, fantasy was widely deemed essential to the psychological health of children. The clinical and popular literature on fantasy proliferated throughout the 1940s and 1950s. By the time that *Wild Things* appeared, the child experts had come to embrace fantasy, whereas librarians were now among the skeptics. "What had happened was twofold," notes Bader.

> With the insights that psychology afforded, fairy tales, myths, legends had come to be seen as other than simple straightforward stories (however little agreement there was as to what, exactly, they represented); and children had come to be seen as rather less simple creatures too, and possessed of dark visions of their own. (Bader 514)

Wild Things, she observes, is at once myth and fairy tale, and recognition of such "catapulted Sendak to prominence as a prime mover, a vital force. He not only had talent, his work had meaning—interest to adults and power over children" (514). Given his individual talent and his particular history, Sendak was uniquely positioned to become our premier picture-book psychologist.

FROM *KENNY'S WINDOW* TO *WILD THINGS*

Although Freud was highly interested in questions of visual-verbal relation, he was writing before the heyday of picture books and thought of such books only as delivery systems for images and scenes formative to individual experience. In picture books, noticed Freud, we encounter powerful scenes that stay with us into adulthood. In *The Interpretation of Dreams* (1900), Freud describes a dream as "a substitute for an infantile scene modified by being transferred on to a recent experience" (585)—including experiences with picture books. In the case of Little Hans, a picture-book illustration helps Freud make sense of a horse phobia. In the Wolf Man's case, the patient's dream of the wolves derives in part from a childhood encounter with "the picture of a wolf in a book of fairy tales," in which, as Freud reports, "the wolf was standing upright, striding out with one foot, with its claws stretched out and its ears pricked" (187). Freud theorizes that the Wolf Man's recollection of this image gets entangled with his (screen) memory of the fairy tales "The Wolf and the Seven Little Goats" and "Little Red Riding Hood." Freud doesn't muse explicitly on the picture book as an image-text form or genre, despite his sense of the dreamwork as a "pictographic script," a "picture puzzle" (*Interpretation* 312). Others, of course, have pushed this line of inquiry.

In *Dreams of Authority*, Ronald R. Thomas reminds us that Freud's theory of the dreamwork is indebted to scenes of dreaming in Victorian and other literature. Moreover, he argues that "the paradigmatic plot" of both literature and psychoanalysis "as mediated by the dream, revolves around questions of authority. Nineteenth-century literary dreams are *always* dreams of authority" (2; emphasis in original). While Sendak doesn't position himself as an authority on the dream, he does self-identify as an authoritative dreamer of childhood and its discontents.

Even as he drew from real life, Sendak styled his work after Winsor McCay, creator of the comic strip *Little Nemo in Slumberland*. In a 1973 tribute to McCay, republished in *Caldecott & Co.*, Sendak remarks, "McCay and I serve the same master, our child selves . . . and neither of us forget our childhood dreams" ("Winsor McCay" 78). "McCay re-created dreams that we all had as children," he continues, "but few of us remember—or care to remember . . . In Slumberland, as in Wonderland, irrational taboos, forbidden places, and terrifying creatures confront our hero at every turn" ("Winsor McCay" 81). In every strip, Little Nemo sleeps, dreams, and awakes—often screaming or falling out of bed, as his dreams are usually nightmares. Once Sendak "did a Rosie"—imagined himself in place of the creative child—Sendak drew kids dreaming as well as drawing. But unlike Little Nemo, and unlike Freud's Wolf Man, Sendak's child dreamers don't typically suffer nightmares. In both *Kenny's Window* and *Wild Things*, Sendak transforms dreams of Wild Things into fortifying experiences for the child inside and outside the text.

The Wolf Man case is the best known or most canonical of all Freud's case histories. In February 1910, a young, wealthy Russian aristocrat named Sergey Pankejeff came to Freud for help with some serious psychological symptoms. The analysis lasted until 1914 and focused on a neurosis that occurred between the ages of four and ten, as suggested by the official case title, *From the History of an Infantile Neurosis*. The case revolves around a "specimen dream" occurring just before the Wolf Man's fourth birthday but recollected during the analysis. Here is the Wolf-Man's account of the dream, as reproduced by Freud:

> *I dreamt that it was night and that I was lying in my bed. (My bed stood with its foot towards the window; in front of the window there was a row of old walnut trees. I know it was winter when I had the dream, and night-time.) Suddenly the window opened of its own accord, and I was terrified to see that some white wolves were sitting on the big walnut tree in front of the window. There were six or seven of them. The wolves were quite white, and looked more like foxes or sheep-dogs, for they had*

big tails like foxes and they had their ears pricked like dogs when they are attending
to something. In great terror, evidently of being eaten up by the wolves, I screamed
and woke up. (186; italics in original)

To accompany this report the Wolf Man gave Freud a drawing of the dream, the
first of many such renderings. In the drawing, against a blank background, five
white wolves perch ominously on the craggy branches of a tree. There are five
wolves instead of the six or seven in the narrated account. Freud used the dream
and the case history more generally to argue for the staying power of early childhood experience and to theorize about the origins of sadomasochism and obses-
sional neurosis. While both Freud and the Wolf Man were satisfied with the course
of treatment, the Wolf Man's symptoms later returned after he lost his wealth in the
Russian Revolution, and he spent the rest of his life in and out of therapy.[3]

And here's the beginning of *Kenny's Window*:

In the middle of a dream, Kenny woke up. And he remembered a garden.
   "I saw a garden in my dream," thought Kenny, "and a tree."
   There was a tree covered white with blossoms. And above the tree shone the
sun and the moon side by side. Half the garden was filled with yellow morning
and the other with dark green night.
   "There was something else in my dream," thought Kenny, and he tried to
remember.
   "A train," he cried, "and a rooster with four feet and he gave me something."
   There was a train puffing its way through the garden and in the caboose sat a
rooster with four feet and he gave Kenny a piece of paper.
   "Here," said the rooster, "are seven questions and you must find all the
answers."
   "If I do," asked Kenny, "may I come and live in the garden?"
   But before the rooster could answer, the dream ended.

Kenny then sets about answering the seven questions, which are: 1. Can you
draw a picture on the blackboard when somebody doesn't want you to? 2. What is
an only goat? 3. Can you see a horse on the roof? 4. Can you fix a broken promise?
5. What is a Very Narrow Escape? 6. What looks inside and what looks outside? 7.
Do you always want what you think you want? Instead of six or seven white wolves
we get seven seemingly absurd questions and a tree covered in white blossoms; in
place of the eerie moonlight scene of Freud we have a split scene of day and night.
While more philosophical than sexual, at least on the surface, Kenny's questions
echo the questions of the Wolf Man and indeed the "researches" of small children.
Beginning his quest, Kenny tries to draw a picture on the blackboard, remarking
that "I'll call it A Dream" (capital letters). "NO!" cried an angry voice. "You cannot
draw on the blackboard today!" "Why not?" asked Kenny. "Because!" said the
voice. The voice belongs to Bucky, Kenny's stuffed animal, who refuses the role of
collaborator or transitional object. Bucky is upset because Kenny has neglected
him, and after Kenny writes a poem for him, he can draw his dream-picture on the
blackboard, a picture featuring Bucky astride the dream-rooster, a distorted image
of the dream we've been told about. As he pursues the other questions, Kenny has

close encounters with a white goat, lead soldiers, his dog Baby, and his friend David. At the book's end, on another dreamy, moonlit night, the rooster returns to hear Kenny's answers. The hardest of all is no. 7: Do you always want what you think you want? "I thought I wanted to live in the garden with the moon on one side and the sun on the other, but I really don't," concludes Kenny. That we don't always want what we think we want is one of Freud's central lessons.

Sendak has never mentioned any direct influence of the Wolf Man case on *Kenny's Window* or *Wild Things*, although he has repeatedly acknowledged the general influence of Freudian analysis on his life and work. Sendak was inspired to write *Kenny's Window* after reading, in a period of depression and on the advice of his analyst, Dorothy W. Baruch's case history *One Little Boy* (1952). Baruch was a psychoanalytically trained child therapist who wrote a number of popular texts on child-rearing as well as books for children. *One Little Boy* is an account of a seven-year-old boy named Kenneth brought into treatment because of failure in school, which turns out to be a symptom for family dysfunction and emotional distress. Dr. Baruch gives the boy play therapy in the tradition of Melanie Klein, working closely with Kenny and even explaining to him the principles of treatment. The book is sometimes mistakenly described as an account of autism; in fact, Kenny's problems are more generic, the result of family dynamics and childhood anxiety generalizable to all children, according to Baruch. Eschewing Freudian terminology, Baruch nonetheless takes us through the usual Freudian story of psychosexual development, explaining how she gave Kenny permission to be bad, such that "he would now be a fraction less afraid of two things: of his own inner feelings running wildly out of hand, and of retribution from me" (Baruch 39). With her help, Kenny learns to express anger, and his parents learn to put aside their own childish fears. His imaginative world is "as illogical and full of fantasy as are all children's," writes Baruch. "From the vantage point of adult logic, they looked as strangely distorted as images seen in the mirrors of funhouses" (103).

As Bader notes, while *Kenny's Window* is not a direct translation of *One Little Boy* into picture-book form, "the seven episodes that answer the questions for Kenny deal figuratively with yearnings of fears that Kenneth confronts and comes to terms with in the course of his therapy" (504–5). By the end of his adventures, Kenny no longer wants to live in isolation in the magic garden and is no longer fearful of himself or others. Sendak aligns himself with Freud and Baruch alike, while taking cue from an earlier generation of picture-book psychologists. Sendak develops his picture book as a therapeutic exercise, a working-through of desire, prohibition, and anger undertaken on behalf of the child subject. It's a fascinating picture book but not a very successful one. Many readers find it enigmatic or too existential in concern. Bader remarks that the book's shape is "unintelligible because Kenny is indistinct" (505); we don't know enough about his situation to understand his experiences. Another, more significant problem is that adult presence hovers in the text, not the presence of parent figures, but rather of the author, who presides over Kenny's recovery not unlike a child therapist. While it's not quite so explicitly bibliotherapeutic as, say, *The Berenstain Bears Visit the Dentist* (1981) or other titles dealing with children's fears, *Kenny's Window* fails in part because its psychological concern is too obvious.

"The picture books that become classics do so," writes Ellen Handler Spitz, "because they dare to tackle important and abiding psychological themes, and because they convey these themes with craftsmanship and subtlety" (8). By this standard, the "classic" status of *Wild Things* should come as no surprise: indeed, the book functions for Spitz (among many others) as the exemplary picture book. *Wild Things* in fact helped set the stage for what makes a picture book a classic; classicism or canonicity isn't a naturally occurring phenomenon but rather the result of particular values and practices. Psychological depth alongside "craftsmanship" and "subtlety" are certainly to be found in *Wild Things*. Unlike *Kenny's Window*, *Wild Things* gets the dreamwork just right. Moreover, there's little sense of authorial presence; the story seems to tell itself.

Sendak made the first dummy for *Wild Things* in 1956, calling it *Where the Wild Horses Are*. Displeased with it, he put the dummy aside until 1963, after he had written several other books of his own and illustrated many others. At that point, he still struggled with the concept, at first writing several horse-themed versions (including one about "nightmares") before finally deciding he couldn't draw horses and revising to the generic and far less threatening "things." On May 25, he composed a new dummy featuring eighteen illustrations and only 380 words, far fewer than in the first version. Given the level of revision that went into *Wild Things*, we might even call it overdetermined, like the dreamwork itself. In one of the best analyses of Sendak's book, Perry Nodelman calls attention to the complexities of its spatial and temporal design, including its alternation of "action" shots with scenes of Max suspended "in a dreamlike stasis" (*Words* 162).

Wild Things is more clearly about the possibility of self-fulfillment, in keeping with broader cultural trends. Steven Mintz and Susan Kellogg note that while American child-rearing literature had previously been dominated by just a handful of manuals—the foremost being Spock's *Baby and Child Care*—the field "rapidly grew more crowded and confused during the 1960s," and by 1981, more than six hundred books on the subject were in print (Mintz and Kellogg 220). The new manuals shifted emphasis away from the child's thinking life and toward her feeling life. By the mid-1960s, notes Eugene Schwartz, books on child care "suddenly have many discussions on 'feelings' (virtually absent from earlier volumes)" (46). The literature remained focused on the mother-child relationship, and there were strong traces of Freudian thought inherited from the so-called Freudian forties, especially to the extent that "feelings" could signify the unconscious. By the 1960s, so-called humanistic or "third force" psychology of Abraham Maslow, Carl Rogers, and Erich Fromm had come to dominate the popular scene, placing great premium on individual happiness and self-realization. Child-rearing discourse since Spock had already imagined a kinder, gentler sort of parenting, setting the stage for further modification. Accounts of this general trend in psychological discourse vary; some welcomed it as a hopeful alternative to the pessimism of psychoanalysis and behaviorism, while skeptics saw it as vacuous and anti-intellectual as well as solipsistic (in Philip Rieff's words, the "triumph of the therapeutic").

In *Wild Things*, published in the middle of this overhaul of child-rearing literature, we see the importance of feelings both in a residually Freudian sense and in the context of humanistic psychology. Sendak is perfectly attuned to the complexities of his time and represents them as we might well expect: through a dream, one that echoes but also revises the Wolf Man's dream and other variants of wolf-boy narrative. Running amok in a wolf suit and making mischief "of one kind/and another," young Max is sent off to bed supperless. His room dreamily becomes a forest—bedposts turning into trees, carpet into grass, the moon escaping the window frame. An ocean tumbles by, and Max sails "off through night and day / and in and out of weeks / and almost over a year / to where the wild things are." Five Wild Things welcome Max as their king. The wild rumpus, which runs several pages and constitutes a centerfold of sorts, is wordless, not unlike the Wolf Man's dream of the wolves. Both "dreams" are moonlit, essentially nonverbal episodes. Post-rumpus, Max grows bored and homesick and sails back "into the night of his very own room" he finds his supper waiting for him—"and it was still hot."

There are of course key differences between the Wolf Man's dream of the wolves and Max's dream of the Wild Things. The situation of the protagonist is particularly crucial. The Wolf Man reports in distress that "it seemed as though [the wolves] had riveted their whole attention upon me" (186). Max, too, is the center of attention, but he's firmly and happily in charge, staring into the Wild Things' yellow eyes until they look away and sending them to bed without supper. Max, notes McGillis, is aggressive and destructive, and "the book is replete with images of phallic aggressiveness: the strong vertical lines of erect trees, bedposts, Max's scepter, his ship's mast, and the horns of some of the Wild Things" (80). Because Max's anger is directly partly toward his mother, explains McGillis, the Wild Things are "parodic of adults" rather than scary (81). Even at their most menacing, the Wild Things have a friendly countenance, their arms extended in welcome and their forms suggestively human. (The Wild Things were reportedly modeled on Sendak's uncles and aunts.) "Whereas Freud's patient feared animals," McGillis points out, "Max is one" (82). McGillis notes that in an early version of the story, Max does not wear a wolf suit; rather, he meets a character who claims to be his mother but who then turns into a rapacious wolf.[4] This aborted plot resonates with the Wolf Man's dream and with wolf-themed fairy tales, whereas in Sendak's version, the mother is firmly linked with care and feeding (rather than child-devouring). Whereas the Wolf Man spends the rest of his life in analysis, never successfully overcoming his phobias, Max works through his anger and returns to a hot supper. Max needs no dramatic intervention, only an understanding mother and some time and space of his own.

While it met with some initial disapproval, *Wild Things* quickly found affirmation as a psychological as well as aesthetic masterpiece. Psychologist Michael Thompson, for instance, proclaims Sendak's text "the best book on boy anger" (165). Whatever its complexities, it has nonetheless been received as a psychological primer. Sendak himself authorized that view in his Caldecott acceptance speech: "Through fantasy, Max, the hero of my book, discharges his anger against his mother, and returns to the real world sleepy, hungry, and at peace with himself" (151). In that speech, Sendak remarks, "I feel like I am at the end of a long apprenticeship," anticipating work even more attuned to "the child's endless battle with disturbing emotions" (154). *Wild Things* has a place in our culture because it made classic the idea of the picture book as hard psychological work.

WHERE THE CRITICS ARE, AND WHERE THEY MIGHT GO: TOWARD A QUEER SENDAK

In 1963, *Wild Things* may have served as the picture-book equivalent of the new child-rearing literature on feelings, but it now stands for a reigning orthodoxy, its reception perhaps too powerfully determined by a larger psychological plot of adventure and mastery. Sendak himself doesn't think it's his best work, but popular opinion and the scholarship both reflect this orthodoxy. Moreover, there's very little critique of Sendak's book. I've found no class-oriented analysis at all, and feminist commentary is decidedly pro-Sendak.[5] Interpretations from a postcolonial studies perspective likewise tend toward affirmation. Both John Clement Ball and Jennifer Shaddock acknowledge the colonialist echoes of *Wild Things* but conclude that Sendak's relation to colonialist narrative is ironic. Both situate the book in relation to psychology as well, Ball developing a psychoanalytic reading and Shaddock arguing that Sendak interrogates the opposition of wild and civilized in the idiom of 1960s psychology. While Shaddock concludes that Sendak's psychological refashioning of wild amounts to a critique, the popularity of the book is likely due to the broader cultural success of such refashioning, likely not so ironic. That is, lovers of *Wild Things* probably don't see it as a child's version of the *Heart of Darkness* (how Shaddock presents the book) but rather as a self-help book for children and their parents. *Wild Things*, in other words, is part of the culture of self-help if also a deconstruction of such.[6] In different ways, Ball and Shaddock raise the question of how to historicize psychology in a culture largely (in)formed by psychological discourse. We are arguably all colonizers of the psyche, even as we are also all its subaltern subjects, which makes all the more difficult a historicist understanding of picture-book psychology.

Offering alternatives to psychological readings of *Wild Things*, Nodelman and McGillis nevertheless leave room for the possibility that Sendak's book performs psychological work (and link that idea to its status as a classic). McGillis speculates that *Wild Things* "touches on each reader's Oedipal experience," remarking that the "experience of reading this book gives us the pleasure of having our fantasies taken care of. We are complicit with the literary text" (179–80). Noting that "many good picture books manage to capture a childlike guilelessness—a sort of defenseless and vulnerable fantasizing that comes very close to dream," Nodelman "can only conclude they do so because they speak symbolically to a level of human understanding that is below consciousness . . ." (*Words* 109).

In his more recent, magisterial study *The Hidden Adult*, Nodelman draws from sociologist Pierre Bourdieu's theories about "habitus," "position," and the "field of cultural production" to rethink children's literature and its study. Returning briefly to the case of *Wild Things*, Nodelman proposes that his "especially intense grasp of the habitus" enabled Sendak to take "a position that was not actually there to be taken in the field of children's literature as it existed at that time"—namely, the position that childhood can itself be monstrous, and usefully so (*Hidden* 122; 121). Sendak's take on the monstrosity theme, in and around a broader refashioning of wildness, made for "startling but acceptable innovation" (*Hidden* 123) within the field of picture books. *Wild Things* in turn made possible further domestications of the monstrous (think Muppets and so forth). In his emphasis on Sendak's intuitive understanding of the psychosocial possibilities of picture books, Nodelman anticipates much of what I've proposed in this essay.

While a queer interpretation of Sendak's work has yet to emerge, a foundation for such has been established by McGillis, who emphasizes the polymorphous libido of Max. Indeed, a queer reading of *Wild Things* might recast many of the observations already made in the scholarship about Max's hybridity, passion, and performativity and perhaps link such to Sendak's own life. Such a reading is tempting in light of Sendak's recent self-outing in the *New York Times* profile piece by Patricia Cohen. Noting that he has given hundreds of interviews over the years, Cohen asks Sendak if there's any question that was never asked in all that time. "He paused for a few moments and answered, 'Well, that I'm gay. All I wanted was to be straight so my parents could be happy. They never, never, never knew'" (no page).

Sendak's depression and adventures in therapy surely had something to do with his life as a closeted gay man in pre-Stonewall New York. Before that, Sendak had what might fairly be described as a queer childhood. Talking with Jonathan Cott, Sendak remarks, "I was miserable as a kid . . . I couldn't make friends, I couldn't play stoopball terrific, I couldn't skate great. I stayed home and drew pictures. You *know* what they all thought of me: sissy Maurice Sendak" (Cott 45). Sendak recalls that as a teenager he began illustrating his own books, beginning with Oscar Wilde's *The Happy Prince* and then moving on to Bret Harte's *The Luck of Roaring Camp*. "It was my favorite story, and what is it about? A baby that is adopted by a lot of rough men, lumberjacks—an illegitimate child abandoned after the death of its mother" (Cott 46). Sendak's creative activity, in other words, was bound up with a queer sensibility and served as a sort of survival or coping strategy. Sendak goes on to discuss the book then in development, *Outside Over There* (1981), also about a baby, albeit with goblins rather than lumberjacks. *Outside Over There* is Sendak's favorite book, not only because it was the hardest to make (as he has often said), but perhaps also because it's a strange and melancholic story, revolving as it does around a baby's abduction by goblins and subsequent rescue by her older sister, Ida.[7] Sendak likens the creative experience to "getting pregnant when you've just gone crazy and you've found out your house has burned down" (Cott 60)—an interesting analogy for a male writer to make. It's worth noting that Sendak identifies just as strongly with his girl protagonists (Rosie, Ida) as with his boy ones.

Max may well be the boy next door in a wolf suit—the exemplary subject of humanist child-rearing and child psychology—but he too is a queer child. Sendak's child characters more generally represent a departure from kid types in prior picture books. Sendak's kids are immigrant kids, Brooklyn kids, "eyes often closed, stiff-gaited, top-heavy, and heavy-footed, smilingly sensual, obviously bright, theatrically temperamental, self-satisfied tiny egoists" (Kushner 9–10). They are at once regular kids and unusual, eccentric, singular kids. Max, of course, is usually described as normal precisely through his wildness, in keeping with the remythification of the feral tale. But the feral tale's energies are historically queer, and even the most civilized Wild Thing remains liminal, neither clearly human or animal, child or adult. The feral child is "Betwixt-n-Between," as J. M. Barrie described another famous feral boy, Peter Pan. Max, it seems to me, is both normal and queer, perhaps a young version of Sendak himself.

Art historian Whitney Davis offers another route to the queerness of Max and Sendak, by way (as it happens) of a provocative reading of the Wolf Man case, titled *Drawing the Dream of the Wolves*. Davis proposes that a whole intersubjective dimension of the case has been missed, one vital to psychoanalysis and also to Freud's influential construction of homosexuality. The Wolf Man, he points out, draws *for* Freud, both literally and through words, hoping to make Freud interested in and happy with him. Freud in turn "draws" the Wolf Man, giving his patient a mythology linked with the "specimen dream" of the wolves and the various sketches produced in its wake. Freud needed the Wolf Man just as much as the other way around. Identifying the Wolf Man as a "latent" homosexual, Freud fails to acknowledge his homoerotic investment in the Wolf Man, holds Davis, and suppresses his own childhood encounters with a suggestive, scary wolf picture. Davis unearths a favorite picture book of Freud's suppressed in but key to the case history. The book in question is Friedrich von Tschudi's *Animal Life in the Alpine World* (1865), which features an illustration of a lupine and menacing-looking rescue dog saving a little boy lost in the snow, its ears pricked and its sharp teeth clearly visible (Davis 200–201). The illustration bears a striking resemblance to the Wolf Man's "memories" of the wolf dream and of the fairy tale illustrations he ostensibly encountered in childhood; in fact, notes Davis, the von Tschudi image looks *more* like the latter than does the scene from the Wolf Man's dream. Freud's concept of latent homosexuality emerges out of his intersubjective, unconscious relationship with the Wolf Man, in and around formative if forgotten images.[8]

We are back, it seems, to the drawing board. In *Wild Things*, Sendak draws a wolf-boy character with none of the Wolf Man's problems, and presumably that's that. But if Freud's case history hinges on an unrealized homoerotic dimension, how might that in turn have influenced Sendak? Was Sendak drawn to the case because it deals so extensively with the question of homosexuality in and around childhood and dreams? Davis emphasizes that for Freud, the theory of latent homosexuality is at root a theory of human intersubjectivity, latency implying the potential for actualization and not only of sexuality. The Wolf Man was based on a real person, and perhaps Max was, too, perhaps on Sendak himself or on an idealized boy whose dreams he hoped to nurture. *Wild Things* is a picture book, but it is also a dream book and a case history, drawn from Sendak's encounters with real children as well as his own memories of childhood.

In one of the few critical assessments of Sendak, Maria Tatar recognizes in more negative terms Sendak's self-fashioning as a picture-book psychologist. "The rhetoric of mastery that permeates Sendak's writings about children's books," she writes, "dovetails neatly with the model of reading as therapy developed by Bruno Bettelheim in his *Uses of Enchantment*" (74). Both Sendak and Bettelheim, she suggests, rely on and promote a male developmental model and "argue for the instrumentalization of fantasy . . . even as they deplore children's literature that takes an explicitly didactic turn" (76). Tatar is right to emphasize their shared ambitions; in fact, it's worth noting that Bettelheim came to view Sendak as a rival expert on childhood, one working creatively rather than clinically.[9] Bettelheim became aware of *Wild Things* in the late 1960s, and in one of his "Dialogues with Mothers" (titled "The Care and Feeding of Monsters") tries to discredit Sendak's work—even as his encounter with Sendak led Bettelheim, I suspect, to take a closer look at the psychological power of fairy tales.[10] Bettelheim's resistance to Sendak helps us understand picture-book psychology as an alternative to official psychology, even as a creative form of lay analysis.

But while Sendak is indeed committed to the instrumentalization of fantasy and perhaps an underlying male development model, and while he certainly self-presents as an authority on childhood, there's more going on in his work than straightforward bibliotherapy and traditionally masculinist storying. I would locate Sendak in a long line of authorial "uncles," not unlike the Bad Boy authors of the late nineteenth century whom I discuss in *Making American Boys*. There I suggest that authors for boys especially tend to adopt an avuncular sort of relation to their young subjects and readers, presenting themselves as lay boyologists or character builders. "Forget the Name of the Father," Eve Kosofsky Sedgwick urges us; "Think about your uncles and aunts" (59). In Sedgwick's reading, the "avunculate" or the social formation of aunt and uncle (which may or may not involve blood relation) can provide relief from and alternative wisdom to the traditionally nuclear family, especially for queer kids. Sendak perhaps functions as an avuncular picture-book psychologist, not unlike other uncles with a powerful presence in children's literature and culture, some queer, some not (Uncle Shel Silverstein or, more sinisterly, Uncle Walt Disney). Being Uncle Maurice gives Sendak a legitimate and safe relation to the child: he is the eccentric, gifted uncle, whose odd stories and drawings are so mesmerizing.

Queerness, of course, extends far beyond the sexual in most understandings of the term and in Sendak's case might apply to everything about his life and work that is nonconformist, difficult, melancholic. Sendak, we might say, is queer because he's gay *and* Jewish *and* irascible.[11] "He is not, as children's book writers are often supposed, an everyman's grandpa," notes Cohen. "His hatreds are fierce and grand, as if produced by Cecil B. DeMille." And if *Wild Things* represents a more assimilationist—more easily assimilated—Sendak, his larger body of work complicates the story, disassociating the picture book from happy endings and even the dream of imaginative mastery. We need only point to *Brundibár* (2003) written by Kushner and illustrated by Sendak and based on a 1938 opera subsequently performed by children in the concentration camp Theresienstadt. Or to *Dear Mili*, the grim Grimm Brothers tale that Sendak illustrated in 1988. Or to Sendak's *We Are All Down in the Dumps with Jack and Guy* (1983), a response to homelessness and AIDS and dedicated to another gay picture-book artist, the late James Marshall. *Wild Things*, while powerful, is but one small part of Sendak's queer achievement.

Picture-book psychology is a many-splendored thing, a constellation of child-centered discourses embodying a widespread belief that picture books fortify the young reader and a creative-professional vocation. Sendak's career has helped authorize faith that the picture book should grapple with the dramas of childhood and that the picture-book creator is an authority on childhood. Building on the traditions he inherited, Sendak has presented the picture book as serious and important psychological business. When asked in an interview with Walter Lorraine, "Can you define what a picture book is for you?" here is Sendak's telling response:

> It's my battleground. It's where I express myself. It's where I consolidate my powers and put them together in what I hope is a legitimate, viable form that is meaningful to somebody else and not just to me. It's where I work. It's where I put down those fantasies that have been with me all my life, and where I give them a *form* that means something. I live inside the picture book; that's where I fight all my battles, and where I hope to win my wars. (193)

NOTES

Warm thanks to Phil Nel, Joan Menefee, Anastasia Ulanowicz, Cari Keebaugh, Julia Mickenberg, and Lynne Vallone for suggestions along the way.

    1. Other manuals that translated Freud into "common sense" include Margaret Ribble's *Rights of Infants* (1943) and Edith Buxbaum's *Your Child Makes Sense* (1951). See Hardyment, 230.

    2. Julia Mickenberg acknowledges Mitchell's importance while identifying two major strains of thinking about the psychological and cultural work of children's books in early twentieth-century America, both heavily influenced by the Lyrical Left movement as well as the popularization of Freud and the rise of progressive education. These two strains or philosophies—what she calls "Liberation through Imagination" and "Liberation through Knowledge"—were not entirely separate and in fact overlapped especially when it came to children's books (33–46).

3. Pankejeff sought Freud's help with his nervous compulsions and inability to have bowel movements without an enema. Freud thought that his patient was resisting full analysis and gave the analysis a one-year deadline, with an ostensibly successful outcome. Drawing heavily upon the wolf dream, Freud came up with two explanations for the Wolf Man's symptoms; first, he concluded that Wolf Man had witnessed his parents having coitus *a tergo* ("from behind") while still very young; later, he suggested that his patient had perhaps witnessed animal sex and had projected anxieties about such onto his parents, in keeping with classic Oedipal formation. Freud emphasized the Wolf Man's identification with his mother as well as his father, underscoring the presence of same-sex identification and desire in early childhood. Because it combined dream interpretation with a focus on infantile sexuality, the Wolf Man case became a cornerstone for Freudian analysis and is still used in the training of analysts.

4. By having Max replace his mother as the wolf, suggests McGillis, Sendak acknowledges the boy's overriding narcissism as well as the dynamics of aggression and sublimation (82). And by making this particular change, he revises the fairy-tale formula behind the Wolf Man's dream (which may also be that of Freud), emphasizing the adaptive power as well as the psychic wildness of the child.

5. Deborah Thacker, for example, argues Sendak "claims the feminine domain as the rightful place of the child" (12). Max's return to Mom represents a triumph of maternal love and feminine domesticity, in her view. Melissa Gross reaches a similar conclusion, reading even the wild rumpus scene as evidence of Max's mastery of "the socializing behavior exhibited by his mother" (151).

6. Roger Sutton starts off his interview with Sendak by noting that in a recent episode of *Queer Eye for the Straight Guy*, "one of the makeover experts made a joke about how the guy's wallpaper looked like *Where the Wild Things Are*. How does it feel to realize that your work—*Wild Things* in particular—is so much a part of public culture?" Sendak responds thus: "I'm not very impressed with being a catchword every time someone needs something to be 'wild'" (Sutton 687).

7. *Outside* completes the "psychological" trilogy made up of *Wild Things* and *In the Night Kitchen* (1971). *Wild Things*, *In the Night Kitchen* (1970), and *Outside* function, in Sendak's own words, as "variations on the same theme: how children master various feelings—anger, boredom, fear, frustration, jealousy—and manage to come to grips with the realities of their lives" (qtd. in Lanes 227).

8. There's also the tree motif, which shows up in the Wolf Man's dream, in *Wild Things* and in Freud's vision of the psyche as "a system or network of branching interconnections. He depended on this image throughout his mature psychoanalytic writings" (Davis 97).

9. Bettelheim earned his doctorate in aesthetics and never underwent formal analytic training. Like Sendak, he was largely self-taught, Jewish, and deeply preoccupied with the emotional and imaginative lives of children. By claiming fairy tales as more genuine psychological texts, the Viennese-born Bettelheim capitalized on their broad popularity and aligned himself with Freud and the classic tradition of fairy-tale analysis. Sendak, too, capitalized on the genre, by illustrating classic fairy tales and by producing fairy tales in picture-book form.

10. This is one example of the "position-taking" within the field of children's literature that interests Nodelman in *The Hidden Adult*.

11. Observes Kushner: "Maurice is a child of the Great Depression and of Jewish Depression, if I may generalize. Jewish Depression is that inherited awareness of the arduousness of knowing God, the arduousness of knowing *anything*, an acute awareness of

the struggle *to know*, the struggle against not knowing; and it is that enduring sense of displacement, yearning for and not securely possessing a home. It is the conviction, passed through hundreds of generations, that true home is elsewhere, promised but not attained, perhaps not even attainable. Maurice's is a *Yiddische kopf*, a large, brooding, circumspect, and contemplative mind, darkened by both fatalism and faith" (190).

WORKS CITED

Bader, Barbara. *American Picture Books from Noah's Ark to the Beast Within*. New York: Macmillan, 1976.

Ball, John Clement. "Max's Colonial Fantasy: Rereading Sendak's *Where the Wild Things Are. ARIEL* 28, no. 1 (1997): 167–79.

Baruch, Dorothy W. *One Little Boy*. 1952. New York: Dell, 1964.

Bettelheim, Bruno. "The Care and Feeding of Monsters." *Ladies Home Journal* (March 1969): 48.

———. *The Uses of Enchantment: The Meaning and Importance of Fairy Tales*. New York: Alfred A. Knopf, 1976.

Cech, John. *Angels and Wild Things: The Archetypal Poetics of Maurice Sendak*. University Park, PA: The Pennsylvania State UP, 1995.

Cohen, Patricia. "Concerns Beyond Just Where the Wild Things Are." *New York Times*, September 10, 2008. Accessed September 11, 2008. http://www.nytimes. com/2008/09/10/arts/design/10sendak.html

Cott, Jonathan. *Pipers at the Gates of Dawn: The Wisdom of Children's Literature*. New York: Random House, 1983.

Cummins, Julie, ed. *Wings of an Artist: Children's Book Illustrators Talk about Their Art*. New York: Harry N. Abrams, 1999.

Davis, Whitney. *Drawing the Dream of the Wolves: Homosexuality, Interpretation, and Freud's "Wolf Man."* Bloomington: Indiana UP, 1995.

Eddy, Jacalyn. *Bookwomen: Creating an Empire in Children's Book Publishing, 1919–1939*. Madison: U of Wisconsin P, 2006.

Freud, Sigmund. *The Interpretation of Dreams*. Translated and edited by James Strachey. New York: Avon Books, 1965.

———. *Three Case Histories: The "Wolf Man," the "Rat Man," and the Psychotic Doctor Schreber*. Edited and introduction by Philip Rieff. New York: Collier-Macmillan, 1963.

Gardner, Howard. *Artful Scribbles: The Significance of Children's Drawings*. New York: Basic Books, 1980.

Gross, Melissa. "Why Children Come Back: *The Tale of Peter Rabbit* and *Where the Wild Things Are*." In *Beatrix Potter's* Peter Rabbit: *A Children's Classic at 100*. ChLA Centennial Studies #1. Edited by Margaret Mackey, 145–58. Lanham, MD: The Scarecrow Press, 2002.

Hardyment, Christine. *Dream Babies: Child Care from Locke to Spock*. London: Jonathan Cape Ltd, 1983.

Hulbert, Ann. *Raising America: Experts, Parents, and a Century of Advice about Children*. New York: Random House, 2003.

Kidd, Kenneth. *Making American Boys: Boyology and the Feral Tale*. Minneapolis: U of Minnesota P, 2004.

Kushner, Tony. *The Art of Maurice Sendak: 1980 to the Present*. New York: Harry N. Abrams, 2003.

Lanes, Selma G. *The Art of Maurice Sendak*. New York: Harry N. Abrams, 1980.

Marcus, Leonard S., ed. *Dear Genius: The Letters of Ursula Nordstrom*. New York: HarperCollins, 1998.

———. *Margaret Wise Brown: Awakened by the Moon*. New York: HarperCollins, 1992.

McGillis, Roderick. *The Nimble Reader: Literary Theory and Children's Literature*. New York: Twayne, 1996.

Menefee, Joan. "The Shape of a Hand: Children's Drawings in 20th-Century Psychology." Unpublished talk, Children's Literature Association Annual Conference, June 2007. Cited with permission.

Mickenberg, Julia. *Learning from the Left: Children's Literature, the Cold War, and Radical Politics in the United States*. New York: Oxford UP, 2006.

Mintz, Steven. *Huck's Raft: A History of American Childhood*. Cambridge, MA: Belknap-Harvard UP, 2004.

Mintz, Steven, and Susan Kellogg. *Domestic Revolutions: A Social History of American Family Life*. New York: The Free Press, 1988.

Nodelman, Perry. *The Hidden Adult: Defining Children's Literature*. Baltimore: Johns Hopkins UP, 2008.

———. *Words about Pictures: The Narrative Art of Children's Picture Books*. Athens: U of Georgia P, 1988.

Rieff, Philip. *The Triumph of the Therapeutic: Uses of Faith After Freud*. New York, Harper & Row, 1966.

Schwartz, Eugene. *Millenial Child: Transforming Education in the Twenty-First Century*. Hudson, NY: Anthroposophic Press, 1999.

Sedgwick, Eve Kosofsky. "Tales of the Avunculate: *The Importance of Being Earnest*." *Tendencies*. Durham: Duke UP, 1993. 52–72.

Sendak, Maurice. "Caldecott Medal Acceptance." 1964. In *Caldecott & Co.: Notes on Books & Pictures*, by Maurice Sendak, 145–56. New York: Farrar, Straus and Giroux, 1988.

———. "A Conversation with Walter Lorraine." In *Caldecott & Co.: Notes on Books & Pictures*, by Maurice Sendak, 185–93. New York: Farrar, Straus and Giroux, 1988.

———. "Really Rosie." In *Caldecott & Co: Notes on Books & Pictures*, by Maurice Sendak, 179–84. New York: Farrar, Straus and Giroux, 1988.

———. *Where the Wild Things Are*. New York: Harper, 1963.

———. "Winsor McCay." In *Caldecott & Co: Notes on Books & Pictures*, by Maurice Sendak, 77–86. New York: Farrar, Straus and Giroux, 1988.

Serlin, David, and Brian Selznick. "Where the Wild Things Were: An Interview with Leonard S. Marcus." *Cabinet Magazine* 9 (Winter 2002/3). Accessed September 14, 2008. http://www.cabinetmagazine.org/issues/9/wherewild.php

Shaddock, Jennifer. "*Where the Wild Things Are*: Sendak's Journey into the Heart of Darkness." *Children's Literature Association Quarterly* 22, no. 4 (Winter 1997–1998): 155–59.

Spitz, Ellen Handler. *Inside Picture Books*. New Haven: Yale UP, 1999.

Sutton, Roger. "A Interview with Maurice Sendak." *Horn Book* (November/December 2003): 687–99.

Tatar, Maria. *Off with Their Heads! Fairy Tales and the Culture of Childhood*. Princeton, NJ: Princeton UP, 1992.

Thacker, Deborah. "Feminine Language and the Politics of Children's Literature." *The Lion and the Unicorn* 25, no. 1 (2001): 3–16.

Thornton, Matthew. "Wild Things All Over." *Publisher's Weekly*, 4 February 2008. 22 October 2008, http://www.publishersweekly.com/article/CA6528120.html.

Thomas, Ronald R. *Dreams of Authority: Freud and the Fictions of the Unconscious*. Ithaca: Cornell UP, 1990.

Thompson, Michael. *Speaking of Boys: Answers to the Most Often Asked Questions about Raising Sons*. New York: Random House, 2000.

FURTHER READING

Adams, Rebecca V. L., and Eric S. Rabkin. "Psyche and Society in Sendak's *In the Night Kitchen*." *Children's Literature in Education* 38, no. 4 (December 2007): 233–41.

Arakelian, Paul. "Text and Illustration: A Stylistic Analysis of Books by Sendak and Mayer." *Children's Literature Association Quarterly* 10, no. 3 (Fall 1985): 122–27.

Bodmer, George. "Arthur Hughes, Walter Crane, and Maurice Sendak: The Picture Book as Literary Fairy Tale." *Marvels & Tales* 17, no. 1 (2003): 120–37.

Goldthwaite, Jonathan. *The Natural History of Make-Believe*. New York: Oxford UP, 1996.

Jones, Raymond E. "Maurice Sendak's *Where the Wild Things Are*: Picture Book Poetry." In *Touchstones: Reflections on the Best in Children's Literature*. Vol. 3, *Picture Books*, edited by Perry Nodelman, 122–31. West Lafayette: Children's Literature Association, 1989.

Keeling, Kara, and Scott Pollard. "Power, Food, and Eating in Maurice Sendak and Henrik Drescher: *Where the Wild Things Are, In the Night Kitchen*, and *The Boy Who Ate Around*." *Children's Literature in Education* 30, no. 2 (June 1999): 127–42.

Lazú, Jacqueline. "National Identity: Where the Wild, Strange, and Exotic Things Are: In Search of the Caribbean in Contemporary Children's Literature." In *Children's Literature: New Approaches*, edited by Karín Lesnik-Oberstein, 189–205. New York: Palgrave, 2004.

Moebius, William. "Introduction to Picturebook Codes." In *Children's Literature: The Development of Criticism*, edited by Peter Hunt, 131–47. London: Routledge, 1990.

Roxburgh, Stephen. "A Picture Equals How Many Words? Narrative Theory and Picture Books for Children." *The Lion and the Unicorn* 7/8 (1983–84): 20–33.

Sipe, Lawrence R. "The Private and Public Worlds of *We Are All in the Dumps with Jack and Guy*. *Children's Literature in Education* 27, no. 2 (1996): 87–108.

Stanton, Joseph. "Maurice Sendak's Urban Landscapes." *Children's Literature* 28 (2000): 132–46.

Sonheim, Amy. *Maurice Sendak*. New York: Twayne, 1991.

Tannenbaum, Leslie. "Betrayed by Chicken Soup: Judaism, Gender and Performance in Maurice Sendak's Really Rosie." *The Lion and the Unicorn* 27, no. 3 (2003): 362–76.

Waller, Jennifer R. "Maurice Sendak and the Blakean Vision of Childhood." *Children's Literature* 6 (1977): 130–40.

....

CHAPTER 11

REIMAGINING THE MONKEY KING IN COMICS: GENE LUEN YANG'S *AMERICAN BORN CHINESE*

....

LAN DONG

GENE Luen Yang began drawing comic strips in fifth grade and started publishing comics under the alias of Humble Comics in 1996. In 1997 Yang received the Xeric Grant, a prestigious comics industry grant, and under its auspice published Gordon Yamamoto and the King of the Geeks *(2004). He is the author of several comic books:* Duncan's Kingdom *(illustration by Derek Kirk Kim, 1999),* The Rosary Comic Book *(2003),* Loyola Chin and the San Peligran Order *(2004), and* The Eternal Smile: Three Stories *(coauthored with Derek Kirk Kim, 2009). His graphic novel,* American Born Chinese *(2006) is the winner of the Printz Award. In 2008 Yang published "The Motherless One," a fourteen-page black-and-white comic tale that appears in* Up All Night, *an anthology of young adult short stories. Beginning November 9, 2008, Yang published an eighteen-week comic series,* Prime Baby, *on the Funny Pages section of the* New York Times Magazine. *In addition, Yang has made many appearances nationwide at conferences, interviews, library festivals, reading events, book signings, and other programs where he has discussed not only his works but also the role of comics, how to use comics in education, Chinese American heritage, and multicultural literature for young adults. He created and maintains his personal website: www.humblecomics.com that includes his profile, publications, links to cartoonists, comics publishers and distributors, and other comics-related websites. He maintains a blog on his website.*

Gene Luen Yang's *American Born Chinese*[1] is an important cross-cultural rewriting of the classic Monkey King story for young adult readers.[2] Through juxtaposing the Monkey King with the toy transformer, the suburban single-family house with the Chinatown herbalist store, American school with Chinese heritage, Yang's book explores the possibility and process for an adolescent to define his or her bicultural identity. As the first graphic novel[3] to win the American Library Association's Michael L. Printz Award for Excellence in Young Adult Literature and to become a National Book Award Finalist in the young people's literature category, *American Born Chinese* enjoyed a stunning success shortly after its publication.[4] In addition to receiving many impressive awards, this work has been praised in numerous book reviews.[5]

Upon first reading, Yang's book seems to include three story lines. Story One reimagines the Monkey King, a popular character originating from Chinese folklore, and retells his story with a contemporary American spin. Story Two traces the experience of Jin Wang, a schoolboy whose parents are immigrants from China. Jin's narrative begins when his family moves from San Francisco's Chinatown to an all-white suburb at the beginning of third grade. Story Three documents a visit by Chin-Kee, a composite of racial stereotypes of Chinese, to his seemingly Caucasian cousin, Danny. Chin-Kee's annual visits mark Danny as an embarrassing "misfit" at school. Although the book presents three tales, a careful reading unites these stories into a coherent whole.

Presenting its intertwined story lines in the form of a graphic novel for young adults, *American Born Chinese* lends itself readily to the study of cultural transformation, identity politics, ethnicity, childhood, and adolescence through textual as well as visual representations. A fiction with autobiographical ingredients, the book incorporates some of the author's personal experiences. There are multiple thematic elements running through the story lines: transformation and identity, prejudice and acceptance, and the dual cultural heritage of being an American-born Chinese.[6] It is worth noting that by choosing the term "American born Chinese" instead of the more inclusive and commonly used "Chinese American," Yang deliberately draws a distinction between the American-born generation and their immigrant parents. Such a choice speaks to the specific struggle over identity and belonging represented by his characters Jin and Danny in the American school environment. Yang's portrayal of the young characters' constant struggle and efforts to "fit in" at school also contributes to its appeal to young adult readers, of Chinese heritage and otherwise. The opening chapter on the Monkey King introduces these primary themes and sets the book's overall narrative tone.

American Born Chinese retells the Chinese folk story of the Monkey King in a new light in terms of both its content and format. This graphic novel transforms traditional Chinese folklore and transplants the celebrated character of the Monkey King into a contemporary Chinese American context. A favorite character for children as well as adults in Chinese folklore, literature, and media, the Monkey King is traditionally perceived as an antiauthoritarian figure who was born out of a rock and who has the capabilities to transform into different shapes, to fly over long distances in an instant, and to fight against various opponents fearlessly. His story has enjoyed long-lasting popularity and has been rewritten in many different genres and forms in China.

Although various cultural elements and sources have enriched the character of the Monkey King, the most important text establishing this figure's far-reaching fame is a one-hundred-chapter novel, *Xi you ji* (*The Journey to the West*, sixteenth century), one of four major classic Chinese novels.[7] Despite the scarce evidence found in premodern versions and differences among contemporary scholars, studies have generally attributed the authorship of this novel to Wu Cheng'en (ca. 1506–ca. 1582).[8] *The Journey to the West* has some loose historical basis in the seventeen-year pilgrimage of the monk Xuanzang (also known as Tripitaka or Tang Sanzang, 596–664) to India in search of Buddhist scriptures from 629 to 645. Xuanzang's historical journey is of significance in setting the terms for the cross-cultural fertilization that the story invokes. After returning from his trip, Xuanzang devoted his time to translating the scriptures. He is a well-known historical figure in Chinese Buddhism.[9] It is believed that Wu Cheng'en developed Xuanzang's story into a colorful novel, most likely based on previous versions, both written and oral.[10] In this novel, the disciples who accompany Xuanzang on his journey are Sun Wukong, Zhu Wuneng, and Sha Wujing (commonly known as Monkey, Pigsy, and Sandy or Sun Xingzhe, Zhu Bajie, and Sha Heshang, respectively).

At once an adventure story, a fantasy, and a satire, *The Journey to the West* contains countless Buddhist elements, practices, and allusions as well as Taoist concepts, ideas, and beliefs. The original plotline of the novel narrates how under the Buddha's instruction the Bodhisattva Guanyin appointed Xuanzang for the pilgrimage to India and gave him three disciples who need to atone their past sins to protect and assist him. The novel portrays dozens of geographical locations and hundreds of characters. Before even introducing the nominal main character, Xuanzang, the book spends seven chapters telling the story of the Monkey King, who will accompany Xuanzang on his journey. The stone-born Monkey followed a Taoist master to acquire outstanding martial skills and the ability to fly and change shape. Because Monkey caused tremendous disturbance in heaven, the Buddha confined him under the Wuxing Mountain for five hundred years until Xuanzang saved him. On their long way to the West, Xuanzang was captured and his life threatened multiple times by various demons, monsters, ogres, humans, and other creatures living in the wild. Monkey, together with Pigsy and Sandy and sometimes with the guidance or assistance of the Bodhisatvva Guanyin, fought against those hostile forces. Most of the calamities turned out to be challenges and tests that Xuanzang had to overcome to attain Buddhahood. At the end, Monkey attained immortality and became a Buddha. It is Wu Cheng'en who portrayed the stone-born Monkey as the "real hero" in his work of "comic fantasy" and defined this heroic character "in terms of his spiritual detachment, his prankish humor, his restless energy, and his passionate devotion to his master" (Hsia 130, 115). *The Journey to the West* sets up the stage for the immense appeal of the character Monkey.

The colorful elements in this novel provide important basis for his characterization, which later versions of the Monkey King have built on, expanded, and rewritten. Through its many variations and incarnations, *The Journey to the West* has
been a favorite for millions of Chinese children and adults and has become known
to English-speaking readers as well through translation and media adaptations
(fig. 11.1).[11]

The tale of the Monkey King has gained a significant position in Asian diasporic
and Asian American communities as a result of numerous literary reconfigurations,
for example: Timothy Mo's *The Monkey King* (1987), Gerald Robert Vizenor's
Griever, An American Monkey King in China (1987), Maxine Hong Kingston's *Tripmaster Monkey: His Fake Book* (1989), and Patricia Chao's *Monkey King* (1997). All
these authors have adapted or alluded to the story of the Monkey King and altered
his character as well as the story line for their respective political and critical agendas.
The Monkey King also has attracted attention from authors of children's literature

Figure 11.1. An illustration of the Monkey King from a seventeenth-century
illustrated version of Wu Cheng'en's novel, *Xiuxiang xi you ji* (Illustrated the
Journey to the West). 1696. 33.

and has been adapted into a number of picture books. Some recent examples include Grania Davis's *The Monkey King: Legend of a Wise and Brave Leader* (1998), Ed Young's *Monkey King* (2001), and Debby Chen and Wenhai Ma's *Monkey King Wreaks Havoc in Heaven* (2001) and *Tang Monk Disciples Monkey King* (2005). These works generally adapt the Chinese folk story for child readers and their parents.[12] In contrast, Yang's book specifically targets a young adult (rather than child) audience and foregrounds issues of race and ethnicity.

Gene Yang's graphic novel takes the Monkey King's story to new levels in terms of its social and cultural connotations. Having heard bedtime stories about the Monkey King from his mother since childhood, Yang retains in *American Born Chinese* some of the basic elements of the original Chinese folk story: the Monkey King's birth out of a rock, his super-heroic skills, his kingdom at the Flower-Fruit Mountain, his rebellion against heaven, and his apprenticeship with Xuanzang and their journey to the West. Yet his work goes well beyond the parameters found in the novel *The Journey to the West*, to reimagine the character of the Monkey King and to reinvent the story line with new twists. In particular, the connection between the Chinese Monkey King (introduced in the first chapter) and the American toy transformer (introduced on the first page of the second chapter) leads the reader to ponder embedded messages about identity, coming of age, and the risk of losing oneself by trying too hard to fit in. Yang claims the super-powered and kung fu fighting Monkey, the transformers, and the American superheroes with their alter egos filled his childhood imagination with colorful plots and characters. Yet it was not until Yang started writing *American Born Chinese* that he connected "the dual nature of the transformers with the dual identities of American superheroes with the shape-shifting abilities of the Monkey King." To some degree, the writing process seems to be his "unconscious trying to work something out" (Yang 2008). Thus the issue of transformation emerges as the key that gives *American Born Chinese* thematic and structural unity, "although transformative acts are not always in the right direction for Yang's characters" (Fu 275).

Yang's book begins with the Monkey King's recognition of himself as a monkey and the consequent transformative actions he takes on in order to change his reality and to alter his identity. The Monkey King, however, cannot escape his monkey identity despite his attempts at transformation, his exceptional skills in kung fu, his mastery of the Four Major Heavenly Disciplines, and his sovereign rule over thousands of loyal subjects on the Flower-Fruit Mountain. One day he waits with eager anticipation to join a deity dinner party in heaven only to be denied entrance because he is a monkey and because he walks without shoes. The Monkey King's "other" nature is exemplified by his lack of footwear. Yang portrays this dramatic moment in effective visual narrative as well as dialogue. Side by side with the Monkey King's boasts about his various deity-like qualities on page 14, the close-up of the bare monkey feet in the upper left panel of the same page clearly indicates his "problem." As the guard emphasizes: "Look. You may be a king—you may even be a deity—but you are still a monkey" (fig. 11.2). In these panels the Monkey King's argumentative gesture is posed in contrast to the guard's smiling face, other deities' snickers, and the exaggerated capitalized font of "HA, HA," emphasizing the fact that other characters do not take him seriously and his defense is futile. Feeling thoroughly embarrassed and enraged, the Monkey King storms across heaven, beats up deities and guards, and destroys the dinner party before returning to Flower-Fruit Mountain, dejected. In an attempt to remedy his humiliation from the deity party and his monkey identity, the Monkey King not only decides to wear shoes after that but also orders all his subjects to follow his lead. After spending his days training and nights meditating, he adopts the title of "The Great Sage, Equal of Heaven" and officially declares: "I am not a monkey" (62). Before this transformation from monkey to "more-than-monkey," the Monkey King is portrayed as visibly shorter than the deities and guards in heaven. Afterward, however, in the panels he appears more human-like, not only wearing shoes but also much taller than his subjects. Then the Monkey King makes an effort to introduce his newly adopted

Figure 11.2. From *American Born Chinese* 14–15. Copyright © Gene Luen Yang, 2006. Reprinted with the permission of First Second Books, an imprint of Roaring Brook Press, a division of Holtzbrinck Publishing Holdings Limited Partnership.

Figure 11.2. (*Continued*)

identity to others by force and consequently causes tremendous chaos in heaven. As a result, he is confined under a mountain of rocks with a seal that prevents him from utilizing his martial skills. He does not gain freedom again until five hundred years later when—although pride makes him nearly lose his only chance for escape—he finally makes peace with his monkey identity and embarks on a pilgrimage to the West as one of Wong Lai-Tsao's disciples. After completing the journey successfully, the Monkey King achieves Buddhahood.

Yang developed his interest in the Monkey King shortly after he started creating comics, but he also realized that this character had been particularly popular among many comic artists who had already created composite images of this character.[13] Eventually, Yang decided to give his story an Asian American spin by reimagining the Monkey King as a character struggling with self-doubt, propelling him to use his transforming abilities as a coping mechanism. The author perceives the Monkey King's struggle as "a stand-in for Asian Americans and anyone else who has been on the minority side of a minority-majority dynamic" (Yang 2008). The exclusion that the Monkey King receives from deity hierarchy in heaven and his ability to transform into different shapes metaphorically echoes the difficulties that Yang's second protagonist, Jin Wang, encounters at school as well as his attempts to solve his identity problem.

Just like the Monkey King, Jin has to figure out how to come to terms with his American-born-Chinese identity, how to face racial stereotypes at school, how to make friends, and how to avoid such labels as "chink" and "geek." Told in a first-person narrative, the story of Jin begins to unfold in the second chapter of *American Born Chinese*. Son of an engineer father and a librarian mother who are both immigrants from China, Jin finds that his life takes a dramatic turn after his family moves out of Chinatown into a predominantly Caucasian neighborhood. The very first morning, though well intentioned, his teacher mispronounces his name, mis-identifies his origin, and promotes stereotypes about people of Chinese heritage. Not surprisingly, from his first day at Mayflower Elementary School (a deliberate reference to the English pilgrim settlement in Massachusetts in 1620 that calls for the reader's attention to the United States' immigration history), Jin is teased and tormented by other children because of his differences. Things go further downhill in seventh grade when he falls in love with a Caucasian classmate, Amelia Harris. Like the Monkey King, Jin strives to deny who he is and to assimilate as much as possible, so much so that he actually becomes a different person. Yang uses one large panel that occupies the whole page to portray Jin's transformation. Incorporating the written character *bian* in traditional Chinese (meaning "to change," "to transform") and the Chinatown herbalist's wife—a character introduced earlier in the book—as part of the visual representation, the panel portrays Jin's transforming process from a yellow-skinned and black-haired boy to a fair-skinned and blonde teenager (fig. 11.3). The character's facial features change from an expression of confusion and sadness to that of surprise. The question, "Now what would you like to become," included in a dialogue balloon speaks of Jin's mentality. At the time, however, he does not realize the risk of taking on the role of a transformer, turning himself into an all-American boy and adopting the new name of Danny.

When Jin's family lived in an apartment near San Francisco's Chinatown, Jin would wait in the front room while his mother visited the herbalist, and he often talked to the herbalist's wife while she figured sums on her abacus. One day, upon hearing Jin's desire to become a transformer, the herbalist's wife revealed a "secret" to the young boy: "It's easy to become anything you wish . . . so long as you're willing to forfeit your soul" (29). Her image and the "click, clack" sound of the abacus incorporated into Jin-turning-into-Danny transforming process reminds the reader of her warning. Just as wearing shoes and creating a new title do not help the Monkey King deny his monkey identity, the all-American appearance and new name do not solve Jin/Danny's problem.

Starting in eighth grade, Danny's Chinese cousin Chin-Kee, a reminder of Danny's Chinese heritage, comes to visit and attends school with him each year. Portrayed as a racial stereotype composite, Chin-Kee has slanted eyes and buckteeth and wears a pigtail hairstyle, Chinese shirt, and cloth shoes; his luggage resembles

Figure 11.3. From *American Born Chinese* 194. Copyright © Gene Luen Yang 2006. Reprinted with the permission of First Second Books, an imprint of Roaring Brook Press, a division of Holtzbrinck Publishing Holdings Limited Partnership.

containers of Chinese takeout food (fig. 11.4). Yang uses a series of "HA HA" and "CLAP CLAP" at the bottom border of the page to highlight the humorous effect of Chin-Kee. This establishing image leads the way to many other panels portraying Chin-Kee's appearance, manners, and actions. Attaching humor to Chin-Kee's character and behavior, Yang plays with the discomfort associated with indulging stereotypes by making Chin-Kee hilarious through exaggeration and deliberate reference to the commonly recognizable racial stereotypes, including those rooted in immigration history from the nineteenth century and more recent examples such as Asian Americans being the model minority particularly with regard to their academic success. When he follows Danny to school, Chin-Kee speaks Pidgin English, eats crispy fried cat gizzards with noodles for lunch, and knows all the academic subjects well; everything about Chin-Kee embarrasses Danny. When the conflict between the cousins escalates toward the end of the book, Chin-Kee and Danny get

Figure 11.4. From *American Born Chinese* 48. Copyright © Gene Luen Yang 2006.
Reprinted with the permission of First Second Books, an imprint of Roaring Brook Press,
a division of Holtzbrinck Publishing Holdings Limited Partnership.

into a fight with each other, ending with Danny beheading Chin-Kee. Chin-Kee attacks with "Mongorian foot in face," "Sooshu fist," "Kung pao attack," "Twice cook palm," "Happy family head bonk," "General Tsao rooster punch," "House special kick in hards," "Peking stike," "Three flavor essence," "Hot and sour wet willy," and "Pimp srap, Hunan style," all of which refer to Chinese food familiar to Americans. Purposefully linking Chin-Kee's moves to food items downplays the implication of violence in these action scenes and more importantly encourages the reader to reconsider racial stereotypes and misconceptions.

By adopting the commonly recognizable racial stereotypes in portraying the character Chin-Kee, Yang unavoidably runs the risk of partaking in the creation of "a new, "alternative" Orientalism" (Ma 95). Chinese American scholar Sheng-mei Ma has criticized Amy Tan and Gretchen Schields's picture book, *The Chinese Siamese Cat* (1994), as an example of racial essentialism that features a mystical landscape filled with Chinoiserie and ethnic stereotypes: "For someone like Tan whose cultural arsenal in launching an oppositional discourse against Orientalism is circumscribed by her American identity, she is bound to duplicate Orientalist practices as often as she repudiates them" (Ma 110). Ma's remarks are arguably applicable to Yang as well who is also of Chinese heritage and American born. Thus, the question arises: in presenting the character of Chin-Kee as a caricature is Yang guilty of reinforcing Orientalist stereotypes in the field of young adult literature?

Presenting the young character Jin's coming of age in a graphic novel, Yang's book lends itself readily to the study of race, ethnicity, and popular culture. Because parts of *American Born Chinese* were originally published as a mini-comic and a web-comic whose audiences are relatively small and usually are made up of seasoned comics readers, Yang did not concern himself about possible misunderstanding and criticism of his portrayal of Chin-Kee, whose beheading happens at a crucial, dramatic moment as the story moves to its closure. Reflecting on this character and the racial stereotypes that he has represented after the publication of *American Born Chinese*, Yang comments: "For me, Chin-Kee was an exorcism of sorts. He was my chance to gather many of the little pains, annoyances, and embarrassments I experienced as a child; put them into a single character; and behead him" (Yang 2008).

In the book Chin-Kee serves as Danny's conscience and a signpost to his soul. Yang uses this provocative character not only to criticize racism with a sense of humor but also to make a connection between history and reality. Historically, political cartoons and graphic propaganda in the United States employed racist depictions of Asians and Asian Americans. Chin-Kee's buckteeth, slit eyes, and pigtail cannot help but remind the reader of the derogatory comic images of Chinese and Chinese Americans in nineteenth-century America; not to mention the fact that his name is obviously a play on the racist term "chinky." Chin-Kee's appearance also bears traces from the detective comics in the 1930s when Fu Manchu–like characters represented the Chinese, and by extension, all Asian American men.[14] In the realm of Asian American children's literature, many writers and artists have been working in their own ways to "replace the stereotypical depictions of the Asians and Asian Americans that children know best, as in what used to pass for Asian American literature" (de Manuel and Davis viii). As an Asian American writer for young adults, Yang exorcises old myths by telling the story of Chin-Kee and reminding the reader of these long-lived racial stereotypes. As Yang's publisher has pointed out:

> There is nothing frivolous about the use of the character Chin-Kee. Gene Yang knew very well—better than most, perhaps—what he was invoking with Chin-Kee. Part of what makes *American Born Chinese* such a persuasive portrait of racism—both external and internalized—is the balance it strikes between the quiet, "socially acceptable" faces of racism, and the hidden truth—the figure that's too embarrassing and too upsetting for most folks to want to look at directly or talk about. Chin-Kee is that figure. And we have to talk about him. (First Second Books)

Yang's usage of easily identified racist images therefore can be viewed as challenging the common misconceptions of Chinese and Chinese Americans that proliferate in both historical and contemporary discourse in the United States. As children's literature author Laurence Yep has stated, it is the interplay between dreams and America's peculiar effect upon dreamers that has defined the Chinese American experience (157). Yang's creation of Chin-Kee stands the enduring images of the "Heathen Chinee" and the Chinaman on their heads and provides criticism in visual as well as textual representations. In *American Born Chinese*, the story climaxes at Chin-Kee's beheading and the revelation that he is actually the Monkey King in a new shape. Embedded in the two-in-one duality of the Monkey King and Chin-Kee is Yang's criticism of the "inherent inferiority" and "inherent distortion" of the Orientalist representations of Chinese Americans.[15]

Ethnic children's literature is "a particularly intense site of ideological and political contest, for various groups of adults struggle over which versions of ethnic identity will become institutionalized in school, home, and library settings; groups and individuals often advance specific reading and purchasing guidelines (Smith 3). Identity pursuit becomes especially pressing in the particular case of Asian American children who are caught in "a triple bind: pressured to remain faithful to ancestral heritage, while at the same time admonished to assimilate and become fully American, but ultimately finding that because of their Asian genes, many Americans will never give them full acceptance" (de Manuel and Davis vi–vii). In order to fully comprehend the challenges facing writers and scholars in Asian American children's literature, it is worth noting some of the specific historical circumstances faced by Chinese Americans in particular and Asian Americans in general in terms of restrictive immigration laws and the racism such legislation implied. The nineteenth-century anti-Chinese hysteria led to the 1882 Chinese Exclusion Act that barred the entry of Chinese to the United States. The act's amendments and other related laws and regulations continued to reinforce anti-Chinese sentiment and restrictions for decades.[16] Pointing out that children's literature has reinforced the perception of Asian Americans as foreigners for generations of Americans, Sandra S. Yamate provides a survey of the history, status, recurring themes, exemplary authors, and texts of Asian American children's literature, as well as teaching strategies and resources (95–128). According to Yamate, by the late 1990s there were still far too few Asian American children's books being published, although the depth and breadth of those that were available had begun to play a significant role in representing the multicultural reality of contemporary American life (98). On the one hand, Asian American children's literature needs to be read "as a multilayered and nuanced attempt to establish the place of Asian American writers for children in American culture, and to creatively engage their marginal positioning." On the other hand, "in-depth criticism and interpretation of the field as a whole is rare" (de Manuel and Davis vi–ix). *The Lion and the Unicorn* special issue on Asian American Children's Literature (2006) was the first critical volume focusing specifically on Asian American writers and works for children.

By presenting a story in the graphic novel format, *American Born Chinese* plays a significant role in recasting the values of this particular generic category.[17]

Historically speaking, political and editorial cartoons recognized Chinese and Chinese Americans as "benign and non-competitive" at the early stage of Chinese immigration when cheap laborers benefited the booming American economy. When anti-Chinese sentiment intensified, the drawings published in magazines and newspapers (for example: *Harper's Weekly*, *The Wasp*, and *Puck*) became useful venues for political satire and generally portrayed Chinese as "caricatures representing 'ugly' and 'irrepressible' heathens" (Choy, Dong, and Hom 21). Such images not only reflect the hostility and tension during the era of exclusion but also helped build up decidedly negative stereotypes of Chinese Americans, and by extension, of Asian Americans in general.

Emerging as a "distinct entertainment medium" in the 1930s, comic books continued to recycle racist stereotypes and to incorporate political propaganda, including strikingly racist portraits of Japanese, Koreans, and Vietnamese in comic books published during World War II and the Korean and Vietnam wars (Wright xiii). When the graphic novel emerged as a popular form in the 1970s, its creators borrowed many conventions from serial comics.[18] While the extreme racism of comics published earlier in the twentieth century is no longer common, until 2006 graphic novels featuring non-Caucasian characters were still rare in the United States (Crawford 240).

Even though the past three decades have witnessed a remarkable increase in its publication, influence, and classroom adoption, the graphic novel lacks a commonly agreed-upon definition, and its legitimacy as serious literature is still under debate. Yang likes to draw and to tell stories, and because comics contain both visual and textual components, he calls them "the most intimate medium" (Cart 43). According to Andy Runton, award-winning author of the *Owly* series, good graphic novels are child friendly because the stories "are essentially wordless" and "give the early readers who can enjoy them 'a sense of accomplishment'" (qtd. in Cart 43).[19] Like many other ethnic children's texts, *American Born Chinese* combines folklore, oral tradition, school knowledge, and personal experiences in structuring its narrative and visual presentation. Not only does the book reflect a common cultural experience for Chinese-American youth, but it also tackles themes that have universal appeal to young adults. "In the new generation of Asian American young adult fiction, heralded by writers like Gene Luen Yang, David Yoo, An Na and Tanuja Desai Hidier, the ethnic identity of many protagonists takes a back seat to typical American teen preoccupations such as social cliques, dating and college" (Macabasco 37). In many respects the character Jin's struggle is that of a typical teenager, regardless of his or her ethnic and cultural background. His shyness and clumsiness in front of his love interest, Amelia, and his joy when she agrees to hang out with him, for example, resonate with many young adult readers. His problem of establishing a relationship with a girl may have as much to do with his "geek" status as his bicultural heritage.

In his use of colorful comic panels to reimagine the traditional tale of the Monkey King with a contemporary American spin, Yang presents a powerful narrative enriched by visual representation and cultural complexity. In 1998 Peter E. Morgan, who teaches young adult literature at the State University of West Georgia, wrote: "There are disturbingly few multicultural texts and even fewer Asian American texts written specifically to serve the young adult market" (18). Yang's work helps fill this gap by providing a visualized text whose main characters may be Chinese American but whose central theme appeals to young adults of various cultural backgrounds. Like many other titles from First Second Books, *American Born Chinese* was targeted to young readers but may appeal to readers of all ages (Bickers 62). The publisher states that although primarily intended for young adults, *American Born Chinese*'s themes of alienation and self-acceptance are so universal that it is hard to identify a target audience *per se* (First Second Books). Yang has reconfigured the genre of the graphic novel and its connection to children's and young adult literature by introducing complex Chinese American characters and themes. On the question of readership, Yang has noted: "I tell people I think *American Born Chinese* is for high school and up, or junior high in moderated settings" mainly because younger children may not fully understand the Chin-Kee character or understand him in the wrong way (Yang 2008).

The toy transformer that Jin plays with at the beginning of the story points to the connections between the dual identities of Jin/Danny and the Monkey King/Chin-Kee as well as the story lines of the characters' multiple transformations. In the end, it is his master Wong Lai-Tsao who tells the Monkey King that "[to] find your true identity . . . within the will of Tze-Yo-Tzuh . . . is the highest of all freedoms" (Yang 2006, 149). The Monkey King finally accepts the fact of being a monkey and accompanies his master "on his journey to the west and served him faithfully," leaving his shoes behind (Yang 2006, 160). After completing the journey, the Monkey King stands in the holy presence of Tze-Yo-Tzuh and becomes one of his emissaries. Similarly after many failed attempts to hide his racial difference in order to blend into the Caucasian student body, Jin eventually understands his position as well. Chin-Kee's annual visit has caused great agony for Danny. After the embarrassing week or two of having Chin-Kee by his side everywhere, Danny has to transfer to another school in order to get away from his identity as Chin-Kee's cousin. Yang's book does not reveal until the end that cousin Chin-Kee is actually the Monkey King in a different shape; his visit is a reminder of Danny's cultural roots and a signpost to finding the youth's lost soul. It is the Monkey King who tells Jin that "I would have saved myself from five hundred years' imprisonment beneath a mountain of rock had I only realized how good it is to be a monkey" (Yang 2006, 223). The book closes with Chin-Kee and Danny transforming back to their original selves, the Monkey King and Jin, respectively (fig. 11.5). As the panels on pages 212-13 show, after Danny beheads Chin-Kee with a punch on the face, the character Chin-Kee changes shape and height from a human to a monkey and reveals his true form—the Monkey King. In the top panel on the next page Danny turns from being curly-blonde-haired with eyes in light hues to having flat black hair and dark eyes. Such an ending indicates the hope that the characters may finally make peace with their true identities.

The success of *American Born Chinese*, to some degree, answers the question: "Can graphic novels—and all young adult literature, really—nurture thought, passion, and understanding within our young people" (Yang 2007, 13). Many librarians and teachers have enthusiastically embraced Yang's message about why graphic novels belong in libraries and classrooms (Yang 2007, 11).[20] According to Yang himself, graphic novels are particularly useful for young adults because comic arts combine two divergent forms—pictures and text—that echo the converging media of the Internet and the digital technology that children grow up with nowadays (Engberg 75). Yang has presented *American Born Chinese* to young adults as well as to other readers with an invitation to rethink the implications of children's literature within the context of identity formation and transnational mythology.

Figure 11.5. From *American Born Chinese* 213–14. Copyright © Gene Luen Yang 2006. Reprinted with the permission of First Second Books, an imprint of Roaring Brook Press, a division of Holtzbrinck Publishing Holdings Limited Partnership.

Figure 11.5. (*Continued*)

NOTES

1. Acknowledgement: I thank First Second Books and Gene Luen Yang for responding to my questions and am very grateful for Gina Gagliano from First Second Books for her help in obtaining copyright permission and getting responses from the publisher and Gene Yang.

2. In Andre Lefevere's study, *Translation, Rewriting, and the Manipulation of Literary Fame* (1992), rewriting comes in many forms and plays a crucial role in addressing the issues of power, ideology, institution, and manipulation.

3. There has not been a commonly agreed definition of the graphic novel, even though the past few decades have witnessed a remarkable increase in its publication and cultural influence. The term "graphic novel," coined by Richard Kyle in 1964 to refer to comic books in general, has been used to "designate publications that differed from comic books only in number of pages and thickness of cover stock" (Harvey 116). I use the term "graphic novel" to refer to both fictional and nonfictional accounts published in the form of book-length comics.

4. *American Born Chinese* has won the Eisner Award for Best Graphic Album, the Reuben Award for Best Graphic Novel, and Chinese American Librarians Association Best

Book Award. It is *Publishers Weekly* Best Book of the Year, *School Library Journal* Best Book of the Year, the *Booklist* Editors' Choice Book, the *San Francisco Chronicle* Best Book of the Year, and Library Media Editor's Choice for 2007.

5. A few such examples include the *Publishers Weekly's* review, "American Born Chinese," on June 12, 2006; Jesse Karp's review for the *Booklist* on September 1, 2006; the *School Library Journal's* review, "American Born Chinese," in fall 2006; Shelley Glantz's review for the *Library Media Connection* in January 2007; the *Current Events's* review, "Beyond Words," on February 5, 2007; and Michele Gorman's review for the February 2007 issue of the *Teacher Librarian*. Overall, these reviewers applauded Yang's book for its clean artistic style, its compelling story line, and its universal appeal to young adult readers.

6. In his interview with Rick Margolis in 2006, Yang talked about some of these common themes as the reason that he abandoned the original plan of writing three separate books and produced one unified work instead (Margolis 41).

7. The other three are *Sanguo yanyi* (The Romance of the Three Kingdoms, Luo Guanzhong, fourteenth century), *Shuihu zhuan* (The Water Margin, Shi Nai'an, seventeenth century), and *Hong lou meng* (The Dream of the Red Chamber, Cao Xueqin, eighteenth century).

8. In his book *The Classic Chinese Novel: A Critical Introduction* (1968), C. T. Hsia provides a brief overview of the scholarly study on the authorship and historical basis of *The Journey to the West* as well as the evolution of the basic story line in different texts before the novel came into being (116–25).

9. Anthony C. Yu provides a brief overview of Xuanzang's experience as well as the historical and literary texts regarding his trip to India in the introduction to his four-volume translation of the novel *The Journey to the West* (1–13).

10. Many scholars have studied the possible origins and models of the character Monkey in *The Journey to the West*. Hu Shi, a renowned Chinese scholar in the early twentieth century, for instance, suggested Hanuman from the Indian epic *The Ramayana* as the prototype of the Chinese Monkey King (1923/1988, 2:902–04). His study of *The Journey to the West* is influential. Whalen Lai's article that traces Monkey's background to a combination of a mythic battle, a medieval Buddhist saint, a folk Zen parody, and an ancient tradition about the Chinese Titans (29–65) and Meir Shahar's study of the monkey lore of the Lingyin Monastery in Hangzhou, China (193–224) are two examples of recent scholarly exploration.

11. In China besides the many different editions of the novel *The Journey to the West*, there have been adaptations of the story in serial picture books, comics, television series, stage plays, animation, and other forms. Monkey's name remains well known in almost every Chinese household today. In English, Arthur Waley's abridged translation, *Monkey, Folk Novel of China* (1943), is widely known and read. Waley's version includes chapters 1–15, 18–19, 22, 37–39, 44–49, and 98–100 of the classic Chinese novel. Anthony C. Yu's four-volume translation, *The Journey to the West* (1977), is the first fully translated text of the one hundred chapters. Both the 2001 two-part television miniseries, *The Lost Empire*, and the 2008 live-action feature film, *The Forbidden Kingdom*, are mixtures of fantasy and martial-arts adventure loosely based on the Chinese novel. All these sources have helped broaden the Monkey King's fame among English speakers.

12. These authors in general sanitize the story of the Monkey King in order for it to be appropriate for child audience and families: the religious aspects of the novel *The Journey to the West* are downplayed; the gothic description of monstrous creatures and bloody battles are eliminated; complicated and intertwined story lines are recast; the Monkey King stands out as the main character.

13. The list of comic books featuring the Monkey King is extensive, including: Hyun-Jong Choi's *Trickster King Monkey Comic* (1988), Chang Book Kiat's *The Birth of the Monkey King* (1999) and *Adventures of the Monkey King* (2006), Kevin Lau and Erik Ko's *XIN: Journey of the Monkey King* (2003), and Katsuya Terada's *The Monkey King* (2005).

14. In his speech at the Printz Award ceremony, Gene Yang said Chin-Kee's outfit, hairstyle, and facial features were inspired by the overtly racist imagery in the late 1800s and, in particular, by a political cartoon of "sanctioned discrimination and violence" against Chinese Americans in the early 1900s and the Fu Manchu–like characters in the detective comics (2007, 12–14).

15. Perry Nodelman uses these terms in analyzing Orientalism, colonialism, and children's literature (29–35).

16. Alexander Saxton's *The Indispensable Enemy: Labor and the Anti-Chinese Movement in California* (1971) and Jean Pfaelzer's *Driven Out: The Forgotten War against Chinese Americans* (2008) are useful sources on this subject.

17. The educational value of graphic novels is of particular significance for young adult readers, as many educators and librarians have noticed. For example, the *Young Adult Library Services Association* sponsored an event in 2002 called "Getting Graphic @ Your Library," which became the best-attended *American Library Association's* preconference of that year (Cart 43). Education professionals have recognized the usefulness of graphic novels and other media in teaching visual literacy, developing comprehension and thinking skills, and achieving the fundamental goal of education: "to teach effective communication" (Frey and Fisher 1).

18. Will Eisner's *A Contract with God and Other Tenement Stories* (1978) is commonly considered one of the first American graphic novels. Although Eisner did not invent the term "graphic novel," he has played a significant role in advocating for this genre and introducing it to a broad range of readers.

19. Andy Runton's *Owly* series won the 2005 Harvey Award for Best New Talent, the 2005 Ignatz Award for Promising New Talent, the 2006 Eisner Award for Best Publication for a Younger Audience, and the 2006 Ignatz Award for Best Series.

20. As an educator himself Gene Yang is an advocate for the educational uses of comics. He has served as a math and computer science teacher, an educational technologist, and the Director of Information Services at Bishop O'Dowd High School in Oakland, California. Yang started to explore the educational values of comics years before he published *American Born Chinese*. For example, when he was a substitute teacher he once drew out the algebra lessons in comics that his students loved; he later wrote his master's thesis on the educational uses of comics based on this experience (Engberg 75).

WORKS CITED

"*American Born Chinese.*" *Publishers Weekly* 253, no. 24 (June 12, 2006): 36–37.
"*American Born Chinese.*" *School Library Journal* 52 (Fall 2006): 66.
"Beyond Words." *Current Events* 106, no. 17 (February 5, 2007): 6.
Bickers, James. "The Young and the Graphic Novel." *Publishers Weekly* 254, no. 8 (February 19, 2007): 62–63.
Cart, Michael. "You Go, Graphic!" *Booklist* 103, no. 14 (March 15, 2007): 43.

Chen, Debby, and Wenhai Ma. *Monkey King Wreaks Havoc in Heaven*. Union City, CA: Pan Asian Publications, 2001.

———. *Tang Monk Disciples Monkey King*. Union City, CA: Pan Asian Publications, 2005.

Choy, Philip P., Lorraine Dong, and Marlon K. Hom, eds. *The Coming Man: 19th Century American Perceptions of the Chinese*. Seattle: U of Washington P, 1995.

Crawford, Philip Charles. "American Born Chinese." *School Library Journal* 52, no. 9 (September 2006): 240.

Davis, Grania. *The Monkey King: Legend of a Wise and Brave Leader*. Berkeley, CA: Dharma Publishing USA, 1998.

de Manuel, Dolores, and Rocío G. Davis. "Editor's Introduction: Critical Perspectives on Asian American Children's Literature." *The Lion and the Unicorn* 30, no. 2 (April 2006): v–xv.

Engberg, Gillian. "The *Booklist* Interview: Gene Luen Yang." *Booklist* 103, no. 13 (March 1, 2007): 75.

First Second Books. Email to the author. 9 December 2008.

Frey, Nancy, and Douglas Fisher, eds. *Teaching Visual Literacy: Using Comic Books, Graphic Novels, Anime, Cartoons, and More to Develop Comprehension and Thinking Skills*. Thousand Oaks, CA: Corwin Press-Sage Company, 2008.

Fu, Binbin. "American Born Chinese." *Multi-Ethnic Literature of the United States* 32, no. 3 (Fall 2007): 274–76.

Glantz, Shelley. "American Born Chinese." *Library Media Connection* 25, no. 4 (January 2007): 65.

Gorman, Michele. "Original Graphic Novels with an Asian Influence." *Teacher Librarian* 34, no. 3 (February 2007): 12.

Harvey, Robert C. *The Art of the Comic Book: An Aesthetic History*. Jackson: UP of Mississippi, 1996.

Hsia, C. T. "Journey to the West." *The Classical Chinese Novel: A Critical Introduction*. New York: Columbia UP, 1968. 115–64.

Hu Shi. "*Xi you ji kaozheng*" (Study of *The Journey to the West*). *Hu Shi gudian wenxue yanjiu lunji* (Collected Work on Classic Literature by Hu Shi). Shanghai: Shanghai guji chubanshe, 1988.

Karp, Jesse. "American Born Chinese." *Booklist* 103, no. 1 (September 1, 2006): 114.

Lai, Whalen. "From Protean Ape to Handsome Saint: The Monkey King." *Asian Folklore Studies* 53, no. 1 (1994): 29–65.

Lefevere, Andre. *Translation, Rewriting, and the Manipulation of Literary Fame*. London: Routledge, 1992.

Ma, Sheng-mei. "The Chinese Siamese Cat: Chinoiserie and Ethnic Stereotypes." *The Deathly Embrace: Orientalism and Asian American Identity*. Minneapolis: U of Minnesota P, 2000. 95–111.

Macabasco, Lisa Wong. "Teens First, Asian Americans Second." *Hyphen Asian America Unabridged* 13 (Winter 2007): 37–39.

Margolis, Rick. "*American Born Chinese*: Gene Yang's Remarkable Graphic Novel Grapples with Racial Prejudice." *School Library Journal* 52, no. 9 (September 2006): 41.

Morgan, Peter E. "A Bridge to Whose Future? Young Adult Literature and the Asian American Teenager." *The Alan Review* 25, no. 3 (Spring 1998): 18–20.

Nodelman, Perry. "The Other: Orientalism, Colonialism, and Children's Literature." *Children's Literature Association Quarterly* 17, no. 1 (Spring 1992): 29–35.

Shahar, Meir. "The Lingyin Si Monkey Disciples and the Origins of Sun Wukong."
     Harvard Journal of Asiatic Studies 52, no. 1 (1992): 193–224.
Smith, Katharine Capshaw. "Introduction: The Landscape of Ethnic American Children's
     Literature." *Multi-Ethnic Literature of the United States* 27, no. 2 (Summer 2002): 3–8.
Waley, Arthur, trans. *Monkey, Folk Novel of China*. New York: John Day, 1943; New York:
     Grove P/Evergreen, 1958.
Wright, Bradford W. *Comic Book Nation: The Transformation of Youth Culture in America*.
     Baltimore: The Johns Hopkins UP, 2001.
Yamate, Sandra S. "Asian Pacific American Children's Literature: Expanding Perceptions
     about Who Americans Are." In *Using Multiethnic Literature in the K-8 Classroom*,
     edited by Violet J. Harris, 95–128. Norwood, MA: Christopher-Gordon Publishers, 1997.
Yang, Gene Luen. *American Born Chinese*. New York: First Second Books, 2006.
———. Email to the author. 9 December 2008.
———. "Printz Award Winner Speech." *Young Adult Library Services* (Fall 2007): 11–13.
Yep, Laurence. "Paying with Shadows." *The Lion and the Unicorn* 30, no. 2 (April 2006):
     157–67.
Young, Ed. *Monkey King*. New York: HarperCollins Publishers, 2001.
Yu, Anthony C., trans. *The Journey to the West*. 4 vols. Chicago: U of Chicago P, 1977.

FURTHER READING

Carpenter, Carole H. "Enlisting Children's Literature in the Goals of Multiculturalism."
     Mosaic 29, no. 3 (September 1996): 53–73.
Carrier, David. *The Aesthetics of Comics*. University Park: Pennsylvania State UP, 2000.
Chinn, Mike. *Writing and Illustrating the Graphic Novel: Everything You Need to Know to
     Create Great Graphic Works*. Hauppauge, NY: Quarto Publishing, 2004.
Chiu, Monica. "The Cultural Production of Asian American Young Adults in the Novels
     of Maries G. Lee, An Na, and Doris Jones Young." *The Lion and the Unicorn* 30, no. 2
     (April 2006): 168–84.
Clark, Beverly Lyon. *Kiddie Lit: The Cultural Construction of Children's Literature in
     America*. Baltimore, MD: Johns Hopkins UP, 2003.
Cooksey, Thomas L. "Hero of the Margin: The Trickster as Deterritorialized Animal."
     Thalia: Studies in Literary Humor 18 (1998): 50–61.
Davis, Rocío G. *Begin Here: Reading Asian North American Autobiographies of Childhood*.
     Honolulu: U of Hawaii P, 2007.
de Jesús, Melinda L. "'Two's Company, Three's a Crowd?' Reading Interracial Romance in
     Contemporary Asian American Young Adult Fiction." *Lit: Literature Interpretation
     Theory* 12, no. 3 (2001): 313–34.
de Manuel, Dolores, and Rocío G. Davis, eds. "Special Issue: Asian American Children's
     Literature." *The Lion and the Unicorn* 30, no. 2 (April 2006).
Eisner, Will. *Comics and Sequential Art*. Tamarac, FL: Poorhouse P, 1985.
———. *Graphic Storytelling and Visual Narrative*. Paramus, NJ: Poorhouse Press, 1996.
Hatfield, Charles. *Alternative Comics: An Emerging Literature*. Jackson: UP of Mississippi,
     2005.
Howes, Craig. "Hawaii through Western Eyes: Orientalism and Historical Fiction for
     Children." *The Lion and the Unicorn* 11, no. 1 (1987): 68–87.

Hynes, William J., and Willian G. Doty, eds. *Mythical Trickster Figures: Contours, Contexts, and Criticisms.* Tuscaloosa: U of Alabama P, 1993.

Knowles, Liz, and Martha Smith. *Understanding Diversity through Novels and Picture Books.* Westport, CT: Libraries Unlimited, 2007.

Kruse, Ginny Moore, and Kathleen T. Horning. *Multicultural Literature for Children and Young Adults: A Selected Listing of Books, 1980–1990 by and about People of Color.* 3rd ed. Madison: Cooperative Children's Book Center, U of Wisconsin-Madison, Wisconsin Department of Public Instruction, 1991.

———. *Multicultural Literature for Children and Young Adults.* Vol. 2, *1991–1996: A Selected Listing of Books by and about People of Color.* 3rd ed. Madison: Cooperative Children's Book Center, the Friends of the CCBC, Inc., and U of Wisconsin-Madison, Wisconsin Department of Public Instruction, 1997.

Louie, Ai-Ling. "Growing up Asian American: A Look at Some Recent Young Adult Novels." *Journal of Youth Services* (Winter 1993): 115–27.

Lutgendorf, Philip. *Hanuman's Tale: The Messages of a Divine Monkey.* Oxford: Oxford UP, 2007.

MacCann, Donnarae. "Multicultural Books and Interdisciplinary Inquiries." *The Lion and the Unicorn* 16, no. 1 (1992): 43–56.

McCloud, Scott. Making Comics: *Storytelling Secrets of Comics, Manga and Graphic Novels.* New York: HarperCollins Publishers, 2006.

———. *Understanding Comics: The Invisible Art.* New York: HarperCollins Publishers, 2004.

"Monkey King: A Record of a Journey to the Western Paradise to Procure the Buddhist Scriptures for the Emperor of China." In *Asian American Folktales*, edited by Thomas A. Green, 38–44. Westport, CT: Greenwood Press, 2009.

Mower, Nancy Alpert. "Who Is the Other? That Is the Question: Orientalism Revisited." In *Re-Placing America: Conversations and Contestations: Selected Essays*, edited by Ruth Hsu, Cynthia Franklin, and Suzanne Kosanke, 122–30. Honolulu: College of Languages, Linguistic and Literature, University of Hawaii and the East-West Center, 2000.

Pearson, J. Stephen. "The Monkey King in the American Canon: Patricia Chao and Gerald Vizenor's Use of an Iconic Chinese Character." *Comparative Literature Studies* 43, no. 3 (2006): 355–74.

Pfaelzer, Jean. *Driven Out: The Forgotten War against Chinese Americans.* Berkeley: U of California P, 2008.

Said, Edward. *Orientalism.* New York: Vintage, 1978.

Saxton, Alexander. *The Indispensable Enemy: Labor and the Anti-Chinese Movement in California.* Berkeley: U of California P, 1971.

Smith, Katherine Capshaw, and Margaret R. Higonnet, eds. "Special Issue: Multi-Ethnic Children's Literature." *Multi-Ethnic Literature of the United States* 27, no. 2 (Summer 2002).

Varnum, Robin, and Christina T. Gibbons, eds. *The Language of Comics: Word and Image.* Jackson: UP of Mississippi, 2001.

Versaci, Rocco. *This Book Contains Graphic Language: Comics as Literature.* New York: Continuum, 2007.

PART III

READING HISTORY/ LEARNING RACE AND CLASS

FROGGY'S LITTLE BROTHER: NINETEENTH-CENTURY EVANGELICAL WRITING FOR CHILDREN AND THE POLITICS OF POVERTY

KIMBERLEY REYNOLDS

FROGGY's Little Brother *(1875), "the most touching story in the English language,"[1] was written by "Brenda," the pen name of Mrs. G(eorgina) Castle Smith (1845–1933). Little known today, in her lifetime this British writer produced many popular children's books.* Froggy *was her second novel, and its immediate success with critics and readers brought Brenda to national attention. Although she wrote twenty-three books over a career spanning fifty-nine years (her last book was published when she was eighty-seven), this sad story of two orphan brothers struggling to survive in Victorian London was the book for which she was remembered (Thiel 149). Throughout her life she received tributes from readers of every kind and station who were moved by* Froggy; *when she died,* The Times *carried a lengthy obituary, praising the way she pulled the nation's heartstrings in its pages.*

*Brenda wrote four other tales about the urban poor, including a sequel—*More About Froggy *(1914)—in which "Froggy" goes to sea and gets married; but most of her novels centered on the experiences of children who lived happy, middle-class lives doing everyday things such as playing in the park and going to the seaside (see Thiel on Brenda's domestic fiction). These stories offer illuminating vignettes of life in a Victorian household of a kind rarely found in more famous "adult" novels of the period.*

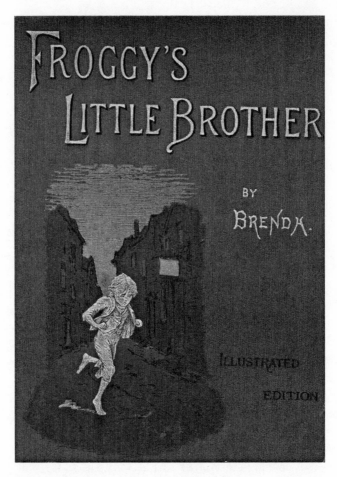

Figure 12.1. Cover of the illustrated edition published by John F. Shaw and Co (London c. 1887). The illustrator is not credited. All the images used in this chapter come from this edition.

STREET ARABS: STRANGERS IN OUR MIDST

Froggy's Little Brother belongs to a genre known as "street arab" fiction. In the nineteenth century, the term "street arab" was frequently used to describe the multitude of children who filled the streets of Britain's cities by day—and often slept on those streets at night. It is no exaggeration to call them a multitude: unlike our own time, when most developed countries have aging populations, during the nineteenth century, Britain saw a huge expansion in its numbers of children and young people, with nearly 40 percent of the total population being made up of children under the age of fourteen (Hopkins 161). The majority of these children lived in cities, and until legislation making education compulsory for all children between five and ten years of age came into being in 1880, they were often unsupervised; many also lacked parents or other caring adults and supported themselves as best they could, which was usually inadequately. It is two such children who Brenda places at the center of *Froggy's Little Brother.*

"Street arab" is a telling label, for it exposes a way of thinking about poor city children that refused to see them either as part of British society or as children (the rural poor were a different matter as they were associated with nature in ways that were entirely consonant with prevailing Romantic discourses of innocent childhood). It marked these street children as outcasts—beings of an entirely different order from the middle and upper classes who were reading about them—and gave rise to an attitude of "domestic orientalism" (Plotz 37), meaning that those in positions of power regularly made pronouncements about poor children that both described and inscribed them in culture in ways that were disempowering and justified their exploitation and neglect. "Domestic orientalism" is a term derived from the work of Edward Said, whose influential study *Orientalism* (1978) argued that the West legitimized its colonization and subjugation of the East through a set of false representations that figured Eastern cultures (and, indeed, all cultures colonized by westerners) and peoples as less developed culturally, physically, intellectually, and morally than those in the West. This view was given power through statements ranging from official documents to sensational articles in the popular press that held such attitudes to be true and self-evident when in fact they were constructions based on a particular view of the world. In the same way, nineteenth-century discourses around the poor in Britain (hence "domestic" orientalism) were symptomatic of a middle- and upper-class mind-set that denied—or failed to recognize—any value to the way the working classes lived and constructed them as beings of a lower order.

It was against this background that Brenda wrote *Froggy's Little Brother.* To evaluate her achievement, and particularly the extent to which she either transcended or perpetuated such colonizing discourses, it is helpful to make use of insights gained from postcolonial theory. Having established that like colonizers abroad, the upper classes justified their behavior toward the poor by designating them inferior and in need of regimes of discipline and education intended to be "civilizing," it follows that other central ideas and approaches from postcolonial theory can fruitfully be applied to a discussion of street children and fiction about them. For example, they alert us to the assumption by those in authority that they have the right to speak for and about all, and so impose a language and way of thinking about themselves on other parts of society. Postcolonial theorists also point to the need to examine issues and information that have been pushed into the background or erased from writing about the colonized, so when reading about street children it will be necessary to look for aspects of life in the poor parts of Britain's cities that are muted or rendered invisible. Beyond identifying mechanisms of repression, postcolonial critics focus on aspects of resistance and change, both as they find expression in writing and - particularly important with regard to a text such as *Froggy's Little Brother*, which was written from a middle-class perspective—in the way it was read.[2] *Froggy* had a readership that spanned social classes and ages; perhaps unsurprisingly, while contemporary middle-class readers of the *Times* found Brenda's story to be "full of pathos and truth," (qtd. in Lennox-Boyd 120), the poor and those outside cities were more mixed in their responses. Charlotte Mary Yonge read *Froggy* to some village children in Hampshire and found their reactions varied markedly from class to class (qtd. in Lennox-Boyd 120).

To read *Froggy's Little Brother* from a postcolonial perspective and to understand it as part of a larger discourse about Britain's poor children, it is necessary to look in some detail at the way street children were written about and constructed in Victorian society. The Member of Parliament and reformer Lord Shaftesbury, who did much to help children living in poverty, not only coined the phrase "street arab" but also provided one of the most graphic descriptions of the real children about whom it was used:

> Everyone who walks the streets of the metropolis must daily observe several members of the tribe [of street arabs], bold, pert, and dirty as London sparrows, but pale, feeble, and sadly inferior to them in plumpness of outline. . . . Many are spanning the gutters with their legs and dabbling with earnestness in the latest accumulation of nastiness; while others, in squalid and half-naked groups, squat about at the entrance of the narrow, foetid courts and alleys that lie concealed behind the deceptive frontages of our larger thoroughfares. Whitechapel and Spitelfields [sic] teem with them like an ant's nest; but it is in Lambeth and Westminster that we find the most flagrant traces of their swarming activity. There the foul and dismal passages are thronged with children of both sexes, and from the age of three to thirteen. Through want and hazard, they are singularly vivacious and engaged in every sort of occupation but that which would be beneficial to themselves and creditable to the neighbourhood. The matted hair, the disgusting filth that renders necessary a closer inspection before flesh can be discerned between the rags which hang about them, and the barbarian freedom from all superintendence and restraint, fill the mind of a novice of these things with perplexity and dismay. (qtd. in Plotz 34)

This account is striking—and a prime example of domestic orientalism at work—for the way it treats its subjects as if they were less than human: the children are compared to birds, insects and, in their half-naked state, implicitly to savages (at the time considered less evolved than "civilized" races such as the British). They roam the same fetid spaces and rubbish heaps as vermin or dogs, and in their "barbarian freedom" are the antithesis of the ideal of Victorian middle-class childhood, safely secured in the routines of the nursery, seen but not heard. While at one level Shaftesbury was undoubtedly using this imagery to shock readers into realizing that in their own time children in Britain were living in this way, the extent to which the children he describes are dehumanized is telling.

Street children belonged to a world that would have been unknown to most of Brenda's readers; despite the fact that such youngsters were regularly working, playing and running amok around the city, they lived in places that members of the middle classes only ventured into when doing charitable work of the kind Lord Shaftesbury himself was known for—in his case trying to improve the living and working conditions of poor children and attempting to educate them so that they could support themselves in such socially approved ways as learning a trade, running errands, or selling goods/offering services on the street. As with Brenda, it is necessary to ask how far his efforts grew from the recognition that the poor were only "other" as a consequence of their circumstances and how far he regarded them as inferiors who needed to be educated to give them at least some semblance of civilization and make their presence tolerable for the rest of society. Either way, his description reflects the sense that there was a separate territory inhabited by primitive hordes that infused Victorian social discourse. The journalist Henry Mayhew captures this attitude perfectly in the sensational opening sections of *London Labour and the London Poor* (1861),[3] a series of interviews with and reflections on the lives and beliefs of the London poor that makes the underlying attitudes and power structures of colonialism in the relations between rich and poor unmistakable. Mayhew compares his forays into the slums of London to travels among primitive people in a foreign land. Like Dante he is reporting back from an underworld; like David Livingstone ("discovered" by Henry Stanley just four years before *Froggy* was published), he is exploring a dark continent, though one located in the very capital of England. He explains the existence of these tribes using the following analogy:

> . . . we, like the Kafirs, Fellahs, and Finns, are surrounded by wandering hordes—
> the "Sonquas" and the "Fingoes"of this country—paupers, beggars, and outcasts,
> possessing nothing but what they acquire by depredation from the industrious,
> provident, and civilized portion of the community;—that the heads of these
> nomads are remarkable for the greater development of the jaws and cheekbones
> rather than those of the head;—and that they have a secret language of their
> own—an English *"cuze-cat"* or "slang" as it is called—for the concealment of
> their designs: these are points of coincidence so striking that, when placed before
> the mind, make us marvel that the analogy should have remained thus long
> unnoticed. (2)

Mayhew goes on to devise a taxonomy of these "others" who live amongst the English that comprises six groups: I. Street-sellers; II. Street-buyers; III. Street-Finders; IV. Street-Performers, Artists, and Showmen (this being the group to which Froggy's family initially belongs); V. Street-Artizans, or Working Pedlars, and VI. Street-Labourers. Among the many shortcomings of the slum-dwellers Mayhew notes are their "repugnance to regular and continuous labour," "want of providence," "inability to perceive consequences," "passion for stupefying herbs and roots, and, when possible, for intoxicating fermented liquors," "immoderate love of gaming," "absence of chastity among [the] women," and "vague sense of religion, rude idea of a Creator, and utter absence of all appreciation of the mercy of the Divine Spirit" (2). The best he can say of them is that they have "extraordinary powers of enduring privation" and a "comparative insensibility to pain" (2). In other words, the poor not only represent the antithesis of respectable Victorian bourgeois values but are seen as congenitally inclined to degenerate behavior.

STREET ARAB FICTION: THE POLITICS
OF POVERTY

Mayhew's diatribe is typical of a widely held view of the poor that regarded their problems as largely of their own making and assumed that they lacked the resolution to help themselves in the way advocated by prominent Victorians such as Samuel Smiles, writer and reformer whose influential book *Self-Help* (1859) embodied the middle-class Victorian ethic of personal responsibility. Responsibility was closely associated with a model and rhetoric of respectability that, particularly in relation to the poor, celebrated characteristics such as honesty, temperance, hard work, steadiness, self-improvement, self-discipline, sexual control, cleanliness, duty, and acceptance of one's social position. Much of the thinking about and energy in promoting respectability came from the evangelical side of the Anglican Church, and so in the public mind there was a strong correlation between behaving "respectably" and being "saved," which meant living in a way that prepared you for a better time in the next life. However, this should not disguise the fact that these are all attributes that make individuals easy to govern, and so much of the support for working-class respectability came from those in positions of authority who, consciously or not, found it a useful form of social control. There is considerable evidence (Thompson 1988; Huggins 2000; Dawson 2007) that the middle and, particularly, the upper classes defined respectability more strictly for the lower orders than they did for themselves.

Against this background, in *Froggy's Little Brother*, Brenda had to navigate the waters of public opinion very carefully. On the one hand, she needed to establish that her impoverished characters are in extremis, and on the other, she needed to make them sympathetic, which meant establishing their respectability. Describing with accuracy the degrading circumstances in which orphans like Froggy and Benny lived risked alienating readers by evoking images such as Shaftesbury's and Mayhew's, so throughout she focuses on such things as the thinness of the boys' clothes rather than the fact that they had no way to wash them, and emphasizes the virtues of the poor while passing lightly over ubiquitous problems such as drunkenness, violence, and prostitution—precisely the debauched spectrum of behavior that the code of respectability was designed to address. Where Shaftesbury notes the "disgusting filth" and inadequate rags of the children he encountered, she shows Froggy attempting to keep himself decent through washing his face and head in freezing water and mending his clothes. In contrast to the image of London's street children disseminated through the tropes of domestic orientalism, Froggy has, it seems, an inbuilt notion of propriety. Illustrators, including Brenda's husband, "Cas," who provided the pictures for the first edition of the novel, also attempted to convey this quality by depicting the boys in picturesquely torn clothing rather than filthy rags, their eager—and evidently clean—faces illuminated by light from the garret window.

Froggy is not the only honorable character in these fictional slums; readers are also called upon to admire acts of kindness and generosity among those who have virtually nothing to call their own. For instance, Mrs. Blunt, mother of the family that lives below the boys, helps them when she can, providing the odd candle so that five-year-old Benny does not have to wait alone in the darkness when Froggy is late, occasionally lending them money for breakfast, and keeping an eye on Benny when Froggy is out. Each time she makes such an intervention, the text reminds readers that her own life is a constant struggle: she has a drunken husband and six children, and she works as a charwoman as well as taking in washing. When Benny

CHAPTER IV.

Supperless.

Figure 12.2. Sparing readers' sensibilities, the illustrator sets the scene for a chapter titled "Supperless" with an image of the brothers eating a relatively substantial meal in the window that illuminates their cheerful stoicism and basic respectability.

is ill—presumably with the same infection that a few days earlier had killed his playmate Debs, Mrs. Blunt's youngest child—she immediately gives Froggy some fuel to make a little fire. The text identifies this as characteristic of "the generosity of her class." There follows one of the most frequently quoted passages from the book, in which Brenda simultaneously characterizes the poor as embodying Christian kindness and prompts her readers to recognize that they have it in their power to do much more for the needy and at less cost to themselves:

> How many beautiful lessons can we learn from the poor—for suffering nobly endured and heavy burdens bravely borne. . . . They show us how to be truly and greatly generous in their willingness to share the last crumb of comfort, whatever that may be, with a neighbour, kindly and ungrudgingly, without hope of return or reward. Theirs is not a generosity which costs them nothing—it often entails going without a meal or sitting by a fireless grate, but a self-sacrifice of some sort, *always*. It is of the highest and truest order, because the nearest to our great Pattern, whose generosity only reached its sublime perfection on the cross at Calvary. . . . We are not called upon to lay down our lives, but we *are* called upon to make very great sacrifices . . . for one another; and in the homes of the poor, I think, we see this answered as a rule more obediently and absolutely than anywhere else. (158)

This encomium to the poor makes explicit a key part of Brenda's agenda; *Froggy's Little Brother* not only presents the poor—and particularly poor children—as admirable people in difficult circumstances rather than as a barbarian race living wild in England's cities, but it also conveys a subtext reminding comfortably situated readers, identified here and throughout the novel as like the narrator through pronouns such as "we" and "our," that it behooved them to attend to the poor before the poor took matters into their own hands. This lesson is characteristic of street arab fiction, which by the time Brenda was writing in the 1870s had a clear set of conventions. Foremost among these are the focus on ragged urban children who endure privation, face and overcome temptation, and whose good behavior, often associated with love for and loyalty to a family member or friend, is finally rewarded when it is discovered by an enlightened philanthropist who is also usually a Christian. Street arab tales tend to have recent or contemporary settings, to be authentic in their depictions of the lives of the poor and to convey a strongly evangelical Christian message about salvation. They almost always feature a "good" child's deathbed scene in which the dying child is assured of being reunited with parents or other loved ones while those left behind find new beginnings that combine improved living conditions and confirmation of their faith in God and his servants in this world.[4]

Froggy's Little Brother makes use of all these conventions to underline the urgent need to attend to the poor. While the message in street arab novels is always couched in terms of Christian duty, it also contains a strong pragmatic element that acknowledges and seeks to address tensions between the classes. Works such as Friedrich Engels's *Condition of the Working Class in England* (1844) and influential exposés such as Mayhew's articles on London's poor and John Hollingshead's *Ragged London in 1861* (1861) had documented the extent to which the poor were living in overcrowded, unsanitary conditions—often in the most abject state of poverty. Unsurprisingly, fear of social unrest was both rife and justified. Through-out the middle decades of the century the working classes agitated for reform and change, most visibly through the efforts of the Chartists, who between 1839 and 1848 presented three petitions demanding working-class suffrage to parliament. All were rejected, but the unrest they represented was recognized as potentially leading to the kinds of civil disturbance—even revolution—that was sweeping across Europe at the time. While most slum-dwellers were unlikely to be involved in such orga-nized protests, the call to alleviate the suffering of the poor found in *Froggy's Little Brother* and other street arab tales can be understood as part of a general recogni-tion of the need to defuse this social time bomb as well as to underscore lessons about being a good Christian. It reflects Brenda's awareness that though some thirty years had passed since the first Chartist petition, the condition of the poor had not improved. The reminder that the poor needed help was not confined to Brenda's own class; in this novel even the Queen is implicitly criticized for turning a blind eye to the suffering of her subjects when she fails to answer the laboriously penned plea for help that "two little chaps wrote her from Shoreditch eight days ago" (135), as Froggy explains to the soldier outside of Buckingham Palace when he tramps there through the cold one day in the belief that the Queen would want to help. The soldier suggests the letter hasn't reached her and that they should try again, but though this offers an explanation for the Queen's silence, the fact that on his return Froggy finds Benny ill from the fever that kills him firmly links the Queen's inac-tivity to Benny's death.

The parlous state of the poor is established from the opening pages of the novel, which describe Froggy's home and way of life. He, his parents, and baby brother, Benny, live in "a very bare garret, at the top of a dark, dingy house, the upper part of which was scorched and blackened from the effects of a fire" (16). One of the ef-fects of the fire has been to damage all the glass in the windows, which Froggy's "careful mother," stops up with what rags she can spare, though even rags, the reader learns, "are precious things in some homes!" (4) Froggy's proper name is Tommy, but he has been nicknamed Froggy because living in these conditions he is often cold and ill and then makes a croaking sound. The family earns its living by performing Punch and Judy shows for wealthy children, and to do this all four—mother carrying Benny, father the show, and six-year-old Froggy on his own thin legs—tramp across London, whatever the weather.

Froggy's family is established as loving and hard-working; although somewhat idealized in their uncomplaining acceptance of the harsh conditions in which they live and well-mannered care for one another, Brenda's portrait of the way they live and the precarious nature of their existence reveals that she had done her research. In line with descriptions and evidence in the numerous reports and investigations into the lives of the poor that appeared in the course of the nineteenth century, Froggy's mother is shown to be the lynchpin of the family; she struggles to improve their lot and keep them "respectable." Despite her efforts, the long-term effects of poverty, exacerbated by the father's tendency to drink much of any day's profits on the way home—a common problem in the parts of London where they live—undermine her health. When she dies of a wasting disease brought about by years of deprivation, Froggy is gratified to learn that she has gone to a "Better Land," while her husband respects her last request and takes the pledge. When he is no longer using his earnings to buy alcohol, the little boys' lives improve: they go to church regularly and Froggy attends a night school similar to the kinds of schools for the poor that Lord Shaftesbury had set up. The combination of religious instruction and rudimentary education laid down in this interlude fortify Froggy in the hard months that come after his father is run over and killed in a street accident. The traumatic loss of both parents in the space of two chapters may today seem implausible, but working and existing on the streets as they did, such accidents among the poor were common and helped swell the numbers of unsupervised children who, like Froggy and Benny, subsisted as and how they could.

Even when he is being looked after by both parents, Froggy's old head on a child's body corresponds closely to the descriptions of street children contained in Henry Mayhew's interviews and similar accounts, further evidence that the author had studied her subject and was familiar with both the facts collected about the poor and the conventions for writing about them. For instance, Mayhew reports that one eight-year-old girl who sold watercress "had entirely lost all childish ways, and was, indeed, in thoughts and manner, a woman. There was" he continues, "something cruelly pathetic in hearing this infant, so young that her features had scarcely formed themselves, talking of the bitterest struggles of life, with the calm earnestness of one who had endured them all" (151). Similarly, the philanthropic entrepreneur who became known as "Doctor" Barnardo recalled being struck when meeting his first street arab, a boy of ten, by the fact that his face "was not that of a child. It had a careworn, old-mannish look, which was only relieved by the bright glances of his small sharp eyes" ("My First Arab," qtd. in Plotz 36). At a critical moment in the novel, when Froggy discovers he has unknowingly been involved with a gang of pickpockets and has to go home to Benny without the money they had expected him to earn, the novel dwells on the extent to which his struggles have prematurely aged him:

> Froggy was feeling something of that craving for deep rest, which is natural for old men and women to feel after they have been tossing on the waves of this troublesome world for a lifetime, but which is very sad to see in a child. Froggy was but eleven, and he should not have been feeling like an old, tired man. . . . London has nothing more sorrowful to show us . . . than its old children, with their shrewd, anxious faces, and knitted brows. (84)

This passage is another example of the careful way in which Brenda constructs Froggy's character. A romantic discourse of childhood as a time of delightful innocence had grown up around middle-class Victorian children, setting up carefree, charming, inexperienced children as "normal." This means the novel must establish that Froggy is still a child but one who is being denied his childhood because of his circumstances. It is vital that he does not seem to have ceased to be a child or deliberately sought out adult experiences, behavior that would render him abnormal and unnatural and so less sympathetic. In this passage, Froggy falls into an exhausted sleep in a doorway and dreams he is a child again, being looked after by loving parents with baby Benny asleep in his cot. In contrast, the ne'er-do-well Mac drinks, smokes, speaks roughly, and steals; by the end of the novel the fact that he is languishing in jail takes no account of his youthfulness or circumstances.

Keeping Froggy appealing and acceptably childlike requires Brenda to negotiate with great care the rhetoric that transformed the poor into savages, for it was grounded in the belief that poor children were precocious and experienced and so could be excluded from the category of "children."[5] Looking again at the passage by Lord Shaftesbury it is notable that even this man who did so much to improve the conditions of poor children never refers to them *as* children, and the delicacy of the operation is evident periodically when the carefully chosen spectacles that Brenda has placed on her readers appear to slip, revealing that though she has created

Figure 12.3. Worn out, Froggy dreams of his mother and happier times.

admirable, lovable individual characters, she is less sanguine about the massed poor. For instance, when Mac is (rightly) suspected of being involved in a robbery and the boys look out their garret window to see what is causing the commotion they can hear in the street, theirs is an oddly middle-class view of the neighborhood and their peers and playmates, who are described as "swarms of dirty little gutter-children" (106).

Significantly, the tendency to present the poor in a negative light becomes more frequent as the story is drawing to a close and readers are being restored to their own comfortable homes after their time among Brenda's fictional poor. When Benny gets ill, for example, he is compared to a "dumb animal" (141; 151), and describing his symptoms he tells Froggy, "I think I's got what the cab-horses has. . . . I's got the staggers, Froggy!" (141–42). Similarly, after Benny's death Froggy is taken into a small orphanage where he volunteers to look after another, younger child who has just been orphaned. The new boy, Billy, reminds Froggy of Benny, but the narrator compares him to the "marmozet monkeys in the Zoological Gardens" and describes his grave face as "truly comical" (193). Although such moments at first seem to be at odds with the rest of the book and to be buying into an orientalizing attitude toward the poor, they are in fact central to its success. If street arab fiction were to be a force for reform, it needed to employ highly emotive plotlines and narrative strategies. *Froggy* is a supreme example of this kind of writing; it is a "tear-jerker" of the highest order. However, books that end on too distressing a note risk undermining their goal, for a great outpouring of emotion tends to be cathartic, releasing all the pity and fear accumulated in the course of the novel. Catharsis can be enervating rather than a spur to action, encouraging readers to luxuriate in the knowledge that they have been spared the kind of suffering about which they have been reading.[6] Since in *Froggy's Little Brother* Brenda specifically sets out to encourage her readers to take action on behalf of the poor, it is crucial that the book ends on an uplifting and energizing note. After the distressing death of Benny, which provides the emotional peak, the narrative begins to pull away from the events. Froggy is left safely in the care of responsible figures with a replacement for Benny and good prospects for the future ahead of him. His energies are no longer concentrated on how to survive, leaving him time to speculate about whether or not the finances of the institution where he is living will stretch to giving the boys a day trip to the country. From this safe position the narrator turns to the reader to make the appeal to which the book has been leading:

> Remember it is the Froggys and Bennys of London for whom your clergyman is pleading when he asks you to send money and relief to the poor East End! They may be street Arabs, but they have immortal souls, and they are our brothers and sisters, though we may not own them. (198)

That Brenda used the conventions of street arab fiction successfully is evidenced by the high regard in which she was held and the many tributes paid to *Froggy's Little Brother* both in her lifetime and at the time of her death. Among these was the observation made by Arthur Jocelyn Charles Gore, the 6th Earl of Arran, who initiated a friendship with Georgina Castle Smith while he was the Hon. Treasurer for the Children's Country Holiday Fund. The appeal at the end of *Froggy* encourages readers to help raise funds to be used, among other things, "to enable poor little East End children to have a day in the country" (199), and clearly the Earl had reason to be grateful for this mention, for he writes that it "must have proved to be the most powerful agent in existence for procuring assistance to many charities for children" (Thiel 158).

EVANGELICAL WRITERS AND THE FICTION OF REFORM

The Earl and the novelist, like the hard-working fictional doctor, clergymen, and benefactors of the institution where Froggy is placed, represent a strong tradition in Victorian society that combined philanthropy, social work, and reform, and in which fiction, not least that written by women for children, played an important role. Charles Dickens was one of the foremost Victorian writers to use novels to call attention to the plight of London's poor, and Dickens was both a model and a supporter of many of those who wrote street arab fiction. His influence is clear in *Froggy*; for instance, after the death of his father, Froggy becomes a crossing sweeper, a job immortalized in fiction by Jo in *Bleak House* (1851–52), who is harried to death by the police who are constantly moving him on and so making it impossible for him to support himself. It is likely that the fictional Jo and his sad end would have been in many readers' minds when Froggy made his choice of occupation and set out to find a suitable crossing. Brenda tries to mobilize sympathy for the real crossing sweepers through requiring readers to empathize with her fictional one, as can be seen when she breaks the illusionism of the text and encourages her readers to behave differently the next time they use the services of children such as Jo and Froggy. As Froggy becomes aware that to many of the people in the metropolis he is effectively invisible, he attempts to compel them to notice his efforts, looking into their faces and asking, "Please, sir, throw us a copper!" The effect is not what he hopes, with one gentleman retorting, "Certainly not! What do we want sweepers for in this fine weather?" The narrator then turns to the reader and asks, "Yes! But did the gentleman remember that poor little sweepers want bread to eat in *fine* weather as well as in bad?" (32).

The shadow of Dickens's Jo would have alerted readers to the troubles ahead of Froggy, although by the time Brenda was writing a number of important changes had come into effect that would in reality have given Froggy more avenues for help than were available to Jo. This may account for the very specific time frame of the novel; Brenda wrote it in 1875 and at one point mentions that it refers to the recent winter of 1873, "one of the hardest the [poor of London] had ever known" due to the effects of a strike by Welsh miners that raised the costs of all the necessaries of life (44). Toward the end of the novel there is another direct address to readers, which asks, "You will like to know what became of poor little Froggy, will you not?" Brenda answers the question in the present tense explaining that he is in a Home, meaning an orphanage, "where he is learning the trade of a carpenter" (189), giving the impression that the story is both absolutely current and based on events from life—standard devices of the genre. The immediacy it provides helps Brenda keep the pathos of her story at a high pitch while simultaneously assuring readers that changes for the better in the way the poor were cared for are in hand.

Dickens began writing *Bleak House* in 1851, a time when the poor were suffering the indignities of the recently revised Poor Law Acts that made the harshness of life in the workhouse forever synonymous with degradation and despair. When *Froggy* was published a quarter of a century later, there had been many improvements to the workhouse regime, particularly as they affected children; nevertheless, Froggy, Benny and all their neighbors still live in fear of being sent to the "House." When at their lowest point Froggy concludes that they will have to go to the workhouse and Benny has

> to gulp down a sob himself at the thought they were going to that terrible place,
> the workhouse, of which he had always heard the neighbours speak with such
> horror and dread, as if being driven to "the House" would be the very last sorrow
> and degradation they could know in their poor lives. (94)

Brenda's reassurance that institutions are now more kindly, the middle classes who operate them genuinely concerned, and the education and opportunities they afford beneficial would have been vital to making middle-class readers believe that any donations they made would be used for good causes. Likewise, any poor children who were read or given a copy of *Froggy* would have taken away the message that there was nothing to be feared and much to be gained by accepting the help of their social superiors. Indeed, the logic of the plot implies that if Froggy had not struggled so hard to keep them independent, Benny would have had a happier and a longer life.

This message was underlined through allusions to another Dickens novel; *Oliver Twist* (1838) is clearly referenced too, notably its encounter between the honest orphan protagonist and a gang of young pickpockets, replayed by Brenda in the disastrous day when Froggy is duped by the wretched Mac into helping him and his gang of pick pockets on the grand occasion when the Queen comes to the East End. Like Oliver, Froggy preserves his innocence, refusing to take his share of the earnings and so returning empty-handed to Benny. Just as Oliver's trials are ended through the intervention of well-intentioned and well-off adults, so Froggy is finally relieved of his burdens when the plight of the two boys is discovered by a charity doctor who is called upon to attend to Benny.

Though Benny dies, it is through no fault of the doctor's, and the book makes this clear by marking Benny out as one of the many Victorian children in fiction who are destined to die young: his is the "good" death in this street arab tale. Preternaturally cheerful and caring, he says his prayers each night, shares what little he has with a mouse, refuses to be angry when the cat steals the first little piece of meat the boys have had for weeks, and, most telling of all, sits in the window in their high garret and stares up to heaven. There he would "gaze up at the foggy sky, and . . . speculate upon the Beautiful City that lies beyond, whither 'gentle Jesus' had carried little Deb, and where she was now 'hearing music more beautifuller than the organs!'" (129). In the semiotics of Victorian fiction and painting, the invalid's gaze out the window invariably heralds approaching death,[7] so Brenda's readers would have been well-prepared for Benny's demise. Tears were shed not only for Benny, who they are assured has gone to meet his parents in the Better Land—the last thing he tells Froggy is that he can hear angels singing and that "everybody's going home" (183)—but also for Froggy, who is now all alone.

The religious symbolism around Benny's death is emphasized by a pointed shift in the way the boys are described. Perhaps as a way of enhancing his vulnerability and appeal, Froggy is given a number of feminine characteristics in the course of the novel: he nurtures Benny, changing and feeding him when he is a baby, and striving as hard as any mother to care for him when they are left alone. He both cooks and sews; indeed, he "could patch and darn almost as neatly as a girl" (104).[8] Once Benny becomes ill, however, the text repeatedly emphasizes the boys' masculine characteristics, using many comparisons with soldiers: when the doctor first calls, "Froggy spoke up and answered promptly, like a little soldier" (164); Froggy sits beside Benny's sickbed "like a grave little sentinel" (176); and in an exhausted dream, while Benny is dying beside him, Froggy hears an organ-grinder playing "When Johnny comes marching home!" (177). Children at the time were trained to read emblematically, and they would have recognized that the boys are being established as Christ's soldiers, fighting for him in life and joining him in death.

The mixture of pathos and religious consolation is much stronger in street arab fiction than in Dickens, possibly because these books tended to be written by middle-class Christian women such as Brenda, for an audience primarily of children. Moreover, many street arab tales were published by religious publishing houses such as the Religious Tract Society (RTS) or the Society for Promoting Christian Knowledge (SPCK), which saw such publications as part of their missionary work at home. Unsurprisingly, then, they tended to overlay pleas for social reform with somewhat heavy-handed evangelical messages, a combination that was popular with organizations such as schools, Sunday schools, and mothers' meeting. Accordingly, street arab stories were often given as rewards or prizes for good behavior or achievement, boosting sales and spreading the message that across Britain destitute children were suffering. The strong sales of such books meant that other publishing houses produced copy-cat books: *Froggy's Little Brother* was in fact published by the firm of John F. Shaw, but it is no less religious in tone or nature than those produced by the RTS and SPCK. The text is punctuated with comments made directly to readers such as:

> What a sad reflection—motherless, fatherless, and friendless! But so it was; and this is the condition of hundreds of our poor little brothers and sisters in great London. Let us think of this next Sunday when the petition comes in our beautiful Litany, "That it may please Thee to defend and provide for the

fatherless children and widows, and all that are desolate and oppressed!"
and say from our hearts on their behalf, "We beseech Thee to hear us, good
Lord!" (29)

To modern eyes and out of context such passages may seem so didactic that it is
hard to understand the appeal of writing of this kind, but the plotting, pathos, and
pace of *Froggy's Little Brother* make it a compelling read still,[9] and in its day many
readers forgot it was a work of fiction (this is clearly what Brenda is striving for
when she offers information about what Froggy is doing now) and longed to do
something for the two little boys. In *Lark Rise to Candleford* (1939–43), her autobiographical account of growing up in rural Oxfordshire in the 1880s, Flora Thompson
recalls many tears being shed over *Froggy*, including by one woman in her village
who lamented, "Poor little mite. If we could have got him here, he could have slept
with our young Sammy and this air'd have set him up in no time" (251). Benny, of
course, is never set up, but in line with the practical education and philanthropic
philosophy of the day, Froggy is taught a skill—he is trained as a carpenter—and so
is able to support himself and cease to be a burden on or a threat to society. This is
the ultimate happy ending for a street arab novel, and though in its day it had the
desired effect of encouraging readers to put their hands in their pockets and find
other ways to help alleviate the suffering of the poor, to modern tastes it may seem
a rather flat ending to an emotionally charged story. Oliver Twist discovers wealth,
family, and social status; Froggy may no longer be on the streets, but he has also
ceased to be a figure of interest. This is fully apparent in the unsuccessful sequel,
which charts his life as a conscientious, "respectable" working man.

The convention in street arab fiction for realistic narratives leading to prosaic
endings in combination with a shift to a more secular society may account for the
fact that this much-loved story and what had been a thriving genre have effectively
disappeared from cultural memory today. Additionally, when poor children were
legislated off the streets and into schools they became less visible and so less of a blot
on the nation's psyche, not least because the landslide election of the Liberal government in 1906 paved the way for the modern Welfare State in Britain by introducing a basic national health service and unemployment insurance. By the
beginning of the twentieth century the workhouse was steadily being consigned to
history, a safety net for the poor was in formation, and various acts including the
Prevention of Cruelty to Children Act (1889) were in place and seeking to ensure
that the welfare of children was officially the responsibility of the State. In theory at
least, no Froggys were ever again going to need to look after their little brothers on
their own, making street arab fiction effectively unnecessary.

Under these circumstances it has to be asked whether there is a need to revive
this woeful tale. Its role today has changed in that its historical setting means that
it is no longer explicitly addressing topical local problems in the way it did for its
original readers. Nevertheless, bringing *Froggy* back into circulation offers some
interesting possibilities for rethinking nineteenth-century experience and fiction
and for interpreting how they were depicted.[10] For instance, it has a clear value for

what it reveals about the composition of Britain's cities and the lived experience of the urban poor in the late nineteenth century. The insights it offers into such policies and practices as the ill-advised slum clearances (responsible for the closure of Froggy's night school and his lack of contact with the teachers who would have helped him after his father's death), charitable work, and the appeal of religion to the poor are more vivid and better contextualized in its pages than in formal histories. As developments in postcolonial studies expose the tenacious legacy of domestic orientalism, it is possible to use texts such as *Froggy's Little Brother* as primary evidence about constructions of the poor that can be put alongside alternative versions such as Stephen Humphries's *Hooligans or Rebels? An Oral History of Working-Class Childhood and Youth 1889–1939* (1981) and Anna Davin's *Growing Up Poor: Home, School and Street in London 1870–1914* (1996). Both works offer firsthand accounts from those who were real-life street children. What they show is that writers of street arab fiction were giving very one-sided views of life in the poor parts of Britain's cities. All was not as desperate as these books make it out to be, for there was a strong working-class culture in which many children thrived and that was the envy of some middle-class children in the freedoms it offered and the value it ascribed to the young. As these corrective voices start to be heard, it is necessary to reread street arab stories to see what they preserve and what they erase of this way of life. *Froggy's Little Brother* may often misrepresent Victorian London's poor children, but it is one of the key texts that sought to carve out a place for them in culture and helped create pathways by which their stories were gathered and told. Brenda's novel is of more than historical interest, however: at a time when countries ranging from the United States and the United Kingdom to many countries in South America, Africa, and parts of the Indian subcontinent have their own multitudes of outcast children like Froggy and Benny, its message of compassion and attempt to make the vulnerable visible and valuable is as relevant as ever.

NOTES

1. This description comes from a letter to Brenda written by the 6th Earl of Arran on rereading the book as an adult, some forty years after first encountering it (Thiel 158).

2. For a more detailed discussion of postcolonial theory, see Bill Aschcroft et al., *The Empire Writes Back: Theory and Practice in Post-Colonial Literature* (1989); Homi K. Bhabha, *Nation and Narration* (1990); Clare Bradford, *Unsettling Narratives: Postcolonial Readings of Children's Literature* (2007).

3. The original newspaper articles on which Mayhew's book is based were published in the *Morning Chronicle* between 1849 and 1850; the first volume of the study appeared in 1851, but it took a further ten years for the work to be completed.

4. Those who have written at length about street arab fiction, also known as "waif stories," include Cutt (1979), Bratton (1981), and Davin (1996; 2001).

5. Henry A. Giroux reveals the same process at work today. In *Stealing Innocence: Corporate Culture's War on Children* (2001) he analyzes institutional bias such as "innocence profiling," which tends to treat white, middle-class children who break the law as ill while those who are, say, black or Latino are designated criminal and deviant. Judith Plotz's *Romanticism and the Vocation of Childhood* (2001) discusses in detail the effects of the way images of the poor child contradicted the ideal of childhood (34–39).

6. Augusto Boal explores this aspect of catharsis in *Theatre of the Oppressed* (1997).

7. For a detailed discussion of this trope, see chapter 4 in Elizabeth Gargano's *Reading Victorian Schoolrooms: Childhood and Education in Nineteenth-Century Fiction* (2007).

8. This kind of feminization is consistent with orientalizing strategies, which often rely on making "others" feminine: for instance, by showing them as dependent, irrational, and good at practical tasks but lacking the ability to analyze or take command of situations.

9. Selecting her top ten reads for the Book Depository blog, writer and journalist Julia Gregson says of *Froggy's Little Brother*, "My sister and I, well fed and nicely brought up, were so utterly gripped by this dark and melodramatic tale of two London orphans struggling to survive, that we slept under our beds for several weeks after we read it." http://www.bookdepository.co.uk/blog/index/cat/tuesday_top_ten (accessed 17 March 2009).

10. While this essay focuses on fiction, many of the insights about representations of poor children pertain equally to the visual arts.

WORKS CITED

Primary Texts

"Brenda." *Froggy's Little Brother*. London: John F. Shaw, 1875. Accessible online at http://core.roehampton.ac.uk/digital/chlit/brefrog/pgs156-158.pdf (accesssed 3 June 2009).

Dickens, Charles. *Bleak House*. 1852–53. New York: The Heritage Press, 1942.

———. *Oliver Twist*. 1838. London: Penguin, 2003.

Thompson, Flora. *Lark Rise to Candleford: A Trilogy*. 1839–43. Boston: David R. Godine, Inc., 2008.

Secondary Texts

Aschcroft, Bill, et.al. *The Empire Writes Back: Theory and Practice in Post-Colonial Literature*. London: Routledge, 1989.

Bhabha, Homi K. *Nation and Narration*. London: Routledge, 1990.

Boal, Augusto. *Theatre of the Oppressed*. 2nd. Rev. ed. London: Pluto Press, 1997.

Bradford, Clare. *Unsettling Narratives: Post-Colonial Readings of Children's Literature*. Waterloo: Wilfred Laurier UP, 2007.

Bratton, J. S. *The Impact of Victorian Children's Fiction*. London: Croom Helm, 1981.

Cutt, Margaret Nancy. *Ministering Angels: A Study of Nineteenth-century Evangelical Writing for Children*. Wormley: Five Owls Press, 1979.

Davin, Anna. *Growing Up Poor: Home, School and Street in London 1870–1914*. London: Rivers Oram Press, 1996.

————. "Waif Stories in Late Nineteenth-Century England" In *History Workshop Journal* 52 (2001): 67–98.

Dawson, Gowan. *Darwin, Literature and Victorian Respectability*. Cambridge: Cambridge UP, 2007.

Gargano, Elizabeth. *Reading Victorian Schoolrooms: Childhood and Education in Nineteenth-Century Fiction*. New York: Routledge, 2007.

Giroux, Henry A. *Stealing Innocence: Corporate Culture's War on Children*. New York: Palgrave Macmillan, 2001.

Hollingshead, John, *Ragged London in 1861*. 1861. London: Dent, 1986. Accessible online at http://www.victorianlondon.org/publications/raggedlondon-thecentre.htm (accessed 22 March 2009).

Hopkins, Eric. *Childhood Transformed: Working-Class Children in Nineteenth-Century England*. Manchester: Manchester UP, 1994.

Huggins, Mike J. "More Sinful Pleasures? Leisure, Respectability and the Male Middle Classes in Victorian England." *Journal of Social History* (Spring 2000): 1–11. Accessible online at http://findarticles.com/p/articles/mi_m2005/is_3_33/ai_61372235/ (accessed 2 June 2009).

Humphries, Stephen. *Hooligans or Rebels? An Oral History of Working-Class Childhood and Youth 1889–1939*. Oxford: Basil Blackwell, 1981.

Lennox-Boyd, Charlotte. "Brenda and Her Works." *Signal* 62 (May, 1990): 114–130.

Mayhew, Henry. *London Labour and the London Poor*. 1861. London: Constable, 1968. Accessible online at http://etext.virginia.edu/toc/modeng/public/MayLond.html (accessed 22 March, 2009).

McGeorge, Colin. "Death and Violence in Some Victorian Reading Books." *Children's Literature in Education* 29, no. 2 (1998): 109–17.

Plotz, Judith. *Romanticism and the Vocation of Childhood*. New York: Palgrave, 2001.

Thiel, Liz. "The Woman Known as Brenda." In *A Victorian Quartet: Four Forgotten Women Writers*, edited by Liz Thiel, Elaine Lomax, Bridget Carrington, and Mary Sebag-Montefiore, 147–208. Lichfield: Pied Piper Publishing, 2008.

Thompson, F. M. L. *The Rise of Respectable Society: A Social History of Victorian Britain, 1830–1900*. London: Fontana, 1988.

Websites

http://www.bookdepository.co.uk/blog/index/cat/tuesday_top_ten (accessed 17 March 2009).

Further Reading

Flegel, Monica. *Conceptualizing Cruelty to Children in Nineteenth-Century England: Literature, Representation, and the NSPCC*. Farnham: Ashgate, 2009.

Garwood, John. "Criminal and Destitute Juveniles; or, the Ragged School Class." In *The Million-Peopled City; or, One-Half of the People of London Made Known to the Other Half*. London: Wertheim and Macintosh, 1853. Accessible online at http://www.victorianlondon.org/publications4/peopled.htm.

Nelson, Claudia. "The Unheimlich Maneuver: Uncanny Domesticity in the Urban Waif Tale." In *Youth Cultures: Texts, Images and Identities*, edited by Kerry Mallan and Sharyn Pearce, 109–21. Westport, CT: Praeger, 2003.

Rodrick, Anne Baltz. "The Importance of Being an Earnest Improver; Class, Caste and
    Self-Help in Mid-Victorian England." *Victorian Literature and Culture* 29, no. 1 (2001):
    39–50.
Smith, Lindsay. *The Politics of Focus: Women, Children and Nineteenth-Century
    Photography*. Manchester: Manchester University Press, 1998.
Wagner, Tamara S. "'We have orphans [. . .] in stock'; Crime and the Consumption of
    Sensational Children" In *The Nineteenth-Century Child and Consumer Culture*, edited
    by Dennis Denisoff, 201–16. Aldershot: Ashgate, 2008.

CHAPTER 13

....

HISTORY IN FICTION: CONTEXTUALIZATION AS INTERPRETATION IN ROBERT LOUIS STEVENSON'S *KIDNAPPED*

....

M. O. GRENBY

ROBERT Louis Stevenson was born in Edinburgh in 1850, the son of Thomas Stevenson, a civil engineer famous for his construction of lighthouses, and Margaret Balfour, the daughter of a Presbyterian minister. Although at first destined to enter the family engineering firm, as a young man Stevenson decided to be a writer, honing his literary style in the production of magazine articles, essays, and travel writing. Having met and married the American Fanny Osbourne, he produced the first of his great successes, Treasure Island *(1883), taking his inspiration from a map he drew for her son, Lloyd.* Treasure Island *was followed by many other novellas, travel accounts, essays, short stories, and volumes of poetry, written for children or adults or both. Many of these have become international classics, widely regarded as masterpieces of their individual genres, including* Strange Case of Dr Jekyll and Mr Hyde *(1886),* A Child's Garden of Verses *(1885), and* The Amateur Emigrant *(1895). Unwell from childhood, Stevenson spent much of his life outside Scotland in search of residences that would be beneficial to his health. Following the death of his father in 1887, Stevenson planned to settle in America, but, after having taken several voyages around the Pacific, he settled in 1890 on Upolo, one of the Samoan islands. Stevenson built himself a house, became involved in local politics, and continued to write. He died there suddenly in 1894 at the age of forty-three.*

THE PROBLEMS OF *KIDNAPPED*

Although perhaps not now as well known as some of his others novels—*Treasure Island*, say, or *Strange Case of Dr Jekyll and Mr Hyde*, both of which appeared in the same few astonishingly productive years in the mid-1880s—*Kidnapped: Being Memoirs of the Adventures of David Balfour in the Year 1751* (1886) is the equal of anything Robert Louis Stevenson wrote. Perhaps the reason it is not so widely read as it once was is that to twenty-first-century readers it can seem a difficult novel. Few children's books now are located quite so brazenly and meticulously in a specific and obscure geographical and historical setting, in this case the Scotland of the mid-eighteenth century. Or rather if they are, more concessions are made to readers. Historical novels for children now often take the form of time-slip fantasies, in which the strangeness of the past is mediated to the reader through the observations and reactions of a visitor from the modern day. There is an element of this in *Kidnapped*, too, for David, the hero, being a Lowland Scot, is almost as much a stranger in the Highlands of Scotland as modern readers are likely to be, and Stevenson delights in showing David's frequent bafflement. Yet it can seem that Stevenson expected his readers to know really rather a lot about the history of eighteenth-century Scotland. After all, his fictional story is organized around a real event—the "Appin murder" of 14 May 1752 (although unaccountably moved by Stevenson to 1751)—and his imagined characters mingle with real historical personages, notably Alan Breck Stewart. There are other alienating factors too. Despite his promise to his American publisher that "the Scotch is kept as low as possible" (*Letters* 5:179), there is Stevenson's plentiful use of archaic and geographically specific dialect. There is the remarkable absence of major female characters (an omission Stevenson tried to rectify in his 1893 sequel, *Catriona*). And there is the novel's curious, perhaps defective, structure, which can seem like two plot lines clumsily jammed together. All in all, it should be no surprise if *Kidnapped* is rather off-putting to modern readers.

To those who have read it, though, *Kidnapped* needs no apology, for once one has plunged in, become accustomed to the idiom and immersed in the story, its many virtues speak for themselves. For G. K. Chesterton, it was "the brisk and bright treatment, the short speeches, the sharp gestures" and "those snapping phrases that seem to pick things off like pistol shots" that characterized Stevenson's style, and that were exhibited most superbly in *Kidnapped* (118–19). Henry James, Jorge Luis Borges, Italo Calvino, Margaret Atwood, and many others have been lavish in their praise of the lightness, precision, and effectiveness of the novel. There can be no doubt of its worldwide literary influence either. *Kidnapped* might be said to stand toward the head of several important subgenres of children's fiction. It seems a direct ancestor, for instance, of many works recounting the flight of children through inhospitable territory, such as Ian Serraillier's *The Silver Sword* (1956), Anne Holm's *I Am David* (1963), and Cynthia Voigt's *Homecoming* (1981). And it provides a fine exploration of the father-son relationship—a theme considered in some detail in the second section of this essay—with clear lines of descent to many modern works, for both children and adults, such as Roald Dahl's *Danny the Champion of the World* (1975), Alan Garner's *Stone Book Quartet* (1979), or even Cormac McCarthy's *The Road* (2006).

These enduring motifs and themes do not somehow float above the novel's specific setting but are firmly enmeshed in the historical and geographical contexts that Stevenson took such care to establish. The principal purpose of this essay is to demonstrate that, far from standing as a bar to our appreciation and understanding, these contexts should increase and enhance our comprehension of the novel's meaning and achievement. As with all good historical novels, contextualization provides us with one of our most valuable interpretative tools. In the case of *Kidnapped*, the first important context is, of course, the mid-eighteenth-century setting. Equally important is the late nineteenth-century milieu in which Stevenson was writing, and from which his first readers were drawn. The final section of this essay shows how an awareness of some of the concerns of 1880s Britain open up the text in important and rewarding ways. As we shall see, when read in this context, *Kidnapped* emerges as a political novel, very deeply concerned with nationhood. To begin, though, it is worth making one or two further points about those features that can dishearten and disconcert the modern reader. Notably, it is these "problems" of *Kidnapped* that best throw into relief Stevenson's chief aims and accomplishments in the novel.

The initial point to make is that it is not only today's readers who can be mystified by the specific historical and geographical setting that Stevenson chose, nor indeed the novel's sometimes abstruse language. A letter to a friend reveals that Stevenson deliberately deployed what he called his "Scōtch" dialect—though not too strongly, he conceded, "for the sake o' they pock-puddens [English], but jist a kitchen o't, to leeven the wersh, sapless, fushionless, stotty, stytering South-Scotch they think sae muckle o'." (*Letters* 5:206) What this jokey comment betrays is that Stevenson (living in Bournemouth when he wrote the novel: about as far away from the Highlands as it was possible to be while being still in Britain) worked hard to strike a balance between clarity and opacity. The apparent impenetrability of his writing, even to contemporary readers, was designed to lend his Highland story an alluringly exotic tone, wholly in harmony with the rage for Highland culture—"tartanry" as it is sometimes called—that was such a feature of Victorian society. Hence the book is full of Gaelic and Scots words, place-names, and customs, seemingly making little concession to the majority of readers unfamiliar with them, then or now, but that never, in fact, compromise the novel's comprehensibility. In one sense, then, Highland Scotland, with its own dialects and complex and rather baroque history and geography, functions for Stevenson as a sort of mythic space, not wholly dissimilar to more obviously fantastical places such as J. R. R. Tolkien's Middle Earth. Like Tolkien, Stevenson deploys contextual detail to give his story a hinterland and to generate verisimilitude. Just as maps of Middle Earth were included in the endpapers of *The Hobbit*, for instance, Stevenson gave precise instructions to an illustrator for a map of the Highlands, showing David's journey "There and Back Again" (as the subtitle of *The Hobbit* puts it, marking another similarity). In both cases, this was cartography designed not only to expound the protagonist's progress but also to emphasize the foreignness and fictiveness of the setting—just like the very long, deliberately archaic full title of *Kidnapped* (designed, Stevenson told his father, to resemble "one of Defoe's" [*Letters* 5:94]).

In another sense, however, the events into which Stevenson launched David were very real and important. *Kidnapped* is set in the aftermath of the Jacobite Rising of 1745–46. The Jacobites were supporters of the Stuart royal dynasty. The Stuarts had been deposed by the "Glorious Revolution" of 1688–89. In their place, William of Orange and Mary II were invited to rule, after whose deaths the throne passed to Mary's sister Anne, and then to George I, the first of the Hanoverian dynasty. The Hanoverians would remain in power for the rest of the century. Meanwhile the Stuarts remained in exile in France. They and their supporters—the Jacobites—made frequent attempts to regain the throne: some historians point to "a continuous series of conspiracies, negotiations and revolts punctuating the history of Britain between 1689 and 1760" (Holmes and Szechi 97). The most important of these events was a large-scale invasion and rebellion in 1745, but this had finally been defeated by the Hanoverian army at the Battle of Culloden in April 1746. In the aftermath of the battle, the Stuart claimant to the throne—Charles Edward Stuart (known as "Bonnie Prince Charlie" or the "Young Pretender")—fled back to France with many of his supporters. Those suspected of Jacobitism who were left in Scotland were subject to harsh repression, with their freedoms severely limited and their traditional culture attacked. This process of pacification has been understood by some historians as a campaign of "state terrorism," pursued even with "genocidal intent," resembling the "ethnic cleansing" of our own era (Macinnes 74–75).

It is tempting to believe that this complex and brutal history would have been better known in late Victorian Britain than it is by today's readers, but this was not necessarily the case. Writing in 1880, when he was researching for a planned history of the period, Stevenson himself considered that this "interesting and sad story . . . is all to be written for the first time" (*Letters* 3:149). Moreover, as Julia Reid has pointed out, those late Victorian historians and anthropologists who did take an interest in eighteenth-century Scotland were largely convinced that if Jacobitism was important it was merely as something that had been overcome in the inevitable and much-vaunted progress of Scotland from "savagery" to "civilization" (122–25). In other words, just as with his use of dialect, Stevenson was strategically deploying his historical *mise-en-scène*. His projected history of the period may never have been completed (or even started), but in writing *Kidnapped* Stevenson understood himself to be an educator, not merely a novelist who had appropriated a known historical setting for his own purposes. Indeed, this essay will be arguing that he understood himself as a campaigner, using history to communicate something about Scotland and Scottishness. In short, the setting of *Kidnapped* was always supposed to be jarring, and rather than daunting us, it should alert us to the novel's underlying purposes. We will return to what Stevenson was trying to say about his nation in the final section of this essay.

First, however, we might return to that other problem, the novel's apparently flawed structure, for this too can point us toward another important dimension of the work. *Kidnapped* has a bipartite plot. The first strand is that of David Balfour, putatively the novel's main story. Newly orphaned, David, a boy on the threshold of adulthood, leaves home with almost nothing, following his dead father's advice to present himself to his uncle Ebenezer. His uncle, a miser who does not welcome a new claimant to his wealth, attempts to kill David by having him climb a ruined stairway in the dark. David survives but, on his uncle's orders, is abducted and taken on the ship *Covenant* to the Carolinas to be sold as an indentured servant. Only in the novel's third-to-last chapter is the previous history of David's family revealed: a quarrel between his uncle and his father, making David the rightful inheritor of the family's estate. He returns to claim it from his uncle. All this takes up only the beginning and the end of the book. In between there is the much longer story of Alan Breck Stewart, formerly a Hanoverian soldier but by 1751 a committed Jacobite, whose task is to collect rents from Highlanders loyal to the Jacobite cause after the Rebellion. While he is returning to France with Jacobite rents, Alan's boat collides with the ship taking the kidnapped David to America. Alan and David form an unlikely alliance against the rapacious crew of the *Covenant*, defeating them in the "Battle of the Roundhouse," young David himself killing two men. The *Covenant* is wrecked. Quickly reunited, David and Alan begin a long journey through the Highlands, which turns into a flight from the Hanoverian soldiers after they witness and are accused of the assassination of Colin Campbell, the "Red Fox," the new landlord and representative of the Hanoverian king in that part of the Highlands. It is Alan who helps David return to receive his inheritance, Alan finally departing for the Continent. Stevenson himself acknowledged that there were problems with this structure. Having begun the book "partly as a lark, partly as a pot-boiler," he wrote self-effacingly to one critic, "David and Alan stepped out from the canvas," but this left "the cursed beginning" and therefore "a cursed end must be appended" (*Letters* 5:313–14). Also open to criticism is the episodic structure of the middle section of the novel—the "flight through the heather"—which sometimes can seem to have little in the way of narrative coherence. Only the chase, it can appear, gives the book momentum here, but occasionally the tension is allowed to drop, the two protagonists at times outpacing their pursuers by some distance.

Individual readers can decide for themselves whether all this impairs the novel or not, but what the problems with structure bring into sharp focus are some of the real strengths of *Kidnapped*. As Stevenson recognized, only "one part" of his novel was truly "alive," and this was the section in which David and Alan travel together through the Highlands (*Letters* 5:313–14). It is their relationship that stands at the center of the novel. The real climax of the novel comes not when David is restored to his inheritance at its end, but when he and Alan quarrel and fight in chapter twenty-four, a tense standoff with a sudden and moving resolution. The narrative never flags, but it is impelled not by the demands of a dénouement-driven plot but by the development of a relationship between an orphan on the edge of adulthood finding out where he belongs in the world and a rather childish man being driven away from his own community. It is this relationship, and the place it occupies in the story of David's development, that the next section of this essay will explore in more detail.

FATHERS AND SONS: *KIDNAPPED* AND COMING OF AGE

Kidnapped is a classic *bildungsroman*, following David from orphanhood to adulthood and charting his psychological development and education in the ways of the world. What is noticeable is the way Stevenson writes this process into the geography of his story—probably the best example of his ability to use the putatively specific and realist setting as a psychological landscape with much more general relevance. For instance, the narrative is dominated by crossings, particularly of water. At the end of the first chapter David fords a stream to begin his journey; thereafter he crosses rivers, lochs, and stretches of sea with remarkable frequency— "a good deal of ferrying" as he calls it at one point (123)—until he finally finds a way to cross the Firth of Forth to escape his pursuers and claim his fortune: "I had come to port," as he puts it (237). All of these crossings are emblematic of his steady, summer-long advance to maturity and his integration into society. The most dramatic crossing is the fearful leap across the Glencoe river in chapter twenty, a "Rubicon" moment when David first understands the gravity of his implication in the murder of the "Red Fox." Probably the most significant crossing comes after he has been shipwrecked on the islet of Earraid. He thinks himself castaway and cut off from the world, only to find, eventually, when he encounters two boatmen and puzzles out what they are trying to tell him in incomprehensible Gaelic, that the tides will allow him to cross to the mainland at certain times. There could be no better emblem of the beginning of a child's socialization. From this moment, and particularly from his meeting again with Alan, the isolated orphan finds himself increasingly integrating with his nation and its communities, his kidnapping having threatened to divide him from them forever.

Despite this narrative of progressive development, Stevenson's triumph in *Kidnapped* is to present and explore the ambiguities of age and maturity and the complications of the transition between childhood and adulthood. We encounter several instances of arrested development, for instance, or of false or forced maturity. The cabin boy Ransome provides a vivid counterpoint to David. He is a boy, perhaps about David's age though he "could not say how old he was, as he had lost his reckoning" (43), who attempts to act as a man—ludicrously and, ultimately, fatally. He shows off his tattoos, boasts "of many wild and bad things that he had done," and "whenever he remembered," swears and curses, "but more like a silly schoolboy than a man" (43). While they are together on the *Covenant*, David attempts "to make something like a man" of Ransome, or rather "something like a boy," for Ransome's brutal apprenticeship on the brig has robbed him of his childhood and thus the possibility of a normal and healthy development. David, by contrast, shifts much more gradually from childhood to adulthood. Part of this process, as Stevenson presents it, is the frequent crossing backward and forward between adulthood and childhood, which the novel presents as a healthier pattern of development. His retrospective account acknowledges that David came to his uncle "little more than a child" (40), but he soon fancies himself an adult. Stevenson is clear that it is David's overconfidence in his maturity that allows him to be kidnapped ("I had a great opinion of my shrewdness" [40]). Once so cruelly disabused of his pretensions to adulthood, the tribulations he encounters often throw him back into childhood. Castaway on the islet, for instance, he frankly confesses that he "wept and roared like a wicked child" (110). Ultimately, his adventures make a man of him, but even at the very end of the novel, when he has gained his estate, David feels like sitting down to "cry and weep like any baby" when he watches Alan depart (240). What emerges is a strong sense of the permeability of the frontier between childhood and adulthood and a conviction that maturity should not be rushed.

Throughout the novel, even the protagonists' ages are uncertain and confused. David tells us that when he set out on his adventure he was sixteen (15), but the date of birth he later admits to makes him seventeen (217), and the handbills describing him as a fugitive from justice call him eighteen (164). Alan is obviously his senior by many years, although David is "a good twelve inches taller" (193)—a fact Alan disputes because of a vanity that David labels "childish" (73). Indeed, David's description of Alan is often pointedly infantilizing: Alan has a "childish propensity to take offence and to pick quarrels" (97), David says, and—just after Alan has ruthlessly passed his sword through each of his fallen enemies following the battle on the *Covenant*—"his eyes were as bright as a five-year-old child's with a new toy" (81). Yet Alan looks after David during their flight across the Highlands like a surrogate father, and David looks up to him, Stevenson insists, with feelings "like what a child may have" (174).

This disordering of age comes to a head in "Cluny's Cage," the hideout of a Jacobite chief in which Alan and a sickly David take refuge. As David describes it, everyone there behaves like a child. Cluny's servants "trembled and crouched away from him like children before a hasty father"; Cluny himself questioned his barber for news "as earnestly as a child"; and even the Young Pretender himself, the leader of the Jacobite Rebellion, though often drunk, had appeared a "spirited boy" during his stay at the Cage (177–78). Stevenson was surely making a political point here, about the infantilization inevitably caused by living life isolated from society, an outlaw existence forced on the Jacobites by the persecution that followed Culloden. But more important to the central strand of the narrative is Alan's immaturity while at the Cage. Encouraged by Cluny he gambles away all his own money, then David's too, wheedling it from him although David is almost insensible with illness. "Alan had behaved like a child and (what is worse) a treacherous child" (185), David summarizes later, and it is this that causes the terrible quarrel between them that stands at the novel's heart. Here their ages seem to fluctuate wildly. Alan is the "treacherous child," but this drives David to insult him with "the rude, silly speech of a boy of ten" (189). He abuses Alan's Jacobite cause. Alan reacts by contemptuously treating David as irksome and immature, hardly worth his notice. In response to this calculated disdain, David, in a show of manhood, draws his sword—and we find in this one moment that he has absorbed much of Alan's reckless courage and his delicate sense of honor. In this same moment we find that Alan, though incensed, cannot bring himself to fight—privileging their relationship over his pride, backing down, throwing his sword away. All their enmity suddenly dissipates when David, almost dying with fatigue and sickness, asks pathetically for help. This rouses Alan's solicitude, and he apologizes for his resentment in paternalistic terms: "I couldnae remember ye were just a bairn" (193).

This paternal relationship requires further investigation, for it lies at the very core of the novel. Published a few years earlier than *Kidnapped*, Stevenson's *Treasure Island* had already been largely concerned with a fatherless boy's search for a paternal figure, and his relationship with Long John Silver in particular has been seen as reflecting the author's own troubled relationship with his father (Sandison 43–44). *Kidnapped* is also very much concerned with fatherhood, something evident even from the rather strange, cross-generational dedication to Stevenson's friend Charles Baxter, telling him that although he himself might not like the novel that "perhaps when he is older, your son will" and "he may then be pleased to find his father's name on the fly-leaf." This prediction is curiously echoed by David's discovery of his father's name on the fly-leaf of a book in his uncle's house, which gives him the first premonition that the proper lines of inheritance have buckled (32). *Kidnapped*'s main plot restores the rights of primogeniture usurped by Ebenezer, the disruption to legitimate inheritance succinctly signified by the unfinished and decaying state of the House of Shaws, which was caused, we learn, by Ebenezer's having, with filial disloyalty, opposed his father's will by halting his plans "to enlarge the house" (30).

Precisely the same themes are carried over into the middle sections of *Kidnapped*, providing the novel with a deeply embedded coherence that goes some way to uniting the two sections of the book. Stevenson's audacious inclusion in a walk-on part of Robin Oig, "one of the sons of the notorious Rob Roy" (a celebrated bandit), makes this clear, especially when Robin, finding that David cannot be sure of his ancestry, dismisses him as "some kinless loon that didn't know his own father" (197–98). This, as Barry Menikoff points out, is "the worst insult" to a Highlander (56), but Stevenson was also surely playing with oxymoron here, for Robin is an outlaw who, ironically, is fixated by legitimacy. So too is Alan, a man completely formed by his notions of patrimony. His obsession with legitimacy is of course most obvious in his keen loyalty to the usurped Stuart dynasty, but his relationship with his father complicates the issue. He proudly admits that, along with the silver buttons about which he is so vain, he has inherited his martial prowess and his prodigality from his father, and he cannot help telling David an anecdote concerning his father's visit to London to demonstrate his swordsmanship. He "showed the whole art of the sword for two hours at a stretch, before King George and Queen Carline, and the Butcher Cumberland," Alan boasts, before he ostentatiously overtipped the palace porter to give an idea of the munificence of Highland gentlemen. "And that was the father that I had," crows Alan, apparently made oblivious by his fervent filial devotion to the fact that his father had been performing for the Hanoverians—the very people against whom the Jacobites were fighting and who are the cause of Alan's present difficulties (91).

If, in this instance, Alan's familial and political loyalties clash (at least after Alan's desertion from the Hanoverian army), there is less dissonance between the personal and the political in his relationship with David. Just like Charles Edward Stuart and his father, the "Old Pretender," David and his father have been usurped from their rightful inheritance. It is easy to see how, for Alan, David is a substitute for the Young Pretender, for as both Jacobite and friend of David, Alan is engaging on a quest to restore the legitimate heir—to a usurped estate, in David's case, and to the throne in the case of the Stuarts. We cannot help thinking also that Alan finds in David a son, someone to whom he can pass on his values and traditions. This is neatly symbolized by Alan's gift to David of one of the few things that his father had left to him, so that David assumes the identity of "The Lad with The Silver Button." Although political enemies then—for David is a "Whig," that is to say, a political supporter of the Hanoverians—the two are brought together in a touchingly filial relationship, as David looks for a father and Alan for a son. In this respect, *Kidnapped*'s examination of the father-son bond goes further than that of *Treasure Island*, for the relationship is considered from the point of view of the father as well as of the child.

If they are, in a way, father and son, David and Alan are also aspects of the same character. Stevenson is one of the undoubted masters of this doubling technique, which allowed him to do two things: to study two sides of the same character and to explore the ramifying and often disastrous consequences of choices precipitately made. He did the first in *Strange Case of Dr Jekyll and Mr Hyde*, which appeared concurrently with *Kidnapped*. He did the second three years later in *The Master of Ballantrae* (1889), a story of two brothers caught up, like David, in the 1745 Jacobite Rebellion and pursing different but intersecting paths. *Kidnapped* itself has several sets of doubles. David's father and uncle were brothers who, like those in *The Master of Ballantrae*, quarreled and parted. David and Ransome are paired figures. And Captain Hoseason is a double-character all on his own, his egregious turpitude oddly balanced against his love for his ship, his fervent church-going when on shore, and his touching filial duty (he fires a gun whenever his ship passes his mother's home). The most important conjoined pair, though, is David and Alan, each representing what the other might have been, or perhaps would like to have been if only they would admit it. Had it not been for his defection to the Jacobite cause, Alan might have been the settled and prosperous gentleman that David will become. David, meanwhile, for all that he is a somewhat dour Presbyterian Whig, clearly admires Alan's flamboyance and élan. Had he been brought up a laird (a member of the Scottish gentry), as his birth entitled him to be, he might easily have become a vain spendthrift, however much he might claim to despise it in Alan. Stevenson hints at this in a number of subtle ways. While on the islet, for instance, David's money drips away through a hole in his pocket. This puts us in mind of the profligacy that he will encounter in Alan and that was exhibited by Alan's father, who gave away his guineas to the king's porter in a grandiose show of liberality, and by David's father, too, who renounced his estate in a quarrel over a love affair.

In *Kidnapped*, then, Stevenson was asking whether it is character, choice, or circumstance that has made his protagonists as they are. In general terms these were questions that were circulating widely in children's books of the 1880s. Mark Twain's *The Prince and the Pauper* appeared in 1881, F. Anstey's *Vice Versa: A Lesson to Fathers* in 1882, and the serialization of Frances Hodgson Burnett's *Little Lord Fauntleroy* overlapped with that of *Kidnapped* in summer 1886. Each of these describes the upsetting of the established order by a temporary reversal of roles—a poor American becoming an English lord, say, or a man metamorphosing into a boy—just as *Kidnapped* has an establishment Whig becoming a renegade Jacobite (and just as the 1688 "Glorious Revolution," by overthrowing the Stuart monarchy, had turned a king and his descendents into impoverished exiles). Each novel, in essence, was asking about who has a legitimate claim to power and privilege and on what basis. Like *Kidnapped*, they offered the hope that greater empathy and social regeneration would result from a restoration of the proper order after a short period of hierarchical confusion.

In making these links with other children's novels of the period we should not lose sight of the specificity of the setting Stevenson chose. Just as David's development maps onto the geographical locations of the novel, so too does the historical context that Stevenson carefully, though sometimes a little anachronistically, constructed. The fundamental difference between David and Alan is that the former accepts the Hanoverian George II as the rightful king and the latter does not. More than mere politics, this also accounts for their approaches to life. By accepting the Hanoverian king, David accepts the "Glorious Revolution." This was an event built on the idea that the people had the right to choose their rulers and that the authority of these rulers could and should be limited and not absolute. Alan rejects this and so too, in fact, did David's Uncle Ebenezer, who, we discover in an aside toward the end of the novel, had also been supporter of the deposed Stuarts during the earlier Jacobite rebellion of 1715 (222). Both these men, and Alan in particular, support the idea of monarchy as sanctioned by God, the people therefore having no right to choose their rulers nor to limit their power. This becomes important when we see Alan and Ebenezer as possible surrogate fathers to David. David is an adolescent boy, on the frontier between childhood and adulthood. He is increasingly conceited, and he confronts the authority of those who are supposedly his superiors—his uncle, with whom he becomes very angry, then his shipmates on the *Covenant*, then Alan. He is determined to deal with these authority figures as an equal and to limit the power that they wish to exert over him, and he is adamant that he will not be ruled by them if he does not agree with their decisions. He is, in this sense, reenacting the "Glorious Revolution" in his own life. We note also that David is not prepared to act the adult simply by emulating his elders, as does the cabin boy Ransome. Rather, he wants to reform authority, not merely to imitate it, comply with it, or simply take its place.

As I have suggested, Twain, Anstey, and Burnett, along with a number of other late nineteenth-century children's writers, all presented children as agents of social regeneration. Stevenson, though, was particularly deft in merging the personal and the political. The complete fusion of his individual characters' narratives and their psychological drama with the complex historical setting was one of his greatest achievements in *Kidnapped*. What we should now turn to is how Stevenson was also contributing to a political debate current at the time he was writing.

KIDNAPPED IN ITS CONTEXTS

"*Kidnapped* says as much about Stevenson as any autobiography," Ian Bell has remarked, noting that in David and Alan, he "gave substance to two sides of his own character, adventurer and rationalist, man of duty and man of passion" (194). The social and psychological topography of Stevenson's native Edinburgh can also seem a contributory factor to his persistent use of doubles, divided as the city was between the respectable, bright, rationally laid-out New Town where his prosperous family lived, and the dark, winding, supposedly amoral Old Town to which he was deeply attracted. His religion may have been relevant too. "Calvinism divided the world into the elect and the damned," Bell reminds us (191). Stevenson's exploration of what has made David and Alan so different, though potentially so similar, was surely at some level putting on trial the Presbyterian theology of Predestination, with its belief that the individual was ineluctably heading for either heaven or hell.

Above all, though, it is the question of nation that underlies *Kidnapped* and its use of doubles. Scotland, for Stevenson, was both historically and geographically a divided nation. Most obviously it was split between the Lowlands and the Highlands. Stevenson himself was a Lowlander. David comes from this same background—his home is in the "Forest of Ettrick", near the border with England—and he is a Presbyterian and "as good a Whig as Mr Campbell could make me" (71). His presentation as cautious and sensible, ethical and introverted, might almost be seen as a caricature of the Presbyterian soul. Stevenson, however, was an imaginative child, and was "willing to be 'kidnapped' any moment by the romance of a vigorous, glamorous warrior culture" that he firmly associated with the Highlands (Harman 315). The Highlands were still popularly imagined as a wild area where lived a savage but noble, extravagant and spirited people, not quite as tame as those who lived in large cities in the south of Scotland or in the quiet, domesticated countryside of the Lowlands. This was a view shared by many Victorians, not least the Queen herself whose affection for the Highlands became increasingly public especially after her purchase and rebuilding of an estate house there—Balmoral Castle—in the 1850s. Queen Victoria, of course, was the descendent of the Hanoverians, and it could be said that the whole solidity and success of the British state, its imperial status and global power, were founded on the Whigs' victory over the Jacobites. Nevertheless, since it was no longer a serious political threat, Jacobitism had become a romantic and glorious cause for Stevenson and some of his contemporaries. As Peter Womack notes in his history of the Highland mythos, "sentimental reconstructions" such as Stevenson's "sanitize the Highlanders' motives by reading that failure back into them," so that the clansmen "support the Pretender not *despite* his disastrous unpreparedness but actually *because* of it" and "one feels that if the enterprise had held out the slightest chance of success they would have superbly refused to take part in it" (53). In the Victorian imagination, the Jacobites were regarded as doomed heroes, whose support for a lost cause seemed to prove themselves brave, generous, honorable, idealistic, and (paradoxically, given that they were rebelling against the Hanoverian regime) loyal. In the novel, all these qualities are seen in Alan, though they are balanced by impetuosity, irresponsibility, and egotism, traits also presented as characteristic of the Jacobite cause more generally.

In the two central characters of *Kidnapped*, then, Stevenson presents the two sides of himself, but also what another of his biographers has called "the struggle for the national soul between the contending traditions of Jacobitism and Calvinism," mapped tidily in the novel onto Highland and Lowland (McLynn 302). Read this way, *Kidnapped* is an historical and national novel in the tradition of Sir Walter Scott, an attempt to validate nationhood after what Jenni Calder has called the "quintessential split of Scotland's historic personality" after the 1745 Rising (17). What follows after the chance meeting of David and Alan and the collaboration forced on them by their adversity onboard the *Covenant* is a long and often faltering process of exchange, misunderstanding, education, resentment, and reconciliation. Alan at first thinks David weak and mean, but he comes to appreciate both him and his values. David comes to respect and admire Alan and to appreciate the nobility, albeit the stubborn, foolish, and self-defeating nobility, of the Jacobites. We see this most especially as David gradually comes to realize the fineness of the double-rents the Jacobites pay—to their Hanoverian landlords *and* to the exiled Stuarts—though it bankrupts them and probably pays only for the extravagant Jacobite court in exile: "I'm a Whig," says David, shocked but impressed, "but I call it noble" (93). Whig and Jacobite, Lowland and Highland, must be reconciled for the nation to thrive, Stevenson insists. If this was so in the mid-eighteenth century, it is implied, it was equally true for the Scots of Stevenson's own day.

Why, though, with Scotland remarkably stable and prosperous in the 1880s, was Stevenson concerned to write this kind of novel of national reconciliation just then? One intriguing context is the surprising revival of interest in Jacobitism that more or less coincided with the appearance of *Kidnapped*. The bicentenary of the "Glorious Revolution" was marked by a "Stuart Exhibition" at the British Museum in London in 1889–90. The "Order of the White Rose" was founded in 1886 to celebrate Jacobite history and ideals. The folklorist Andrew Lang, like David, born and brought up near the Forest of Ettrick, was a member, giving his well qualified opinion that "Jacobitism was a fairy-tale, perhaps the greatest one of all" (qtd. in Pittock 123–24). The more earnest "Legitimist Jacobite League" followed in 1891, and although it had negligible political impact, its establishment demonstrates that Jacobitism was, at least for some, more than a quaint cause to be supported only out of nostalgic sentimentality. One persuasive interpretation is that this recrudescence of Jacobite feeling represented a "reaction by the artistic and literary classes against the values of material progress, and the burgeoning worlds of imperial and industrial power" that characterized late Victorian Britain (Pittock 120). This clash of traditional and modern was felt particularly in Scotland, where the big industrial cities—most especially Edinburgh, Dundee, and Glasgow and its satellites—were all well south of the "Highland Line" that separated them from the still largely rural and economically deprived north and west. Nineteenth-century industrialization may have left the cities of southern Scotland prosperous and important, hubs of a global empire, but it had also reemphasized the schism into two nations that the Jacobite rising and its aftermath had wrought, or at least made much more obvious, in the eighteenth century.

Something else had brought the division of the nation into sharp focus in the period leading up to the publication of *Kidnapped*: the so-called Crofters' War. The long process known as the "Highland Clearances" had been underway for much of the later eighteenth and the nineteenth century. During that time, as a result of the modernization of agricultural methods, particularly the increasing preference for sheep farming on big estates, huge numbers of men and women had been forced off the land they had rented as smallholdings. In the Highlands this was exacerbated by the acquisitiveness of the large property owners who had inherited land and power after the suppression of the old clan structures in the wake of the 1745 Rising. The clearances led to great waves of migration to the cities of southern Scotland and to North America. By and large, there was little organized opposition to this process, either from the displaced Highlanders themselves or the political classes in Edinburgh or London. In the 1880s, however, a number of acts of resistance did take place, which came to be known rather hyperbolically as the Crofters' War. These began with the "Battle of the Braes" in 1882, a mildly violent confrontation on the Isle of Skye between crofters and their landlord about grazing rights. Quickly a campaign of rent strikes, destruction of fences, and mutilation and killing of livestock had spread to other parts of the Highlands. The protest remained small-scale and, ultimately, rather futile, but the newspapers often exaggerated the extent of the clashes. The *Scotsman* of 15 October 1884 reported that "men are taking what does not belong to them, are setting all law at defiance, and are instituting a terrorism which the poor people are unable to resist" (qtd. in Devine 219).

Reading this kind of account, comparisons with the aftermath of the 1745 Rebellion would have been difficult for Stevenson and others to resist. There was the issue of rents, the Jacobite clansmen having nobly paid double while the crofters refused to pay any. There was the link between the "terrorism" of the crofters and of the renegade Jacobites, who (as seen in *Kidnapped*) had gone so far as to assassinate the unpopular new landlord Colin Campbell. And there was the question of how the activism should be dealt with. Just as Stevenson was writing *Kidnapped*, the British government was being forced to contemplate sending an expeditionary force to the Highlands—"the first since the time of the last Jacobite rebellion in the eighteenth century," as the historian of the Crofters' War points out (Devine 219).

Although a violent armed confrontation between troops and crofters was eagerly anticipated in sections of the press, none in fact took place. What happened instead was that, for the first time in the history of the Clearances, public opinion moved behind the crofters, forcing the government to legislate to protect their tenure. It was a concessionary measure taken for fear that the situation in Scotland would become as serious as in Ireland, where agitation for Home Rule had led to several acts of terror, including political assassinations that must have invited comparisons with the murder of Colin Campbell. Stevenson's own political opinions were seldom very pronounced. He was in many ways a conservative figure, and certainly a Unionist, adamant that the union of England, Scotland, and Ireland should be maintained. The very few of his letters that do mention politics reveal little more than a hostility to William Gladstone, the Liberal prime minister who favored Irish Home Rule. Indeed, most scholars have seen Stevenson exhibiting "virtually no interest in the present" (Cowan 195), a deliberately apolitical figure who steadfastly refused to "tackle the social realities of Scotland of his own day" (Harvie 124). Moreover, Stevenson's letters make no mention of the Crofters' War (although they do show opposition to the aims and tactics of the Irish National Land League who agitated for rent reforms and redistribution of land, sometimes violently).

Given its context, though, we should surely read *Kidnapped* as an intervention in a debate on the future of the Highlands, perhaps also on the Irish Question. It was published in the very year that Gladstone was forced to introduce a Home Rule bill for Ireland and that the Crofters' Holdings (Scotland) Act was passed, which finally protected their rights. *Kidnapped* even includes a brief but moving vignette of the Clearances when David, traveling through the Highlands, encounters a beach "quite black with people . . . crying and lamenting one to another so as to pierce the heart" as they prepare to embark for the "American colonies." Stevenson surely wanted his readers to understand that the "great sound of mourning" David hears echoes not only across the loch but also down the decades, for he has David pointedly say, "How long this might have gone on I do not know, for they seemed to have no sense of time" (121–22).

It would be foolish to argue that *Kidnapped* was written expressly as political propaganda or even as a direct response to the Crofters' War. After all, Stevenson had, as he confided to his friend Sidney Colvin, been planning to write the "most interesting and sad story" of the 1745 Rising and its aftermath and of "the odd, inhuman problem of the great evictions," since at least 1880 (*Letters* 3:149). This was originally to be a work of history, not fiction, and he drafted a title—"The Transformation of the Highlands"—and a list of contents that included chapters on "The Forfeited Estates . . . and the admirable conduct of the tenants," "The Evictions," and "Emigration," culminating in an investigation of the Highlands' "Present State"

(Cowan 188–89). The history was never to appear, but it is surely quite clear that the project metamorphosed into *Kidnapped*. Whatever narrative mode he was employing, his aim in rewriting Scottish history was to jolt his contemporaries out of their complacent assumption that Scotland was progressing smoothly in the right direction. Its cities might be growing more prosperous, but, as the Crofters' War showed, the old divisions of the eighteenth century, exhibited in the novel, were reappearing. In this sense, David functions perfectly as a personification of the readers Stevenson was hoping to reach and a fantasy of how he hoped they would respond.

At first David is naive about the unity of the nation. Following the assassination in which he is implicated, David, smugly thinking that he can give Alan "a little lesson," tells him that "I have no fear of the justice of my country." Alan scoffs, pointing out that because it is a Campbell who has been killed, and that since judge and jury will be Campbells sitting in the "Campbell's head place," a trial would be little better than a lynching. "It's all Scotland," David protests, but he admits to the reader that his experiences will show him "how nearly exact were Alan's predictions" (138).

What, then, was Stevenson's solution to the problem he was exposing? Certainly he was no political agitator, and *Kidnapped* was not a political polemic for either side. What Stevenson advocated was not resistance (like the Jacobites in the 1740s and '50s or the crofters in the 1880s) or repression (as practiced by Colin Campbell's Whigs and threatened by William Gladstone's Liberals) but the kind of empathy that David and Alan develop over the course of the novel. This empathy is personal but also political. When David admits that "we ourselves might take a lesson by these wild Highlanders" (138), he speaks not only for eighteenth-century Whigs but also, Stevenson hoped, for his own late nineteenth-century readers. He and his contemporaries had been too blind to the plight of the Highlanders, he felt, in the period leading up to the Crofters' War. He was advocating neither the crofters' cause, nor the landlords', and still less the violent tactics used either in Scotland or Ireland, but rather mutual understanding and acceptance, and through these a renewed national unity.

To view *Kidnapped* merely as a response to particular nineteenth-century political events and anxieties would be reductive, and there are many other ways in which the novel could and should be read. But the specific contexts of its production *are* important, as is an awareness of some of the complexities of the novel's eighteenth-century Scottish setting. It is certainly possible to enjoy Stevenson's writing without knowing much about either, but to investigate the ways in which *Kidnapped* was both formed by, and was a contribution to, several pressing cultural and political debates of the late Victorian period surely enriches our appreciation of the novel. The distant and rather bewildering setting that Stevenson chose for his novel turns out to be more pertinent than we might initially have thought: not merely an exotic and exciting backdrop, but an intrinsic part of his achievement. It is essential to his depiction of the complex relationship between Alan and David, and therefore to his careful revision of the coming-of-age novel. And it is essential to his intervention in the political and cultural debates echoing through Scotland and further afield as he was writing. In *Kidnapped*, the picturesque was both political and psychologically crucial, as only a full investigation of the novel's multiple contexts can reveal.

WORKS CITED

Bell, Ian. *Robert Louis Stevenson: Dreams of Exile*. Edinburgh: Mainstream, 1992.

Calder, Jenni. "The Eyeball of Dawn: Can We Trust Stevenson's Imagination?" In *Robert Louis Stevenson: New Critical Perspectives*, edited by William B. Jones, 7–20. Jefferson, NC: McFarlane and Co., 2003.

Chesterton, G. K. *Robert Louis Stevenson*. London: Hodder and Staughton, n.d.

Cowan, Edward J. "'Intent upon my own race and place I wrote': Robert Louis Stevenson and Scottish History." In *The Polar Twins*, edited by Edward J. Cowan and Douglas Gifford, 187–214. Edinburgh: John Donald, 1999.

Devine, T. M. *Clanship to Crofters' War: The Social Transformation of the Highlands*. Manchester: Manchester UP, 1994.

Harman, Claire. *Robert Louis Stevenson: A Biography*. London: HarperCollins, 2005.

Harvie, Christopher. "The Politics of Stevenson." In *Stevenson and Victorian Scotland*, edited by Jenni Calder, 107–25. Edinburgh: Edinburgh UP, 1981.

Holmes, Geoffrey, and Daniel Szechi. *The Age of Oligarchy: Pre-Industrial Britain 1722–1783*. Harlow: Longman, 1993.

Macinnes, Allan I. "Scottish Gaeldom and the Aftermath of the '45: The Creation of Silence." In *Jacobitism and the '45*, edited by Michael Lynch, 71–83. London: Historical Association, 1995.

McLynn, Frank. *Robert Louis Stevenson: A Biography*. London: Hutchinson, 1993.

Menikoff, Barry. *Narrating Scotland: The Imagination of Robert Louis Stevenson*. Columbia: U of South Carolina P, 2005.

Pittock, Murray G. H. *The Invention of Scotland: The Stuart Myth and the Scottish Identity, 1638 to the Present*. London: Routledge, 1991.

Reid, Julia. *Robert Louis Stevenson, Science, and the* Fin de Siècle. Basingstoke: Palgrave, 2006.

Sandison, Alan. *Robert Louis Stevenson and the Appearance of Modernism: A Future Feeling*. London: Macmillan, 1996.

Stevenson, Robert Louis. *Kidnapped: Being Memoirs of the Adventues of David Balfour in the Year 1751*. London: Capuchin Classics, 2008.

———. *The Letters of Robert Louis Stevenson*. Edited by Bradford A. Booth and Ernest Mehew. 8 vols. New Haven and London: Yale UP, 1994–95.

Womack, Peter. *Improvement and Romance: Constructing the Myth of the Highlands*. Basingstoke: Macmillan, 1989.

FURTHER READING

Calder, Jenni, ed. *Stevenson and Victorian Scotland*. Edinburgh: Edinburgh UP, 1981.

Colley, Ann C. *Robert Louis Stevenson and the Colonial Imagination*. Aldershot: Ashgate, 2004.

Ekirch, A. Roger. *Birthright: the True Story that Inspired Kidnapped.* New York: W. W. Norton, 2010.

Federico, Annette. "Books for Boys: Violence and Representation in *Kidnapped* and *Catriona.*" *Victorians Institute Journal* 22 (1994): 115–33.

Kucich, John. *Imperial Masochism: British Fiction, Fantasy, and Social Class.* Princeton: Princeton UP, 2007.

Kiely, Robert. *Robert Lewis Stevenson and the Fiction of Adventure.* Cambridge: Harvard UP, 1965.

CHAPTER 14

TOM SAWYER, AUDIENCE, AND AMERICAN INDIANS

BEVERLY LYON CLARK

BORN *in 1835 to Jane Lampton Clemens and John Marshall Clemens, Samuel Langhorne Clemens grew up in Hannibal, Missouri. After his father died in 1847, he worked as a typesetter and a river pilot, and in 1861 he served briefly in a local militia loosely allied with the Confederacy. In the 1860s he moved to Nevada, then California, prospecting for silver and writing for newspapers; during this time he started to use the pen name Mark Twain. His 1865 story "Jim Smiley and His Jumping Frog" gave him national visibility, and in 1869 he published* The Innocents Abroad, *an irreverent travelogue based on a tour of the Mediterranean. He married Olivia Langdon in 1870 and moved with her the year after to Hartford, Connecticut. During the next decade they would have a son, who died very young, and three daughters. In the 1870s and 1880s Twain published* The Adventures of Tom Sawyer, The Prince and the Pauper, Life on the Mississippi, Adventures of Huckleberry Finn, *and* A Connecticut Yankee in King Arthur's Court, *among other works. The 1890s, however, were difficult. His daughter Susy died. And thanks in part to investing in the failed Paige typesetting machine, he went bankrupt, though a world lecture tour eventually enabled him to pay off all his creditors. Twain also managed to publish a couple of books, including* The Tragedy of Pudd'nhead Wilson. *The leonine, white-suited image that many now have of Twain dates from the following decade, when he received such accolades as honorary doctorates from Yale and Oxford. He died in 1910, survived only by a daughter—and by* The Mysterious Stranger, *compiled and published posthumously.*

In writing *The Adventures of Tom Sawyer* Mark Twain was charting new territory for himself. He had previously written brief sketches and travelogues but not, on his own, a novel. So he had to decide what kind of longer narrative to write, how to structure it, and, importantly, who his audience was. Was it children? Adults? Children and adults? A family audience that included young and old, male and female? What he didn't consciously decide was the race of his audience; an unquestioned assumption was that he was not addressing, for instance, American Indians.

Reception study in the United States has long focused on the study of audience, including the changing reception of works over time, canonicity, popularity, the encoding of the reader within a text, and the responses of individual readers and interpretive communities of scholars. Children's literature lends itself to the study—and indeed the interrogation—of such topics. Often excluded from the "canonical," for instance, it has been considered "popular," yet must popularity preclude canonicity? It is, furthermore, a literature defined by its primary audience, yet those who write and publish it are almost never members of this audience. To cite just a few examples of the kinds of reception criticism children's literature scholars have undertaken: Zohar Shavit has explored the double address of children's literature, to children and adults; Perry Nodelman, the surface simplicity of its texts but also elements that bespeak a "hidden adult." Barbara Wall has examined the encoding of readers within the text; Michael Benton, the responses of actual child readers. Educators Maria José Botelho and Masha Kabakow Rudman discuss how to encourage such readers to do critical multicultural analysis. Psychoanalytic critic Karen Coats provides a Lacanian view of how literature shapes children's subjectivities. I myself have undertaken a reception history of children's literature in the United States.

Extensions of reception study, what James L. Machor and Philip Goldstein call postmodern reception study, assume "that the epistemological critique of foundational theory reveals the biases or local interests that have always governed criticism"—which is to say that one should examine "women's, African-American, and multicultural literatures, popular culture, the ordinary reader, the history of the book, and so on" (xii, xiii). Some critics of children's literature have attended to such critiques and perspectives, yet a tendency to focus on an abstract child as audience has sometimes obscured the differences among children, including differences of race. My intention in this essay is to do what Machor and Goldstein might consider a postmodern reception study, in two movements: in one I examine some overt questions about the audience for Twain's book; in the other I attempt to unpack some of "the biases or local interests" that govern his novel, focusing specifically on the biases that inform his discursive treatment of Native Americans. Indeed the figure of the Indian becomes, for Twain, a way of mediating between child and adult.

FIRST MOVEMENT

Twain blurred some of the audience distinctions, or market niches, that now seem natural to us, as he helped to create a new genre—transforming the British school story into the American boy book—and also helped shape an audience, happily addressing young and old, male and female. I've argued elsewhere that *The Adventures of Tom Sawyer* (1876) and *Adventures of Huckleberry Finn* (1884) were seen as having equivalent audiences in the nineteenth century, both young and old, and the two also received equivalent critical acclaim; only in the early twentieth century did *Tom Sawyer* come to be seen as a book for children, and *Huckleberry Finn* as a novel for adults, indeed a classic, the great American novel (Clark 77–101). I'll briefly recapitulate some of that argument here. In the nineteenth century, books were not sharply divided into those for children and those for adults, as they usually are now. The most important cultural gatekeepers, the editors of literary magazines such as the *Atlantic Monthly*, devoted considerable space to reviewing and discussing what we would now consider children's literature. That changed in the early twentieth century, when cultural gatekeeping largely shifted to professors, and writings by women and also those for children mostly dropped out of the canon of important literature, and works by Twain and, for instance, Melville were elevated. Nineteenth-century commentators, however, almost always mentioned *Huckleberry Finn* and *Tom Sawyer* in the same breath, not finding one infinitely better or more important than the other, or indeed than any other work by Twain, as has since been the case. Nineteenth-century valuations of Twain's merits were simply different. Consider a readers' choice poll of the "best" forty American books, a list published in 1893 in the journal *The Critic* (a list that includes, by the way, *Little Women* [1868] and *Little Lord Fauntleroy* [1885]). A title by Twain appears, as would probably be the case in a poll undertaken by, say, the *New York Review of Books* today. But in the 1890s the "best" Twain work was *The Innocents Abroad*, not *Huckleberry Finn*.

Or consider the histories of Twain's last two published stories featuring Tom. *Tom Sawyer Abroad* first appeared in a magazine that primarily targeted children, *St. Nicholas* (in 1893–94); *Tom Sawyer, Detective* first appeared in *Harper's Monthly* (in 1896), whose primary audience we consider to be adults. Both were published in a single volume a few months later. Imagine a modern author publishing a long story in the children's magazine *Cricket* two years ago, one in the *New Yorker* last fall, and the two together as a book this fall. It simply wouldn't happen.

As for *The Adventures of Tom Sawyer*, Twain waffled for several months as to whether it was for boys or adults, finally concluding, in his preface,

> Although my book is intended mainly for the entertainment of boys and girls, I
> hope it will not be shunned by men and women on that account, for part of my
> plan has been to try to pleasantly remind adults of what they once were
> themselves, and of how they felt and thought and talked, and what queer
> enterprises they sometimes engaged in. (5)[1]

What I especially like about this combined address is that he is not condescending to children, as the split market now too readily encourages one to be.[2]

In the twentieth century, unlike the nineteenth, critics often condescended to children's literature. For one thing, they often ignored it. When they did attend to what they classified as children's literature they mentioned it in passing as frivolous or lamented that an author wasted his time with it. Or, in the case of *Tom Sawyer*, they tended to praise it as something that nevertheless doesn't require or even bear close analysis. Commentators often echoed Twain's statement that the book was "simply a hymn, put into prose form to give it a worldly air" (Paine, *Letters* 476), without offering much further analysis.

In some ways the flexibility of the readership is mirrored by the flexibility of Tom's age. For he is "a boy of no determinable age" (Doctorow xxxv). Most of his activities, including his being one of two generals in the boys' play armies, argue an age of eleven or twelve. Yet Tom also loses one of his front teeth, as if he were about six. Or consider Judge Thatcher "put[ting] his hand on Tom's head and call[ing] him a fine little man," and the fact that Muff Potter's hand is too large to pass through the bars of the jail but Tom's and Huck's are small enough (32, chap. 4). Tom's romantic interest in Becky, however, suggests an older age: E. Anthony Rotundo's research into "boy culture" indicates that such an interest was not characteristic of prepubescent boys in nineteenth-century America. It was only as they moved out of the boys' world of mock armies, games, pranks, codes of loyalty, and, more generally, evasions of domesticity that boys seemed to take an interest in the opposite sex: "the customs and habits of boy culture started to lose their luster" as youths took care not to muss their clothes and to keep their faces clean (220). Indeed an early reviewer of *Tom Sawyer* finds Tom's "love for the school-girls" out of character, calling Tom "preternaturally precocious" (Review 56).

Tom Sawyer is, in fact, a tonal pastiche, drawing on a variety of discursive modes; and it's the conjunction of such modes that obscures Tom's age.[3] An early rehearsal of some of the novel's incidents was a parody of a love story, between juveniles; Twain also incorporates a nostalgic evocation of "a vanished past," a parody of Sunday school stories, and elements of a melodramatic thriller, as Henry Nash Smith argued (75, 82). Sometimes Twain uses satire to poke fun at adult society; sometimes he pokes fun at Tom. Sometimes the narrative presents Tom's perspective on events, fostering reader identification and granting Tom agency; sometimes it presents a detached observer, using a circumlocutory and florid phrasing that Twain elsewhere satirizes, perhaps condescending to Tom and his friends as "little waifs" (76, chap. 13). Twain has not yet found the more consistent, first-person vernacular voice that he will use in *Huckleberry Finn*.

Similar incongruities appear in Twain's approach to childhood. Is the book simply a paean to childhood? Or is it a satire? Or something else? Critics have debated whether Tom matures or stays the same, whether the book is a *bildungsroman* or a boy book.[4] I have to admit that I'm not in the *bildungsroman* camp. I don't see Tom as significantly maturing by the end. He's still playing games and he's still hustling. Unlike Horatio Alger's Ragged Dick, who overcomes minor vices and works hard to get ahead, going from rags to relative riches, Tom acquires a fortune almost by chance—thus validating the treasure-hunting game in which he and Huck have indulged. But *Tom Sawyer* as a boy book, a celebration of boyhood— that I can see. And that might make some sense of the ambiguity of Tom's age: he could then represent all boyhood.[5] Still, such ambiguity does a disservice to children. Tom embodies a generalized image of boyhood, a stereotype, if you will. Even though some children find resonance in it, I'm troubled that it's not a particularized portrait but a nostalgic amalgamation of traits.

Twain's blurring of latter-day audience distinctions, however unintentional, reflects the state of children's literature at the time: it was not yet sharply differentiated from literature for adults. And in mapping new territory—for himself and for literature as a whole—he drew on a variety of preexisting discourses, leading to inconsistencies that could lend power to the work but also to potential stereotyping. It's to another strand of discourse, and its potential for stereotyping, that I turn next.

SECOND MOVEMENT

Like other white Americans, many Twain critics have tended to think of race dualistically, as black and white: they have paid much attention to blacks in Twain's work, but little to American Indians. In nineteenth-century children's literature, as in nineteenth-century literature more generally, Indians were generally either evil or noble (Stott 4; Sundquist). Susan Scheckel points out the need, early in the nineteenth century, to create a sense of national origins; and Americans turned to Indians even though the actual history of whites' relationships with Indians questioned the legitimacy of a national identity founded on liberty (7–9). Portrayals of Indians, often with contradictions that could be symbolically resolved through narrative closure, performed important cultural work. The evil Indian was hideous, dishonest, vengeful, and cruel; the noble one was honest, generous, and loyal—to whites, that is. The former figure appeared in early captivity stories and later dime novels; the latter, in such a story as Louisa May Alcott's "Onawandah" (1884), whose hero gives his life as he rescues two white children from captivity, loyally serving the white family that took him in when he was starving. Both figures are stereotypes that do a disservice to American Indians.

What Twain does with Native Americans in *Tom Sawyer* is rather different from what he does with the largely invisible African Americans. Blacks and Indians were situated rather differently in the national imaginary in the late nineteenth century. If, as Toni Morrison has argued, black slavery helped define a new nation's sense of liberty, by establishing its opposite (see esp. 3–28), American Indians provided the country with an honored past. Hence, in addition to the negative stereotype of the evil Indian—the one who still needed to be quashed in the nineteenth century, whether through removals like the ones that led to the Trail of Tears in the 1830s or through massacres like the one at Wounded Knee in 1890—there was also the stereotype associated with nobility, even with the regal.[6] If, furthermore, the Indian was seen as vanishing, the noble image could be allowed even freer play, certainly more than noble images of African Americans could. An African American could be imaged as loyal and perhaps generous, but necessarily subservient: as the mammy rather than the Indian princess. As Eric J. Sundquist points out regarding rebel figures, contrasting Black Hawk's *Autobiography* (1833) and Nat Turner's *Confessions* (1831), "the African American rebel remained a specter of terror whereas the Indian rebel by then could more easily be absorbed into the narrative of Romantic nationalism" (212). Twain, however, reversed the valences. Although raised in a slave-holding community, he learned over the years to respect African Americans. His portrait of Jim in *Huckleberry Finn*, at least in the early pages, shows respect for the slave's humanity; and in the 1880s Twain helped defray expenses for an African American studying law at Yale, someone who would go on to mentor civil rights lawyer and Supreme Court Justice Thurgood Marshall (Fishkin 104–5). Twain seems never to have overcome a distaste for Indians, however, a distaste—even revulsion—fostered by his early prospecting and work as a journalist in the West. Despite opportunities to dismantle negative images, despite almost flirting with such opportunities, Twain declined to do so in *Tom Sawyer*.

Consider the chapter detailing miscellaneous events in Tom's summer. We learn that the fourth of July was disappointing in part because "the greatest man in the world (as Tom supposed) Mr. Benton, an actual United States Senator, . . . was not twenty-five feet high" (112, chap. 22). Thomas Hart Benton was, in fact, a five-term senator from Missouri, best remembered now perhaps for espousing "manifest destiny," the idea that it was the clear destiny of the United States to expand its territory to the Pacific Ocean. Westward expansion by whites, of course, meant running roughshod yet again over American Indians, already pushed westward through broken treaties and removals. During the Second Seminole War of the 1830s Benton learned that U.S. troops were violating flags of truce. Yet, far from being outraged with the U.S. soldiers, he was so upset that Seminoles were resisting removal that he invented details to claim that the troops were justified: he posited that a white flag, the recognized sign for asking to talk or for surrender, might be a bit of cloth "stripped, perhaps, from the body of a murdered child, or its murdered mother" and hence should not be allowed to "cover the insidious visits of spies and enemies. A firm and manly course was taken" (*Congressional Globe*, qtd. in Rogin 240). The "manly course"? Seminoles carrying white flags were shot. So much for the rules of war. It might be tempting to think that, in deflating Benton (not, after all, "twenty-five feet high"), Twain wanted to swerve from the popular and populist embrace of the United States expanding ever westward and making the Indian eventually disappear.

It might also be tempting to think that, in the graveyard scene in *Tom Sawyer*, Twain is playing subversively with Indian themes as well. There we have an Indian who has agreed to desecrate a grave but who kills the instigator of such desecration and in the name of revenge: he kills the doctor who hired him to obtain a corpse, arranging for the blame for the murder to fall on his partner, Muff Potter. The discourse that Twain is overtly invoking here is that of the nineteenth-century controversy over the study of anatomy: doctors learned how to treat illness and injury by studying cadavers—indeed they were often required by law to undertake such study—but there were also laws preventing them from having access to corpses, and thus they sometimes employed rather shady means to remedy this lack (see, e.g., Draper 201). Yet perhaps Twain is also invoking another, subtextual discourse.

In the 1860s there were several now-notorious cases in which Army surgeons rushed to the fields of battle or massacre in Colorado, Kansas, and the Dakotas to collect and deflesh the bodies, especially the heads, of slain Indians, in order to ship the skulls and other bones to the Army Medical Museum in Washington, D.C. (see, e.g., Thomas 53–58). The surgeons had to use deception, often at night, to slip past the Cheyenne or Pawnee or Lakota who might be guarding their dead. The purpose of the thefts was to provide skulls for scientific study, presumably to enhance the collection of skulls of many races. Yet by the 1890s, at a time when Native Americans comprised about half of one percent of the population of the United States, Indian skulls constituted 54.4 percent of the collection then stored at the National Museum of Natural History of the Smithsonian Institution (Smits 43; Gulliford 126): one has to consider the possibility of racist motivations. Certainly Indians did not appreciate being the objects of such study: nineteenth-century travelers frequently noted what one called "that veneration for their remains which is a characteristic of the American Indians" (John Bradbury [1819], qtd. in Bieder 18). In the words of the father of Chief Joseph of the Nez Perce (Nimíipuu), "Never sell the bones of your father and mother," to which Chief Joseph added, "A man who would not love his father's grave is worse than a wild animal" (qtd. in Echo-Hawk and Echo-Hawk 17). Native Americans also often objected, when they were told that they would have to move west to make room for eager white settlers, that they did not want to leave the land where their ancestors were buried (see, e.g., Rogin 214–16, citing none other than Andrew Jackson, the prime engineer of Indian removal). It's tempting to think that Injun Joe's interest in revenge is not just personal—not just because the doctor once turned him away when Joe begged for something to eat and the doctor's father had Joe "jailed for a vagrant" (57, chap. 9)—but reflects a broader sense of injustice. The themes in the graveyard incident are not strictly aligned for such a case—there's no indication that Hoss Williams, whose body was being disinterred, was Indian—but the conjunction of American Indian, grave desecration, and revenge could bespeak a conjunction that was in the air at the time, an available discourse. Twain could conceivably be rehearsing such a conjunction in order to question popular opinion.

Such a benign possibility is not supported, however, when one looks elsewhere in Twain's writings. Carter Revard, for instance, points to the racism in Twain's *Roughing It* (1872), in which Twain says, among other things, "The Bushmen and our Goshoots are manifestly descended from the self-same gorilla, or kangaroo, or Norway rat, whichever animal-Adam the Darwinians trace them to" (qtd. in Revard 342). Another repository of Twain's attitudes is an 1870 essay, "The Noble Red Man," published six years before *Tom Sawyer*, and it's this repository that I'll focus on here. Now it's possible to argue that Twain, ever fond of tall tales, was exaggerating in this essay; certainly other work that he published in this venue, such as "The Story of the Good Little Boy," was satirically exaggerated. It's also important to note that Twain was reacting against a literary image of American Indians: part of his vituperation was directed at the success of James Fenimore Cooper and others, whose Indians exuded a "kingly presence," with hair "as black as the raven's wing" and an "eagle eye," and spoke in metaphors and exhibited "peerless faithfulness" and "knightly magnanimity," to cite the essay itself ("Noble Red Man" 426–27). Yet none of these possible explanations really excuses the vitriol of Twain's ensuing portrait. For he writes that the Indian "is a good, fair, desirable subject for extermination if ever there was one" (427). The "Noble Aborigine," he argues, is "little, and scrawny, and black, and dirty," "base and treacherous," "greedy," "a skulking coward and a windy braggart, who strikes without warning"—in short, "a poor, filthy, naked scurvy vagabond, whom to exterminate were a charity to the Creator's worthier insects and reptiles which he oppresses" (427, 428, 427).

Then, in *Tom Sawyer*, there is Injun Joe. Twain isn't just conveying the attitudes of small-town whites as a backdrop, representing the temper of the times, as he might conceivably be said to be doing regarding African American slaves in this book. Instead he consciously chose to make his villain Native American. James C. McNutt claims, as part of an argument that Twain increasingly embraces cultural relativism in his thinking about American Indians, that the seriousness with which Twain treats Injun Joe represents some progress: Joe is "one of the few Indians accorded the status of a full character in any of Twain's works" (232).[7] Yet with virtually no redeeming backstory or moments of humanizing indecision, this unabashed villain kills the doctor, is willing to let Muff Potter die for the crime, and seeks to avenge having been horsewhipped by Justice Douglas by scheming to slit the nostrils and notch the ears of the man's widow. As an otherwise admirable character comments regarding these latter plans, "white men don't take that sort of revenge. But an Injun! That's a different matter, altogether" (143, chap. 30). The idea that Indians were vengeful was a nineteenth-century stereotype, one of the few that Twain failed to enumerate in "The Noble Red Man."

Curiously, though, Joe's death inspires the narrator's most magniloquent flight of fancy, as he descants on the drop of water that falls on a stalagmite every three minutes, in the cave where Joe dies, and

> was falling when the Pyramids were new; when Troy fell; when the foundations of Rome were laid; when Christ was crucified; when the Conqueror created the British empire; when Columbus sailed; when the massacre at Lexington was "news." . . . It is many and many a year since the hapless half-breed scooped out the stone to catch the priceless drops, but to this day the tourist stares longest at that pathetic stone and that slow dropping water when he comes to see the wonders of McDougal's cave. (156–57, chap. 33)

Twain's use of temporal distances here—the past of Western civilization, the pastness of what the tourist views—simultaneously invokes the American Indian past and erases it. No mention here of the ancient Mound Builders, for instance. Instead there is a generalized pastness that may hint at the past of an ancient race—also a doomed race, pathetic really. After the Red Man has safely vanished, whites can think of him with what Renato Rosaldo calls imperialist nostalgia, masking the processes of domination with a species of regretful tenderness, translating "transformations of other cultures" into "personal losses" (70).

Again, it may be tempting to think that in this scene Twain is reimagining a trope, in this case that of the captivity of whites by American Indians. Indian captivity narratives had been a staple American literary genre—and Indian captivities a frequent trope in other works—since Mary Rowlandson's *Soveraignty and Goodness of God, Together with the Faithfulness of His Promises Displayed; Being an Account of the Captivity and Restauration of Mrs. Mary Rowlandson* (1682). These tales, whether nonfictional or fictional, tell the story of a white captured by Indians during a time of war, subjected to duress, sometimes adapting, but often escaping. Early in the colonial era the narratives played out fears of the effects of the wilderness on European, especially Puritan, sensibilities and enacted a drama of being tested or punished by God; later they enacted a national fantasy of overcoming the wilderness and Indians, justifying violence and dispossession.[8] When Tom and Becky are lost in the cave that turns out to be Injun Joe's hideout, they enact a displacement of such a narrative, caught more by the cave than by the Indian, and successfully escape. That Injun Joe should himself get sealed into the cave could almost be an inversion of the trope, a possible way of according some sympathy and respect to the vanishing Indian, especially since he is now securely vanquished—in this case, starved to death, having uselessly scratched at the foundation of the blocked door with his knife, his eyes "fixed, to the last moment, upon the light and cheer of the free world outside" (156, chap. 33).

Yet Twain does not allow dripping nostalgia to linger long. In the paragraph after the Pyramids-and-Troy one cited above, his narrator describes Joe's funeral: people flocked there with "their children, and all sorts of provisions, and confessed that they had had almost as satisfactory a time at the funeral as they could have had at the hanging" (157, chap. 33). In the next paragraph the narrator relates that Joe's death fortunately quashes "a committee of sappy women" who had started a petition to the governor to pardon Joe, imploring the governor, in the words of the narrator, "to be a merciful ass and trample his duty under foot" (157, chap. 33). Twain effectively displaces his narrator's sentimentality about Joe's death onto sappy women pleading for Joe's life. He thereby undermines his sentimentally poetic flight, without fully erasing its poetry, I would argue, simply disinfecting it: as if made anxious by his own poetic soaring, or perhaps to quash the Indian even more fully while getting in a dig at white women, too tenderhearted and weak toward evildoers, he demolishes the outbreak of sentiment.

Glenn Hendler has traced the alternations between sentimental identifications and antisentimental distancing in *Tom Sawyer*, the multiplicities of what it means to be a boy, culminating in a projection of the destabilizing elements onto Becky, who is then effectively expelled from the world of the novel: Tom can then finally represent stable, autonomous, self-possessed masculinity. I would add to the gender politics that Hendler describes a racial one: something similar happens with Injun Joe. Throughout the novel Tom has flirted with the ultimate disintegration of the self that is death, returning from the grave, as it were, but actually from Jackson's Island, to appear at his own funeral, and more nearly dying in actuality when he and Becky become lost in McDougal's Cave. His hypothetical and potential deaths are effectively projected onto Injun Joe, whom we first encounter disinterring a body and who finally dies in the cave that nearly entombs Tom (as if Twain is playing yet more with the trope of Indian burials; indeed Injun Joe's bones are disinterred by whites). If Tom achieves a kind of white masculine individuality at the end, it's by abrogating not just the feminine but the racial Other, this racial Other who is also internally destabilized by being a half-breed.

Half Indian, half white, Joe is called a half-breed—*breed* being an animal-based term frequently applied to nineteenth-century Native Americans. When he isn't referring to Joe as a "bloody-minded outcast" or a "human insect" (156, 157, chap. 33), Twain uses "half-breed," eight times in the novel. Revard suggests that the term would have implied bastardy and also that the Indian mother was "used as prostitute. 'Half-breed' carried not only racist but legal, moral, social, and religious sting; half-breeds were not only 'naturally' apt to be of poor character by being products of miscegenation, but apt to be really bad people because they were children of society's 'dregs,'" drunks as well as prostitutes (346). Or to map the body onto the nation, as Sundquist does, "the theme of mixed blood became . . . a means of generating the horror of transgressed or collapsed boundaries in the body comparable to boundaries violated and crossed by actual Indian warfare and Removal" (224). At times in nineteenth-century cultural representations, a half-breed could assume a tragic nobility similar to that of the tragic mulatto. A mulatto was sometimes viewed as tragically torn between two worlds—hence the power of the literary theme in works ranging from Lydia Maria Child's "The Quadroons" (1842) and William Wells Brown's *Clotel* (1853) to Nella Larsen's *Passing* (1929). Occasionally a half-breed could assume a similar tragic nobility, as in Child's *Hobomok* (1824). Yet often in popular thinking a half-breed was worse than a full-blooded American Indian: he (and the figure was usually male in the popular imagination) presumably combined the cunning of a white with the treachery of a savage. The politics of slavery and race in the nineteenth century made one black according to a precise formula, such as having one's heritage be one-eighth black, thereby creating a binary system: one was either black or not. The divide was more ambiguous for Native Americans—not strictly binary. After all, many of the First Families of Virginia, as they styled themselves, were proud to claim the seventeenth-century Pocahontas as an ancestor (see Tilton 172). Policing the nineteenth-century boundaries of racial purity seemed to require strong sanctions against further miscegenation: the offspring was thought to be more tainted than a full-blooded Indian, who could at times be depicted as noble even though savage. Francis Parkman wrote in *The Oregon Trail* (1849) that the half-breed was "a race of rather extraordinary composition, being, according to the common saying, half Indian, half white man, and half devil" (qtd. in Brown 100). Other nineteenth-century writers described various mixed-race individuals as having "all the vices of the whites and Nascapees, without one of their virtuous qualities," "none of the redeeming traits of the full-blooded

Indian, and none of the virtues of the white man"—as, in short, a "monstrous abor-tion" (qtd. in Scheik 19, 21, 35).[9]

In *The Adventures of Tom Sawyer*, this misbegotten figure of the Indian legiti-mates two white boys' ill-gotten gains. The treasure that Tom and Huck find "under the cross" in the cave, Injun Joe's stash, is theirs to keep. It's not as if it was the Welshman's secret hoard, or even that of the dead doctor. In a law review article Elmer M. Million cleverly mounts a case that, according to 1835 Missouri statutes, and assuming that Injun Joe and his confederate, the "ragged man," died intestate, Huck and Tom are entitled to the money. Yet there is no evidence that the possi-bility of heirs or previous owners crosses the minds of anyone in St. Petersburg: no one tries to find Injun Joe's legitimate heirs or his victims or the victims of Murrel's gang, whose treasure Joe seems to have appropriated. Indeed Scott Michaelsen argues that Tom "seeks to steal gold legitimately found by Injun Joe, and then 'for-gets' (rather actively, perhaps) to tell the town that Joe is trapped in the cave" (135). Joe's villainy justifies Tom and Huck in keeping his tainted lucre, the very taint affording legitimacy—much as white settlers could feel justified about keeping Indian lands if they could consider Native Americans ignoble savages. Joe functions as a scapegoat for negative features of nineteenth-century adult masculinity: the potentially murderous competition for wealth that gave rise to robber barons becomes, in him, literally cutthroat. Tom and Huck don't need to kill for cash, at least not directly—Joe does that for them and then is himself "accidentally" but conveniently killed off.

One more note about Injun Joe before I move from the literal representation of the American Indian in Twain's text to more figural ones. Scores of nineteenth- and especially twentieth-century critics writing about *Adventures of Huckleberry Finn*, including Twain's biographer Albert Bigelow Paine in 1912 and novelist Pat Conroy in 1999, have referred to Huck's companion on the raft as Nigger Jim.[10] Twain never calls Jim by that title in the text. The closest he comes are phrases in which "Jim" functions as an appositive: "Miss Watson's nigger, Jim," who "had a hair-ball," and Huck's letter describing "your runaway nigger Jim" (19, chap. 4; 169, chap. 31). Yet white critics have felt licensed to attach a derogatory epithet to Jim's name. Twain knew better. In *The Adventures of Tom Sawyer*, however, he attaches the derogatory epithet—"Injun" was a degraded dialect form of "Indian"—to the character's name himself.

Then there are less literal appearances of Indians, in the texture of the text. Early on after Tom wishes he could make his aunt remorseful by dying, tempo-rarily, he imagines going off to be a soldier . . . no, better to be an Indian . . . no, better still to be a pirate. If an Indian, he could return from buffaloes and warpaths as "a great chief, bristling with feathers, hideous with paint, and prance into Sunday-school, some drowsy summer morning, with a blood-curdling war-whoop, and sear the eye-balls of all his companions with unappeasable envy" (51, chap. 8). But it would be "gaudier" to be a pirate, to become the Black Avenger of the Spanish Main. And that hierarchy of play—pirates over Indians—would seem to reassert itself later on, when Tom, Huck, and another boy seek ways to spend their time as runaways on Jackson's Island. It's only after they play pirates and more pirates and circus clowns and marbles, and they smoke, that they decide to "be Indians for a change" (91, chap. 16). They strip, stripe themselves with mud ("like so many zebras"), attack an English settlement ("all of them chiefs, of course"), then attack one another as separate hostile tribes "and darted upon each other from ambush with dreadful war-whoops, and killed and scalped each other by thousands. It was a gory day. Consequently it was an extremely satisfactory one" (91, chap. 16). They have to end by smoking a peace pipe, of course; and Tom and Joe are thankful that previously "they had gone into savagery" (91, chap. 16)—that they had already practiced the "savagery" of smoking—so they can now smoke without getting sick. Such play bears little relationship to what it actually means to be Indian: as Philip Deloria has noted of Indian play more generally, it "was perhaps not so much about a desire to become Indian . . . as it was a longing for the utopian experience of being in between, of living a paradoxical moment in which absolute liberty coexisted with the absolute" (185)—a longing to preserve stability while enjoying freedom, as the boys are attempting to do on Jackson's Island. Once again Tom can enact the freedoms associated with multiplicity, but only in play, projecting the destabilizing elements onto the figure of the Indian. Still, for Tom, Indian play is second best, at best. And that's despite the fact that it seems to lend itself to more of Twain's favorite "humorous" effects (the boys all chiefs, scalping one another by the thousands) than piracy does.

As for other submerged discourse invoking Native Americans, when Tom shows off to attract Becky's attention he is "'going on' like an Indian; yelling, laughing, chasing boys, jumping over the fence at risk of life and limb, throwing hand-springs, standing on his head—doing all the heroic things he could conceive of" (71, chap. 12). The linking of heroism and handsprings is particularly humorous if the audience believes that Indians and heroism can be yoked together only violently. Injun Joe, of course, enacts the adventure stories that Tom likes to playact: if the game does not include a real pirate then a real Indian will do, or rather a half-breed, half-projection. Twain turns to projection onto a nonwhite adult male to broker the chasm between childhood and adulthood that the book attempts to bridge.

Later in the book Huck is relieved to learn that what villagers found at the Temperance Tavern where Injun Joe had stayed was only liquor, not treasure; thus Huck can fall back on his sickbed, thinking that "there would have been a great pow-wow if it had been the gold" (147, chap. 30). In short, there would have been so much noise that even Huck in his sickbed would have heard something. The *Oxford English Dictionary* (*OED*) gives a subsidiary or occasional meaning of "powwow" as "bustle, activity," citing a reference in Twain's *Following the Equator* (1897) to "energy and confusion and pow-wow." The usage in *Tom Sawyer*, not referenced by the *OED*, seems to have a similar meaning—resembling Twain's earlier use of "going on" when Tom shows off in front of Becky, indicating certainly a bustle and possibly something more, an unruly ruckus.[11] A term used more or less respectfully by other nineteenth-century whites (as cited in the *OED*), to refer to a Native medicine man, a ritual ceremony, or a meeting or gathering, is here degraded certainly to bustle, possibly to mere noise. Twain may not have single-handedly stretched the meaning of "powwow," helping erase what it meant to Natives, but he mightily contributed.

Earlier when Tom is whitewashing the fence and wants to get his friend Ben to do some, Tom feigns reluctance to relinquish the brush and says, "Ben, I'd like to, honest injun; but . . ." (20, chap. 2). A curious phrase that, "honest injun." Tom's proceeding is part of a ruse to get others to whitewash the fence. And the implied audience should know better than to trust the honesty of Indians: as Twain says in "The Noble Red Man," the Indian's language is not figurative but "very simple and unostentatious, and consists of plain, straightforward lies" (427). For Twain, "honest injun" would be an oxymoron, hinting at Tom's dishonesty. The OED glosses the term straightforwardly—"honour bright: perh. orig. an assurance of good faith extracted from Indians"—though in most of the ten cited examples the honesty of the user seems to be under question.[12] Tom, of course, uses the phrase not altogether honestly, as part of a con. But then this is a novel in which honesty is undermined, or at least revalued, a novel in which Judge Thatcher eventually praises Tom for his "magnanimous lie" in taking the blame for Becky's tearing of the anatomy book—"a lie that was worthy to hold up its head and march down through history breast to breast with George Washington's lauded Truth about the hatchet!" (166, chap. 35). Then again, the story about young George admitting to chopping down the cherry tree was invented in 1806 by Mason Weems[13]: this Truth, too, is a lie.

But back to "honest injun." When, near the end of the book, Tom tells Huck that Joe's money is in the cave, an incredulous Huck asks, "Tom,—honest injun, now—is it fun, or earnest?" (158, chap. 33). In this instance, Tom is in earnest. Honest: the money is in the cave. But the treasure hunt has been in fun, too, as well as earnest. Tom works hard at playing. Indians, of course, don't: Twain claims in "The Noble Red Man" that the Indian "never works himself" (428)—his wife does all the work.[14] Yet here, just two pages after the discovery of Injun Joe's body in the cave—followed by Twain's magniloquence on dripping water and his excoriation of sappy women—Indian and other play is transmuted into the white middle-class seriousness of getting money; all are mediated by a figure (honest? injun?) whom Twain and other whites assumed could not be trusted. James M. Cox argues that Tom undertakes "play which converts all serious projects in the town to pleasure and at the same time subverts all the adult rituals by revealing that actually they are nothing but dull play to begin with" (141). I'd argue that there is two-way traffic here, between play and seriousness—in Peter Messent's words, "Tom is simultaneously both playful boy and apprentice businessman" (71)—mediated by an Indian who can be played but is also deadly serious. At the end of Tom's adventures, once the literal Indian is dead, Tom can swear by him in all honesty as he collapses the distinction between play and work.

Much of the power of Twain's writing derives from the way he would seem to collapse boundaries as he plays with audience, rethinking genre and switching tones. In his portrayal of race in The Adventures of Tom Sawyer, however, he was

very much of his time—or even worse, given that Helen Hunt Jackson would
shortly write *Ramona* (1884), a novel acknowledging some of the wrenching difficulties faced by Native Americans, even if she does not fully realize their perspectives. Twain may have contributed to the transformation of a genre and the creation
of the boy book; he may in so doing have crossed what we have since come to see as
audience boundaries, inviting readers of all ages. Yet in his portrayals of race in this
book that has become a touchstone of nineteenth-century children's literature, he
was not inviting to readers of all races. Indeed he used the figure of the Indian to
mediate between child and adult in the book and in its audience, the Indian
becoming a child's projection that can then be expelled, making the book simultaneously appealing to and what adults would consider safe for a white child audience.
White and Indian remain markedly twain in *Tom Sawyer*, their boundaries crossed
only metaphorically; Indians and especially Injun Joe simply mark the sign of the
cross, simply enable other crossings, before they disappear altogether.

NOTES

1. Subsequent references to the text include chapter and page numbers. In an
exchange of letters with William Dean Howells, Twain claims in July 1875 that *Tom
Sawyer* is "*not* a boy's book," but then Howells urges him to treat the story "explicitly *as*
a boy's story," and Twain agrees, admitting that it is "professedly & confessedly a boy's
and girl's book" (3 July 1875, Smith and Gibson 1:90; 21 November 1875, 1:110; 18 January
1876, 1:122).

2. He also includes girls as part of his audience: his prefatory inclusiveness was in
part a marketing ploy, but he invites and hence creates at least some space for female
readers. Almost half of the nineteenth-century reviews that twentieth-century scholars
have located followed Twain's lead in the preface and stressed that the book was for young
and old; the reviewers were less likely than Twain was, however, to embrace girls as part of
his audience.

3. For a defense of "the contest for narrative authority" in the novel, see Wonham.

4. For an influential early argument that Tom does indeed mature, see Blair.
Trensky provides an excellent brief account of formal and thematic characteristics of the
boy book (including the "separate, timeless, unchanging aspect of the boy's world" [515]),
as does Gribben.

5. In the preface, Twain notes that Tom "is a combination of the characteristics of
three boys whom I knew, and therefore belongs to the composite order of architecture"
(5). He would seem to be composite with respect to age as well.

6. The many insightful studies of the functions of American Indians in the national
imaginary include those by Abrams, Berkhofer, Deloria, Huhndorf, Pearce, Scheckel, and
Trachtenberg.

7. McNutt goes on to admit that Twain "never totally refrained from using the
Indian's savagery as a club whenever convenient" (238). For arguments that Twain's views
ameliorated over time, see Denton, Hanson, and Newquist. For less exculpatory accounts
of Twain's attitudes, see Brown, Camfield, Coulombe, Harris, L. Morris, and Revard. Few

devote much attention to the portrayal of Native Americans specifically in *Tom Sawyer*, however.

8. Insightful accounts of the genre include those by Burnham, Castiglia, Faery, Faludi, Namias, Slotkin, and Strong.

9. Scheick is quoting James McKenzie, journal (1808); Mary Howard, *The Black Gauntlet* (1860); and a character in Walt Whitman's "The Half-Breed" (1846).

10. As early as 1884, a year before the book appeared, when Twain was giving readings based on it, a journalist noted that "Huck Finn, a white boy, and Nigger Jim ran away from the plantation" ("Some of Mark Twain's Fun"). It's possible that Twain himself referred to Jim orally as "Nigger Jim," but he did not do so in the text.

11. Most of the eight appearances of "powwow" later in *Adventures of Huckleberry Finn*, whether it's "a pow-wow of cussing" or the barking of dogs "making pow-wow enough for a million" (78, chap. 16; 215, chap. 40), seem to make the term synonymous with "ruckus." I am grateful to Stephen Railton's excellent "Mark Twain in His Times" website (http://etext.lib.virginia.edu/railton/) for providing searchable texts of Twain's works.

12. As is the case in ten additional quotations in Lighter. Although Mathews provides a citation of "Honest Indian" from the 1851 San Francisco *Pioneer*, the first clear example of the phrase in the *OED* is the cited quotation from *Tom Sawyer*. An 1892 dictionary notes the term's use as "a pledge of faith" but claims, "Originally, no doubt, the reference to Indian honesty was sarcastic" (Walsh). William and Mary Morris note, "Originally it was probably an expression of sarcastic derision—'as honest as an Indian.' But later it came to mean the same thing as the British *honor bright* or the American *Scout's honor*—a pledge of truth and honesty"

13. For the fifth edition of his biography of Washington (see, e.g., Marling 306).

14. In Twain's lexicon, Indian women are not Indians but squaws.

WORKS CITED

Abrams, Ann Uhry. *The Pilgrims and Pocahontas: Rival Myths of American Origin*. Boulder, CO: Westview, 1999.

Alcott, Louisa M. "Onawandah." *Spinning-Wheel Stories*, 77–98. 1884. New York: Grosset, 1908.

Benton, Michael. "Readers, Texts, Contexts: Reader-Response Criticism." In *Understanding Children's Literature*, edited by Peter Hunt, 81–99. London: Routledge, 1998.

Berkhofer, Robert F., Jr. *The White Man's Indian: Images of the American Indian from Columbus to the Present*. New York: Knopf, 1978.

"The Best American Books." *The Critic* 19 (3 June 1893): 589.

Bieder, Robert E. *Brief Historical Survey of the Expropriation of American Indian Remains*. N.p.: Native American Rights Fund, 1990.

Blair, Walter. "On the Structure of *Tom Sawyer*." *Modern Philology* 37 (August 1939): 75–88.

Botelho, Maria José, and Masha Kabakow Rudman. *Critical Multicultural Analysis of Children's Literature: Mirrors, Windows, and Doors*. New York: Routledge, 2009.

Brown, Harry J. *Injun Joe's Ghost: The Indian Mixed-Blood in American Writing*. Columbia: U of Missouri P, 2004.

Burnham, Michelle. *Captivity and Sentiment: Cultural Exchange in American Literature, 1682–1861*. 1997. Hanover, NH: Dartmouth College, UP of New England, 1999.

Camfield, Gregg. "Native Americans." In *The Oxford Companion to Mark Twain*, 389–91. Oxford: Oxford UP, 2003.

Castiglia, Christopher. *Bound and Determined: Captivity, Culture-Crossing and White Womanhood from Mary Rowlandson to Patty Hearst*. Chicago: U of Chicago P, 1996.

Clark, Beverly Lyon. *Kiddie Lit: The Cultural Construction of Children's Literature in America*. Baltimore: Johns Hopkins UP, 2003.

Coats, Karen. *Looking Glasses and Neverlands: Lacan, Desire, and Subjectivity in Children's Literature*. Iowa City: U of Iowa P, 2004.

Conroy, Pat. "A Muddied Mississippi Misadventure." *New York Times Magazine*, November 1999. American Enterprise Institute, 1999. Accessed 19 November 2005. http://www.geocities.com/lowenstein1992/mississippi.html

Coulombe, Joseph L. "Mark Twain's Native Americans and the Repeated Racial Pattern in *Adventures of Huckleberry Finn*." *American Literary Realism* 33, no. 3 (Spring 2001): 261–79.

Cox, James M. *Mark Twain: The Fate of Humor*. Princeton: Princeton UP, 1966.

Deloria, Philip. *Playing Indian*. New Haven: Yale UP, 1998.

Denton, Lynn W. "Mark Twain and the American Indian." *Mark Twain Journal* 16, no. 1 (1972): 1–3.

Doctorow, E. L. Introduction. In *The Adventures of Tom Sawyer*, by Mark Twain, xxxi–xxxviii. New York: Oxford UP, 1996.

Draper, John. "Dissection of the Dead." *New York Times*, 18 October 1853, 2. Reprinted in Twain, *Tom Sawyer* 201–4.

Echo-Hawk, Roger C., and Walter R. Echo-Hawk. *Battle Fields and Burial Grounds: The Indian Struggle to Protect Ancestral Graves in the United States*. Minneapolis: Lerner, 1994.

Faery, Rebecca Blevins. *Cartographies of Desire: Captivity, Race, and Sex in the Shaping of an American Nation*. Norman: U of Oklahoma P, 1999.

Faludi, Susan. *The Terror Dream: Fear and Fantasy in Post-9/11 America*. New York: Metropolitan, 2007.

Fishkin, Shelley Fisher. *Lighting Out for the Territory: Reflections on Mark Twain and American Culture*. New York: Oxford UP, 1997.

Gribben, Alan. "Boy Books, Bad Boy Books, and *The Adventures of Tom Sawyer*." In Twain, *Tom Sawyer* 290–306.

Gulliford, Andrew. "Bones of Contention: The Repatriation of Native American Human Remains." *Public Historian* 18, no. 4 (1996): 119–43.

Hanson, Elizabeth I. "Mark Twain's Indians Reexamined." *Mark Twain Journal* 20, no. 4 (1981): 11–12.

Harris, Helen L. "Mark Twain's Response to the Native American." *American Literature* 46, no. 4 (January 1975): 495–505.

Hendler, Glenn. "Masculinity and the Logic of Sympathy in *The Adventures of Tom Sawyer*." In Twain, *Tom Sawyer* 306–31.

Huhndorf, Shari M. *Going Native: Indians in the American Cultural Imagination*. Ithaca, NY: Cornell UP, 2001.

Lighter, J. E., ed. *Random House Historical Dictionary of American Slang*. 2 vols. New York: Random House, 1994–.

Machor, James L., and Philip Goldstein. Introduction. In *Reception Study: From Literary Theory to Cultural Studies*, edited by James L. Machor and Philip Goldstein, ix–xvii. New York: Routledge, 2001.

Marling, Karal Ann. *George Washington Slept Here: Colonial Revivals and American Culture, 1876–1986*. Cambridge: Harvard UP, 1988.

Mathews, Mitford M. *A Dictionary of Americanisms on Historical Principles.* 2 vols. Chicago: U of Chicago P, 1951.

McNutt, James C. "Mark Twain and the American Indian: Earthly Realism and Heavenly Idealism." *American Indian Quarterly* 4, no. 3 (August 1978): 228–42.

Messent, Peter. *Mark Twain.* New York: St. Martin, 1997.

Michaelsen, Scott. "Tom Sawyer's Capitalisms and the Destructuring of Huck Finn." *Prospects* 22 (1997): 133–51.

Million, Elmer M. "SAWYER et al. v. ADMINISTRATOR OF INJUN JOE." *Missouri Law Review* 16, no. 1 (January 1951): 27–38.

Morris, Linda A. "*The Adventures of Tom Sawyer* and *The Prince and the Pauper* as Juvenile Literature." In *A Companion to Mark Twain*, edited by Peter Messent and Louis J. Budd, 371–86. New York: Blackwell, 2005.

Morris, William, and Mary Morris. *Morris Dictionary of Word and Phrase Origins.* New York: Harper, 1971.

Morrison, Toni. *Playing in the Dark: Whiteness and the Literary Imagination.* Cambridge: Harvard UP, 1992.

Namias, June. *White Captives: Gender and Ethnicity on the American Frontier.* Chapel Hill: U of North Carolina P, 1993.

Newquist, David L. "Mark Twain among the Indians." *Midamerica* 24 (1994): 59–72.

Nodelman, Perry. *The Hidden Adult: Defining Children's Literature.* Baltimore: Johns Hopkins UP, 2008.

Oxford English Dictionary. 2005. Oxford UP. Accessed 18 November 2005. http://dictionary.oed.com/

Paine, Albert Bigelow. *Mark Twain, a Biography.* 2 vols. New York: Harper, 1912.

———, ed. *Mark Twain's Letters.* 2 vols. New York: Harper, 1917.

Pearce, Roy Harvey. *Savagism and Civilization: A Study of the Indian and the American Mind.* Rev. ed. Berkeley: U of California P, 1988.

Revard, Carter. "Why Mark Twain Murdered Injun Joe—and Will Never Be Indicted." *Massachusetts Review* 40, no. 4 (Winter 1999–2000): 643–70. Reprinted in Twain, *Tom Sawyer* 332–52.

Review of *The Adventures of Tom Sawyer. New York Times*, 13 January 1877, 3. Reprinted in Scharnhorst 54–57.

Rogin, Michael Paul. *Fathers and Children: Andrew Jackson and the Subjugation of the American Indian.* New York: Knopf, 1975.

Rosaldo, Renato. "Imperialist Nostalgia." In *Culture and Truth: The Remaking of Social Analysis*, 68–87. Boston: Beacon, 1989.

Rotundo, E. Anthony. "Boy Culture." In *American Manhood: Transformations in Masculinity from the Revolution to the Modern Era.* New York: Basic Books, 1993. Reprinted in Twain, *Tom Sawyer* 213–20.

Scharnhorst, Gary, ed. *Critical Essays on "The Adventures of Tom Sawyer."* New York: Hall, 1993.

Scheckel, Susan. *The Insistence of the Indian: Race and Nationalism in Nineteenth-Century American Culture.* Princeton: Princeton UP, 1998.

Scheick, William J. *The Half-Blood: A Cultural Symbol in 19ᵗʰ-Century American Fiction.* Lexington: UP of Kentucky, 1979.

Shavit, Zohar. *The Poetics of Children's Literature.* Athens: U of Georgia P, 1986.

Slotkin, Richard. *Regeneration through Violence: The Mythology of the American Frontier, 1600–1860.* Middletown, CT: Wesleyan UP, 1973.

Smith, Henry Nash. *Mark Twain: The Development of a Writer.* Cambridge: Belknap P–Harvard UP, 1962.

Smith, Henry Nash, and William M. Gibson, eds. *Mark Twain–Howells Letters: The Correspondence of Samuel L. Clemens and William D. Howells, 1872–1910*. 2 vols. Cambridge: Belknap P–Harvard UP, 1960.

Smits, David D. "'Squaw Men,' 'Half-Breeds,' and Amalgamators: Late Nineteenth-Century Anglo-American Attitudes Toward Indian–White Race-Mixing." *American Indian Culture and Research Journal* 15, no. 3 (1991): 29–61.

"Some of Mark Twain's Fun: He and Mr. Cable Amuse an Audience by Turns." *The Sun* (New York), 19 November 1884. Mark Twain in His Times. Accessed 19 November 2005. http://etext.lib.virginia.edu/railton/huckfinn/twinsnyt.html

Stott, Jon C. *Native Americans in Children's Literature*. Phoenix: Oryx, 1995.

Strong, Pauline Turner. *Captive Selves, Captivating Others: The Politics and Poetics of Colonial American Captivity Narratives*. Boulder, CO: Westview, 1999.

Sundquist, Eric J. "The Literature of Expansion and Race." In *The Cambridge History of American Literature*. Vol. 2, *1820–1865*, edited by Sacvan Bercovitch, 125–328. Cambridge: Cambridge UP, 1995.

Thomas, David Hurst. *Skull Wars: Kennewick Man, Archaeology, and the Battle for Native American Identity*. New York: Basic Books, 2000.

Tilton, Robert S. *Pocahontas: The Evolution of an American Narrative*. Cambridge: Cambridge UP, 1994.

Trachtenberg, Alan. *Shades of Hiawatha: Staging Indians, Making Americans, 1880–1930*. New York: Hill, 2004.

Trensky, Anne. "The Bad Boy in Nineteenth-Century American Fiction." *Georgia Review* 27 (1973): 503–17.

Twain, Mark. *Adventures of Huckleberry Finn: An Authoritative Text, Backgrounds and Sources, Criticism*. Edited by Sculley Bradley, Richmond Croom Beatty, E. Hudson Long, and Thomas Cooley. 2nd ed. New York: Norton, 1977.

———. *The Adventures of Tom Sawyer: Authoritative Text, Backgrounds and Contexts, Criticism*. Edited by Beverly Lyon Clark. New York: Norton, 2007.

———. *Huck Finn and Tom Sawyer among the Indians and Other Unfinished Stories*. Edited by Dahlia Armon, Paul Baender, Walter Blair, William M. Gibson, and Franklin R. Rogers. Berkeley: U of California P, 1989.

———. "The Noble Red Man." *Galaxy*, September 1870, 426–29.

Wall, Barbara. *The Narrator's Voice: The Dilemma of Children's Fiction*. 1991. Houndmills, Basingstoke, Hampshire: Macmillan, 1994.

Walsh, William Shepard. *The Handy-Book of Literary Curiosities*. 1892. Detroit: Gale, 1966.

Wonhan, Henry B. "Undoing Romance: The Contest for Narrative Authority in *The Adventures of Tom Sawyer*." In Scharnhorst 228–41.

FURTHER READING

Benton, Michael. "Readers, Texts, Contexts: Reader-Response Criticism." In *Understanding Children's Literature*, edited by Peter Hunt, 81–99. London: Routledge, 1998.

"Books to Avoid." *Oyate*. 2008. Accessed 22 November 2009. http://www.oyate.org/books-to-avoid/index.html

Fox, Dana L., and Kathy G. Short, eds. *Stories Matter: The Complexity of Cultural Authenticity in Children's Literature*. Urbana: NCTE, 2003.

Reese, Debbie. *American Indians in Children's Literature*. 2009. Blog. Accessed 22 November 2009. http://americanindiansinchildrensliterature.blogspot.com/

Seale, Doris, and Beverly Slapin, eds. *A Broken Flute: The Native Experience in Books for Children*. Berkeley: AltaMira and Oyate, 2005.

Stott, Jon C. *Native Americans in Children's Literature*. Phoenix: Oryx, 1995.

Twain, Mark. *The Adventures of Tom Sawyer: Authoritative Text, Backgrounds and Contexts, Criticism*. Edited by Beverly Lyon Clark. New York: Norton, 2007.

CHAPTER 15

··

LIVING WITH THE KINGS: CLASS, TASTE, AND FAMILY FORMATION IN *FIVE LITTLE PEPPERS AND HOW THEY GREW*

··

KELLY HAGER

MARGARET *Sidney is the pen name of Harriett Mulford Stone Lothrop (1844–1924). Born in New Haven, Connecticut to Sidney Mason and Harriett Mulford Stone (both of whom could trace their ancestry back to the Mayflower), she published under a pseudonym because, as her daughter recounts in* The Wayside: Home of Authors, *her father "looked with disfavor upon young women who wrote for publication." "She did not wish to bring opprobrium upon her father's name" but was loathe "wholly to desert it, since she dearly loved him." So she chose Sidney for her father, and Margaret "not because it means 'Pearl' and 'Daisy' but because it means Truth."*

Her first published writings were "Polly Pepper's Chicken Pie" and "Phronsie Pepper's New Shoes," which she sent to Wide Awake, *a children's magazine published by D. Lothrop Publishing Company, in 1878. These stories were so popular that the head of the firm, Daniel Lothrop, asked for more. She wrote twelve installments in 1880 and collected the tales as* Five Little Peppers and How They Grew, *which Lothrop published in 1881, the same year Daniel Lothrop married the author. They had one daughter, Margaret, in 1884. They lived in Boston and summered at The Wayside in Concord (Hawthorne's home and, before that, the Alcotts'), which they purchased from Hawthorne's daughter in 1883.*

In addition to the Pepper books, Lothrop wrote regional travel guides, novels and stories for children, and novels for adults, all under the name Margaret Sidney. After Daniel Lothrop died in 1892, she ran his publishing firm for two years and then sold it in 1894. She helped found the Concord chapter of the Daughters of the American Revolution in 1894 and the National Society of the Children of the American Revolution in 1895. Harriett Lothrop is buried next to her husband in Sleepy Hollow Cemetery, Concord.

Margaret Sidney's *Five Little Peppers and How They Grew* is a classic of children's literature in that its publication history reveals how deeply the book "resonates for readers past, present and future," to borrow Wai Chee Dimock's formulation (1064). But we might also recall Myra Jehlen's assertion that "classics typically mediate a culture's founding contradictions" (113). For to read *Five Little Peppers* today is to be struck most forcefully by its attempt to reconcile the contradictions of the founding principles of democracy and equality revealed by its depiction of the poverty-stricken Peppers and their aristocratic benefactor, Mr. King. Living up to his name, Mr. King acts as if "he owned the whole of the Peppers and could dispose of them all to suit his fancy" when he adopts them and moves them out of their home and into his (201). A kind of Horatio Alger story in which the whole family goes from rags to riches, *Five Little Peppers* provides the opportunity for an exploration of assumptions about class, birth, and taste operative at the end of the nineteenth century in U.S. culture.

Contemporary reviewers praised the novel as "a real study of life" and found its "plot most naturally developed." Lauded for its "sympathy and fidelity," the novel reminded an anonymous reviewer in March of 1885 "here and there . . . of Mark Twain, anon of Dickens, and often of George Eliot" (21). Perhaps most pertinent in terms of the novel's treatment of social class is Norma Bright Carson's 1910 assessment of the Peppers:

> They are just the unspoiled, unspotted children that belong to a world in which
> imagination must supply what fortune withholds, and in which honest aspiration
> uplifts in the midst of the ordinary course of good and ill. Everything that
> happened to the Peppers might happen to any similar family, and their
> characteristics are those of thousands of youngsters and homes. They deserve all
> the good that comes to them, and they are sensible enough to appreciate the
> "sweets of adversity." (414)

These assessments emphasize the novel's verisimilitude and realism; they point to its quintessential plot and characters ("Everything that happened to the Peppers might happen to any similar family, and their characteristics are those of thousands of youngsters and homes"). This kind of endorsement suggests yet another way in which this novel is a classic in the sense of representative, typical, paradigmatic. Indeed, Carson insists the "appeal" of the Pepper series "is universal, for they are typical of the brightness, the vivacity, the wholesomeness, the resourcefulness, of the average American boy and girl" (414). It is also worth noting that the reviewer in March of 1885 twice describes the novel as "bracing" and also praises it as "strengthening," a set of adjectives that point to the novel's work as a conduct book of sorts, a text that uplifts and encourages its readers to adopt what Carson calls "the happy optimism of the little Peppers" (21, 414). Like Horatio Alger tales that promise financial and familial rewards to those who work hard, *Five Little Peppers* depicts, according to these reviews, a family rescued from poverty because "they deserve all the good that comes to them," because they are "sensible," optimistic, and happy. Similar happy endings are, it is implied, in store for readers who follow the "bracing" good example of the "wholesome" Peppers.

Comparing this instructive tale to a Horatio Alger story is revealing in a way that has to do with a specifically American confusion over class as a marker of breeding and birth versus class as an indicator of financial standing. The prototypical plot of *Five Little Peppers*—"a real study of life"—and characters that "depict the true type," as Carson would have it, is quite similar to the popular view of Alger's narratives as stories of opportunity that encourage and inspire their readers. Alger describes his heroes' rise to fortune with a kind of gritty realism and pays lip service to the notion that all who work hard can prosper in America, the land of opportunity, where birth is no obstacle to success. In this sense, his tales chronicle the adventures of an Everyboy and present themselves as at once representative, democratic, and hortatory. Similarly, the first reviewers of *Five Little Peppers* describe it as the story of a typical family who struggles with adversity and is rewarded for their good attitude and their hard work, a reward that is, like those accorded to Alger's heroes, marked as American and as attainable by all who seek to earn it.

But on the other hand, and as many recent critics of Alger have noted, the success of his heroes has as much, if not more, to do with luck than it does with pluck.[1] Almost magical tales of wish fulfillment, fortuity, and incredibly good timing, novels like *Ragged Dick* (1867), its sequel, *Fame and Fortune* (1868), and *Struggling Upward* (1868) reveal that hard work alone does not guarantee success. "Rather than presenting an example of 'rugged' and competitive individualism," Michael Moon insists, "they show boys 'rising' through a combination of genteel patronage and sheer luck" (89). The hero must also have the good fortune to encounter what Glenn Hendler calls an "affluent observer": he "must constantly be waiting for an opportunity to attract the attention of a wealthy male" (423, 422). "No matter where he is," Hendler reminds us, "the books lead us to expect that someone he does not know is always watching and waiting to reward virtue or even the appearance of virtue" (423). "He must also," as Hendler points out, "demonstrate by means of his physiognomy and his actions that he is (at least) a cut above his peers." The fact that he can immediately and clearly "be read as attractively virtuous is at the origin of the Alger hero's success" (Hendler 420). Or as Michael Moon puts it, "'luck' comes to them, and 'pluck' they exhibit when it is required, but their really defining attribute is good looks," and he goes on to argue that "the good looks revealing themselves despite the physical evidence of poverty—dirt and rags—is the infallible sign that one of Alger's boy characters is likely to emerge from his outcast condition to become a 'gentle/dangerous' boy" (94).[2]

The distinction here between poverty ("dirt and rags") and breeding (the "gentle" boy) is crucial to the plot of success in both Alger and Sidney. The stereotypical understanding of Alger novels as rags-to-riches tales masks the fact that their plots are dependent on coincidence and that their heroes must reveal their innate good character in order to flourish, in order to escape the economic and social conditions that do not match their inherent worthiness. This, more accurate, version of an Alger tale also has much more in common with *Five Little Peppers*, for while the Peppers do work hard, like Alger's Ragged Dick or Luke Larkin, who struggle upward, they, like Alger's future tycoons, are also lucky enough to encounter their own magical patron, in the form of Jasper King, and it is that patron, not their hard work, who ensures their financial future. And like Ragged Dick, who looks as "frank and honest" as he in fact is, the Peppers also have a look about them that reveals their inherent good breeding (84).

What this paradox exposes is that *Five Little Peppers*, like most Alger novels, wants to have it both ways: it tells what is, in fact, a Cinderella story, disguised as a celebration of Yankee grit and determination.[3] Alger and Sidney promise in their novels that anyone can move from poverty to riches, but an attentive reading of their plots reveals that that rise depends on good fortune, happy accident, and a legible physiognomy (what Glenn Hendler calls "an ideal of transparent legibility") that bring to light how very much the poverty-stricken deserve better (419). Peter Stoneley, who reminds us that "the rescue of the [Peppers] is as fortuitous as was their initial fall," argues that this plot "points to a contemporary awareness . . . that in a radically unstable financial environment, the fact of either success or failure has little to do with being 'deserving'" and that the novel's drama is "intensified by the fear that morality and social power are not securely wedded" (53). His argument suggests we need to attend to the economic context of the novel's publication in 1881,[4] and he anticipates my interest in what the novel reveals about class, birth, and taste when he points to the uneasy relationship between "morality and social power" that lies at the heart of the novel's concerns.

It is important at this point to remember that this novel, with its vexed revelations about the operation and understanding of class at the end of the nineteenth century, belongs to one of the most capacious genres of children's literature, the family story. Chronicling the challenges and adventures of the five fatherless Pepper children and their saintly, hard-working Mamsie, the novel is a fairly traditional instance of what Richard Brodhead, in *Cultures of Letters*, calls "disciplinary intimacy"; it reveals the power of love not only to nourish and discipline the children, but also, quite literally to feed them, for it is made clear on every page of the novel that all the work they do is a labor of love for their family. " 'To help mother' was the great ambition of all the children," the narrator tells us in chapter 1 (2). But this novel goes beyond the celebration of family and the ennobling of hard work, for the Peppers are not just poor, but in quite immediate peril of running out of money entirely.[5] Breakfast is mush and cold potatoes, supper is typically bread and leftover potatoes, with "very weak milk and water" to drink, a piece of stationery is a treasured luxury, and when the two oldest children (ages ten and eleven) come down with measles and cannot make their usual contribution to the household's earnings, Mamsie is afraid she will not have enough money to pay the rent (8). Yet no sooner do we become acquainted with their dire, if picturesque, poverty than the young gentleman who will save them from their financial distress, even as they will save him from his emotional poverty, appears on the scene. A motherless, only child, Jasper King not only befriends the Peppers, but he also becomes so attached to them that his wealthy and autocratic father arranges for the family to make an extended visit to his mansion in the city and ultimately adopts them.

Sociological studies of class such as Pierre Bourdieu's *Distinction* and Anthony Giddens's *The Class Structure of the Advanced Societies* help unpack the novel's emphasis on the disconnect between the Peppers' financial predicament and their innate appreciation of education and the arts—between what Bourdieu refers to as material wealth and symbolic capital (what Thomas Otten identifies as the "cognates" of class, "like taste and refinement" [40]). The ease with which the Peppers slip into what Bourdieu would call the Kings' "lifestyle practices" suggests their refinement, and what Mr. King's daughter refers to as the "look about them" suggests their "good blood" (202).⁶ Their social identity is at odds with their economic identity, to use Giddens's terms, an opposition that alerts us to the novel's participation in what Mary Poovey calls "the debate over what the term *class* describes—an objective set of material conditions, or a mode of understanding one's place in a social hierarchy, which only became available in the nineteenth century" (15). Like the March family in *Little Women* (1868–69), the Peppers are impoverished gentlefolk, but the narrator makes it abundantly clear that while they are poor, and the family that befriends them and ultimately serves as their benefactors is rich, "both are still—just about—of the same class," as Stoneley observes. "There can be no 'betters,'" he points out, "on the social plateau of gentility, even though there may be richer and poorer" (57).

Similarly, Amy Schrager Lang's analysis of the nineteenth-century "doctrine of harmony"—which insisted that the interests of capital were identical to those of labor—helps contextualize the novel's determination to treat Mr. King's child, Jasper, and the Pepper children as equals (69). Because the Peppers are apparently members of "the class that labors" and their benefactors clearly belong to "the class that lives by others' labor" (the terms are Martin J. Burke's, from his *The Conundrum of Class*), the postbellum *Five Little Peppers* seems to illustrate the harmony of interests between those raised on hard work and the child of privilege who so wants to be a part of the Peppers' makeshift family fun that his father eventually makes that family a part of his (qtd. in Lang 70). But the novel's account of that harmony is more complicated. While the Peppers eventually live with and as if they are Kings, even when she lives in the Kings' mansion as a member of the family, Mrs. Pepper does the mending, while her daughter Polly serves as voluntary governess to Jasper's nephews, Percy, Van, and Dick Whitney, and Ben works at Cabot & Van Meter's store, indicating, it would seem, that they must continue to behave as befits their class status, as those that labor.⁷ But it is revealed in the novel's last chapter that the Peppers are related to the Kings (albeit by marriage), a detail that suggests that while the Peppers do labor, they are not necessarily of "the class that labors."[8] Unlike the doctrine of harmony's insistence on the shared interests of the two classes, the denouement of *Five Little Peppers* suggests that this understanding of class is imprecise, that work and poverty are not indicators of class, and that even those who do not need to work may choose to. Jasper, though a King by birth, chooses himself to work (against his father's wishes and in the poorly paid field of publishing, no less) in the third novel in the series, *Five Little Peppers Grown Up* (1892), and while Polly's younger brothers, Joel and Davie, go to Harvard thanks to Mr. King's generosity, Polly studies to become a music teacher, so that she (like her older brother Ben and her future husband Jasper) can support herself and, just as importantly, do the work she finds so satisfying.

But it is not just that Polly "loves her work so" or that Jasper finds it "jolly to explain business intricacies" to anyone who will listen (*Five Little Peppers Grown Up* 122, 129). In addition to the fact that the characters we most admire (Mrs. Pepper, Polly and Ben, Jasper) find joy and satisfaction in their work, nostalgia for the "Little Brown House" (a phrase that is almost always capitalized) and all it represents runs throughout the series. The Peppers remember with fondness and a keen sense of longing the house they lived in when they were poor, the stove they had to stuff with boot-tops so it would burn, the games they played to disguise their poverty, and the strategies they employed to supply what they lacked. The Peppers talk of their life in the Little Brown House so often and with such longing and affection that these stories become the ones the Kings and the Whitneys most want to hear; "Let's talk of the Little Brown House. Do tell us what you used to do there—that's best," exclaims Percy, the oldest Whitney boy (244). "So 'tis!" agrees his brother Van, while Jasper insists that Mrs. Pepper "couldn't tell *all* the nice times if she had ten years to tell them in" and declares the Little Brown House "the very nicest place in the whole world!" (244, 245). The Peppers' nostalgia for the Little Brown House and the Whitney boys' envy of "the perfectly *elegant* times" the Peppers had there become so strong that they organize a trip back to the house in the second novel of the series, *Five Little Peppers Midway* (1890) (246). And this trip does not disappoint; not one of the characters that go back to Badgertown with the Peppers (Mr. King and Jasper, the Whitney boys, and their mother, Marian) finds it to be any less wonderful than the stories they have heard have led them to expect. In fact, they try to recreate scenes from all the stories they have been told about the Little Brown House: they have "a baking frolic," go for a drive in Deacon Brown's horse-drawn wagon, visit Grandma Bascom, try some of the legendary doughnuts at Mr. and Mrs. Beebe's shoe shop, and go sledding (158).

This fetishizing of their former life of poverty exists in tension with the novel's description of all they enjoy thanks to the generosity of their benefactors, but at no point in the novel is this version of their Little Brown House life called into question or revealed be a matter of false pride or a romanticized version of all they endured. Rather, the novel takes pains to celebrate both the joys of life in the Little Brown House and the advantages of life in the Kings' mansion (chief of which is the education Mr. King provides the Pepper children, an advantage their mother has been trying to provide for them since the third paragraph of the novel—"I must get learning for 'em someway; but I don't see *how*!") (2). Indeed, while the Peppers receive a formal education thanks to the largesse of their benefactors, the Pepper family also provides the children of privilege (who turn out to be their cousins) with an education the novel reveals to be just as important as that which comes from books: what the novels calls "the Little Brown House teachings" (*Five Little Peppers Grown Up* 211). Polly's first reaction when she sees the Whitney brothers fighting is that she "could never remember such goings-on in the Little Brown House." Similarly, Jasper reminds her that "we've always found that when a thing had to be done, it was done. You know the little brown house taught us that," and Polly reflects that people "who've never had a little brown house" don't have the same "duty to be good" as had the Peppers, thanks to the good influence the Little Brown House and the life of hard work it represents has been on them (*Five Little Peppers and How They Grew* 193; *Five Little Peppers Midway* 75, 179–80). The novels thus reveal the advantages the Peppers enjoy because, not in spite, of their poverty. From Joel's exclamation, "weren't those good days, though, in the little brown house, when we had all outdoors to work in!" to Jasper's employer's pronouncement that Jasper has had "the misfortune to be born into a rich family, and your father probably never had to raise his hand to earn a penny," the series is just as dedicated to describing the delights and benefits of work as it is to depicting the advantages that money can provide (*Five Little Peppers Grown Up* 299, 383). Indeed, the narrator takes similar pleasure in describing the Kings' mansion as she does in describing Marian Whitney's pleased reaction to Badgertown: "How restful it all is here, and so quaint and simple," she thinks to herself, as she sits in the sun and knits (*Five Little Peppers Midway* 184).

Peter Stoneley calls *Five Little Peppers* a "drama of exclusion" and argues that it reveals "the social paranoia generated by economic uncertainty" (52–53). Insisting that "this novel and its sequels are more openly hungry than precursors by Dodge or Alcott, in that they show an almost desperate readiness to merge with the monied, urban class and to acquire its advantages," Stoneley's reading of the novel would seem to be the exact inverse of mine (56).[9] But his analysis of the disjunct between the Peppers' class status and their financial predicament reveals, rather, the degree to which our readings agree. For in his careful demonstration of how strenuously Mrs. Pepper refuses to be the object of Mr. King's charity, he uncovers the important fact that Mrs. Pepper "will not surrender her claim to gentility to her present need for money" (57). What the narrator describes as her "independent soul" keeps her from accepting that which she considers "a favor to her child" (181, 180). Similarly, she will not allow Mr. King to provide her children with an education unless she can provide something in return. Indeed, Mr. King only manages to convince Mrs. Pepper to move her family into his mansion by pointing to the way in which his interests are intertwined with hers: "Don't you see it's for the children's advantage? They'll get such educations, Mrs. Pepper, as you want for them. And it accommodates me immensely" (249). It will "accommodate" him because, as he explains, "I must have somebody who will keep this house" (248). While that role is filled by his daughter now, who, along with her three sons, has moved into her father's mansion while her husband is out of the country on business, Mr. King knows, and reminds his daughter, that his son-in-law will be coming "back in the fall, and then I suppose you'll have to go with him" (248). Mr. King thus makes it clear that his need is both real and imminent. The introduction and conclusion of Stoneley's chapter suggest otherwise, but the heart of his argument illustrates not the Peppers' "desperate readiness" to move in with the Kings but rather, as Stoneley himself puts it, the "delicate negotiation between independence and patronage" that both Mr. King and the novel "manage so well" that they all become one big happy family. (Remember that the position Mr. King offers Mrs. Pepper is one now occupied by his daughter.) The Peppers do not "become indebted," as Stoneley would have it, and they avoid that status not because "their lack of a fortune is off-set" by their "good blood" but rather because, as I have suggested above, they have as much to offer the Kings as the Kings have to offer them.

One of the seemingly intangible benefits the Peppers offer the Kings is, as Stoneley points out, "the domestic hubbub of a less wealthy household," a benefit also conferred on Laurie Laurence by the March girls in *Little Women* (57). But Alcott's readers remember that Laurie is also attracted to the March girls' industry, to their frank acceptance of their impoverished financial status, and to what I would call, paraphrasing Stoneley, "the domestic hubbub of a more loving family." Indeed, as the fact that Peppers, Kings, and Whitneys live together under one roof as members of one extended family, united by distant ties of blood and closer ties of affection, suggests, *Five Little Peppers* is one of the many novels of the period that celebrates the notion of a family based on choice, on ties of affection, as well as those of blood.[10] The novel's understanding of class is thus both dependent on and interwoven with a plot that celebrates "a paradigm of family based on chosen affections" and "biologically determined ones" and suggests that what Nina Baym identifies as the "self-made or surrogate family" is a legitimate variation on the consanguineous family (Weinstein 45, Baym 38). I have been using the word "adopt" throughout this essay to describe how Mr. King makes the Peppers part of his family, and I mean thus to emphasize that he makes their family part of his, that he seeks to make them part of the same kinship system, that he wants to turn a tie of affection into one that is taken as seriously as a blood relationship. Like class, family relations are coming to be seen as flexible and malleable at mid-century, as the first U.S. adoption law (enacted in Massachusetts in 1851) and the fact that adoption itself moves from an economic to an emotional relationship in the second half of the century suggest. Part of what Cindy Weinstein calls "a widespread cultural examination of the family," *Five Little Peppers* is evidence of the "paradigm shift" that replaces blood with "freely given love" "as the invincible tie that binds together individuals in a family" (8, 9). Think, for instance, of the way in which Polly immediately becomes a part of the King family, on her first visit to them, long before the rest of the Peppers join her at what will become their home for the rest of the series: Marian Whitney, "just because she couldn't help it, gathered Polly up in her arms" mere moments after meeting her, "in two or three minutes it seemed as if Polly had always been there," and at the end of dinner, the youngest Whitney boy, "flinging himself into her arms, declared: 'I love you—and you're my sister!' " (188, 190). "Nothing more," the narrator concludes, "was needed to make Polly feel at home" (190). We see here an exclamation of spontaneous affection, a sense of natural belonging, a declaration of love, and then an assertion of kinship. This progression not only describes Polly's first moments in the mansion, but it is also an accurate delineation of Jasper's first encounter with the Peppers, of Mr. King's introduction to Phronsie, and of the way in which each member of the Pepper family is swiftly, naturally, and lovingly made a part of the King-Whitney clan, and vice versa.

In thus combining these three families, the novel also reveals the extent to which one of the most basic *topoi* of children's literature—the child in search of a family to which she can truly belong—is reunderstood in the nineteenth century in legal terms and as a way of getting at the inherent refinement of the misplaced child.[11] But in *Five Little Peppers*, this plot, which celebrates the recent codification of children's rights[12] and restores the patrician child to her rightful place in the social hierarchy, involves an entire family. Claudia Nelson finds that "child placement is the stuff of which engrossing narratives are made," and that story becomes even more fascinating (and reassuring) when it involves the rescue of a sainted, hard-working mother along with her children, when it re-places mother and child in a family that loves and appreciates them and in a society that pays tribute to their well-bred tastes and talents (4). *Five Little Peppers* goes even further though, for it also supplies Jasper and his father with a loving and affectionate clan of relations, it gives Marian a sister (who turns out to be her cousin-in-law) and a daughter (who also turns out to be a kind of cousin), and it gives the Whitney children a much-needed dose of "Little Brown House teachings," affectionately administered by the very individuals they claim as family long before they learn that they are truly, not just affectionately, related. What Nina Baym says with respect to those novels in which "a network of surrogate kin gradually defines itself around the heroine, making hers the story not only that of a self-made woman but that of a self-made or surrogate family" applies even more strikingly to Sidney's novel, for *Five Little Peppers* chronicles not only the self-made but also the surrogate family; the synonymous "or" in Baym's account becomes a more flexible and inclusive "and" in Sidney's hands, a modification that calls attention to the fact that "self-made" is no longer understood as depending on substitution but rather offers a supplement to that logic of adoption and replacement (38).

Illustrating just how imbricated (and expansive, as opposed to substitutive) the novel's depiction of this ideal family is, Mrs. Pepper turns out to be Mr. King's son-in-law's cousin. Mr. King of course has no idea that Mrs. Pepper is related to his daughter's husband when he makes the Pepper family a part of his own. And while affective ties are thus ultimately (but not until the novel's final chapter) revealed to be blood ties, this biological relationship exists in both very specific and quite comprehensive ways. The Peppers are not related to the Kings, but rather to their in-laws, to Mr. Whitney, the man Mr. King's daughter marries. "You are all cousins," Mr. King grandly announces, revealing that the affective ties that brought them together as a kind of family are also biological ties that make them family in the legal sense (272). Yet when he tries to clarify that they are not all related— "Everybody but Jasper," he hastens to explain. "You and I, my boy, are left out in the cold"—Jasper's exclusion from the newly expanded family so distresses Joel Pepper that Jasper falls back on the flexible notion of family he employed when he first befriended the Peppers: "I'll tell you how we'll fix it! I'll be your brother," he says (273). In that same spirit, Phronsie Pepper takes to calling Mr. King her "gran-papa," while in the sequels to *Five Little Peppers*, Mr. King calls Joel his grandson. What Weinstein argues with respect to Maria Cummins's *The Lamplighter* (1854), then, could just as appropriately be said of *Five Little Peppers*: it "profoundly waver[s] about affirming the very reconstitution of the family that [its] narrative seem[s] to advocate" (46). Like the "almost" and "sort of" that typically modify the descriptions of Cummins's heroine as daughter, sister, or cousin to those who befriend her, the fact that the Peppers are related to the Whitneys but not to the Kings suggests the novel wants to celebrate the ability to choose your own family as much as it wants to shore up the importance of blood and kinship. By the same token, there must be some explanation for the Peppers' exquisite taste and tact; the novel cannot accept that such "very nice" children could be the products of their working-class environment (202). Or as Cindy Weinstein says about *The Lamplighter* (a novel that, like *Five Little Peppers*, celebrates a family formation that is as affectionate as it turns out to be consanguineous), "it is not, however, the case that consanguinity simply disappears from *The Lamplighter*'s understanding of family, but rather that it disappears just long enough so that the novel can begin to lay the groundwork for an affective rather than an economic foundation upon which the family can be redefined" (12). Like Mrs. Pepper's refusal to take any favors from the Kings, her decision to let Polly visit Jasper only when she understands that his "failing health" requires Polly's cheering presence reveals her similar determination to "lay the groundwork for an affective rather than an economic foundation" for the relationship between the two families (180).

It is, of course, the Peppers' "breeding" that accounts for Mrs. Pepper's intense dislike of what the narrator describes, in quotation marks, as "putting one's self under an obligation," and the conditions of the Peppers' birth are also literally, as well as figuratively, what is at stake in the novel's twin interests in their refined tastes and their family tree (181). While the novel may seem, as Alger tales so often do, to celebrate U.S. culture's democratically open, "rags to riches" approach to class and status, the fact that the Peppers are quite easily assimilated into Kings, that their father was "an Englishman by the name of Pepper," and that they are related to the man Marian King marries indicate that what they endure in the first half of the novel is a kind of shabby-genteel poverty rather than a working-class existence (270).[13] This novel is then more of a Cinderella story than a Horatio Alger tale: the Peppers do not rise from poverty to a life of ease but rather are reinstated in the appropriate environment when their true class origins are intuited (and later uncovered). While I would not go so far as to denounce the novel as an instance of "bad faith or hypocrisy," as Stoneley does, the fact that, as he points out, "the narrative hastens to ensure that the genteel are also wealthy" does point unmistakably to the tension that runs throughout all the *Five Little Peppers* books about the relationship between manner(s) and money.[14]

Focusing on the ways in which class and family come to be understood in the last half of the century, then, allows us to see that the novel offers the Peppers' reinstatement as members of the cultural elite as both an acceptable (and very popular) resolution to the discrepancy between their economic situation and their social identity *and* as a response to what Weinstein identifies as sentimental fiction's "profound awareness of the relative fragility of the biological family" (4). This classic of children's literature "mediate[s]" the "founding contradictions" of U.S. culture by fashioning a plot that is resolved by a "merger between class as conduct and class as financial power" combined with a "commitment to strengthening and redefining [the family] according to the logic of love" (Stoneley 58, Weinstein 4). In other words, the surrogate family is created not by a kind of cozy magic or a version of domestic wish fulfillment. It happens as a part of writing class in the last decades of the century, a pairing that suggests that *Five Little Peppers* is also a classic in Matthew Arnold's sense of the term in that it is "a work of synthesis and exposition" and that what Arnold would call its "gift" "lies in the faculty of being happily inspired by a certain intellectual and spiritual atmosphere, by a certain order of ideas," "of dealing divinely with these ideas, presenting them in the most effective and attractive combinations,—making beautiful works with them, in short" (11–12). The concepts of family and of class that are so contested in the 1880s and 1890s are, in *Five Little Peppers*, synthesized into a work "not of analysis and discovery," as Arnold puts it, but rather into one that is "beautiful" in that the story it tells is "effective" and "attractive"—so "effective" and "attractive," in fact, that the novel, as befits a classic, has never been out of print (and is currently in print in at least three trade paperback editions, innumerable print on-demand editions, and as both a CD-ROM and a Kindle Book). Over 125 years later, in 2010, the idea(l) of the family is still a work in progress, and any consideration of class in U.S. culture is still marked by a discomfort that discomfits. Little wonder, then, that *Five Little Peppers and How They Grew* has proven to be such a resonant text for over two generations. Smaller wonder still that my students come to class with their parents' (and their grandparents' and great-grandparents') copies of the novel, eager to read the text they have so carefully preserved and what that not-so-innocuous tale has to reveal about nineteenth-century constructions of the happy and prosperous family.

NOTES

1. See Michael Zuckerman, "The Nursery Tales of Horatio Alger," Michael Moon, "'The Gentle Boy from the Dangerous Classes,'" and Glenn Hendler, "Pandering in the Public Sphere," for three examples of this approach to Alger's fiction.

2. The phrase "gentle/dangerous" boy points to what is perhaps the crucial distinction between Alger and Sidney, for unlike the boys who rise to fortune in Alger, the Peppers are decidedly not of the dangerous classes; they are just poor.

3. *The Bay State Monthly* for November of 1885 lauds Sidney's "delineation" of "the New England type" (16).

4. *The Portrait of a Lady* was serialized in 1880–81 in the *Atlantic Monthly*, and twelve Peppers stories appeared in *Wide Awake* in 1880, before being collected as *Five Little Peppers and How They Grew* in 1881. I mention this correspondence because the plots of both novels (and of many others written in the 1880s and 1890s) are inaugurated when a father who has spent all his capital dies and leaves his family in financial distress. Isabel Archer's father has "squandered a substantial fortune," leaving behind him "very little money" at his death; similarly, when *Five Little Peppers* opens, Mr. Pepper has been dead only a year or two, and since his death, "Mrs. Pepper had had hard work to scrape together money enough to put bread into her children's mouths and to pay the rent of the little brown house" (*Portrait* 49, 43; *Peppers* 1). While Isabel is rescued almost immediately after her father's death by her aunt, the Peppers have to wait a bit longer to be taken up by Mr. King, but the contours of both plots depend on and depict an economic state of affairs described by Andrew Carnegie in his *North American Review* essay of 1889 entitled "Wealth." "The problem of our age is the proper administration of wealth, so that the ties of brotherhood may still bind together the rich and poor in harmonious relationship," he insists, bringing to mind both the adoption of Isabel by her aunt and of the Peppers by the Kings. And he goes on to account for the need for this kind of adoption by describing "the contrast between the palace of the millionaire and the cottage of the laborer" (conjuring up a picture of the Kings' mansion and the Peppers' Little Brown House) and pointing to that contrast as a "measure of the change that has come with civilization" (653).

5. It's worth noting, though, that what it would mean to run out of money is left unexplored. Some possibilities, as the editors of this collection point out, are that they would lose their house or Polly would have to go out to service or the family would be split up. But the narrator is silent about the precise nature of the peril the Peppers face.

6. Thomas Otten argues, following William James, that "something constructed and contingent like class can assume the appearance of something incontestable and inevitable if it can be redescribed as physiology," which is precisely what Sidney is doing here (52).

7. He works so hard that Mr. Cabot tells him, "If you work on as you have done these two years since you came in here as errand boy, Ben, I'll make you a power in the house" (279).

8. The narrator implies that they must "labor" because Mr. Pepper is dead; in chapter 1 we learn that "times were always hard with them nowadays; and since the father died, when Phronsie was a baby, Mrs. Pepper had had hard work to scrape together money enough to put bread into her children's mouths, and to pay the rent of the little brown house" (8). We learn later in the chapter that Polly and Ben work as hard as their mother does to earn money, and even Joel, the scapegrace of the family, is eager to do what he can to contribute to the family finances.

9. Stoneley here alludes to Mary Mapes Dodge's novel *Hans Brinker, or The Silver Skates* (1865) and Alcott's *Little Women*. He finds *Hans Brinker* to be, like *Five Little Peppers*, a novel that "stage[s] the spectacle of a sudden and apparently irrecoverable loss of status" and describes *Little Women* as a novel that, unlike *Five Little Peppers* and *Hans Brinker*, "provides a robust reassurance for readers, in that the girl-heroine's moral independence and hard work will enable her to reassert her worth" (52). In Dodge and

Sidney, however, "the heroine is still good and resourceful, but this is no longer enough to counteract the social paranoia generated by economic uncertainty" (52–53).

10. It is also worth noting that the March family makes not only Laurie but also the orphaned John Brooke and the expatriate Professor Bhaer a part of their family, and they do so by marriage—a tie of affection that is also legal and produces its own ties of blood.

11. We see this plot in Cinderella, in Maria Cummins's *The Lamplighter*, when it is revealed that Gerty is the child of privilege, not of the slums in which we find her on the novel's first page, and in Frances Hodgson Burnett's *A Little Princess* (1905), when Sara Crewe is rescued from her attic and her life of drudgery by the man who bankrupted her father, just to name a few of its compelling iterations.

12. For an account of the codification of children's rights and the emergence of adoption law that emphasizes "the idea that family relationships could be as much about contractual relationships as blood relationships," see Cindy Weinstein's chapter "'A sort of adopted daughter': Family Relations in *The Lamplighter*" in her *Family, Kinship and Sympathy in Nineteenth-Century American Literature* (56). For an analysis of "representations of adoption and foster care in writings produced between 1850 and 1929" and "the rhetorical uses to which such children were put," see Claudia Nelson's *Little Strangers* (2). These two studies should be read together; Weinstein's emphasis on children's rights and Nelson's concern with the way that orphan fiction, legal writings, and sociological studies of child placement take up "the question of how these children might be made productive Americans" and the role that "displaced children have played in the reshaping of American childhood and the American family" are complementary pieces of the adoption puzzle (4).

13. That Mr. Pepper is British has, of course, much to do with the Peppers' perceived breeding and refinement; as the editors to this collection point out, a kind of inherent gentility gets attached to England, and I would also suggest that Mr. Pepper's nationality confers a pedigree of sorts on his American-born children.

14. For instance, in *Five Little Peppers Midway*, Mr. King's cousin, the society matron Eunice Chatterton, refers to the Peppers as "that low, underbred family," and while the narrator (and the plot) take pains to point out how superficial her judgment is, it is striking how often she herself is described as "well-bred" and "high-bred" (31). She makes Polly feel "unusually awkward and shy," she treats Polly and Phronsie as if they were her maids, and, on the whole, her character brings to mind the way Mr. King tried to arrange the Peppers to his liking in the first novel of the series (25). Like Mr. King, she learns that they must be treated with respect, of course, and the novel's final paragraph takes the form of a note in which she makes Phronsie "her sole heir" and entreats "may God bless Phronsie" (512). But the disjunct between her bearing and theirs and the theme of breeding runs throughout the novel, like a constant refrain, underlying the novel's explicit plot of harmony and its willed ignorance of class difference.

WORKS CITED

Alger, Horatio. *Ragged Dick* and *Struggling Upward*. 1867, 1868. Edited by Carl Bode. New York: Penguin, 1985.

Arnold, Matthew. "The Function of Criticism at the Present Time." 1864. In *The Function of Criticism at the Present Time by Matthew Arnold and An Essay on Style by Walter Pater*. New York: Macmillan, 1895. 1–86.

Baym, Nina. *Woman's Fiction: A Guide to Novels by and about Women in America, 1820–70.*
    1978. Urbana: U of Illinois P, 1993.
Bourdieu, Pierre. *Distinction: A Social Critique of the Judgments of Taste.* Translated by
    Richard Nice. 1984. Cambridge: Harvard UP, 2007.
Brodhead, Richard. *Cultures of Letters: Scenes of Reading and Writing in Nineteenth-
    Century America.* Chicago: U of Chicago P, 1993.
Carnegie, Andrew. "Wealth." *North American Review* 391 (June 1889):
    653–64.
Carson, Norma Bright. "'Margaret Sidney' The Writer of the Famous Polly Pepper Books."
    Book News Monthly 28 (February 1910): 407–14.
Dimock, Wai Chee. "A Theory of Resonance." *PMLA* 112 (1997): 1060–71.
Giddens, Anthony. *The Class Structure of the Advanced Societies.* 1973. New York: Harper
    and Row, 1975.
Hendler, Glenn. "Pandering in the Public Sphere: Masculinity and the Market in Horatio
    Alger." *American Quarterly* 48 (1996): 415–38.
James, Henry. *The Portrait of a Lady.* 1880–81. Edited by Nicola Bradbury. New York:
    Oxford UP, 1995.
Jehlen, Myra. "Banned in Concord: *Adventures of Huckleberry Finn* and Classic American
    Literature." In *The Cambridge Companion to Mark Twain*, edited by Forrest G.
    Robinson, 93–115. Cambridge: Cambridge UP, 1995.
Lang, Amy Schrager. *The Syntax of Class: Writing Inequality in Nineteenth-Century
    America.* Princeton: Princeton UP, 2003.
Lothrop, Margaret M. *The Wayside: Home of Authors.* 1940. New York: American Book
    Company, 1968.
Moon, Michael. "'The Gentle Boy from the Dangerous Classes': Pederasty, Domesticity,
    and Capitalism in Horatio Alger." *Representations* 19 (1987): 87–110.
Nelson, Claudia. *Little Strangers: Portrayals of Adoption and Foster Care in America,
    1850–1920.* Bloomington: Indiana UP, 2003.
"Notices of Recent Publications." *The Bay State Monthly*, March 1885, 21.
Otten, Thomas J. *A Superficial Reading of Henry James: Preoccupations with the Material
    World.* Columbus: The Ohio State UP, 2006.
Poovey, Mary. "The Social Constitution of 'Class': Toward a History of Classificatory
    Thinking." In *Rethinking Class: Literary Studies and Social Formations*, edited
    by Wai Chee Dimock and Michael Gilmore, 15–56. New York: Columbia UP,
    1994.
"Recent Books by Well-Known Authors." *The Bay State Monthly*, November 1885. 16.
Sidney, Margaret. *Five Little Peppers Grown Up.* Boston: D Lothrop Company, 1892.
———. *Five Little Peppers and How They Grew.* 1881. New York: Grosset &
    Dunlap, 1982.
———. *Five Little Peppers Midway.* 1890. Boston: Lothrop, Lee & Shepard
    Co., 1893.
Stoneley, Peter. "Dramas of Exclusion." In *Consumerism and American Girls' Literature,
    1860–1940*, 52-58. Cambridge: Cambridge UP, 2003.
Weinstein, Cindy. *Family, Kinship, and Sympathy in Nineteenth-Century American
    Literature.* Cambridge: Cambridge UP, 2004.
Zuckerman, Michael. "The Nursery Tales of Horatio Alger." *American Quarterly* 24 (1972):
    191–209.

FURTHER READING

Alcott, Louisa May. *Little Women.* 1868–69. Edited by Anne K. Phillips and Gregory Eiselein. New York: W.W. Norton, 2004.

Alger, Horatio. *Fame and Fortune.* Philadelphia: John C. Winston Co., 1896.

Cummins, Maria. *The Lamplighter.* 1854. Edited by Nina Baym. Piscataway, NJ: Rutgers UP, 1988.

Dodge, Mary Mapes. *Hans Brinker, or The Silver Skates.* 1865. Mineola, NY: Dover, 2003.

Homans, Margaret. "Adoption and Essentialism." *Tulsa Studies in Women's Literature* 21, no. 2 (2002): 257–74.

———. "Adoption Narratives, Trauma, and Origins." *Narrative* 14, no. 1 (2006): 4–26.

Kermode, Frank. *The Classic: Literary Images of Permanence and Change.* Cambridge: Harvard UP, 1983.

Kornfield, Eve, and Susan Jackson. "The Female *Bildungsroman* in Nineteenth-Century America: Parameters of a Vision." *Journal of American Culture.* 10, no. 4 (1987): 69–75.

Sidney, Margaret. *Phronsie Pepper.* 1897. New York: Grosset & Dunlap, 1937.*

———. *The Stories Polly Pepper Told.* Boston: Lothrop Publishing Company, 1899.

———. *The Adventures of Joel Pepper.* Boston: Lothrop Publishing Company, 1900.

———. *Five Little Peppers Abroad.* Boston: Lothrop, Lee & Shepard Company, 1902.

———. *Five Little Peppers at School.* Boston: Lothrop, Lee & Shepard Company, 1903.

———. *Five Little Peppers and Their Friends.* Boston: Lothrop, Lee & Shepard Company, 1904.

———. *Ben Pepper.* 1905. Boston: Houghton Mifflin Company, 1937.

———. *Five Little Peppers in the Little Brown House.* Boston: Lothrop, Lee & Shepard Company, 1907.

———. *Our Davie Pepper.* Boston: Lothrop, Lee & Shepard Company, 1916.

Singley, Carol. "Adoption and Nineteenth-Century American Children's Literature." In *Expectations and Experiences: Children, Childhood and Children's Literature*, edited by Clare Bradford, Valerie Coghlan, and Kimberley Reynolds, 40–55. Lichfield, Staffordshire: Pied Piper Publishing Ltd., 2007.

———. "Building a Family, Building a Nation: Adoption in Nineteenth Century Children's Literature." In *Adoption in America: Historical Perspectives*, edited by Wayne Carp, 51–81. Ann Arbor: U of Michigan P, 2002.

———. "Teaching American Literature: The Centrality of Adoption." *Modern Language Studies* 34 (2004): 76–83.

Phronsie Pepper is the last of the chronological series. As Sidney explains in the preface to that novel, "as Phronsie Pepper was the only one of the 'Five Little Peppers' who had not had a chance to become a 'grown-up' in the three books that form the Pepper Library, it seemed (to judge by the expressions of those persons interested in this family) a little unfair not to give her that opportunity." Sidney goes on to write that after this novel, she will "draw the curtain over the 'little brown house' and the 'Five Little Peppers,' never more to rise" (vii). The following eight volumes (from *The Stories Polly Pepper Told* through *Our Davie Pepper*) circle back to fill in the blanks and tell more stories about the Peppers before Phronsie grew up; in the preface to each of these novels, Sidney explains that she is writing yet another Pepper novel because of pressure from her readers.

....

CHAPTER 16

A DAUGHTER OF THE HOUSE: DISCOURSES OF ADOPTION IN L. M. MONTGOMERY'S *ANNE OF GREEN GABLES*

....

MAVIS REIMER

Lucy Maud Montgomery was born in Prince Edward Island, Canada, in 1874. Her mother died before little Maud was two years old, and she was left to be raised by her maternal grandparents, whom she later characterized as stern and reserved. When she was six, her father left the Island to begin a new life in western Canada. Maud lived with his second family in Saskatchewan for a year during her mid-teens but returned to PEI after realizing that her stepmother valued her primarily as unpaid domestic labor.

Montgomery trained as a teacher and taught school in a number of Island communities until 1898, when she once again returned to Cavendish after the death of her grandfather, to ensure that her grandmother could remain in the family home. These experiences clearly inflected the story of Anne of Green Gables, *published by the firm of L.C. Page in Boston in 1908. The book quickly became an international bestseller. In 1911, after the death of her grandmother, she married the Presbyterian minister Ewan Macdonald and moved with him to Leaskdale, Ontario. The Macdonalds had two sons—Chester and Stuart. Despite the multiple demands on her time, Montgomery wrote steadily, producing not only twenty novels, but also short stories, poetry,*

letters, and the journals that now comprise a primary resource for scholars of her
work. The journals reveal a darker life narrative than the stories she staged for her
publics. Montgomery struggled with depression for much of her adult life; family
members believe that she chose to end her life in 1942. Her first novel has been trans-
lated into more than thirty languages and continues to be read avidly by readers
around the world. In Canada, she is regarded as being among the first generation of
writers to separate themselves from European literary models to write distinctively
North American fiction.

In September 1907, *The Delineator* of New York—a family magazine edited by
author Theodore Dreiser in which L. M. Montgomery had published both poetry
and stories—began a series of articles featuring the stories of children available for
adoption. The magazine's Child Rescue Campaign had a national impact, according to Claudia Nelson, contributing to the creation of the U.S. Children's Bureau
in 1912 (116). Taking as its slogan, "For the child that needs a home
and the home that needs a child," the series explained that the connection between
the home and the child is a "natural" one: "Each needs the other to lead it to
the highest happiness" (*The Delineator* 715). As Irene Gammel observes, the campaign might be seen "to encapsulate the motto of *Anne of Green Gables*" and the
novel in turn seen to "promote the idea of adoption as we understand it today"
(238, 239).

Questions of how the line between nature and culture is drawn have occupied
critical theorists at least since the early decades of the twentieth century. If the connection between the happy home and the happy child appears to be a natural one,
structural and post-structural theorists contend, it is because it has been naturalized; in other words, social ideology has obscured the process of the construction of
this linkage in a specific time and place. To the extent that Montgomery's famous
first novel was part of the process of naturalization, we can expect that it, too, will
move into the background the elements that might perform such a conceptual and
emotional linkage.

The existing criticism on Montgomery's first novel confirms that scholarly
readers have found a number of other matters to be of more obvious interest.
Foremost among these analyses are essays on the construction and critique of gender in *Anne of Green Gables*, on the relation of Montgomery's first novel to her life,
and on the place of the novel in literary history. In various ways, each of these
critical approaches is predicated on the location of the novel in history. The contexts assumed are either social and aesthetic constructions shared across a wide
range of societies derived from European, and particularly British, models, or the
narrower question of the uptake of these ideas in a specific life and writing career.
Less often considered in Montgomery scholarship is the situation of the novel
within determinate political and social histories.[1] Montgomery begins her writing
career at a particular cultural moment, that of Canada in the early decades of its
nationhood. While Canada is granted self-governance through the British North
America Act of 1867, popular history in Canada takes World War I as the moment

at which the colony truly becomes a nation. *Anne of Green Gables*, in other words, is among the texts that stand between the legal formation of the nation and the felt formation of the nation, what we might call the national "structures of feeling," to use Raymond Williams's analytic term for the relation between "formal or systematic beliefs" and "meanings and values as they are actively lived" (132). Arguably, literary texts such as Montgomery's supply some of the terms of those structures of feeling.

The nation, in Benedict Anderson's well-known phrase, is "an imagined community." The distinctiveness of the nation as a kind of community is that, while it is dispersed over space, it is linked through shared understandings of the meanings of simultaneous actions in that space. According to Anderson, the novel and the newspaper "provided the technical means" for representing this community because these forms fuse the "interior" time of the text to the "exterior" time of the reader (25). As Anderson implies in his exemplary readings of nation-building novels, communities at all levels in these texts can be understood as analogues of one another. The title of *Anne of Green Gables* indicates the primary context for Anne's identity as the member of a community—that of the house and the family in the house. From the opening scene of the novel, however, as Rachel Lynde surveys "everything that passed" on "the Avonlea main road," it is clear that the homing of Anne depends not only on her acceptance by Matthew and Marilla Cuthbert, but also on her integration into the larger, overlapping communities that surround her (53). As the novel proceeds, these are shown to include church, school, town, island, and nation.

Anne's story moves her from the condition of being a "stray waif" whom "nobody ever did want" to being Anne of Green Gables, Marilla's adopted and loved child, a popular teacher in the local school, and the daughter who saves the house from its creditors (78, 74). Discussions of this fairy-tale plot of transformation often have focused on the person of Anne, but the function of community and the terms of communal identity in the Anne series also have been addressed in a thread of Montgomery scholarship over the years.[2] For Susan Drain, Anne's incorporation into Green Gables and Avonlea more generally is one of "mutual adaptation," the communities around Anne reformed by her as much as Anne is reformed by her adoptive communities (120). This observation suggests the questions around which I develop the reading of the novel that follows. What makes Anne suitable for adoption in this novel? What is the nature of the home that learns to want her?

A principal source for answering these questions is the archive of public discourses surrounding foster care and adoption, discourses underway in North America at the end of the nineteenth century and the beginning of the twentieth century. I have focused here on the circulation of these ideas in mainstream Canadian newspapers of the period.[3] This method seems particularly appropriate to criticism of this novel. Montgomery's occupation as assistant postmistress in Cavendish during the time that she was writing *Anne of Green Gables* gave her the opportunity to see all of the papers and periodicals to which people in her community subscribed. She unabashedly read many of them before passing them on to their addressees (Gammel 25–26). This reading habit is evident in the text. From Rachel Lynde's opening citation of "the paper" as her authority for her knowledge of the ways of orphans (59) to the "folded paper" reporting the failure of the Abbey Bank found in Matthew Cuthbert's hand when he dies (319), newspapers and magazines index the connections between the interior events of the novel and exterior events in society.[4] The method also seems appropriate at a theoretical level. If newspapers and novels are forms that produce the nation, as Anderson has proposed, then considering the discourse of novel and newspapers together should make visible some of the "structures of feeling" being set in place to support the idea of the national Canadian home.

Conditions of Possibility

Earlier in this essay I suggested that the elements of a social ideology that a text works to naturalize typically are moved into the background or obscured by other elements that are moved into the foreground. At the same time, however, these obscured elements must be present in the text. Film theorists and critics sometimes use the verb "screen" to convey this double action of displaying and hiding in texts. In literary theory, Pierre Macherey describes a similar process in terms of gaps and margins. Every work, he maintains, "has its *margins*, an area of incompleteness from which we can observe its birth and its production" (90). It is within these margins that a critical reader can find the "conditions of the possibility" of the created textual world (92). After the question of how a work coheres is answered, the second question of criticism for Macherey is that of the conditions of possibility, "to bring out . . . what the work is *compelled* to say in order to say what it *wants* to say" (94). In short, it is in the margins of the text where a reader can glimpse the terms that the text needs in order to make the connections that it wants to display. For Macherey, these terms are always immanent to the work itself—the work is "haunted" by them, he says—but also lead to "that which haunts it," "the play of history beyond its edges, encroaching on its edges" (94).

If we assume, with Irene Gammel, that the motto of *Anne of Green Gables* is that the home needs a child and the child needs a home, we might ask what conditions make the performance of the linkage of happy home and happy child possible. In the first chapter of the novel, in the conversation between Rachel Lynde and Marilla Cuthbert about the child who is expected at Green Gables, some of these conditions briefly become visible. The child who is to be brought into the household, Marilla insists, is not one of "those stupid, half-grown little French boys" who are so hard to get "broke into your ways and taught something"; not "a Barnardo boy," a "London street Arab"; not an English or an American child; but rather "a native born . . . a born Canadian" (58, 59). This chapter ends with the narrator allowing the reader a brief, pathetic glimpse of "the child who was waiting patiently at the Bright River station at this very moment," a child whose vivid and loquacious entrance into the text in the next chapter works to divert readerly attention from the xenophobia of the conversation that has announced her imminent appearance (61). As Macherey predicts, looking at this textual margin points to the connection of the text to a specific "undisguised (which does not mean innocent) relation with history" (92). What can we see and hear if we fail to follow the textual diversion and consider more closely some of these children whose exclusion from the house at Green Gables permits Montgomery's text to produce its understanding of home?

A full reading of the encroachments of history on *Anne of Green Gables* would require a consideration of each of these kinds of excluded children. The history of the Acadians after 1763, when they were forced from their lands as the colony of Canada was transferred to British governance, is replete with instances of classist and racialized constructions of French Canadians in relation to Canadians descended from British—and particularly Scottish—people.[5] Canadians' understanding of their national identity as triangulated with English and American national constructions has been, and continues to be, the subject of much political, literary, and historical commentary. Although the presence of Aboriginal Canadians is erased from the novel, there may be a trace of an historical haunting in Marilla's need to specify that "native born" means "born Canadian."[6] But, as a demonstration of how a reading of the conditions of possibility can be used to seek what Macherey calls "not the meaning that [the work] gives itself but the meaning that seizes hold of it," I focus here on the Barnardo children and the larger group of young immigrant "street Arabs" of whom they were the largest and most readily identifiable group (95).[7]

Between 1868 and 1925, historians estimate, eighty thousand British children, most under the age of fourteen, were relocated to Canada through one of more than a dozen child emigration schemes, thirty thousand through the regular transportations of girls and boys from the London rescue homes established by the Evangelical minister and medical student Thomas Barnardo (Bagnell 9, 122, Parr 11). Typically, they were taken first to institutional homes in towns and cities, from which they were dispersed to family homes across Canada, most to farmers who had applied to the institutions for young people to help with field and domestic labor. Barnardo was legendary in England for the energy and self-assurance that saw him opening one institution after another, beginning in 1870, to care for various populations of vagrant, abandoned, indigent, relinquished, and foundling children of London. So great was the success of his various social missions that the homes were soon overcrowded. He recognized that the time inevitably would come when he would be unable to accept any new children into them. "To secure the open door in front," Barnardo told the trustees of his Barnardo's Homes in 1876, a rescue home "must maintain its exit door in the rear" (qtd. in Bagnell 121).

Canada seemed an ideal "exit door" to Barnardo and other British social reformers like him. As historian Joy Parr explains, there were both negative and positive reasons for this view, often argued simultaneously: "Child emigration was to be both a safety-valve for internal disorder [in Britain] and a path to salvation [for the children]" (27). Legal restrictions on the scope of children's labor in Britain after the 1830s, which increased the number of unemployed young people in urban areas; a cholera epidemic in London in the 1860s, which swelled the numbers of orphaned children; and the British financial crises of the 1860s, which exacerbated pauperism among the working class, were among the historical conditions that made child emigration appear to be a desirable remedy for social troubles in Britain (Parr 29, Parker 6). Many of the child-saving reformers were religious workers: while they supplied the material wants of the children—at least at minimal levels— they often saw their spiritual wants as equally pressing (Parr 27, Parker 8). Because the child emigration schemes focused on placing children with Canadian families, invariably requiring that such families be recommended by their clergymen, the assumption was that what Victorians understood as the most important context for children's moral and spiritual development—a family—was assured them (Parr 37). Canada, moreover, advertised itself in Britain as a new country of limitless op-portunity. "You need CANADA needs you," ran the slogan of one advertising cam-paign sponsored by the Canadian government in London, the chiasmic structure of the rhetorical figure emphasizing the mutual benefits of immigration (Parker, no page number). The labor of good men and women—and, apparently, also that of boys and girls—was much needed to build the young country, particularly its agri-cultural sector; it was implied, too, that the dispossessed of the old country could find places and property for themselves in the new land. Both the Canadian cam-paigns and the British child-savers exploited the views of idyllic rural life and its "natural" association with healthy children, especially as contrasted to degenerate urban life and its corruption of children, views that British children's literature of the period, among other cultural documents, produced (Rooke and Schnell 226, Parker 20). The separation of children from their former unsatisfactory conditions was made visible and thorough in the emphasis on the geographical distance between the old and new locations (Rooke and Schnell 200, Parr 33, Parker 20).

Within Canada, however, public reaction to the presence of the children was mixed. The evidence of applications from farmers showed they clearly were needed in the new country. E. A. Struthers, the manager of Barnardo's industrial farm in Manitoba, observed in an 1893 letter to the editor that "our colonists are in such demand where they are known, that one-fifth only of the applications for farm help is supplied from the numbers available—a practical answer in itself to the com-plaint that 'the lads are not wanted in this country.'" An 1895 editorial in the *Mani-toba Morning Free Press* reported the claim that the demand for boys as farm laborers was "three or four times in excess of the supply" ("Those Terrible Boys!"). Historian Roy Parker calculates that the actual numbers exceed even those sug-gested by Struthers, with between five and sixteen times the number of applicants for the British child immigrants as there were children available for placement (135). That the young workers provided "a crucial and significant addition to the agricul-tural labour force" in Canada is an "inescapable" conclusion, he says (134). It was a conclusion also acknowledged by some Canadians at the time, such as the writer of a letter to the editor quoted in an 1897 editorial in the *Manitoba Free Press*: the vast majority of these children, "who are scattered all over the Dominion," the correspondent remarks, are "faithfully working their part in the development of this great country" ("The Barnardos Again").

But there were also many protests against the importation of so many "British waifs," as they were often called in the newspapers, and the terms of those protests are consonant with the racism and classism evident in Marilla's and Rachel's opening conversation. A letter to the editor of *The Globe* in Toronto on the subject of "the unwisdom of importing into our country, or rather of allowing to be deported into it, the paupers and waifs picked up elsewhere" begins from the assumption that it is a "scientific law that like begets like, that blood tells, and especially bad blood" (Blue). This linkage of poverty, orphans, race, and otherness is assumed, as well, in Marilla's description of these children as "London street Arabs." "Street Arabs," a common label for urban homeless children in the nineteenth century both in Britain and in Canada, is a racializing term, marking the children as being ideologically "outside the category of whiteness," as Cecily Devereux puts it in her note to this comment in her edition of the novel (58n2). By adding the designation "London," middle-class homemaker Marilla makes it clear that these children are multiply foreign—homeless, urban, and not Canadian. A writer to the *Stratford Beacon* in 1895 provides a more elaborate description of the practice of allowing Home boys to enter the country as immigrants, a description clearly inflected by the eugenics discourses circulating in the late nineteenth century in Europe and North America (Rooke and Schnell 239–40): "Stunted, starved, dwarfed in body and mind and associated with poverty, vice and sin . . ., they are picked out of England's social gutters and engrafted on strong, healthy Canadian society" (Allan). Even in reporting the 1895 case of George Greene, a Barnardo boy apparently starved and beaten to death on a farm in rural Ontario by his employer, Ellen Findlay, mainstream newspapers of the day reported that Greene was "lame, knock-kneed, hump-backed, short-sighted, and weak of intellect" ("A Repulsive Boy") at the same time that they deplored the "awful death" he suffered ("An Awful Death").

For many Canadians, the solution to this dilemma—their need for cheap agricultural and domestic labor conflicting with their fear of the physical and moral "taint" of the little emigrants—was the one at which Marilla Cuthbert arrives. "Give me a native born at least," Marilla reports that she has told Matthew, "There'll be a risk, no matter who we get. But I'll feel easier in my mind and sleep sounder at nights if we get a born Canadian" (59). George Greene's death and the subsequent trial of Findlay was one of the events around which this consensus crystallized (Bagnell 64–65). The *Stratford Beacon* editorial writer in 1896 summed up a common judgment in his assertion that the juvenile emigration schemes were a clear case of "misdirected philanthropy": in his estimation, the "vague notion that the unfortunate waifs and strays of English society can be made sound in mind and body by sending them away 'somewhere'" is demonstrably wrong (*Stratford Beacon*). Many public commentators greeted the appointment of J. J. Kelso to the office of superintendent of neglected and dependent children for Ontario in 1893 as a signal that

Canada, properly, was showing a new interest in its own orphaned and indigent children. In its report of the appointment, a Kingston newspaper manages simulta-neously to represent English child emigrants as less than human and to represent Canada as an open-hearted and open-handed mother of vulnerable children:

> Canada is ever welcoming and clasping to her bosom the waifs of other lands,
> nourishing and protecting them, whilst in her every village, town and city may be
> found destitute and homeless little ones. . . . How can we in justice to ourselves,
> our children and our country, permit our shores to be used as a dumping ground
> for little outcasts, when we are already surrounded by wretched suffering little
> ones appealing to us for pity and protection? . . . There is a great work lying at
> our doors in the removal of children from the street and slums into comfortable
> homes, under healthful influences. . . . When we have accomplished this noble
> work, then will we be in a position to extend our missionary labors to other
> countries. ("To Save Little Ones")

The media accounts rhetorically separate the British children and the Canadian chil-dren into undeserving and deserving recipients of places in Canadian homes. Yet it was the British juvenile emigration schemes, which instantiated new theories about child culture under debate in England, that served as models for the new "system of care for neglected and dependent children" being established in Canada by Kelso and the children's aid societies, according to historian Neil Sutherland (34).

A primary argument for the placement of children into families in the British context, note historians Patricia Rooke and R. L. Schnell, was that the "observa-tion of regular and respectable laboring family life led to the breaking of the chain of dependency and contributed to the depauperization of society" (191). The "healthful influences" in "comfortable homes" extolled by the Kingston paper clearly included expectations that the "suffering little ones" in Canada also would contribute to the work of the household. As a Toronto newspaper explicitly noted in reporting the meeting of the Children's Aid Society at which Kelso's appoint-ment was announced, "Mr. Kelso . . . will be in a position to assist farmers and others in obtaining Canadian boys and girls as household helps" ("Canadian Waifs"). For, whether British or Canadian, orphaned or relinquished, children "placed out" into foster homes typically were regarded as workers or as workers in training. In an 1893 interview with *The Evening Telegram* of Toronto, Kelso is quoted as remarking that children who are "boarded out in the homes of working people . . . early assimilate themselves to their surroundings and become self-supporting through a natural process," so that, by the age of twelve or thirteen, they can be expected to be "wage-earners." The great danger that is thereby avoided is "encouraging the dependent or pauper spirit" in children. As evidence for his claim, Kelso enthusiastically refers his interviewer to the success of "placing out" schemes in New York ("Children in Orphanages"), schemes that had already been highly influential in the formation of similar home-placement and fostering plans throughout the United States (Zelizer 172).

It is just such a situation from which Anne has come and to which she is almost returned in Montgomery's novel. After her schoolteacher parents die of "fever" within a few days of one another. Anne is rescued from being raised in an orphanage by Mrs. Thomas, "a poor woman who came in to scrub" for her mother (89). Although Anne's placement with the Thomases is a fall in class status, her accommodation within a family home rather than in an institution is understood as the preferable situation in the context of the discourse of the child-protection reformers at the end of the nineteenth century. For Kelso and the children's aid societies he shaped, placing children into family homes, particularly family homes in the country, was not only an economically but also a morally sound practice. As he explained in 1893 to the World's Congress of American Humane Associations in Chicago, "the real happiness of childhood is a quality that is not and cannot be developed in the institution," which tends to suppress children's "natural exuberance of spirit" (qtd. in Jones and Rutman 83). Anne assists in raising four Thomas children before she is eight years old, when she is passed on to the backwoods Hammond family, which has eight children who need "looking after," after which she is returned to the orphanage at age eleven. It is her obvious stamina as a worker rather than any "natural exuberance of spirit" that recommends her as a foster child to Mrs. Blewett. Mrs. Blewett clearly has no intentions of encouraging a "pauper spirit" in Anne: "if I take you you'll have to be a good girl, you know—good and smart and respectful. I'll expect you to earn your keep, and no mistake about that" (96).

That orphaned children in general are dangerous elements to bring into a family is emphasized at the beginning of Montgomery's novel. As Rachel Lynde reminds Marilla, "You don't know what you're getting. You're bringing a strange child into your house and home and you don't know a single thing about him nor what his disposition is like nor what sort of parents he had nor how he's likely to turn out" (59). She has read in the papers, she goes on to say, that these strange children have been known to burn families "to a crisp in their beds," "to suck the eggs," and "to put[] strychnine in the well" (59, 60). The accusations of arson, theft, and poisoning Mrs. Lynde levels against orphans can indeed be found in the newspapers of the day but usually attached specifically to Barnardo children rather than to orphans in general. For example, a story about Charles Bradbury, a boy brought from England who set fire to the house and barn of his employer, circulated widely, some of the newspapers lingering on the details of the "simmering" bed mattress discovered in the house ("The Dead Barnardo Boy"). Charles was not able to tell his side of the story, because he was himself discovered dead in the barn. His employer conceded at the inquest that the fire followed a quarrel between them, with Charles apparently protesting "the terms of agreement under which [he] was engaged" ("A Mysterious Holocaust"); the "quarrel" ended in the employer "severely assault[ing] the lad" ("The York Mills Tragedy"). Tales of attempts to poison employers reappeared from time to time. A boy is accused of attempting "to murder his benefactor" by putting "Paris green," a form of arsenic, into the teapot ("Barndardo Boy Tries to Murder His Employer"), while an almost identical story told about a young girl identifies the poison of choice as carbolic acid ("To Poison Stepmother"). Yet another girl accused of threatening to poison the hired hand and to hang herself is returned to the institution from which she had been placed into a family home. In this last case, the superintendent of one of Dr. Barnardo's homes wrote to local papers to note that he could confirm that the girl was definitely not a Barnardo girl and that there was, in general, "an absence of fact about this little story" (Owen, "Not a Barnardo Girl"). He makes no attempt to fill in the specific absence in the "little story" that might explain the girl's motivation, although the autobiographical accounts of Home children collected by modern historians give readers reason to suspect that she might have been, or feared that she would be, assaulted by the hired man.[8] Stories of the theft of food were also repeated, as in the case of George Greene, stories suggesting that some of these children were chronically underfed by employers and foster families.

Agents for the Barnardo homes repeatedly wrote Canadian newspapers to protest misrepresentations of child emigrants as particularly likely to commit criminal acts. Alfred Owen, a Toronto agent for Barnardo, for example, observes in 1893 that "the statement that there are a 'goodly number'" of the children who end up in "Canadian penal institutions" has been often made, but "has yet to be verified" (Owen, "A Few Inaccuracies"). One such claim appears in a letter to the editor in 1894, the writer asserting that, "while the unfortunate waifs probably do not exceed one half of one per cent. of the juvenile population, they represent more than half the juvenile criminals at the police courts" ("Care of Children"). Owen specifies rather different numbers: according to the Barnardo records, less than one percent of their children have been "convicted for crimes" ("The Barnardo Boys"). E. A. Struthers, Barnardo's agent in Manitoba, writes the *Free Press*, also in 1893, to observe that it is a "young fellow" from "our native juvenile population" who has recently been convicted of "murder by the use of strychnine placed in the food of the friend who fed, clothed, and housed him," and not a Barnardo boy as reported. The editorial writer of the *Manitoba Free Press* was among the few who exposed the faulty logic underlying the public commentary of many of his compatriots: "A good many of our people have the impression that every Barnardo boy is a bad boy, and even worse than this, that every bad boy is necessarily a Barnardo boy." Such prejudices had become so entrenched that they had attained the status of truth in Canada, he observed, a truth that served the "double duty" of explaining juvenile crime as the result of the "inherent badness" of Barnardo boys, "while at the same time we display our own superior sagacity" ("A Needed Inquest"). In the context of this national conversation, Mrs. Lynde's attribution of criminality to orphans in general, rather than the Barnardo children in particular, can be seen as aligning her with the liberal end of the spectrum of public opinion. Marilla's comment about the little British immigrants, "They may be all right.—I'm not saying they're not," opens the possibility, although warily, that "the papers" may be inaccurate in their characterization of Barnardo children (58).

The Island communities of Montgomery's novel recognize that foster parents and employers are sometimes guilty of inciting the pauper children they take into their homes to violence and theft. Marilla's first qualms about whether Mrs. Blewett represents "an unexpectedly good chance to get this unwelcome orphan off her hands" are recorded before the "small, shrewish-faced woman without an ounce of superfluous flesh on her bones" even appears on the scene (94). Marilla knows Mrs. Blewett "only by sight," but she has heard that she has a temper, is stingy with her servants, and is, in general, "[a] terrible worker and driver" of them (94). Indeed, Marilla's description of Mrs. Blewitt resonates with the newspaper accounts of the employer of George Green, Ellen Findlay, who is said to be "of very masculine appearance" and with "an unenviable reputation in the neighborhood" of cruel treatment of her workers ("A Single Woman"). Marilla finally decides not to "hand over" Anne to Mrs. Blewett, after seeing in Anne's expression "the misery of a helpless little creature who finds itself once more caught in the trap from which it had escaped" (97). It is a decision that her brother, Matthew, has anticipated before Marilla's failed attempt to send Anne away. When Marilla rhetorically asks, "What good would she be to us?" Matthew retorts, "We might be some good to her" (80).

The contradictory views of "good" evident in Matthew's and Marilla's reasoning point to another discourse emerging in Canada, as in other Anglo-American societies, at the end of the nineteenth century, the discourse of what Viviana Zelizer has called "the priceless child" (14). Claudia Nelson has observed that, among the "rhetorical uses" to which "displaced, adopted, and fostered children" were put at this time in the United States was "the reshaping of America's understanding of itself" (2, 4). In Canada, I have been arguing, the discussion about unattached children was one site for the articulation of the structures of feeling of the new nation. The substantial presence of "the London street Arabs" in homes and newspapers provided a ready source of examples for commentators against which to define the Canadian child. Indeed, the "double duty" served by the Barnardo children in public conversations was even more significant than the *Free Press* editorial writer supposed: the assignment of the dangers and evils of orphan children to these outsiders allowed Canadians to claim Canadian orphans for the purpose of displaying their valuation of the priceless child.

Residual and Emergent Practices

In *Marxism and Literature*, Raymond Williams, developing methods of literary analysis that account for "the complexity of a culture" and changes within a culture, argues that it is important for analysts to recognize that a culture is more than its dominant or hegemonic ideology (121). Rather, at any moment, analysts can expect to find evidence also of "residual" and "emergent" sets of ideas actively shaping responses within societies. Residual processes are those that have been "effectively formed in the past" but that continue to "be lived and practised" in the present (122). Sometimes such processes become archaic and are practiced only in isolated pockets of a society; rarely they continue to carry "alternative and oppositional meanings and values" within a culture; usually they are incorporated into the dominant culture (122). Indeed, some such incorporation is necessary, "if the effective dominant culture is to make sense in these areas" (123). The emergent modes of a culture are more difficult to identify, according to Williams, since what may look like "new meanings and values, new practices, new relationships and kinds of relationship" may, in fact, turn out to be "really elements of some new phase of dominant culture," merely novel and not truly emergent (123). As with residual modes, moreover, there will always be pressure within a social formation to incorporate or co-opt emergent modes, rather than to permit them to oppose or transform that formation. Despite his cautions about too-easy ascriptions of subversive cultural practices, Williams concedes that it is "the fact of emergent cultural practice . . . together with the fact of actively residual practice" that account for changes in societies (126). Such change often will be registered first in the shifts in the "affective elements of consciousness and relationships" or "structures of feeling" (132) and present itself in these forms in art and literature (132).

The opening chapters of *Anne of Green Gables* make it clear that the place of unattached children in society is a site at which change is being negotiated in the communities inside the novel and in the communities outside the novel to which it is tied. Evidently there are various positions available at this time to "ordinary" people in the community. For Mrs. Lynde, orphans are dangerous strangers who should not be invited into family homes but, presumably, kept in institutions. For Mrs. Blewett, it seems that orphans can be useful additions to family homes, if they are kept in their place and made to contribute to the household labor. For Marilla, distinguishing between "born Canadians" and "London street Arabs" is a way of significantly reducing the risk to the family home while continuing to garner the benefits of unpaid labor. Mrs. Spencer, by contrast, assumes that orphans are suitable subjects for adoption.

The disquiet and sometimes outrage expressed in the newspaper articles about the ill treatment of children—particularly Canadian orphans and other "native-born" children, but also occasionally the young British emigrants—parallel Marilla's and Matthew's reactions to Mrs. Blewett. Marilla says only that she does not "fancy her style myself," but Matthew's vehement exclamation, "I wouldn't give a dog I liked to that Blewett woman," borrows the rhetoric of animality often used in the Canadian papers to describe the abject conditions in which children were sometimes found by neighbors or police and to register the horror of mainstream society at such abuse (97).[9] But the moral distaste Marilla expresses about Mrs. Blewett's style does not change the fact that she shares Mrs. Blewett's view of the function of orphans at the beginning of the story. That view—that orphans are workers who should be grateful to find themselves in a family home—was, as I've already demonstrated, the dominant view of Canadians as expressed in the media of Montgomery's day. It is, rather, the implications of Mrs. Lynde's view (that orphaned children should be kept in institutional homes) and Mrs. Spencer's view (that orphaned children can be made members of the family) that represent residual and emergent ways of thinking about the relationships of unattached children to their society.

The specialized institutions for indigent and abandoned children established by various religious and charitable societies in England from the early nineteenth century and in Canada from the mid-nineteenth century were regarded in their time as significant advances over the workhouses, poorhouses, factories, or streets in which these children might otherwise be found. The children certainly were expected to help maintain the institutions with their labor and to prepare themselves for useful futures as workers, but the fact that they were housed, fed, and clothed seemed great moral and physical goods (Bagnell 98–99, Parr 37). Perhaps most important, the residential refuges, asylums, and orphanages allowed for the segregation of indigent children from adult paupers. As Rooke and Schnell observe, "the creation of the orphan asylum meant the possibility of a completely controlled environment." The implementation of "the dual conditions of 'rescue' and 'restraint'" was "the logical extension of assumptions regarding the vulnerability, malleability, and ultimately the 'educability' of children" hegemonic in the nineteenth century (74–75). By the end of the century, however, the system of congregate care came to be seen as undesirable. "Children in institutions lead an artificial existence," J. J. Kelso told the *London Citizen and Home Guard* in 1894, "they are marked off from the rest of the community, are looked upon as objects of pity, and do not undergo the ordinary experiences of happy and growing childhood" ("Our Neglected Children Act"). Rather than "crowding [dependent children] into asylums," Canada was looking forward to being able to adopt a practice whereby all children would be "placed in private families," he told a conference group in 1896. He had no doubts that this "is certainly the best [plan], and is accepted [as such] by all educators and sociologists" ("A Review of the Charity Conference"). It was claimed that the saddest deprivation of institutional life is the absence of "the petting and fondling" of a mother, for whom a child has "a great, constant, aching, instinctive longing" ("Organization of Conference"). Sometimes the word "home" is set into quotation marks when it is used to refer to institutions in the newspaper articles, in order to mark its status as an artificial, rather than natural, home ("A Good Work," Jones and Rutman 83). Many of these attitudes were shared across Anglo-American societies: as I noted earlier, it was because children were to be settled in good Canadian homes that British philanthropists and the public that funded them were persuaded to support the child emigration schemes (Parr 46–47, Parker 20, 69).

Asylums and institutions increasingly came to be regarded as places to which only the insane, the morally reprobate, the incorrigible and uneducable, or the crippled child should be confined (Sutherland 143, Rooke and Schnell 21, 276). All of the fostering and "placing out" plans assumed that "deficient" children could be returned to their institutional homes if they did not fit into the family home to which they'd been assigned (Parker 216–21). Indeed, Canadian newspapers regularly reported on Barnardo children in their districts who had been "sent back" for a variety of perceived defects and offences. In Montgomery's novel, Anne seems to be well aware that the asylum marks its residents as the unwanted and unfit when she pleads with Marilla to let her stay at Green Gables: "I'll try to do and be anything you want me, if you'll only keep me" (97). On one occasion early in the novel, Anne acknowledges her culpability for a mistake by telling Marilla that she may have to be sent back to the asylum after all (131). The comic excess of this scene—Marilla's belated discovery that Anne has appeared in church with real rather than artificial flowers decorating her hat—makes the exchange primarily an indication of Anne's increasingly secure place at Green Gables. But the possibility of such a return in the communities outside the novel functions as a reminder inside the novel that a family home is, as Beverly Crockett has observed, a "contingent" place for those children Kelso often calls the "dependent" children of Canada (70).

The institutionalization of children, while an ongoing practice in Canadian society at the time Montgomery writes her novel, is becoming what Williams calls an active residual mode, limited to pockets of society. The emergent practice is adoption. The first Canadian laws governing adoption were passed in New Brunswick in 1873 and in Nova Scotia in 1896. Prince Edward Island formalized and regularized the relation of adopted child and adoptive parent in 1916 in an act that, according to historian Veronica Strong-Boag, retained the vestiges of the conceptualization of "disadvantaged youngsters" as laborers (28). Many orphaned children were adopted as members of a family before the passage of these laws, often by the mutual consent of the adults and the children, but the meaning of these relationships were variable (Strong-Boag 9–16). In Montgomery's novel, Mrs. Spencer goes to the orphanage with the intention of finding a young girl to adopt, something she sees as a charitable service to the asylum, it is implied, and "under the impression" that the Cuthberts also want "a little girl to adopt" (95), something she readily agrees to undertake on their behalf although she has only a confused idea of their motives. When Marilla finally agrees to keep Anne, she too relinquishes the rhetoric of the child as worker she has used in her first conversation with Rachel and substitutes the language of adoption in her self-reflections: "Marilla Cuthbert, you're fairly in for it. Did you ever suppose you'd see the day when you'd be adopting an orphan girl?" (98). At this point, she understands her decision as the taking up of "a duty" to train Anne to be "a useful little thing" (97, 98). Both Mrs. Spencer and Marilla, in fact, could be listed among the "laudable" Canadians praised in a 1902 *Ottawa Evening Journal* article for receiving orphan and dependent children into their homes and giving them "useful and kindly training for future citizenship" ("An Interesting Work"). In the eyes of the children's aid societies established in the 1890s, these "philanthropic" people are distinguishable from "persons whose plain object is to make of an unfortunate child a little slave," in large part by their commitment to the schooling of the children ("Twelve Little Folks"). When Marilla agrees to allow Anne to prepare for the entrance exam to college, she confirms the Cuthberts' early resolution to "do the best we could for you and give you a good education" (274). Such good folk are constantly being sought through Canadian newspaper notices describing the "bright," "active," "happy" children available for placement in family homes, descriptions often accompanied by photographs, as they were in the 1907 *Delineator* campaign.[10]

Alongside the discourse of child-rescue, adult benevolence, and the natural benefits of family homes, there is an emerging discourse of the emotional benefits children bring to a home. In an 1894 report on its work published in many Canadian papers, for example, the Toronto Children's Aid Society alternatively deploys the rhetoric of love and the rhetoric of service in its solicitation of foster parents:

> If any reader has a childless home and longs to hear the patter of the little feet and to feel the caress of chubby, grateful arms they should send their names to the Children's Aid Society. . . . Apply for a baby or a little tot of four or five and then you have a human soul that you can train, a little heart you can teach to love you and call you by the sweetest of all names—"mother." There is no better service anyone can render to church or state than the training of a child for good citizenship. ("To Protect Children")

Later notices from the societies emphasize the emotional gifts brought by children "who would certainly be a treasure in some quiet home where the prattle of children is not known" (*Erin Advocate*) or children whose presence would bring "brightness and sunshine" to bereaved homes or happiness and brightness to childless homes ("A Great and Noble Work"). The emerging structure of feeling evident in such rhetoric is one in which, to use Zelizer's terms, the child is "economically worthless but emotionally priceless" to adults (14).

The plot of *Anne of Green Gables* spans the distance Marilla travels from understanding the child who is to enter her home as a farm worker with economic worth to understanding the child in her home as an emotional resource. Even before she has conceded to herself that she has taken on the task of adopting a child, Marilla finds herself moved to "a reluctant smile" at Anne's verbal flourishes, to a pity "stirring in her heart" for the child whose past life is one "of drudgery and poverty and neglect," and to a "softening" conviction that Anne has a moral right to a home (76, 92, 96). Several of the "softening" moments of the novel, during which Anne becomes more securely tied to the home at Green Gables, notably, are incidents in which she demonstrates her ineptness for domestic work and her aptitude for emotional work to the adults in her community. Matthew, for example, is enthralled by her interesting "chatter" during the "odd half-hours she was allowed for play," and her liniment-flavored cake is dismissed as "a funny mistake" by Mrs. Allan, who takes the loveliness of the decorated tea table and Anne's flower garden to be the markers of her true worth (111, 214). As Anne progresses toward the "pruned down and branched out" self she achieves by the end of the novel, Marilla progresses toward a place where she both knows and says that she loves Anne "as dear as if you were my own flesh and blood" (304, 322). Margaret Atwood has observed that one way to read *Anne of Green Gables* is to assume that the central character is Marilla: "Only Marilla unfolds into something unimaginable to us at the beginning of the book. Her growing love for Anne, and her growing ability to express that love . . . is the real magic transformation" (R7). The "catalyst" for the magic is the economically worthless but emotionally priceless child.

That it is a female child who enables Marilla's transformation is not surprising. It is clear from the notices of children available for fostering and adoption posted in newspapers as the discourse of the priceless child took hold that girls are considered more adoptable than boys. In a letter to the editor describing ten boys available to "a good home," for example, J. Stuart Coleman of the Toronto Children's Aid Society notes that "we have so many applications for girls from six to sixteen, as yet unfilled, that it will be quite useless for any of your readers to apply for such at present." Zelizer suggests that "established cultural assumptions of women's superior emotional talents . . . made girls so uniquely attractive for sentimental adoption" (194). If boys were particularly wanted by families looking for cheap labor, little girls were most desirable to families looking for priceless children. Anne confirms that such a situation prevails at the Hopetown asylum to which she was relinquished. She was not sent to Green Gables, she assures Marilla, because of a lack of available boys; in fact, there "was an abundance" of boys (77). As Anne is acutely aware, she is not like the "very beautiful" little Lily whom Mrs. Spencer adopts (77); she does, however, manifest the "natural exuberance of spirit" that J. J. Kelso invokes in his public rhetoric as the mark of the happy child suitable for home placement (qtd. in Jones and Rutman 83).

Kelso offered an explanation different from Zelizer's for the preference for girl babies: female foundlings, he observed, were generally assumed not to come "from a line of criminals" but to be "simply the offspring of some unfortunate girl who makes a mistake" ("Girl Babies Wanted"). The logical links among class, heredity, and gender in the reasoning Kelso reports may be difficult to reconstruct for a contemporary reader, but the conclusions Marilla draws about Anne's class and heredity are based on similarly tortured reasoning. The narrator judges Marilla to be a "shrewd" reader of history. "Reading between the lines" and "divin[ing] the truth," Marilla concludes well before she decides to keep Anne that Anne likely is telling the truth about her parents being married and being teachers because "there's nothing rude or slangy in what she does say. She's ladylike. It's likely her parents were nice folks" (92).

A Daughter of the House

What makes Anne suitable for adoption in this novel? What can be said about the nature of the home that learns to want her? Anne can make a mother of a spinster "of narrow experience and rigid conscience" (57) and can bring "joy and comfort" to a "painfully clean" and underused home (56) because, among other things, she is a white, English-speaking, Canadian orphan; she is the legitimate descendent of middle-class people; and she is an emotionally priceless girl child (57, 56). But this chosen child can be celebrated only by obscuring the presence of other unattached children also resident in the home of the nation—displaced child emigrants, racialized lower-class children, child laborers, institutionalized children—who are rarely imagined in place inside happy family homes. The iconic status of *Anne of Green Gables* as a text in and of Canada suggests the naturalized power of this image of the happy daughter of a happy house. As Clare Bradford has observed about Montgomery's novel, among a number of enduring children's texts from "the homely nations of Canada and Australia," these powerful narratives propose "versions of nationhood where citizens are nurtured and loved insofar as they conform to the will of the national imaginary" (192).

The happy home formed around the happy child is explicitly understood by the Canadian newspapers to be a microcosm of the nation, and the unproductive priceless child, ironically, its guarantor of a prosperous future. "The child, from the standpoint of national life, is our most valuable asset" and the "safeguard [of] our material resources," declares one editorial writer in 1909 ("Value of the Child"). Anne herself, of course, proves the truth of this maxim, saving the house and farm from being sold at the end of Montgomery's novel and affirming that "nothing could be worse than giving up Green Gables" (328). In a striking instance of the congruence of the interior time of Montgomery's novel with the exterior time of the nation, two years after the publication of *Anne of Green Gables*, J. J. Kelso tells the dramatic story of a son who hears that the home and farm of his foster parents will have to be sold to "satisfy a mortgage." Arriving unannounced at the auction at "the last moment," he purchases the farm himself: "The old people . . . continued to reside there in peace and plenty, lovingly sheltered by the boy whom they had 'taken to raise'" (Kelso, "The Destiny of a Child"). Kelso promises in 1911 that, if we only hedge the child around "with saving influences," "this Canada of ours" will prosper (Kelso, "Save the Children"). That the figure of the singular child and the plural first-person pronouns put to such stirring use in the public rhetoric are built on select inclusions and systematic exclusions is forgotten in the swelling hymn to the happy child in the happy home: "Home, Sweet Home is a beautiful thing. What a great deal we owe to home life!" ("The Great Asset of this Nation").

NOTES

1. Notable exceptions are the essays by Beverly Crockett, Cecily Devereux, Erika Rothwell, Christiana Salah, and Gavin White cited below.

2. See, for example, Claudia Mills, "Children in Search of a Family: Orphan Novels Through the Century"; Susan Drain, "Community and the Individual in *Anne of Green Gables*: The Meaning of Belonging"; and Laura Robinson, "'A Born Canadian': The Bonds of Communal Identity in *Anne of Green Gables* and *A Tangled Web*."

3. Brenna McGregor, my research assistant on this project, undertook the archival research in the Archives of Manitoba and the Archives of Ontario on which this reading of the novel is based. The Manitoba archives house the journals and letters of E. A. Struthers, the manager of Dr. Barnardo's Industrial Farm in Russell, Manitoba. The items from

Manitoba newspapers can be found on the Internet site, NewspaperARCHIVE.com. The Ontario archives house scrapbooks of J. J. Kelso, who was appointed the superintendent of neglected and dependent children for Ontario in 1893. His influential public service for children in a variety of roles spanned forty years, including from 1897 the position of inspector of juvenile immigration agencies in Ontario. The scrapbooks consulted for this project contain his clippings of newspaper articles related to the child emigrants in Canada, foster care, and adoption between 1893 and 1940, although we focused our work on newspaper articles published before 1915.

4. In her edition of the novel, Cecily Devereux notes textual references to actual periodicals being published in Canada when Montgomery wrote the novel. I have used Devereux's edition for my citations of the novel.

5. See Gavin White, "L. M. Montgomery and the French," and Laura Robinson, "'A Born Canadian,'" for discussions of Montgomery's representation of French Canadians.

6. White speculates that the description of the Barrys' babysitter, Mary Joe, as "broad-faced" might also "hint at Indian ancestry" (65). The *Oxford English Dictionary* confirms that "native" was commonly used to refer to Canadians of Aboriginal ancestry at the end of the nineteenth century.

7. In "Outlaws, Outcasts, and Orphans: The Historical Imagination and *Anne of Green Gables*," Beverly Crockett also reads Montgomery's novel beside the story of the young emigrants to Canada. Crockett focuses on autobiographical accounts of the Home children, collected in the 1970s, while I focus on the public media discourses about the child emigration schemes during the period when Montgomery wrote and published the novel. Crockett's essay would usefully be read beside mine.

8. See *The Home Children: Their Personal Stories*, ed. Phyllis Harrison, and Margaret McNay's "Immigrants, Labourers, 'Others': Canada's Home Children" for some of these accounts.

9. As, for example, in the 1903 article about the proceedings of a Hamilton conference of charities and correction, which details "some shocking instances" of "cruelty and vice," including the story of a young girl from an affluent family who is made to eat from her plate "like a dog" ("Neglect of Children"). This rhetoric doubtlessly would be recognizable to contemporary, as to contemporaneous, readers of Montgomery's novel: it continues to be widely used in child-protection discourse.

10. Anne's description of the little girl adopted by Mrs. Spencer mimics these notices, which typically list the children's names, ages, hair and eye color, and distinctive characteristics: "Lily is only five years old and she is very beautiful. She has nut-brown hair" (77).

WORKS CITED

Allan, Charles. "Pauper Immigrants." *[Stratford] Beacon*, June 24, 1895. RG 29-75. Reel 1. Scrapbooks on Child Welfare Issues, 1893–1940. Archives of Ontario, Toronto.

Anderson, Benedict. *Imagined Communities: Reflections on the Origin and Spread of Nationalism*. 1983. Rev. ed. London: Verso, 1991.

"An Awful Death." N.d. Newspaper article. RG 29-75. Reel 1. Scrapbooks on Child Welfare Issues, 1893–1940. Archives of Ontario, Toronto.

Atwood, Margaret. "Bewitched By an Antique Orphan." *[Toronto] Globe and Mail*, April 5, 2008, R1, R7.

Bagnell, Kenneth. *The Little Immigrants: The Orphans Who Came to Canada.* 1980. New ed. Toronto: Dundurn, 2001.

"Barnardo Boy Tries to Murder His Employer. He Put Paris Green in the Tea." N.d. Newspaper article. RG 29-75. Reel 1. Scrapbooks on Child Welfare Issues, 1893–1940. Archives of Ontario, Toronto.

"The Barnardo Boys. Interesting Conversation with the Canadian Agent." *Globe*, October 27, 1894. Newspaper article. RG 29-75. Reel 2-4. Scrapbooks on Child Welfare Issues, 1893–1940. Archives of Ontario, Toronto.

"The Barnardos Again." *The Manitoba Morning Free Press*, February 25, 1897. Newspaper-ARCHIVE.com.

Blackford, Holly, ed. *100 Years of Anne with an "E": The Centennial Study of* Anne of Green Gables. Calgary: U of Calgary P, 2009.

Blue, A. "Importing Paupers." *[Toronto] Globe*, June 1, 1895. RG 29-75. Reel 1. Scrapbooks on Child Welfare Issues, 1893–1940. Archives of Ontario, Toronto.

Bradford, Clare. "The Homely Imaginary: Fantasies of Nationhood in Australian and Canadian Texts." In Reimer, *Home Words* 177–93.

"Canadian Waifs Must Come First. The Children's Aid Society Will Find Homes for Friendless Children." c.1893. Newspaper article. RG 29-75. Reel 2-4. Scrapbooks on Child Welfare Issues, 1893–1940. Archives of Ontario, Toronto.

"Care of Children." *The Intelligencer.* November 20, [1894]. Letter to the Editor. RG 29-75. Reel 2-4. Scrapbooks on Child Welfare Issues, 1893–1940. Archives of Ontario, Toronto.

"Children in Orphanages, Some Sound Ideas." *The [Toronto] Evening Telegram.* December 7, 1893. RG 29-75. Reel 2-4. Scrapbooks on Child Welfare Issues, 1893–1940. Archives of Ontario, Toronto.

Coleman, J. Stuart. "Do You Want a Child?" *The Templar*, April 25, 1896. Letter to the Editor. RG 29-75. Reel 2-4. Scrapbooks on Child Welfare Issues, 1893–1940. Archives of Ontario, Toronto.

Crockett, Beverly. "Outlaws, Outcasts, and Orphans: The Historical Imagination and *Anne of Green Gables*." In Novy, *Imagining Adoption* 57–81.

"The Dead Barnardo Boy." N.d. Newspaper article. RG 29-75. Reel 1. Scrapbooks on Child Welfare Issues, 1893–1940. Archives of Ontario, Toronto.

"*The Delineator* Child-Rescue Campaign." *The Delineator*, November 1907, 715–19.

Devereux, Cecily. "'Canadian Classic' and 'Commodity Export': The Nationalism of 'Our' Anne of Green Gables." *Journal of Canadian Studies* 36, no. 1 (2001): 11–28.

———. "Not One of Those Dreadful New Women: Anne Shirley and the Culture of Imperial Motherhood." In Hudson and Cooper, *Windows and Words* 119–30.

———. "'Writing with a Definite Purpose': L. M. Montgomery, Nellie L. McClung and the Politics of Imperial Motherhood in Fiction for Children." *Canadian Children's Literature* 99 (2000): 6–22.

Drain, Susan. "Community and the Individual in *Anne of Green Gables*: The Meaning of Belonging." *Children's Literature Association Quarterly* 11 (1986): 15–19. Reprinted in Reimer, *Such a Simple Little Tale* 119–30.

The Erin Advocate, November 13, 1902. Newspaper clipping. RG 29-75. Reel 2-4. Scrapbooks on Child Welfare Issues, 1893–1940. Archives of Ontario, Toronto.

Gammel, Irene. *Looking for Anne of Green Gables: The Story of L. M. Montgomery and Her Literary Classic.* New York: St. Martin's P, 2008.

Gammel, Irene, and Elizabeth Epperly, eds. *L. M. Montgomery and Canadian Culture.* Toronto: U of Toronto P, 1999.

"Girl Babies Wanted." *News*. c.1896. Newspaper clipping. RG 29-75. Reel 2-4. Scrapbooks on Child Welfare Issues, 1893–1940. Archives of Ontario, Toronto.

"A Good Work." N.d. Newspaper article. RG 29-75. Reel 1. Scrapbooks on Child Welfare Issues, 1893–1940. Archives of Ontario, Toronto.

"A Great and Noble Work." *The Goderich Star*. September 11, 1903. Newspaper article. RG 29-75. Reel 2-4. Scrapbooks on Child Welfare Issues, 1893–1940. Archives of Ontario, Toronto.

"The Great Asset of this Nation." *The Hamilton Spectator*, January 23, 1912. Newspaper article. RG 29-75. Reel 2-4. Scrapbooks on Child Welfare Issues, 1893–1940. Archives of Ontario, Toronto.

Harrison, Phyllis, ed. *The Home Children: Their Personal Stories*. [Winnipeg]: Shillingford, 1979.

Hudson, Aïda, and Susan-Ann Cooper, eds. *Windows and Words: A Look at Canadian Children's Literature in English*. Ottawa: U of Ottawa P, 2003.

"An Interesting Work." *The Ottawa Evening Journal*, August 2, 1902. RG 29-75. Reel 2-4. Scrapbooks on Child Welfare Issues, 1893–1940. Archives of Ontario, Toronto.

Jones, Andrew, and Leonard Rutman. *In the Children's Aid: J. J. Kelso and Child Welfare in Ontario*. Toronto: U of Toronto P, 1981.

Kelso, J. J. "The Destiny of a Child." N.d. Newspaper article. RG 29-75. Reel 2-4. Scrapbooks on Child Welfare Issues, 1893–1940. Archives of Ontario, Toronto.

———. "Save the Children." July 15, 1911. Newspaper article. RG 29-75. Reel 2-4. Scrapbooks on Child Welfare Issues, 1893–1940. Archives of Ontario, Toronto.

Lerner, Loren, ed. *Depicting Canada's Children*. Waterloo, ON: Wilfrid Laurier UP, 2009.

Macherey, Pierre. *A Theory of Literary Production*. 1966. Translated by Geoffrey Wall. London: Routledge and Kegan Paul, 1978.

McNay, Margaret. "Immigrants, Labourers, 'Others': Canada's Home Children." In Lerner, *Depicting Canada's Children* 153–72.

Mills, Claudia. "Children in Search of a Family: Orphan Novels Through the Century." *Children's Literature in Education* 18 (1987): 227–39.

Montgomery, L. M. *Anne of Green Gables*. 1908. Edited by Cecily Devereux. Peterborough, ON: Broadview, 2004.

"A Mysterious Holocaust. Charles Bradbury Burnt to Death at York Mills." N.d. Newspaper article. RG 29-75. Reel 1. Scrapbooks on Child Welfare Issues, 1893–1940. Archives of Ontario, Toronto.

"A Needed Inquest." *Manitoba Morning Free Press*, December 18, 1893. NewspaperARCHIVE.com.

"Neglect of Children." *[Hamilton] Spectator*. Hamilton, Ontario. September 24, 1903. Newspaper article. RG 29-75. Reel 1. Scrapbooks on Child Welfare Issues, 1893–1940. Archives of Ontario, Toronto.

Nelson, Claudia. *Little Strangers: Portrayals of Adoption and Foster Care in America, 1850–1929*. Bloomington: Indiana UP, 2003.

Novy, Marianne, ed. *Imagining Adoption: Essays on Literature and Culture*. Ann Arbor: U of Michigan P, 2001.

"Organization of Conference of 1898." N.d. Newspaper article. RG 29-75. Reel 1. Scrapbooks on Child Welfare Issues, 1893–1940. Archives of Ontario, Toronto.

"Our Neglected Children Act: Some Interesting Facts from the New Provincial Superintendent." *[London] Citizen and Homeguard*. February 12, 1894. Newspaper article. RG 29-75. Reel 2-4. Scrapbooks on Child Welfare Issues, 1893–1940. Archives of Ontario, Toronto.

Owen, Alfred B. "A Few Inaccuracies." *Telegram*. December 14 [1893]. Letter to the Editor. RG 29-75. Reel 2-4. Scrapbooks on Child Welfare Issues, 1893–1940. Archives of Ontario, Toronto.

———. "Not a Barnardo Girl." N.d. Letter to the Editor. RG 29-75. Reel 1. Scrapbooks on Child Welfare Issues, 1893–1940. Archives of Ontario, Toronto.

Parker, Roy. *Uprooted: The Shipment of Poor Children to Canada, 1867–1917*. Bristol: Policy P, 2008.

Parr, Joy. *Labouring Children: British Immigrant Apprentices to Canada, 1869–1924*. Toronto: U of Toronto P, 1980.

Reimer, Mavis, ed. *Home Words: Discourses of Children's Literature in Canada*. Waterloo, ON: Wilfrid Laurier UP, 2008.

———. *Such a Simple Little Tale: Critical Responses to L. M. Montgomery's* Anne of Green Gables. Metuchen, NJ: Scarecrow, 1992.

"A Repulsive Boy." N.d. Newspaper article. RG 29-75. Reel 1. Scrapbooks on Child Welfare Issues, 1893–1940. Archives of Ontario, Toronto.

"A Review of the Charity Conference." New Orleans, Ontario. March 1896. Newspaper article. RG 29-75. Reel 1. Scrapbooks on Child Welfare Issues, 1893–1940. Archives of Ontario, Toronto.

Robinson, Laura. "'A Born Canadian': The Bonds of Communal Identity in *Anne of Green Gables* and *A Tangled Web*." In Gammel and Epperly, *L. M. Montgomery* 19–30.

Rooke, Patricia T., and R. L. Schnell. *Discarding the Asylum: From Child Rescue to Welfare State in English-Canada (1800–1950)*. Lanham, MD: UP of America, 1983.

Rothwell, Erika. "Knitting Up the World: L. M. Montgomery and Maternal Feminism in Canada." In Gammel and Epperly, *L. M. Montgomery* 133–44.

"A Single Woman." [1895]. Newspaper article. RG 29-75. Reel 1. Scrapbooks on Child Welfare Issues, 1893–1940. Archives of Ontario, Toronto.

Salah, Christiana. "A Ministry of Plum Puffs: Cooking as Path to Spiritual Maturity in L. M. Montgomery's Anne Books." In Blackford, *100 Years of Anne with an "E"* 193–210.

Stratford Beacon. c.1896. Newspaper clipping. RG 29-75. Reel 1. Scrapbooks on Child Welfare Issues, 1893–1940. Archives of Ontario, Toronto.

Strong-Boag, Veronica. *Finding Families, Finding Ourselves: English Canada Encounters Adoption from the Nineteenth Century to the 1990s*. Don Mills, ON: Oxford UP, 2006.

Struthers, E. A. "The Barnardo Boys. To the Editor of the Free Press." *Manitoba Morning Free Press*, December 14, 1893. NewspaperARCHIVE.com.

Sutherland, Neil. *Children in English-Canadian Society: Framing the Twentieth-Century Consensus*. 1978. Waterloo, ON: Wilfrid Laurier UP, 2000.

"Those Terrible Boys!" *Manitoba Morning Free Press*, December 10, 1895. NewspaperARCHIVE.com.

"To Poison Stepmother." N.d. Newspaper article. RG 29-75. Reel 2-4. Scrapbooks on Child Welfare Issues, 1893–1940. Archives of Ontario, Toronto.

"To Protect Children. The Good Work of the Children's Aid Societies." Syndicated Newspaper article. RG 29-75. Reel 2-4. Scrapbooks on Child Welfare Issues, 1893–1940. Archives of Ontario, Toronto.

"To Save Little Ones. The Door to Canada Should Close for a Time." *The Daily British Whig*. c. May 4, 1894. Special correspondence. RG 29-75. Reel 2-4. Scrapbooks on Child Welfare Issues, 1893–1940. Archives of Ontario, Toronto.

"Twelve Little Folks Awaiting a Home." N.d. Newspaper Article. RG 29-75. Reel 2-4. Scrapbooks on Child Welfare Issues, 1893–1940. Archives of Ontario, Toronto.

"Value of the Child." N.d. Newspaper Clipping. RG 29-75. Reel 2-4. Scrapbooks on Child Welfare Issues, 1893–1940. Archives of Ontario, Toronto.

White, Gavin. "L. M. Montgomery and the French." *Canadian Children's Literature* 78 (1978): 65–68.

Williams, Raymond. *Marxism and Literature.* Oxford: Oxford UP, 1977.

"The York Mills Tragedy. Further Details of Charles Bradbury's Death." N.d. Newspaper article. RG 29-75. Reel 1. Scrapbooks on Child Welfare Issues, 1893–1940. Archives of Ontario, Toronto.

Zelizer, Viviana A. *Pricing the Priceless Child: The Changing Social Value of Children.* New York: Basic Books, 1985.

FURTHER READING

Edwards, Gail, and Judith Saltman. *Picturing Canada: A History of Canadian Children's Illustrated Books and Publishing.* Toronto: U of Toronto P, 2010.

Galway, Elizabeth A. *From Nursery Rhymes to Nationhood: Children's Literature and the Construction of Canadian Identity.* Children's Literature and Culture. New York: Routledge, 2008.

Montgomery, L. M. *The Selected Journals of L. M. Montgomery.* Edited by Mary Rubio and Elizabeth Waterston. 5 vols. Toronto: Oxford UP, 1985–2004.

Rubio, Mary Henley. *Lucy Maud Montgomery: The Gift of Wings.* [Toronto]: Doubleday Canada, 2008.

CHAPTER 17

WHERE IN AMERICA ARE YOU, GOD?: JUDY BLUME, MARGARET SIMON, AND AMERICAN NATIONAL IDENTITY

JUNE CUMMINS

JUDY *Blume is one of the best-known and most widely read children's authors in the United States today. Famous for books for older children like* Are You There God? It's Me, Margaret; Then Again Maybe I Won't; *and* Deenie; *she is also beloved for her books for younger readers, including* Tales of a Fourth-Grade Nothing *and* Super- fudge. *More than eighty million copies of her books have been sold, and they have been translated into over thirty languages. Born in Elizabeth, New Jersey, in 1938, Blume grew up in a Jewish household. She graduated from New York University in 1961. Much of her writing for children was groundbreaking, as she was the first to deal frankly with topics such as menstruation and masturbation. From the beginning of her career, she was censored, as adults objected to the treatment of subjects that were thought by some to be taboo. Today she is one of the most highly censored children's authors of all time. In response, Blume has worked closely with the National Coalition against Censorship. She also founded The KIDS Fund, a charitable organization. Today, Blume is still writing and enjoys spending time with her family, which includes her husband, three grown children, and one grandchild. She has won several awards, including the American Library Association's Margaret A. Edwards Award for Lifetime Achievement, the Library of Congress Living Legends Award, the 2004 National Book Foundation's Medal for Distinguished Contribution to American Letters, and, most recently in 2009, the University of Southern Mississippi Medallion for her lifelong contributions to the field of children's literature.*

Are You There God? It's Me, Margaret is a book whose readership far outstrips the amount of critical scholarship addressing it. Although millions of children have read *Are You There God?* since it was published in 1970, very few scholars have written about it, and most of the criticism concerns censorship of the book.[1] A fine example of scholarship not focused on censorship is Michelle Martin's "Periods, Parody, and Polyphony: Fifty Years of Menstrual Education through Fiction and Film," an article concerned with what *Are You There God?* is primarily known for— frank discussions of puberty and, more specifically, menstruation. Most readers, when asked what they remember about the book, will mention breasts, sanitary napkins, and other items and issues related to Margaret's and her friends' changing bodies, the physical aspects of their early adolescence. As a work of literature, the book has not received much critical praise (Martin describes it as "literary mediocrity") and has been outright maligned for its portrayal of girls (such as in R. A. Seigel's, "Are You There, God? It's Me, Me, ME!: Judy Blume's Self-Absorbed Narrators"). I think the focus on puberty and the criticism of Blume's writing skill elide deeper issues in this book that merit critical attention. If we widen the lenses we apply to the novel, we see that Margaret is concerned not just with her changing body but also with the question of where she fits into American society. She is as focused, if not more so, on the topic of choosing a religion as she is on buying her first bra. These issues, which we might call sociological, are revealed if we move our focus from puberty to the republic and consider the novel not only in terms of an adolescent girl's physical growth but also within the greater context of the novel's production and its conversation with theorists of American identity.[2] For at times in this book, Blume was grappling as much with the question of a postwar American identity as were contemporary sociologists, and in some ways, her book envisioned a national culture of the future that her contemporaries could not yet imagine.

As the book opens, Margaret and her parents are experiencing their first day in their new home in a New Jersey suburb. By making this move, the Simon family joined millions of Americans who relocated to the suburbs after World War II and experienced one of the primary tensions in American identity—individualism/idealism versus conformism/materialism—in new ways. This tension, historian David Potter explains, can be seen through the difference between Alexis de Tocqueville and Thomas Jefferson. Tocqueville observed that Americans' propensity for living in groups, not in isolation, spurred their conformity and led to materialism. Thomas Jefferson believed that "the model American was a plain, straightforward, agrarian democrat" who lived in isolation (233). America's foremost theorist of this tension in the mid-twentieth century was sociologist David Riesman, whose book *The Lonely Crowd* was strongly influenced by Tocqueville.[3]

The Lonely Crowd was extremely popular throughout the 1960s, the decade during which Judy Blume became an author and wrote *Are You There God? It's Me, Margaret*. Its popularity extended throughout the twentieth century, becoming the best-selling sociological study of all time (cf. Gans). Today, it is described on Amazon.com as "considered by many to be the most influential book of the twentieth century." Although millions read the book, Riesman described his "principal audiences" as "teachers, liberals, Negroes, women, Jews, intellectuals, and so on" (qtd. in Larrabee 60). Blume, an education major, belonged to all of these categories but one. While Blume informed me that she was not aware of Reisman's book at that time, she was attending college (she graduated from New York University in 1961) in a milieu that would have been full of people who were reading or talking about it. It formed an essential part of the *zeitgeist*.

In her communication to me, Blume noted that *The Lonely Crowd* was first published in 1950 and that she herself was eleven, Margaret's age, in that year: "When it was published in 1950 I'd have been in 6th grade (Margaret's age). The character of Margaret shares some of my 6th grade experiences and concerns" (2 June 2009). And in a recent online article by Shauna Miller, Blume declared succinctly, "I was Margaret." With these comments, Blume reveals that while Margaret seems a very contemporary character in 1970, she is based in part on a child of her age (Blume herself) in 1950.

Blume's recognition of her childhood connection to Riesman's work is telling, for Riesman focuses recurrently on children throughout his book. Centrally concerned with the question of children's socialization, Reisman turns to children's literature to make one of his most salient points. In his comments regarding the 1945 Little Golden Book *Tootle*, about a young train engine that learns not to go off the track to find flowers, Riesman argues that the popular children's book performed a role in encouraging conformity among its readers. That Riesman saw the importance of children's literature to his overarching analysis of American culture demonstrates the reciprocal relationship between sociology and children's texts. Blume's work further helps us see this connection.

Reisman's view of American Character hinges on his understanding of conformity. Briefly, Riesman felt that the rapid rise of the suburbs after WWII was causing a fundamental change in Americans' personalities. He argued that Americans were transitioning from what he called an inner-directed society to an other-directed society. In an inner-directed society, people were motivated to believe what their parents told them to believe and to behave the way their parents taught them to behave. After the war, Riesman believed, young people increasingly turned away from the older generation and toward their peers for instruction as to how to fit in. Seeing this change occur primarily in big cities and in the new suburbs, Riesman called these younger Americans "other-directed" and was concerned that they were too easily influenced by their peers, teachers, and the media and too quick to cast aside their parents and grandparents. The other-directed person, for Riesman, is particularly an American type: "my analysis of the other-directed character is thus at once an analysis of the American and of contemporary man" (19). In *Are You There God?* Blume often seems to argue with Riesman as she develops characters and situations that demonstrate constant negotiations of the tension between individualism and conformity in American identity rather than simply illustrate them.[4]

From the first page of the book, conflict between individualism and conformity is established as Margaret's parents, despite moving to the suburbs, seem to exhibit the desire to reject conformity as they begin to demonstrate strains of the Jeffersonian American. When she returns to her New York City apartment from summer camp, Margaret is surprised to learn that her parents, Herb and Barbara Simon, have bought a house in Farbrook, New Jersey. Margaret groans, "Why New Jersey?" (1) and her parents respond, "Long Island is too social—Westchester is too expensive—and Connecticut is too inconvenient" (2). Margaret seemingly disavows her parents' explanation and declares to the reader, "I think we left the city because of my grandmother, Sylvia Simon. I can't figure out any other reason for the move. Especially since my mother says Grandma is too much of an influence on me" (2). Despite her protest, Margaret expresses that she does understand her parents' drive for independence (they reject life in a "social" suburb), but at this point she sees their departure as facilitating independence from her grandmother rather than independence from overbearing neighbors.

Margaret notices, also, that her mother is suddenly interested in nature. Ruminating over the decision to move, Margaret thinks, "So Farbrook, New Jersey it was, ... where my mother could have all the grass, trees and flowers she ever wanted. Except I never knew she wanted all that stuff in the first place" (2). Perhaps hinting at what she perceives as her parents' hypocrisy, Margaret nonetheless is aware that her mother is striving for something new. Margaret's father, for his part, wants to move to Farbrook so he can develop his inner agrarian. When Margaret tells him a neighborhood boy has offered to cut their grass, her father says, "No, thanks ... I'm looking forward to cutting it myself. That's one of the reasons we moved out here. Gardening is good for the soul" (13). Herb's new interest in his yard and in gardening is at least in some part related to the "back to the land" movement popular in the late 1960s and through the 1970s, but it also speaks to his very American desire to work his own land. The "back to the land movement" was itself anticonformist and antimaterialist. As historian Ryan Edgington explains, this movement captured Americans' desires for "freedom, independence, and self-reliance" (287) and contemporized Jefferson's belief that "cultivators of the earth are the most virtuous and independent citizens" (279). Margaret is confused by her parents' new interests and desires—"They were really driving me crazy with all that good-for-the-soul business. I wondered when they had become such nature lovers!" (13)—and cannot understand the impetus behind their recent decision to move toward the country.[5]

Even as her parents announce their plans to do their own things, Margaret notices immediately upon their move that "every house on our new street looks a lot the same. They are all seven years old. So are the trees" (2). She remarks on this conformity again when she first sees her new neighbor's house: "Nancy lives six houses away, also on Morningbird Lane. Her house looks like mine but the brick is painted white and the front door and shutters are red" (5). On this first day in the new neighborhood, Margaret is immediately confronted with the individuality versus conformity debate. She has already detected the conflict between what her parents seek and what they have found. And before she knows it, she will be struggling with the conflict herself.

The day of the move, Margaret comes up against what her parents meant by the dangers of the "too social," even though they chose New Jersey instead of Long Island. Less than an hour after the Simons move in, Nancy comes over. "Hi. . . . I'm Nancy Wheeler. The real estate agent sent out a sheet on you. So I know you're Margaret and you're in sixth grade. So am I" (4). Margaret thinks dryly, "I wonder what else she knew," demonstrating her initial reluctance to be completely open and available to this Farbrook neighbor (4). Within a few minutes, Margaret feels scrutinized and intruded upon as Nancy comments on Margaret's as-yet undeveloped chest—"Oh, you're still flat"(6)—and remarks that she has noticed that Margaret's ears "stick out" (8). Uncomfortable, Margaret thinks "I got the feeling that Nancy noticed *everything*" (9).

Moments later, the invasion continues, as Nancy introduces Margaret to her mother, who "[takes] off her glasses" the better to scrutinize Margaret. Mrs. Wheeler wants to know exactly where in New York City the Simon family had lived and exactly what occupation Mr. Simon holds. Margaret answers automatically; as she describes it—"I sounded like a computer" (9). Margaret is not interested in feeding Mrs. Wheeler's other-directed curiosity.

Margaret's answer to Mrs. Wheeler's next question, which is actually stated as a command, reveals that she understands her parents', or at least her mother's, individualistic streak better than she initially realized. Says Mrs. Wheeler: "Please tell your mother I'm looking forward to meeting her. We've got a Morningbird Lane bowling team on Mondays and a bridge game every other Thursday afternoon and a. . . ." Margaret interrupts this list of suburban housewives' activities with, "Oh, I don't think my mother knows how to bowl and she wouldn't be interested in bridge. She paints most of the day" (10). Mrs. Wheeler persists in her questioning, but Margaret refuses to agree that her mother might be interested in joining neighborhood activities.

Undaunted, Mrs. Wheeler continues her campaign: "Tell your mother we're making our car pools early this year. We'd be happy to help her arrange hers . . . especially Sunday school. That's always the biggest problem" (10). Whether or not Margaret is aware that Mrs. Wheeler mentions Sunday school in order to determine Margaret's religious affiliation, Margaret answers that implied question—but not in a way that Mrs. Wheeler expects. "I don't go to Sunday school." Mrs. Wheeler can only reply, "You don't?" before Nancy shouts "*Lucky!*" (10). The conversation is cut short, but Margaret will soon learn that the question of her religious identity will not die quietly. On this, the first day in her new neighborhood, she has been confronted with the two central issues explored over the course of the book: her changing body and her religious identity. From the beginning, both are fraught with the conformity/individualism tension as Margaret feels pressured to fit in both physically and culturally, yet at the same time she desires to do certain things her own way.

Before the end of this chapter, Margaret speaks to God for the first time, addressing him in the italicized paragraphs that indicate the private monologues to which he is the only audience (other than the readers, of course). In this first communiqué, Margaret expresses her immediate concerns:

> *Are you there God? It's me, Margaret. I'm in my new bedroom but I still have the same bed. It's so quiet here at night—nothing like the city. I see shadows on my wall and hear these funny creaking sounds. It's scary God! Even though my father says all houses make noises and the shadows are only trees. I hope he knows what he's talking about! I met a girl today. Her name's Nancy. She expected me to be very grown up. I think she was disappointed. Don't you think it's time for me to start growing God? If you could arrange it I'd be very glad. Thank you.* (14)

With this monologue, Margaret demonstrates her unhappiness over the move to the suburbs—the quietness and creaking trees, that is, nature, scare her—and her worry that she has not met Nancy's expectations. In her quick segue from her father, whose authority she is questioning, to Nancy, whose approval she seeks, Margaret enacts one of the social changes Riesman discusses at length in *The Lonely Crowd*. In his construct, Margaret represents the typical child growing up in a society changing from inner-directed to other-directed: such a child is more influenced by her peer group than by her parents. Riesman explains: "In the smaller families of urban life, and with the spread of 'permissive' child care to ever wider strata of the population, there is a relaxation of older patterns of discipline. Under these newer patterns the peer-group (the group of one's associates of the same age and class) becomes much more important to the child [than] the parents" (21). In her plea to God, Margaret reveals how quickly she has capitulated to Nancy's expectations and judgments. Before the first day in her new house has ended, Margaret has begun to experience the shifts she has seen in her parents, but while they seem to be moving in the direction of individualism, Margaret is falling under the spell of conformity. When Nancy tells Margaret that she must wear loafers without socks on the first day of school—"otherwise you'll look like a baby"—Margaret at first hesitates but then says she will remember the rule after Nancy insists, "Besides, I want you to join my secret club and if you're wearing socks the other kids might not want you" (13). "I'll remember," says Margaret (13). Margaret's quick acquiescence signals she has learned the first lesson of suburban conformity.

Loafers without socks becomes a point of conflict between Margaret and her mother, who thinks this fashion is "dumb" (24). The ensuing heated conversation between the two vividly illustrates how the drive for conformity and approval creates conflict between mother and daughter and suggests the peer group is winning the battle. Mrs. Simon gives up trying to reason with Margaret, allowing her to leave the house without further comment. But very soon after, Margaret declares, "By the time I got to Room Eighteen of the Delano Elementary School my feet hurt so much

I thought I wouldn't make it through the day. Why are mothers always right about these things? As it turned out, half the girls had on knee socks anyway" (25).

The loafers-without-socks incident indicates that Blume is well aware of the pull an other-directed society exerts on a child to move away from parents and toward peers. At the same time, Blume credits Mrs. Simon through Margaret, revealing that contemporary children continue to see that their parents can be right and that their wisdom should not be so easily discounted. Another character, Sylvia Simon, Margaret's grandmother, also enables Blume both to demonstrate and critique the other-directed society Riesman describes.

Riesman gives special consideration to grandmothers in *The Lonely Crowd*, arguing that the other-directed society is "eliminati[ng]" them (57). Riesman claims that parents feel this older generation has become "less and less endurable," and they no longer want grandmothers living in their homes or close by (56):

> While the parents try to keep up with their children, both as a means of staying young and as a means of staying influential, this is seldom possible for the grandparents. Hence their role in the formation of the other-directed character is negligible. Far from presenting the child with a relatively consistent "family portrait," standing in the back of the parents and strengthening them, grandparents stand as an emblem of how little one can learn from one's elders about the things that matter. (57)

Sylvia Simon, however, does not fit Riesman's mold; she seems to have a lot of influence on her granddaughter. Thus, her son and daughter-in-law try to make her more like the grandparents Riesman thinks are everywhere. Margaret's hunch that her parents are leaving New York City to escape Sylvia is correct, as the text makes clear. Early in the morning on Labor Day, shortly after the move, Margaret is very surprised when her grandmother shows up at their front door. When she goes upstairs to announce the visitor, both parents are dumbfounded that Sylvia has found her way to Farbrook. After hearing the news from Margaret, Herb relays it to his wife, Barbara, who swallows her toothpaste either in surprise or distress or both. They must compose themselves before going downstairs to greet Sylvia and marvel at "how clever [she is] to take a train and taxi to our new house when she'd never been to Farbrook before" (22).

Sylvia is well aware that her son and his wife want to limit her involvement with Margaret. During a private conversation in which Sylvia suggests that she and Margaret converse each night on the phone, and that these calls must remain a secret, Margaret readily agrees, demonstrating not only that she is willing to go against her parents' wishes to be able to interact with her grandmother, but also that she does value, *pace* Riesman, her grandmother's role in her life.

Why do Margaret's parents want to minimize Sylvia's presence in Margaret's life? Partly, they are avoiding her influence in matters of taste, as Sylvia indicates when she begins to make suggestions for decorating Margaret's room and then realizes with a sigh, "But I guess your mother wants to fix it up herself" (22). They also seem to want to lessen the impact of Sylvia's money on Margaret, as Margaret explains. "My mother says Grandma is too much of an influence on me. It's no big secret in our family that Grandma sends me to summer camp in New Hampshire. And that she enjoys paying my private school tuition (which she won't be able to do any more because now I'll be going to public school)" (2). But it seems most of the Simons' anxiety comes from something deeper than who picks the bedspreads and curtains or who pays for Margaret's summer camp—something that Margaret does not quite understand:

> Anyhow, I figure this house-in-New-Jersey business is my parents' way of getting me away from Grandma. She doesn't have a car, she hates buses *and* she thinks all trains are dirty. So unless Grandma plans to walk, which is unlikely, I won't be seeing much of her. Now some kids might think, who cares about seeing a grandmother? But Sylvia Simon is a lot of fun, considering her age, which I happen to know is sixty. The only problem is she's always asking me if I have boyfriends and if they're Jewish. Now *that* is ridiculous because number one I don't have boyfriends. And number two what would I care if they're Jewish or not? (3)

Margaret's father is Jewish, and her mother is not. For most of her life, this difference between her parents has not affected Margaret very much. Presumably, she knew other children from mixed-heritage households, or the people she knew in New York City simply did not care. But in New Jersey, Margaret is suddenly forced to confront the issue of her own religious identity, as the conversation with Mrs. Wheeler about Sunday school makes clear. The topic heats up during the first meeting of Nancy's private club, soon to be known as the "Four PTS's"—the Pre-Teen Sensations.

This name is Nancy's suggestion, and as she is the alpha girl, the other three girls in the club—Gretchen, Janie, and Margaret—quickly agree to it. At first, the club meeting has nothing to do with religion. It's mostly about Nancy making sure Nancy is in charge. Extremely invested in establishing and asserting authority, Nancy makes rules right and left, including the rule that everyone has to wear a bra. Since neither Margaret nor Janie need bras yet, Nancy's rule embarrasses them. When it is Margaret's turn to make a rule, she tries to make one as innocuous as possible: "We meet on a certain day each week" (34). Margaret does not realize that this rule will reopen up the religious school topic as Gretchen has to go to Hebrew school twice a week. The question again arises over what religious school Margaret attends, and again, the news that she doesn't go to any is met with surprise and gaiety, more this time than before. Hearing the news that Margaret is "not any religion," Gretchen's "mouth [falls] open" (34). When Margaret reveals that her parents also do not have religion, Gretchen declares emphatically, "How positively neat!" (34). The girls are entranced by the romantic story of Margaret's parents' courtship, seeing only glamour in the tale of star-crossed lovers and hostile parents. But the story Margaret tells operates on deeper levels, suggesting, on the one hand, the intense conflict Margaret will soon experience and, on the other hand, acknowledging ongoing anti-Semitism. Margaret explains:

This was the first time they were interested in anything I had to say. "Well, my mother's parents, who live in Ohio, told her they didn't want a Jewish son-in-law. If she wanted to ruin her life that was her business. But they would never accept my father for her husband."
"No kidding!" Gretchen said. "How about your father's family?"
"Well, my grandmother wasn't happy about getting a Christian daughter-in-law, but she at least accepted the situation."
"So what happened?" Janie asked.
"They eloped."
"How romantic!" Nancy sighed.
"So that's why they're not anything."
"I don't blame them," Gretchen said. "I wouldn't be either." (35)

Had the conversation stopped there, Margaret would have remained the center of attention with her dramatic story, but Janie asks a pragmatic question: "But if you aren't any religion, how are you going to know if you should join the Y or the Jewish Community Center?" (35). Margaret says she does not know and adds, "I never thought about it. Maybe we won't join either one." Nancy, certain that one must affiliate and conform, declares, "But *everybody* belongs to one or the other" (35). Later that evening, when Margaret calls to God, she reveals that fitting a bra and fitting into her group have become her central concerns.

> Are you there God? It's me, Margaret. I just told my mother I want a bra. Please help me grow God. You know where. I want to be like everyone else. You know God, my new friends all belong to the Y or the Jewish Community Center. Which way am I supposed to go? I don't know what you want me to do about that. (37)

Riesman would have considered Margaret a typical other-directed child and could have used this paragraph to provide proof of the mid-twentieth-century suburban's child need to conform and be accepted. He might not have known, however, what to say about Margaret's statement, "I don't know what you want me to do about that." Believing that children of his time do not struggle with issues of identity and self-definition, Riesman instead views them as wanting identities ready made for them. In his preface to the 1969 reprint of *The Lonely Crowd*, composed just as Blume was writing *Are You There God?*, Riesman states, "I see many young people today who expect to *fall* into a commitment or into an identity or into a meaning for their lives, the way romantic young people expect to fall in love" (xxix).

Margaret will prove herself to be unlike the "many young people" Riesman discusses, but it takes her teacher, Mr. Benedict, to prompt her into a course of self-investigation. Mr. Benedict, a member of one of the three main groups of people that Riesman argues influence children in contemporary society (including teachers, peers, and the media), is a young, relatively progressive teacher who asks his students to do a year-long, self-directed project on a topic of their own choosing. He realizes that something is amiss with Margaret and her chosen topic—religion—when he reads the responses Margaret has written on the getting-to-know-you papers the students completed on the first day of school. In response to the prompt "I hate," Margaret had written "pimples, baked potatoes, when my mother's mad and religious holidays" (27-28). In the conversation Margaret has with Mr. Benedict about the last part of this answer, two intertwined issues that deeply affect Margaret's developing sense of identity, religion and suburbanization, are revealed when she tells him, "None of those holidays are special to me. I don't belong to any religion" (39). Mr. Benedict is intrigued, as if he has "uncovered some deep, dark mystery":

> "I see. And your parents?"
> "They aren't any religion. I'm supposed to choose my own when I grow up. If I want to, that is."
> Mr. Benedict folded his hands and looked at me for a while. Then he said, "Okay, Margaret. You can go now."
> I hoped he decided I was normal, after all. I lived in New York for eleven and a half years and I don't think anybody ever asked me about my religion. I never even thought about it. Now, all of a sudden, it was the big thing in my life. (39)

With this thought, Margaret conveys her awareness that the move to the suburbs has forced the issue of religious identity upon her. In the city, no one cared how Margaret affiliated or, indeed, whether or not she affiliated in the first place. In the suburbs, everyone seems to care how Margaret defines herself and wants to know to which groups she belongs.

Intent on figuring out a way to fit in, Margaret doesn't consider the choices her own parents have made. For Barbara and Herb decided long ago that they did not need to fit into the traditional categories of an inner-directed society. Through their intermarriage, the Simons have chosen what Werner Sollors describes as a *consent*-based identity, which he believes to be the basis or defining feature of American national identity. According to Sollors, the terms "descent" and "consent" refer to those aspects of our identities that we cannot and can choose, respectively, such as our relatives and blood ties on one hand, and our spouses, politics, and other affiliations on the other. To Sollors, ethnic identity in America is based on the ambiguity swirling around these terms. For if the country itself was founded on the notion of consent—"the concept of a new American citizenship emerged in the American Revolution and was based on the 'idea of volitional allegiance'" (150)—then national identity was seen as something one could choose, which left ethnic identity to be something that one has happen to him or her.[6] Hence, "in American social symbolism ethnicity may function as a construct evocative of blood, nature, and descent, whereas national identity may be relegated to the order of law, conduct, and consent" (151). People like Herb and Barbara Simon,[7] however, demonstrate in their own choices that they assume ethnic identity can become something one chooses when one is the offspring of an intermarriage.[8]

From early in the twentieth century, intermarriage was viewed by some as the route to a truly consenting American identity. Sollors discusses at length the Israel

Zangwill play *The Melting-Pot*, first performed in 1908 (66). It was Zangwill's play that popularized the term "melting pot" and by doing so "more than any social or political theory . . . shaped American discourse on immigration and ethnicity" (66). While "melting pot" is a highly contested term, at many points in American history, the blending of ethnicities and races was seen as an ideal. In Zangwill's play, the image of the melting pot was offered as not only a cure for the tensions created by the polyphony of America's diverse peoples but also as the very definition of an American nation. What Zangwill calls "hardness," Sollors explains, "is related to the past and the boundaries of *descent*" (69), while the coming together of opposites in the melting pot is about looking forward and dissolving boundaries through *consent*. The play asserts that "the past may be anchored in old-world hardness, but the future in America is identified with the melting pot" (71). The vehicle Zangwill uses to make these points is intermarriage. His two main characters, a non-Jew and a Jew, fall in love, overcome obstacles, and marry in a move that argues that Jews and Gentiles must come together for America to be a strong and united country. While American literature and popular imagination, not to mention actual historical reality, demonstrate that other historically opposed groups, such as Native Americans and Anglo-Americans, also came together through intermarriage, the image of the intermarried Jew and Gentile became, through Zangwill's play, the highest emblem and very definition of a melting-pot mentality.

From this perspective, we can see how Sollors's view is reflected in Margaret's parents' marriage. Their decision not to privilege either of their religious backgrounds in raising Margaret speaks to their desire to overcome the "hardness" of descent. Riesman, however, might ascribe the Simons's decision to the social pressures of other-direction. Riesman believes that contemporary parents who have rejected the seemingly rigid and unfeeling practices of inner-directed parents of the previous generation end up being unable to supply their children with any clear sense of direction. He explains, "Inhibited from presenting their children with sharply silhouetted images of self and society, parents in our era can only equip the child to do his best, whatever that may turn out to be" (47).

Margaret, not particularly aware that her parents' intermarriage may be performing an American ideal, focuses on the choice she feels she must make. Although she has told Mr. Benedict that her parents have said she can choose *if she wants to*, meaning she can choose not to choose, as her parents have, Margaret feels compelled to make a choice of religious identity. The approach she takes to making the decision is intellectual and pragmatic: like an anthropologist, she will visit as many houses of worship and do as much reading as she can. Margaret believes that this academic approach, the work of her year-long project, will yield to her a "correct" answer.

Margaret's forays into varying religions are both funny and touching. When Margaret tells her grandmother that she would like to attend synagogue with her on Rosh Hashanah, Sylvia is ecstatic. Despite Margaret's explanation that her decision to attend synagogue does not mean that she has chosen to be Jewish, Sylvia chooses to interpret her granddaughter's curiosity as a sign she has found her roots: "I'm thrilled! I'm going right home to call the rabbi" (55). But her smile quickly disappears when she suddenly realizes that Margaret's parents may blame her for Margaret's new interest: "Grandma slapped her hand against her forehead. 'Be sure to tell them it's not my idea! Would I be in trouble!'" (56).[9] Margaret tells Sylvia not to worry, but as it turns out, Barbara Simon is very upset when she hears the news. The conversation between Barbara and Margaret not only contrasts the one between Sylvia and Margaret but also reveals that perhaps Barbara is not as indifferent to the subject of Margaret's religious identity as she had believed herself to be:

> "That's ridiculous!" my mother said when I told her. "You know how Daddy and I feel about religion."
> "You said I could choose when I grow up!"
> "But you're not ready to choose yet, Margaret!"
> "I just want to try it out," I argued. "I'm going to try church too, so don't get hysterical!"
> "I am *not* hysterical! I just think it's foolish for a girl of your age to bother herself with religion." (56)

When confronted with the prospect of Margaret choosing Judaism, Barbara relapses into an inner-directed parent, one who "cannot be sure of what the adult working role and mode of life [his or her] children will be, [but cannot let] conformity to that role be left to chance and behavorial opportunism" (Riesman 41). When Margaret calls her mother on what she perceives to be hypocrisy, it takes Barbara only a second to come back to her present. After her mother's remark that it's "foolish" for Margaret to be concerned with religion, Margaret asks, "Can I go?" Her mother answers: "I'm not going to stop you" (56). The next time Barbara is mentioned, it is in the context of Margaret describing her new clothes, purchased because "my mother said everyone wears new clothes for the Jewish holidays" (58). It seems Barbara has accepted her child's wishes to explore her Jewish background.

Margaret describes her trip to New York and her visit to her grandmother's synagogue in some detail, devoting three full pages to discussion of the synagogue, the service, the rabbi, the flowers, the organ music, and so on. Margaret is struck by the "beautiful" music and the "very pretty" silver bowls filled with flowers. When she meets the rabbi, he asks if she enjoyed the service, and Margaret answers "Oh, yes . . . I just loved it" (60). It's hard not to notice that when Margaret visits Janie's Presbyterian church, she spends less than a page describing the experience, and when she goes with Nancy to her family's United Methodist Church on Christmas Eve, she dispatches the description in less than half a page. Addressing God after each visit, Margaret says of Janie's church, "*I didn't feel anything special in there God. Even though I wanted to. I'm sure it has nothing to do with you. Next time I'll try harder*" (63). And about Nancy's church she tells God that although she "loved" the "beautiful" choir songs, "*Still, I didn't feel you God. . . . I'm trying hard to understand but I wish you'd help me a little. If only you'd give me a hint God. Which religion should I be? Sometimes I wish I'd been born one way or another*" (94).

Margaret's third experience with Christianity occurs unexpectedly after Laura Danker, a girl whose tallness and developed breasts are the target of Nancy's nasty gossip, tells off Margaret when Margaret accuses her of going behind the A&P with boys to let them "feel" her (116). Laura's furious reaction to the accusation makes Margaret suddenly realize that she could be wrong about Laura and that it's possible Nancy has spread false information. For the first time, we see Margaret putting herself into someone else's shoes and breaking away from the enforced conformity Nancy has imposed on her. She apologizes to Laura and follows her to confession.

Hiding in the Catholic church so Laura won't see her, Margaret decides she will confess after Laura leaves. She enters a confession booth and sits down, not knowing what to do. When a disembodied voice says, "Yes, my child," Margaret is startled. "At first I thought it was God. I really and truly thought it was, and my heart started to pound like crazy and I was all sweaty inside my coat and sort of dizzy too" (118–19). Even after she realizes it was not God who spoke but a priest, and even though the priest speaks gently to Margaret, she is dismayed and overwhelmed. "I flung open the door and ran down the aisle and out of the church. I made my way back to school, crying, feeling horribly sick and scared stiff I would throw up" (119). While in some ways, Margaret's excursion to confession has produced for her the most authentic and deeply felt religious experience she has had so far, it is also the most negative and upsetting. Margaret's sickened reaction is based on a combination of fear, shock, shame, and guilt, but the implication that Catholicism is not going to work for her is clear. The moments in confused and fearful conversation with the priest are very different from the pleasant conversation she has with the rabbi of her grandmother's temple.

Margaret may not notice that she is somewhat privileging her Jewish experience by spending more time discussing her experiences in synagogue, by perceiving church-going as negative, and by expressing great fondness for and connection to her grandmother, but her mother, it seems, notices Margaret's developing preference. After 14 years of estrangement from her own parents, Barbara decides to send them a Christmas card, a decision she does not announce but which Margaret discovers by looking through the outgoing stack of cards. When these parents write back and announce they plan to make a visit, Herb "hit[s] the roof" (121), demanding to know how they could have known the Simon family's new address, and Barbara is forced to confess. Margaret describes the angry argument between her parents, which reaches a dramatic peak when Herb yells, "They want to see *you*, not me! They want to see Margaret! To make sure she doesn't have horns!" (121).

The visit of Margaret's maternal grandparents is terrible in many ways. From the outset, Margaret is enraged because she has to cancel her plan to spend her spring break in Florida with Sylvia. When her grandparents arrive, they prove to be old and stodgy, nothing like the fun, lively grandmother Margaret is used to. A strained politeness prevails at the dinner table the first night of the Hutchinses' visit until, once again, the subject of Margaret's religious identity comes up and the grandparents express consternation and dismay at learning that Margaret is not a practicing Christian. Barbara tries gently to reason with her parents, but they refuse to understand the decision to raise Margaret outside of the Christian faith. When she explains that Margaret will be able to choose a religion when she's older, Mrs. Hutchins cries, "Nonsense! . . . A person doesn't choose religion" (133). And her husband "boom[s]," "A person's born to it!" (133). Mrs. Hutchins agrees. "Grandmother smiled at last and gave a small laugh. 'So Margaret is Christian!' she announced, like we all should have known" (133).

With these pronouncements, the Hutchinses align themselves not only with the inner-directed older generation Riesman describes but also to the type of person Sollors calls an "ethnic purist." Such descent-oriented people fear intermarriage and other forms of ethnic mixing because they believe their own ethnicity will be lost through the transmission: "The dream of the ethnic purist is the eternal likeness of all after-generations to his or her own image. . . . The purists' own unwillingness to accept the mixed after-generations as theirs is seen as the 'loss' of the children, and the projection of this self-constructed loss upon the descendants of mixed marriages is the cultural belief—widespread in nineteenth and early-twentieth century America—that [children of mixed marriages] were sterile" (224). Casting the Hutchinses as ethnic purists both explains the source of their fear and renders them unpleasant characters. In describing them as old and boring, as rigid and dogmatic, and as anti-Semitic, Blume quietly favors Margaret's paternal grandmother, Sylvia, who does yearn for Margaret to be Jewish but is far more attractive, vivacious, and interesting.

At the same time she makes the Hutchinses and their perspectives unsympathetic, Blume also, to a certain degree, shows that they may be right in an odd way. Although Barbara tries valiantly to stop her parents, Mrs. Hutchins persists, claiming "But a child is always the religion of the mother. And you, Barbara, were born Christian. You were baptized. It's that simple" (133). Enraged, Herb bursts out, "Margaret is nothing!" (133). Although Margaret herself has described herself as "not being anything," her father's abrupt statement is shocking and hurtful. She keenly feels the threat to her selfhood in her father's "nothing." "I didn't want to listen anymore. How could they talk that way in front of me! Didn't they know I was a real person—with feelings of my own!" (133). The description of Margaret as "nothing" demonstrates the outer limit of Riesman's critique of other-directed parents—they are so concerned with not imposing on their children that they offer them no mechanisms for becoming their own people (what Riesman describes as "autonomy") and leave them adrift, unable to find a place to drop an anchor. To Reisman, the utterly rootless child is in danger of becoming a nonentity. He ends *The Lonely Crowd* with the powerful sentence (in both senses of the word), "The idea that men are created free and equal is both true and misleading: men are created different; they lose their social freedom and their individual autonomy in seeking to become like each other" (307). The Simons, fearful of overconformity, strived for independence and individuality, but they cannot overcome the forces of the suburb, the time period, and their own choices. Not wanting to prescribe identity to Margaret, they ultimately send her a message that she is "nothing."

Aware at some level that her parents and grandparents, haggling over her identity, have stripped her of selfhood, Margaret rejects religion altogether and resolves to stop talking to God. The climax of Margaret's search for religious identity occurs in the penultimate chapter. When Mr. Benedict announces that the year-long projects are due, everyone turns in a "thick booklet with a decorated cover" (143) while Margaret only writes a letter: "Dear Mr. Benedict, I have conducted a year-long experiment in religion. I have not come to any conclusions about what religion I want to be when I grow up—if I want to be any special religion at all" (142). She then lists the three books she has read about Christianity, Judaism, and Catholicism and the names of the various churches and one synagogue she has visited. She explains she did not try being a Buddhist or Moslem because she doesn't know people who are those religions. She then concludes:

> I have not really enjoyed my religious experiments very much and I don't think
> I'll make up my mind one way or the other for a long time. I don't think a person
> can decide to be a certain religion just like that. It's like having to choose your
> own name. You think about it a long time and then you keep changing your
> mind. If I should ever have children I will tell them what religion they are so they
> can start learning about it at an early age. Twelve is very late to learn. Sincerely,
> Margaret Ann Simon. (143)

Here Margaret seems to admit defeat. After she gives Mr. Benedict the letter, Margaret runs from the room and starts to cry. She seems traumatized by her experience, and the issue of her religious identity remains unresolved.

The last chapter of the novel switches to its most memorable topics: maturation, puberty, and boys. The climax of the puberty aspect of the novel becomes the climax of the whole book when Margaret discovers she has finally gotten her period. Crying and laughing, Margaret calls to her mother who rushes to help her. Margaret is relieved and jubilant, and she reconciles with her mother. The last non-italicized words of the book express her happiness at having finally gotten her period. "How about that! Now I am growing for sure! Now I am almost a woman!" (148). But these are not the actual last words of the book.

In the final, italicized paragraph, Margaret talks to God again. *"Are you still there God? It's me, Margaret. I know you're there God. I know you wouldn't have missed this for anything! Thank you God. Thanks an awful lot . . ."* (149). With this final address to God, Margaret demonstrates that she has figured out her identity. She is not Christian, and she is not Jewish. She is a person who believes in God her own way. Her conviction that God is still there for her, demonstrated in her renewing her dialogue with him, reveals she has always had her own kind of spirituality, and now she accepts it.

Scholar David Hollinger would call Margaret's discovery "postethnicity." Critical of 1950s sociologists and other thinkers like Riesman who viewed people as more or less the same, and who grouped together all Americans under one definition, Hollinger, writing at the turn of the twenty-first century, instead focuses on how people's differences become the fabric of American national identity.

Hollinger emphasizes choice, which he views as similar to Sollors's concept of "consent," but his analysis goes further than the consent/descent paradigm. He defines postethnicity as a perspective that "favors voluntary over involuntary affiliations, balances an appreciation for communities of descent with a determination to make room for new communities, and promotes solidarities of wide scope that incorporate people with different ethnic and racial backgrounds" (3). While Margaret has no friends who are not white, her mention of Buddhists and Moslems in her letter to Mr. Benedict reveals her understanding that the world is much wider than the makeup of Farbrook, New Jersey, might suggest. Her own sense of difference that comes from being the child of a mixed marriage deepens her understanding of others' valuable differences.

Hollinger maintains that two main tenets of postethnicity are "affiliation by revocable consent" and "choice over prescription" (13). Over and over again, Margaret voices or enacts her belief in choice and rejection of prescription as she moves from church to church to synagogue to confessional. In countering her grandparents, she explicitly rejects the identities they hope she will choose, but she does not give up her affiliation with them. This positioning is much more clearly seen in her relationship with Sylvia than in her relationship with the Hutchinses, since that elderly couple leaves the Simon home before Margaret has a chance to build a relationship with them. But Margaret does firmly reject Sylvia's efforts to make her a Jewish girl—all the while maintaining her affiliation with her. In this way, she bears out Hollinger's argument that "a postethnic perspective challenges the right of one's grandfather or grandmother to determine primary identity" (116).

The last conversation that takes place between Sylvia and Margaret exemplifies the ability Margaret has both to reject labels and to maintain a seemingly contradictory stance at the same time. Rushing from Florida to New Jersey in order to counteract the Hutchinses' influence, Sylvia insists, "Just remember, Margaret . . . no matter what they said . . . you're a Jewish girl." Margaret denies this: "'No I'm not!' I argued. 'I'm nothing, and you know it! I don't even believe in God!'" (140). Ironically, Margaret says to herself after making this declaration, "I wanted to ask God did he hear that! But I wasn't speaking to him and I guess he knew it!" (140), revealing to the reader she hasn't really given up on believing in God but wants to keep her belief to herself. Still, Margaret closes the chapter with these thoughts: "Sometimes Grandma is almost as bad as everybody else. As long as she loves me and I love her, what difference does religion make?" (141). Margaret has revoked formal Judaism, but not her Jewish grandmother.

Ultimately, Hollinger argues that through postethnicity, Americans can claim a national identity. Tracing the twentieth-century history of the notion of an American national identity, Hollinger explains that the 1950s studies of national character, such as that of Riesman, were "widely discredited in later decades" (189). By the 1980s and 1990s, "'American identity' was understood to be a shallow concept that masked diversity and implied a conformist mentality" (189). Yet, Hollinger argues, ethnic groups such as Asian Americans and African Americans did want to claim a group identity, and he asks his readers to consider what could be a workable reconfiguration of American identity, a postethnic American identity. From the beginning of the 1995 edition of his *Postethnic America* in which Hollinger claims, "I defend the notion of a national culture as an adhesive enabling diverse Americans to see themselves as sufficiently 'in it together' to act on problems that are genuinely common" (14–15), to the end of his 2000 postscript in which he goes further, stating that "a stronger national solidarity enhances the possibility of social and economic justice in the United States" (201), Hollinger presses for a new understanding of American identity. Of course people debate the issue of an American national identity for a large variety of reasons, and many do not like the concept at all. But I am asking that we briefly accept Hollinger's notion of a national culture so as to consider what Margaret reveals to us about late 1960s and early 1970s America and, in particular, about the place of sociological concepts in popular discourse.

Margaret's final act of accepting God on her own terms, of refusing the consent-based identity of either parent, and of living in peace with some unresolved identity issues is not unrelated to her rejection of Nancy's rules concerning how to treat girls who develop earlier than other girls. In other words, Margaret has rejected conformity and decided that one can be just who one is without fitting into anyone else's definition. Absent from her final address to God is the line she repeated over and over again earlier in the book: "*Please . . . let me be like everybody else*" (101). Instead, she thanks him for her period and asserts that she knows he is there. Margaret has dropped the plea to be like "everybody else."

By the end of the book, the terms of the debate have shifted. Margaret does not have to choose either conformity or individuality. With foresight, Blume renders Margaret an early-edition postethnic American. Without giving up either of her parents or rejecting any of her friends, but instead widening the pool of people with whom she will associate no matter what Nancy says, Margaret confirms the possibility of an escape from the individualism/conformity debate and a movement toward a postethnic future. The enduring popularity of *Are You There God? It's Me, Margaret* has much to do of course with the universal interest in puberty, but that is only one part of the picture. If *Are You There God?* was groundbreaking for its open discussion of menstruation and bras, it was also groundbreaking in its frank discussion of religious identity and its evocation of what might be called the post-other-directed child. With her character Margaret, Blume does not merely reject implicitly Riesman's claims about conformity, nor does she presciently scoff at Sollors's desires for a consent-driven society. She gently demonstrates the limitations of these theorists of national culture and anticipates the postethnicity posited more recently by Hollinger. Blume envisioned a progressive, tolerant America and voiced her ideal through the preteen character Margaret Simon. The enduring cultural interest in *Are You There God? It's Me, Margaret* may have originated in curiosity about puberty, but it resulted in creating a readership that participated in forming a new American identity.

NOTES

....

1. One recent exception is Joseph Michael Sommers, "Are You There, Reader? It's Me, Margaret: A Reconsideration of Judy Blume's Prose as Sororal Dialogue."

2. Studies that argue for a unified national identity or an "American Character" are considered outmoded today. Popular from the 1930s through the 1960s, such studies began to lose credibility with the advent of the civil rights movement, feminism, and ethnic studies that argued for particularity in American experience. I will be arguing that *Are You There God?* enters American society at a pivotal point, as scholarly paradigms of identity transition from embracing national character to insisting on diversity and multicultural experience.

3. Tocqueville's influence on Riesman is discussed in Nathan Glazer, "Tocqueville and Riesman."

4. Although Riesman's book was and still is the most widely read, it was not the only study published in this era that expressed fears of conformity and loss of individuality. People were also reading C. Wright Mills's *White Collar: The American Middle Classes* and William Whyte's *The Organizational Man*. A popular novel (and film) of the time, *The Man in the Gray Flannel Suit*, also dealt with the perils of conformity.

5. The "back to the land" movement was of course also related to the rising counter-culture of the mid- to late 1960s. While Margaret's parents were certainly not hippies or radicals, they were echoing one of the tenets of the counterculture movement, according to Bruce Schulman, which was "a new relationship to nature" (17). People younger than the Simons "planted organic gardens, experienced with food production and communal living, and emulated romantic versions of Native American tribal culture" (90).

6. Sollors attributes the idea of "volitional allegiance" to James Kettner and para-phrases Kettner's statements in *The Development of American Citizenship, 1608–1870* (150).

7. The Simons are actually on the cusp of a radical change in American culture in terms of the rates of intermarriage between Jews and non-Jews. If Margaret is eleven in the late 1960s, then we can assume her parents were married in the early to mid-1950s, a time period during which intermarriage was only starting to become common. According to Keren McGinity, "Authors commented in 1956 that intermarriage had become 'an everyday occurrence'" (78). In fact, intermarriages between Jews and non-Jews almost tripled between 1956 and 1965. From 1956 to 1960, 5.9 percent of American Jews married non-Jews; from 1961 to 1965, 17.4 percent of Jews married non-Jews (219). This percentage continued to rise until it hit nearly 50 percent in 2001 (219).

8. Although the word "ethnicity" was not commonly used in the 1960s, it was not unheard of. Interestingly, the 1972 Supplement to the *Oxford English Dictionary* cites David Riesman himself in its first example of the usage of the word. The essay cited is Riesman's "Some Observations on Intellectual Freedom" (1953). Sollors explains, "What is striking, however, is that in the article Riesman uses the word 'ethnicity' without any self-con-sciousness and without a hint of semantic innovation. In 1977, Riesman reacted with surprise to the suggestion that he invented 'ethnicity'" (23).

For the purposes of this paper, I will treat Judaism as both a religion and an ethnicity, reflecting how many Americans view it.

9. Sylvia's excitement that Margaret may choose Judaism reveals that Sylvia herself is progressive. In traditional Orthodox Judaism, religion is conferred matrilineally. Sylvia is aligning herself with Reform Judaism, a more liberal form of the religion, by her willing-ness to see Margaret as Jewish if Margaret chooses to be Jewish. She also aligns herself with Sollors's notion of a consent-based American.

WORKS CITED

Blume, Judy. *Are You There God? It's Me, Margaret.* 1970. Atheneum Books for Young Readers ed. New York: Simon & Schuster Children's Publishing Division, 2001.

———. Email. "Question for article." (Email to author.) 2 June 2009.

Edgington, Ryan. "'Be Receptive to the Good Earth': Health, Nature, and Labor in Countercultural Back-to-the-Land Settlements." *Agricultural History* 82, no. 3 (2008): 279–308.

Gans, Herbert J. "Best-Sellers by Sociologists: An Exploratory Study." *Contemporary Sociology* 26,no. 2 (1997): 131–35.

Glazer, Nathan. "Tocqueville and Riesman." *Society* 37, no. 4 (2000): 26–33.

Hollinger, David. *Postethnic America: Beyond Multiculturalism.* 10th Anniversary Edition. New York: Basic Books, 2006.

Larrabee, Eric. "Reisman and His Readers." *Harper's Magazine,* June 1961, 59–65.

Martin, Michelle H. "Periods, Parody, and Polyphony: Fifty Years of Menstrual Education through Fiction and Film." *Children's Literature Association Quarterly* 22, no. 1 (1997): 21–29.

McGinity, Keren. *Still Jewish: A History of Women and Intermarriage in America.* New York: New York UP, 2009.

Miller, Shauna. "Judy Blume: 'I Was Margaret': An Interview with the YA Writer Who Couldn't Wait for Puberty." *doubleX.* 2 October 2009. Accessed online: http://www.doublex.com/section/arts/judy-blume-i-was-margaret

Potter, David. "The Quest for National Character." *The Reconstruction of American History.* Edited by John Higham, 197–220. New York: Humanities P, 1962. Reprinted in *History and American Society: Essays of David M. Potter.* Edited by Don E. Fehrenbacher, 229–55. New York: Oxford UP, 1973.

Riesman, David, with Nathan Glazer and Reuel Denney. *The Lonely Crowd.* 1950. Revised and abridged edition. 1961. New Haven: Yale UP, 2001.

Schulman, Bruce. *The Seventies: The Great Shift in American Culture, Society, and Politics.* New York: The Free Press, 2001.

Sollors, Werner. *Beyond Ethnicity: Consent and Descent in American Culture.* New York: Oxford UP, 1986.

FURTHER READING

Cody, Diablo. "In Praise of Judy Blume." *EW.Com* (online version of *Entertainment Weekly*) September 27, 2008. http://www.ew.com/ew/article/020229048,00.html

Sammond, Nicholas. *Babes in Tomorrowland: Walt Disney and the Making of the American Child, 1930–1960.* Durham, NC: Duke UP, 2005.

Sommers, Joseph Michael. "Are You There, Reader? It's Me, Margaret: A Reconsideration of Judy Blume's Prose as Sororal Dialogue." *Children's Literature Association Quarterly* 33, no. 3 (Fall 2008): 258–79.

Ulanowicz, Anastasia. "Sitting Shiva: Holocaust Mourning in Judy Blume's *Starring Sally J. Freedman as Herself. Children's Literature* 36 (2008): 88–114.

Wise, Gene. "'Paradigm Dramas' in American Studies: A Cultural and Institutional History of the Movement." *American Quarterly* 31, no. 3 (1979): 293–337.

CHAPTER 18

LET FREEDOM RING: LAND, LIBERTY, LITERACY, AND LORE IN MILDRED TAYLOR'S LOGAN FAMILY NOVELS

MICHELLE H. MARTIN

Mildred Taylor was born in 1943 in Jackson, Mississippi. When she was a baby, her father moved the family to Toledo, Ohio, both because of a racist incident and because he wanted better opportunities for his children. In Toledo, Taylor's family owned a large duplex, where Mildred and her sister grew up surrounded by family—most of them originally from Mississippi. After spending many hours absorbing family lore, Taylor decided, at an early age, to become a writer. She graduated from high school in 1961 and attended the University of Colorado. She spent 1965 to 1967 as a Peace Corps Volunteer in Yirgalem, Ethiopia, an experience that had a powerful impact on her. As a result of winning a writing contest sponsored by the Council on Interracial Books for Children, Taylor received her first book contract from Dial for the novella Song of the Trees. *She won the Newbery Medal in 1977 for* Roll of Thunder, Hear My Cry, *becoming only the second African American to win the award (following Virginia Hamilton who won it for* M. C. Higgins the Great *two years prior).* Roll of Thunder *was the first full-length novel about the Logan family, and Taylor says that her novel* Logan, *which had not yet been published at the time of this writing, will complete the series. Taylor has built a successful career as a children's writer of African American historical fiction around this compelling saga.*

Mildred Taylor's Newbery Medal–winning novel, *Roll of Thunder, Hear My Cry*, details the trials and conflicts of the Logan family as they survive in racist 1930s

Mississippi. Throughout Taylor's Logan family saga, consisting of the novels *Roll of Thunder, Hear My Cry* (1976), *Let the Circle Be Unbroken* (1981), *The Road to Memphis* (1992), and *The Land* (2001), and the novellas *Song of the Trees* (1975), *Mississippi Bridge* (1990), *The Well: David's Story* (1995), *The Friendship* (1997), and *The Gold Cadillac* (1998), Taylor fictionalizes her own family's history to expose readers to African American life after Reconstruction and during the early twentieth century.

In these texts, Mildred Taylor offers a unique window into African America not only because these works of historical fiction deliver a seven-book[1] longitudinal study of a black family struggling through significant eras in black American history, but also because Taylor composed them to tell personal and particularized stories that help young readers understand and experience history that mainstream texts, such as school textbooks, omit. In the Author's Note to *The Friendship*, Taylor comments that she was born in the South but grew up in the North and came to know the South both through annual trips to Mississippi and through

> the stories told whenever the family gathered, both in the North and in the South. Through the stories I learned a history about my family going back to the days of slavery. Through the stories I learned a history not then taught in history books, a history about the often tragic lives of Black people living in a segregated land. (48)

Critic Suzanne Rahn posits that writers of historical fiction, the only genre Taylor has written for young people, "want to bring the culture of some former age to life for a generation with little or no knowledge of it; they are less interested in great historical events and figures than in showing children what it was like to live and grow up then" (3). Clearly, Taylor's purpose in writing these stories, beginning in the 1970s, is to teach young readers about black history in a way that will make them care about that history. She draws readers into her stories by creating compelling characters and realistic conflicts, but she teaches readers about the trials of African American life in the late nineteenth and early twentieth centuries by defining freedom in very specific terms. In the historical worlds that Mildred Taylor creates, all of which she sets after emancipation, true freedom does not come with manumission alone. For Taylor, African Americans in general and the Logan family in particular obtain true freedom only through owning land; actively fighting injustice, even as children; pursuing an education, which includes acquiring literacy both in the traditional sense and in the sense of cultural literacy; and understanding their own history through family oral traditions.

Most of Taylor's work cannot rightly be called "autobiographical" since she writes about her ancestors rather than her own generation. However, given the intersections between Taylor's life and work, knowledge of how her background influenced the vision of freedom that surfaces in her novels helps readers appreciate the impetus behind her work. Clearly, the Logans' four avenues to pursuing freedom—land ownership, struggling for civil rights, pursuing an education, and learning family oral history—have been central in Taylor's own life. She came to understand as a child that a certain measure of power and security comes with land ownership. Taylor's father, Wilbert, grew up in the South, but when Taylor was still a baby, he moved the family to Ohio specifically to escape the racism of Mississippi and to give his children better opportunities than he had had growing up (*CLR* 90:119). Shortly after moving to Ohio, Wilbert purchased a large duplex that eventually accommodated Mildred's uncles and their wives as well as other cousins and relatives (Crowe, *Presenting* 4–5). Taylor had been surrounded by family while living in the South, and her father's establishment of a "homestead" in Ohio enabled her, once again, to live among many family members. Chris Crowe notes that Taylor's parents, as much as they could, sheltered her as a child from harmful racist encounters and "surrounded her with relatives, bathed her with love and attention, and taught her self-respect and pride in her family" (117). The Ohio duplex not only gave the extended Taylor family a home but also connected them with a network essential for employment opportunities and success in their new lives. When Taylor was in fifth grade, her family moved from the duplex in a black neighborhood to a house in a newly integrated neighborhood of Toledo[2] where Taylor and her sister began attending a majority-white school. As she grew up, Mildred's father made sure that his children never knew what it meant to be a renter or a sharecropper[3] because for Wilbert Taylor, owning land and owning a home meant having the security to raise his family on his own terms, not on the terms of a landlord who had the power to deprive them of the most basic human need for shelter and to keep them in perpetual poverty. This strong value of land ownership has translated directly into a touchstone of Logan family ideology in Taylor's novels.

Taylor also absorbed her family's commitment to actively resisting oppression. In her 2004 acceptance speech for University of Oklahoma's first NSK Neustadt Prize for Children's Literature, Taylor said, "Toledo gave us opportunity, but the South was still home" (Taylor, "My Life" 9). And even though Taylor loved the beauty of the Mississippi landscape, she despised the racism she encountered there and took an active role in the fight for civil rights to secure the freedom that the U.S. Constitution promises to every American. In her southern homeland, Taylor encountered racism firsthand:

> I experienced not being able to try on clothes in department stores . . . not being waited on by store clerks until all white customers had been waited on . . . being told to go to the back door of ice-cream parlors, just to get an ice-cream cone. I experienced derogatory remarks because I am black, and I experienced the signs. Signs that read WHITE ONLY, COLORED NOT ALLOWED. Signs on hotel windows, signs on restroom doors, signs on restaurant windows, signs above water fountains. Signs, signs, everywhere.
>   WHITE ONLY, COLORED NOT ALLOWED.
>   They hurt my soul. (Taylor, "My Life" 9)

The impetus for Taylor's participation in the struggle for African Americans' civil rights came not only from her family's values but also in response to horrific events that occurred during her childhood. One of these, the brutal murder of four-teen-year-old Emmett Till, happened in August of 1955, when Taylor was almost twelve years old. Till traveled from his home in Chicago to Money, Mississippi, for a summer visit to see his uncle Moses Wright and other relatives. Till and his cousins went to Bryant's Grocery & Meat Market to purchase candy and sodas, and Till al-legedly entered the store on a dare and asked Carolyn Bryant, wife of store owner Roy Bryant, out on a date and then wolf whistled at her. When Roy Bryant returned to town, a black male shopper told him what had happened, and Roy and J. W. Milam (and perhaps several others) went to Moses Wright's house in the middle of the night and forced Till into their car. They beat Emmett Till to death, gouged out one of his eyes, dislocated the other, crushed his skull, castrated him, shot him in the head just above the right ear, tore off the other ear and, after tying a 100-pound cotton gin fan around his neck with barbed wire, dumped his mutilated body into the Tallahatchie River (Crowe, *Getting Away with Murder* 64).[4] This senseless and barbaric act of murder, for which the perpetrators were acquitted, impacted Afri-can Americans all over the country. Taylor's fictional story of T. J. Avery in *Roll of Thunder* and *Let the Circle Be Unbroken* echoes the Till murder, and through it, she emphasizes to readers that despite their age, young people just as often fall prey to crimes of injustice as do adults and ought therefore to fight prejudice wherever they find it—even if they happen to be, like protagonist Cassie Logan in *Roll of Thunder*, only nine years old. As a student at the University of Colorado, Taylor became ac-tive in the Black Student Alliance, "which in the 1960s worked to establish black pride and to overcome discrimination" (Crowe, *Presenting* 132), but her most en-during stance against racism has been through educating children and young adults through the Logan family novels.

Taylor focuses on the importance of land and liberty, but in Taylor's historical fiction, land and liberty mean little without the third "L"—literacy—for literacy prepares one to become an engaged citizen. Though Taylor had always been a good student, when she began attending the majority-white school in Toledo as a fifth grader, she felt compelled to excel academically, fearing "that if she failed, people would say she had failed because she was black" (Crowe, *Presenting* 16). Feeling as though she were "representing the race" in the white school contributed to the pressure she felt to perform well academically, but the high expectations of her parents as well as her dream of one day becoming a writer and serving in the Peace Corps in Ethiopia compelled her to do her best. Taylor graduated from Scott High School in 1961 and entered the University of Toledo the next fall (18). A college ed-ucation satisfied her thirst for knowledge, but it did nothing to dampen her desire for cultural literacy about her African ancestry. Only time in Africa would do that. With the exception of her sister Wilma and her paternal grandmother, Taylor's family members were adamantly opposed to her going to Africa; they argued that it was too far, that a young, single female would have no protection there; and several of her relatives also felt that she should not volunteer to serve a country that had treated its black citizens so poorly (19). At one point, her father even promised her a new car for graduation if she would abandon her plan to go. Unmoved by their resistance, Taylor spent 1965 to 1967 in Yirgalem, Ethiopia, as a Peace Corps volunteer, time she has characterized as the two best years of her life. Taylor felt at home among the Ethiopians:

> Though her Peace Corps training had prepared her to expect some prejudice from the Ethiopians, Taylor discovered instead that she was the first black American most of the people from the mountain village had met, and she was accepted by them as a long-lost daughter, a descendant of the people who had been forced into slavery hundreds of years earlier. (21)

Ethiopia reminded Taylor somewhat of the South, but "removed from the racism of the United States, she felt good about herself, and she admired the solid sense of identity of the Ethiopians and the pride they had in themselves" (21).

It's no coincidence that Taylor went to Africa in the midst of the U.S. civil rights movement. "Freedom Summer" came in 1964, when thousands of young people flocked to Mississippi to register black voters and to contribute to other projects in black communities—the same summer that President Lyndon B. Johnson passed the Civil Rights Act that prohibited discrimination in public places, provided for school integration, and made employment discrimination illegal. That fall, the first group of students integrated the Montgomery, Alabama, schools. In 1965, the year Taylor went to Ethiopia, Malcolm X was slain, thousands participated in the five-day march from Selma to Montgomery to demand voting rights, and President Johnson signed the Voting Rights Act into law, outlawing discriminatory practices that kept many African Americans from voting. And in 1968, after her return, Martin Luther King, Jr. was assassinated. Thus, while the United States was finally beginning to establish civil rights for African Americans, Mildred Taylor was finding her own sense of self as a descendent of Africa and receiving the nurturing in Ethiopia that she needed to grow stronger, to find her own voice, and to decide on a profession that would enable her to make a difference in the lives of others. Hence, this time in Africa had a profound effect on shaping Taylor's adult identity as an *African* American and as a writer, strengthening her commitment to American citizenship but also putting her in touch with her ethnic and cultural "roots."

Taylor felt a similar kinship with the Ethiopians that she felt with her own relatives in part because they placed the same importance on family oral history as did Taylor's extended family. When the Taylors took summer trips South, Mildred particularly enjoyed the story-telling sessions that would occur in the evenings when she would hear relatives—especially her father, a master storyteller—recount black history that she never found in school textbooks. In her 1977 Newbery Medal acceptance speech, Taylor said:

> And at night when neighboring relatives would gather to sit on the moonlit porch or by the heat of the fire . . . talk would turn to the old people, to friends and relatives who then seemed to have lived so long ago. As the storytellers spoke in animated voices and enlivened their stories with movements of great gusto, I used to sit transfixed, listening, totally engrossed. It was a magical time. (Taylor, "Newbery" 401)

"I never tired of hearing those stories," Taylor commented (Taylor, "My Life" 9). Given this early cultivation of valuing family lore and her renewed immersion into stories in Africa, when Taylor returned to the United States, her love of writing and storytelling, her knowledge of African American history through family stories, and her desire to teach children about black history that had systematically been excluded from textbooks coalesced in Taylor's first efforts to publish historical fiction for children.

Despite many rejections, in February of 1974, Taylor finally succeeded in publishing her first book. As a result of winning a contest for minority writers sponsored by the Council on Interracial Books for Children, an organization established for the express purpose of publishing the work of minority children's authors and illustrators and raising "consciousness about racism, sexism, militarism, class bias, and other issues in children's literature" (Mickenberg 274),[5] she received a contract with Dial for the novella *Song of the Trees*. Published in 1975, this was the first of the Logan stories. It is appropriate that Taylor began her career with a story that illustrates how vehemently the Logans value the land. This longing for a place of their own begins with young Paul Edward Logan in *The Land*, prequel to the other books, and continues throughout the series. As the protagonist of most of the novels, Cassie Logan absorbs this value of land ownership at a very early age.

Cassie learns as a child that land-owning black people enjoy freedoms that sharecropping families do not. The Logans have owned property since Cassie's paternal grandfather, Paul Edward, purchased their first parcel of land in 1887. Though Cassie is a third-generation land-owning Logan, she does not fully appreciate what this means until conflicts between her family and the white community arise. The Logans understand the injustice of the sharecropping system and make a concerted effort to undermine this unfair practice through a shopping boycott. While Mary, Cassie's mother, organizes the boycott to encourage poor blacks to fight economic and racial injustice, Cassie learns how little power sharecroppers have to resist the multiple levels of oppression they face. The Wallaces, the racist white family who own the community store, have lynched black citizens without fear of punishment from authorities or retaliation from blacks, and they corrupt black youth by encouraging them to drink alcohol, smoke, and gamble at their store. This degradation of black children serves a twofold purpose: it entertains the Wallaces and their white customers while it drives the parents of these sharecropping children further into debt with the Wallaces.

When David Logan, Cassie's father, comes home for Christmas from his railroad job in Louisiana, he discusses with the adults in the family the emerging plan for the boycott. David acknowledges the dangers to his family's livelihood if they use their property to back the credit of black shoppers. The Logans could lose their land since the Wallaces and Harlan Granger, on whose land the Wallace store sits, can pressure the bank that holds the Logans' mortgage to "call in the loan." David has further cause for concern because Harlan Granger has been trying for years to reacquire the Logans' four hundred acres, which were once a part of the Granger family's six thousand acres. Granger regularly makes veiled threats to the Logans in an effort to intimidate them into selling their land. Hence, in both direct and indirect ways, pursuing this boycott would put Logan land at risk. Nine-year-old Cassie, who should be asleep when David consults the family about the boycott, overhears the adults' conversation and gets up to ask, "Papa, we gonna lose our land?" In response, "Papa reached out and softly touched my face in the darkness. 'If you remember nothing else in your whole life, Cassie girl, remember this: We ain't never gonna lose this land. You believe that?'" (Taylor, *Thunder* 152). Reassured, Cassie answers affirmatively and drifts back to sleep.

This announcement from Papa should have come as no surprise to Cassie because earlier in the novel, David has already expounded upon the importance of the land. When Cassie complains about David's having to work laying railroad track in Louisiana and wonders aloud why the land is so important, her father takes her outside to survey the fields and tells her:

> Look out there, Cassie girl. All that belongs to you. You ain't never had to live on nobody's place but your own and long as I live and the family survives, you'll never have to. That's important. You may not understand that now, but one day you will. Then you'll see. (Taylor, *Thunder* 7)

Puzzled over how Papa could say all of the land belongs to her when she has three brothers to whom it also belongs, Cassie concludes:

> But Papa never divided the land in his mind; it was simply Logan land. For it he would work the long, hot summer pounding steel; Mama would teach and run the farm; Big Ma, in her sixties, would work like a woman of twenty in the fields and keep the house; and the boys and I would wear threadbare clothing washed to dishwater color; but always, the taxes and the mortgage would be paid. (7–8)

This passage suggests that owning land is worth the sacrifice of every family member, from the youngest to the oldest. It also indicates that despite the land's value, it cannot produce enough to support the family, making it necessary for both Mary and David to work off of the farm.

Hence, in this post-Reconstruction era, David owns land on which he cannot live because of a lack of available local employment. He has the freedom to work elsewhere and to earn his own money—in contrast to both slaves of previous generations and sharecroppers of the current time who are bound to another's land by ownership or debt, respectively—but must regularly face the intrusions of white people who resent what the Logans own and who sometimes try to take what is rightfully theirs. The tension between David's freedom to travel to find work and to earn wages to send home constantly pulls against his desire to be physically present on the land to help protect his family and the acreage his ancestors fought so hard to obtain. David's decision to have Mr. Morrison, a coworker on the railroad, live with the family in his absence settles some of this tension he feels since the stature of Morrison, who is over seven feet tall, gives intruders—especially white intruders with nefarious intentions—pause before trespassing on Logan land.

Verbal discussions between Logan adults and their children like those above make explicit the values the adults want the children to hold about the land, but Taylor's novels also offer evidence of the adults' actively *showing* their children what the land means and the children's internalization of these values.

When the bank requires the Logans to pay their property taxes long before they should be due, Hammer, David's brother, sells his shiny new Packard to obtain the tax money. Taken aback by this decision, family members ask how he could have done this, and in his response, Hammer prioritizes what he values: "What good's a car? It can't grow cotton. You can't build a home on it. And you can't raise four fine babies in it" (Taylor, *Thunder* 236). In other words, anything that does not sustain and support family is not worth keeping—and notably, this comes from a single man with no children of his own.

In *Song of the Trees*, a prequel to *Roll of Thunder*, Cassie and her siblings show their own commitment to the land by physically attacking a white man, Mr. Andersen, and his lumbermen for attempting to log a beautiful grove of old-growth trees on their land without the permission of Caroline (known to the children as Big Ma), the family's matriarch, who actually owns the property at the time. Cassie loves these trees, which both she and her father believe sing. After receiving $65 for the trees but fearing Mr. Andersen will take many more trees than he has paid for, Caroline and Mary send Stacey overnight to Louisiana to get David. When he returns, David secretly plants sticks of dynamite in the grove before dawn, and when Mr. Andersen and the loggers return to haul the fallen trees away, David threatens to blow up the grove and all of the men in it if they refuse to leave. David tells Andersen, "You ain't taking one more stick out of this forest" (51), and when Andersen reminds him that he won't always have the black box, David retorts: "That may be. But it won't matter none. Cause I'll always have my self-respect" (52). In this scene, rather than telling them, David *shows* his children that the land is worth great sacrifice as he informs the stunned Andersen: "One thing you can't seem to understand . . . is that a black man's always gotta be ready to die. And it don't make me any difference if I die today or tomorrow. Just as long as I die right" (49).

In this episode, which Taylor based on an actual account from her family history (*SAA* 135, 207), David teaches his children the importance of integrity and also places the value of their land above that of human life—both the lives of the white men and of himself. He would rather die than allow them to strip his land of some of its value. Critic Hamida Bosmajian comments that Taylor shows Cassie growing up "in the context of the middle-class values of life, liberty and the pursuit of property (happiness)" (144), and in this scene, David illustrates his commitment to this "American dream," despite the risks. Given that the Logans own four hundred acres of land, the logging of this grove of trees would not likely have done the family much long-term financial damage, even if Andersen had taken more of the trees than he had said he would, as Caroline expects he will. In fact, David's accepting the additional money Andersen offers might have helped them in the short term since this takes place during the Great Depression, when every penny counts. At times, the Logans even have to ration flour to feed their children; they clearly need additional income. David, however, understands that if Andersen intrudes on their property uninvited and takes what he wants from their property against the will of the family in exchange for a price far below market value, this act issues an open invitation for other whites in the community to do likewise. Rather than let this happen, he employs a reckless and dangerous threat that enhances his reputation as a "crazy fool" (in Andersen's words) and as a man who always means what he says (in David's words). If individuals within the Logan family were to compromise small parcels of their land in exchange for short-term gain, such decisions would eat away at the integrity of the land and of the family. Big Ma knows this and acknowledges that because of her gender and advanced age, she might no longer be the best person to make financial decisions and transactions concerning the land. As a result, in *Roll of Thunder*, she transfers ownership of the land to David and his brother, Hammer, making them the responsible parties with whom men in power such as Mr. Andersen will have to deal in the future.

At the same time, David's threats of bodily harm to a white man—even a white man guilty of trespassing and attempting what amounts to theft—is likely a far more dangerous way for a black man to defend a piece of property in the 1930s than would have been historically advisable. Statistics from the archives of Tuskegee Institute show that of the 3,446 lynchings of blacks that occurred in the United States between 1882 and 1968, the highest incidence—539—occurred in Mississippi (Linder). In *Roll of Thunder*, even the children become aware of the prevalence of lynching when Mary takes them to visit the Berry family, one member of which is so badly burned by the "night men" (Ku Klux Klan) that he eventually dies.

Given that Taylor carved the logging incident from *Song of the Trees* out of a true story from her own family history, and also given that this was the first published book in the Logan family series, told from an eight-year-old child's perspective, Taylor drives home the point that protecting Logan land is worth a great deal of sacrifice—even sacrifice on the part of children. Since this episode precedes those in *Roll of Thunder* and even explains the history behind the grove of trees that Big Ma visits in *Thunder*, readers who have absorbed this backstory in *Song of the Trees* understand the strength of his conviction when David tells Cassie in *Thunder* that "We ain't never gonna lose this land" (Taylor, *Thunder* 152).

In the same way that Taylor illustrates a multigenerational commitment to the land through the actions of both the adults and the children, she also shows both the elder and the younger Logans fighting injustice to suggest that obtaining and maintaining one's freedom requires active struggle at all walks of life. In the climactic incident in *Roll of Thunder*, David sacrifices his cotton to save the life of a troubled neighbor boy, T. J. Avery, whom the "night men" are preparing to lynch. Although Stacey and T. J. were once good friends, T. J. has betrayed the Logan children repeatedly and even contributed to Mary's being fired from her teaching job at Great Faith Elementary. Hence, David would have had good reason not to interfere, for T.J. has increased his own family's economic hardship. But like Emmett Till, T. J. Avery has fallen into a situation in which he does not understand the social and racial forces to which he is subject as a young black male in the Jim Crow South, and David understands that T. J.'s lack of wisdom and his family's inability to protect him should not subject him to the abuse and violence of a lawless band of racists.

Like Till, T. J. is "guilty" of crossing the line that separates whites and blacks. Hamida Bosmajian comments that "T. J.'s 'crime' is that he has tried to deny *difference*, that he has confused the boundaries the black community must insist on for their survival" (150). Earlier in the novel when T.J. begins to associate with Melvin and R. W. Simms, lower-class whites in the town, he considers them his friends when they are really only using him for their own benefit. T. J. does not have the wise counsel or fatherly advice David gives Stacey when he warns him not to try to befriend white people because "right now the country ain't built that way" (Taylor, *Thunder* 158). T. J.'s spineless father, who seems to have lost control of his son long before, does not advise his children as David does his. Setting T. J. up, R. W. and Melvin convince him to help them steal a pearl-handled pistol T. J. has been admiring at the Barnetts' store in the town of Strawberry. During the attempted robbery, the Barnetts walk in on the break-in, and an altercation occurs. When T. J. threatens to tell the authorities of the Simms brothers' role in the robbery, the boys first beat him and then frame him for Mr. Barnett's murder. By the time T. J gets to Stacey for his help in getting home, the "night men" have already arrived. They intend to lynch T. J. and perhaps also attack Mr. Morrison and the Logans, whom many whites in the community resent for their indepence and property. David anticipates this escalation of violence and diverts attention from T. J. by setting his own cotton crop on fire. Fearing that the fire will spread to the rest of the town and to their own properties, the men abandon their plan to lynch T. J. and run to help put out the fire.

David's desperate act has financial consequences for his family, but it has greater social and racial implications for the community in which he lives. Despite the conflicts T. J. has had with both the Logan children and the Logan adults, David considers T. J. something of a son because of the boy's friendship with Stacey and the Logans' friendship with the Averys. He also acknowledges that T. J. needs the mentorship of a strong adult male figure, which he lacks at home. In this community where most whites employ extraordinary means to destroy or at least oppress black people in general but black males in particular, T. J. desperately needs this support. For this reason, David chooses to risk his family's financial viability rather than stand idly by while this neighbor boy gets lynched. David's sacrificial act demonstrates that the Logans are willing to fight injustice not only when it is directed against Logans; when they fight for and with others in the black community, as with the boycott and with their struggle for black suffrage in *Let the Circle be Unbroken*, they preserve the freedom of all African Americans in the community. Furthermore, in saving T. J., David sends a message to the rest of the community that black adults have a responsibility to all black children—even ones not their own and even ones who have strayed from the community's most important core values. Bosmajian labels T. J. the sacrifice or scapegoat for Stacey (150), emphasizing that Stacey could easily be in T. J.'s position. This sheds light on why David employs such extreme measures to protect T. J.: if the mob were not pursuing T. J. as a lynching victim, they could instead be coming for Stacey or even for David himself.

David's confrontation with Mr. Andersen in the grove of trees in *Song of the Trees* and his burning of his own crops to save T. J.'s life in *Roll of Thunder* both illustrate how David, now the family's patriarch, imparts his own values concerning the Logans' land and freedom. But for Cassie, protagonist and narrator of the majority of the Logan family novels, to grow into young adulthood, she must grapple with learning to balance these concepts herself. According to Roberta Seelinger Trites's *Disturbing the Universe, Power and Repression in Adolescent Literature* (2000):

> Although the primary purpose of the adolescent novel may appear to be a
> depiction of growth, growth in this genre is inevitably represented as being linked
> to what the adolescent has learned about power. Without experiencing gradations
> between power and powerlessness, the adolescent cannot grow. . . . During
> adolescence, adolescents must learn their place in the power structure. They must
> learn to negotiate the many institutions that shape them. . . . They must learn to
> balance their power with their parents' power and with the power of the other
> authority figures in their lives. And they must learn what portion of power they
> wield . . . (x)

More specifically, in her confrontation with Lillian Jean Simms, Cassie tests how much power the racist system in which she lives will allow her to wield in a conflict with a white person whose age, intelligence, and social class resemble her own. In addition, Cassie's experimentation with power in this conflict best reveals how she views her responsibility for making society a more just place for black people. When Big Ma finally takes Cassie to the town of Strawberry where she will sell the family's produce and transact business with Mr. Jamison, the family's lawyer, Cassie accidentally bumps into Lillian Jean Simms, sister of R. W. and Melvin, while walking on the sidewalk. Lillian Jean demands that Cassie apologize, and when she fails to exhibit the deference the white girl expects, Lillian Jean orders Cassie to get down on the road. Cassie refuses, and Mr. Simms knocks Cassie off of the sidewalk for disrespecting his daughter. To keep matters from worsening, Big Ma forces Cassie to apologize, which Cassie considers the greatest public injustice she has ever suffered. At this point, Cassie's awareness of her own "double consciousness" leads to what Victor Turner describes as "a sense of enclosure that may reach claustrophobic proportions" (Stepto 69). Cassie does not understand even as a nine-year-old that white people consider her and all black people inferior, suggesting that Mary and David have insulated Cassie from racism—perhaps to a fault. What functioned as sheltering at home becomes a handicap in the racially mixed environment of Strawberry—a handicap that feels like entrapment to Cassie, who now glimpses how little she knows about the social systems to which she is subject.

The response to this incident of each of the four Logan adults—Caroline, Mary, Hammer, and David—offers Cassie different perspectives on prejudice and power, and each helps her settle into her own ethos concerning the balance between self-respect and self-preservation. Cassie scorns Big Ma's approach to racial conflict: in Caroline's view, whites have all the power, blacks have none; therefore blacks must bow to the will of whites. Though Mary encourages her to empathize with Big Ma, Cassie flatly rejects this approach because, in her opinion, it obliterates self-respect.

True to his name, Uncle Hammer resists racism by exerting his power overtly. This tactic Cassie admires. When she tells Hammer what happened in Strawberry, she hopes he "knocks his [Mr. Simms'] block off" (Taylor, *Thunder* 125). Fearing Hammer's temper will lead to violence, the older Logans warn Cassie not to tell him what happened, but Cassie persists. Predictably, when Hammer learns of the incident, he gets his gun and zooms off in the Packard toward the Simms farm, but Mr. Morrison goes along to "talk him down" from his rage. In the morning, the children learn that Mr. Morrison and Mary stayed up most of the night with Hammer to avert a situation that would likely have threatened both the land and the lives of the Logans. Though Cassie feels disappointed that Hammer didn't beat up Mr. Simms, she thinks better of her expectations of immediate retaliation when Stacey tells her that Hammer could have gotten killed had he gone to the Simms farm. Once she begins to understand fully the dangers of overt revenge, however justified, she is better prepared for the lesson in respect that Mary offers.

While Hammer's temper and risky behavior around southern white people illustrate why he had to move North, Mary's conversation with Cassie after the Strawberry incident demonstrates how she has managed to function in this racist region. Mary explains that Big Ma did what she did only to protect Cassie. Mary also explains racism to Cassie—something her daughter never encountered so personally before. She tells Cassie that Mr. Simms thinks his daughter is better than she because their family is white. She then tells her about American slavery and how the racial dynamics between blacks and whites came to be the way they are as a result of whites having owned blacks for hundreds of years. Clearly, Taylor includes this speech more for inexperienced child readers than for this nine-year-old who has been hearing stories of her slave ancestors all her life. Mary concludes:

> White people may demand our respect, but what we give them is not respect but fear. What we give our own people is far more important because it's given freely. Now you may have to call Lillian Jean "Miss" because the white people say so, but you'll also call our own young ladies at church "Miss" because you really do respect them. . . . Baby, we have no choice of what color we're born or who our parents are or whether we're rich or poor. What we do have is some choice over what we make of our lives once we're here. (Taylor, *Thunder* 129)

From this conversation, Cassie begins to understand that she exists as only a small part of an unjust system. The fact that she is nearly a teenager before she learns and understands this lesson is both a problem—because she is ill-equipped to behave in socially appropriate ways around white people—and a testament to the fact that David and Mary have raised her with a strong sense of self and a belief in her own value. After learning from watching the family's response to Hammer's temper that open retaliation only invites the wrath of white racists, and after this talk with Mary, who teaches her that she must make her own choices about how she will live her life, Cassie is primed to act on what she learns from David. This lesson in racial power dynamics marks *Roll of Thunder* as both a product of the civil rights movement and also, though written for somewhat younger readers, of the newly emergent genre of Young Adult literary realism that exploded in the 1970s.

David teaches Cassie the art of subversion and the benefits of patience. He tells her that she'll encounter many things in life she doesn't want to do but must do to survive. He says he resents Charlie Simms's actions but:

> I had to weigh the hurt of what happened to you to what could've happened if I went after him. If I'd've gone after Charlie Simms and given him a good thrashing like I felt like doing, the hurt to all of us would've been a whole lot more than the hurt you received, so I let it be. I don't like letting it be, but I can live with that decision. (175)

Cassie knows that white people—such as the driver of the white school bus and Mr. Barnett, the store owner who serves his white customers before he serves Cassie, who entered first—have wronged her before, and David assures her that Lillian Jean won't be the last, but Cassie must decide whether retaliation against Lillian Jean is worth the risk. Ultimately, she feels strongly enough about the injury she has suffered to craft a plan for revenge that will avoid open confrontation.

To gain power over Lillian Jean Simms, Cassie works hard to cultivate the white girl's trust, and she does so by becoming Lillian Jean's "slave" for the entire month of January, carrying her books, making conversation with her, and feigning friendship (177). Cassie comments: "When friends of hers walked with us, she bragged about her little colored friend and almost hugged herself with pleasure when I called her 'Miz' Lillian Jean" (177). Lillian Jean even begins to divulge her secrets to Cassie. When Cassie decides she has successfully gained power over Lillian Jean, she lures her into a clearing in the woods, pretending to show her something special, and gives her a sound thrashing. When Lillian Jean threatens to tell her father, Cassie promises her that if she tells anyone, "everybody at Jefferson Davis [School] is gonna know who you crazy 'bout and all your other business . . . and you know I know. Besides, if anybody ever did find out 'bout this fight, you'd be laughed clear up to Jackson. You here going on thirteen, getting beat up by a nine-year-old" (181). Cassie's plan works. Though she must do so privately to ensure her own safety, Cassie gets even with Lillian Jean, who is shocked to discover that Cassie never was her friend. What's more, she neither threatens the safety of Logan land nor requires the intervention of Logan adults. In this way, Cassie uses her "power over" Lillian Jean to seize her "power to" exact revenge in one small way against an injustice that has left her feeling dehumanized and wronged (Trites 6). Furthermore, Cassie incorporates all of the wisdom of Logan adults into her decisions about how to retaliate against her enemy without putting herself or her family in danger.

In *Narrative of the Life of Frederick Douglass*, Douglass overhears his master say, "Learning would spoil the best nigger in the world . . . if you teach that nigger how to read, there would be no keeping him. It would forever unfit him to be a slave" (45). Accordingly, literacy, which constitutes a third necessary component of freedom in the Logan family saga, makes the young Logans dissatisfied with mediocrity and oppression and opens a window to the white world, exposing them to ideas of which they would otherwise have remained ignorant. Little Man, Cassie's youngest brother, illustrates this point when he stomps on his textbook the first day of school after reading in the front cover of his book that the white school district has given them to the "nigras" at Great Faith only when their condition is "poor." Even as a preschooler, Little Man uses his reading abilities to gain a greater understanding of the prevailing social conditions, and once he understands them, he rejects the inferior role his teacher—also a Negro—and the school district administrators expect him to play. Nothing that Mary and David Logan have taught Little Man and his siblings prepares him to accept marginality.

Both the Logan children's sacrifices to acquire literacy and their attitudes toward books reveal that the family values literacy. In sunshine and rain, Cassie and her siblings walk several miles to and from school every day and suffer humiliation from the white bus driver and riders to get an education. They attend a vastly overcrowded school in old buildings that they know are far inferior to the white school. Even though they sometimes grumble about the sacrifices they make for learning, at Christmastime all of the Logan children demonstrate their passion for reading. When David comes home for the holidays and brings gifts, the children enjoy the fruit, candy, and clothing they receive, but "nothing compared to the books," says Cassie. David tells them that Alexander Dumas, the author of *The Three Musketeers* and *The Count of Monte Cristo*, was a black man. When he bought them, he bragged to the salesman, who considered these books "right hard reading for children": "They can't read 'em now . . . they'll grow into 'em" (Taylor, *Thunder* 153). The family's excitement about the books is to be expected since this family has several generations of educated individuals. Mary has a college degree, and Cassie's grandfather, Paul Edward, learned to read and write as a child and suffered aggression from whites and blacks alike both because he was a mulatto who looked white and because of his level of education at a time when few blacks could read and write. Like those who would come after him, Paul Edward used literacy to his advantage and relied on it to help him reach his goal of owning land some day.

Finally, learning family lore helps maintain the Logans' freedom because understanding the successes and failures of the past gives them wisdom about their present. Some stories teach the children *African-American* history, while others teach them *Logan* history—and Taylor makes clear that knowledge of both is important for the children to survive and to gain a deeper understanding of who they are as black people and as young Logans. One night, when Mr. Morrison begins to tell the children about his experience with the Ku Klux Klan, Mary tries to stop him, but David tells her, "These are things they need to hear, baby. It's their history" (148). Mr. Morrison not only tells them of how the "night men" came into his home when he was a child, killed his sister, attacked his mother, and burned the house down because Morrison's father tried to protect two boys who were accused of molesting a white woman, but he explains that his parents were much bigger than average because they had been bred for size as slaves. This story exposes Cassie and her siblings to the truth that slavery was a business, and to keep it lucrative, some slave masters used tactics not unlike those of cattle farmers who breed their stock to encourage desirable physical characteristics. Though the Logan children may not absorb the importance of ideas such as these immediately, hearing them prepares them to understand why whites interact with them as they do.

Unlike Morrison's story, the one that Big Ma tells Cassie about the grove of trees conveys particular Logan family history that gives Cassie a glimpse of the love story between Big Ma and the late Paul Edward and reveals to her what her grandfather accomplished because of the power of his dream. Cassie's interactions with Big Ma during this conversation make clear that she has heard it repeatedly. Notably, Big Ma also takes time to make sure Cassie understands who all the players are in her story since most of the families in the historical story still live in the community. She takes time with the craft of the telling. She says of Paul Edward:

> He put his arms 'round me and looked out at his new piece of land, then he said 'zactly the same thing he said when he grabbed himself that first two hundred acres. Said, "Pretty Caroline, how you like to work this fine piece of earth with me?" Sho' did . . . said the 'zact same thing. (Taylor, *Thunder* 93–94)

Clearly, storytelling plays an important role in the Logans' lives, and whether it be tales of David and Hammer stealing watermelons from a neighbor's field as children or the somber recounting of a lynching, every story serves a purpose that contributes to the growth of the Logan children.

Mildred Taylor commented in her 1977 Newbery acceptance speech for *Roll of Thunder*:

> If people are touched by the warmth of the Logans, it is because I had the warmth of my own youthful years from which to draw. If the Logans seem real, it is because I had my own family upon which to base characterizations. And if people believe the book to be biographical, it is because I have tried to distill the essence of Black life, so familiar to most Black families, to make the Logans an embodiment of that spiritual heritage; for, contrary to what the media relate to us, all Black families are not fatherless or disintegrating. (Taylor, "Newberry" 403)

Taylor has based her entire literary career as a children's author on this close connection between life and literature, and through these works, she has made a substantial contribution to the shaping of the genre of contemporary African American children's literature. Like Mrs. Amelia E. Johnson, author of *Clarence and Corinne* (1890), widely recognized as the first children's novel written by an African American, Taylor draws readers into the story with compelling characters. Like Langston Hughes, she makes music and song important foci in her writings. Like Arna Bontemps, she makes history accessible to young readers. Like Virginia Hamilton, Tom

Feelings, and Walter Dean Myers, the "thumbprint" of the civil rights movement is on everything she writes because she lived through it. And like many other contemporary African American authors of children's and young adult literature, Taylor succeeds in showing black children a reflection both of who their ancestors might have been and how this legacy contributes to who they may become.

NOTES

1. *Logan*, the eighth and final novel of the saga, was scheduled for 2002 publication but has not yet been published (Crowe, *Presenting* 64).

2. The Taylors were the third black family to move into this neighborhood. Due to "white flight," this neighborhood became all black within five or six years of the Taylors' move (Scales 241).

3. Sharecropping was a system in which poor people (and in the context of these novels, poor *black* people, many of whom were former slaves) lived on the land of white landowners (some of whom were former slave owners) and farmed the land with seed and tools provided by the landowner in exchange for a high percentage of the crop yield. Through this system many African Americans remained indebted indefinitely to white landowners. Sharecropping, in a sense, perpetuated a slightly altered form of slavery.

4. Chris Crowe's *Getting Away with Murder* offers young adult readers more information about Emmett Till's life and death.

5. For a rich discussion of the impact of the Council on Interracial Books for Children on the genre, see the epilogue (273–82) of Julia Mickenberg's *Learning from the Left: Children's Literature the Cold War, and Radical Politics in the United States.*

WORKS CITED

Bosmajian, Hamida. "Mildred Taylor's Story of Cassie Logan: A Search for Law and Justice in a Racist Society." *Children's Literature* 24 (1996): 141–60.

Children's Literature Review (CLR), vol. 90, *s.v.* Mildred D(elois) Taylor. Detroit: Gale Research Company (2004):119–49.

Crowe, Chris. *Getting Away with Murder: The True Story of the Emmett Till Case.* New York: Dial, 2003.

——. *Presenting Mildred D. Taylor.* New York: Twayne, 1999.

Douglass, Frederick. *Narrative of the Life of Frederick Douglass, an American Slave.* New York: The Modern Library, 2004.

Johnson, A. E. *Clarence and Corinne, or God's Way.* Philadelphia: American Baptist Publication Society, 1890.

Linder, Douglas O. "Lynchings: by State and by Race, 1882–1968. 17 May 2009. http://www. law.umkc.edu/faculty/projects/ftrials/shipp/lynchingsstate.html.

Mickenberg, Julia. *Learning from the Left: Children's Literature the Cold War, and Radical Politics in the United States.* New York: Oxford UP, 2006.

Rahn, Suzanne. "An Evolving Past: The Story of Historical Fiction and Nonfiction for Children." *The Lion and the Unicorn* 15, no. 1 (1991): 1–26.

Scales, Pat. "Mildred D. Taylor: Keeper of Stories." *Language Arts: The Journal of the Elementary Section of the National Council of Teachers of English* 80, no. 3 (2003): 240–44.

Something about the Author (SAA), vol. 135, *s.v.* Taylor, Mildred. Detroit: Gale Research Company (2003): 205–9.

Stepto, Robert. *From Behind the Veil: A Study of Afro-American Narrative*. Urbana: U of Illinois P, 1979.

Taylor, Mildred D. *The Friendship*. New York: Scholastic, 1997.

———. *The Gold Cadillac*. Illustrated by Michael Hays. New York: Puffin, 1998.

———. *The Land*. New York: Phyllis Fogelman, 2001.

———. *Let the Circle Be Unbroken*. New York: Dial, 1981.

———. *Mississippi Bridge*. New York: Dial Books for Young Readers, 1990.

———. "My Life as a Writer." *World Literature Today: A Literary Quarterly of the University of Oklahoma* 78, no. 2 (2004): 7–10.

———. "Newbery Acceptance Speech." *The Horn Book* 53 (1977): 401–9.

———. *The Road to Memphis*. New York: Puffin, 1992.

———. *Roll of Thunder, Hear My Cry*. New York: Dial, 1976.

———. *Song of the Trees*. New York: Bantam, 1975.

———. *The Well: David's Story*. New York: Dial Books for Young Readers, 1995.

Trites, Roberta Seelinger. *Disturbing the Universe: Power and Repression in Adolescent Literature*. Iowa City: U of Iowa P, 2000.

FURTHER READING

Children's Literature Review, vol. 9, *s.v.* Mildred D(elois) Taylor. Detroit: Gale Research Company (1985): 223–29.

Children's Literature Review, vol. 59, *s.v.* Mildred D(elois) Taylor. Detroit: Gale Research Company (2000): 154-75. [Detroit: Gale Research Company, 2000.]

Davis-Undiano, Robert Con. "Mildred D. Taylor and the Art of Making a Difference." *World Literature Today: A Literary Quarterly of the University of Oklahoma* 78, no. 2 (2004): 11–13.

Fisher, Leona W. "'Bridge' Texts: The Rhetoric of Persuasion in American Children's Realist and Historical Fiction." *Children's Literature Association Quarterly* 27, no. 3 (2002): 129–35.

Harper, Mary Turner. "Merger and Metamorphosis in the Fiction of Mildred D. Taylor." *Children's Literature Association Quarterly* 13, no. 2 (1988): 75–80.

Harris, Marla. "'A History Not Then Taught in History Books': (Re)Writing Reconstruction in Historical Fiction for Children and Young Adults." *The Lion and the Unicorn* 30, no. 1 (2006): 94–116.

Levine, Ellen. *Freedom's Children: Young Civil Rights Activists Tell Their Own Stories*. New York: G.P. Putnam's Sons, 1993.

"The Murder of Emmett Till: American Experience." http://www.pbs.org/wgbh/amex/till/index.html. PBS Online.

Nelson, Marilyn. *A Wreath for Emmett Till*. Illustrated by Philippe Lardy. Boston: Houghton Mifflin, 2005.

Nordan, Lewis. *Wolf Whistle: A Novel.* Chapel Hill, NC: Algonquin, 1993.

Scales, Pat. "Mildred D. Taylor: Keeper of Stories." *Language Arts: The Journal of the Elementary Section of the National Council of Teachers of English* 80, no. 3 (2003): 240–44.

Smith, Karen Patricia. "A Chronicle of Family Honor: Balancing Rage and Triumph in the Novels of Mildred D. Taylor." In *African-American Voices in Young Adult Literature: Tradition, Transition, Transformation,* edited by Karen Patricia Smith, 247–76. Metuchen: Scarecrow P, 1994.

"WHAT ARE YOUNG PEOPLE TO THINK?": THE SUBJECT OF IMMIGRATION AND THE IMMIGRANT SUBJECT IN FRANCISCO JIMÉNEZ'S *THE CIRCUIT*

PHILLIP SERRATO

FRANCISCO *Jiménez was born in Tlaquepaque, Mexico, in 1943. In 1947, his family migrated to California and became migrant farmworkers. When he was in the eighth grade, he and his family were caught by the Border Patrol and deported to Mexico. Soon, however, the Jimenezes managed to secure visas and return to the United States to resume their pursuit of a stable life. Jiménez eventually graduated high school, completed an undergraduate degree in Spanish at Santa Clara University, and obtained an M.A. and Ph.D. in Latin American Literature at Columbia University. With his doctorate in hand, Jiménez returned to Santa Clara University in 1973 as a professor. During his tenure at SCU, where he continues to teach, he has occupied several administrative posts, including Chair of the Department of Modern Languages and Literatures, Director of the Ethnic Studies Program, and Associate Academic Vice President.*

Besides numerous scholarly articles, books, and edited collections, Jiménez has published The Circuit: Stories from the Life of a Migrant Child *(1997), Breaking*

Through (2001), and Reaching Out (2008), a trilogy of autobiographical works that chronicle his life from his childhood experiences in a migrant farmworker family to his years at SCU. In addition, he has published two picture books for children based on stories from The Circuit, La Mariposa (1998) and The Christmas Gift/El Regalo de Navidad (2000).

> What are young people to think about the issues that con-
> front them in daily newspaper headlines and on prime-time
> news? How can young people begin the educational process
> that will enable them to become more empathetic, rational,
> and reasonable about such a complex issue as immigration?
> How can they begin to develop an understanding of the
> struggles and human suffering of immigrants and of undoc-
> umented persons who have no legal stature in this country
> but who wish to participate more fully?
>
> —Oralia Garza de Cortés, "Behind the Golden Door:
> The Latino Immigrant Child in Literature and Films
> for Children"

In 1997, the University of New Mexico Press published Francisco Jiménez's The Circuit: Stories from the Life of a Migrant Child, a collection of autobiographical short stories that provide a compelling firsthand account of a Mexican family's migration to the United States.[1] With a forthright, almost confessional writing style, Jiménez shares with readers a series of episodes from his childhood that enable an understanding and appreciation of the material realities and psychological stress that many undocumented immigrants face as they work to gain a foothold in American society. It begins in 1947 in Tlaquepaque, Mexico, with the narrator as a four-year-old child ("Panchito") who at first is confused by the talk he overhears about "la frontera" ("the border"). However, he quickly becomes excited when he learns that his family will be moving to the United States to "leave our poverty behind" (1). The text depicts the family's travel north, their entry into California's agricultural labor economy, and the various harsh realities that, alongside other migrant families, they encounter on the margins of the U.S. national community. In a powerful reenactment—and indictment—of the exclusion of the Mexican immigrant from American civic life and the American Dream, the final story of the collection ends with Panchito arrested at school by a Border Patrol officer and deported with his family back to Mexico.

Notably, as Jiménez recounts the grueling nature of life on "the Circuit"—the circular route in California's Central Valley traveled by migrant farmworkers following the crops that become ready for harvest at various times of the year—the text manages to speak to multiple audiences with distinct yet equally important outcomes.[2] Certainly, readers from migrant backgrounds who can see their own story or their family's history in Jiménez's book constitute one crucial audience.

For these readers, the book validates their experiences by rendering them worthy of representation and acknowledgment. Moreover, by attesting not just to the struggles and resiliency of migrant families but also to their hopes, anxieties, and fears, *The Circuit* registers the subjectivity of a population that has a lengthy history of dehumanization and demonization in popular media. It is thus not surprising to hear Jiménez report that over the years he has received numerous letters from "children who come from migrant parents or grandparents [who] express gratitude to me for writing about their families' experiences. They usually say, 'Your story is the story of my family'" (Carger 16).[3]

For readers who do not necessarily share Jiménez's background or just lack an acquaintance with the conditions and circumstances that some immigrants face, *The Circuit* provides an unprecedented glimpse into an existence "rarely noticed by American readers" (Carger 14). To be sure, in recent years several books for children on Mexican immigration in general and on migrant laborer experiences in particular have appeared in the marketplace of children's literature, but these works (most of which are picture books) do not always provide the detailed, emotionally nuanced treatment that *The Circuit* provides.[4] With *The Circuit*, Jiménez creates an opportunity for readers to get to know his story—an undocumented migrant farmworker child's story—in a uniquely personal manner and, in the process, gain insight into a social phenomenon about which they may know little or nothing. Importantly, by providing insight into the challenges and ordeals that some immigrants must surmount as they pursue their hopes for a better life, *The Circuit* encourages younger readers, possibly under the guidance of their school teachers, to undertake further, more compassionate research into immigrant lives.

The intensification and proliferation of xenophobic and racist discourses about Mexican immigration and Mexican immigrants over the past few decades make Jiménez's text especially valuable. As noted by sociologist Leo Chavez, within the United States there exists a "grand tradition of alarmist discourse about [Mexican] immigrants and their perceived negative impacts on [American] society" (*Latino Threat* 3). Allegations abound in particular about undocumented or "illegal" Mexican immigrants taking jobs away from (legitimate) "Americans," poisoning United States society with criminal activity, and voraciously siphoning the economic vitality out of the country by abusing a host of public services. Obviously, claims such as these render Mexican immigrants irredeemably inassimilable and inadmissible to the U.S. national community.[5] Yet another terrible side effect of such propaganda is the dehumanization of this social group. Chavez points out as much when he emphasizes that media coverage of Mexican immigration has been sensationalized and "limited at best," serving more to incite paranoia and stoke xenophobia than to impart information that could provide "a more complete picture of undocumented immigrants" (*Shadowed Lives* xi). Because of contemporary media's tendency to ignore questions and concerns "about [undocumented immigrants'] lives, their motivations, and their aspirations for the future," Chavez asserts, "What [is] missing [is] a sense of their everyday reality and experiences" (*Shadowed Lives* xi).

By sensitively describing and humanizing the experiences of Panchito and his family, *The Circuit* supplies that which Chavez rightly insists has been "missing." In contrast to the dehumanization of undocumented immigrants in popular media, Jiménez's text renders life on the Circuit materially and emotionally palpable. Among other things, deliberate pacing, thorough description, and a frank honesty allow *The Circuit* to impress upon readers the stress and hardship that Panchito and his family suffer. For readers far removed from the kinds of situations and experiences that Jiménez recounts, such narrative "completeness" makes the material at hand comprehensible and compelling. The patient style, measured manner, and sincere tone with which Jiménez tells his stories also prove to be invaluable narrative features, for they allow the author to reach out and engage younger readers of diverse backgrounds. This makes it possible for a broad audience to learn about immigrant experiences and think critically about the status of migrant workers in U.S. society and U.S. popular media. Ultimately, as Jiménez pushes younger readers outside of egocentrism, xenophobia, and racism and into more nuanced, more sympathetic understandings of the details of migrant workers' lives, *The Circuit* becomes a crucial contact zone within which the relationship of readers to the subject of immigration and to immigrant subjects is reconstituted.[6]

A FRIEND FROM THE OTHER SIDE

In creating an autobiography . . . a writer transforms the
complex interaction of self and society into a literary form.
—James Craig Holte, *The Ethnic I: A Sourcebook
for Ethnic-American Autobiography*

An autobiographical work such as *The Circuit* is uniquely capable of interrupting the ongoing construction of Mexican immigrants as "less legitimate, marginalized, and stigmatized Others" (Chavez, *Latino Threat* 6). First of all, as Julia Watson mentions in an essay on the social and cultural politics of autobiography, the publication of autobiographies "giv[es] cultural status to particular lives" (61). With the premise that a published autobiography constitutes a privileged "means of self-inscription . . . written by persons whose lives are culturally endorsed, that is, 'worth' writing" (60), Watson posits that the marketplace of autobiography—wherein, for an assortment of reasons, some life stories enjoy publication and publicity and others do not—monumentalizes some identities and experiences while maintaining the subaltern status of others. In the case of *The Circuit*, the simple fact that an undocumented immigrant's autobiography has been deemed worthy of publication—as well as inclusion in school libraries and school curricula—conveys to younger readers that reasons exist for reading about this individual. In turn, the parameters of "worthy" reading and "worthy" lives expand.[7] The fact that autobiography provides a platform or venue for an autobiographer to express him/herself as a speaking subject also allows the text of The Circuit (for the first time in a work of nonfiction accessible to younger readers) to recover and assert the lived reality and the subjectivity of a Mexican migrant worker. Such a recovery and assertion is a significant departure from the preponderance of contemporary "media spectacles [that] transform immigrants' lives into virtual lives, which are typically devoid of the nuances and subtleties of real lived lives" (Chavez, Latino Threat 5–6). By foregrounding Jiménez's subjective experience, The Circuit redresses the dismissal, the disparagement, and the distortion of undocumented Mexican immigrants and thereby assumes the potential to neutralize their alienated, abject status in American society.

The capacity of Jiménez's work to deconstruct the otherness of undocumented Mexican immigrants and thus subvert a lynchpin of xenophobia and racism begins with its creation of a safe, welcoming space for any and all readers to learn and think about the experiences of a hitherto maligned and disregarded population. In the opening lines of the opening story ("Under the Wire"), a willingness to accommodate a diverse readership through a balance of specificity and exposition reveals itself:

> "La frontera" is a word I often heard when I was a child living in El Rancho
> Blanco, a small village nestled on barren, dry hills several miles north of
> Guadalajara, Mexico. I heard it for the first time back in the late 1940s when Papá
> and Mamá told me and Roberto, my older brother, that someday we would take
> a long trip north, cross la frontera, enter California, and leave our poverty behind.
>
> I did not know exactly what California was either, but Papá's eyes sparkled
> whenever he talked about it with Mamá and his friends. (1)

On one level, the touch of Spanish, the geographical references, and the allusion to the reason the family considers migration serve as points of contact for readers who may share elements of Jiménez's background. For these readers, this opening strategy provides a precious relatability and a personal validation that they may not be accustomed to finding in literature. On another level, this opening passage carefully broadens the horizons of readers encountering for the first time the kind of content that The Circuit contains. Children's limited life experience necessarily forecloses—to varying degrees, of course—their familiarity with other people and other places. Likewise, a panoply of social variables, including but not limited to economic class, ethnic background, national origin, and quality of education, circumscribe, inflect, and otherwise determine children's knowledge and perspective of the world and its inhabitants even further. For this reason, teachers and scholars often extol literature (especially nonfiction) as a powerful means for exploding egocentrism and "[giving] children a glimpse of other lives, other places, and other times" (Huck 573). At the very least, the opening references in "Under the Wire" to El Rancho Blanco and Guadalajara create opportunities for unfamiliar readers to consult a map and expand their geographical knowledge.

More important, the setting of the story in such a locale, replete with intimations of the family's poverty as well as an introduction to the subject of immigration, takes readers outside of the intrinsically parochial bounds of their own perspective and life circumstances and into the perspective and life experience of another/an "other."

The Spanish that Jiménez integrates into the opening passage and throughout *The Circuit* is an artistically and politically pointed gesture that adds to the deconstruction of unfamiliar readers' egocentrism by confronting them with alternative discursive and cultural registers. As Manuel Martín-Rodríguez explains in *Life in Search of Readers: Reading (in) Chicano/a Literature* (2003), the linguistic choices that Chicano/a authors make carry a host of implications. In literature produced in the 1960s and 1970s amidst the Chicano Movement, authors "[explored] multifold linguistic combinations" (Martín-Rodríguez 109). They wrote in Spanish, English, and varying mixtures of Spanish and English (and even Caló), a diversity that Martín-Rodríguez suggests not only "replicated the real-life speech patterns of Chicanos/as" but also "[reflected] what kind[s] of [audiences] writers were looking for" (109). While Movement writers tended to target Chicano/a audiences, many contemporary Chicano/a authors aspire to reach heterogeneous readerships and so strategically work "to transcend [the] barriers and borders that could impede" some readers' engagement with their works (Martín-Rodríguez 123). As exemplified by the opening passage of "Under the Wire," Jiménez manages in his linguistic choices to be subtly subversive yet maintain accessibility. The fact that the first words of the first story are in Spanish deftly undermines the primacy of the English language and demonstrates immediately the author's refusal to abide by any rules or expectations that "literature" in the United States must be written in English. In fact, in light of widespread efforts in the 1990s to eliminate bilingual education and declare English the official language of the United States, Jiménez's incorporation of Spanish into his stories constitutes a rather clever snub of English-only zealotry as well as a defiant assertion of authorial agency over the discursive and cultural terms of his storytelling.[8]

Alongside such politically provocative implications, Jiménez's linguistic choices and discursive maneuvers bespeak a parallel desire to accommodate multiple audiences. By and large, the presence of Spanish in the text does not stand in the way of comprehension. Jiménez only uses it occasionally and in ways that do not overwhelm a reader. For instance, in the course of the first paragraph of "Under the Wire," *la frontera* is repeated twice, which on a practical level gives a reader who may lack Spanish-language competency not only two shots at context-meaning making but also two opportunities to look the word up in a Spanish-English dictionary. In terms of the relationship of the text to the reader, the repetition of *la frontera* and the couching of it in descriptive, deliberately paced prose signals a patient willingness on the part of the author/narrator to carefully escort readers through the potentially unfamiliar geographic, linguistic, and experiential terrain of this autobiography. In addition, the fact that not even Panchito, the child narrator, fully understands what *la frontera* means removes any pressure from the child reader to know its definition. If anything, the ignorance that the reader may share with Panchito creates a kind of suspense that entices and encourages a reader to follow the boy's narrative lead so they can find out together the location and meaning of *la frontera* and its significance to the boy's life.[9]

As the text proceeds, it takes readers into experiences increasingly particular to migrant worker families and thus becomes more and more illuminating and challenging. Shedding light on the methods by which some families cross into the United States, Jiménez describes his family's arrival at the U.S.-Mexico border and explains how they entered California by crawling through a hole in the border fence and then riding with a smuggler, "for a fee, to a place where we would find work" (5). Shortly thereafter, readers share in the disillusionment and desperation that the family immediately faces. When Panchito's father learns from the foreman of a strawberry field that work will not be available for two weeks, he cries out, "That can't be! We were told we'd find work right away" (6), leaving readers to wonder (and worry), like Panchito, how the family will manage. While this moment elicits concern from the reader and begins to instruct readers on the sorts of challenges faced by undocumented immigrants trying to break into the agricultural labor economy, it leads into a very humanizing portrayal of dignity, optimism, and resilience. Panchito narrates,

> After a long silence, Mamá said, "We'll manage, *viejo*. Once work starts, we'll be fine."
> Roberto was quiet. He had a sad look in his eyes.
> During the next two weeks, Mamá cooked outside on a makeshift stove using rocks and a *comal* Doña Lupe had given her. We ate wild *verdolagas* and rabbit and birds, which Papá hunted with a rifle he borrowed from a neighbor. (7)

The ease and unexpectedness with which the family finds itself homeless and facing an uncertain future could be a startling dose of social realism for readers who may take for granted their own secure life situations and the comforts of home. Moreover, through the trying turn of events, readers are positioned to realize that in contrast to popular proclamations that "opportunistic" Mexicans flock to the United States to partake of "the benefits of the welfare state" (Schuck and Smith 109), life for Mexican immigrants, especially undocumented farmworkers, is actually a humbling and risky undertaking that requires tremendous strength of character.

The depiction of the family's homelessness is part of Jiménez's overarching effort to direct attention to the marginal, invisible spaces of American society and the people who, unbeknownst to many readers, reside there. In this manner *The Circuit* becomes nothing less than a child-accessible version of a sociological study such as Chavez's *Shadowed Lives: Undocumented Immigrants in American Society* (1992). Like Chavez, Jiménez exposes the liminal status of undocumented migrant workers to complicate unenlightened readers' understanding of American society.

In the story "Miracle in Tent City," Jiménez takes readers to rural Santa Maria, describing a labor camp dubbed "Tent City," which, according to Panchito, "was neither a city nor a town. It was a farm labor camp owned by Sheehey Strawberry Farms" (27). In this explanation, a reader encounters not only potentially unfamiliar living conditions but also a befuddling liminality, for the fact that Tent City is "neither a city nor a town" conflicts with popular insistences fed to children that the world can be neatly organized into discrete continents, countries, cities, and towns. Subsequent lines then push readers to accommodate even more unfamiliar realities:

> Tent City had no address; it was simply known as rural Santa Maria. It was on Main Street, about ten miles east of the center of town. A half a mile east of it were hundreds of acres of strawberries cultivated by Japanese sharecroppers and harvested by people from the camp. Behind Tent City was dry wilderness and a mile north of it was the city dump. Many of the residents in the camp were single men, most of whom, like us, had crossed the border illegally. There were a few single women and a few families, all Mexican. (27)

The fact that "Tent City had no address" and so is outside of the national symbolic order underscores the liminal status of the site. Set apart from and unacknowledged by larger American society on multiple levels, the residents of Tent City remain an underclass of "outsider[s], foreigner[s], and stranger[s]" (Chavez, *Shadowed Lives* 18). There is an important irony, however, in the fact that Tent City is on "Main Street." If we visualize Main Street as a continuum upon which membership in mainstream society can be plotted, the distance of Tent City from the center, combined with its proximity to such marginal zones as the wilderness and the city dump, suggests its alienation from the mainstream of American society. Nonetheless, Tent City is on and not off or otherwise detached from Main Street. The idea thus emerges that Tent City and the undocumented workers assembled there are actually connected to and present in American society in ways that some people might not realize or just might not want to acknowledge. Through *The Circuit*, an opportunity arises for readers to formulate a new understanding of the American national community that accommodates individuals and experiences that, Jiménez notes, have yet to be recorded or accepted as "part of the American experience" (Day 267).

Jiménez's portrayal of the living conditions that the family endures in Tent City and other places once they become part of the Circuit makes the very difficult (and probably very different) realities of migrant workers' lives all too clear. Although the Jimenezes are never again homeless once they break into the Circuit, the various temporary residences that they inhabit illustrate the deplorable housing that is a fact of life for farmworkers. In "Death Forgiven," Panchito mentions that the family lived in a "dilapidated garage . . . while harvesting Mr. Jacobson's vineyards" (57); in the title story he says of another garage that they occupied while working for Mr. Sullivan,

> [It] was worn out by the years. It had no windows. The walls, eaten by termites, strained to support the roof full of holes. The dirt floor, populated by earth worms, looked like a gray road map. (77)

Again reminiscent of the work of sociologists like Chavez, Jiménez compels readers to confront sordid realities that largely remain out of sight and out of mind for mainstream America. Interestingly, reflective of the dignity of the family, the Jimenezes always do their best to turn their substandard housing into a home, regardless of how temporary their stay may be. When the family moves into Mr. Sullivan's garage, for example, readers see the lengths to which they go to transform its uninhabitable state:

> That night, by the light of a kerosene lamp, we unpacked and cleaned our new home. Roberto swept away the loose dirt, leaving the hard ground. Papá plugged the holes in the walls with old newspapers and tin can tops. (77)

To be sure, in this description of the bustle that ensues when the family moves in, Jiménez manages to reiterate the miserable condition of the structure, which enables an even more complete understanding and appreciation of what the family endures. But above all else, the portrayal of the family's effort to tidy up the space simultaneously foregrounds the perseverance with which they strive to live in dignity even in the most humbling of situations and contradicts stereotypical associations of Mexican immigrants with squalor.[10]

Other details about the struggles of the family simply to survive document the terribly precarious situation of undocumented migrant workers. In "Miracle in Tent City," a story in which Panchito's baby brother nearly dies from illness because the family cannot afford medical care for him, Panchito reveals, "To make ends meet Mamá cooked for twenty farm workers who lived in Tent City. She made their lunches and had supper ready for them when they returned from picking strawberries at the end of the day. She would get up at four o'clock every morning, seven days a week, to make the tortillas for both meals" (28). At other points, the family has to take particularly desperate measures to get by. In "Christmas Gift," Panchito explains that during one stay in Corcoran (where the family regularly picked cotton),

> Sometimes, in the evenings, we went into town in our *Carcachita* to look for food in the trash behind grocery stores. We picked up fruits and vegetables that had been thrown away because they were partly spoiled. Mamá sliced off the rotten parts and made soup with the good vegetable pieces, mixing them with bones she bought at the butcher shop. She made up a story and told the butcher the bones were for the dog. The butcher must have known the bones were for us and not a dog because he left more pieces of meat on the bones each time Mamá went back. (51–52)

Since many children would likely find the idea of scavenging for food unfathomable, Jiménez's frank account of the family finding itself in such dire straits is likely to touch a nerve with readers forced to process the genuine vulnerability and desperation of migrant workers in the United States. Importantly, once readers are touched, empathy, compassion, and understanding across potentially alienated social, economic, and ethnic subject positions become possible.

The emotional toll that migrancy and farmwork take on the individual family members throws the difficulty of this life into especially stark relief and is an equally potent means by which the text secures the empathy of readers. For example, a great deal of responsibility and frustration befalls Roberto, Panchito's slightly older brother, because he cannot go to school. Although Panchito has to help the family by working in the fields, he is at least able to attend school most of the year. Roberto, however, only goes to school a few months out of the year because the family depends upon his full-time labor. In an exceptionally poignant moment in the title story, Panchito describes Roberto's disappointment (as well as his own feelings of guilt):

> Since I could not sleep, I decided to get up and join Papá and Roberto at breakfast. I sat at the table across from Roberto, but I kept my head down. I did not want to look up and face him. I knew he was sad. He was not going to school today. He was not going tomorrow, or next week, or next month. He would not go until the cotton season was over, and that was sometime in February. (80)

The boys' father, meanwhile, is constantly anxious given the unstable work opportunities available to his family. In *"El Angel de Oro,"* Panchito remarks that "Papá passed most of his time worrying. He smoked one cigarette after another and complained about the rain because we could not pick the cotton when it was wet" (46). Similarly, in "Death Forgiven," Panchito reveals that "[Papá] had been in a terrible mood the last few days because he was not sure where we would work now that the grape season was almost over" (59). Usually Papá's anxiety has him reaching for a cigarette or the bottle of aspirin that he always keeps nearby, but in the latter instance, Papá erupts violently. Panchito relates that at the time he had a parrot that one of the other farmworkers gave to him to keep as a pet. On this fateful occasion, unfortunately, his pet had been throwing a tantrum that grated too much on his father's tense nerves:

> The noise [from *El Perico*] struck my father like lightning. . . . Covering his ears with his hands, he bolted to the corner of the garage [where we lived], grabbed the broom, and swung with all his might at my friend who was perched on the wire. Red, green, and yellow feathers scattered everywhere. *El Perico* hit the dirt floor like a wet rag. (59)

To say that Papá's outburst indexes his stressed condition in this particular moment would be an awful understatement. Frustration and anxiety boil over here into an unexpected and unprecedented volatility that suddenly threatens to ravage the family that has so far met adversity with dignity, optimism, and resilience.

At the same time, the murder of *El Perico* illustrates the fact that as much as anyone else Panchito has his own set of stressors to manage. It goes without saying that the death of *El Perico* upsets him tremendously not only because he has witnessed the murder of his pet but because of the emotional intensity of the ordeal:

> Instantly Roberto, Mamá, and I started wailing. My father shouted at all of us to stop. Seeing a stream of blood dribble from *El Perico*'s silent beak, I felt as though someone had ripped my heart out. I threw the garage door open and darted out, running as fast as I could toward a storage shed that was about half a mile away. The shouting, screaming, and crying from our home chased me. (59)

Between the ghastly sight of the dead bird and the traumatizing maelstrom of "shouting, screaming, and crying" that "chase" Panchito, the scene is an emotionally overwhelming one for Panchito and the reader alike. Of course, this incident is only one of a string of stressful events that the boy encounters. Elsewhere in the text readers are privy to the isolation that he experiences at school, the taxing demands of farmwork on his small body, and his increasing weariness over his family's transience. Once readers factor into their understanding of Panchito all of the various stressors that arise in the boy's life—and drive him at one point as a mere seventh grader to need to take "two of Papá's aspirins and lay down" (85)—a stunning matrix of hardship takes shape.

GROWING UP IN AND THROUGH *THE CIRCUIT*

> By participating in this fluid space (the classroom) in which
> contradictions and conflict are played out, we can create an
> empathetic moment in which the classroom participants feel
> what it might be like to cross into the borderlands.
>
> —Teresa McKenna, *Migrant Song: Politics and Process in*
> *Contemporary Chicano Literature*

All children grow up, and for many children growing up is hard to do, but Panchito grows up under unusually arduous conditions that precipitate in him a combination of resilience, wisdom, and compassion unusual in one so young. The numerous difficulties that he faces distress the boy but end up eliciting from him a strong and mature capacity for coming to terms with adversity. After fleeing his father's yelling in "Death Forgiven," Panchito explains that he ran to a storage shed where he could settle himself down:

> I fell to my knees and prayed and prayed for *El Perico*. The repetition of "*Santa María, Madre de Dios, ruega Señora por nosotros los pecadores ahora y en la hora de nuestra muerte, amen*," slowly comforted and soothed my soul. Then I prayed for my father. (60)

Rather than let himself be emotionally broken by the incident, Panchito manages to cope with it. He recomposes himself and pursues a course of action that offers some productive form of resolution for himself and, he hopes, for his father (against whom he could easily hold a grudge). In "To Have and to Hold," the boy's resilience is again tested. First, his little sister, Rorra, spoils his penny collection by spending his cherished 1865 and 1910 pennies on gumballs. Later, a fire burns down the decrepit house in which the family had been living while in Orosi and destroys a treasured notebook that holds a cumulative list of the spelling rules Panchito hoped would help him develop his English competency. By the end of this story, Panchito again manages, with some help from his mother, to resolve his distress and put events in a mature perspective. He accepts that at the age of four his sister cannot be completely blamed for her actions, and he realizes that since he already had memorized what was in his notebook, "It was not all lost" (112).

Undoubtedly, the presence in Panchito's life of other people who model resilience contributes to the development of his own strength.[11] Although his father is increasingly inclined to lose his composure as life on the Circuit wears on him, in general Panchito finds himself surrounded by examples of sacrifice, perseverance, and strength of character in the face of duress. One such person is Don Gabriel, who is introduced in "Learning the Game." He is a worker whom Papá, Roberto, and Panchito meet in the fields one day and who, it turns out, has left his family (including his three children) behind in Mexico in an effort to earn a better income in the fields of California. Over lunch, he reveals,

> I haven't seen [my children] for months. I didn't want to leave them, but I had no choice. We have to eat, you know. I send them a few dollars every month for food and things. I'd like to send them more, but after I pay Díaz for room and board and transportation, little is left. (89)

In this and in other instances, Panchito sees individuals working desperately hard for a better life for themselves and for their families. Consequently, he gleans from these individuals values that are integral to the development of resilience, such as sacrifice, hard work, and perseverance. Moreover, through the examples of these individuals he arrives at progressively more encompassing, more compassionate understandings of immigrant realities. As he bears witness to his mother "always [being] tired from all the work she did" (29), Roberto longing to go to school like other children, and Don Gabriel yearning to be reunited with his own children, Panchito becomes aware of and sensitive to the disappointment and suffering of other people. In the process, he progressively moves out of the naïveté of childhood, transcends childhood egocentrism, and actually begins formulating a rudimentary class consciousness.

In particular, Panchito becomes increasingly sensitive to the unfair, arbitrary distribution of privilege and power that leaves migrant workers an exploited and degraded social group. In "*El Angel de Oro*," he first stumbles into a foundational lesson on the arbitrary nature of privilege when a rainstorm floods a creek near the family's cabin in Corcoran and leaves several common gray fish suffocating in puddles left behind by the receding waters. All the while, a neighbor's goldfish swims comfortably in its bowl in a window that overlooks the puddles. Admittedly, in the desperation of the moment, Panchito is not fully conscious of the social and philosophical implications of the disparity between the fates of the gray fish and the goldfish, but he begins to realize not only the existential injustice of it all but also the potential for the coexistence of the two. After frantically working to save the dying fish by returning them to the creek, he decides to place the last of the rescued in the fishbowl where, to his contentment, he sees "The goldfish [swim] peacefully alongside the little gray fish" (50).

By the time readers reach "Learning the Game" a few stories later, they see Panchito's critical awareness becoming more pointed and more explicit when Don Gabriel confronts the foreman of a strawberry field who instructs him to tie around his waist a rope affixed to a plow so he can till the furrows in the same way an ox would. Panchito narrates that when Don Gabriel expresses his resentment over being reduced to doing the work of an animal, "The *contratista* walked up to Gabriel and yelled in his face, 'Well this isn't your country, idiot! You either do what I say or I'll have you fired!'" (91). Moments later, the confrontation becomes physical. After Don Gabriel begs that he not be fired because he has to support his family, Panchito relates:

> "I don't give a damn about your family!" the *contratista* replied, grabbing Gabriel
> by the shirt collar and pushing him. Gabriel lost his balance and fell backwards.
> As he hit the ground, the *contratista* kicked him in the side with the tip of his
> boot. Gabriel sprung up and, with both hands clenched, lunged at the *contratista*.
> White as a ghost, Díaz quickly jumped back. "Don't be stupid . . . your family," he
> stammered. Gabriel held back. His face was flushed with rage. (91–92)

Shaken, Panchito confesses, "I felt scared. I had not seen men fight before" (92), but afterward he says, "All day, while Gabriel and I hoed weeds, I kept thinking about what happened that morning. It made me angry and sad. Gabriel cursed as he hacked at the weeds" (92). The fact that Panchito is initially scared reflects the fact that the development of critical awareness can be an intimidating, even shocking experience because the secure—and naive—paradigms for understanding that the individual previously held have been shattered. After some reflection, however, Panchito transcends the initial shock that gripped him and begins to arrive at a complicated realization of the mistreatment and oppression of (fellow) fieldworkers.

As usually occurs in children's literature, the maturation of Panchito in *The Circuit* parallels and enables the maturation of the child reader. With and through Panchito, younger readers learn about the experiences of undocumented migrant workers and are positioned to feel compassion and empathy for a social group that has historically been subjected to vitriolic xenophobia and racism. Notably, the combination of enlightenment and empathy that becomes possible for younger readers allows for a transcendence of egocentrism that carries socially and politically progressive implications. Applicable to both Panchito and younger readers of *The Circuit*, in fact, is the idea explained by psychologists Dante Cichetti and Donald Cohen that "as youth develop and interact with elders and peers, their perceptions and behaviors change with social and cognitive development. They move from having an egocentric to a more sociocentric view of their world as they develop into more social beings" (632). While Panchito comes into an awareness of his own and other workers' standing within the migrant labor economy, younger readers of *The Circuit* begin to formulate more complicated, more compassionate, and more macrocosmic understandings of American society and the realities contained therein.

In a classroom setting or other such workshop venue, *The Circuit* can also serve as the basis for sophisticated critical conversations about the social and political issues that arise in the text. With some guidance, for example, even readers in middle school can critically press on the twofold consequences of the liminality that Jiménez depicts. First of all, the social invisibility of undocumented migrant workers constrains any possibility of concern and activism within the larger national community on their behalf. Migrant workers' being out of sight and out of mind results in obliviousness and apathy within the social mainstream and thereby results in the persistence of the status quo for the conditions in which migrant workers live and work. Second, as a socially alienated population, migrant workers are a silent population, estranged as they are from the means of media production. Thus disenfranchised, they are perfectly vulnerable to disparagement and distortion in dominant media venues ranging from talk radio to newspaper op-ed pieces to websites such as *Glenn Spencer's American Patrol Report*. Through a discussion of the historical correlation between social marginalization, economic disempowerment, and technologies of representation, young readers can interpret the reasons why, in dominant media, "the undocumented immigrant's image consists of a conglomeration of negative values and missing qualities" (Chavez, *Shadowed Lives* 18). Critical awareness of the fact that within the sphere of representation undocumented immigrants are powerless and subject to the whims of dominant society allows students to parse the direct relationship between social status and representational power and in essence arrive at Guy Debord's conclusion in *The Society of the Spectacle* (1994) that "the spectacle is capital accumulated to the point that it becomes images" (17).

With the final story, "Moving Still," younger readers can additionally explore the constitution of imagined communities and interrogate the "problem" of defining American identity. The scene revolves around a homework assignment that requires Panchito to memorize and recite an excerpt from the Preamble to the Declaration of Independence. On the day of his recitation, Panchito is at his desk doing his final preparations, repeating to himself, "We hold these truths to be self-evident: that all men are created equal; that they are endowed by their creator with certain inalienable rights; that among these are life, liberty, and the pursuit of happiness" (134). At that instant, however, an immigration officer enters the classroom with the school principal. In a narration of what Jiménez cites as one of the most traumatizing ordeals of his childhood (Fischer 4), Panchito relates:

> The instant I saw the green uniform, I panicked. I wanted to run but my legs would not move. I began to tremble and could feel my heart pounding against my chest as though it wanted to escape too. Miss Ehlis and the immigration officer walked up to me. Putting her right hand on my shoulder, and looking up at the officer, she said sadly, "This is him." My eyes clouded. I stood up and followed the officer out of the classroom and into his car marked "Border Patrol." I sat in the front seat as the officer drove down Broadway to Santa Maria High School to pick up Roberto. (134)

A difficult irony arises in the scene as a collision between the lines that Panchito has memorized and the de facto status of undocumented migrant laborers unfolds. At once, readers must reconcile the fact of the nation's dependence on undocumented farm labor, the fact of immigration laws, the spirit of the Declaration of Independence, and the humanity of those individuals such as Panchito and his family who migrate to the United States. There is, of course, no easy way to adjudicate these issues, which in and of itself allows readers to realize that the matter of Mexican immigration is far more complicated than popular discourses tend to acknowledge. In addition, the closing scene of *The Circuit* prods sophisticated critical thinking and critical conversations about the nature of imagined communities and the parameters and the policing of the American national community. In reading about the arrest and deportation of Panchito and his family, readers bear witness to a succinct dramatization of the systematic and relentless "excision of the Mexican body from the American body politic" (Lima 25) that scholars such as Lázaro Lima and Suzanne Oboler identify as the ongoing legacy of 1848. As the alienated yet complex relationship of Mexican immigrants to the American national community thus becomes starkly legible to younger readers, the opportunity arises for further research into the unstable, arbitrary, and oppressive ways that "America" and "American" have been defined over the course of the nation's history.

By thus nurturing a rather savvy and sophisticated critical acumen at the same time that it imparts sociological insight, *The Circuit* emerges as an unusually effective and productive text for younger readers. Most immediate, it makes clear the nature of life for migrant workers, but over and above enabling an awareness of hitherto suppressed realities, the text allows for a challenging (re)examination of the function, the effects, and the inadequacy of contemporary discourses about Mexican immigration, Mexican immigrants, and the American national community. Fortunately, although the text elicits empathy and compassion for migrant worker experiences, it does not simply recycle the idealized myth of the United States as a beacon of hope for homeless and hopeless Mexicans. As noted by Lauren Berlant, a self-righteous sense of the United States as a land of unbridled freedom and opportunity often undergirds rhetoric about immigration. Drawing attention, in fact, to the flipside of the alarmist discourse that Chavez describes, Berlant argues that "immigration discourse is a central technology for the reproduction of patriotic nationalism: not just because the immigrant is seen as without a nation or resources and thus as deserving of pity or contempt, but because the immigrant is defined as *someone who desires America*" (*The Queen of America* 195). To be sure, the Jimenezes migrate to the United States in search of a better life, but rather than contribute to what Berlant calls "the symbolic implication immigration has on national vanity" (*The Queen of America* 196), *The Circuit* prompts critical questions and realizations that unsettle naive nationalism. In turn, younger readers of *The Circuit* end up uniquely equipped to read, assess, and respond to the fraught discourses about Mexican immigration, Mexican immigrants, and the American national community that presently abound and that they will certainly encounter as they continue to grow up.

NOTES

···

1. Though the book was originally categorized as fiction and even garnered, among other distinctions, the Boston Globe-Horn Book Award for Fiction, Jiménez has indicated that *The Circuit* is indeed an autobiography of his childhood. In a rather endearing manner, however, he always insists on pointing out that the text features moments where he has drawn upon imagination and creativity to compensate for forgotten details of his childhood. Ever cautious about avoiding any possible deception of readers, when asked whether *The Circuit* is fact or fiction, he always explains, "My stories are approximately 90 percent fact and 10 percent fiction. Some of the smaller details are fiction, but the experiences are real" (Fischer 4). When pressed on what is fact and fiction, he draws attention to minor details that only underscore the autobiographical nature of the text. For example, in one interview, Jiménez reveals, "In the title story, 'The Circuit,' I could not remember the number of the school bus [that picked me up and consequently I made up a number]. I also invented [in the same story] page 125, the number of the page I was asked to read in Mr. Lema's class" (Fischer 4). If "inventions" such as these are all that keep the text from being certified as unqualified nonfiction (which of course is an impossible ideal anyway), the author need not worry about becoming the next James Frey (the now-disgraced author of the now-debunked "memoir," *A Million Little Pieces* [2005]).

2. Interestingly, Jiménez has mentioned that when he began writing *The Circuit*, he did not have a child audience in mind (Carger 15). He cites his wish "to voice the experiences of a large sector of our society that has been frequently ignored" (Fischer 3) without any particular regard for the possible age range of his readership. Likewise incognizant of the potential of *The Circuit* to reach younger readers, the University of New Mexico Press initially marketed Jiménez's book as an immigrant narrative more suited to undergraduate Chicano Studies courses than to middle-school curricula. Soon enough, however, and to Jiménez's surprise (Carger 15), teachers, librarians, and reviewers welcomed *The Circuit* as a much-needed "multicultural" autobiography appropriate for younger readers due to the age of the narrator as well as its stylistic accessibility.

3. Jiménez has actually found that *The Circuit* resonates with immigrant readers from a variety of backgrounds. In an interview, he reveals, "I get letters [of appreciation] not only from Mexican Americans but from other immigrants. One I received recently was from a Japanese girl. I've gotten them from Vietnamese too. And when I speak in public places and meetings, I've had Asian Americans and East Asian Americans say that their experience is very similar to the one I describe in [the story] 'Inside Out'" (Carger 16).

4. Recent books for children that depict the experiences of Mexican immigrants include picture books such as *Calling the Doves* (1995) and *The Upside Down Boy* (2000) by Juan Felipe Herrera, *Friends from the Other Side* (1993) by Gloria Anzaldúa, *Tomás and the Library Lady* (1997) by Pat Mora, *América Is Her Name* (1998) by Luis Rodríguez, and *My Diary from Here to There* (2002) by Amada Irma Pérez. Irene Beltran Hernandez's *Across the Great River* (1989), Pam Muñoz Ryan's *Esperanza Rising* (2000), and Ann Jaramillo's *La Linea* (2006) are a few of the longer works available for older readers that portray Mexican immigration. For a more complete listing and review of picture books about migrant farmworkers, see Scott Beck's "Children of Migrant Farmworkers in Picture Storybooks: Reality, Romanticism, and Representation."

5. To borrow a neologism from Lisa Lowe, Mexican immigrants have historically had an "alien-nated" relationship to the American national community. As Lowe says of Asians in America, Mexican immigrants have been figured in terms of a "critical apposition" (12)

to the American national community that has been "refracted through images, memories, and narratives—submerged, fragmented, and sedimented in a historical unconscious" (12). Arnoldo de León's *They Called Them Greasers: Anglo Attitudes toward Mexicans in Texas, 1821–1900* (1983) and William Nericcio's *Tex{t}-Mex: Seductive Hallucinations of the "Mexican" in America* (2007) offer comprehensive overviews of the historical emergence, evolution, and sedimentation of the alienated status of Mexicans in America. In *Operation Gatekeeper: The Rise of the "Illegal Alien" and the Making of the U.S.-Mexico Boundary* (2002), Joseph Nevins provides an illuminating and focused discussion of the nefarious machinations and ramifications of popular discourses about Mexican immigration.

6. In this formulation of *The Circuit* as a site of an encounter between individuals of potentially different subject positions, I am consciously drawing upon and modulating Mary Louise Pratt's conceptualization of contact zones as "the space of colonial encounters, the space in which people geographically and historically separated come into contact with each other and establish ongoing relations, usually involving conditions of coercion, radical inequality, and intractable conflict" (6–7).

7. While anything that the Houghton Mifflin Company does must be understood as motivated by profit potential, the decision of this major publisher to reissue *The Circuit* in 1999 and to publish two sequels, *Breaking Through* (2001) and *Reaching Out* (2008), is a highly significant turn of events because it has made greater visibility and wider distribution possible for Jiménez's autobiographical trilogy.

8. English-only efforts hit a high point in 1995 when in Congress alone five such initiatives were put forth (Anderson A1). Susan Headden et al. provide an overview of the fervor for monolingualism that swept the United States that year in their article, "One Nation, One Language?"

9. My reading of shared ignorance between Panchito and what Martín-Rodríguez would call a "culturally distant reader" is informed by Martín-Rodríguez's delineation of similar dynamics in Rudolfo Anaya's *Bless Me, Ultima* (1972) (115).

10. De León's overview of nineteenth-century conceptualizations of "Mexicans [as] a dirty, putrid people" (17) provides an informative background for understanding the origins of contemporary figurations of Mexican immigrants as hygienically depraved. Discussions by scholars such as Lauren Berlant ("National Brands"), Robyn Wiegman, and Karen Coats on the imbrications of race, the body, and the constitution of the (white) American nation are worth consulting for thinking through the machinations and implications of the ongoing abjection of Mexican immigrants, especially the construction of them as inconsistent with—and a threat to—the (white, hygienic) American national body politic.

11. Incidentally, several sociological studies have found the development of resilience a common—and crucial—attribute amongst migrant workers in the United States. Studies by Ellen Ernst Kossek et al. and José Rubén Parra-Cardona et al. provide useful overviews of this phenomenon.

WORKS CITED

Anaya, Rudolfo. *Bless Me, Ultima*. Berkeley, CA: Tonatiuh, 1972.
Anderson, Curt. "Speaking of English—House GOP Discusses Official Language Bills."
    The Press-Enterprise, 19 October 1995, A1.

Anzaldúa, Gloria. *Friends from the Other Side*. San Francisco: Children's Book P, 1993.

Beck, Scott A. "Children of Migrant Farmworkers in Picture Storybooks: Reality, Romanticism, and Representation." *Children's Literature Association Quarterly* 34, no. 2 (Summer 2009): 99–137.

Berlant, Lauren. "National Brands/National Body: *Imitation of Life*." In *Comparative American Identities: Race, Sex, and Nationality in the Modern Text*, edited by Hortense J. Spillers, 110–40. New York: Routledge, 1991.

———. *The Queen of America Goes to Washington City: Essays on Sex and Citizenship*. Durham, NC: Duke UP, 1997.

Carger, Chris Liska. "Talking with Francisco Jiménez." *Book Links* (December 2001/January 2002): 14–19.

Chávez, Leo R. *The Latino Threat: Constructing Immigrants, Citizens, and the Nation*. Stanford: Stanford UP, 2008.

———. *Shadowed Lives: Undocumented Immigrants in American Society*. Fort Worth, TX: Harcourt Brace, 1992.

Cicchetti, Dante, and Donald J. Cohen. *Developmental Psychopathology: Theory and Method*. Hoboken, NJ: Wiley, 2006.

Coats, Karen. *Looking Glasses and Neverlands: Lacan, Desire, and Subjectivity in Children's Literature*. Iowa City: U of Iowa P, 2004.

Day, Deanna. "Persevering with Hope: Francisco Jiménez." *Language Arts* 83, no. 3 (January 2006): 266–70.

Debord, Guy. *The Society of the Spectacle*. Translated by Donald Nicholson-Smith. New York: Zone Books, 1994.

De León, Arnoldo. *They Called Them Greasers: Anglo Attitudes toward Mexicans in Texas, 1821–1900*. Austin: U of Texas P, 1983.

Fischer, David Marc. "Your Story Is the Story of Our Family." *Writing* 23, no. 5 (February/March 2001): 3–5.

Frey, James. *A Million Little Pieces*. London: John Murray, 2003.

Garza de Cortes, Oralia. "Behind the Golden Door: The Latino Immigrant Child in Literature and Films for Children." In *The New Press Guide to Multicultural Resources for Young Readers*, edited by Daphne Muse, 446–52. New York: The New P, 1997.

Glenn Spencer's America Patrol Report. 6 July 2009. <http://www.americanpatrol.com>.

Headden, Susan, Linda Rodriguez Bernfield, Sally Deneen, Missy Daniel, Monika Guttman, Barbara Burgower Hordern, Scott Minerbrook, Debra A. Schwartz, and Jill Jordan Sieder. "One Nation, One Language? Would Making English the Nation's Official Language Unite the Country or Divide It?" *U.S. News & World Report* 25 Sep 1995: 38-42.

Hernandez, Irene Beltran. *Across the Great River*. Houston: Arte Público, 1989.

Herrera, Juan Felipe. *Calling the Doves*. San Francisco: Children's Book P, 1995.

———. *The Upside Down Boy*. San Francisco: Children's Book P, 2000.

Holte, James Craig. *The Ethnic I: A Sourcebook for Ethnic-American Autobiography*. New York: Greenwood, 1988.

Huck, Charlotte S. *Children's Literature in the Elementary School*. New York: Holt, Rinehart, and Winston, 1976.

Jaramillo, Ann. *La Linea*. New York: Square Fish, 2006.

Jiménez, Francisco. *Breaking Through*. Boston: Houghton Mifflin, 2001.

———. *The Christmas Gift/El Regalo de Navidad*. Boston: Houghton Mifflin, 2000.

———. *The Circuit: Stories from the Life of a Migrant Child*. Albuquerque: U of New Mexico P, 1997.

————. *La Mariposa.* Boston: Houghton Mifflin, 1998.

————. *Reaching Out.* Boston: Houghton Mifflin, 2008.

Kossek, Ellen Ernst, Darrell Meece, Marguerite E. Barratt, and Beth Emily Prince. "U.S. Latino Migrant Farmworkers: Managing Acculturative Stress and Conserving Work-Family Resources." In *Work and Family: An International Research Perspective,* edited by Steven A.Y. Poelmans, 47-70. Mahwah, NJ: Lawrence Erlbaum, 2005.

Lima, Lázaro. *The Latino Body: Crisis Identities in American Literary and Cultural Memory.* New York: New York UP, 2007.

Lowe, Lisa. *Immigrant Acts: On Asian American Cultural Politics.* Durham, NC: Duke University Press, 1996.

Martín-Rodríguez, Manuel. *Life in Search of Readers: Reading (in) Chicano/a Literature.* Albuquerque: U of New Mexico P, 2003.

McKenna, Teresa. *Migrant Song: Politics and Process in Contemporary Chicano Literature.* Austin: U of Texas P, 1997.

Mora, Pat. *Tomás and the Library Lady.* New York: Dragonfly, 1997.

Nericcio, William Anthony. *Tex{t}-Mex: Seductive Hallucinations of the "Mexican" in America.* Austin: U of Texas P, 2007.

Nevins, Joseph. *Operation Gatekeeper: The Rise of the "Illegal Alien" and the Making of the U.S.-Mexico Boundary.* New York: Routledge: 2002.

Oboler, Suzanne. *Ethnic Labels, Latino Lives: Identity and the Politics of (Re)Presentation in the United States.* Minneapolis: U of Minnesota P, 1995.

Parra-Cardona, José Rubén, Laurie A. Bulock, David R. Imig, Francisco A. Villarruel, and Steven J. Gold. "'Trabajando Duro Todos los Días': Learning from the Life Experiences of Mexican-Origin Migrant Families." *Family Relations* 55, no. 3 (Jul 2006): 361–75.

Pérez, Amada Irma. *My Diary from Here to There.* San Francisco: Children's Book P, 2002.

Pratt, Mary Louise. *Imperial Eyes: Travel Writing and Transculturation.* New York: Routledge, 1992.

Rodríguez, Luis J. *América Is Her Name.* Willimantic, CT: Curbstone P, 1998.

Ryan, Pam Muñoz. *Esperanza Rising.* New York: Scholastic, 2000.

Schuck, Peter H., and Rogers M. Smith. *Citizenship without Consent: Illegal Aliens in the American Polity.* New Haven: Yale UP, 1985.

Watson, Julia. "Toward an Anti-Metaphysics of Autobiography." In *The Culture of Autobiography: Constructions of Self-Representation,* edited by Robert Folkenflik, 57–79. Stanford: Stanford UP, 1993.

Wiegman, Robyn. *American Anatomies: Theorizing Race and Gender.* Durham, NC: Duke UP, 1995.

FURTHER READING

Bradford, Clare. *Unsettling Narratives: Postcolonial Readings of Children's Literature.* Waterloo, ON.: Wilfrid Laurier UP, 2007.

Day, Frances Ann. *Latina and Latino Voices in Literature for Children and Teenagers.* Portsmouth, NH: Heinemann, 1997.

McGillis, Roderick, ed. *Voices of the Other: Children's Literature and the Postcolonial Context.* New York: Garland, 2000.

Reséndez, Gerald A. "Chicano Children's Literature." In *Chicano Literature: A Reference Guide*, edited by Julio A. Marínez and Francisco A. Lomelí, 107–21. Westport, CT: Greenwood P, 1985.

Saldívar, Ramón. *Chicano Narrative: The Dialectics of Difference.* Madison: U of Wisconsin P, 1990.

Smith, Angela. "Paddington Bear: A Case Study of Immigration and Otherness." *Children's Literature in Education* 37, no. 1 (March 2006): 35–50.

PART IV

INNOCENCE AND AGENCY

"MY BOOK AND HEART SHALL NEVER PART": READING, PRINTING, AND CIRCULATION IN THE *NEW ENGLAND PRIMER*

COURTNEY WEIKLE-MILLS

THE New England Primer *taught early Americans how to read, selling approximately five million copies between the seventeenth and nineteenth centuries. Though no concrete evidence confirms the primer's existence before the earliest extant copies of 1727, it is likely that the text was printed decades earlier and not in New England. An entry for the "New England Primer" appeared in the London Stationers Registry in 1683, and a letter sent to the colonies in 1685 declared that it was out of stock throughout the city (Cohen 55).[1] The first colonial version was probably compiled by nonconformist printer Benjamin Harris between 1687 and 1690, using the least inflammatory bits of his anti-Catholic Protestant Tutor (1679) as well as materials written by New England divines. By the eighteenth century, the text's ubiquity was well known, but it is difficult to pin down because it was always changing. Few of its many editions were exact copies of one another, but together they form a repository of early children's reading materials and a catalog of colonists' beliefs and rituals. Because even the earliest versions of the* Primer *were composed of works that had been published elsewhere, the* Primer—*like the child made in God's image—can be said to have always been a copy. It is fitting, then, that the major theme of the* Primer *is replication, a further instantiation of its pages within the heart of the child reader.*

At the heart of the *New England Primer*, within its distinctive but frequently revised pictorial alphabet, stands a line that rarely altered. "My Book and Heart Shall Never Part," referring to the Bible but more immediately to the *Primer* itself, is the text's most direct articulation of its pedagogy (9).[2] Yet, despite its implication of stability, the "H" couplet, from which this line is taken, reflects several reading practices and modes of authority that faded into and out of currency during the *Primer*'s nearly two-hundred-year history. On one level, the line describes traditional methods of teaching reading through repetition. Using an instructional technique that stemmed from catechizing, children memorized verses "by heart" so that they could reproduce them exactly in recitation.[3] This teaching method was tied to a patriarchal social model, in which clergymen and fathers transmitted elementary religious knowledge to those in their care.

But just as strongly, the couplet reflects the emerging notion that children should read to develop and nurture an interior realm of experience, sometimes figured as "the closet of the heart." This imperative stemmed from the Protestant idea that each believer should have unmediated contact with God and his word. Over the course of the seventeenth and eighteenth centuries, this belief gave rise to emotional and personalized modes of reading. As David D. Hall observes, "To read was to feel; the act of reading involved the affective self" (*Worlds of Wonder* 40). Such contemplative reading influenced the expansion of print culture in the new world, as book production developed in order to meet the growing need for devotional materials. The *Primer*'s inclusion of joyous prayers and solemn meditations on death suggest that these individual rituals were central to its pedagogy. While solitary reading practices had long been available to clergy, they now involved the most unpracticed readers. A poem that appeared in a 1750 version of the *Primer* envisions the child reading alone: "Though I am young, a little one / If I can speak and go alone / Then I must learn to know the Lord / And learn to read his holy word" (*The New England Primer* 18).[4]

The connection between reading and solitary reverie opened the possibility for new interactions between readers and their books. Though the *Primer* arose within a culture founded on patriarchal authority and the strict interpretation of biblical texts, its emphasis on the literacy of the individual believer anticipated a shift toward self-government and the reader's participation in the creation of meaning. The *Primer*'s connection between children's learning and the feelings of the heart anticipates John Locke's argument that children must be taught to read "as a Thing of Delight" (51) so as not to impinge upon their sense of liberty, a pedagogical technique that later appeared in John Newbery's books as a command to "learn to love your book" (*The Child's New Play-Thing* 73).

The *Primer* bears the traces of several reading practices and ideological investments in part because it was a heavily redacted text, compiled by several authors from a variety of sources. But it was also a book that was constantly evolving.[5] As I argue in this essay, the *Primer* is best understood as a transitional text between patriarchal subjecthood and modern subjectivity, oral and textual culture, and ancient and early modern understandings of spirituality and the heart. These shifts, though uneven and gradual, grant child readers more room to engage freely with their books, supplementing the wisdom of parents and clergymen with the authority of their own convictions. But the transition from patriarchalism to individualism must also be understood as messy and incomplete, creating new bonds for the child reader. The *Primer*'s lasting emphasis on the love between child and book likely stems from the emotion's ability to liberate *and* constrain, which allowed early pedagogues to represent learning to read simultaneously as a devotional activity unregulated by traditional church hierarchies and as a lesson on how to "love" and submit oneself to the less tangible authorities of God, school, book, and state.

This pedagogy of autonomy through attachment corresponds with larger efforts in the text to wed authorization with control, self-making with textual conscription. An example of the *Primer*'s attempt to balance these aims can be found in the earliest 1727 version, which included the poem "The Child's Complaint." While the poem begins by chastising the child for loving play over prayer, it promises that if the child learns to surrender to God, he can have a voice: "For God will lend a gracious Ear / To what a Child can say" (68). Placed at the end of the text, the poem suggests that the power of self-expression was seen as the natural result of learning and submission. This lesson would become crucial to the American ideal of self-governance, which offered citizens liberty, but required that they learn to police their own actions and actively create their identities in line with established social codes. The quintessential early American schoolbook, the *Primer* eventually inaugurated a transition from subjecthood to citizenship, which was not so much a clear transition from patriarchal subjection to individual freedom, as the creation of individuals who, in the words of one nineteenth-century columnist, make liberty and restraint "love each other" ("From the Charleston Courier" 339).

In addition to providing an encapsulation of the *Primer*'s transitional politics, the couplet is relevant to current debates within children's literature studies between seeing children's books as transmitting adult authority and as validating children's potential for self-determination. Pointing to a history and theory of children's reading in which these functions are not mutually exclusive, the book-heart image brings together at least two ways of understanding children's reading in general, based on metaphors of "printing" and "circulation." While the notion that reading could be a means of "writing" upon the heart is a biblical trope, print metaphors first became attached to children's education during the Renaissance. Embracing the technology of the printing press, pedagogues argued that reading could be a means of stamping lessons onto the child's heart. Evoking a side-by-side comparison, "My Book and Heart Shall Never Part" elicits the child's promise to replicate the book faithfully so that her interior recesses render a copy of the text. A similar image of reading appears in the John Rogers poem, in which he asks his children to keep his words "within your heart, / and print them in your thought" (30).[6]

As recent conversations in children's literature studies have noted, these comparisons between reading and printing have led to assumptions that children's identity formation through reading is primarily passive. Karen Sánchez-Eppler observes that the child represents "the strongest exemplar of how reading might shape identity and character, precisely because children are viewed as least able to evaluate or resist" what they read (10). The *Primer* is often read through these assumptions as a text that coerces its readers into adopting rigid religious identities. Yet, as Sánchez-Eppler goes on to say, beginning in the eighteenth century, child readers were also considered "repositories of feeling and fantasy" (13). The idea that children are passively "printed upon" by texts is complicated by the attachments and insights that children are meant to form as readers.

In the early American context, the print trope was complicated by scientific investigations of the active functions of the heart, as well as the *actual* composition and printing of books such as the *Primer*, which had not achieved the uniformity of recent printing technology. In a notable point of correlation, the expansion of print circulation accompanied discoveries about the heart's role in the body's circulation. From ancient times, the heart had been understood as a source of human emotion and sensation. Stemming from this classical trope, the Bible imagined the heart as a surface of the body on which God could write divine law and religious passion. Correspondingly, physicians assumed that the heart only produced and stored blood, a parallel to the metaphorical notion of the heart as a storehouse of learning. With William Harvey's publication of *Exercitatio Anatomica de Motu Cordis et Sanguinis in Animalibus* (1628), scientists came to understand that blood actually returned to the heart to be renewed and recirculated.[7] While Eric Jager has argued that this idea of the heart as a pumping organ demystified understandings of the heart as a seat of knowledge and feeling, the book and heart metaphor in the *Primer* suggests that these medical advancements also gave rise to new understandings of heart as a site of reciprocal, emotionally charged interaction between reader and text.

Though the exegesis of texts had long been available to clergymen, the modes of reading inculcated by the *Primer* opened the possibility that readers would not simply be "written upon" by reading, but would learn to interpret their books and recirculate their messages in new forms. In this way, "My Book and Heart Shall Never Part" does not describe a one-way transmission, but a circuit. Children came to act as the living hearts of their books, keeping them alive by adapting their contents to fit their lives and closets. Printers, in turn, revitalized texts by changing elements that had gotten stale or outdated. At the same time, as suggested by the other bookish primer line, "Thy Life to Mend / This Book Attend," books were understood as a source of spiritual renewal, mimicking the cleansing function of the heart-as-organ (8).

This idea of reading as a site of renewal is reflected in the actual circumstances of printing and circulation in early America, which made a text such as the *Primer* anything but stable. While most versions of the *Primer* included a few common elements, including the syllabarium, lexicon, and alphabet couplets, these features were frequently rewritten over the course of the book's circulation. In addition to these central features, the *Primer* contained a variety of poems, dialogues, and prayers, such as the John Rogers poem, "The Dialogue between Christ, Youth, and the Devil," and Isaac Watts' "A Cradle Hymn," but the exact selection differed from edition to edition. Due to the virtual nonexistence of copyright laws in the colonies, as well as to the habits and limitations of early printers, these constituent parts were frequently edited, reordered, omitted, or supplemented with new material. Printers—many of whom probably read the book as children—rewrote the alphabet couplets, changed the woodcuts, added new religious materials, and interspersed features from different children's genres, including conduct books, fables, almanacs, chapbooks, spelling books, bestiaries, and playbooks.

As it became important within Protestant religious culture for readers to have access to books of their own, it was increasingly difficult for authorities to control the versions of the texts to which readers might be exposed. Throughout the eighteenth century, there were over twenty different versions of the *Primer* printed in Boston alone, with more variation occurring farther afield. Charles Hartman's bibliography lists 278 different editions of the *Primer* in fifty-nine cities, which in addition to Boston, New York, and Philadelphia include small centers of commerce such as Portsmouth, Pittsburgh, and Worcester. Though not every edition was unique—especially after 1830 when printers adopted an archival approach to the text—multiple variants arose based on the whims and resources of bookmakers. Through circulation, the text's elements were reimagined and renewed.

Though we have only a few records of how readers experienced the text (most of which come from late in its reign as the American schoolbook of choice) what we can surmise about the *Primer*'s readership suggests that its replication in the child's heart likely mirrored its inexact reprinting: some things inscribed faithfully upon the memory, others adapted to fit the specific needs and visions of readers. Like the *Primer*, the child reader is best understood as a hybrid, shaped by the variety of discourses circulating in New England and blending the cultural expectations of religious culture with an individual experience of the world. Though colonial New England is often portrayed as a monolithic Calvinist religious culture, Anna Mae Duane has suggested that colonists saw hybridity as an inevitable, though threatening, result of children's contact with the new world. The *Primer* emerged and thrived during a time in which the culture was being increasingly destabilized. The Halfway Covenant of 1662, which preceded the *Primer* by a few decades, was designed to address settler children whose distance from old world customs had made them unwilling to accede to the beliefs of their parents.[8] The *Primer* represents both an attempt to rein in this new generation through education and the difficulties in doing so. As the colonies were transformed into provinces and then U.S. states, orthodox religious culture was further diluted and the *Primer* was subject to more and more variations. The text's composition and readership resembles Hall's description of cultural transmission as a "muddied, multilayered process," in which individuals collect and assemble "bits and pieces of past belief" from a "loosely bounded set of symbols and motifs" (*Worlds of Wonder* 11, 18).

Resembling the innovations and changes made by printers in the early American period, the child reader's self-creation through reading meant choosing from and reworking a set of possibilities. Notably, John Rogers's injunction to children to "print" his words on their thought envisions them not only as the raw material for printing, but as printers, allowing them to imagine participating in the incessant rewriting and reassembling of the book. A list of occupations in a 1750 Boston version of the *Primer* further urges children to take on the role of "book-binder" and "PRINTER" (the only trade in all caps). In some rare cases, child readers literally did this work; Isaiah Thomas, one of the most important early American printers, set the type for the *Primer* as an apprentice at age eight and later sold at least three different versions in his print shop (Thomas 143). In the *Primer*'s later years, child readers imitated the work of printers by engaging in their own in-text revisions in crayon and pencil.

Even if children did not write in their books, we might imagine that the multiple reprintings of the *Primer* had similar effects as Ann Howey's recent interpretation of "retellings" of children's stories. Even as retellings limit "the ways in which new meanings might be constructed," they "suggest the power of readers—even child readers—to construct meaningful self-narratives" (86–87). Howey's argument is indebted to the work of reception theorists, who have long argued that a single text may take on multiple meanings, so that each reader essentially reads a different text. The *Primer*'s various printings no doubt point toward the even greater variation in the ways that it was read and interpreted by the several generations who used it as a textbook and companion. Thus, while the *Primer* insists upon the authority of texts, its continual reimagining suggests that books are also dependent for their meaning upon the books that readers understand themselves to be reading: the ones that appear in their hearts.

As the book-heart couplet suggests, what was meant to keep children from abandoning their books altogether was love. As an emotion that was considered at times compulsory, involuntary, and volitional, love unsettles the usual way of thinking about child readers, since its voluntary quality denies the complete domination of the reader by the text and its insistence on attachment complicates the reader's freedom to diverge from its lessons. Seen in this way, "My Book and Heart Shall Never Part" registers the reader's acceptance of constraint in not departing *fully* from the text and forges a partnership in the creation of its meanings. The book-heart couplet demands, as Katherine Jones does in her article on Childhood Studies, that scholars recognize "the [child] reader and the text as both acting upon and constraining each other" (290–91). Tracing the *Primer* from the seventeenth to the nineteenth century, I argue that the book continued to circulate because it was continually reconstituted, urging children to integrate their reading rituals into the structures validated by the community while reimagining its contents in light of their changing experiences.

Children's reading has long been understood as a site of cultural reproduction. This idea was especially important in the new world given that "the American Puritans looked to the child to reflect the future of their parents' errand"

(Duane 64). Arguing that their learning could not be "buried in the grave of [their] forefathers," the Massachusetts General Court instituted laws requiring reading instruction for children and apprentices in 1642 and 1647.[9] Reading was taught as part of the transmission of religious beliefs. The word "primer" first meant a book of basic religious knowledge and only later came to signify alphabets and primary reading materials. Children became familiar with the *Primer*'s contents within the context of family worship services, which regularly included recitation and drilling in the catechism. As late as 1790, a woodcut appeared in the frontispiece of the *Primer* with children praying on their knees to God and also kneeling before their parents, with their books in hand. As the positioning of this picture at the beginning of the *Primer* suggests, these deferential practices were considered important aids to literacy.

Though most settlers' first contact with religious books was aural, colonial authorities devoted so much attention to reading instruction because New England was becoming an increasingly textual culture. As Matthew P. Brown has shown, ministers assumed that their congregations had access to at least a few religious books and used text-based practices to structure rituals at home, church, and school (21). In addition, printed books were central to the community's imagination of itself as a new incarnation of the Bible in the new world, which created a constant referential flipping back and forth between text and experience. New Englanders imagined living individuals as extensions of the Bible, such as the new Moses or Nehemiah. An elegy written for John Cotton in 1653 described him as an entire "living breathing Bible [in which] Gospel and law, in's heart, had each its column" (Woodbridge 28). As implied by another *Primer* line that rarely changed, "In Adam's Fall, We Sinned All," children were also thought to embody biblical books, most closely the book of Genesis and its tragic hero, Adam. These typological connections prompted children to see themselves as "copies" of older events and persons, mirroring the reproductive similitude of print.

As the phrase "we sinned all" implies, the major biblical event that was "copied" in each generation was original sin, which was often described using metaphors from print culture. For instance, in the Rogers poem, "I know I am a sinner born / From the original" imagines the inheritance of original sin in each new individual as comparable to the processes of print reproduction (35). The widespread propagation of printed texts provided an apt metaphor for the omnipresence of sin and the inescapable need for repentance. Individuals were thought to be shaped and constrained through these processes of textual replication. For instance, David H. Watters argues that the child reader of the *Primer* is meant to "[enclose] an authoritative text in his heart and then ['publish'] it in prayers and holy behavior" (203).

In the seventeenth-century imagination, Adam was the source not only of sin but also of subjugation, both for the child and the political subject. Robert Filmer claimed in 1680 that the "children of Adam" could not "be free" because their filial subjection had been replicated in each new person over time (*Patriarcha* 7). This patriarchal logic affected all levels of society. Cotton's *Milk for Babes* catechism, frequently included in the *Primer*, argues that the fifth commandment applies to "all . . . superiours, whether in family, school, church and commonwealth" (45). Print was a means of continuing these hierarchies in generations to come. Cotton Mather, who wrote over four hundred religious books in his lifetime, imagined children as sponges who would soak up the lessons of their books. In a 1705 sermon, he demands that they "look . . . into the Bible that lies open before you, and Matter or Prayer will pour in upon you" (*The Religion of the Closet* 10). By becoming copies of their books, children were meant to ensure the replication of the existing social order.

Yet, by late seventeenth century, these patriarchal notions of children as copies of biblical texts came to coexist with emerging ideas of children as "blank slates."[10] These ideas were attractive because they provided a new metaphor for transmitting authority through print, but they also complicated the replication of patriarchal hierarchies by suggesting that children could play a part in self-writing. The blank slate metaphor is traceable even within the earliest versions of the *Primer*, but it would become more prominent in the mid-eighteenth century due to the Great Awakening, which prompted evangelical revisions to the text.[11] The revivalist ministries of this period associated sinful biblical characters with their redeemed counterparts, such as Adam with Jesus, and Eve with Mary. While this Christ-based iconography did not fully replace the *Primer*'s preoccupation with original sin, the older elements blended with imagery recognizing the voice of the child as a believer shaped by her own choices. For instance, a 1735 evangelical edition of the *Primer* suggests that the child may yet be innocent of sin, like Christ: "I must not Sin as others do, Lest I lie down in Sorrows too" (*The New-England Primer, Enlarged for the More Easy Attaining the True Reading of English* 70).

The evangelical revisions of the *Primer* were part of an ongoing shift within New England religious culture from patriarchal hierarchy to individual spiritual responsibility. While in a strictly patriarchal system children were thought to inherit the beliefs of their parents, most eighteenth-century divines argued that parents' authority over their children's souls was limited.[12] This shift was the logical result of the doctrine of "free grace," which understood each individual's fate as already printed in God's book, but in practice, the doctrine granted individuals more autonomy in *discovering* their salvation and receiving the grace of God. In this light, typological comparisons between children and Adam or Christ suggest the beginning of a new, revised "draft" of biblical events, in which the child might be simultaneously constrained by humanity's sinful past and given the freedom to act anew.[13] In addition to ensuring the replication of biblical events and the perpetuation of human sin, reading brought about the renewal of mankind. As children made their hearts in the image of their books, book and child became *like* hearts in that they were instruments for the recirculation of the traditional beliefs, as well as a locus of regeneration between old and new, sin and rebirth, ancient traditions and modern contexts.

Because children were seen as spiritually independent of their parents, ministers recognized the importance of their conversion experiences, which were memorialized in books such as *A Token for Children* (1700) by James Janeway and Cotton Mather and *Early Piety, Exemplified in Elizabeth Butcher of Boston* (1725). These conversion narratives, like the *Primer*, prompted children to replicate "examples" of pious youth, but they also recognized the importance of children's experiences and were frequently presented as representations of children's voices. For instance, the author of *The Compleat Scholler* (1666) insists that Caleb Vernon's narrative consists of "relicks at last . . . faithfully set down for you and yours in writing from his mouth" (1). *A Legacy for Children: Being Some of the Last Expressions, and Dying Sayings, of Hannah Hill* (1717) is "signed" H. H., even though Hannah was dead by the time the text was published (22). As the adult compilers' role in collecting, editing, and authoring these narratives suggests, children's lives were still made to conform to adults' expectations and biblical conventions. Nonetheless, the texts assume children's participation in writing their own stories.

The *Primer*'s compiling of multiple genres indicates that the child's worldly inheritance was not limited to sin but was composed of texts, which could be selectively copied into their hearts. The poem attributed to John Rogers provides a model for this selective self-writing. Despite his frequently cited metaphor of printing on the child's thought, the actual "book" that he leaves his children is a compilation of his experiences, as personal as a face: "I leave you here a little book / for you to look upon, / That you may see your father's face / when he is dead and gone" (30). Using Rogers's face-book as a model, child readers were encouraged to use books to create their own interior texts by meditating upon verses that they found meaningful. For instance, Mather supplied all of his children with commonplace books in which they could reflect upon their reading. Thomas White's 1702 children's book, *A Little Book for Little Children*, printed a large selection of an eight-year-old boy's commonplace, including eighty-four bible verses he deemed important (60). The church fathers perhaps failed to fully anticipate the consequences of these practices in authorizing children to interpret texts in accordance with their lives. The conversion narratives occasionally even license child readers to disobey the commands of their parents if they conflict with their own interpretation of their spiritual requirements. For instance, in one story, a child with poor eyesight disobeys his parents' order not to read the Bible and is lauded for his devotion, even though it causes him to go blind. By expressing both respect for and anxiety about children's literacy and authority, this story represents a culture that was coming to terms with new notions of the individual's right and ability to define his place in the world through reading.

This newfound emphasis on the importance of self-examination led authority figures to notice drawbacks in the usual ways of teaching reading through recitation. Clergymen feared that children might adopt "ceremonial piety" in which they would perform lessons in the sight of authority figures without integrating them into their hearts. They were horrified to find that, when they switched the order of their questioning, children would give perfectly memorized answers for the wrong questions. The first recorded account of a reader's response to the *Primer* reflects an even more anxious image of oral drilling, suggesting that there was some ambivalence about forcing children to repeat the contents of their primers. In 1693, the strange "performances" of Katherine Branch, a servant girl, were offered as testimony against Elizabeth Clawson, who was being tried as a witch in Connecticut. Kate claimed that she was put under the control of Clawson's spirit, who ordered her to sing, dance, and recite from her primer. Commissioner Johahn Sellack testifies,

> Kate rehersed a great many verses, which are in some primers, & allsoe ye dialoge between Christ, ye yoong man & the dieull . . . & sayd why doe I say these things; you do not loue them. (qtd. in Taylor 115–16)

Reflecting the colonists' belief that they were battling the devil for their children's hearts, Kate's recitation signified to the court not her piety but her possession by a *demonic adult*, who was forcing her to say its contents aloud. This public uproar over a demon turned schoolmaster reflects the culture's emerging distrust of parental domination and traditional reading practices, as well as ambivalence about children's newfound, sometimes accusatory voices.

The antidote to "ceremonial piety" was "heart-piety," a devotion that would be performed within the invisible workings of the heart. Accounts of pious children from the period imagined that children would learn to read in private spaces, such as in the closet, in the corner, or even in bed. These imperatives granted children unprecedented autonomy as readers, though their freedom was of course limited by their containment within easily monitored spaces and by their use of approved texts. The *Primer*'s composition of prayers and meditations in addition to alphabets and lexicons suggests that it could be used for these private kinds of reading practices in addition to recitation, providing both a progressive curriculum of oral mastery and a constant companion for one's early years.[14]

Both progressive and ruminative types of reading, which Brown labels the "pilgrim and the bee," were common in early New England. "Pilgrim" reading structured texts such as *Pilgrim's Progress* (1678), in which the child takes a journey alongside the book's characters. Some elements of the *Primer* approximate a pilgrimage. For instance, the text often, though not always, begins by introducing children to the letters and then gradually introduces more difficult spiritual material. As Watters has observed, the first two alphabet couplets move from sin to regeneration, suggesting that "the act of reading" the *Primer* from beginning to end imitates "the passage of human life, and the grand drama of human history" (201).

What Brown calls "bee" reading, conversely, encourages readers to cycle back through the text's elements, reciting or praying some parts each day and returning to others as touchstones of faith. The *Primer*'s sequence, which changed from edition to edition, largely provides index-based alphabetical order, rather than story-based chronology. For instance, after the first two letters, the alphabet couplets typically bring biblical characters, animal fables, and proverbs into discontinuous succession. When used alongside the Bible, the couplets support the arrangement of stories for reflective purposes as much as a progressive reading of the Bible in course. The instructions for the section on the books of the Bible in the same 1727 edition claims that "the numeral Letters and Figures . . . serve for the ready finding of *any* Chapter, Psalm, and Verse in the Bible" (24, emphasis added).

The *Primer* invites readers to use the text on a regular basis by including prayers that are meant to be performed daily, such as "A Short Prayer for Children in the Morning." Likewise, many versions, such as the 1750 Boston edition, begin with oft-repeated elements of worship services, such the Creed, providing an opening for restarting the book. There were theological reasons for such cycling; as Brown observes, "devotional experience was cyclical as well as teleological . . . a lifelong process that was a linear growth in grace and a static meditation on sin" (30).

Because New Englanders' adherence to religious culture was ultimately, as Hall puts it, "partial, ambiguous, and even contradictory," the need for change of the *Primer*'s contents was ongoing (*Worlds of Wonder* 3). Depending on where children stood in relation to their faith at any given moment, their repeated contact with the *Primer* encouraged them to use the text to meet their spiritual needs. Printers' changes suggest possibilities for personal reordering. The "never" in the phrase "My Book and Heart Shall Never Part" implies that the child could continue reading the text even after learning its basic lessons, shifting their meanings to ever-new contexts.

Colonists' belief in the universal relevance of the *Primer* provides a way of understanding its often conflicting messages. For instance, the alphabet couplets ask child readers to navigate a world in which a lion and lamb may peacefully lie down together, at the same time that a cat kills mice and God eventually sends death to all. While religious exegesis posits that these competing meanings are held together by the sovereignty of God's will, the inconsistent images also suggest that the *Primer* recognizes the plurality of contexts to which his will might be applied by readers. In this way, the *Primer* reinforces the lessons of biblical exegesis found in captivity narratives such as Mary Rowlandson's *The Sovereignty & Goodness of God* (1682), which uses the Bible to explain her harrowing experiences with the Wampanoag Indians, as well as such seemingly unchristian acts as stealing a horse foot from a starving child's mouth (46). Though Puritan theology did not invite readers to freely associate meanings from texts, the Puritans' perchance for personalizing biblical readings to fit their own lives and to explain historical events may have been what opened the *Primer*'s contents to the inclusion of secular or unorthodox materials, which made its contents more applicable to the changing world.

Yet, even if its range of meanings could not be ultimately controlled, the *Primer* envisions that books could play a role in continually molding the child's heart to fit the structures valued by the community. In "Verses for Young Children," the child speaker casts God as the ultimate editor of his heart, ensuring that his internal text is compatible with God's larger book of grace: "Make my Heart in thy Statutes found, / And make my faith and love abound. / Lord circumcise my heart to love thee, / And nothing in the World above thee" (74). In another book-heart metaphor, the Alphabet of Lessons exhorts "Keep thy heart with all Diligence, for out of it are the issues of Life" (14). The word "issues" equates the circulation of blood and of texts, envisioning the child's heart as a printing press that produces book-shaped nourishment in various forms, keeping the text in circulation. "My Book and Heart Shall Never Part" was not just a statement of fact but a promise to continually revise the book of the heart in collaboration with the divine Author.

The *Primer*'s mutability secured its place in the changeable universe of early America. The American Revolution gave way to the most intensive revision of the *Primer*. For instance, the king, who was, in the early primers, "no man of blood," came to be reimagined as an enemy thwarting America's maturity and indepen-dence, requiring printers to rewrite the couplets. These revisions reflect changing American sentiments—from "Kings Should be Good / No Men of Blood" in the 1779 *Newest American Primer* (38) to "The British King / Lost States Thirteen" in the 1788 New York edition (*The New-England Primer, Improved, for the More Easy Attaining the True Reading of English* 21). Postrevolutionary versions, such as an 1809 *Boston Primer*, introduce words such as "voluntarily," "sympathetically," and "theologically," giving children a vocabulary for considering the changing contexts in which meaning might be made and for switching between different interpretive lenses (22). New materials added to the *Primer* suggest that the text was even adapt-able to the secular concerns of the early nation, allowing children to identify prob-lematic figures in a republican society such as the sluggard and the libertine. Borrowing a page from the 1770 *Royal Primer*, animal pictures in a 1790 version teach lessons such as "The Butterfly in gaudy dress / The worthless coxcomb doth express" (*The New England Primer, Enlarged and Improved* 29). The *Boston Primer* tells a seduction tale, warning female readers that "the silver tongue of *flattery* is hollow, and loaded with guile," a lesson that was also considered increasingly important for citizens in resisting the ploys of slick-tongued politicians (47).

The *Primer*'s positioning of the child's heart as a site of change was compatible with the formation of a liberal political system, which mirrored religious volunta-rism in arguing that each generation should have the liberty to consent to the law independently.[15] The beginnings of this shift in political authority are traceable even in the *Primer*'s earliest editions, which include the "Dutiful Child's Promises." While the promises seem to bolster a patriarchal model, they also suggest that the child, so long a model for obedience across various hierarchical relationships, could no longer be automatically linked with the replication of existing traditions.

The title, with its once redundant phrase, "the dutiful child," conveys the pos-sibility that some children will not be dutiful and thus that the child reader must *pledge* to fulfill his duties. Reading much like a social compact, the passage declares:

> Now the Child being entred into his Letters and Spelling, let him learn these and
> such like Sentences by Heart, whereby he will be both intrusted in his Duty, and
> encouraged in his Learning . . . I will fear God, and honour the King. I will
> honour my Father & Mother.
>   I will obey my Superiours. I will Submit to my Elders. I will Love my
> Friends. (10)

Though the promises create a relentless parallelism between authority figures, they also reflect the reimagination of authority by Locke, who argued that political power and parental power were distinct. The text attributes to each authority a *different* ruling passion, progressing from involuntary fear to honor, which was coming to be understood as a feeling that had to be earned by authority figures, and finally to love, that reciprocal sentiment of brotherhood and citizenship. The contractual element of the promises resembles republican documents such as the Declaration of Independence (1776). The emphasis on the reader's promise mirrors the political argument that in order to be legitimate, authority required the "consent of the governed." Though the king was still in place in 1727, in the 1771 and 1779 versions, he is missing, with no substitute added (*The New England Primer Enlarged* 12; *The Newest American Primer* 41). Even so, the patriarchal elements of the text were never fully discarded. After all, what Jay Fliegelman has called a "revolution against patriarchal authority" also gave rise to the idea of the founding fathers, and often, as in Washington Irving's "Rip Van Winkle" (1819), the pictures of King George were replaced with George Washington with no alteration.

The repetition of the child's "will" captures the culture's attempt to cling to the notion that the child's obedience to authority was inevitable, while simultaneously giving voice to the child's volition. In "My Book and Heart Shall Never Part," the word "shall" has a similar function as this "will," embodying both compulsion and volition. Reflecting the emerging idea of an "age of consent," the "will" also has the effect of postponing the consequences of the child's promises to a future time when he can be said to have consented with reason.[16] The claim that the child must learn the letters before consenting begins to articulate a preliminary (though childlike) concept of informed consent through reading. The lexicon of the 1750 version of the *Primer* reflects the growing emphasis on the child's role as a participant in the processes of consent and unification. Words such as "fornication" are abandoned in favor of words like "author" and "calculate," which suggest active ways of bringing about social "harmony."

The 1750 *Primer* also teaches the word "affection." The juxtaposition of love with the more constraining language of submission and fear suggests that affection was coming to be understood as a chosen feeling, reserved for forging bonds of equality between citizens. As such, "My Book and Heart Shall Never Part" provides a preliminary model for the formation of a national community, which was, at least partially, established through texts. As Benedict Anderson has argued in *Imagined Communities*, modern nations relied on print culture, such as newspapers, to create associative bonds between citizens. With its wide circulation and nominally American roots, *The New England Primer* became an obvious site of national identification, as well as religious association. In the early republic, its name was sometimes changed to the *American Primer*. As Michael Warner has argued, the social compact was mediated through printed texts such as the Constitution so that individuals could imaginatively include themselves in its promises (106). Because of the nation's growing size, individuals increasingly had to manifest their patriotism in attachments to *texts*, rather than directly confronting the bodies of other citizens. For instance, Noah Webster remarked that every person in America "should *know* and *love* their laws," a mode of reading that was already familiar to readers of the *Primer*

(65). Here, as in early versions of the text, the connection between book and heart is a way of simultaneously authorizing individuals and ensuring their continued attachment to the nation and its founding narratives.

In the nineteenth century, the *Primer* competed for the reader's affection with "lovelier" books. As the weariness of one mid-century reflection suggests, some readers had mixed feelings about the text's capacity for rejuvenation. *The Youth's Companion* claimed in 1843 that "every one of [our] readers . . . has, no doubt, heard and read [the *Primer*], a hundred times" ("Editorial" 135A). Caroline Cowles Clarke was one such reader, who, writing in her diary in 1853, records that her grandmother bribed her with ten cents to learn the John Rogers poem. She reports that this contractual agreement ended when her sister Anna mocked the evangelical couplet, "Zaccheus he Did Climb the Tree / His Lord to See," by adding her own tercet: "the tree broke down and let him fall and he did not see his Lord at all" (10).[17] The nursery-rhyme style of Anna's addition, which echoes the themes of "Hush-a-by Baby," testifies to the growing popularity of secular children's books such as *Mother Goose's Melody* (1785), which no doubt shaped the way these later readers interacted with the *Primer's* rhyming couplets.

Despite the Cowles children's impatience with the *Primer*, several nineteenth-century printers attempted to restore the text to popularity—perhaps due to nostalgia or, just as likely, to a desire to profit from selling an artifact of New England history.[18] For instance, in 1813, Quaker children's bookseller Samuel Wood produced a cheap pamphlet, *Beauties of the New England Primer*, which was intended partially as an archival endeavor. Yet, despite their preservationist aims, nineteenth-century printers were no more faithful than earlier printers in copying its pages. Though Wood's version of the text begins with a poem pledging the fixity of the child's heart, Wood changed the alphabet couplet for "H." While Wood's version, "Wrought by the hand / Great works do stand," makes a similarly weighty claim of the text's durability, it also demotes the *Primer* from the centrally located heart to the comparatively peripheral and disembodied divine hand, distancing it from the hearts of readers (5).

Wood abridged the text drastically and gave the other couplets a rewrite, undermining the seriousness of earlier versions. For instance, the weightiness of "Time cuts down all / Both great and small" is undercut by the verse for U, which states that "Urns hold," not ashes, but "Coffee and Tea" (7). One extant bound copy of *Beauties* represents a tension between a desire to preserve the text for future readers and a newfound levity toward books, promoted by the expansion of the book market and new possibilities for extensive reading. Though the "original" text is preserved in a richly clad volume with marbled cover and gilded leather spine, the reader has chosen to combine it with lighter materials such as "A Pleasing Toy" and "The Book of Riddles."

A story from Lydia Maria Child's the *Juvenile Miscellany*, "Alice Reed" (1832), also contrasts imagery of fixity with levity in its depiction of a child "rewriting" the *Primer*. The child protagonist, Alice attends school, where she has to sit "as still as a mouse" (62). As a result of her feeling of constraint, she misapprehends the proverb included in many editions of the *Primer*: "Train a child up in the way he will go, and when he is old he shall not depart from it," replacing it with the phrase, "Chain up a child and away she will go" (62). Alice's version voices a warning to parents against excessive discipline, which Child was attempting to replace by an ethos of gentle correction.[19] It is also inflected by a rising awareness of the many children in slavery, whose plight Child frequently dramatized in her magazine. In addition to adapting the book's meaning to a new context, however, Alice's phrase mimics the revisionary dynamic that had long characterized the history of the *Primer*. Like the book-heart couplet, the original phrase suggests the child's exact replication of her lessons, but Alice's rendition imagines possibilities in between a rigid internalization of the primer's lessons and the imaginative free play implied by the child's flight. Alice's phrase, which encompasses both constraint and freedom, is neither wholly like nor wholly different from the proverb. Indeed, its implication that children must be taught by engaging their affections rather than through overt constraint is very much in line with the *Primer*'s heart-centered pedagogy, even if the textbook seemed stodgy compared to the emerging class of colorful children's books.

The memories of nineteenth-century readers record similar acts of playful meaning-making from the *Primer*. The illustration for the evangelical couplet, "Young Timothy Learnt Sin to Fly," shows a young boy being chased by a dragon-like creature, meant to represent sin. An 1882 article in the *Sunday School Times* reports that "a distinguished professor" of Harvard University "could never divest himself of the idea which first struck him when studying the New England Primer . . . 'Sin' he took to be a little dog whom the boy had helped to a pair of wings and *taught to fly*" ("The New England Primer" n. pag.) The professor's imagination of the image, which resides in his heart next to a more orthodox interpretation of the wages of sin, is another example of the ways that readers both revise and reproduce the lessons of their books. Like Alice, what the professor adds to the image is the power to fly away, a sign that escape is a common topic for the daydreams of schoolchildren. But even though his interpretation gives the image a new meaning, the professor does not fully "part" from the text's lesson. In fact, the image of the dog flying away seems to have worked as a memory aid, helping him keep his book in his heart.

Children's writing and drawing in some extant copies suggest that the continual revision of the text inspired actual children to take a turn at rewriting the *Primer* themselves. In one version from 1827, a child reader has scribbled, as if to "write," in the blank spaces in the catechism section. This reader has also edited John Rogers out of his own picture by scribbling on top of his head, enacting the line that his children would no longer see his face now that he was "dead and gone." Other nineteenth-century child readers of the *Primer* made use of the art supplies sold in the era's bookshops, sometimes complicating the transmission of a text's meanings. For instance, in another antebellum copy of the *Primer*, a reader has done an elaborate drawing of a fashionable woman with puffed sleeves—a worldly image that contrasts with the spiritual meaning of the text.

The most interesting drawings in the American Antiquarian Society's collection are from an 1854 cheap paper copy from Hudson, Ohio, that appears to have been owned by a child of former slaves. A blank centerfold is inscribed in pencil, "A slave. My father and my mother." On a page of the alphabet couplets, the child has colored the people brown. The coloring perhaps records an attempt to recolor the world, and the book, from the child's point of view. The people in the John Rogers poem are also colored brown, though Rogers' executioners are left white. One might imagine that the image of a man being tortured to death in front of his children would have had new resonance in the context of slavery. The recoloring of the picture changes the text's meaning, but it also evokes the original lesson of the text in its paralleling of the injustice of slavery with religious persecution.

Though readers eventually abandoned the *Primer* for other books, the text's long life demonstrates the power, not necessarily of its message, but of its adaptability. Recently, the text has resurfaced in print due to historical interest, as well as the millennial wave of evangelical Christianity. While working with fifth-grade students at Heninger Elementary School in Santa Ana, California, Andrew Newman discovered that the text still provides a basic format from which new meanings can be made. Students in his class composed couplets such as "God will give you a good job" and "Cuida tus libros / son tus amigos." In general, the text's history is instructive for scholars of children's literature because it shows how a text can be both loved and reimagined, consistent and flexible. The reading practices inaugurated by the *Primer* are perhaps best summarized by a reader who in 1849 asked, "whose brain has not been effectually confused by copious and involuntary draughts of John Cotton's 'Spiritual Milk for Babes' [and been] reminded, in a moment of despondency, that his 'Book and Heart Must *Never* Part'?" ("The New England Primer" 209). But the author simultaneously reflects:

> The hymns and prayers contained in this unpretending little volume . . . [are]
> graven upon the heart's innermost surface, and there they remain, fresh as ever,
> buried, it may be, under the mass of selfish and worldly cares and troubles . . . but
> still they are there, ready to pour a flood of tenderness through the soul, at the
> calm hour of twilight, or when the world is hushed in slumber. (209–10)

This passage suggests that readers continued to think of the text as a site of personal renewal, even as new ideas and desires came to be written upon the child's heart.

NOTES

1. No extant copies from this printing have been found, causing scholars to speculate that the English version of the *Primer* was registered and never printed. As Daniel Cohen points out, however, "the sixpence fee for registration would tend to make the entry of a spurious title unlikely" (55). It is equally possible that no English copies remain due to "the ravages of time and careless owners" (Cohen 53). The difficulty of locating

existing copies has also been a limitation in studying the American versions. The more than 450 extant copies available at the American Antiquarian Society do not come close to the number printed. In one specific case, Philadelphia printers Benjamin Franklin and David Hall record that between 1749 and 1766 they sold over thirty-seven thousand copies of the *Primer*, but only a single copy from this firm is known to have survived.

2. For the sake of consistency, unless otherwise noted, the citations in this essay are from the earliest extant 1727 "Milk for Babes" Boston edition of the *Primer* printed by S. Kneeland and T. Green. This *Primer*, however, should not be seen as the definitive version. Reflecting the diversity of the *Primer*'s content even from its earliest printings, the only other version extant from 1727, also published by Kneeland and Green, follows the same basic sequence until page 32 and then includes different materials in different order, including the Assembly of Divines catechism. The fact that the same printer published two different versions of the text in the same year suggests that the variation in *Primers* was deliberate and that readers were likely aware of the existence of multiple versions.

3. See David D. Hall's *Worlds of Wonder* for an account of these practices (32–37). See also sixteen-year-old Chloe Bridgman Conant Bierce's letter to her younger brother in 1819: "Do you continue committing to memory the Scripture and what is contained in the evangelical primer, going to meeting, and reciting it?" (151).

4. Child conversion narratives, though not necessarily unbiased reports, also suggest that children engaged in solitary reading beginning in this period. For instance, as described in *Early Piety*, six-year-old Elizabeth Butcher took "her Catechism or some other good Book to Bed with her, and in the morning she would be sitting up in her Bed Reading before any of the Family were awake besides her" (2).

5. Because scholars do not have access to an original version of the *Primer*, no authoritative edition exists, only copies that cannot be considered perfect renderings. The earliest scholarship by Charles F. Heartman and Paul Leicester Ford necessarily focused on its bibliography. Subsequent criticism has engaged in closer textual analysis but has focused mainly on the eighteenth-century evangelical versions; for instance, Watters restricts his otherwise compelling analysis to a "group of *Primers* whose contents reflect a period of consensus" (209). Such analyses are limited because the *Primer* is not just one book, but many books, which do not reflect an entirely consistent message. Instead, it was the book's ability to hold together disparate readings and to change that ensured its continued appeal. Patricia A. Crain has shown more recently that even in a single copy of the *Primer*, one finds traces of various "texts" deriving from animal fables and tavern signs in addition to religious works.

6. The metaphor of the heart as a book-like storehouse of knowledge stems from classical writing (the word "record" comes from the Latin "cor" or heart), but subjectivity became even more strongly correlated with print by Locke and other Protestant writers, who described children as blank slates. See Eric Jager, *The Book of the Heart*, for an extensive discussion of the book-heart trope.

7. Cotton Mather's writing shows that he was familiar with this scientific development. In *Sober Sentiments*, he writes, "The *Blood-Vessels* must . . . be drawn asunder, and then crouded again together, that so the *Blood* contained therein may be duly broken, and by a communution into very small Parts, be rendered fit for the Circulation, and pass the better thro' all the Strainers of the Body" (16).

8. The descendants of the original settlers were increasingly unable or unwilling to testify to election. Because both community and civic rights were tied to church membership, the church had to compromise, allowing access to baptism and property ownership, while voting and communion were reserved for those who had testified. The Halfway

Covenant, as the compromise was known, was the subject of much controversy and was blamed for violent events such as King Phillip's War (1675–76).

9. See E. Jennifer Monoghan, *Learning to Read and Write in Colonial America* for a discussion of how these laws affected actual literacy rates in the colonies. Though the law does not specify whether "children" included girls as well as boys, I would argue that girls were meant to be included because the law goes on to say that girl apprentices under age eighteen will be removed to the care of the state if they were not being educated. A later 1703 law specified that girls were required to learn to read, while boys must learn to read and write. While Native American and slave children were not included in any of these laws, the colonists regularly used reading instruction in their attempts to convert these children. Predating the *New England Primer* by nearly twenty years, the first primer printed in the colonies was John Eliot's *Indian Primer* (1669), which contains some of the basic elements of the *Primer*, such as a syllabarium and catechism.

10. The traditional understanding of this concept by Aristotle matched the patriarchal notion of infant depravity, in which the child is plagued by sin from birth. The philosopher conceives of the mind as a palimpsest-like text, in which the bad must be blotted out through discipline before the good can be "written" in its place. Protestant writers, however, were beginning to reshape the concept of the *tabula rasa* into an understanding of the mind as "a white sheet of Paper in which little is written," which should not be "blotted" or "besmeared" with "defilements" (Vincent n. pag.).

11. During the 1760s, the alphabet couplets were entirely rewritten to refer only to biblical events. These evangelical editions were so popular that nineteenth-century critics believed that faithful renditions of the earliest copies of the text were actually bowdlerized copies of these later religious versions.

12. Mather argued that only infants were saved by the faith of their parents, while other ministers, such as Jonathan Edwards, refused to guarantee elect status even to children who died in infancy, further emphasizing children's responsibility for their own souls.

13. Thomas Hartwell Horne explains, "A type, in its primary and literal meaning, simply denotes a rough draught, or less accurate model, from which a more perfect image is made" (qtd. in Landow 22). This concept of revision is reflected in biblical typology, which suggests that the events of the Old Testament are rectified by those of the New Testament. The New England Protestants believed that the new world presented the opportunity for yet another rendition of the events of the Bible, leading to the second coming of Christ. As the future generation of believers, children were central to this vision, providing an opportunity for renewal of mankind's covenant with God.

14. Because the *Primer* was one of a few books that a family might own, it was likely subject to what Rolf Engelsing calls "intensive reading." In Hall's evidence on seventeenth-century book ownership in Middlesex County, Massachusetts, two thirds of homes owned the Bible and 60 percent had a few other books ("Readers and Writers in Early New England" 124). Hall argues that by the early eighteenth century "most persons [in New England] had the use of, or owned, a Bible, psalmbook, primer and catechism" (*Cultures of Print* 57).

15. See Jay Fliegelman's *Prodigals and Pilgrims* for a discussion of the American Revolution's effect on child rearing.

16. See Holly Brewer for a discussion of consent and reason in early America as it relates to children.

17. While the Cowles children mocked the *Primer* as a result of the book being forced upon them, there are suggestions that other nineteenth-century children embraced the

text. Writing in 1859, Ralph Waldo Emerson's daughter, Ellen Tucker Emerson, records a conversation that she had with her friends about "books we had when we were young" and notes that they discussed the *Primer* and other early children's textbooks with affection (174).

18. Several articles in 1849 celebrated the revival of the *Primer*, citing a press run by the Massachusetts Sabbath School society of 100,000 copies. See, for instance, "The New England Primer" in *The New-England Historical and Genealogical Register*.

19. This reaction likely represents nineteenth-century concern about the *Primer*'s harsher moments, such as the continuous threats that children may go to hell if they do not experience conversion. In 1829, "The Essayist" similarly criticizes the pedagogy of the *Primer* as antithetical to children's natural "buoyancy" (281).

WORKS CITED

Anderson, Benedict. *Imagined Communities: Reflections on the Origin and Spread of Nationalism*. London: Verso, 1991.

Beauties of the New England Primer. New York: Printed and Sold by S. Wood, 1813.

Bierce, Chloe Bridgman Conant. "Letter from Chloe Bridgman Conant Bierce, August 12, 1819." In *Journal and Biographical Notice of Chloe B. Conant Bierce*. Cincinnati, Ohio: Elm Street Printing Co., 1869.

The Boston Primer; Being an Improvement of the New-England Primer. Boston: Printed and Sold by Manning & Loring, No. 2, Cornhill, 1809.

Brewer, Holly. *By Birth or Consent: Children, the Law, and the Anglo-American Revolution in Authority*. Chapel Hill: U of North Carolina P, 2005.

Brown, Matthew P. *The Pilgrim and the Bee: Reading Rituals and Book Culture in Early New England*. Philadelphia: U of Pennsylvania P, 2007.

Child, Lydia Maria. "Alice Reed." *The Juvenile Miscellany* 3, no. 1 (1832): 59–64.

The Child's New Play-Thing. Boston: Printed by J. Draper, for J. Edwards in Cornhill, 1750.

Clarke, Caroline Cowles Richard. "Diary of Caroline Cowles Clarke, March, 1853." *Village Life in America 1852–1872 Including the Period of the American Civil War as Told in the Diary of a School-Girl*. New York: Henry Holt & Co., 1913.

Cohen, Daniel A. "The Origin and Development of the New England Primer." *Children's Literature* 5 (1976): 52–57.

The Compleat Scholler, or Relation of the Life, and Latter-End Especially, of Caleb Vernon. London: Printed for J. W. and W. S., 1666.

Crain, Patricia A. *The Story of A: The Alphabetization of America from The New England Primer to The Scarlet Letter*. Stanford: Stanford UP, 2000.

Duane, Anna Mae. "Casualties of the Rod: Rebelling Children, Disciplining Indians, and the Critique of Colonial Authority in Puritan New England." In *Messy Beginnings: Postcoloniality and Early American Studies*, edited by Malini Johar Schueller and Edward Watts, 63–77. New Brunswick, N.J.: Rutgers P, 2003.

Early Piety Exemplified in Elizabeth Butcher of Boston. Boston: Printed by S. Kneeland, for Samuel Gerrish, and Sold at his Shop Near the Old Meeting House, 1725.

"Editorial," *The Youth's Companion* 17, no. 34 (1843): 135A.

Emerson, Ellen Tucker, "Letter from Ellen Tucker Emerson to Edith Emerson Forbes, March 3, 1859." In *The Letters of Ellen Tucker Emerson*. Vol. 1, edited by Edith W. Gregg, 174–76. Kent, Ohio: Kent State U P, 1982.

"The Essayist," *Gospel Advocate and Impartial Advocator* 7, no. 18 (1829): 280–81.

Filmer, Sir Robert. *Patriarcha and Other Writings*. Edited by J.P. Sommerville. Cambridge: Cambridge U P, 1991.

Fliegelman, Jay. *Prodigals and Pilgrims: The American Revolution Against Patriarchal Authority 1750–1800*. Cambridge: Cambridge UP, 1982.

Ford, Paul Leicester. *The New England Primer: A History of Its Origin and Development*. New York: Columbia UP, 1962.

"From the Charleston Courier." *Weekly Visitor, or Ladies' Miscellany* 3, no. 43 (1805): 339.

Hall, David D. *Cultures of Print: Essays on the History of the Book*. Amherst: U of Massachusetts P, 1996.

———. "Readers and Writers in Early New England." *A History of the Colonial Book in America*. Chapel Hill: U of North Carolina P, 2007.

———. *Worlds of Wonder; Days of Judgment: Popular Religious Belief in Early New England*. Cambridge, Mass.: Harvard UP, 1989.

Harvey, William. *Exercitatio Anatomica de Motu Cordis et Sanguinis in Animalibus*. Frankfurt: Sumptibus Guilielmi Fitzeri, 1628.

Heartman, Charles F. *The New-England Primer Issued Prior to 1830*. New York: R.R. Bowker, 1934.

Howey, Ann. "Reading Elaine: Marjorie Richardson's and L. M. Montgomery's Red-Haired Lily Maids." *Children's Literature Association Quarterly* 32, no. 2 (2007): 86–109.

Irving, Washington. "Rip Van Winkle." In *The Sketch-Book*, 56-94. New York: Printed by C.S. Van Winkle, 1819.

Jager, Eric. *The Book of the Heart*. Chicago: U of Chicago P, 2000.

Janeway, James, and Cotton Mather. *A Token for Children. Being an Exact Account of the Conversion, Holy and Exemplary Lives and Joyful Deaths of Several Young Children. To Which is Added, A Token, for the Children of New England*. Boston: Printed for Nicholas Boone, 1700.

Jones, Katherine. "Getting Rid of Children's Literature." *The Lion and the Unicorn* 30 (2006): 287–315.

Landow, George P. *Victorian Types, Victorian Shadows: Biblical Typology in Victorian Literature, Art, and Thought*. Boston: Routledge & Kegan Paul, 1980.

A Legacy for Children: Being Some of the Last Expressions, and Dying Sayings, of Hannah Hill. Philadelphia: Printed by Andrew Bradford, 1717.

Locke, John. *Some Thoughts Concerning Education*. Edited by Ruth Weissbourd Grant and Nathan Tarcov. Indianapolis, Ind.: Hackett Publishing, 1996.

Mather, Cotton. *The Religion of the Closet*. Boston: Printed by T. Green, 1705.

———. *Sober Sentiments in an Essay upon the Vain Presumption of Living & Thriving in the World; which Does Too Often Possess and Poison the Children of This World*. Boston: Printed by T. Fleet in Pudding-Lane, 1722.

Monoghan, E. Jennifer. *Learning to Read and Write in Colonial America*. Amherst: U of Massachusetts P, 2005.

The New England Primer. Boston: Printed by S. Kneeland and T. Green, 1750.

"The New England Primer." *The New-England Historical and Genealogical Register* 3, no. 3 (1849): 209–10.

"The New England Primer." *The Sunday School Times*. Philadelphia, 29 April 1882.

The New-England Primer Enlarged: For the More Easy Attaining the True Reading of English. To which is Added, Several Chapters and Sentences of the Holy Scriptures. Germantown, Pa.: Printed and Sold by Christopher Sower, 1771.

The New England Primer, Enlarged and Improved: Or, an Easy and Pleasant Guide to the Art of Reading. Adorned with Cuts. Newburyport: Printed by John Mycall for John Boyle, 1790.

The New-England Primer, Enlarged for the More Easy Attaining the True Reading of English. To which Is Added, Milk for Babes. Boston: Printed and Sold by S. Kneeland & T. Green, 1735.

The New England Primer Enlarged for the True Reading of English. To Which Is Added, Milk for Babes. Boston: Printed by S. Kneeland & T. Green, 1727.

The New-England Primer, Improved, for the More Easy Attaining the True Reading of English. To which is Added, the Assembly's Shorter Catechism, New York: Printed by S. Loudon, 1788.

The Newest American Primer, for the Easy Attaining of the True Reading of English. Philadelphia: Printed by Styner and Cist, 1779.

Newman, Andrew. "Literacy Then and Now." *The Common-Place* 2, no. 3 (2002). Web. 12 July 2010<http://www.common-place.org/vol-02/no-03/school/>.

Rowlandson, Mary. *The Soveraignty & Goodness of God, Together, with the Faithfulness of His Promises Displayed; Being a Narrative of the Captivity and Restauration of Mrs. Mary Rowlandson.* Cambridge: Printed by Samuel Green, 1682.

The Royal Primer. Or, An Easy and Pleasant Guide to the Art of Reading. Authorized by His Majesty King George II. To Be Used Throughout His Majesty's Dominions. Boston: Printed by William M'Alpine for, and Sold by John Boyles, 1770.

Sánchez-Eppler, Karen. *Dependent States: The Child's Part in Nineteenth-Century American Culture.* Chicago: U of Chicago P, 2005.

Taylor, John. *The Witchcraft Delusion in Colonial Connecticut, 1641–1697.* New York: Grafton Press, 1908.

Thomas, Isaiah. *The History of Printing in America.* Worcester, Mass.: Published from the Press of Isaiah Thomas, 1874.

Vincent, Thomas. *Words of Advice to Young Men.* London: Printed for Thomas Parkhurst, 1668.

Warner, Michael. *The Letters of the Republic: Publication and the Public Sphere in Eighteenth-Century America.* Cambridge, Mass.: Harvard UP, 1990.

Watters, David H. "'I Spake as a Child': Authority, Metaphor and The New-England Primer." *Early American Literature* 20, no. 3 (1985): 193–213.

Webster, Noah. "On the Education of Youth in America." *Essays on Education in the Early Republic.* Edited by Frederick Rudolph. Cambridge, Mass.: Belknap Press of Harvard U P, 1965.

White, Thomas. *A Little Book for Little Children.* Boston: Reprinted, by T. Green, for Benjamin Eliot, at his Shop, under the West-End of the Exchange, 1702.

Woodbridge, Benjamin. "Elegy of John Cotton." *American Poems (1625–1892).* Edited by Walter Cochrane Bronson. Chicago: U of Chicago P, 1912.

FURTHER READING

Avery, Gillian. "Origins and English Predecessors of the New England Primer." *Proceedings of the American Antiquarian Society* 108, no. 1 (1998): 33–61.

Brown, Gillian. *The Consent of the Governed: The Lockean Legacy in Early American Culture.* Cambridge, MA: Harvard UP, 2001.

Carr, Jean Ferguson, Stephen L. Carr, and Lucille M. Schultz. *Archives of Instruction: Nineteenth-century Rhetorics, Readers, and Composition Books in the United States.* Carbondale: Southern Illinois UP, 2005.

Fessenden, Tracy. "Protestant Expansion, Indian Violence, and Childhood Death: *The New England Primer.*" In *Culture and Redemption: Religion, the Secular, and American Literature,* 34-59. Princeton, N.J.: Princeton UP, 2007.

Lerer, Seth. "'Thy Life to Mend, This Book Attend': Reading and Healing in the Arc of Children's Literature." *New Literary History: A Journal of Theory and Interpretation* 37, no. 3 (2006): 631–42.

Marten, James, ed. *Children in Colonial America.* New York: New York University Press, 2006.

New, Elisa. "'Both Great and Small': Adult Proportion and Divine Scale in Edward Taylors' 'Preface' and The New-England Primer." *Early American Literature* 28, no. 2 (1993): 120–32.

CHAPTER 21

....

CASTAWAYS: *THE SWISS FAMILY ROBINSON,* CHILD BOOKMAKERS, AND THE POSSIBILITIES OF LITERARY FLOTSAM

....

KAREN SÁNCHEZ-EPPLER

JOHANN *David Wyss (1743–1818) spent his professional life as one of the pastors attached to the cathedral in Bern, Switzerland. During the early 1790s he began reading Daniel Defoe's* The Life and Strange Surprising Adventures of Robinson Crusoe of York, Mariner *(1719) to his four sons. After enjoying these stories of survival on a deserted island, the family improvised their own similar tale narrating the exploits of a father, mother, and four boys shipwrecked en route to Tahiti, and the pastor recorded this story as it was told. The second son, Johann Rudolf Wyss (1781–1830), a professor of philosophy at the University of Bern and a noted folklorist, edited this rambling family manuscript into an immediately popular children's book:* Der Schweizerische Robinson. *He released a second volume of adventures the next year, also culled from his father's manuscript. The books were translated into French in 1814 by the prolific Swiss author Mme le Barronne Isabelle de Montolieu, who included some episodes of her own invention. That same year William and Mary Godwin published an English version of* The Family Robinson Crusoe *that drew from both the French and German versions. De Montolieu continued the tale, publishing five volumes of new adventures between 1824 and 1826. Later translators have felt similarly free to embellish the story, so that*

there really is no definitive English text, and many of the most beloved incidents were
created by translators and editors.

> When I was a child I did not want to know that *The Swiss Family Robinson* had an
> author. To me it seemed a collection of words fallen from the sky into my hands.
> Those words allowed me access to a pre-existing world of people and their
> adventures. . . . I saw through the words to what seemed to me beyond them and
> not dependent on them, even though I could get there in no other way than by
> reading those words. I resented being told that the name on the title page was that
> of the "author" who had made it all up.
>   Whether many other people have had the same experience, I do not know,
> but I confess to being curious to find out. It is not too much to say that this whole
> book has been written to account for this experience. Was it no more than
> childish naiveté, or was I responding, in however childish a way, to something
> essential about literature? (Miller 14–15)

This essay takes up J. Hillis Miller's charming provocation, though in somewhat
different terms. In *On Literature* (2002), Miller proffers his "childish" experiences
with *The Swiss Family Robinson* as a model for grasping the very nature of the
literary, and along the way he offers one of the very few critical engagements with
this chaotic, compendious, family adventure story. Like Miller I want to see what
might be learned about literature by taking seriously children's responses to their
reading, by heeding the "childish way." This essay reflects my ongoing efforts to
retrieve writing by nineteenth-century American children, and so to make it possible for their voices to be part of childhood studies. I have learned in my reading
of children's diaries, school essays, letters, poetry, and fiction to look through
children's socialization, to recognize traces of agency in even the most supervised
of these texts, and in this way to chart children's collaboration in the processes of
cultural production (*Dependent States*). This essay details how two generations of
children in the same Boston family drew upon *The Swiss Family Robinson* in their
own bookmaking. In telling this nineteenth-century U.S. reception story I hope
to demonstrate how as scholars of children's literature we can use children's writings as a means of understanding not only children's perspectives on the specific
books they read, but even more the role such reading plays in children's imagination, activities, sense of self, and ultimately their participation in the social
world.

The Swiss Family Robinson, first published in Zurich in 1812, is surely one of
the most adapted and adaptable of childhood texts, and so proves a perfect site for
this inquiry. This narrative of survival on a deserted island, through God's grace
and the family's own ingenious efforts, endlessly reiterates the process of making
up a world. Beginning with ten-year-old Jack's suggestion that the family might
get from broken ship to rocky shore by fashioning rowing boats out of the sailor's
wooden washtubs, the family's island life depends on their capacity to reimagine
and reuse the flotsam of European civilization with which they are marooned.
Thus the concept of the castaway so central to *The Swiss Family Robinson* offers a
particularly apt site for this investigation, since children's writing itself so often

depends on scavenging—from the imitation of plot and genre to the very scraps of paper on which it is inscribed. The methodology I am suggesting here, of approaching children's literature through the traces books leave in children's writing, entails an archival salvage operation that mirrors not only children's own writing practices, and the survival strategies of the Swiss family itself, but also the extraordinarily complex textual history of the book that recounts their adventures.

CASTAWAY: ASSEMBLING *THE SWISS FAMILY ROBINSON*

All literature is constructed out of flotsam. But this children's classic proves unusual for how self-consciously and emphatically it presents itself as a salvaged text, constantly made and remade in homage, translation, and pastiche. Walt Disney has led modern readers, viewers, and amusement park enthusiasts to think of "Robinson" as the family's name. But it is not; the original novel never mentions the family surname, rather the title emphasizes the secondhand status of this tale: *Der Schweizerische Robinson* (The Swiss Robinson) proclaims itself an alpine and familial rendition of Daniel Defoe's *Robinson Crusoe*.

During the founding years of the English novel, literature for children was only beginning to be differentiated, and critics often cite the publication of *Robinson Crusoe* (1719) as an inaugural text both for the English novel and for children's literature. "We will have dealt with this character from our earliest years," Hubert Damisch affirms, "this book which figures among the great pedagogical tools of our civilization, is multiply tied to our own origins" (18). The colonizing impulses at the root of this novel permeate not only literary culture generally, but also children's literature in particular. In tracking young readers' responses to *The Swiss Family Robinson*, and the Crusoe story that stands behind it, this essay explores how the colonial impetus to remake the world to our desires is inculcated through childhood reading.

The profound formative appeal of *Robinson Crusoe* always included young readers as well as adults, and new world readers as well as old world ones. By 1830 well over a hundred different editions of *Robinson Crusoe* had been printed in the United States.[1] Moreover, almost immediately, imitations, abridgements, and parodies proliferated in Europe and America, many using the word "Robinson" in their title—creating the literary category of the "Robinsonade" (Fisher). One of the most influential was explicitly intended for younger readers; Joachim Heinrich Campe's *Robinson der Jungere* (1779, first translated into English in 1788) spawned versions throughout the United States.[2] Many of these featured Americanizing adaptations: an 1810 version of Campe's *The New Robinson Crusoe* printed in

Manhattan, for example, casts Crusoe as an American youth and begins with him no longer "Robinson Crusoe of York, Mariner" but rather "walking around the port of New-York" (3).

The Swiss pastor Johann David Wyss was thus doing nothing at all unusual when, in the early 1790s, he began reading *Robinson Crusoe* aloud to his four sons. "There is no book that has been more universally read and approved, for the opening of the infant mind, than *The Adventures of Robinson Crusoe*," the second of these boys, Johann Rudolf Wyss, affirms in his 1812 preface to *Der Schweizerische Robinson* (3). When the reading of Defoe's long novel finally came to an end, the pastor and his children began to improvise the family's own version of this island survival story, making up adventures for a mother, father, and their four boys ship-wrecked on an uninhabited land as the lone Crusoe had been.

This scene of family instruction, of stories as a shared familial bond, suffuses the novel. As nineteenth-century reviewers frequently noted, the presence of a family proves one of the crucial ways that Wyss's castaway story differed from Defoe and Campe:

> The "Swiss Robinson" of M. Wyss is "Robinson Crusoe" in the bosom of his family. Instead of the rash and obstinate sailor who struggles against death in a prolonged agony, it is a father, a mother, and their charming children. . . . The new author's combination has changed the entire economy of his fable; it transports you from the final abode of a solitary adventurer to the cradle of human society. (Nodieck 9)

Johann David Wyss appears to have written down these episodes as he told them, filling 841 manuscript pages between 1792 and 1798 with accounts of the family's various efforts to produce shelter, food, and other amenities and the lessons in natural history and personal behavior that could be wrung from them. Wyss refers to the manuscript he produced in these years as a "Charakteristik meiner kinder in einer Robinsonade" [a characterization of my children in the form of a Robinson-ade] (Green 66). The novel's initial presentation of the family describes them as they are arranged in those lifeboat tubs: "Sweet" six-year-old Francis; ten-year-old "enterprising, audacious, generous" Jack; twelve-year-old Ernest, a boy "of a ratio-nal reflecting temper, well informed, but somewhat disposed to indolence and the pleasures of the senses"; the eldest "handsome" Fritz, "full of intelligence and vivacity"; and their "exemplary" mother all appear as character types (23).[3] The boys' adventures stem from the traits assigned to them here and often serve to cor-rect them: "I had fixed upon Ernest for my assistant," the father narrator explains, "thinking that his indolent temper required to be stimulated to exertion" (195). In Wyss's telling both father and mother remain nameless, or rather named only by their familial roles.

The book itself was clearly a family endeavor. There is every reason to suspect that the boys suggested incidents and animals as the story unfolded. The third son, Johann Emmanuel, drew pictures to illustrate the manuscript. The family com-bined these evenings of storytelling with more active games and experiments, actual hunting expeditions, and tamer imitations of island construction projects (Green 69). In 1812 Johann Rudolf Wyss—the second son, model for the bookish Ernest, and by then a professor of philosophy at the University of Bern—edited this manuscript of the stories first told in his childhood and had it published to quick celebrity. Still drawing upon his father's manuscript, he published a second volume of these family adventures the next year.

As all readers have surely noticed, *The Swiss Family Robinson* has little by way of overall plot or form. It entails many accounts of journeys to the ship to salvage useful and desirable objects, the building of various houses (the tent house, the tree house of "Falcon's Nest," the salt rock house, two farm cottages), and experiences with endless new varieties of plants and animals. "The wild animals encountered," as Miller puts it, "must either be shot or tamed, sometimes some of each" (84). Thus, when the family's European dogs attack a large jackal and devour most of its litter, ten-year-old Jack gains permission to train the one remaining pup into a hunting dog of his own. The book itself, with its multiple reiterations of these scenes of taming, is of course just such an experiment in the education of the young: domesticating the boys as well as the landscape and creatures that surround them. The pleasure young readers are presumed to take from these stories stems less from wildness than from the family's success at making wildness yield. In one of the most carefully detailed narratives of taming, the onagra (a beautiful wild ass) becomes docile when father "seized with my teeth one of the long ears of the enraged creature, and bit it till it bled" (368). Such taming is precisely what the book hopes to achieve, not just for the boys in it, but for its child audience, to take control of them by the ears and both enliven and domesticate the imagination.

Endlessly episodic in the first instance, the text, like its predecessor *Robinson Crusoe*, has proved immensely inviting to adaptation. Nothing in the structure of the book inhibits the discovery of a new plant, an encounter with a new animal, the descriptive pleasures of a new view, the advantages of another trip to the wreck to salvage more things, or the opportunity to build another house. The book was translated into French in 1814 by the prolific Swiss writer Mme le Barronne Isabelle de Montolieu, and in the translation process she added a few incidents of her own invention. That same year William and Mary Godwin published the first English edition of *The Family Robinson Crusoe* as part of their Juvenile Library, drawing from both the Wyss and de Montolieu versions.[4]

The Godwin story ends after two years of life on the island, with father musing about whether they will ever encounter any other human beings, but concluding: "We encourage serenity and thankfulness in each other, and wait with resignation the event" (429). Such resignation, satisfied in the isolated nuclear family, echoes the claim at the end of the second volume of Defoe's narrative that "having lived a life of infinite variety seventy-two years" Crusoe had "learned sufficiently to know the value of retirement, and the blessing of ending our days in peace" (591).[5] This serenity did not, however, long satisfy readers of the *Swiss Family Robinson*. Isabelle de Montolieu soon published an expanded edition, stretching island life to a decade filled with increasingly dangerous adventures and an ever more exotic array of animals (the ostrich, the whale, the boa constrictor that swallows their donkey whole, and finally even lions all come from de Montolieu's pen). She gave "mother" the name "Elizabeth," and for a hint of romance she added a treasure trove of pearls and another castaway, a young English girl ready to be rescued by handsome Fritz.

Subsequent English editions drew upon all these texts and often indulged in creating new adventures of their own and excising ones of which they disapproved. Thus, for example, the dogs' gruesome savaging of the litter of jackals was deleted from Godwin's 1826 version, leaving the origins of Jack's pet jackal inexplicable in later chapters.[6] William Henry Giles Kingston's translation of 1879 proved the most popular of the late nineteenth-century English versions. Claiming to be based on the original, it nevertheless included de Montolieu's second volume and increased the menagerie with elephants and hippopotami: "It has been translated," Kingston affirmed, "by members of my family from the German, with the omission of the long sententious lectures found in the original, and some slight alterations calculated to enliven the narrative" (ii).[7] John Seelye notes, "*The Swiss Family Robinson*, as a text, resembles the adventures of the family themselves, in that it is a communal, even corporate, product" (viii–ix). There is not, never was, and really never can be a definitive English text of *The Swiss Family Robinson*. It is itself a wild conglomeration of incidents, and much of its appeal stems from the implicit invitation to imagine more, and so participate in the world-building adventures of this insulated family. Thus, Seth Lerer explains, *The Swiss Family Robinson* presents authorship as a "collective performance, bequeathed to the child" (147).

SALVAGE: THE HALE CHILDREN'S LIBRARIES

In mid-nineteenth-century Boston, Massachusetts, on a different continent and in a different century, the children and grandchildren of Nathan and Sarah Hale amused themselves by making books. The Hales' modes of familial bookmaking have much in common with the narrative collaborations of the Wyss family that produced *The Swiss Family Robinson*. Nathan Hale owned *The Boston Daily Advertiser*, which often operated from the ground floor of the family house. His seven children grew up learning to set type and run presses. As Susan Hale would satirically note in her fictionalized autobiographical essay, "Straw into Gold," "This family was so literary that the children were fed entirely with alphabets and multiplication-tables. They sat upon dictionaries when the chairs were not high enough for the table and they had newspaper aprons to protect them from the soup" (754–55).

In 1839, six-year-old Susan and her two brothers Alexander (Elly), aged ten, and Charles, then eight, with a little help from their older siblings and a few cousins and friends, founded "The Franklin Circulating Library." By 1846 they had produced 183 small homemade books. In publishing these manuscript books, just three or four inches high, the children carefully imitated printing conventions, feigning leather bindings with strips of tape and marking the publication date and publishing house on each little volume. They were similarly elaborate in developing the rules and regulations of their circulating library. None of the Franklin Library "proprietors," as they called themselves, had children of their own, but their older brother, the Unitarian minister and popular author Edward Everett Hale, fathered eight children. His two eldest, Ellen (Nelly), born in 1854, and Arthur, born in 1859, were inspired by the Franklin Library to create a similar literary venture. Together with some participation from their younger brothers and much help from a large group of friends, they ran the "Charlieshope Library" from 1865 to 1869. The volumes in this library are even tinier, each book less than two inches square, yet sixty-one of them have survived.[8] In their nearly 250 combined volumes, these libraries of homemade books are unusual in scope, but throughout the nineteenth century the act of making one's own books appears to be a fairly widespread behavior among both children and adults in the literate middle and upper classes. Thus insights garnered from the Hale books carry wider relevance. In spanning two generations, with stories written by boys and girls, and addressing a broad array of subject matter, genre, and style, the Hale libraries provide an extraordinary resource for assessing children's attitudes toward books.

The Hales offer a particularly vivid instance of literary salvaging. They truly did make their books out of scraps of discarded paper, many pages crossed by ledger lines, and in producing the Charlieshope Library they employed bits of patterned wallpaper and even the marbled end pages of bigger books to fashion covers for their tiny volumes. Similarly, the content and plots of these books often derive from and comment on books the children had read. In all these ways the Hale children's scavenger methods of bookmaking recapitulate the strategies through which Fritz, Earnest, Jack, and Francis build their island home.

The Swiss Family Robinson is explicitly named and frequently alluded to in the Hale children's homemade books, and sea travel, shipwrecks, and deserted island survival stories are a favorite genre for these children. The Franklin Library contains thirty-four books of sea adventure, many of which include castaway survival strategies. In the Charlieshope Library, pressures of authorship and historical period made the shipwreck plot somewhat less popular. Produced primarily by girls in the years directly after the Civil War, stories of conflict with rebel soldiers dominate the library's adventure genre. Even so, the Charlieshope Library contains at least five castaway stories, including one with a tree house. Overall, the Hale books reveal the multitudinous forms the Robinsonade took in mid-nineteenth-century Boston. For example, in his 1842 Franklin Library book *Adventures of Bill and Tom with their Dog Jack* (in six volumes), Charles Hale describes their shipwreck in verse:

> The ship rocked and tossed till about 3 o'clock Friday morn when
> 'the ship with a shock

Came plump against a rock'
And smashed to pieces." (1:7)

The rhyme comes from a popular song, "Robinson Crusoe," whose relevant verse goes

You've read in a book of a voyage he took,
While the raging whirlwinds blew so,
That the ship, with a shock, fell plump on a rock,
Near drowning poor Robinson Crusoe. (*Selected Songs* 59–60)

The 1844 Franklin Library book on *The Settlement of the Island of Regia* suggests that the Hale children had probably read Joachim Campe, since the castaways of Regia herd llamas like Campe's Crusoe rather than goats like Defoe's Crusoe.[9] Awash in castaway stories, the Hales simply pick and choose amongst them as they please, salvaging this abundant literary material for use in the construction of their own literary communities.

For the Hale families as for the Wysses these island adventures seem to gird their domestic formation—thus the notion of being castaways becomes a means of intensifying the family bond. In *The Swiss Family Robinson*, if the family disperses to engage in various daily explorations and inventions, the chapter often concludes with family members recounting their separate escapades: "the story of our different adventures served for the amusement of the evening" (328). Similarly, the Hale children treat storytelling as a favorite amusement; clearly the family's pleasure in narrative motivated the creation of these libraries, so it is appropriate that storytelling itself should prove a prime activity to depict within these homemade books.

In the 1842 Franklin Library book *New Years Day*, thirteen-year-old Elly Hale describes a family's holiday celebrations, recounting the abundant food and presents with detailed delight, and surely a bit of wishful exaggeration: "Peter had a kite. George had a box of sugar plums come from France not common confectionary but chocolate & such things in a box about two feet square" (3). The narration of the holiday encompasses not only such extraordinary treats but a large range of celebratory activities, including various games and, of course, storytelling:

George told the following story. Once there was a boy who was very fond of the
sea so he went to sea. One night a severe storm arose and the ship began to sink
he ran up onto the stern and held his life preserver in one hand and he leaped
into the sea he swam until he came to an island where he lived "in peace and died
in a pot of grease." (5–7)

The ending is a traditional period close for fairy tales "of the good old Mother Goose Style" and some other Franklin Library stories employ it as well (Duer).[10] George's shipwreck story is an obviously rushed telling, in a tale within a tale, where the conventional couplet serves as an excuse not to have to write the details of this boy's survival. After all, Elly's concern in this volume centers on recording the elaborate pleasures of the holiday party. Still, even this abrupt story asserts its mastery of ship lore with its talk of the boat's "stern" and the good advice to grab a life preserver. In any event it represents castaway stories as just as much a part of family festivities as games or candy.

In *Peggy's Stories*, a book thirteen-year-old Nelly Hale created in 1867 for the Charlieshope Library, the heroine is herself a storyteller: "One day Margaret was sitting on a rock dipping one foot in the water and stroking the other lazily, thinking of taking a nap, when the rest of the children except Arthur came up, and began to beseech her to tell them a story" (5) (fig. 21.1). The Civil War tale Peggy tells is interrupted when Arthur arrives with a plan that they all "row over to Hog Island" (9). That night they camp out on the island, engaging in such castaway-style activities as cooking over open fires. During the row home "the children saw a flash of lightening, and then heard the thunder. The waves rose very high and a good deal of water got into the boat which Margaret bailed out with a chocolate pot as best she could" (14). The boat does not flounder, after all, the children had already enjoyed a night of island adventures; instead Nelly describes how they reach home wet and tired to be "welcomed with delight and griddlecakes" (14). This story totters on the edge of turning playing at castaways into an actual shipwreck—but happily such

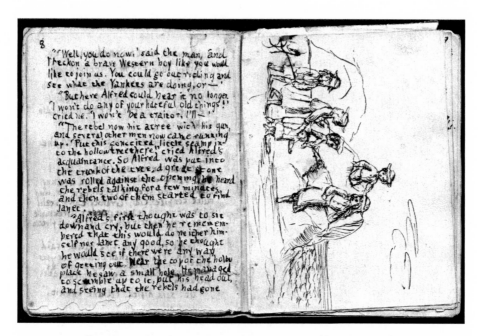

Figure 21.1. Ellen Day Hale, who grew up to become a professional artist and art teacher, was the most prolific author and illustrator for the Charlieshope Library. This drawing shows Margaret at the water's edge telling stories to her siblings from *Peggy Stories* (1867), 8–9, in the Hale Family Papers. Courtesy of the Sophia Smith Collection, Smith College, Northampton, Massachusetts.

dangers can be held at bay by a well-wielded chocolate pot. Thus in both generations the children recognize the story of island survival as a kind of marker for communal play and imagination. The presumed deprivations of island life come integrally linked to the telling of stories and the consumption of sweets. Sugar cane, honey, and coconuts always figured large in *The Swiss Family Robinson* itself, and one of de Montolieu's additions for the second half is the discovery of cocoa on the island.

The sense of playing at being castaways, so prominent in the Hale libraries, was in fact an actual family game. In the article "The Book *Robinson Crusoe*" that Edward Everett Hale wrote for a popular juvenile magazine in 1868, just a year after Nelly penned the *Peggy Stories*, he describes the combination of autonomy and safety that made these imaginative activities so satisfying: "enterprising girls and boys generally have some opportunity for playing Robinson and Friday on some desert island, in the pasture, or in the pond,—or in the midst of the hills— separated from the rest of the world, for the convenience of hut-building, but still not so wholly insulated but one can go to dinner when the bell rings" (187). Clearly his account of these "enterprising girls and boys" celebrates his own busy and inventive brood. In a letter to his wife from the summer of 1873, Edward Everett Hale details the pleasures of a beach holiday in Matunuck, Rhode Island:

> The older children are constantly talking of Swiss Family Robinson. As we came five of us from the beach the other day, they said Papa was "I," Nelly the good Elizabeth, Arthur Fritz, Edward Ernest, Philip Jack and Berty Francis. Then they seemed conscious that Edward and Ernest did not fit well and tried to recast their characters. You will guess that the whole imagination originated with Edward. (Hale Jr. 2:183)

That last sentence rather oddly suggests that Edward would indeed make a good Ernest, even if it registers that the more active characters were more attractive to children than this most reflective and well-read of the Swiss boys. In the remainder of this essay I strive to eavesdrop on the Hale family's game of "constant talking of *Swiss Family Robinson*," by putting scenes from the books the Hale children made into conversation with this beloved childhood novel, and adding their words and drawings to the long tradition of building island homes in the pages of a book.

ISLANDS: BOOKS, HOUSES, AND COLONIES

Johann Rudolf Wyss's preface to this book voices a distinctly troubled attitude toward reading, or at least to solitary reading outside the succor of the family:

> In reality, it is very rarely, and perhaps never, proper that children should read by themselves; few indeed are the individuals in those tender years that are not either too indolent, too lively, or too capricious to employ themselves usefully upon this species of occupation. (5)

Such anxiety about books permeates the novel. Little Francis in particular responds to the island through a lens of fantasies and fears fostered by books: "Do you know, papa, I have been thinking that this must be an enchanted forest, like those I have read about in my little books," he exclaims (315). But even though young readers encounter this marvelous island world through their own little books, *The Swiss Family Robinson* represents such interpretations as wrong-headed. As the father repeatedly explains, the abundant pleasures of their island home are not marks of fiction's enchanting imagination but rather proof that "the whole scheme of nature is a perpetual tissue of wonders proceeding from the hand of a beneficent creator" (314).

Many critics have noted that the relation between book knowledge and natural experience proves hopelessly circular and paradoxical in *The Swiss Family Robinson*, as in the following discussion:

> [Ernest:] if I am not mistaken he is named the *agouti*.
>
> Ah! Ha! said Fritz, here is a learned professor profound in the subject of natural history!
>
> And who this once is not mistaken? cried I. Spare your raillery Fritz, for it is really an agouti. I do not myself know anything of the animal: but by his description in books or engravings, with which his appearance perfectly corresponds; he is a native of America, lives underground on the roots of trees, and is, as travellers report, excellent food. But of this we will judge for ourselves. (33–34)

Jean-Jacques Rousseau's *Emile* (1762) asserts that true education derives from lived experience rather than from book knowledge.[11] *The Swiss Family Robinson* obviously prizes the boys' direct experience with nature, gleeful that they can trust their own tongues rather than travelers' reports for judgment on the agouti's relative tastiness. Still, father's and Ernest's detailed knowledge of the agouti comes explicitly from books, and many editions of *The Swiss Family Robinson* intersperse images of the family's more dramatic adventures with precise realistic engravings like this one with its Latin species nomenclature (fig. 21.2) and thus offer this fictional book as precisely the sort of reference work father and Ernest have relied on for their knowledge of the agouti.

The Hale children literally treat *The Swiss Family Robinson* as a reference book. In the 1843 volume from the Franklin Library, *The Unsuccessful Voyage to America*, two boys starting off on a journey "had read *Robinson Crusoe, Swiss Family Robinson*, and *The French Cabin Boy*. In case they should be wrecked they provided themselves with a chest of which more will be told here after" (2). The boys are, of course, shipwrecked, at which point the book lists the tools they have prudently brought with them in that chest, having been well prepared by their reading. In the 1842 Franklin Library book *Adventures of Bill and Tom with their Dog Jack*, Charles Hale enumerates, in a carefully laid out footnote ranged in columns, the contents of the "gunners chest" that Bill and Tom recover from their shipwreck. His list contains not only six entries for guns and ammunition but also a library, including "1 Robinson Crusoe,"

WHAT IS IT ?   37

THE AGOUTI (*Dasyprocta*).

been saved, and that some vessel has picked them up *en
route.*"

I made no answer, for I knew better than my wife the perils of
a stormy sea and crowded boats; but I was unwilling to disturb
my family with sorrowful and unavailing reflections. Frederick
then resumed the narration of his adventures.

"I descried several animals of this species," said he; "I saw it
leaping among the grass, and sometimes squatting in the grass on
its hind-legs, and rubbing its snout with its fore-paws. Had I not
been afraid it might escape me, I should have endeavoured to catch
it alive, for it appeared to me tolerably tame."

Meanwhile Ernest examined the animal in question.

"It does not belong to the porcine race," he remarked; "for
though it has a bristly skin, it has not the teeth of a hog, but only
incisors like the rodents.* It closely resembles an animal which
I have noticed in the engravings of my Natural History, and if

[* The *Rodentia, Rodent,* or *Gnawing Animals,* is an order forming a connecting link
between the flesh-eating and herbivorous Mammals, and distinguished by the peculiar
conformation of their teeth; having two long chisel-shaped incisors in each jaw, admirably adapted for gnawing vegetable substances. They rather leap than walk, and most
of them have the habit of sitting upon their haunches, using their fore-feet to carry the
food to their mouths. The squirrel, marmot, beaver, rabbit, hare, rat, lemming, cavy,
capybara, jerboa, porcupine, mouse, are all *Rodents.* —*Translator.*]

Figure 21.2. Detailed illustration of the agouti with scientific Latin tag in *The Swiss
Family Robinson* (London and New York: T. Nelson and Sons, 1870), 37. This edition was
first sold in New York in 1865 and so is contemporaneous with the Charlieshope Library.

"3 Bibles," and a number of history books, as well as paper and ink. "You may be sure
these things were very acceptable," Charles concludes (4:2). Both *Robinson Crusoe*
and *The Swiss Family Robinson* emphasize the excessive arsenal enlisted in the settling of deserted islands, and Crusoe took similar relish in the making of lists. I will
say more about the lessons of colonization at stake in these castaway tales, but that
these book-making children value not only armaments but also writing implements
highlights the extent to which they understand these accounts as literary adventures
and recognize that their islands are in fact made of paper.

Nelly Hale makes similar use of Wyss's novel in the Charlieshope Library book *Mary Lowell or the Desert Island* (1865). When the shipwrecked Mary returns to the boat from which she seems to be the only human survivor, she rescues cows, horses, cats, and fowl "so that," as she modestly puts it, "I was well provided with animals" (17); she also "packed some of my plainest dresses into a chest with some pens and ink, my work-box, some books, and some pencils and paper, among the books was the Swiss Family Robinson" (14). Gender distinctions mark the boys' chest full of guns and influence both Mary's care in collecting her sewing kit and her tender pleasure in the kittens, as well as Nelly's focus on the pragmatic selection of only the "plainest" dresses. As an instructor in gender norms *The Swiss Family Robinson* itself offers a very limited role for women. The father narrates, knows, and does, while the "exemplary" mother mostly cooks and worries (Green 69–70, Miller 141). In contrast, although the shipwreck stories Nelly and her girlhood friends write for the Charlieshope Library often contain rather heroic cooking (think of Margaret and the chocolate pot), and even some worrying, they are characterized by a sense of female possibilities largely lacking in Wyss's novel and most renditions of the castaway plot.[12] When Mary first finds herself alone on the abandoned ship she bursts into tears but "soon remembered that crying makes no difference, so I stopped and began to think how to save myself" (4). Ultimately the provisions Mary salvages from the ship include "a gun (for my father had taught me how to use one) some powder and shot." Thus while island life may be better suited to plain dresses than to lace, and Mary's resilience and prowess require explanations that the boys never need to provide, the similarities of these castaway tales, the fact that both boy and girl authors evoke *The Swiss Family Robinson* as a narrative model and a source of expertise, suggest that one of the pleasures of island adventures may lie precisely in the opportunities these literary fantasies offer to flout gender conventions.

Shawn Thomson convincingly argues that as the most beloved of boyhood reading "*Robinson Crusoe* served as a platform from which young men broke from the hold of the sentimental family and met the opportunities and blunt realities of Jacksonian America" (147). Edward Everett Hale acknowledged in his essay on *Crusoe* that "the girls do not like it so well as the boys" and explains this is "because they are afraid of the 'Savages,' and do not like the idea of roasting people and eating them; so they have to skip the parts of the book that are most entertaining to their brothers" (187). Despite the satirical gendering of his published essay (who is being ridiculed here, the skittish girls or the boys entertained by cannibalism?), this father's observations of his own children's reading and play seem to recognize that girls could be fascinated by this castaway story and suggest how narratives of island survival might actually function to fortify the sentimental family. In a letter to his then-ten-year-old daughter, Edward Everett Hale describes how he reads "Robinson Crusoe to Arthur every morning" and adds that the little boy "is very much delighted with it. We have come today as far as the goat in the cave" (Hale Family Papers, February 11, 1864). The letter implies that father and daughter had once shared this same delight. It enacts a complex familial function, inviting Nelly to participate both in the childhood pleasure of remembering Crusoe's adventures and in the more parental pleasure of observing her five-year-old brother's excitement about this beloved book. The *Crusoe* plot might be, as Thomson argues, "a map to manhood," but the sharing of it inside the family charts familial bonds (146). As Andrew O'Malley notes, abridgements of *Robinson Crusoe* intended for children devote disproportionate space to Crusoe's domestic arrangements (341). One of the attractions of *The Swiss Family Robinson*, of course, is that in marooning the whole family together it produces not the isolated individual but the insular family. It is Wyss's novel that Mary Lowell salvages, and perhaps not surprisingly this Charlieshope book ends with Mary discovering her family safely ensconced on another part of the island.

Michael Seidel notes that *Robinson Crusoe* is "not only a primer on how to live on a remote island, but on how to write the experience up" (79). *The Swiss Family Robinson* includes occasional moments in which father remarks on his journal keeping, but the places of most chaotic contradiction between the various versions rest on awkward attempts to provide frame scenarios with Russian ships or British ones that can bring the journal of these adventures back to civilization and readers. In a sense the novel's own ambivalence about textual versus experiential knowing hampers the moments that acknowledge the novel's status as writing. Charles Hale's *A Voyage to Patagonia*, written for the Franklin Library in 1841, betrays no such insecurities. Peter is abandoned with just "the long boat of the ship . . . with six oars in it and also a sheet of paper and some pens and ink. He then began to write a Journal of this event and after he had finished it he got into the boat and rowed to Boston" (7–8). As the Hale children see it, first you write up your adventure and only then can you row home.

These stories very self-consciously depict their own production: in painstakingly imitating the genre traits and material form of published books the children broadcast their mastery of bibliographic conventions (fig. 21.3). For example, in creating the 1842 Franklin Library book *Bill Pumpkin*, the children lavished much care on the decorative initial capitals at the beginning of chapters. The footnote appended to this drawing suggests both a lack of confidence that the picture of a billowing sail will be recognized as the B of BILL, as well as a proud delight in this punning device. With this note the bookmakers call attention to their brilliant use of printerly conventions, not wanting to risk that any reader might miss it. The attempt to cram page numbers, chapter numbers, a map, and its legend onto these tiny sheets tends toward chaos, but it makes clear how much the effort of constructing these books is the Hale children's own equivalent to the castaways' labor of producing and organizing a coherent island home. The 1845 Franklin Library story of *Jack Tokera* sports better page layout, a firm grasp of eighteenth-century titling conventions, and a sense of irony (fig. 21.4). Parodying the bookish tendencies of their adventure stories, the Hale children wittily proffer school learning as the best "life preserver": the boy thrown overboard without it drowns.

The Swiss Family Robinson calls attention to the ties between the construction efforts that build their island home and the work of imagination. The preface to an 1836 Boston edition of the novel asks: "What youthful reader of lively dispositions,

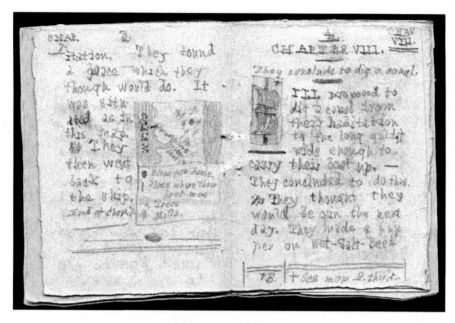

Figure 21.3. The pages of this Franklin Library book overflow with the Hale children's efforts to demonstrate their knowledge of publishing conventions. *Bill Pumpkin* (1842), 3–4, in the Hale Family Papers. Courtesy of the Sophia Smith Collection, Smith College, Northampton, Massachusetts.

would not try to possess, or dream of the possession of, a saw, a hammer, and some nails, and hurry, in fancy, to the contrivance of a Family Bridge, a staircase to Falcon's Nest, or a parlor, a bedroom, and a kitchen, in a Rock of Salt?" (v). This preface assumes that like the Swiss family themselves, the child readers' strongest desire will be to build houses. It is surprising to realize how much this adventure story dwells on the construction of domestic spaces; castaway *The Swiss Family Robinson* is nevertheless the most homebound of texts. The family's first island home, Tent House, is a quickly built and clearly makeshift structure. Though Tent House continues to be useful, and eventually gets improved and fortified, there is never anything very marvelous about it, and almost immediately the book occupies itself with imagining something better. That better is, of course, Falcon's Nest—the famous tree house.

But the rest of the book works to contain this fantasy nest of a house, ultimately bringing it to the ground. First father and mother become anxious that their children might fall in clambering up the ladders, and so construct the staircase to Falcon's Nest. Spiraling inside the hollow tree to reach the beds in the branches, this staircase is the novel's most complicated construction project. It takes two chapters to complete while most chapters hold two or three different undertakings. The boys work hard at it, of course—labor is one of the delights of *The Swiss Family Robinson*—but the impetus for this construction stems from parental fear, not boyish desire. When the rainy season comes the family must abandon the tree house altogether or at least till summer.

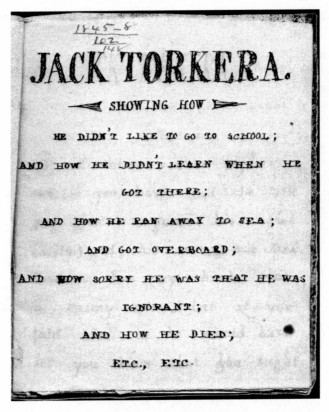

Figure 21.4. Title page of the Franklin Library book *Jack Torkera* (1845), in the Hale Family Papers. Courtesy of the Sophia Smith Collection, Smith College, Northampton, Massachusetts.

Wyss represents this hardship as a blessing. The easy abundance of the island poses a threat to the Swiss character, which the father suggests requires some bad weather:

> None of these valuable fruits are indigenous or native in the colder parts of Europe: yet this ungrateful and rough climate it is that operates on the European so as to distinguish him from the inhabitants of other parts of the world, by his intelligence, his fitness for toil, and his skill in agriculture. There exist abundant means for rendering man effeminate and indolent, but necessity and want stimulate him to industry and useful inventions and by these blessings the inconveniences of climate are amply compensated. (348)[13]

By the end of the book the family has not only constructed an underground rainy season home in a salt cave but also built two more regular houses on their various farms: "The whole had really the appearance of a European cottage, and was finished in the short space of six days" (424).

The six volumes of Charles Hale's *Adventures of Bill and Tom with their Dog Jack* (1842–43) features the boys' construction of a tree house, following some of the building strategies Wyss describes. In volume 3 Charles changes the format of his story in imitation of Crusoe's log, "We present to our readers [if we have any—] a journal which Bill kept" (3:4). As the adventures continue Charles has a hard time keeping track of which narrative mode he is using, sometimes erasing "they" and replacing it with "we" but in other places carelessly writing in the third person. Just as making homes fills the pages (and years) of *The Swiss Family Robinson* and *Robinson Crusoe*, house-building fuels this narrative. Once Bill and Tom have constructed their tree house, there seems little more to tell. Consequently in the last volume the boys abandon this island and set off for another, thus gaining the opportunity to build a new teepee home. A comparison of these two books reveals how much more careful and competent a draftsman Charles Hale has become at twelve than he was at eleven years old. This self-correcting tendency, in houses, in artistry, or in narrative form, suggests that the pleasure of these island fantasies stems largely from the opportunity to make the world anew: the colonizing instinct.

Unapologetic, the *Swiss Family Robinson* touts its colonizing stance: "We who are founders of a new colony!" (73) Father proclaims, and he and the boys talk repeatedly about how they are living in the "Patriarchal mode" (126) like Adam or Abraham. In his letter about the children playing *Swiss Family Robinson*, Edward Everett Hale makes light fun of that stance, noting how while "our life here is absolutely perfect . . . There is a patriarchal side to it which has an element of humor" (Hale Jr. 182–83). Of course in their games "Papa" Hale himself gets cast as the paternal "I."

Defoe's *Robinson Crusoe*, where the ill-fated journey begins as a slaving expedition, stands as one of the most cogent accounts of the economic structures of colonialism and capitalist expansion. Wyss's novel of island survival importantly revises Defoe's narrative, not only by providing a family, but also by making his island completely empty of any other human inhabitants. There may be animals to tame or kill, but there are no native peoples. References to "savages" are frequent in the novel however: many of the family's methods for preparing foods or climbing trees are learned from "savages" and "negro slaves" (312), or at least from reading about their practices. Thus all the savages found in *The Swiss Family Robinson* are imagined and literary: "Little Francis was terribly afraid that it must be the savages come to eat us up, like those described in Robinson Crusoe's island" (104), but the frightening sounds the boy hears are just father and Fritz returning from the wreck laden with more salvaged European goods.

The Hale books share Francis's sense that islands are likely to hold cannibals:

Tom. Do you suppose this island is inhabited?
Bill. Why—I don'o
Tom. I don't think it is or we should have seen them
Bill. Why they might be savages
Tom. Cannibals!
Bill. They might be

Tom. And they might be kind to us

Bill. Yes. I almost wish we were drowned! (*Bill and Tom* 2:3)

The Hales wrote during a period of great racial tension in the United States. The second generation's library includes a goodly collection of Civil War stories, but these tales rarely if ever mention slavery or race; they generally tell of children's heroic clashes with rebel soldiers. The Hales' shipwreck stories, however, are loaded with savages and slavery and suggest that, like little Francis, fear of racial others and conceptions of their own colonial and racial power is one thing that white child readers take from the castaway plot.

Sometimes these encounters are purely ethnographic, as in a series of Franklin Library books of island exploration: *Account of the Island of Buhue, Account of the I. of Logu,* and the like.[14] Generally, however, the libraries feature otherness as threat: Tom's thought that "they might be kind to us" hardly registering in their exchange. Still, Tom and Bill don't encounter savages and in the Charlieshope Library book *Clara Andrews and Her Friend who Lived in a Tree,* when Clara finds that communication with the natives on the island where she first lands "was no use . . . [s]he went away and landed on another part of the island where there were no savages" and she could safely build her *Swiss Family Robinson*–style tree house (21). The Hale children seem to recognize how their book-making and world-making activities entail colonizing conflict and power, but the islands of their imagination are flexible, with room for all. Despite the many guns they pack and their negative accounts of "savages," the Hales' island adventures never actually require human bloodshed.

Instead, just as shipwrecks enabled the Hale girls to loosen gender norms, imagining island life seems, at least occasionally, to invite the Hale children to forgo racial hierarchies. The 1841 Franklin Library book *The Negro Slave* by the Hales' cousin Robert Durivage, begins with "a negro slave" who "set out to run away he went aboard a ship and was wrecked and was drifted ashore he lay sick and exhausted. At last he got up and walked along and at last he came to a cavern in a rock where he crawled into and at last fell asleep" (2–3). After this anomalous and unusually grim landing ("at last, at last"), for the rest of this little book the shipwrecked runaway slave has precisely the kinds of adventures other castaways do: he kills a hare with a stone and cooks it on a spit over a fire, which he makes with ease because, lucky boy, "he found a match" (7). In this auspicious island life the book seems to lose all track of its racial, antislavery opening, becoming simply another castaway tale. *The Negro Slave* concludes: "he staid on the island five years and then he came over in a ship to America," as if it had no recollection at all that for this boy America threatened bondage and required escape (7). This slippage reflects the disquieting ease with which the black body might be erased in the antebellum imagination, but it also, and more hopefully, exemplifies the democratizing effect of participation in such a highly formulaic genre. The familiar patterns of the castaway story prove easy to adapt: even girls or slaves can inhabit a desert island and make it their own.

The island world of *The Swiss Family Robinson* celebrates domesticity, ingenuity, and abundance and equates colonial power with the power of the imagination. It prompts the Hale children, like generations of readers before and after them, to enter into the island world of this novel and lay claim to their own version of island life. Both for the Wyss family as father and sons collaborated in the creation of this narrative, and for the Hale siblings as they produced their libraries, the castaway plot allows children to see themselves and their scavenger ways as culturally productive. John Gillis and other scholars have written about the "islanding of childhood" as the often negative or nostalgic process of segregating children's spaces and cultures. The trajectories I have described in this essay focus rather on the elasticity of the island as a cultural trope. As the books produced by Defoe, Campe, Wyss, de Montolieu, and the Hale children build upon the castaway stories that come before them, they reveal the island to be less a site of isolation than of connection. In my reading of *The Swiss Family Robinson* and the Hale libraries, I treat children as participants in cultural formation, creatively deploying flotsam salvaged from the adult world. I am interested, then, less in how the castaway plot separates children on an island of childhood, however imaginative, than in the complex interconnectivity of these island stories and how they mark children and their books as part of a larger cultural project.

NOTES

1. A World Cat search (http://www.worldcat.org/) for editions of Daniel Defoe's *Robinson Crusoe* published in the United States by 1830 produces around 350 entries, including, of course, some reprintings of the same edition, all of them abridgements or adaptations, often for children. The earliest book version appears to be the edition printed in New York "by Hugh Gaine, at his book-store in Hanover-Square, where may be had a great variety of little books for young masters and misses, 1774." Besides editions produced in the major publication centers of New York, Boston, and Philadelphia, there were also many pre-1830 editions printed by booksellers in far smaller communities like Windsor, Vermont, and Cooperstown, New York.

2. For a fascinating account of Campe's pedagogical and philosophical concerns, see Erlin. In addition to children's books, the Crusoe story permeated American culture in virtually every literary genre: plays, songs, poetry, and more.

3. Unless otherwise indicated, all quotations from *The Swiss Family Robinson* refer to the Penguin edition, based on the 1816 edition of the Godwins' English translation.

4. Holden's unpublished M.A. thesis remains the best source for comparing the many English versions of this novel. The Godwins published additional editions in 1816 and again in 1818, now under the title *The Swiss Family Robinson*, and offered further modified versions in 1826 and 1828. The 1828 text, the seventh London edition, was used as

the basis for the first two U.S. editions, both published in New York in 1832. Harper and Brothers claimed that theirs was "improved by the author of 'Uncle Philip,'" the Episcopalian Minister Francis Hawks. The J. J. Harper 1832 imprint, published as part of their *Boys and Girls Library*, boasts that it is "sold by booksellers throughout the United States" and produced "from the 7th London edition, greatly improved."

    5. Modern editions rarely include the second volume of Crusoe's narrative and so do not end with him valuing peace but rather setting out on new adventures. Throughout the nineteenth century, however, children as well as adults generally read *Crusoe* in the two-volume version. Defoe's third volume has rarely been included in editions of the novel although some material from it often made it into even the abridgements for children. The Boston edition from which this quote is taken was intended for young readers. Even Aiken's *Robinson Crusoe in Words of One Syllable*, though greatly shortened and simplified, includes Crusoe's travels in Asia and ends with his serene account of approaching death. Aiken would also produce a "words of one syllable" version of *The Swiss Family Robinson*.

    6. The contemporary Oxford edition of *The Swiss Family Robinson* combines the 1826 Godwin text with J. D. Clinton Locke's 1848 translation of the de Montolieu addition, including Locke's introductory note.

    7. The elephants and hippopotami appear in chapter 15. Miller suspects that as a child he read a text based on Kingston's version, and most contemporary editions of the book aimed at young readers are still adaptations of the Kingston text.

    8. For a fuller account of these libraries, see my essay "Practicing for Print." The volumes of both libraries are in the Hale Family Papers. When referring in this essay to any of these handmade books I note the library to which it belongs, and give the title, date, and author of the volume if known (a good number of the books are anonymous, and some of the Charlieshope books have no date). In quoting from these books I have preserved the children's spelling, grammar, and punctuation.

    9. Erlin explains that Campe made this correction so as to more accurately reflect the South American location of Crusoe's island (369).

    10. See also Ramble, where the narrator claims "that couplet completed every story I ever heard on a sand-box, or in the porch of a corner store." Charles Hale uses the rhyme to end another castaway story, the Franklin Library book *History of Timothy Trumpet and Jack Fiddle* (1842), 4.

    11. *Robinson Crusoe* is the first and for a long time the only book Rousseau has Emile read since it "supplies the best treatise on an education according to nature" (205). Green discusses the influence of Rousseau's pedagogical theories on attitudes toward the "Crusoe Story" (34–47). Seelye's introduction notes Johann David Wyss's interest in Rousseau and his effort to follow the French philosopher's educational experiments in creating "a schoolhouse environment without perceptible walls" (xi–xii). For a provocative unmasking of Rousseau's relation to *Crusoe*, see Damisch.

    12. Interestingly, of the 128 German Robinsonsades, sixteen published in the eighteenth century have female protagonists, and like the books produced for the Hale libraries, these anonymous texts tend to imagine more elastic and utopian possibilities of what island life might offer women (Blackwell).

    13. In the rainy season's darkest pages of *The Swiss Family Robinson* Fritz finds a copy of *Robinson Crusoe* at the bottom of a chest of clothes and hails it as "our best counselor and model" (381); thus in the one scene in the novel that truly does seem like a trial Defoe (and his cave-building) becomes a resource.

    14. I discuss these ethnographic books in "Practicing for Print" (198–99).

WORKS CITED

Aiken, Lucy [Mary Godolphin, pseud.]. *Robinson Crusoe in Words of One Syllable.* New York: George Routledge and Sons, 1868.

——. *The Swiss Family Robinson in Words of One Syllable.* New York: George Routledge and Sons, 1869.

Blackwell, Jeannine. "An Island of Her Own: Heroines of the German *Robinsonades* from 1720 to 1800." *German Quarterly* 58 (1985): 5–26.

Campe, Joachim Heinrich. *Robinson der Jünger.* 1779. Stuttgart: Reclam, 1981.

——. *The New Robinson Crusoe.* 1788. New York: Garland Publishers, 1976.

——. *The New Robinson Crusoe, Designed for Youth.* New York: Thomas Powers, 1810.

Damisch, Hubert. "Robinsonnades I: The Allegory." Translated by Rosalind Krauss. *October* 102 (1998): 18–27.

Defoe, Daniel. *The Life and Adventures of Robinson Crusoe, of York, Mariner, with an Account of His Travels Around Three Parts of the Globe.* Boston: Munroe and Francis, n.d.

Duer, John. "Chinese Sketches." *Knickerbocker Magazine* (April 1860): 403.

Erlin, Matt. "Book Fetish: Joachim Heinrich Campe and the Commodification of Literature." *Seminar a Journal of Germanic Studies* 42 (2006): 355–76.

Fisher, Carl. "The Robinsonade: An Intercultural History of an Idea." In *Approaches to Teaching Robinson Crusoe*, edited by Maximillian E. Novak and Carl Fisher, 129–39. New York: Modern Language Association, 2005.

Gillis, John. "The Islanding of Children—Reshaping the Mythical Landscapes of Childhood." In *Designing Modern Childhoods: History, Space, and the Material Culture of Children*, edited by Marta Gutman and Ning De Conick-Smith, 316–30. New Brunswick, NJ: Rutgers UP, 2008.

Green, Martin. *The Robinson Crusoe Story.* University Park: Pennsylvania State UP, 1990.

Hale, Edward Everett. "The Book 'Robinson Crusoe.'" *The Riverside Magazine for Young People* 2 (1868): 187–90.

Hale, Edward, Jr. *The Life and Letters of Edward Everett Hale.* 2 vols. Boston: Little Brown, 1917.

Hale Family Papers. Ms. 71. Sophia Smith Collection. Smith College, Northampton, MA.

Hale, Susan. "Straw into Gold." *Old and New* 1 (1870): 754–55.

Holden, Philip. "A Textual History of J. R. Wyss's *The Swiss Family Robinson.*" M.A. thesis, University of Florida, 1986.

Kingston, Henry Giles. "Note." In *The Swiss Family Robinson*, by Johann David Wyss, ii. New York, London: George Routledge, 1879.

Lerer, Seth. *Children's Literature: A Reader's History, From Aesop to Harry Potter.* Chicago: U Chicago P, 2008.

Locke, J. D. Clinton. "Preface to the Translation of De Montolieu's Continuation." In *The Swiss Family Robinson*, by Johann David Wyss, 5. New York: Oxford UP, 1991.

Miller, J. Hillis. *On Literature.* New York: Routledge, 2002.

Nodiek, Charles. "Introduction." In *The Swiss Family Robinson.* London and New York: T. Nelson and Sons, 1870.

O'Malley, Andrew. "Crusoe at Home: Decoding Domesticity in Children's Editions of *Robinson Crusoe.*" *Journal for Eighteenth-Century Studies* 29 (2006): 337–359.

Ramble, Lincoln. "Chalkmarks." *The United States Magazine and Democratic Review* (November 1846): 451.

Rousseau, Jean-Jacques. *Emile: On Education*. 1762. Translated by Barbara Foxley. Charleston SC: Bibliobazaar, 2006.

Sánchez-Eppler, Karen. *Dependent States: The Child's Part in Nineteenth-Century American Culture*. Chicago: U of Chicago P, 2006.

———. "Practicing for Print: The Hale Children's Manuscript Libraries." *Journal of the History of Childhood and Youth* 1 (2008): 188–209.

Seelye, John. "Introduction." In *The Swiss Family Robinson*, by Johann David Wyss, vii–xxvi. New York: Oxford UP, 1991.

Seidel, Michael. *Robinson Crusoe: Island Myths and the Novel*. Boston: Twayne, 1991.

Selected Songs Sung at Harvard College from 1862–1866. Cambridge: Press of John Wilson and Sons, 1866.

Thomson, Shawn. "Robinson Crusoe and the Shaping of Masculinity in Nineteenth-Century America." In *Enterprising Youth: Social Values and Acculturation in Nineteenth-Century American Children's Literature*, edited by Monika Elbert. 133-148. New York: Routledge, 2008.

Wyss, Johann David. *The Swiss Family Robinson*. New York: Harper and Brothers, 1832.

———. *The Swiss Family Robinson*. New York: J. J. Harper, 1832.

———. *The Swiss Family Robinson*. Boston: Munroe and Francis, 1836.

———. *The Swiss Family Robinson*. Translated by Henry Giles Kingston. New York, London: George Routledge, 1879.

———. *The Swiss Family Robinson*. New York: Oxford UP, 1991.

———. *The Swiss Family Robinson*. New York: Penguin, 2007.

Wyss, Johann Rudolf. "Preface." In *The Swiss Family Robinson*, by Johann David Wyss, 1–5. New York: Penguin, 2007.

FURTHER READING

Alexander, Christie, Julie McMaster, and Gillian Beer. *The Child Writer from Austen to Woolf*. New York: Cambridge UP, 2005.

Armstrong, Michael. *Children Writing Stories*. New York: Open UP, 2006.

Goodenough, Elizabeth, Mark Heberle, and Naomi Sokoloff, eds. *Infant Tongues: The Voice of the Child in Literature*. Detroit, MI: Wayne State UP, 1994.

Hager, Kelly. "Betsy and the Canon." In *The American Child: A Cultural Studies Reader*, edited by Caroline F. Levander and Carol J. Singley, 106–27. New Brunswick, NJ: Rutgers UP, 2003.

Steedman, Carolyn Kaye. "The Tidy House." In *The Children's Culture Reader*, edited by Henry Jenkins, 431–55. New York: New York UP, 1998.

....

TOM BROWN AND THE SCHOOLBOY CRUSH: BOYHOOD DESIRE, HERO WORSHIP, AND THE BOYS' SCHOOL STORY

....

ERIC L. TRIBUNELLA

THOMAS *Hughes was born in Uffington, England, on October 20, 1822. He attended a private preparatory school as a boy before being sent to board at the elite Rugby School when he was eleven. In 1842 he left Rugby to attend Oriel College, Oxford, and in 1847 he married Frances Ford, with whom he had nine children. He began studying law a year later, and while living in London, he helped found Christian Socialism, which sought cooperation between social classes and between the church and workers. He also became an advocate for "muscular Christianity," a social movement for men that promoted the combination of spiritual devotion with athleticism and physical health, and in 1879 he published a book called* The Manliness of Christ. *He wrote a number of additional nonfiction works and biographies, but his most critically and commercially successful work was the 1857 publication of* Tom Brown's Schooldays, *to which he added a sequel,* Tom Brown at Oxford, *in 1861. Set at his beloved Rugby School, the novel was well received in both Britain and the United States and helped popularize the genre of the boys' school story. From 1865 to 1874 Hughes served in Parliament, and in 1880 he helped found a utopian community in the United States, in the state of Tennessee. The village, which he named Rugby, was established especially for the younger*

sons of upper-class families, who struggled to find work during the recession of the
1870s. Financially drained by this American venture, Hughes accepted an appointment
as a county judge in Chester County, England, in 1882. He lived there until his death
in 1896.

Tom Brown and the Boys' School Story

To label a sentiment or desire a "childhood infatuation" or "adolescent crush"
is effectively to dismiss it. Such phrases suggest adult disdain for youth and inexperience, and they play off of the pejorative connotations of "childhood" and
"adolescent" in contrast with adulthood and its supposedly more temperate
passions. However, feminist and queer studies have taught us to attend carefully
to the discursive formations of sexuality and to reevaluate otherwise overlooked
or devalued forms of desires, identities, and pleasures. The schoolboy (or school-
girl) crush is one of those affectional dynamics that is experienced frequently
and intensely by children and adolescents and yet remains largely ignored or
denigrated by adults as infantile and thus unimportant. To the extent that the
crush is indeed a common feature of childhood and adolescence, being attuned
to its operation is helpful when examining books for young readers. The field of
children's literature shares with queer studies an interest in reclaiming previously
overlooked or marginal subjects of study, refusing to dismiss works for children
as "mere" kiddie fare, so a queer theoretical approach to children's literature is
especially useful for considering undervalued forms of childhood desires, pleasures, and relationships. It is in this spirit that I reconsider the schoolboy crush
as an often-overlooked form and practice of desire that nonetheless constitutes
a frequent and important feature of both nineteenth-century boyhood and the
boys' school story, and I examine the importance of the schoolboy crush and
its power to make or break the moral, social, and spiritual successes of boys
and men, especially in Thomas Hughes's landmark school story *Tom Brown's
Schooldays* (1857). I consider the historical record regarding the schoolboy crush,
sometimes referred to in terms of hero worship, in order to explore the importance of Tom Brown's feelings for a relatively minor character, Brooke, an
older boy whom Tom admires from afar. I argue that schoolboy crushes promote
the ideals of same-sex bonding while avoiding the danger that romantic friendships might cross the line into prohibited relationships of sex, contamination,
and vice.

F. J. Harvey Darton, the venerable historian of children's literature, claims that
nineteenth-century writers established a "definite image of Young England: the
Public School Boy for males, the Woman in the Home for females" (286), and John
Reed notes that "public schools were of paramount importance in the development
of a special ethos in Victorian society" ("The Public Schools" 58). British "public

schools," exclusive private schools with a tradition of educating the upper classes, include such well-known institutions as Eton and Rugby. The latter provides the setting for Hughes's *Tom Brown's Schooldays*.[1] Founded in 1557 for the education of local boys in the town whose name it bears, Rugby School, along with its peer institutions, became increasingly exclusive over the course of the seventeenth and eighteenth centuries. Reed notes that by the mid-nineteenth century, these schools were used to educate the new ruling class (*Old School* 4). Alongside the increasing prominence of the public schools, the school story emerged as an important subgenre of children's fiction during the nineteenth century, marking the significance of the public schools within British Victorian society and their key role in socializing the ideal British gentleman.

Although not the first school story, *Tom Brown* embodies many of the elements that would both establish the model for all subsequent boys' school stories and inspire countless imitators in the decades that followed its 1857 publication. According to Reed, "It was Hughes' novel that established permanently the traditional characters, topics, and situations of the public school novel" (*Old School* 26), and contemporary readers of more recent school stories like *Harry Potter* will recognize some of these characteristics, such as the emphasis on sports, the oversight of a benevolent and wise headmaster, the exploits of a gang of friends, and so on. The influence of *Tom Brown* was such that it would come to be imagined as a key prototype of the genre, and along with Frederic Farrar's *Eric, or Little by Little* (1858), Talbot Baines Reed's *The Fifth Form at St. Dominic's* (1881), and Rudyard Kipling's *Stalky and Co.* (1899), it is often cited as one of the most important examples of the boys' school story. Of the four, it is probably the best known and most frequently read. It has remained in print since its initial publication and has been made into four feature films, most recently in 2005 by Dave Moore.

Written for the occasion of Hughes's son's impending departure for school, *Tom Brown's Schooldays* serves not only as a warning to new schoolboys about the difficulties of school life but also as a guide to negotiating its complex social, political, and sexual dynamics. Hughes himself had attended Rugby, so he knew firsthand the culture of meanness, violence, and vice his son would encounter there. The novel begins by providing a glimpse of Tom Brown's childhood before he is sent away to Rugby, and Hughes extols the virtues of the English countryside and people like the Brown family, on whose backs the English empire is built. The structure of the novel is mostly episodic as it follows Tom through his experiences with various schoolboy rituals including dealing with bullies, participating in sports, struggling with the temptation to cheat, and forming friendships with other boys. The central narrative arc involves Tom's declining behavior as he adjusts to the violence of the school and his subsequent reformation through his relationship with a smaller, weaker student named George Arthur, whose spiritual influence and dependence on Tom compel the stronger, pluckier boy to improve his behavior. Over the course of the novel, Tom matures into a fine young man, finally leaving school for Oxford.

HOMOEROTICISM IN SCHOOLS
AND SCHOOL STORIES

One of the key qualities widely recognized by readers and critics alike is the homoeroticism, or homoaffectionalism, of school stories—including *Tom Brown's Schooldays* (Lane 208, Martin 494–95 and 498–99, Quigley 126–27). As single-sex institutions, boarding schools engender a range of same-sex relations, from homosocial friendships to actual sexual explorations and romantic relationships between boys. Given the primacy of men's relationships with other men during the nineteenth century in domains ranging from business and government to education and the military, schools became important sites for fostering intimate or romantic friendships among boys, as well as crushes on older boys and men. While sex between boys would remain officially prohibited and mostly clandestine in practice, the circumstances and culture of the public schools encouraged intimate homo*social* friendships between boys. Eve Kosofsky Sedgwick's groundbreaking study *Between Men: English Literature and Male Homosocial Desire* (1985) defines homosociality as "the spectrum of male bonds that includes but is not limited to the 'homosexual'" (85), including same-sex friendships. The public schools were crucial in the formation of these homosocial bonds, as Sedgwick points out (176). Historian Matt Cook describes the tradition of men's clubs that "formed a continuation of the homosocial worlds of public schools and university" (30). These all-male spaces provided opportunities to escape the world of women, just as the boarding school removed boys from the influence of mothers and nurses and exposed them to communities of other boys and male schoolmasters. Thus, public schools were key sites for the establishment of these intense same-sex bonds that would form the foundation of men's lives, especially ruling-class men, who would draw on those relationships and connections for the work of business and commerce, law, government, and empire. *Tom Brown's Schooldays* includes the formation of such bonds as one of its most salient features.

Given the homosocial environment of the school, boys inevitably formed close friendships with other boys. Reed observes of former public school students, "Men who had no particular love for their schools fondly remembered friendships begun there" ("The Public Schools" 63). Carolyn Oulton argues that "at mid-century, the public school system was largely responsible for fostering same-sex attachment among both boys and girls in the name of public morality" (73). So-called romantic friendships—intimate, affectionate, intense, though *ostensibly* platonic friendships between persons of the same sex—were one of the hallmarks of public schools and of the broader culture of nineteenth-century Britain, which promoted the segregation of sexes into separate social spheres both as an ideal and a common practice.[2] Historians of sexuality explain that for most of the nineteenth century even the most ardent displays or statements of affection would not have implied either a sexual relationship or the notion of a discrete or biological homosexual essence. Indeed, the language of homosexuality and the perception of a strict divide between homosexuality and heterosexuality were only in the process of coming into being over the course of the latter half of the nineteenth century. At the time of the publication of *Tom Brown* and *Eric*, readers would not have understood the population as being divided into different types of persons based on romantic or sexual desire, and the notion that anyone might experience same-sex desire without being totally defined by it would have been consistent with the more common understanding of sex between boys or men as a moral lapse into which anyone might be tempted, rather than as marking a biological or psychological condition distinguishing only certain individuals. Thus, the schoolboy crush or romantic friendship, in the absence of actual sexual activity, would not have resulted in the kind of stigma that would be associated with homosexuality, which implies sex or sexual desire.

THE SCHOOLBOY CRUSH

The boys' school story records a variety of same-sex relations, ranging from depictions of platonic, intimate friendships between boys to intimations of actual sexual activity. In this essay I will concentrate specifically on discussing the schoolboy crush. I differentiate the crush from romantic friendships, and I argue the crush is characterized by an intense and passionate desire that usually remains unrequited or unreciprocated by the object of affection, who is admired, sometimes even anonymously, from afar. While critics who have discussed the homoeroticism of school stories have understandably focused on romantic friendships, I propose that what would come to be known as the crush also plays an important role in the lives of schoolboys and in landmark school stories such as *Tom Brown's Schooldays*.[3] Crushes encouraged boys to emulate and submit to older boys and men, thereby creating bonds of loyalty and service essential to Victorian society. These passionate schoolboy crushes might therefore have constituted an ideal of same-sex devotion essential to the kinds of homosocial relations described by Sedgwick, and because the schoolboy crush could occur without direct contact between boys, unlike romantic friendships, it circumvented many of the obstacles designed to prevent more sexual or physically intimate relations.

In 1897, British sexologist Havelock Ellis published *Sexual Inversion*, one of the first major studies of homosexuality in the English language. In it, Ellis claims to have amassed evidence of "the prevalence of homosexual and auto-erotic phenomena in public and private schools (46), and he notes their reputations as "hot-beds of vice" (45).[4] The subject of Case XIII provides one actual account that bears striking similarities to the crushes described in *Tom Brown's Schooldays*. He is described as a thirty-four-year-old artist, who attended boarding schools as a child, including a major public school, and he explains being unprepared for the sexual environment of the school: "The earliest sex-impression that I am conscious of is at the age of 9 or 10 falling in love with a handsome boy who must have been about two years my senior. I do not recollect ever having spoken to him, but my desire, so far as I can recall, was that he should seize hold of and handle me. I have a distinct impression yet of how pleasurable even physical pain or cruelty would have been at his hands" (71). The subject goes on to describe all manner of sexual contact as taking place at the public school he attended, but it is notable that he recollects so strongly his schoolboy crush on a fellow with whom he never spoke. Firsthand accounts of nineteenth- and early twentieth-century school crushes, such as those reported by the subject of Case XIII, suggest the prevalence of the crush in schools, which is characterized by five qualities: the passionate admiration for an older student by a younger one, minimal contact between boys, the initial eruption of this desire as a result of a passing word or gesture, the relative anonymity of the younger boy, and the lack of reciprocity from the older one.[5]

Because the crush appears to be a common feature of youth and of literature about young people, contemporary feminist and queer scholars have begun to examine the historical and literary significance of the crush in ways that illuminate works such as *Tom Brown's Schooldays*. In her research on schoolgirl crushes in nineteenth-century English boarding schools, historian Martha Vicinus distinguishes between romantic friendships between same- or near-age girls and the kind of crushes I am exploring. Of the latter, she explains, "The emotions were concentrated on a distant, inaccessible, but admired student or teacher; differences in age and authority encouraged and intensified desire" (216). As a special kind of same-sex relationship, the crush holds its own possibilities and pleasures. It becomes clear that the crush on a distant, inaccessible figure constitutes a distinct species of childhood desire, and Vicinus suggests that the particular benefits associated with this experience include facilitating self-definition and community socialization. She writes, "An essential pleasure for those who loved a remote figure was the very distance itself, which gave room, paradoxically, for an enriched consciousness of self. Without gratification, countless fantasies could be constructed, a seemingly continuous web of self-examination, self-inspection, self fulfillment" (218). Responding to Vicinus, Sherrie A. Inness argues in her study of same-sex crushes in women's turn-of-the-century college fiction that "the schoolgirl crush as represented in women's college fiction is an important element in the socialization of the new student into her peer community" (50). Inness argues that while medical and sexological discourse at the turn of the century increasingly discussed the crush as dangerous or pathological, school fiction countered such claims with depictions of same-sex crushes as beneficial: "According to these novels, an acceptable crush socializes outsiders into the community and spreads the hegemonic codes of the institution" (56). As Inness explains, the community exercises this socializing function through the crush by identifying the desirable characteristics that make the desired object worth admiring.

Paul Fussell's study of World War I and its literature provides a way of thinking about the broader implications and uses of the schoolboy crush, revealing at least three connections between the Great War and the public schools of boys' school stories: both involve single-sex experiences and environments, both are violent and notoriously brutal, and many of the British military officers of the war had themselves been public-school boys. In many ways, the circumstances of war replicate public school life, and the respect and adoration of soldiers for their officers and officers for their men reproduce the dynamics of the schoolboy crush. As Fussell explains, "Given this association between war and sex, and given the deprivation and loneliness and alienation characteristic of the soldier's experience—given, that is, his need for affection in a largely womanless world—we will not be surprised to find both the actuality and the recall of front-line experience replete with what we can call the homoerotic" (272). He notes that rather than overt homosexual relations, seen were "something more like the 'idealistic,' passionate but non-physical 'crushes' which most of the officers had experienced at public school" (272). Fussell quotes author J. R. Ackerley, who writes, "the Army with its male relationships was simply an extension of my public school," and Fussell notes that with regards to the objects of battlefield crushes, "as at school, one generally admired them from a distance" (273). Fussell confirms that "it was largely members of the upper and upper-middle classes who were prepared by public-school training to experience such crushes," thereby connecting the school experience directly to war and suggesting how the stakes of the schoolboy crush might extend beyond the school (273). According to Fussell, the crush prepared boys for the bonds between men required to maintain the British public sphere and support the success of the British empire, and *Tom Brown's Schooldays* makes clear that the boys of Rugby are training for precisely this kind of work.

TOM BROWN, ERIC, AND THE USE
OF THE SCHOOLBOY CRUSH

The boys' school story confirms these social benefits of same-sex crushes discussed by Vicinus, Inness, and Fussell. The culture of schools promoted the crush as a means of socializing young people by offering them models to emulate and valorize from afar. We see the dynamic of the schoolboy crush at play in *Tom Brown* between Tom and old Brooke, a sixth-form boy who only briefly and casually acknowledges the much younger protagonist.[6] Tom is the outsider socialized into school life through his admiration for Brooke, who is constructed as a useful object of boyhood desire constituted by an intense mixture of admiration for the desired object and longing for some reciprocal expression of attention, especially a word or gesture of affection. This sentiment is felt at a distance and remains unknown or unrecognized even by the object of the crush. In contrast, Farrar's *Eric, or Little by Little*, from the same period, highlights the dangers of the crush that becomes a full-blown romantic friendship, and while Tom attains successful manhood at the conclusion of Hughes's novel, Eric is corrupted through his friendship with an older boy (and later a younger one) and ultimately perishes.

Brooke is introduced in a pivotal scene on Tom's first day at Rugby. East introduces Tom to the traditions of the school and explains that a crucial game of what would come to be known as rugby football is to be played that day.[7] The traditional event pits School-house, the dormitory in which Tom and East lodge and from which they derive a sense of a community and identity, against all of the other houses of the school. While the young Tom is meant only to watch, he eventually demonstrates his pluck by throwing himself into the game.[8] Brooke leads the School-house team, and when Tom asks about him, East replies, "Why, that big fellow who called over at dinner, to be sure. He's cock of the School, and head of the School-house side" (98). The game brings much of the school out to watch, so the eleven-year-old Tom is given the opportunity to examine his schoolmates, and the older boys in particular, "surveying them from a distance with awe" (100). Hughes describes in detail the football match, which puts the boys' bodies and athletic prowess on display and provides opportunities for the heroic feats that inspire crushes. Hughes's idealization of Brooke is further signaled by the intrusive narrator, who confesses his own desire for a leader like Brooke: ". . . but over all is old Brooke, absolute as he of Russia [Czar Alexander II], but wisely and bravely ruling over willing and worshipping subjects, a true football king. His face is earnest and careful as he glances a last time over his array, but full of pluck and hope, the sort of look I hope to see in my general when I go out to fight" (104). Hughes's language reflects the boys' feelings for Brooke, which are only intensified when he actually pays them individual attention, however slight. During the game Tom heroically throws himself on the ball, and many of the older and bigger boys pile on top of him. It is Brooke who picks him up and dusts him off, feeling Tom's limbs to make sure nothing is broken. "Well, he is a plucky youngster, and will make a player," Brooke says of Tom (113). After the conclusion of the match Brooke again addresses Tom and East, and Hughes's description of the encounter reflects the burgeoning of a schoolboy crush:

> Old Brooke caught sight of East, and stopped; put his hand kindly on his shoulder and said, "Bravo youngster, you played famously; not much the matter, I hope?"
>
> "No, nothing at all," said East, "only a little twist from that charge."
>
> "Well, mind and get all right for next Saturday;" and the leader passed on, leaving East better for those few words than all the opodeldoc [a medical cure-all] in England would have made him, and Tom ready to give one of his ears for as much notice. Ah! light words of those whom we love and honour, what a power ye are, and how carelessly wielded by those who can use you! (114)

This is the most substantial and direct contact Hughes represents the two younger boys having with old Brooke.

This passage constitutes an explicit acknowledgement of how hero worship benefits boys. East is made better by old Brooke's attention, and Tom, too, desires to be noticed. This demonstrates the power of even the most casual gesture of an aloof hero. The narrator confirms the significance of the schoolboy crush with an enthusiastic intrusion into the narrative that also suggests adult nostalgia for these boyhood relationships. Later, Tom does enjoy the privilege of serving Brooke as a fag, a younger student who is expected to run errands and provide services, such as cleaning, for the sixth-form boys: "Tom, in the first blush of his hero-worship, felt it a high privilege to receive orders from and be the bearer of the supper of old Brooke" (145).[9] The language of love, craving, and hero worship indicates that we are in the realm of the schoolboy crush, which the novel clearly represents as having a positive effect on the younger boy.

Brooke is an especially valuable object of the schoolboy crush because he embodies qualities of the ideal boy or young man, including athletic prowess, moral virtue, and skillful leadership. Brooke demonstrates his leadership both on and off of the sports field. The boys refer to him as "Pater [father] Brooke," and at the celebration on the evening of the big match, he addresses his house, to the delight of all the boys present. Brooke condemns bullying and drinking and encourages more unity among the School-house boys. He supports Dr. Arnold's reforms and endorses the discipline that Arnold, and later the public school system in general, would come to embody. His support of the new headmaster and the changes to tradition instituted by Arnold prove controversial with the boys; however, Brooke's popularity allows him to win them over, thereby ensuring that the support of School-house would be thrown behind Arnold. When the under-porter of the house arrives to break up the proceedings for the night, even this adult must look to old Brooke for support, and it is at Brooke's instigation that the boys clear the room. The term ends successfully, with the house "ruled well and strongly" by Brooke (144). To the extent that a large part of the school's function is to make boys into good men, promoting the crush of a younger boy on an ideal older specimen of young manhood helps socialize the boys into effective and respected leaders.

Fussell's connection between the public-school experience of British officers and the Great War provides more perspective on the scene from *Tom Brown* in which old Brooke is introduced and established as a leader. Hughes explicitly likens the Rugby game to a battle, and Brooke to an officer. The narrator addresses the reader directly: "My dear sir, a battle would look much the same to you, except the boys would be men, and the balls iron; but a battle would be worth your looking at for all that, and so is a football match" (106). Hughes understands or anticipates the significance of the schoolboy crush to the kinds of homosocial bonds necessary for the establishment and defense of the empire. As Robert Aldrich explains, "The virtues seen as necessary for the success of the colonial endeavor—bravery, endurance, loyalty, a winning spirit and a sense of fair play—were those ascribed to men. Such ideals were inculcated at all-male boarding schools and military academies, in the predominantly male environment of universities, and on the playing fields where boys competed against each other in preparation to fight for empire" (56). Crushes on officers and administrators would promote, if not ensure, a respect for the military and imperial hierarchy amidst both the bewildering carnage of war and the struggle of the colonial frontier, and the affection of officers for their men would help inspire a sense of protectiveness and respect for the lives they oversaw. The crush from a distance provides a way to encourage these passionate attachments to other men while minimizing the risk of sexual vice and incontinence.

Moreover, Hughes's novel does allude explicitly to specific anxieties about sex between boys, as Claudia Nelson observes. In what she rightly notes is a famous passage in the novel, Tom and East discuss young boys who are known to be sexually available to older ones, referring to one particular boy who has been sent on an errand to enlist the services of a few younger students: "He was one of the miserable little pretty white-handed curly-headed boys, petted and pampered by some of the big fellows, who wrote their verses for them, taught them to drink and use bad language, and did all they could to spoil them for everything in this world and the next" (233). The notion that the boys are being spoiled in this world and the next by their relationships with the older boys obliquely refers to spiritual damnation as a result of homosexual activity. This sentence occasions the only footnote provided by Hughes in the novel, which reads, "there were many noble friendships between big and little boys, but I can't strike out the passage; many boys will know why it is left in" (233). It is left in surely because Hughes wants to include noteworthy features of school life, including the possibility of sexual relations, but given Tom and East's disgust, the passage also serves to warn schoolboy readers away from sex with other boys. Nelson also explains, "For Hughes it seems that the threat of the 'white-handed boys' of pre-reform Rugby was not that they might grow up homosexual, but that introduced to sex in a context in which purity and repression played no part, they would grow up corrupt, to patronize prostitutes or overtax their wives" (546). Introducing the pretty, curly-headed boy allows Hughes to acknowledge the possibility of sexual vice and provides Tom and East the opportunity to disavow any imputations that they are themselves implicated. In fact, Tom calls the boy the "worst sort we breed," and he tells East, "Thank goodness, no big fellow ever took to petting me" (235). East reassures Tom and the reader, "You'd never have been like that" (235).[10] East confirms that Tom is sufficiently masculine to avoid being similarly spoiled by an older boy, but Tom's anxieties nonetheless betray the fear that any same-sex relationship between older and younger boys could be sexually dangerous.

In contrast to big fellows who take to petting younger ones, the novel presents old Brooke as set apart from the other boys, who are free to admire him from a distance without risk of being tempted into a more physical relationship. Brooke is so idealized and respected that he becomes socially inaccessible to younger or less accomplished boys who cannot approach him, and his lofty "virtue" presumably renders him unlikely to temp younger boys into sexual vice.

These references in *Tom Brown* to the dangers of romantic and sexual friendships between boys, especially of different ages, are relatively brief and seemingly inconsequential in the context of the novel, yet they provide a useful indicator as to why the crush as a form of desire for a distant and inaccessible object is superior. Frederic Farrar's *Eric*, another important school story, provides a more significant exploration of these dangers, linking Eric's moral decline and ultimate death to his romantic friendships with both an older and younger boy. Published one year after *Tom Brown's Schooldays*, Farrar's novel is considered far more sentimental than Hughes's, and thus ripe for mockery (Darton 286). Kipling makes the novel a subject of parody in *Stalky and Co.* (1899), in which the boys repeatedly lampoon Farrar's novel and his protagonist. While the readership of *Tom Brown* might now be reduced primarily to scholars and students of children's literature, *Eric* has become even more obscure, as Terence Wright explained in 1982: "The gloomy, introverted and somewhat morally rigid tone of the book is extremely distasteful to mid-twentieth century ears" (62). Wright describes Reverend Farrar's language as "rather syrupy and decidedly stilted" (62) and the overall effect as obsessively evangelical (64). As children's literature moved away from this kind of overt, sentimental, and insistent didacticism over the course of the nineteenth century, a work like *Eric* increasingly failed to resonate or attain the influence of Hughes's book. Nevertheless, it provides a useful perspective on Hughes novel in that it demonstrates in even starker terms the dangers of same-sex intimacy and thus the benefits of the less-threatening crush.

Over the course of the novel, the protagonist, like Tom Brown, declines in virtue and vitality, but unlike Tom, who is eventually rehabilitated by his "noble friendship" with Arthur and his crush on old Brooke, Eric grows more and more corrupt, in part because he indulges in the kinds of relationships with other boys demonized in *Tom Brown*. Like Tom, Eric crushes on an older boy, but the difference here is that the older boy, Upton, returns the affection and the boys develop a romantic friendship. At the point when the relationship begins, Eric is about thirteen or fourteen, and Upton is a few years older: "Upton was a fine sturdy fellow of eighteen, immensely popular in the school for his prowess and good looks. He hated bullying, and often interfered to protect little boys, who accordingly idolised him, and did anything he told them willingly. He meant to do them no harm, but he did great harm" (56). Eric is described as "just the boy to take [Upton's] fancy, and to admire him in return," a reference especially to his pluck, but surely also to his physical attractiveness. Just prior to this scene Eric is described as having the sort of features few can resist. Their relationship looks very much like a romance, complete with tiffs and the occasional attempt to make the other boy jealous: "From this time Eric was much in Upton's study, and constantly by his side in the playground. In spite of their disparity in age and position in the school, they became sworn friends, though, their friendship was broken every now and then by little quarrels, which united them all the more closely after they had not spoken to each other perhaps for a week" (57). The boys are used to taking Sunday strolls together, and when Eric declines Upton's invitation one afternoon in order to speak to another boy, Upton acts like a scorned lover: "'Oh *very* well,' said Upton, in high dudgeon, and, hoping to make Eric jealous, he went a walk with Graham, whom he had 'taken up' before he knew [Eric]" (66, emphasis in original). However, the boys shortly make up, and both their peers and the schoolmasters begin to worry about the effects of their relationship.

As in *Tom Brown's Schooldays*, the headmaster of Roslyn School, Dr. Rowlands, decides to intervene in a friendship deemed to be detrimental. Dr. Rowlands notices that Eric, who had come to Roslyn School an upright boy, is consistently getting into trouble. Catching Upton sneaking away from Eric's room one night leads the headmaster to connect Eric's bad behavior with the older boy's influence. Upton is ultimately described as teaching Eric a number of unspecified "dangerous lessons" (100). When Dr. Rowlands suggests to Eric that his friendship with Upton does him harm, Eric, bitter about being caned, "passionately" resents the notion and determines in "obstinate perversity, to cling more than ever to the boy" (77). The terms with which Farrar describes Eric's feelings for Upton—the language of passion and perversity—hint at the moral and sexual threat the relationship poses to the boy. Eric's refusal to separate from his friend is linked directly to his decline, whereas Tom Brown is rescued by accepting his separation from East. Unlike in Hughes's novel, the headmaster in *Eric* fails to achieve a separation of the boys or to address Eric's decline before it becomes irreversible.

Those of Eric's classmates who refrain from such relationships discuss their suspicion about the "taking up" of young boys by older ones, despite the fact that such relationships are described as common, typically exciting little notice. Montagu and Russell, both Eric's age, condemn his relationship with Upton:

> "Your cousin Upton has 'taken up' Williams," said Montague to Russell one afternoon, as he saw the two strolling together on the beach, with Eric's arm in Upton's.
> "Yes, I am sorry for it."
> "So am I. We shan't see so much of him now."
> "O, that's not my only reason," answered Russell, who had a rare habit of always going straight to the point.
> "You mean you don't like the 'taking-up' system."
> "No, Montagu; I used once to have fine theories about it. I used to fancy that a big fellow would do no end of good to one lower in the school, and that the two would stand to each other in the relation of knight to squire. You know what the young knights were taught, Monty—to keep their bodies under, and bring them into subjection; to love God, and speak the truth always. That sounds very grand and noble to me. But when a big fellow takes up a little one *you* know pretty well that *those* are not the kind of lessons he teaches." (57, emphasis in original)

Russell is fairly explicit here about the dangers of the "taking-up" system in his reference to the failure of boys to replicate the bodily subjection of squires in an earlier era. Nevertheless, Russell thinks Eric will be able to resist the worst dangers because "it's chiefly the soft self-indulgent fellows, who are all straw and no iron, who get spoilt by being 'taken up'" (58). The narrator confirms Russell's opinion of Eric: "Russell was partly right. Eric learnt a great deal of harm from Upton, and the misapplied hero-worship led to bad results. But he was too manly a little fellow, and he had too much self-respect, to sink into the effeminate condition which usually grows on the young delectables who have the misfortune to be 'taken up'" (58). The risk that a romantic friendship, characterized by passionate attachment and intimacy of contact, might lead to an "effeminate condition" is clear to Russell and Montagu, who avoid such relationships. Eric, however, fails to recognize the danger, and his moral character sinks so low he runs away from school, acquires work on a ship, returns home further corrupted by life at sea with coarse sailors, and dies knowing the shock of his sins has killed his mother. The different conclusions of *Tom Brown's Schooldays* and *Eric* indicate that schoolboy crushes are to be recommended when they occur at a distance and feature inaccessible objects of desire.

The intimate friendship between Tom and George Arthur is met with similar suspicion in *Tom Brown's Schooldays*; nevertheless, Tom's relationship with Arthur manages to circumvent this danger. Though the relationship is encouraged by Dr. Arnold, Tom is teased by his peers, who recognize the possible peril and refer to Tom as Arthur's "dry-nurse" (231). East especially warns Tom, and his criticism is articulated in gendered terms: "He'll never be worth a button, if you go on keeping him under your skirts" (232). East suggests that the relationship between Tom and Arthur threatens to feminize both boys, and he worries that a sensitive boy like Arthur will "only spoil" at Rugby (232). This scene is contiguous with Tom and East's encounter with the "pretty white-handed, curly-headed" boy who *is* spoiled—the same word is used—by being "petted and pampered" by the six former for whom he fags (233). In contrast to the romantic friendship between Eric and Upton, which is discouraged by Dr. Rowlands, Tom and Arthur are deliberately paired by Dr. Arnold and remain under his watchful gaze. Tom is meant to benefit from taking responsibility for the newer and weaker boy, while Arthur should profit from the mentorship and protection of the physically stronger and more athletic Tom. Arthur's spiritual purity and insistent morality make him unavailable to being spoiled, or used sexually, and Tom's scrupulous sense of responsibility prevents him from taking advantage of Arthur. Notably, Tom's other near-age friendship, that with East, is deliberately broken up by the headmaster, who worries about the effect the boys are having on each other. Though the relationship between Tom and Arthur is central to the novel, as the novel reaches its conclusion and the boys graduate to the sixth form themselves, Arthur recedes to the background. He is replaced as the object of Tom's ardent affections by Dr. Arnold himself, and the temporary intimacy of boyhood friendship is replaced with Tom's distant crush-like admiration for his headmaster.

Conclusion: The Schoolboy Crush and Spiritual Salvation

Ultimately, the schoolboy crush functions as an outlet for boyhood passion and desire and promotes gendered socialization by encouraging the crushing boy to emulate his idealized and desired object. The trajectory of *Tom Brown's Schooldays* bears this out. By the conclusion of the novel, Tom is described as "grown into a young man nineteen years old, a praeposter and captain of the [cricket team]" (351). In the final passages of the novel Tom learns that his old headmaster has died, and he returns to Rugby School to mourn. By now Tom has learned that Arnold took a specific interest in his affairs, orchestrated his separation from East and his relationship with Arthur, and ensured that Tom developed into a fine man. He is greatly moved by Arnold's efforts on his behalf and amazed by Arnold's ingenuity. Tom's greatest crush is therefore on Arnold himself, and Tom is described as "a hero-worshipper" willing to follow Arnold in everything with the blindest faith.[11]

Thomas Arnold was best known for inspiring reform of the British public schools through his work at Rugby, and his reputation was made in part through the popularity of A. P. Stanley's *Life and Correspondence of Thomas Arnold* (1844). One of his main innovations was establishing the praeposter system whereby older boys like old Brooke would help monitor and discipline younger ones. This put older boys in positions of power and authority that would likely have encouraged schoolboy crushes. Moreover, Stanley's characterization of Arnold can also be understood in terms of what would later be called "muscular Christianity," a phrase coined by T. C. Sandars in a review of Charles Kingsley's *Two Years Ago*, published the same year as *Tom Brown*. Sandars writes of Kingsley, "His ideal is a man who fears God and can walk a thousand miles in a thousand hours" (qtd. in Hall, *Muscular Christianity* 7). According to James Eli Adams, Stanley's biography helped craft the almost mythological reputation of Arnold as embodying Kingsley's ideal Christian man (66). Hughes's novel, published thirteen years after Stanley's biography, reinforced this perception of Arnold and popularized muscular Christianity, a social and religious movement in the mid-nineteenth century that sought to combine religious devotion and pastoral care with robust manliness and athleticism.

Muscular Christianity involved understanding strength and courage as both spiritual *and* physical. Nelson notes that to be manly for Hughes meant an "androgynous blend of compassion and courage, gentleness and strength, self control and native purity" (530). For Tom Brown to be manly, he must demonstrate moral virtue in addition to physical toughness. Thus, Nelson argues that in Hughes's novel "asexuality is an explicit and essential component of the anti-masculine manliness he upholds" (538). To be sexually incontinent by engaging in masturbation or nonprocreative sex is to risk one's mind, by being egocentric or narcissistic, and soul, by engaging in sexual sins that constitute moral corruption and lead to damnation. Hughes, as a key proponent of muscular Christianity, used the boyhood crush as a mechanism for propagating his notion of the Christian man and manly Christian.

The didactic strands of *Tom Brown's Schooldays* converge on this figure of the muscular Christian, and Tom becomes this ideal Christian man over the course of the novel through his various relationships with other boys and men—from his sanctification through his intimate friendship with the saintly George Arthur, to his emulation of old Brooke's mature leadership. This process of moral and gendered maturation culminates in his respect for Thomas Arnold, but even that relationship becomes a stepping-stone to yet another experience of devotion to an idealized "masculine" figure at a distance.[12] We can understand Arnold's prominence in the Victorian imagination in terms of Thomas Carlyle's notion of the heroic clergyman, which he offers as a model of virtuous manhood in *On Heroes, Hero-worship, and the Heroic in History* (1841). The availability of the heroic spiritual leader who mediates between man and God explains Tom's feelings for Arnold at the conclusion of the novel and points to an even greater use of the schoolboy crush in the nineteenth century: it leads to spiritual sanctification through one's love for God.

Thus, Hughes's novel fittingly concludes with Tom's transforming his schoolboy crush on old Brooke into his hero worship of Arnold and then the very worship of God. In the preface to the sixth edition of *Tom Brown's Schooldays*, Hughes confesses that "my whole object in writing at all, was to get the chance of preaching!" (xxxix), and in the final paragraph of the novel, Hughes explicitly addresses Tom's passionate admiration of Arnold from afar and its even more important function: "Such stages have to be gone through, I believe, by all young and brave souls who must win their way through hero-worship, to the worship of Him who is the King and Lord of heroes" (376). This passage echoes one from Carlye's *On Heroes*, in which he writes, "Hero-worship, heartfelt prostrate admiration, submission, burning, boundless, for a noblest godlike Form of Man,—is not that the germ of Christianity itself?" (17). Thus, the concept of hero worship connects the notion of the crush with the spiritual sanctification experienced by Tom Brown over the course of *Tom Brown's Schooldays*, which suggests continuity between same-sex crushes and Christian devotion for men. More than just a mechanism for gender development or the making of good soldiers or colonial administrators who respect social and military hierarchies and worship manhood, the ordinary schoolboy crush is meant to model, and to be converted into, the spiritual and religious worship of God, thereby saving not only the nation but also the very soul.

NOTES

1. John Reed explains the potentially confusing designation "public school" thusly: "The public schools were originally created to provide educational facilities for those unable to afford private education (here meaning tutorial education or education at special boarding schools restricted to the aristocracy)" (*Old School* 3). Though the public schools gradually became increasingly exclusive and are supported privately, in contrast to government schools, they retain their traditional designation as "public schools."

2. The term "romantic friendship" was coined in the eighteenth century and seems to have been used more frequently with reference to women's friendships than with men's friendships (see Mavor 88, Kauth 90). However, historians now commonly use the term to refer to passionate friendships between women *or* between men. For instance, Oulton notes, "Romantic friendship among young men in the nineteenth century is associated largely with the institutions of which it was a tradition, namely the major public schools and Oxford and Cambridge universities" (33).

3. In the context of *Tom Brown's Schooldays*, the term "hero worship" is sometimes used to refer to what I am calling a crush. Thomas Carlyle's 1840 lecture series, published as *On Heroes, Hero-worship, and the Heroic in History*, helped circulate the term, and Carlyle is mentioned explicitly in *Tom Brown*. Whereas Carlyle's hero worship is an almost spiritual ideal, the crush is a far more quotidian expression of schoolboy desire. Given both the use of the term to refer to the feelings of boys for older youths and the romantic and passionate language used to describe them, the concept of the crush provides a useful framework for thinking about hero worship even though "crush" was not popularized until the twentieth century.

4. Reed notes that "references to homosexuality in the schools are frequent—so common, in fact, that simple allusions are easily understood in the fiction of the time. Sex, to most boys under the private educational system, meant masturbation or homosexuality; and the intimations of doom attached to these school crimes made them at the same time vile and wickedly attractive" (*Old School* 68). Alisdare Hickson's *The Poisoned Bowl: Sex and the Public School* (1995) contains more than one hundred anecdotal accounts of relations between boys in British public schools that confirm these assumptions about actual sexual practices in boarding schools.

5. Hickson notes that many of his informants, who attended public schools between the 1920s and the 1960s, confirmed that "the schoolboy crush was one of the common denominators of everyday conversations" (104). He explains that "as opposed to ordinary friendships which usually evolved slowly, a boy 'crashed' into a 'crush.' The realization of a new burning obsession came suddenly and had about it a delicious sensation of phenomenal import" (74). The material reviewed by Hickson demonstrates over and over again that crushes tended to occur at a distance. One man who had grown up in an orphanage reports being rescued from a bully by an older boy who casually intervened and walked away. The man recalls, "I was too small for him to bother about but I admired him from afar" (Hickson 77).

6. In keeping with the common practice of referring to boys by their last names, Hughes uses the designations "old" and "young" to differentiate between the elder Brooke brother and the younger. The sixth form coincides with years 12 or 12 and 13 and was designed to allow boys an extra year of preparation before entering university.

7. Though the sport is referred to in the novel as "football," it is closer to what is now known as rugby. This new form of football, or soccer to American readers, was innovated at Rugby to permit both handling the ball and running with it toward the other team's goal, and, according to Tony Collins, the sport as developed at Rugby School was known to be especially violent (Collins 5–6). During the time when *Tom Brown* is set, the rules for rugby football, including team sizes, had not yet been standardized, and the publication of Hughes's novel is sometimes credited with popularizing the new sport of rugby. In the novel, School-house possesses the most skilled players, which is why it is pitted against all of the rest of the school.

8. One of Thomas Arnold's reforms at Rugby School was to strengthen the house system, whereby boys were grouped in boarding houses, each with its own house master, athletic teams, activities, and sense of identity. One's house provided a smaller community within the school and constituted a basis for athletic rivalries (see Sheldon 59–61).

9. By all accounts the term "fag" was not yet used as a homophobic epithet at this point, even though the system of fagging was known to be conducive to sexual relations between boys and sometimes the abuse of younger ones. The *Oxford English Dictionary* indicates the first recorded use of "fag," as an abbreviation of "faggot," to mean "homosexual" was in 1923, while the first recorded use of "faggot" itself in this way was 1915. The

OED also indicates that the use of the term "fag" as a homophobic epithet is of American origin, and there is no evidence connecting its use at British public schools with the later American use as a slur.

10. Donald E. Hall notes that "it is the younger, passive boys who are the object of his most intense interest and disdain; they are the miserable ones, and even though the 'big fellows' are implicated in their abuse, Hughes's anxiety seems to hover around the figure of the feminized male" (Hall, *Fixing Patriarchy* 147). Indeed, Tom's concern is that he might have been petted, not that he might be tempted to pet.

11. Not coincidentally, Thomas Arnold is widely reputed to be a major figure in the reform of public schools in the early nineteenth century, by which time they had come to be known as brutal places overrun with bullying and vice, and Hickson credits Arnold with striving to eliminate "schoolboy homosexuality." He explains that "he was the first public school headmaster to launch a crusade against sexual experimentation between school boys" (173). Moreover, Stanley's biography of Arnold, influenced by Thomas Carlyle's writings on heroes and hero worship, transformed the figure of the learned clergyman-educator and Arnold himself into objects of admiration that would provide social and spiritual guidance.

12. Donald Hall reads this trajectory in the more sinister terms of Tom's socialization into his patriarchal role as a man (Hall, *Fixing Patriarchy* 142).

WORKS CITED

Adams, James Eli. *Dandies and Desert Saints: Styles of Victorian Manhood.* Ithaca, NY: Cornell UP, 1995.

Aldrich, Robert. *Colonialism and Homosexuality.* New York: Routledge, 2002.

Carlyle, Thomas. *On Heroes, Hero-worship, and the Heroic in History.* 1841. Oxford: Oxford UP, 1907.

Collins, Tony. *Rugby's Great Split: Class, Culture and the Origins of Rugby League Football.* London: Routledge, 1998.

Cook, Matt. *London and the Culture of Homosexuality, 1885–1914.* Cambridge: Cambridge UP, 2003.

Darton, F. J. Harvey. *Children's Books in England: Five Centuries of Social Life.* 3rd ed. Revised by Brian Alderson. New York: Cambridge UP, 1982.

Ellis, Havelock. *Sexual Inversion (Studies in the Psychology of Sex).* 1897. Honolulu, HI: UP of the Pacific, 2001.

Farrar, Frederic. *Eric, or Little by Little.* 1858. Gloucester: Dodo Press, 2007.

Fussell, Paul. *The Great War and Modern Memory.* New York: Oxford UP, 1975.

Hall, Donald E. *Fixing Patriarchy: Feminism and Mid-Victorian Male Novelists.* New York: New York UP, 1996.

———, ed. *Muscular Christianity: Embodying the Victorian Age.* Cambridge: Cambridge UP, 1993.

Hickson, Alisdare. *The Poisoned Bowl: Sex and the Public School.* London: Duckworth, 1995.

Hughes, Thomas. *Tom Brown's Schooldays.* 1857. Oxford: Oxford World Classics, 1999.

Inness, Sherrie A. "Mashes, Smashes, Crushes, and Raves: Woman-to-Woman Relationships in Popular Women's College Fiction, 1895–1915." *NWSA Journal: A Publication of the National Women's Studies Association* 6, no. 1 (spring 1994): 48–68.

Kauth, Michael R. *True Nature: A Theory of Sexual Attraction*. New York: Springer, 2000.

Lane, Christopher. *The Ruling Passion: British Colonial Allegory and the Paradox of Homo-sexual Desire*. Durham, NC: Duke UP, 1995.

Martin, Maureen M. "'Boys Who Will Be Men': Desire in *Tom Brown's Schooldays*." *Victorian Literature and Culture* 30, no. 2 (2002): 483–502.

Mavor, Elizabeth. *The Ladies of Llangollen: A Study in Romantic Friendship*. London: Michael Joseph, 1971.

Nelson, Claudia. "Sex and the Single Boy: Ideals of Manliness and Sexuality in Victorian Literature for Boys." *Victorian Studies* 32, no. 4 (summer 1989): 525–50.

Oulton, Carolyn. *Romantic Friendship in Victorian Literature*. Burlington, VT: Ashgate, 2007.

Quigly, Isabel. *The Heirs of Tom Brown: The English School Story*. London: Chatto, 1982.

Reed, John R. *Old School Ties: The Public Schools in British Literature*. Syracuse, NY: Syracuse UP, 1964.

———. "The Public Schools in Victorian Literature." *Nineteenth Century Fiction* 29, no. 1 (1974): 58–76.

Sedgwick, Eve Kosofsky. *Between Men: English Literature and Male Homosocial Desire*. New York: Columbia UP, 1985.

Sheldon, Henry Davidson. *Student Life and Customs*. New York: D. Appleton, 1901.

Vicinus, Martha. "Distance and Desire: English Boarding-School Friendships." In *Hidden from History: Reclaiming the Gay and Lesbian Past*, edited by Martin Duberman, Martha Vicinus, and George Chauncey, Jr., 212–32. New York: New American Library, 1989.

Wright, Terence. "Two Little Worlds of School: An Outline of a Dual Tradition in Schoolboy Fiction." *Durham University Journal* 75, no. 1 (1982): 59–71.

FURTHER READING

Bamford, T. W. *Rise of the Public Schools: A Study of Boys' Public Boarding Schools in England and Wales from 1837 to the Present Day*. London: Thomas Nelson, 1967.

Clark, Beverly Lyon. *Regendering the School Story: Sassy Sissies and Tattling Tomboys*. New York: Routledge, 1996.

Cohen, Ed. *Talk on the Wilde Side: Toward a Genealogy of a Discourse on Male Sexualities*. New York: Routledge, 1993.

Kidd, Kenneth. "Introduction: Lesbian/Gay Literature for Children and Young Adults." *Children's Literature Association Quarterly* 23, no. 3 (Fall 1998): 114–19.

Kutzer, M. Daphne. *Empire's Children: Empire and Imperialism in Classic British Children's Books*. New York: Routledge, 2000.

Mack, Edward C. *Public Schools and British Opinion, 1780–1860*. Methuen: London, 1938.

———. *Public Schools and British Opinion Since 1860*. New York: Columbia UP, 1941.

Mangan, J. A. *The Games Ethic and Imperialism*. New York: Viking, 1986.

Musgrave, P. W. *From Brown to Bunter: The Life and Death of the School Story*. London: Routledge, 1985.

Petzold, Dieter. "Breaking in the Colt: Socialization in Nineteenth-Century School Stories." *Children's Literature Association Quarterly* 15, no. 1 (1990): 17–21.

Richards, Jeffrey. *Happiest Days: The Public Schools in English Fiction*. Manchester, UK: Manchester UP, 1988.

———. "The School Story." In *Stories and Society: Children's Literature in Its Social Context*, edited by Dennis Butts, 1–21. New York: St. Martin, 1992.

....

CHAPTER 23

PETER PAN AS CHILDREN'S THEATRE: THE ISSUE OF AUDIENCE

....

MARAH GUBAR

AUTHOR of more than forty plays as well as numerous novels and short stories, James Matthew Barrie (1860–1937) was born and raised in Scotland. After moving to London in 1885, he befriended Sylvia and Arthur Llewelyn Davies and their sons, engaging the boys in the kind of dramatic games that he himself had enjoyed as a child. The figure of Peter Pan emerged from these story-telling and acting sessions; his first appearance in print was in The Little White Bird *(1902), a fictionalized account of Barrie's relationship with the Davies family. Two years later, the play* Peter Pan; or The Boy Who Wouldn't Grow Up *debuted on the London stage (Duke of York's 1904); the first New York production quickly followed (Empire 1905). Despite its phenomenal popularity, no script was published at this time. Instead, the chapters of* The Little White Bird *that focused on Peter were republished as* Peter Pan in Kensington Gardens *(1906), with illustrations by Arthur Rackham. A novelized version of the play, entitled* Peter and Wendy *(1911), also appeared; adding to later confusion about the story's publication history, this novel's title was eventually changed to* Peter Pan. *The play itself did not appear in print until 1928.*

Something about J. M. Barrie's work inspires extreme reactions. Lionized as a genius during his own lifetime, Barrie was dismissed in the decades after his death as a "sexless sentimentalist," an "artistic failure" whose writing reflected "a generally sick sensibility" (Daiches, Coveney 249, 242). Critics such as Leonée Ormond and R. D. S. Jack have since offered more measured assessments of his artistic achievements, and *Peter Pan*, Barrie's most famous play, has always garnered serious attention from children's literature critics—though their discourse on Barrie has also tended toward extremes. Early children's literature scholars such as F. J. Harvey Darton celebrated Barrie as the originator of Anglo-American children's theatre, routinely referring to *Peter Pan* as the first play written "specially for children" (312).[1] Recent critics, inspired by Jacqueline Rose's *The Case of Peter Pan* (1984), have insisted that, on the contrary, "Barrie wrote it for adults" (Zipes et al. 1294).[2] Noting *Peter Pan*'s links to past productions aimed at grown-ups, and pointing out that the audience on the first night consisted mainly of adults, Rose argues that it was their intense enthusiasm that led to *Peter Pan*'s establishment as a so-called children's classic: "*Peter Pan* did not found a new type of drama so much as revivify a number of old ones. . . . Children are not the cause of this literature. They are not the group for whom it is created" (102). The real function of plays such as *Peter Pan*, Rose contends, is to enable adult voyeurism (98), a point seconded by Anne Varty, who declares that such dramas provide "a constant succession of children's bodies to delight the carnal interests of their spectator, the consuming adult" (*Children* 50).

It is no wonder that the issue of audience has engendered such debate, since the original script of *Peter Pan* was as much a "Betwixt-and-Between" as its main character, a messy hybrid of several different types of drama (*Peter Pan in Kensington Gardens* 17).[3] As Rose suggests, aspects of Barrie's play recall the phenomenon referred to by the Victorians as "the child drama," plays centered on child characters but aimed primarily at adults (96–97).[4] Moreover, as Roger Lancelyn Green and other critics have demonstrated, Barrie also drew on the conventions of nineteenth-century pantomime, a raucous form of entertainment that featured elaborate spectacle, cross-dressing, and risqué jokes and songs.[5] But *Peter Pan* also has strong connections to a category of Anglo-American drama whose early history has received almost no critical attention: professional children's theatre, commercial productions designed specifically to attract young people and their caretakers to the playhouse. As early as the 1870s, adults were beginning to entertain the idea that children should attend simplified, sanitized shows designed especially for them; by the late 1880s, the English stage had witnessed the success of so many dramas performed "by children for children" that such shows had ceased to be regarded as a novelty (Gubar, *Artful* 182–83, 191). Adapted versions of familiar works of children's literature were frequently offered up as a series of "Christmas Matinees for Children":[6] productions of this type included *Alice in Wonderland* (Prince of Wales 1886); *Little Goody Two Shoes* (Court 1888); *The Rose and the Ring* (Prince of Wales's 1890); *Shock-Headed Peter* (Garrick 1900); *A Little Unfairy Princess* (Shaftesbury 1902); and *The Water Babies* (Garrick 1902)—all of which preceded *Peter Pan*.

This essay does not attempt to establish literary links between these dramas and *Peter Pan*. Instead, because professional children's theatre is such an undertheorized category of children's literature, it tackles more basic questions. What factors led to the emergence of Anglo-American children's theatre? What role—if any—did young people play in this process? What kind of evidence qualifies a drama to count as a children's play? *Peter Pan* cannot be regarded as the paradigmatic example of this subgenre since (as I will argue) it both subverts and participates in the children's theatre tradition. Yet according to the criteria detailed below, it can be categorized as a children's play, and it serves here as a case in point for my contention that young people had more to do with the development of children's theatre than we think, not only as intended and actual audience members, but also as active participants in a thriving tradition of private theatricals that helped inspire the production and shape the form and content of professional children's plays.

The impulse to create a special subcategory of dramas aimed specifically at children arose partly out of adults' anxiety that pantomimes—which many children were taken to see during the Christmas season—were inappropriate for young playgoers.[7] Victorian commentators routinely complained that the convoluted plotting, slangy topicality, and garish spectacle of such shows rendered them unsuitable for children. They worried that the common practice of jumbling together characters from different fairy tales in the same pantomime ruined the simplicity of the source material, even as they fretted that the sexual content of such shows would soil the pure minds of children.[8] In 1882, for example, W. Davenport Adams vehemently protested against the "rows of infinitesimally-clothed" ballet dancers and the cross-dressed women who traditionally played the lead male roles in pantomimes, showing their legs in the process: "[They] are not the sort of spectacle to which it is judicious to introduce the 'young idea,' especially when it is at that age at which curiosity concerning the forbidden is beginning to display itself" (89).

Playwrights who helped pioneer the creation of productions aimed explicitly at children often echoed these objections, and reviewers routinely praised them for offering a more innocent and refined form of drama. For example, after complaining that contemporary pantomime was all "legs and limelight" (qtd. in Wilson 169), E. L. Blanchard composed *Little Goody Two Shoes; or, Harlequin Little Boy Blue* (Adelphi 1876), which he advertised as "a Children's Pantomime, performed entirely by Children . . . At Morning Performances only . . . at Children's Prices" (*Little Goody*). Though many of the characteristic features of pantomime remained in place, the substitution of child performers in place of adults and the tighter focus on a familiar children's story delighted reviewers because they made the show seem less like an unruly pantomime and more like "a fairy play . . . full of pretty thoughts, graceful sentiment, and poetry" (review of *Little Goody*).[9] Similarly, before the debut of *Alice in Wonderland*, both Lewis Carroll and playwright Henry Savile Clarke (who adapted *Alice* for the stage) expressed their objection to the practice of having "two or three nursery legends hashed up so as to become unintelligible" (Clarke 11); they aimed to create a simpler, less "coarse" form of drama (Carroll, qtd. in Lovett 37), and most reviewers felt they had succeeded, praising *Alice* for its lack of spectacular display, its "refined and delicate" tone (review of *Alice*, Era).

Clearly, adult investment in the ideology of childhood innocence was one of the key factors that drove the development of professional children's theatre. According to Rose and Varty, young people themselves played no significant role in this process. Adult protestations about childhood purity and simplicity were deployed not out of genuine attentiveness to what actual children wanted or enjoyed, but merely to assuage adult needs and desires, including the voyeuristic longing to gaze at "a child always innocent and yet sexualised by that very focusing of attention" (Rose 98). These critics focus solely on adults partly because they consider children's responses to cultural artifacts "more or less impossible to gauge" (Rose 9). And indeed, any discussion of the preferences and practices of child playgoers raises serious epistemological problems: even if we establish that shows were designed to draw children into the theatre, and that they were in fact present in large numbers during the run of a show, what can we know about what brought them there, or how they responded to what they saw?

Rather than assuming that we cannot know anything or pretending to know the whole story, I propose that we follow the example of recent theatre historians and performance theorists who openly admit the impossibility of attaining anything close to complete, decisive knowledge about past productions, without giving up on the attempt to find out as much as they can. Because performance (like childhood) is transient and evanescent, "our study is of something which is always-already irrecoverably lost," as theatre historian Jacky Bratton observes (7). To aid in efforts to piece together what information we can about individual productions, Richard Schechner has suggested that we distinguish between drama (the written text or score), script (the drama plus "all that can be transmitted from time to time and place to place" by a teacher), theatre ("the event enacted by a specific group of performers"), and performance (everything that happens from the moment the first spectator arrives to see a show until the time the last one leaves) (71). To this list, Bratton helpfully proposes that we add the idea of "intertheatricality" (37). Taking an intertheatrical approach involves looking beyond the specific occasion of a single performance "to include an awareness of the elements and interactions that make up the whole web of mutual understanding between potential audiences and their players" (37). Just as an intertextual interpretation insists that no act of reading or writing occurs in isolation from others, an intertheatrical reading "seeks to articulate the mesh of connections between all kinds of theatre texts, and between texts and their users" (Bratton 37).

For a variety of reasons, the study of early children's theatre demands an intertheatrical approach. To begin with, many of the categories that nineteenth-century playwrights used to identify their dramas—pantomime, fairy play, musical dream play—tell us next to nothing about who the intended and actual audience was. For instance, pantomime was not originally associated with children or the Christmas season; it became an intergenerational holiday tradition over the course of the nineteenth century. Blanchard's *Little Goody Two Shoes* was both a pantomime and a contribution to the emerging genre of children's theatre. How do we know which other productions can be included in this second category? There is no single decisive criterion, just a list of questions to consider. What did the creators say about their intent? Did advertisements characterize the production as a children's show and mention daytime performances and reduced prices? Does the script of the show owe anything to previous productions aimed explicitly at children, or to the thriving tradition of plays written for children to perform for their peers and relatives at home or at school? Did reviewers emphasize how child-oriented the performance was and dwell on the question of how children might (or did) react? Do we have proof that children actually attended in large numbers, and can we gather together evidence from various sources—fan letters; diaries; memoirs of actors, playwrights, producers, and playgoers—in order to build up a picture of what aspects of the production appealed to individual young people?

In other words, in order to explore the issue of audience, we must look past particular scripts and performances to a constellation of texts that help illuminate the shifting relationship between children and theatre during this period. In making claims about whether specific dramas were aimed at and enjoyed by children, we must try to collate different kinds of corroborative evidence, even as we acknowledge that our conclusions can only ever be tentative, since our knowledge is inevitably fractional, incomplete. Different children undoubtedly reacted in different ways to different productions, and most left no record at all of their responses. For others, writing long after the fact in memoirs, nostalgia may have distorted their recollections of youthful playgoing. Yet these problems should not arrest our inquiry; after all, they affect all attempts to trace audience reaction to productions from the distant past, since it is rare to have a large archive of first-person responses recorded just after a performance takes place. For this reason, a cautious humility should govern the kinds of claims we make about adult spectators as well. While it is currently fashionable to characterize adult interest in child performers solely in terms of lascivious ogling, such a response oversimplifies the various motivations that seem to have attracted grown-ups to these shows, including an appreciation for the skills—not just the bodies—of child actors and the desire to share a less ribald brand of drama with their children.[10]

Another reason why it is necessary to take an intertheatrical approach when studying the role that nineteenth-century children played in the rise of children's theatre is that a key part of this story occurred not in public playhouses but at home. Throughout the nineteenth century, many young people enthusiastically participated in private theatricals, the popularity of which helped bring about the rise of professional children's theatre.[11] Indeed, Blanchard and other early creators of children's theatre modeled their holiday shows on a preexisting tradition of home theatricals in which children performed for other children at Christmas parties, either on their own or under the direction of adults. Catering to this craze, British and American authors produced innumerable guidebooks for home theatricals containing scripts of short plays designed to be enacted by children for children. These dramas, which sold briskly from the middle of the century onward, anticipated both the format and content of professional children's theatre: long before producers in London and New York began hiring all-child casts to enact plays based on a single children's story, guidebook writers such as Julia Corner, Mrs. George MacDonald, and George Bradford Bartlett had already popularized this practice.

More often than not, authors of these manuals stated that they produced their dramas to satisfy a "home demand," as when J. Barmby noted that his *Plays for Young People* (1879) had been "written, with no view for publication, for the entertainment of the writer's own children and their friends for Christmas. . . . They are now published in the order in which they were written and acted, and thus show signs of the advancing age of the actors originally concerned" (iii). Similarly, Corner declared that her efforts had been inspired when she observed how cleverly "a party of young people, from about eight to twelve years of age, contrived to amuse themselves" by acting out elaborate charades at Christmas (209). Indeed, children growing up in the nineteenth century seem to have taken a surprisingly active role in initiating such activities. In their memoirs, M. V. Hughes, George Arliss, and Ernest H. Shepard all recount how they and their young relatives organized private theatricals on their own, rather than having this activity foisted on them by adults. Hughes's brother Tom and Shepard's sister Ethel wrote and directed the annual Christmas play performed by their siblings and cousins. Bored adults were dragooned into serving as audience members: "Father, having had some experience of our theatricals, had provided himself with an evening paper. However, we children all enjoyed it immensely" (Shepard, *Drawn from Life* 26). Noted nineteenth-century children's authors such as Carroll, Barrie, and Louisa May Alcott likewise composed and performed dramas in their youth.

As the Christmas playacting scene in Alcott's *Little Women* (1868) suggests, such performances were not merely opportunities for adult voyeurism, since children in the audience often outnumbered grown-ups. Shepard attended many children's parties of this kind, including one that featured a play starring his young friend Mamie: "I had a crush on Mamie at that time, which got worse when she appeared, made up and looking quite bewitching, on the stage. . . . It all went off swimmingly, and the audience was delighted. My cup of happiness brimmed over when Mamie chose me to take her in to supper and the red paint on her mouth got all smudged with trifle. My only regret is that I was too shy to kiss her" (*Drawn from Memory* 161–62). Shepard was eight years old at the time; his account reminds us that adults are not the only ones who indulge their scopophilia at dramatic events.

From the 1870s onward, contemporary commentators noted the tremendous popularity of both spontaneous and scripted home theatricals among children and used this fact as a rationale for why producers should develop professional children's plays.[12] Indeed, private productions repeatedly preceded and paved the way for public ones. For example, Blanchard borrowed the idea of creating an all-child pantomime from a guidebook for home theatricals that he contributed to six years before the debut of *Little Goody Two Shoes*; this collection featured a

"Juvenile Pantomime" by Tom Hood that had already been performed in private by "a company of little folk" before it appeared in print (Scott 37, 52). Similarly, the first recorded dramatic adaptation of *Alice* was "The Mad Tea Party," a private theatrical presented by young people; then, six years before Clarke's production opened, Kate Freiligrath-Kroeker published *Alice and Other Fairy Plays for Children* (1880), which included a short dramatic version of *Alice* for children to act out at home. "Like most plays of this kind," Freiligrath-Kroeker declared in her preface, "these fairy dramas were originally written to satisfy a 'home demand'" (vii). As children, Susy and Clara Clemens surprised their father, Mark Twain, by acting out scenes from his novel *The Prince and the Pauper* (1881). Delighted by this performance, Twain pressed forward with plans for a professional dramatization and became a vocal supporter of the children's theatre movement. Susy, who had written numerous plays during her youth, was inspired to write another one after viewing the first New York production of *The Prince and the Pauper* (Broadway 1890).

As the case of *The Prince and the Pauper* suggests, there was a lot of back-and-forth flow between private theatricals and public productions during the nineteenth century, as domestic dramas performed by children spurred the production of professional ones, and professional ones in turn inspired children to engage in private reenactments and other kinds of creative activity. *Peter Pan* provides another excellent example of this phenomenon. Despite its formal hybridity, Barrie's drama can be categorized as children's theatre because an array of intertheatrical evidence related to its creation and reception links it to this tradition. As many critics note, the tale of Peter Pan grew out of story-telling and play-acting sessions that Barrie engaged in with the Llewelyn Davies brothers (Birkin 66, 83–93). Captain Swarthy, the prototype for Captain Hook, emerged during the summer of 1901, when Barrie and the boys acted out a series of adventures involving pirates and natives set on an imaginary island. Barrie preserved a record of these private theatricals by taking photographs of the boys enacting various incidents, which he bound together into a booklet entitled *The Boy Castaways of Black Lake Island* (1901). The headings that accompanied these images, he later declared, "anticipate[d] much of the play of *Peter Pan*" ("To the Five" 82). To be sure, Barrie told other stories about the play's origins as well, but they, too, involved amateur theatricals: he called the "tiny old washing-house" in which he had acted out plays as a seven-year-old "the original of the little house the Lost Boys built in the Never Land" ("To the Five" 78); and he described the long evenings he and his fellow pupils at Dumfries Academy spent pretending to be pirates as "a sort of Odyssey that was long afterwards to become the play of *Peter Pan*" (qtd. in Green 8).

Peter Pan bore numerous traces of its private prehistory. Barrie incorporated the names of all five Llewelyn Davies boys into the *dramatis personae* and gave the costume designer a basketful of their clothes so that he could base his designs for the Darling children and the Lost Boys on them. According to Andrew Birkin, Peter Pan's famous declaration that "To die will be an awfully big adventure!" had originally been uttered by George Llewelyn Davies, and the script featured numerous "private jokes intelligible only to the author and the Davies family" (69, 104). Moreover, Barrie's stage directions attest to his desire to make the professional production resemble the kind of domestic theatricals that he enjoyed so much, both as a child himself and as an adult who enjoyed performing with and for children. Barrie appended a list of notes, "On the Acting of a Fairy Play," to the manuscript of *Peter Pan*, which read in part: "The difference between a Fairy Play and a realistic one is that in the former all the characters are really children with a child's outlook on life . . . Pull the beard off the fairy king, and you would find the face of a child. The actors in a fairy play should feel that it is written by a child in deadly earnestness and that they are children playing it in the same spirit. The scenic artist is another child in league with them" (qtd. in Green 105). When he reworked this material for the published script of the play, Barrie stated that all the actors "whether grown-ups or babes, must wear a child's outlook on life as their only important adornment. If they cannot help being funny they are begged to go away" (88).

Without denying the essentialism and sentimentality about childhood that inform these statements, we can also acknowledge that in these notes Barrie set forth for professional actors the model of private theatricals in which the players are more concerned with communal play than public display. Indeed, this ethos of improvisation pervades *Peter Pan*. Barrie greatly admired the writings of Robert Louis Stevenson, who had characterized children as inveterate actors in his essay "Child's Play" (1878): "'Making believe' is the gist of [the child's] whole life" (36). Yet Stevenson also insists that children's dramatic play is highly imitative: dependent on "external aid" because their own minds and memories are "so ill-provided," young people pilfer characters and incidents from stories written by adults, such as *Robinson Crusoe* (34). In shaping the plot of *Peter Pan*, Barrie mixes together pirates borrowed from Stevenson's own *Treasure Island*, "redskins" lifted from the pages of Mayne Reid, animal tricks stolen from Kipling's *Jungle Books* (1894, 1895), and so on. The effect, as contemporary reviewers recognized, was to make the play seem like a (Stevensonian) child's creation. Thus, rather than condemning Barrie for creating a pantomimic mishmash, numerous critics praised him for composing an "artfully artless, go-as-you-please play which has all the pretty inconsequence of an imaginative child's improvisation, all the wild extravagance of a youngster's dream" (review of *Peter Pan*, *Illustrated*). The story of *Peter Pan*, they agreed, was "just the sort of tale one would expect a child to tell, and such a jumble of fairies and children, and pirates and redskins one never met before. I suppose Miss Ela Q. May, who is set down as the author, is the inventor of this wonderful story, which Mr. Barrie has written and dramatised in his own inimitable fashion" (review of *Peter Pan*, *Judy* 44).

Such reviews are revelatory in that they invite us to move past our current critical practice of merely decrying Barrie's habit of attributing authorship of his own work to children. Besides arranging to have the opening night program for *Peter Pan* identify tiny Ela May (who played Liza) as the author of the play, Barrie also pretended that Peter Llewelyn Davies had written the introduction to *The Boy*

Castaways and "The Greedy Dwarf," a play Barrie wrote for home performance. And years later, in "To the Five," a dedicatory essay addressed to the Davies boys that prefaces the published script of *Peter Pan*, Barrie declared that he had "no recollection of having written" his most famous play, adding that "any one of you five brothers has a better claim to the authorship than most, and I would not fight you for it" (75, 77). Rose, Peter Hollindale, and others have characterized such statements as deeply disingenuous, reading them either as an attempt to obscure the fact that an adult wielded total control over the writing process or as "mock self-abnegation," a tongue-in-cheek gesture since, of course, children could not possibly function as the creators of such works (Hollindale xviii).

Yet while Barrie's decision to pretend that various young people authored his own work is certainly fraudulent, it is not necessarily insincere. In my opinion, it was partly motivated by a desire to acknowledge that his work was inspired by interaction with actual children and a creative genre (private theatricals) that did in fact allow young people to function as authors and actors. Indeed, "To the Five" fairly aches with Barrie's desire to publicize *Peter Pan*'s roots as an extended acting game he played with the five Davies boys. Barrie's opening assertion that he cannot recall having written *Peter Pan* makes room for him to reminisce nostalgically about how it evolved through collaborative play:

> We had good sport of [Peter Pan] before we clipped him small to make him fit the boards. . . . Have you, No. 3, forgotten the white violets at the Cistercian abbey in which we cassocked our first fairies . . . or your cry to the Gods, "Do I just kill one pirate all the time?" Do you remember Marooners' Hut in the haunted groves of Waverly, and the St. Bernard dog in a tiger's mask who so frequently attacked you . . .? What was it that made us eventually give to the public in the thin form of a play that which had been woven for ourselves alone? (75)

What was once private has now been transformed into a public spectacle: not just "the play of Peter" (75), but also the extent of Barrie's emotional involvement with the boys. "To the Five" reads like a very personal letter addressed to the boys, yet it also broadcasts the details of their intimacy to the outside world in order to support Barrie's opening contention that *Peter Pan* "never would have existed" if not for them (75). Without denying that adult desire drove the creation of *Peter Pan*, and that an adult wrote it, we can still acknowledge that actual children did participate in its genesis and that their contribution to this process is relevant not just biographically but formally, in that it links *Peter Pan* to the children's theatre tradition that grew out of private theatricals.

Barrie identified children as a crucial target audience for *Peter Pan* both before and after he drafted it. After taking the Llewelyn Davies boys to see *Bluebell in Fairyland* (Vaudeville 1901), a rather derivative children's play written in response to the tremendous success of *Alice in Wonderland*, Barrie announced to his friend and future biographer Denis Mackail that "he wanted to write a fairy play for children, too" (319). Then, in a letter written just after he finished drafting *Peter Pan* in April 1904, he again made his intent clear: "I have written a play for children," he declared to Maude

Adams, who later originated the role of Peter in New York (qtd. in Birkin 103). Perhaps because of its links to *Bluebell* and the pantomime tradition (which by this time was strongly associated with children), the first reviewers easily recognized *Peter Pan* as "a play for children" and routinely speculated about which aspects of it would—or would not—successfully appeal to young people (review of *Peter Pan, Times*).[13]

How, then, do we account for the fact that the audience on the opening night of *Peter Pan* "was made up of London's theatre-going élite, and there was hardly a child among them" (Rose 32)? Here is an instance in which an intertheatrical approach proves invaluable. Only by looking beyond the occasion of a single anomalous performance can we hope to derive a detailed picture of the elusive relationship between text and audience, playwright and playgoers. Reading a broad spectrum of contemporary reviews reveals that opening-night audiences were traditionally dominated by reviewers, theatrical insiders, and other adults. Critics of children's plays such as *Alice in Wonderland* and *Shock-Headed Peter* recognized this and even cited it as a reason for reserving judgment: given that *Alice* was "specially written for children," declared one critic who attended the first night, it was "impossible to say if [it will be] successful or not . . . until we see, as we may next week, the Prince of Wales's Theatre filled with juveniles, accompanied, of course, by their parents . . . but still themselves constituting *the* audience" (review of *Alice, Era*).[14] Describing the crowds of adults who attended the opening night of *Peter Pan*, Mackail matter-of-factly remarks that "of course a lot of them were professional critics" (366). Since evening shows ran late, many parents avoided them; recalling her trip to see the original production of *Peter Pan* as a child, Audrey Lucas notes, "I went . . . not to the first performance, which was probably at night, but to the first matinée" (76).

What evidence do we have about how young playgoers responded to *Peter Pan*? Numerous actors who took part in the first production and subsequent revivals attested to having received large amounts of fan mail from children, some of which has been preserved.[15] Also, well-connected children from theatrical families grew up and wrote memoirs in which they described their childhood reactions to the play. Strikingly, in both archives, we hear about children adoring the show, seeing it multiple times, and reenacting it at home. For instance, Angela du Maurier, the daughter of the first man to play Hook, recalled "those heavenly happy days of childhood when our annual Peter Pan Day came round, and it was time to go to . . . the Duke of York's Theatre and collect our ticket from the 'Wendy House' which the Box Office was always transformed into . . . Lights went out—Crook's music began . . . I should think by the time I was seven I could certainly have prompted all the cast" (15).[16] Du Maurier put this knowledge of the play to good use at home; as she recounts, "Barrie used to visit us in our nursery and we used to act it for him by the hour. Daphne always bagged Peter, and I was Wendy and Mrs. Darling and several of the pirates, Jeanne was Michael and I rather think Eliza [*sic*]. It was quite easy to act *all* the parts in turn, and we flew from chair to chair and swam as mermaids on the floor" (15).

Du Maurier was encouraged to attend and reenact the play by the author himself, but other children with no connection to the show or its author offered remarkably similar accounts of their engagement with Barrie's work. In their fan letters to Pauline Chase, who took over the role of Peter in London in 1906, many children say that they have seen the show numerous times and acted it out at home. For instance, one young fan writes to tell Peter that "We have just finished acting Peter Pan over again but we could not do it properly because there were only four of us I had to be John in the first scene and a lost boy and James Hook at the same time. My brother had to be Michael and a lost boy . . . I have been to see Peter Pan twice and think it is absolutely beautiful and hope it will be on again next year."[17] Similarly, a girl named Helene explains that "I've seen you twice, once last year and again this . . . I envy you acting Peter . . . I am preparing to act Peter Pan on a doll's stage, but I can't get any nice dolls down here, so I think I shall draw some figures and stick them on cardboard. I shall never get tired of seeing Peter Pan because the more you see him the sweeter he gets" (30–31). Indeed, while the letters collected by Chase may not be representative in this regard, almost one third of them mention the writer's interest in acting: "When we play at Peter Pan I am always you" (47); "We have been acting Peter Pan this afternoon" (11–12); "Could you tell me if the words are published as we are getting up 'Peter Pan' here and are going to act it in the servants hall, and I like acting very much" (57–58).

Barrie was tremendously pleased to discover that young fans were reenacting *Peter Pan* at home. Indeed, he was so delighted by this phenomenon that he actually rewrote the play to acknowledge it. By 1908, Hook's soliloquy in Act Five featured the lines: "No little children love me. I am told they play at Peter Pan, and that the strongest always chooses to be Peter. They would rather be a Twin than Hook; they force the baby to be Hook. The baby! that is where the canker gnaws" (139). Barrie also made a point of mentioning such activity in "To the Five"; pondering the question of who really wrote the play, he notes that "a large number of children whom I have seen playing Peter in their homes with careless mastership, constantly putting in better words, could have thrown it off with ease. It was for such as they that after the first production I had to add something to the play at the request of parents . . . about no one being able to fly until the fairy dust had been blown on him; so many children having gone home and tried it from their beds and needed surgical attention" (77). While we may be inclined to doubt that this was a genuine problem, the letters collected by Chase reveal that many children were indeed transfixed by this aspect of the show and tried to emulate it: "I have been trying to fly like you all day" (3); "we all had paper wings on this morning and tried to fly" (8); "I'am always trying too fly like you but I cant" (sic, 24). This is pure speculation, but I have often wondered if Barrie's persistent unwillingness to publish the script of *Peter Pan* arose in part from his desire to allow such play to continue on, unconstrained by a specific, fixed text.[18]

Memoirs by actors involved in early productions of *Peter Pan* provide corroborative evidence that many children not only enjoyed *Peter Pan* but also used it as material for their own creative efforts. For example, Maude Adams (the first American Peter) includes in her recollections not only the standard anecdotes about receiving lots of fan mail and hearing children in the audience call out comments, but also observations about the imaginative activity children engaged in after seeing the show. Describing their domestic reenactments, she recalls that "very few children who saw the play wanted to be Indians . . . No, the children preferred to remain themselves and kill the Pirates. Of course, they liked to play the principal parts and there were a few who liked to play the Lion, but I never heard of any child who volunteered for the Crocodile" (qtd. in Robbins 96). More generally, Adams observed that "the play had the extraordinary effect of inspiring the children who saw it to do work of their own. If their bent happened to be painting, they would tell the story in painted pictures. If they happened to be young sculptors, they would make little figures of the Crocodile or Captain Hook. Those whose fancy turned to writing gave the story of the play in their own words with their own embellishments. Some set the play to music. It was astonishing the urge to creative work the play was to them" (96).

While Adams's examples of artistic endeavors do sound surprisingly elaborate, it actually makes sense that *Peter Pan* would engender such activity, since Barrie's play relentlessly prods children to view themselves as performers. In his very first line, John announces to his mother, "We are doing an act; we are playing at being you and father"; Wendy follows up with, "Now let us pretend we have a baby" (89). Even after flying away to Never Land, the children continue performing domesticity, with Wendy again playing mother and Peter "the Great White Father" (128). The preening, "artful" Peter is the ultimate actor; he travels with his own spotlight—Tinkerbell, twice described as "a ball of light"—and "is so good at pretend" that he is genuinely pained by an imaginary injury (99, 93, 124). Over the course of the play, Peter performs a series of eerily perfect imitations (of Hook, Tiger Lily, a mermaid, a bird, and ultimately, the crocodile). In other words, the plot of the play hinges on his uncanny acting ability. Barrie even suggests that one of Peter's core characteristics—his commitment to boyishness—is in fact only another act; immediately after the line, "I want always to be a little boy and to have fun," Barrie's stage direction reads, "(*So perhaps he thinks, but it is only his greatest pretend*)" (151). Indeed, the idea that "child" and "adult" are roles that anyone can play pervades *Peter Pan*. The precocious Wendy often acts like an adult, while her parents behave like babies, "pouting" and fussing and calling each other names (93).

Barrie's investment in blurring the line between adult and child can also be seen in his casting choices. In the original British and American productions, some of the child parts were played by young actors—Michael, John, Liza—but the main roles of Peter and Wendy were not. Why didn't Barrie arrange for all the children's roles to be played by children? After all, many child-centered dramas in the nineteenth century—*Alice in Wonderland*, *Little Lord Fauntleroy* (Terry's 1888)—featured child actors in leading roles, despite the extremely demanding nature of these parts. As many critics have noted, this choice was partly motivated by a desire to adhere to the risqué pantomime tradition of casting a cross-dressed woman as the principal boy; ignoring the pleas for purity issued by commentators such as W. Davenport Adams, Barrie gleefully exulted in his stage directions that Peter was hardly "dressed at all" (97). But it also owes something to children's theatre. Many dramatists working in this subgenre chose mixed casts over all-child ones on the grounds that "by admitting grown up performers you will certainly get a much higher sum total of skill, & probably much greater success" (Carroll, qtd. in Lovett 38). Carroll used these words to convince Clarke that a mixed cast would be better for *Alice*; both men had originally considered employing an all-child cast but changed their minds. The role of Alice was entrusted to a series of children until 1900, when, for the first time, an adult actress took over: Ellaline Terriss, who went on to play Bluebell in *Bluebell in Fairyland*, and whom Barrie invited to originate the role of Peter. But Terriss was pregnant, so he instead chose Nina Boucicault, who was thirty-seven years old when she originated the role of Peter. Maude Adams was about to turn thirty-three when the show opened in New York.

Such casting choices problematize the common critical assumption that dramas centered around child characters necessarily set up the child as the eroticized object of the adult gaze. In the case of *Peter Pan*, the premiere object of desire was not a child actor but an adult pretending to be a child—not a static icon of innocence but a decidedly liminal figure who blurred the line between adult and child, male and female. If we insist on reading *Peter Pan* biographically (a problematic yet perasive practice) and agree that Peter functions as the most devastatingly attractive figure in the play, then we must admit that what gets presented for erotic consumption is not the Davies brothers—their stand-ins, the Darlings boys, are mere comic side-kicks—but an avatar of Barrie himself: an adult who *acts* like a child, who stage-directs elaborate games, adventures, and "let's pretend" play with actual children.[19] The impulse to blur the line between adult and child is, as I have argued elsewhere, a defining component of the cult of the child that intensified in the late nineteenth century.[20] During this time, as Angela Sorby observes, many adults began to view childhood less as a fixed condition than as "a performative option: a way of acting, a way of thinking, a way of [being] that was open to all" (xxi). In playing Peter, actresses such as Boucicault and Adams modeled this practice for adults in the audience. Many reviewers felt the play succeeded in helping adults to follow their lead: "Grey-bearded grandfather though I am," one marveled, "I felt as I looked at 'Peter Pan' that I renewed my youth" ("First Impressions" 245). By the same token, children were invited to have an "adult" reaction to Peter, if we consider sexual attraction the province of grown-ups; Wendy's erotic interest in Peter provided a model that children in the audience could and apparently did follow (Birkin 118; Gubar, *Artful* 200–201).

As we might expect given such boundary blurring, even as Barrie participates in the children's theatre tradition, he also subverts it. Creators of children's plays generally aimed to preserve (or create) a strict dividing line between children and adults by serving up more innocent and less spectacular fare—something Barrie pointedly refused to do, presenting instead a circus-like production that featured wild animals, flying actors, cross-dressing, and a highly sexed fairy. Rather than policing the adult-child line, *Peter Pan* muddles it, not just thematically (through its characterization of children and adults), but also practically (in terms of casting) and formally (by mixing up aspects of adult-oriented and child-oriented drama). Reacting negatively to precisely this feature of *Peter Pan*, drama critic Max Beerbohm objected to the inclusion of what he viewed as adult content in a play that purported to address children. Young people, he opined, were incapable of appreciating the subtle wit and pathos of Barrie's play ("Pantomime" 118–20). Both he and Bernard Shaw suggested that adult desire was driving the ticket sales: "children cannot go alone to theatres. An adult must accompany the over-excited party. Naturally the adult tries to persuade himself that, in choosing the entertainment least likely to bore himself, he is choosing also that which will most enrapture his dear little friends" (Beerbohm, "Pantomime" 117).

Though Beerbohm's insistence that children could not grasp the finer points of Barrie's play is condescending, he and Shaw were attuned to a genuine problem that haunts any discussion of children's theatre: the vexed issue of the child playgoer's personal agency. Both men acknowledged that early twentieth-century playgoers considered *Peter Pan* a children's play and that children attended in large numbers. What they questioned was whether young people were present of their own free will or had been coerced into coming by adults. In other words, they anticipate the concern expressed by Rose and other critics who emphasize how much power adults wield over children. Like Rose, they admit the impossibility of decisively settling this question. But that does not stop them from investigating the subject of how young people were reacting to *Peter Pan*; it merely prompts them to couch their claims in admirably cautious terms. Does *Peter Pan* enrapture children as well as adults? "I am not at all sure," admits Shaw (1481). "To a certain extent, I daresay," Beerbohm muses, "they are affected by the magnetic currents in the adult crowd around them. But I suspect their thoughts of straying" ("*Peter Pan*" 335).

Notably, Beerbohm and Shaw were not exceptional in their circumspect treatment of this issue. "It should be remembered," observed the author of "Children's Plays" (1899), "that children are not free agents in the choice of their theatrical amusements. As a matter of fact, they have no choice at all, for they have to go where they are taken." All the way back to Blanchard's all-child pantomimes, productions that purported to please children had prompted critics to wonder whether their primary appeal was not to adults. For example, the *Times* described Blanchard's *Little Goody Two Shoes* as "a pantomime played by children for children, for whose amusement ostensibly, but perhaps not actually, such entertainment is put forward" (review of *Little Goody*). Precisely because they were so keenly attuned to this issue, Victorian and Edwardian journalists made a genuine effort to find out what individual children thought about productions that styled themselves as children's plays.

To begin with, there was the phenomenon of the follow-up review: because children did not generally attend opening night, critics sometimes revisited a production after it had been running for some time in order to ascertain whether children were actually attending and how they were reacting.[21] Moreover, critics included detailed descriptions of the reactions of children in their reviews, even when they did not match the reviewer's own expectations about how young people would respond (Gubar, *Artful* 186–98). Then, too, commentators frequently quoted remarks made by young playgoers. For instance, a reviewer of the original London production of *Peter Pan* informed his readers that a puzzled child sitting behind him inquired, "What's it all about?" when the actor who played Hook began to mimic several famous actors of the day, a bit of business that was later cut, probably because more than one critic complained that it was too adult-oriented ("W. T. S." 19). Employing all three of these tactics, the *New York Times* reviewer who covered the final matinée performance of *Peter Pan*'s first American run recounted how mobs of children threw confetti and flowers at Maude Adams and called for a post-performance speech "so insistently" that she was forced to comply, after which "several hundred children" rushed to the stage door and attempted to unharness the horses attached to her carriage so that they could pull it to her home themselves ("Children Admirers"). To illustrate his point that the poor Irish boys in the top-most gallery "had quite as keen [a] perception of the beauties" of Barrie's play as "'de silk stockin's' down below," this reviewer quotes the boys' conversation about fairies at some length ("Children Admirers").

As professional children's theatre companies began to be formed after the turn of the century, journalists and theatrical producers on both sides of the Atlantic came up with another way of recording the reactions of young playgoers: they began to sponsor contests that invited children to try on the role of reviewer. *Pinkie and the Fairies* (His Majesty's 1908), *Alice in Wonderland* (Savoy 1910), and Frances Hodgson Burnett's *Racketty-Packetty House* (Century Children's 1912) all engendered competitions of this kind—and so, eventually, did *Peter Pan*. In 1920, the *Bookman* ran a contest to determine "What the Audience Thinks," inviting children under fourteen to review that year's revival of *Peter Pan*. Many of the successful contestants observe that both adults and children enjoy Barrie's play, and like their professional peers they attempt to explain why. Third-prize winner Bernard Collins, age eleven, is no exception, though his essay is notable for offering criticism as well as praise. Despite its "somewhat unmeaning title," he tartly explains, "*Peter Pan* is very interesting and hence very popular" with everyone from children to old men. Why? Because Barrie's play "has a part for everyone—fairies for the girls; pirates and Indians for the boys, and literary skill, which is very appealing to the grown-ups. A great feature of the last-named is the way the words are put so that a child can understand them; and yet not tiring and babyish to the older people" (120). And yet, Bernard adds, "Although it has its good points, this tale might have a few improvements made: for instance . . . in the end Mr. and Mrs. Darling should come and settle and start a colony on an island not far from the 'Never, never land,' where they could easily communicate with Peter" (120).

What can and can't we learn from tracking down statements such as this one? Obviously, we cannot learn what children as a group thought about *Peter Pan*: Bernard speaks only for himself, a male, English, and (probably) fairly well-to-do child growing up in the 1920s—not as the spokesperson for a coherent constituency who all responded in the same way to Barrie's play. Yet, however scattered and unrepresentative such testimony may be, it can nevertheless enrich our scholarly conversations about children's literature and culture. In this case, my hope has been that including it as one element of an intertheatrical reading might put to an end critical seesawing on the issue of audience. As Bernard and many of his peers and predecessors realized,

Peter Pan was written neither for children nor for adults, but for both; it is, among other things, a children's play. At the same time, I have suggested that we cannot study the history of children's theatre—still one of the most marginalized subgenres in children's literature studies—without attending to the practices and discourses of young people (which perhaps explains *why* this subfield remains so neglected). To ignore the statements of children such as Bernard is to replicate the silencing that makes such evidence so rare in the first place: the low valuation placed on young people's discourse that ensures that children's writing is rarely preserved, archived, and analyzed.

Although such testimony may tempt us to make unjustifiably sweeping statements about young people, it also has the capacity to disrupt such generalizations. For instance, when Bernard winds up his essay by announcing that "in the book I think that Mr. Darling is the best character" whereas "Wendy is the best in the play," he reminds us that we cannot assume that children "could not read" the 1911 novelized version of *Peter Pan* because of its complex, highly allusive prose (Rose 6). Bernard's unsteady adherence to sexual stereotypes is also illuminating. In the fragment quoted above, he adheres to gender norms in his account of *Peter Pan*'s appeal (just as he reveals his relaxed familiarity with imperialist tactics when he suggests that Mr. and Mrs. Darling should become colonists). And yet, despite his causal sexism, Bernard also expresses a desire to domesticate Barrie's hero by providing him with substitute parents and calls Wendy—a dedicated homebody—one of his favorite characters. Such fluctuation might serve as a check to commentators who demonize Wendy and characterize the cozier, more realistic aspects of *Peter Pan* as a hindrance to the real action;[22] or it might enable us to discuss how even dominant ideologies to which children are exposed do not always penetrate them completely. Either way, it reminds us not to generalize about children and their responses to cultural artifacts, a lesson we can also learn from sharp-eyed reviewers such as Beerbohm. Writing about a revival of *Alice* (Vaudeville 1900), Beerbohm announces that he will take a "wild shot" at guessing what child playgoers are thinking ("*Alice*" 111). Yet at the same time, he observes that "it is not safe to dogmatise about their tastes" since "children are probably as different as are adults" (111). Present in the theatre, paying attention to how actual children respond, he nevertheless admits that he is working in the dark. We can never fully know what young people—or, for that matter, adults—thought about such productions, and yet we can make use of a surprisingly rich array of intertheatrical evidence in order to recognize and theorize about the role that children played in the development of children's theatre.

NOTES

1. Some recent accounts of children's theatre continue to posit *Peter Pan* as a point of origin: see for example England (17) and the entry "Youth, Theatre for" in the *Oxford Encyclopedia of Theatre and Performance* (2003).

2. Sale (1) and Kincaid (283) take this position as well.

3. See Birkin (104), Rose (chapter 4), and T. Davis (70–77), all of whom characterize *Peter Pan* as an amalgam of different dramatic subgenres. For different reasons, however, none of them investigate the play's links to children's theatre.

4. For more on *Peter Pan*'s relationship to the child drama, see chapter 6 of my book *Artful Dodgers*.

5. On the topic of *Peter Pan*'s relation to pantomime, see Green (55–69, 82, 99), Rose (95–96), White and Tarr (x–xix), and T. Davis (70–77).

6. This phrase appeared in an advertisement in the *Era* for the double bill of *The Piper of Hamelin* and *Sandford and Merton* (30 December 1893, 14).

7. For more background on the development of pantomime, a category of drama that was not originally designed for children, see J. Davis, Mayer, O'Brien, Speaight (with Alderson), and Wilson. See Bedard (2, 23) and Senelick (xiii–xvi) for information about the American pantomime tradition.

8. For a critical discussion of the erotic elements of pantomime, see Mayer ("Sexuality").

9. Varty offers a detailed and helpful account of this production (*Children* 86–92).

10. I make this argument at length in chapters 5 and 6 of *Artful Dodgers* and in "The Drama of Precocity."

11. As Halttunen, Foulkes, and Dawson have shown, various kinds of private theatricals took place in middle-class Anglo-American homes in the nineteenth century, including plays performed by and for adults; intergenerational events directed by adults but enacted by and for a mixed group of young and old; and theatricals created and performed entirely by children for their own enjoyment.

12. See for example "Music and the Drama" (1875) and "Children's Plays" (1899).

13. The reviewer for *Judy* called it "an ideal play for children" (44); see also "First Impressions" (245).

14. In contrast, critics who attended the daytime performances that followed the first night of *Alice* could and did attest to the presence and positive reactions of child playgoers, whom they declared were "greatly delighted" by the show (review of *Alice*, *Lloyd's*).

15. Hilda Trevelyan, who originated the role of Wendy, recalled that she received "letters from countless numbers of children" (109). See also Chase (in *Peter Pan's Postbag* vi–vii), Robbins (96–97), and Fields (194).

16. Future actress Margaret Webster responded just as ecstatically to *Peter Pan* as a young child (Barranger 10).

17. All the fan mail quoted in this section comes from *Peter Pan's Postbag: Letters to Pauline Chase* (1909). This particular letter was reproduced at the front of Chase's book in an unpaginated section.

18. Victorian and Edwardian dramatists routinely published the "book of the words" during the original run of their plays, yet Barrie delayed for twenty-four years before publishing the script of *Peter Pan*. Another factor in this decision may have been Barrie's unusually flexible attitude toward the text of his plays within the context of professional productions. As Green (80), Ormond (87), and others note, he was a fabulous collaborator who was willing to make all manner of changes based on the input of actors, directors, and others involved in the production process. *Peter Pan* therefore changed as different performers took on the lead roles, and Barrie perhaps did not want to shut down the possibility of those kinds of revisions, either.

19. For an illuminating account of how Barrie wove references to various playground and parlor games into *Peter Pan*, see Varty ("Locating Never Land").

20. See the introduction and chapter 5 of my book *Artful Dodgers*.

21. See, for example, "A Children's Pantomime" (1877) and "The Children's Choice" (1887).

22. Barrie's contemporary H. H. Munro reacted this way to *Peter Pan* (qtd. in Gubar, *Artful* 25); so, too, in his own way, does Kincaid (285–86).

WORKS CITED

Adams, W. Davenport. "The Decline of Pantomime." *Theatre*, 1 February 1882. Reprinted in *Theatre* new ser. 5 (January–June 1882): 85–90.

Arliss, George. *Up the Years from Bloomsbury: An Autobiography*. Boston: Little, Brown, and Company, 1930.

Barmby, J. *Plays for Young People, with Songs and Choruses, Suitable for Private Theatricals*. Music by T. Rogers. New York: Dick and Fitzgerald, 1879.

Barranger, Milly S. *Margaret Webster: A Life in the Theatre*. Ann Arbor: U of Michigan P, 2004.

Barrie, J. M. *Peter Pan in Kensington Gardens* and *Peter and Wendy*. 1906 and 1911. Edited by Peter Hollindale. Oxford: Oxford UP, 1991.

———. *Peter Pan and Other Plays*. Edited by Peter Hollindale. Oxford: Oxford UP, 1995.

———. "To the Five: A Dedication." In Barrie, *Peter Pan and Other Plays* 75–86.

Bartlett, George Bradford. *Parlor Amusements for the Young Folks*. Boston: James R. Osgood and Company, 1875.

Bedard, Roger L., ed. *Dramatic Literature for Children: A Century in Review*. New Orleans, LA: Anchorage Press, 1984.

Beerbohm, Max. "*Alice* Again Awakened." *Saturday Review*, 22 December 1900. Reprinted in *Around Theatres*, 109–12. New York: Simon and Schuster, 1954.

———. "Pantomime for Children." *Saturday Review*, 14 January 1905. Reprinted in *Last Theatres 1904–1910*, 116–20. London: Rupert Hart-Davis, 1970.

———. "*Peter Pan* Revisited." *Saturday Review*, 28 December 1907. Reprinted in *Last Theatres 1904–1910*, 334–37. London: Rupert Hart-Davis, 1970.

Birkin, Andrew. *J. M. Barrie and the Lost Boys: The Love Story that Gave Birth to Peter Pan*. New York: Clarkson N. Potter, 1979.

Bratton, Jacky. *New Readings in Theatre History*. Cambridge, UK: Cambridge UP, 2003.

"Children Admirers Routed Peter Pan." *New York Times*, 10 June 1906, 9.

"The Children's Choice." *Punch*, 29 January 1887, 60.

"A Children's Pantomime." *Era*, 7 January 1877, 12.

"Children's Plays." *Era*, 16 December 1899, 7.

Clarke, Henry Savile. "Christmas Entertainments." *Examiner*, 3 January 1880, 11–12.

Corner, Julia. *Beauty and the Beast*. 1854. Reprinted in Levy, *The Gymnasium of the Imagination* 207–38.

Coveney, Peter. *The Image of Childhood*. 1957. Rev. ed. Baltimore: Penguin Books, 1967.

Daiches, David. "The Sexless Sentimentalist." *Listener*, 12 May 1960, 841–43.

Darton, F. J. Harvey. *Children's Books in England: Five Centuries of Social Life*. 3rd ed. Revised by Brian Alderson. Cambridge: Cambridge UP, 1982.

Davis, Jim. "Boxing Day." In *The Performing Century: Nineteenth-Century Theatre's History*, 13–31. Basingstoke: Palgrave Macmillan, 2007.

Davis, Tracy C. "'Do You Believe in Fairies?': The Hiss of Dramatic License." *Theatre Journal* 57 (2005): 57–81.

Dawson, Melanie. *Laboring to Play: Home Entertainment and the Spectacle of Middle-Class Cultural Life, 1850–1920.* Tuscaloosa: U of Alabama P, 2005.

du Maurier, Angela. *It's Only the Sister: An Autobiography.* London: Peter Davies, 1951.

England, Alan. *Theatre for the Young.* New York: St. Martin's Press, 1990.

Fields, Armond. *Maude Adams: Idol of American Theater, 1872–1953.* Jefferson, NC: McFarland & Co., 2004.

"First Impressions of the Theatre.—V. My First Musical Comedy and Children's Play." *Review of Reviews,* March 1905, 245–48.

Foulkes, Richard. *Lewis Carroll and the Victorian Stage: Theatricals in a Quiet Life.* Burlington, VT: Ashgate, 2005.

Freiligrath-Kroeker, Kate. *Alice and Other Fairy Plays for Children.* London: W. Swan Sonnenschein and Allen, 1880.

Green, Roger Lancelyn. *Fifty Years of Peter Pan.* London: Davies, 1954.

Gubar, Marah. *Artful Dodgers: Reconceiving the Golden Age of Children's Literature.* New York: Oxford UP, 2009.

———. "The Drama of Precocity: Child Performers on the Victorian Stage." In *The Nineteenth-Century Child and Consumerism,* edited by Dennis Dennisoff, 64–78. Burlington, VT: Ashgate, 2008.

Halttunen, Karen. *Confidence Men and Painted Women: A Study of Middle-Class Culture in America, 1830–1870.* New Haven: Yale UP, 1982.

———. "The Domestic Drama of Louisa May Alcott." *Feminist Studies* 10, no. 2 (Summer 1984): 233–54.

Hollindale, Peter. Introduction. In Barrie, *Peter Pan and Other Plays* vii–xxxiv.

Hughes, M. V. *A London Child of the 1870s.* Oxford: Oxford UP, 1934.

Jack, R. D. S. *The Road to the Never Land: A Reassessment of J. M. Barrie's Dramatic Art.* Newcastle-upon-Tyne: Aberdeen UP, 1991.

Kincaid, James. *Child-Loving: The Erotic Child and Victorian Culture.* New York: Routledge, 1992.

Little Goody Two Shoes; or, Harlequin Little Boy Blue. Advertisement. *Era,* 17 December 1876, 10.

Lovett, Charles C. *Alice on Stage: A History of the Early Theatrical Productions of Alice in Wonderland.* Westport, CT: Meckler, 1990.

Lucas, Audrey. *E. V. Lucas: A Portrait.* Port Washington, NY: Kennikat Press, 1939.

Mackail, Denis. *Barrie: The Story of J. M. B.* New York: Charles Scribner's Sons, 1941.

Mayer, David. *Harlequin in His Element: The English Pantomime, 1806–1836.* Cambridge, MA: Harvard UP, 1969.

———. "The Sexuality of Pantomime." *Theatre Quarterly* 4 (February–April 1974): 55–64.

"Music and the Drama." *Appletons' Journal of Literature, Science and Art,* 5 June 1875, 729–31.

O'Brien, John. *Harlequin Britain: Pantomime and Entertainment, 1690–1760.* Baltimore: Johns Hopkins UP, 2004.

———. "Pantomime." In *The Cambridge Companion to British Theatre, 1730–1830,* edited by Jane Moody and Daniel O'Quinn. New York: Cambridge University Press, 2007. 103–27.

Ormond, Leonée. *J. M. Barrie.* Edinburgh UK: Scottish Academic Press, 1987.

Peter Pan's Postbag: Letters to Pauline Chase. London: Heinemann, 1909.

Review of *Alice in Wonderland. Era,* 25 December 1886, 9.

Review of *Alice in Wonderland. Lloyds Weekly Newspaper,* 26 December 1886, 8.

Review of *Little Goody Two Shoes*. *Times*, 27 December 1876, 5.

Review of *Peter Pan*. *Times*, 28 December 1904, 4.

Review of *Peter Pan*. *Illustrated London News*, 7 January 1905, 5.

Review of *Peter Pan*. *Judy: The London Serio-Comic Journal*, 25 January 1905, 44–45.

Robbins, Phyllis. *Maude Adams: An Intimate Portrait*. New York: G. P. Putnam's Sons, 1956.

Rose, Jacqueline. *The Case of Peter Pan: or, The Impossibility of Children's Fiction*. 1984. Rev. ed. Philadelphia: U of Pennsylvania P, 1992.

Sale, Roger. *Fairy Tales and After: From Snow White to E. B. White*. Cambridge, MA: Harvard UP, 1978.

Schechner, Richard. *Performance Theory*. 1977. Rev ed. Routledge: New York, 2003.

Scott, Clement, ed. *Drawing-Room Plays and Parlour Pantomimes*. London: S. Ribers and Company, 1870.

Senelick, Laurence. *The Age and Stage of George L. Fox, 1825–1877*. Hanover, NH: UP of New England, 1988.

Shaw, Bernard. "The Unhappy Years of Barrie." *Sunday Graphic and Sunday News*, 20 June 1937. Reprinted in *The Drama Observed*. Vol. 4: *1911–1950*. Edited by Bernard F. Dukore 1479–81. University Park: Pennsylvania State UP, 1993.

Shepard, Ernest H. *Drawn from Life*. New York: E. P. Dutton and Company, 1961.

———. *Drawn from Memory*. Philadelphia: J. B. Lippincott Company, 1957.

Sorby, Angela. *Schoolroom Poets: Childhood, Performance, and the Place of American Poetry, 1865–1917*. Durham: U of New Hampshire P, 2005.

Speaight, George, with Brian Alderson. "From Chapbooks to Pantomime." In *Popular Children's Literature in Britain*, edited by Julia Briggs, Dennis Butts, and M. O. Grenby. Burlington, VT: Ashgate: 2008. 87–97.

Stevenson, Robert Louis. "Child's Play." In *R. L. Stevenson on Fiction: An Anthology of Literary and Critical Essays*, edited by Glenda Norquay. Edinburgh: Edinburgh UP, 1999. 29–39.

Trevelyan, Hilda. "Maggie, Wendy, Cinders, and Some Others." *Bookman*, December 1920, 109–10.

Varty, Anne. *Children and Theatre in Victorian Britain: "All Work, No Play."* New York: Palgrave Macmillan, 2008.

———. "Locating Never Land: *Peter Pan* and Parlour Games." *New Theatre Quarterly* 23 (November 2007): 393–402.

"What the Audience Thinks. 'Mary Rose' and 'Peter Pan' Prize Competition Results." *Bookman* (U.K.), December 1920, 114–22.

White, Donna R. and C. Anita Tarr. *J. M. Barrie's* Peter Pan *In and Out of Time: A Children's Classic at 100*. Lanham, MD: Scarecrow Press, 2006.

Wilson, A. E. *King Panto: The Story of Pantomime*. New York: Dutton, 1935

W. T. S. "Peter Pan." *Academy and Literature* 7 (January 1905): 19–20.

Zipes, Jack, Lissa Paul, Lynne Vallone, Peter Hunt, and Gillian Avery, eds. *The Norton Anthology of Children's Literature: The Traditions in English*. New York: Norton, 2005.

FURTHER READING

Bedard, Roger L., and C. John Tolch. *Spotlight on the Child: Studies in the History of American Children's Theatre*. New York: Greenwood Press, 1989.

Crozier, Brian. "Notions of Childhood in London Theatre, 1880–1905." Diss., U of Cambridge, 1981.

Davis, James Herbert. *The Happy Island: Images of Childhood in the Eighteenth-Century French Théâtre d'Education*. New York: Peter Lang, 1987.

Davis, Tracy C. "What Are Fairies For?" In *The Performing Century: Nineteenth-Century Theatre's History*, 32–59. Basingstoke: Palgrave Macmillan, 2007.

Doolittle, Joyce, and Zina Barnieh. *A Mirror of Our Dreams: Children and the Theatre in Canada*. Vancouver: Talonbooks, 1979.

Hollindale, Peter. "Drama." In *International Companion Encyclopedia of Children's Literature*, edited by Peter Hunt and Sheila G. Bannister Ray, 206–19. 1st ed. New York: Routledge, 1996.

Levy, Jonathan. *The Gymnasium of the Imagination: A Collection of Children's Plays in English, 1780–1860*. Westport, CT: Greenwood Press, 1992.

Levy, Jonathan, and Martha Mahard. "Preliminary Checklist of Early Printed Children's Plays in English, 1780–1855." *Performing Arts Resources* 12 (1987): 1–97.

Maier, Barbara Jo. "'A Delicate Invisible Hand': Frances Hodgson Burnett's Contributions for Theatre for Youth." In *In the Garden: Essays in Honor of Frances Hodgson Burnett*, edited by Angelica Shirley Carpenter, 113–29. Lanham, MD: Scarecrow Press, 2006.

McCaslin, Nellie. *Theatre for Children in the United States: A History*. Norman: U of Oklahoma P, 1971.

O'Malley, Andrew. "Acting Out Crusoe: Pedagogy and Performance in Eighteenth-Century Children's Literature." *Lion and the Unicorn* 33, no. 2 (April 2009): 131–45.

Salazar, Laura Gardner. "The Emergence of Children's Theatre, a Study in America's Changing Values and the Stage, 1900–1910." *Theatre History Studies* 7 (1987): 73–83.

Smith, Katharine Capshaw. *Children's Literature of the Harlem Renaissance*. Bloomington: Indiana UP, 2004.

Swortzell, Lowell, ed. *International Guide to Children's Theatre and Educational Theatre: A Historical and Geographical Source Book*. New York: Greenwood Press, 1990.

Water, Manon van de. *Moscow Theatres for Young People: A Cultural History of Ideological Coercion and Artistic Innovation, 1917–2000*. New York: Palgrave Macmillan, 2006.

Zipes, Jack. "Political Children's Theater in the Age of Globalization." *Theatre* 33, no. 2 (2003): 3–25.

———. Political Plays for Children: The Grips Theater of Berlin. St Louis: Telos Press, 1976.

....

CHAPTER 24

JADE AND THE TOMBOY
TRADITION

....

CLAUDIA NELSON

BORN *in 1924 in Seattle, Sally Watson remarks in a 2009 interview in the Santa Rosa Press-Democrat that she initially assumed that a career as a novelist was impossible, as "ordinary people couldn't write books." But when she learned in the mid-1950s that a high school friend had recently published a children's story, "I rushed home and started* Highland Rebel *that night," as she puts it in her author's blurb for Image Cascade Publishing.* Highland Rebel, *a blend of fact and fiction woven around Bonnie Prince Charlie's escape after the failed rising of 1745, was quickly written and as quickly accepted by a major publishing house. After that milestone, Watson oscillated for a time between the United States and England (where she lived from 1963 to 1987), studied Highland dancing, earned her black belt in judo, gardened, raised cats, and, by 1972, had written twelve novels with settings ranging from present-day Israel to sixteenth-century London. The author line "by Sally Watson" on a cover signaled for her fans an appealing blend of factual information, exciting plots, and tough-minded heroines.*

In 1972, changes in publishers' handling of their backlists sent all twelve of Watson's novels out of print. Interest among fans still remained high decades later, however, with Internet auctions of her books yielding prices close to $1000 for discarded library copies. Image Cascade, a reprint house specializing in mid-twentieth-century girls' authors, republished seven of her novels in the early 2000s; in 2006, Watson published her first new title in thirty-five years, following it with eight more as of 2009. These titles include some reworkings of previously published material but consist primarily of new stories. Their settings—among them ancient Egypt, seventeenth-century England, and frontier Missouri at the time of the New Madrid earthquake—reflect the same capacious interests that characterize Watson works of the 1950s and '60s.

Sally Watson's fiction, which she began to publish in 1954, both participates in and exaggerates an important trend in earlier twentieth-century writing for girls, namely, the ratifying of the feisty tomboy protagonist.[1] As Michelle Abate notes, "tomboyism as both a cultural phenomenon and [a] literary convention had become ubiquitous in the United States" by the late nineteenth century, with the 1930s "often seen as the final phase of the 'golden age' of tomboy literature" (ix, 137). Writers who preceded Watson in creating strong, active, nonconformist heroines often achieved canonical status; works including Caroline Dale Snedeker's *Downright Dencey* (1927, Newbery Honor book), Rachel Field's *Calico Bush* (1931, Newbery Honor book), Laura Ingalls Wilder's nine-volume Little House series (1932–1971,[2] five Newbery Honor books), Carol Ryrie Brink's *Caddie Woodlawn* (1935, Newbery Medalist), Ruth Sawyer's *Roller Skates* (1936, Newbery Medalist) and *The Year of Jubilo* (1940), and, somewhat later, Elizabeth George Speare's *The Witch of Blackbird Pond* (1958, Newbery Medalist) garnered major prize recognition and in some cases a continued presence in the classroom for their depictions of latter-day Jo Marches impatient with the constraints placed upon women. Clearly, the reviewers, librarians, educators, and publishers who identified and promoted "good books" to the girl reader of the tomboy "golden age"—in effect, shaping a girls' canon whose main characters would model acceptable behaviors and outlooks—were prepared not merely to tolerate but to reward young protagonists' difficulties enacting conventional femininity.

As the preceding sentence implies, the canonical children's book is by no means identical to the popular children's book, although the two categories sometimes overlap. Canonicity, a focus of the present chapter, is connected to (perceived) quality; popularity is connected to the size of a book's readership, often measured by sales figures. When children have purchasing power, they can be the dominant force in determining popularity, but adults, the traditional masters of reviewing outlets, book awards, school book lists, and library collection building, are the arbiters of canonicity. Moreover, the children's books that adults deem worthy are typically seen as performing some desirable social function: "classics" provide access to cultural capital and enable shared experiences across generations (thus a mother may be motivated to give her daughter *Little Women* by a belief that every American girl should read *Little Women*, and/or that the daughter will like the novel because her mother did at the same age), while newly published "good books" may promise educational or moral benefits of other kinds.

We may view the formation of the adult-approved girls' canon of the 1920s and 1930s, with its many tomboy texts, as connected to a perceived need for strong, educated, professional women ready to shoulder responsibility in the post-suffrage and Depression eras and, more generally, to a widespread interest in forming American tastes, whether child or adult, in a way that would benefit the nation. The 1920s and 1930s gave birth, for instance, to the Book-of-the-Month Club, founded in 1926, which promised, in effect, to build a better reader; the Junior Literary Guild, founded three years later, whose similar project was directed at children; the Motion Picture Production Code of 1930, which sought to create a more morally uplifting Hollywood; the film appreciation movement, designed to turn 1930s high school students into more savvy consumers of popular culture; and, most significant to this chapter, the Newbery Medal, first awarded in 1922. As Kenneth Kidd points out, from the outset, the founders and movers of the Newbery saw themselves as "shaping their public," especially by participating in "character building through books," and "by the 1930s, the Medal had come to be as closely associated with the educational mission as with library work" (172, 174).[3] Simultaneously, as librarians, teachers, mothers, and writers and (increasingly) editors of children's books, women were perceived as particularly powerful arbiters of children's culture and were expected to use that power in a way that would shape future citizens—a socializing role that remained women's most potent public role until at least the 1970s.

That Dencey, Caddie, Laura, and their fictional sisters received the Newbery imprimatur identifies them as desirable role models for their era. Yet Watson titles such as *Jade* (1969), which boasts a protagonist who takes feistiness a step further by shipping with the female pirates (and historical figures) Anne Bonney and Mary Read, did not become canonical, despite high literary quality, generally favorable notices, and engrossing plots; indeed *Jade*, along with *Witch of the Glens* (1962), appears to have been a particular favorite for Watson readers (Watson, personal communication, 8 July 2008). And while *Witch of the Glens*, whose outsider protagonist is slowly integrated into an aristocratic Highland family in the seventeenth century, made the *Horn Book* honor list in 1963 and, like *The Mukhtar's Children* in 1969, was named a "*Horn Book* Fanfare Best Book of the Year," the only other prize listed under Watson's name in her *Contemporary Authors* entry is the Brooklyn Community Woodward School's annual book award for 1959 ("Sally [Lou] Watson").[4]

To be sure, only one book a year can win a Newbery, and success or lack of success in that competition is by no means the only marker of canonicity for children's books. In this chapter, I use the Newbery Medal more as shorthand for cultural approval than as an absolute—but a convenient shorthand, both because recognition via that prize had earlier gone to a significant number of tomboy books and because *Jade* seems to have been entirely out of the running. The Book Evaluation Committee of the American Library Association's Children's Services Division omitted *Jade* from its list of sixty-four "Notable Children's Books of 1969" (in effect, the Newbery quarterfinalists),[5] while *School Library Journal*'s editors left it off their list of "Best Books of the Year." Nor was the novel recognized in other prize competitions, such as the *Boston Globe-Horn Book* Award, the children's books division of the National Book Award, or the Christopher Award for books that "affirm the highest values of the human spirit." This chapter proposes that reading *Jade* against its more canonical, more socially approved predecessors provides insight into the parameters of the tomboy tradition and what those parameters imply about twentieth-century understandings of femininity. In terms of both chronology and content, *Jade* was somewhat out of step; not only did it appear after the heyday of the tomboy as an approved figure in American girls' fiction, and, not coincidentally, at a moment when the qualities associated with the tomboy were coming to look newly radical, it also goes further than the Newbery tomboy texts in its suggestions about female gender roles, especially where the family is concerned.

Readers unfamiliar with Watson's novel may find a brief summary helpful. *Jade* opens in 1719, when its heroine is sixteen. Born to an upper-class family in colonial Williamsburg and christened Melanie Lennox, Jade prefers her nickname; since in the eighteenth century "jade" was a derogatory term for disreputable or otherwise hard to control women, this preference matches her rebellious behavior. Her father, who otherwise considers that he has his family in order, is baffled by his eldest child's abolitionist and feminist sentiments and her defiance of the conduct and principles ratified by mainstream Virginia society. With the revelation that Jade has for years been studying fencing with Monsieur Maupin, a French émigré who sympathizes with her unpopular ideas, her father decides that the family will be more comfortable if he escorts her to Jamaica to stay with relatives. Jade is accompanied on her travels by her longtime slave, Joshua, and by a gift thoughtfully provided by Monsieur Maupin, a trunk whose false bottom conceals a compartment containing a rapier, shirt, and breeches.

Jade enjoys the voyage, although she is irked by the scornful demeanor of the second mate, Rory MacDonald (grandson of an earlier Watson heroine, Kelpie of *Witch of the Glens*). She is less taken with Jamaica: her aunt is ineffectual and easily flustered by nieces inclined toward tree-climbing and dress reform, her uncle smugly authoritarian, and "good" society no more congenial to Jade than its counterpart in Williamsburg. Before her father's departure, however, and at her earnest request, he buys Jade a second slave, the African-born Domino, whose unconquered hatred for the system that has made her a captive has identified her to Jade as a kindred spirit. While Jade's efforts teaching Domino to fence go unnoticed, the short haircut that she gives herself one rebellious afternoon cannot be overlooked,[6] and her relationship with her uncle rapidly deteriorates. All greet with some relief the news of a yellow fever outbreak, which will necessitate Jade's return to Virginia on the same ship that brought her out.

But on this voyage, the *Pearl* is carrying a cargo of slaves. Revolted, Jade dons her fencing garb and releases them one night while the ship is moored near an island. The escape is interrupted and traced to Jade, but to her astonishment, Rory admits to having been implicated as well. At the captain's order, both are flogged; immediately afterward, the *Pearl* is taken by Anne Bonney's pirate crew, the remaining slaves set free on the Cuban coast, and the unconscious Jade and Rory transferred to the *Queen Royal*. In due course they recover, become friends, acclimate to pirate society (which, comparatively color- and gender-blind, is much more to their taste than the respectable colonies), and set about breaking laws—though Jade will commit piracy only when it permits her to free the enslaved. The revelation that a crew member known to all as Mark Read was actually christened Mary, and that Mary is so in love with Tom, a neophyte pirate recruited from the *Pearl*'s crew, that she will duel to the death to protect him, begins a series of weddings, the first two based on historical fact: Mary to Tom, Anne to Michael (a physician liberated from a convict ship, where his captain nearly killed him for standing up for the prisoners), Domino to Joshua. Before Jade and Rory have realized that they too would like to marry, the *Queen Royal* is wrecked in a hurricane, with the consequence that most of the pirates are dead or missing, save for a handful—Jade, Anne, Mary, Tom, and a few drunken layabouts, including the *Queen Royal*'s nominal captain, Calico Jack Rackam—who were ashore at the time of the storm.

This small group's efforts to continue a life of piracy come to little, and soon they are captured (Tom is killed in the fight), tried in a Jamaican court, and condemned to death. The men are executed but the women temporarily reprieved, as Anne and Mary are pregnant and Jade has caught the fancy of the populace; although Mary dies of jail fever, Anne and Jade weather their captivity better, in part because Michael, Rory, Domino, and Joshua turn up in the courtroom, unexpected survivors of the shipwreck. Meanwhile, Jade has forged a new identity as a Frenchwoman in order to protect the Lennox name. The masquerade does not attract the attention of her family back in Williamsburg, but it is penetrated by Monsieur Maupin, who comes to Jamaica and negotiates with the governor for Jade's and Anne's release. Anne, a reformed character, will accompany her husband to the American backwoods and disappear from history, but the happy ending for Jade, Rory, Joshua, Domino, and Monsieur Maupin is not to fade into the Western sunset, but to become a breed of pirates preying only upon slavers.

It should be noted that Watson reports that "it never once occurred to me that I was writing in a tradition," and that while Snedeker was a favorite childhood author, she disliked the Little House books and the ending of *Caddie Woodlawn* (personal communication, 8 July 2008). This chapter does not argue that any direct influence or indebtedness exists,[7] but rather that Watson's work contains and magnifies characteristics that may also be found in earlier examples of what I am calling the "tomboy tale." Most obviously, all are classifiable as historical fiction, though in some cases there is a strong admixture of fact. Wilder's novels mythologize her own childhood and youth; *Caddie Woodlawn* is based on Brink's grandmother's reminiscences; *Roller Skates* incorporates Sawyer's recollections of growing up around notables such as composer Edward MacDowell and restaurateur Louis Sherry; and even the novels set in the more distant past sometimes contain historical figures: Governor Andros, Captain Talcott, Eleazer Kimberley, and Reverend Bulkeley in *The Witch of Blackbird Pond* and the Caribbean governors and all the pirates except Jade, Rory, Joshua, and Domino in *Jade*.[8]

Within the tradition of American children's fiction, the historicity of these works provides an appropriate venue for their high-spirited heroines. Critic Anne Scott MacLeod notes that the late nineteenth century produced a spate of novels about girls in their early teens leading what one memoirist calls a "free, joyous life" before settling down to domesticity (12). MacLeod's examination of nineteenth-century women's autobiographies leads her to conclude that *Caddie Woodlawn* errs in implying that the vigorous activity of Caddie's childhood was unusual for nineteenth-century American girls; rather, a frequent pattern was for girls to lead a tomboyish existence until puberty, after which they were required to adopt a more sedate deportment. MacLeod attributes to the shock of this change the affection for the past visible in the novels that she considers, which hint at "women's resentment of their lot" even when they were "written with conscious intent to perpetuate the conventional ideal" (28). Fashions in child-rearing change, of course, and even the oldest of the present chapter's group of Newbery authors (Wilder, born in 1867, and Snedeker, born in 1871) do not belong to the generation that MacLeod has in mind. Nevertheless, the very existence of a vibrant tomboy tradition emanating from an earlier moment than 1927–43, when most of the Newbery tomboy tales were published, may have helped to establish a sense that the past could plausibly be used as a setting for the expression of girls' rebelliousness or wildness. *The Witch of Blackbird Pond*, published in the 1950s, and *Jade*, published in the 1960s, are late additions to a line that has its origins, MacLeod suggests, in the immediate post–Civil War period.[9]

Yet even if for many historical girls preindustrial America was a comparatively permissive environment for the prepubescent, another quality that the tomboy novels share is their protagonists' perception that they are out of step with their families or surrogate families, especially where the performance of femininity is concerned. Snedeker's Dencey, an early nineteenth-century Nantucket Quaker, runs, climbs trees, throws stones, and swims, but these activities attract criticism; her community finds it problematic that her natural affinity is not with her disciplined mother but with her father, a whaling ship captain frequently absent from home. Brink's Caddie Woodlawn, who, like Dencey, is closer to her father than to her mother, has at his urging been allowed to run wild on the Wisconsin frontier to improve her health and consequently lacks the feminine accomplishments that her mother and older sister prize. In Sawyer's *Roller Skates*, Lucinda's closest familial bond is not to a female relative but to her Uncle Earle, while her aunt disapprovingly measures her against her own "docile, ladylike daughters" (34); in the sequel, *The Year of Jubilo*, Lucinda's brothers are again nonplussed by her liveliness, enterprise, and failure to conform to upper-class feminine stereotypes. Laura Ingalls's sisters seem to have been born well-behaved and bonded to their mother, unlike Laura, yet another "Daddy's girl" with a gift for getting into trouble. And Speare's Kit Tyler and Field's Marguerite are literally aliens in colonial society. In *The Witch of Blackbird Pond* Kit, who has emigrated from Barbados to Connecticut after her beloved grandfather's death to live with her maternal aunt, shocks the Puritans around her by her Royalist sympathies, ability to swim, familiarity with frivolous literature such as Shakespeare plays, and lack of domestic skills. Similarly, *Calico Bush*'s Marguerite, a bound-out orphan living in Maine in the 1740s, is French and Roman Catholic and thus an object of suspicion to her English employers, who recognize her competence and ability to function in a crisis but find her background a serious flaw.[10]

Difference in these works is often marked in part by physical distinctions. Kit's opulent wardrobe in Speare's novel—seven trunks of expensive, colorful, fashionable clothes—instantly sets her apart from her new family, as does Marguerite's French accent in Field's tale. Dencey's complexion is so dark that her peers taunt her with racist epithets, while Lucinda, who is considered "homely" within her family, has "close-cropped, black hair," very different from the long blonde tresses of her friends Trinket and Aleda (Sawyer, *Skates* 33). Similarly, Laura Ingalls's "ugly" brown hair contrasts with the "golden curls" of her older sister, Mary, with whom she competes for adult approval through several volumes of the series (Wilder, *Woods* 168). And Caddie Woodlawn is a redhead like her brothers, as opposed to "the dark-haired side of the family where Mother and Clara and all the safe and tidy virtues were" (Brink 3). Coloring has traditionally been a way for American literature to embody female personality. Nineteenth-century domestic novels contain many brunette/blonde sister pairs in which the brunette is spirited and the blonde placid, and in *Tomboys*, Abate traces the affinity between "tomboyishness and blackness" (xiii). In these twentieth-century renditions, however, the common factor is not the prevalence of dark hair but the way in which each girl fails to meet the standard set by her household, even in such basic matters as appearance or (in Marguerite's case) vowel quantities.

Jade's exterior, to be sure, does not initially deviate from the fashionable norm; in Williamsburg, her difference is marked not by her looks but by her behavior. As her father muses, "She looked like such a sweet young girl, with soft honey-brown ringlets hanging thickly about a slender neck, with long lashes and furtive dimples and a soft round chin—which was now sticking out at him like the vanguard of an army" (3). Similarly, the people of Williamsburg and even her family think of her as Melanie and never use the nickname bestowed by her dead grandparents, and her body looks sweetly feminine but is secretly athletic: "Such softly rounded little arms, such slender, shapely legs, giving no hint at all of the trained muscles beneath! And only two people knew. No one else even suspected—how should they?—unless one counted the puzzled glances William Howe had been giving her ever since that day he had tried to kiss her and she knocked him flat and bloodied his nose" (13). Once she cuts her hair, her appearance more closely reflects her personality, since "the soft, oval, feminine face of Melanie, no longer framed by all that hair, had changed its shape, become pointed, all mouth and eyes and ears and cheek bones, not in the least soft or feminine or even pretty" (84). The trope of the closeted presence of something not "feminine"—a name, a muscular body, a readiness to question authority—resurfaces during the attempt to free the cargo of slaves on the *Pearl*, when Jade, who has been wounded (but not recognized) in the melee, hastily bandages her arm and covers bandage and male garb with a dress in order to stand among the innocent passengers. The eventual penetration of her disguise causes consternation; it disrupts the worldview of the captain and his followers to discover the discrepancy between their expectations about this well-born girl and the reality.

The reader, of course, is familiar with the inner Jade from the outset and is not expected to emulate the discomfiture of the captain (and assorted other male authority figures) that she is not a tractable, "good" girl in the mold of Mary Ingalls or Clara Woodlawn. Indeed, unless we refuse to share the narrator's obvious affection for Jade, we will like her for the very qualities that, we are told, the dominant society of her era disapproves. As Janice M. Alberghene sees it, the titles most frequently chosen by the early Newbery committees were those that clarified for young readers "that which is American—even when the books are ostensibly about other cultures" (qtd. in Kidd 177). Jade's nonconformity, energy, and principled commitment to liberty and the rights of the outsider might all be claimed as "American" values, and indeed these qualities are also evident in the protagonists I have identified as coming earlier in the tradition. Snedeker's Dencey secretly teaches a social outcast to read; Sawyer's Lucinda hobnobs with Italian immigrants, Irish cabbies, and trash collectors; Brink's Caddie protects the local Indians from massacre by the white settlers; Speare's Kit befriends a neglected child and a persecuted Quaker; Field's Marguerite makes a life for herself in a hostile world. Even Laura, in a series not notably focused on the rights of such outsiders as Native Americans, moves over the course of Wilder's novels "from obedience to autonomy," as Claudia Mills puts it (139), and eventually finds herself "lighted up" by the realization that "there isn't anyone else who has a right to give me orders. I will have to make myself be good" (Wilder, *Town* 76). Wherein, then, lies the difference? I suggest that it is one less of kind than of degree and timing.

In this regard, it is important to note that the forty-odd years between the publication of *Downright Dencey* and that of *Jade*—marked by upheavals including the Great Depression, American involvement in three lengthy wars, and national anxiety about maintaining superpower status in the face of domestic conflict and international menace—witnessed major social change, including shifting beliefs about appropriate gender roles for children and teenagers. Whereas the economic circumstances of the 1930s and the manpower shortage of the early 1940s influenced many women to work outside the home and to engage in traditionally male activities, the period immediately after the Second World War was characterized by heightened gender anxiety. Women were encouraged to return to home and housekeeping, and as Steven Mintz observes,

> Childrearing practices heavily emphasized gender distinctions. In articles like "Raise Your Girl to be a Wife" and "How to Raise Better Husbands," childrearing experts urged parents to respond promptly to signs of "sissiness" in boys and masculine behavior in girls. . . . tomboyish behavior might lead girls to "give up their femininity." . . . In an age when fitting in was the desired goal, parents were happy to have their children be like the others rather than conspicuous.[11] (281)

Nicholas Sammond notes that while the "natural child" of the 1950s emerged in part to "moderat[e] the conformist excesses of postwar American mass culture and society," it was thought that "the way to achieve that noncomformity was to help the child conform to its gender—to provide an environment in which it could harmonize its sensual impulses with its role in a tightly gendered culture" (252).

MacLeod, similarly, argues that from the end of the war through the mid-1960s (when the adolescent "problem novel" emerged), the dominant note in American novels for girls was one of insistence upon traditional gender roles: "postwar adolescent fiction glorified the domesticated woman," while "Books were full of generalizations, half-jocular (but only half), which began with 'men always' and 'women never'" (55, 56).[12]

In this milieu, it is not surprising that fifteen years intervene between the wartime publication of the last Little House book to appear during Wilder's lifetime and the next Newbery tomboy book, *The Witch of Blackbird Pond*. And while feminist activism was increasingly noticeable by the late 1960s (the National Organization for Women, or NOW, was formed in 1966, for example), it shows up only rarely in the children's books of that era; as Elizabeth Segel points out, "Tomboy heroines were scarce in the late sixties and the seventies" (59). Segel suggests that the tomboy's absence may have been a sign of feminist success, in that androgynous girlhood no longer seemed like an "aberration," but if the feminist battle had been won in the pages of American children's literature, the Newbery list provides little evidence of the victory. While the historically grounded Newbery titles of *Jade*'s generation include some works that reflect the civil-rights ferment of the times (such as the 1969 Honor Book *To Be a Slave*, by activist Julius Lester), they focus more on racial inequity than they do on sexism.

Thus, one of the few negative reviews of *Jade*, by Lillian Gerhardt, reveals deep discomfort with the novel's approach to female gender roles, which Gerhardt believes sets an unfortunate example: "The confusion and reluctance that can attend the acceptance of sex roles is rough enough on girls reaching puberty without Jade," who "automatically always does the opposite of everything that is expected of a girl"; *Jade* constitutes "overt pandering to the idea of unattractively aggressive and prolonged tomboy attitudes" (93). The source of this review is suggestive, since Gerhardt, with two other editors of *School Library Journal*, was responsible for compiling that periodical's "Best Books of the Year" list and was to serve in 1978–79 as president of the Association for Library Service to Children, which controls the Newbery Award. Conversely, a particularly glowing notice in a less influential periodical, *Young Readers Review*, notes with pleasure, "Few girls will be able to resist Jade's aggressive feminism. All those ten, eleven, and twelve-year-olds who always are wishing they were boys have a heroine here whose exploits will thrill them" ("Jade by Sally Watson," n. pag.).[13]

More commonly, however, reviewers sidestep the issue of Jade's convictions about gender equality, although many mention her antislavery views. This emphasis suggests that reviewers felt that abolitionism (a question, after all, decided in the United States more than a century earlier, although racism had hardly been laid to rest) was less controversial in a children's-book heroine than feminism. It is striking that a word often used in the favorable reviews of *Jade* and other Watson novels is "romantic," as in "Add a love story to the romance of the high seas, and this is an adventure novel of great appeal" ("Watson, Sally") or "[Jade's] adventures are wildly romantic" (Sutherland; see also Buell, Goodwin, Jackson, and P. M.). While this term speaks to the swashbuckling aspect of Watson's plots, in the context of postwar fiction for girls it also emphasizes the incipient marriages with which they end and thus hints that the works should be read as endorsements of traditionalism. Watson herself comments that she "never liked 'romantic' as a description. I suspect it was perceived as a requisite for teen-agers—and for that matter, what little romance there was, I put in for the same reason" (personal communication, 8 July 2008).

But in many ways *Jade* reads neither like a conventional romance nor like the earlier tomboy novels. For instance, while courage is presented as a desirable virtue in all the works discussed in this chapter, only in *Jade* does the narrative license its female protagonist to use violence. Although Jade is "sickened" and refuses to participate on moral grounds when she first witnesses a pirate attack that does not involve "reform, or justice, or even vengeance" (149–50), when they encounter a Dutch slave ship, "the ferocity of Jade's fighting this time was awesome. The Quartet [Jade, Rory, Domino, and Joshua] . . . launched itself in a wedge across the deck, annihilating all opposition, driven by devils of scarlet rage. They could probably have taken the slaver alone" (183). This readiness on the part of a young person to back up her principles with her sword would have had uneasy resonances for adult readers in 1969. *Jade* appeared early in the year, before the October "Days of Rage" vandalism, the November diktat by Weathermen leader Bill Ayres to "Bring the revolution home, kill your parents," and the wave of Weather Underground bombings in the early 1970s, but youth protests in Paris, Mexico City, and New York, among other major metropolitan areas, had punctuated 1968, and Chicago *Tribune* reviewer Polly Goodwin, for one, found it advisable to begin her favorable notice of *Jade* by distancing Watson's protagonist from "dissident students."[14]

Moreover, Jade's invasion of masculine territory through fencing is reminiscent of what Bonnie Dow identifies as second-wave feminism's "advocacy of martial arts." As Dow notes, the argument that women should learn self-defense skills was "troubling for feminism's public image" just after *Jade*'s publication; media representations of feminism from 1969 and 1970, when the movement first attracted substantial attention from the mainstream press, implied that "martial arts [were] an outlet for women's rage, and men had better beware" ("Fixing Feminism" 72). Although Watson's own interest in judo (mentioned in the author blurb for the first edition of *The Hornet's Nest* [1968] as well as in that for *Jade*) predates this kind of negative coverage, women's participation in karate and judo would become later in 1969 a metonymy for feminism's distance from the American mainstream, a way for unsympathetic journalists to paint the movement as radical. Dow quotes Susan Brownmiller's 1970 comment that male editors were instructing reporters on Women's Lib to "get the bra burning and the karate up front" ("Fixing Feminism" 72). In this context, Jade's resentment of stays (the eighteenth-century's version of girdles, which, along with bras, were "tossed into a 'freedom trash can'" by feminists protesting the Miss America pageant in September 1968 [Dow, "Feminism" 130]) and her love of swordplay would increasingly have had contemporary resonances in the months after the novel's publication, resonances that might well have dismayed the established professional women who dominated the Newbery committee.

The Newbery heroines use their courage in more traditionally feminine ways. In *Calico Bush*, for instance, Marguerite induces a party of potentially marauding Indians to join in a Maypole dance instead of massacring the household; in *Roller Skates* Lucinda stands her ground when frightened by the appearance of the disreputable-looking Rags-an'-Bottles (with whom she quickly makes friends). In *The Witch of Blackbird Pond* Kit helps Hannah elude the witch hunters and swims out to attract the attention of a ship for the getaway, while in *Caddie Woodlawn* Caddie rides secretly to the Indian camp to warn John and his people of an impending preemptive strike by cowardly white men, her intent not to fight on the Indians' side but to stop the violence by removing the opportunity for it: "Some white men are coming to kill you. You and your people must go away. You must not fight. You must go away" (120). And observing in Wilder's *These Happy Golden Years* that her mentally unstable landlady is threatening her husband with a butcher knife, the adolescent Laura Ingalls can show her courage only by rigid self-control—not reacting, not mentioning the episode to her parents, and certainly not intervening. While *Jade* indicates that sometimes the truest courage lies in enduring difficult situations (in displaying, indeed, a Laura-like discipline) and that swordplay is not always an option, that it is ever possible for her distinguishes Jade from her predecessors and may go some distance toward explaining why so many reviewers, liking the novel, felt the need to cast it in the acceptable light of a romance.

Another important distinction is that the Newbery books discussed here are not only historical novels but also domestic novels: stories of family life with a primary focus on what *Caddie Woodlawn* refers to as "just a lot of everyday adventures" (241). Isolated episodes may be dramatic, such as the witch hunt and subsequent trial in *The Witch of Blackbird Pond* or the murder of the exotic "Princess Zayda" in *Roller Skates*, but the preponderance of attention is on the fabric of daily life. This emphasis, with the concomitant implication that family life may be most pleasurable when it is not exciting, is well suited to the exploration of the "long process of socialization into acceptance of feminine values," as Anita Clair Fellman puts it in discussing the Little House books (105).[15] *Jade* shares the other novels' interest in growing up, but Jade's maturation is not accomplished through an embrace of the values of "gentleness and courtesy and love and kindness" recommended by Caddie's father (Brink 216) or the similar "much gentling and more wisdom" prescribed by Lucinda's Uncle Earle (Sawyer, *Year* 266), but rather through self-knowledge and a readiness to take the consequences of her actions. Tellingly, Watson's narrative is not a domestic novel but a female adventure story— and Anne Bonney, who does ultimately embrace traditional feminine values, sewing baby clothes, announcing her desire to be "nothing more than . . . a good wife and mother," and opting out of adventure, excites Jade's "disgusted" comment, "Even Williamsburg would approve of you now. You've got no spunk left" (258).

Jade's slighting reference to Williamsburg, which may function here as a synecdoche for her family of origin, points to the implications of the novel's shift from domestic tale to adventure. For one thing, like many of the "dissident students" of 1969 and unlike her Newbery tomboy predecessors, Jade appears to have left her country behind; instead of finding new ways to be an American, she heads for the African coast to bring the war against slavery to its epicenter. For another, she rejects the grudging "acceptance of feminine values" that Fellman and others see in the socially approved tomboy narrative. Abate notes that conventionally, tomboyism "is not often seen as a lifelong identity," and that "by far the most compelling reason for young women to abandon tomboyish behavior was pressure to get married and become a mother" (xix)—the route that Anne takes in *Jade*. Jade, then, is unusual in managing to have things both ways, entering into marriage (a rite of passage signifying that adulthood has been reached) without relinquishing her rebellion against the values of her parents' generation.

In contrast, while the Newbery tomboy novels frequently show friction between the protagonist and her household, they also suggest that permanent rupture of the domestic relationship is so undesirable as to be impossible. Punished by her mother for her unfeminine behavior, Caddie considers running away from home but instead listens to her father's loving sermon about the responsibilities of womanhood. Field's orphaned Marguerite, whose relationship with her dour employers has warmed over the course of *Calico Bush*, opts to stay with the family rather than taking the opportunity to return to her culture. While Speare's Kit accepts a proposal from a sailor who does not share her uncle's Puritanism, the marriage will involve an oscillation between the Caribbean, site of Kit's upbringing, and her second home in Connecticut, so that it suggests expansion rather than estrangement. Laura Ingalls's affection and respect for her parents never waver; Sawyer's Lucinda spends *The Year of Jubilo* learning to shape a productive and satisfying family life; and Snedeker's Dencey will marry the outcast Jetsam, but only after he has so embraced her family's faith and outlook that even before the proposal his future mother-in-law undertakes to outfit him for his first voyage: "He should have all from her hands as any son would in starting from home" (310). These denouements are very different from that of *Jade*, which stresses how important Jade considers it that her family never learn that she is still alive. While this permanent separation is ostensibly mandated by her desire to spare them embarrassment, she also perceives that "Virginia's only another kind of prison with a longer sentence" (224).

One reason that pirate life is to be preferred to conventional domesticity is that it lacks the authority structures governing the traditional patriarchal family—structures that the Newbery heroines seem readier than Jade to accept. Each young woman feels a strong attachment to an older person, often male: Laura Ingalls to her father, Sawyer's Lucinda to Uncle Earle (and, in *The Year of Jubilo*, to the memory of her father, who dies after the end of *Roller Skates*), Snedeker's Dencey to her father and Aunt Lovesta, Speare's Kit to her deceased grandfather and the

Quaker "witch" of the title, Brink's Caddie to her father, and Field's Marguerite to an elderly neighbor, Hepsa Jordan. Jade's principal attachment of this sort is not to a family member, since her grandparents have been dead for years and are mentioned only in passing, but to Monsieur Maupin. While all these senior figures are represented as free spirits of some sort, willing to condone a degree of unconventional behavior in the protagonists, in the Newbery novels the adults' very progressivism functions to validate the power vested in the family: when an Uncle Earle or a John Woodlawn administers correction, even the most rebellious girl will listen because she sees him as an ally, not an enemy.[16] In contrast, in *Jade* Monsieur Maupin's mentorship works to undermine paternal authority, not only because the fencing lessons horrify Jade's father, but also because the Frenchman cannot be made subservient to the Lennox family structure; when Mr. Lennox confronts him in the guise of "the angry father" about his association with Jade, Monsieur Maupin laughs that "he found it very much uncomfortable because I kept reminding him of when he was a naughty boy and his father and I used to fish him out of the river and smack his bottom" (12).

In place of the authoritarian family of Mr. Lennox's desire (replicated on the law-abiding ships, whose captains' right to levy punishment is absolute), Jade initially finds on the pirate ship an alternative family structure based on sibling bonds rather than on hierarchy. "Anne and Mark and Pierre in particular," Jade observes, "were like brothers and sisters, laughing and thinking up mischief, and protective of one another" (158). This combination is suggestive, in that the three people most interested in surrogate siblinghood are also the foremost gender rebels among the pirates at this point in the novel. Anne, who insists upon women's right to lead (and kill), first achieved notoriety for "burn[ing] down her own father's house" (56), a clear declaration of war against patriarchal authority; Mark is actually Mary Read, a woman raised as male and still passing as such; and Pierre, dress designer and hair stylist to the women on board, is an effeminate man who, Watson notes, "was undoubtedly gay," a detail based upon her reading of the historical sources (personal communication, 8 July 2008).[17]

Clearly these are the pirates to whom the conventional rules governing gender roles would be most inimical. Not coincidentally, they are also the pirates for whom Jade seems to feel the greatest kinship, inasmuch as they are both prominent in the narrative and presented as more attractive than most of the other longtime pirates. While both Anne and Mary are shown asserting authority over male crew members—Mary challenges the murderous Barton to a saber duel and kills him so that his projected duel with the inexperienced Tom will not take place, while Anne forces the cowardly Calico Jack at gunpoint to return to a battle from which he is escaping and subsequently shoots a pirate who challenges her right to act as captain—no one on the *Queen Royal* attempts to exercise quasi-parental power where Jade is concerned, and her freedom from the dominant strictures of family life surely contributes to her love for her shipboard existence. One way in which the *Queen Royal* differs from the environments in which our Newbery protagonists function, in other words, is that it does not house a wise and admirable adult mentor to furnish guidance for Jade. Although Monsieur Maupin is necessary to Jade's release from prison (since the governor of Jamaica, more traditionally minded than Watson's narrator, considers that she needs a male authority figure) and will accompany her to African waters, he does not play a significant role in her maturation after her departure from Williamsburg and never sets foot on the *Queen Royal*. Much more than, say, Dencey or Caddie, Jade is on her own.

Appropriately, then, the dominant image pattern of Watson's novel is the alternation between images of punishment, confinement, and physical malaise on the one hand and freedom on the other. Philip Greven notes that while families in Jade's social class tended not to practice the harsh child-rearing methods that we associate with Puritanism, the offspring of well-to-do slaveholders in early America nevertheless

> shared a crucial experience [with the offspring of evangelicals], though with a fundamental difference: what the evangelicals did to their own children, the genteel Southerners did only to their slaves. . . . Hence it was possible, in the course of maturing, for both evangelicals and many genteel Southerners to share a special concern with the whole issue of enslavement and of having the will and self rendered submissive. (277)

Jade, who insists to her father that "I won't turn into a rabbit, whatever you say!" (6), is "transfixed" by her first sight of Domino, during which she has "the dizzy sensation of meeting herself in someone else's skin" (61). While the narrative rewards this identification by permitting both girls to attain their freedom, the process is by no means without pain. *Jade* is punctuated with depictions of whippings and floggings witnessed and/or experienced by its heroine, as well as hangings that occur offstage; each transition to a new stage in Jade's life is preceded by chastisements that become more severe once she leaves her family.

Imprisonment is another frequent occurrence in Jade's world, though it is not always intended punitively; in addition to Jade's stints in jail and, earlier, in her own room as a consequence of misbehavior, we have the social assumption that dominant beings (white men) are entitled to deprive subordinate beings of their liberty. That the novel's first scene involves Jade's illicit liberation of a captive fox and swiftly moves to a consideration of the wrongs of slavery encourages readers to notice the ways in which women, even upper-class white women, are confined as well: by fashion (Domino hypothesizes that Jade's whalebone and steel stays may represent "an odd form of punishment" [75]), by custom, and most of all by "the body [they] happened to get born into," as Jade complains (192), which so limits the actions permitted to them that they are, in effect, imprisoned in the wrong social role. And while punishment, confinement, and physical weakness (e.g., jail fever or convalescence from flogging) are all temporary states, freedom, here represented primarily by ocean voyages and fencing, likewise carries with it no promise of permanence.

Punishment is by no means absent from the earlier tomboy narratives. Wilder shows Pa beating Laura with a strap (*Woods* 183), for instance, while Snedeker's

Dencey is whipped by her grandfather (a Congregationalist of the Jonathan Edwards school) and confined to her room, and Caddie Woodlawn receives similar treatment from her mother. Speare's Kit is even jailed overnight before her witchcraft hearing. But punishment in *Jade* is fiercer and more prominent than is the case in any of the other novels, leaving scars both physical and emotional. While many factors help shape this difference, from the period in which the novel is set to that in which it was written,[18] perhaps the harshness of the trope in Watson's novel is in some measure an acknowledgment of the greater risk that Jade is taking in not ultimately acquiescing, as the earlier protagonists do, in the values of domesticity. Readers will understand that the stakes are higher here.[19]

Contemporary sexuality theory sees gender and sexuality as fluid, social constructs rather than absolutes. Leaders in this field such as Judith Butler, Judith Halberstam, and Eve Sedgwick argue against gender as a simple or "natural" binary; Butler, for instance, describes dominant genders and sexualities as perennially threatened by, and tied to, their alternatives, while Halberstam and Sedgwick discuss masculinity as detachable from maleness. These ways of framing matters seem congenial to *Jade*, with its pattern of women who don't fit the feminine stereotype pairing up with men who don't fit the masculine one: Mary fights Tom's duel with Barton, while Tom spends this time locked up for his own protection, a mimicry of the traditional female role; Domino, born free, must bring Joshua, socialized into compliance by having been born into slavery, to an understanding that one can fight injustice instead of automatically submitting to it; Anne and Michael invert the pattern prescribed within the cult of domesticity, in which association with a virtuous woman reforms the wild, antidomestic man. That Jade's rebellious spirit matches Rory's emphasizes the equality of their partnership but also reminds readers that "the body you happened to get born into" is a matter of chance: Jade is female, Rory male, but they feel, think, and behave similarly. If conventional society insists upon confining Jade (and Domino, Anne, and Mary) to roles mandated by their bodies, the narrative suggests that these women are justified not only in seeking more congenial, because more flexible, environments but also in waging war against rigidity. And while *Jade* seems in some ways to accept convention, inasmuch as it sorts the fictional as well as the historical major characters into married pairs, before we reach that stage this nod to tradition has been thoroughly undermined by the lengthy critique of socially dominant approaches to gender.

Jade's Newbery-winning predecessors engage in some of these critiques as well—but not to the same extent. While their protagonists are brave, strong, and individualistic, they also learn to adapt to the strictures of the worlds within which they live. Indeed, a reader might reasonably conclude that a common point of these fictions is to demonstrate that a brave, strong, and individualistic girl can and should learn to exist in harmony with the domestic ethos and that both domesticity and the individual will be better thereby. Like Jo March, whose early longing to be a boy and enjoy the increased mobility and activity belonging to that role is transformed in adulthood to running a boys' school and encouraging the pupils to grow into responsible men, the feisty Newbery protagonists will be assets to their society—and good wives and mothers. Since they must learn to accommodate society rather than vice versa, rewarding their creators with Newbery recognition does not look like a radical act, especially during decades when female individualism was not perceived as particularly threatening to the social fabric.

Adding *Jade* to the approved canon, and thus sanctioning a new model of tomboy so at odds with her era that she is prepared to face stringent punishment in order to jettison not only convention but also family, might have been a different matter. *Jade*, I suggest, is a radical novel that appeared at a moment radical in some ways and conservative in others; to be palatable to those working within establishment venues such as public libraries and mainstream review outlets, it had to be presented—not altogether successfully—as a traditional romantic swashbuckler whose progressivism had more to do with race than with gender. By way of contrast, we might contemplate a later Newbery Honor protagonist created by a male author, the title character of Avi's 1990 *The True Confessions of Charlotte Doyle*.[20] Charlotte has some similarities to Jade, in that she too challenges patriarchal authority, dressing in male clothing and becoming the titular captain of a mutinous ship. Media commentary characterizes her as "spunky" and "daring" (Bauer, Fleming). Yet arguably Charlotte is less of a rebel and less of a feminist than Jade; she comes to rebellion reluctantly, her self-appointed task not to elude masculine power altogether but to learn to identify and support the best manifestations of that power, which in this case means leaving captain and father to side with a lower-class and racially mixed male crew. When she abandons her home, it is apparently to accept the permanent authority of multiple substitute fathers. The success of *Charlotte Doyle*, which has moved from Newbery Honor book and classroom favorite to big-budget film project directed by Danny DeVito, might suggest that a generation after *Jade* as with a generation before, the girls' canon was readiest to accommodate a comparatively gender-conservative text—now to be marketed in mainstream outlets as progressive.

NOTES

My thanks to Sally Watson for her gracious responses to my questions and for the pleasure that her books have given me over the years; to Kenneth Kidd for helpful references; to the students in my spring 2008 graduate class on Literature for Children for their insights into *Jade*; and to Anne Morey, Julia Mickenberg, and Lynne Vallone for comments and suggestions on this essay.

   1. Autobiographical remarks by Watson are available on the Image Cascade website at http://www.imagecascade.com/MM011.ASP?pageno=60. In brief, she was born in Seattle in 1924, the daughter of an electronics engineer and a teacher. After serving in the Navy from 1944 to 1946, she attended Reed College, graduating in 1950; four years later, she began her writing career. Between 1954 and 1971, she published twelve novels, most of them

interconnected works tracing the adventures of a single family from Elizabethan England to nineteenth-century Washington State. These novels appeared under the aegis of a major children's publishing firm, Henry Holt, and gained a modest but devoted following among young readers, some of whom remain Watson aficionados; a Yahoo! group of now-adult fans has formed, eBay auctions of first editions have resulted in prices in the upper three figures for discarded library copies, and the early novels have been restored to print by admirers at Image Cascade, a reprint house specializing in girls' books from the 1950s and 1960s. Encouraged by the continued interest, Watson returned to marketing her writing in 2006, self-publishing both revisions of early productions and wholly new novels. The unusual features of this trajectory—the move from mainstream to alternative outlet, the decades-long hiatus followed by a new burst of creativity—provide another context for considering her output.

2. Wilder died in 1957; the last installment of the series published during her lifetime was *These Happy Golden Years* in 1943. *The First Four Years* appeared in 1971.

3. Newbery recognition is a major factor in subsequent classroom adoption. As Kidd notes, "Although the Medal carries no cash prize, it can more than double the sales of a book, as well as increase sales of the author's other books. More important, the Medal keeps titles and authors in circulation for decades" (168). Kidd adds that winning first place tends to be considerably better for sales than being a runner-up (and that potentially controversial titles are more likely to be runners-up than Medalists), but Honor Book status nonetheless confers some degree of canonicity.

4. Watson's Wikipedia entry adds that *Magic at Wychwood* was recommended by *Library Journal* in 1970, while *Linnet* was a Junior Literary Guild selection in 1971 (http://en.wikipedia.org/wiki/Sally_Watson, accessed 25 July 2009).

5. The Children's Services Division was renamed the Association for Library Service to Children (ALSC) in 1976. According to the criteria posted on the ALSC website (http://www.ala.org/ala/mgrps/divs/alsc/awardsgrants/childrensnotable/notablechibooks/index.cfm), "notable should be thought to include books of especially commendable quality, books that exhibit venturesome creativity, and books of fiction, information, poetry and pictures for all age levels (birth through age 14) that reflect and encourage children's interests in exemplary ways." Although the Newbery criteria state that the medal "is not for didactic intent," singling out books that "encourage children's interests in exemplary ways" suggests a dimension of social engineering.

6. Cropped hair is a common marker of the tomboy. The most famous haircut in American literature is surely that undergone by Louisa May Alcott's Jo March, but Abate offers numerous additional examples of short bobs worn by androgynous girls, from Harriet Wilson's *Our Nig* (1859) to the Tatum O'Neal character in *Paper Moon* (1973).

7. Unless a negative one. Watson has expressed displeasure at *Caddie Woodlawn*'s ending multiple times: in a 2007 posting to her Yahoo! fan group, for instance, and in her comments for *Contemporary Authors*, where she notes that "even adventurous girls like Caddie Woodlawn tended to sell out for tame domesticity at the end. (*My* heroines may ultimately marry, but they don't get tame)" ("Sally [Lou] Watson").

8. Watson derives much of her historical information from the 1724 bestseller *A General History of the Robberies and Murders of the Most Notorious Pirates*, by Captain Charles Johnson, whose identity remains uncertain but whose account is accepted by historians as accurate in many particulars. Johnson's text proved lastingly influential upon subsequent pirate narratives by authors such as Sir Walter Scott (*The Pirate* [1821]), Robert

Louis Stevenson (*Treasure Island* [serialized 1881–82]), J. M. Barrie (*Peter Pan* [1904]), and Rafael Sabatini (e.g., *Captain Blood* [1922]). Notably, however, while Johnson profiles both Anne Bonny [sic] and Mary Read, most nineteenth- and twentieth-century contributors to the pirate tradition present it as exclusively masculine.

9. Abate pushes back the origins of the literary tomboy to as early as the 1820s, with *The Last of the Mohicans* (1826) and *Hope Leslie* (1827). Abate's *Tomboys* moves away from tomboy fiction for girls to adult fictions about tomboys such as Carson McCullers's *The Member of the Wedding* (1946) and Ann Bannon's lesbian pulp "Beebo Brinker" series (1957–62) before concluding in Hollywood.

10. Because her low social standing does not permit her the leisure to run wild and her duties are centered on the home, Marguerite is the least tomboyish of the protagonists discussed in this chapter. Still, in personality she is clearly related to the others, as *Calico Bush* emphasizes her strength of character, ingenuity, capacity for endurance, independence, and courage, all virtues typical of the group.

11. Mintz is writing here about adult desires vis-à-vis the young, not about what children themselves wanted. He adds, "In fact many of the role models that middle-class girls embraced during the decade [of the 1950s] were assertive and self-confident, and one can see the roots of mid-1960s feminism planted in the increasingly autonomous and self-assured girl culture of the 1950s" (283).

12. In *The Feminine Mystique* (1963), Betty Friedan diagnoses in popular reading for adult women the same kind of movement away from anything smacking of female assertiveness. In 1939, Friedan records, large-circulation women's magazines printed fiction about career women of "spirit and character," in whom "individuality was something to be admired" (38). By 1960, a typical women's magazine was representing woman as "young and frivolous, almost childlike, fluffy and feminine, passive, gaily content in a world of bedroom and kitchen, sex, babies, and home" (36).

13. In a 2003 article posted on Salon.com, Adrienne Crew offers reminiscences about her childhood reading, as a "black geek" growing up in Los Angeles, that suggest that Watson's young fans did indeed appreciate the nonstandard vision of femininity that her novels offered. While Crew did not encounter Jade (now "a new Watson favorite" for her) in her youth, she notes, "When I was a kid, I repeatedly checked out Watson's 'Mistress Malapert,' a tale about an aristocratic Englishwoman who masquerades as a boy in order to join William Shakespeare's theatrical troupe. . . . I figured that if I was such a misfit, I wanted to be a spectacular misfit like Watson's heroines."

14. The "dissident students," according to Goodwin, are fond of the concept of "amnesty"; in contrast, "If [Jade] broke the rules for a proper young lady in Colonial Williamsburg, she expected to pay for it—with a parental whipping, if necessary." Gerhardt's negative review likewise addresses the issue of law-abiding behavior, finding particularly distasteful the "weird unacceptable apologia for the pirate ethic." Intergenerational violence, whether viewed in the light of student extremism or in that of excessive force on the part of the authorities, made headlines worldwide in the late 1960s.

15. Fellman adds that the reader is likely to feel "ambivalence" about this socialization process (106)—as many readers of Alcott's March family series have responded to Jo's development and as the young Watson, for one, responded to Caddie Woodlawn's.

16. *The Witch of Blackbird Pond* provides a variation on the usual pattern, as Kit's grandfather becomes less emotionally important to her than the uncle into whose house she moves. Initially Uncle Matthew appears rigid, censorious, and

highly traditional, but by the end of the narrative he emerges as a sympathetic character, since he testifies to her innocence and virtue before the witch hunters even though she has disobeyed him. It is chiefly through Matthew, a more overt patriarch than his counterparts in the other texts, that this novel conducts its defense of patriarchal values.

17. Pierre's sexuality, which excites no overt comment within the narrative, would be invisible to most young readers even today, and adult reviewers may well also have failed to notice it—unless, perhaps, they read *Jade* after the Stonewall riots of June 1969, which are now seen as a pivotal episode in the gay rights movement and brought a new visibility to mid-twentieth-century homosexuality.

18. For instance, as contemporaneous media critics were well aware, the late 1960s witnessed an outpouring of films, to name one medium, that were much more violent than had hitherto been deemed permissible in American popular culture. Literature for young readers was not immune to this trend; although S. E. Hinton's *The Outsiders* (1967), which features gang warfare and both threatened and actual fatalities, represents a different sort of teen novel than *Jade*, the two works address a similar age group.

19. As reviewer Patience M. Canham observed in 1969, "Some may find the values it presents too rough, the justice too ready," although Canham, noting the historical authenticity at work here, was not of that number. I have encountered (in the 1990s) at least one adult who was shocked at the flogging episodes, which did not fit her notions of what might suitably be incorporated into a book for young readers. By contrast, the punishment scenes in the earlier tomboy novels come across as largely symbolic—a hint that the transgressions at issue in those narratives are minor as well and that these protagonists are not really at odds with their societies, for all that the narratives stress their deviation from the cultural norms.

20. Another, more recent male-authored work with some similarities to *Jade* is L. A. Meyer's *Bloody Jack: Being an Account of the Curious Adventures of Mary "Jacky" Faber, Ship's Boy* (2002), first installment in what has become a lengthy series about a cross-dressing and adventurous heroine. More picaresque than *Charlotte Doyle*, the Jacky Faber series has eluded Newbery notice, although the back cover of the paperback edition of *Bloody Jack* notes that the novel is "A Book Sense 76 Pick[,] A *Booklist* Editors' Choice[,] A *Bulletin* Blue Ribbon Book[,] A Junior Literary Guild Selection[, and] A New York Public Library Book for the Teen Age." This list may be said to illustrate what James F. English has termed "the logic of proliferation," in which "Prizes, an instrument of cultural hierarchy, would themselves come increasingly to describe a hierarchical array, a finely indexed system of greater and lesser symbolic rewards, the negotiation of which constitutes a kind of . . . subsidiary cultural marketplace" (50, 54). With enough of the "lesser symbolic rewards," a text may advance toward the kind of widespread acceptance that marks canonicity, and that also includes cultural signifiers such as being taught in children's literature classes—another venue in which *Jade*, which was out of print for approximately thirty years before its 2003 Image Cascade reissue, has thus far had little success. But as a reader review posted on amazon.com by "Cate" on 2 April 2008 puts it, Watson's novels are "still interesting and fun and full of history that the author has managed to make interesting without you realizing you're actually learning history, and the young women portrayed in their pages are still role models for the girls of today." This description suggests that twenty-first century teachers might well wish to contemplate adding *Jade* to their classroom reading lists.

WORKS CITED

Abate, Michelle Ann. *Tomboys: A Literary and Cultural History*. Philadelphia: Temple UP, 2008.

Bauer, Mary Blandin. "Choosing the Newbery Winner." *Washington Post*, 12 May 1991, X16. Available online through Lexis/Nexis. Accessed 7 December 2008.

Brink, Carol Ryrie. *Caddie Woodlawn*. 1935. New York: Simon & Schuster, 1997.

Buell, Ellen Lewis. "Young Reader's Shelf: A Selection from Recent Titles." *New York Times*, 14 April 1963, 382. Available online through ProQuest Historical Newspapers. Accessed 9 June 2008.

Canham, Patience M. "Old Plots for Young Girls." *Christian Science Monitor*, 1 May 1969, B6.

Crew, Adrienne. "Geek Reads." *Salon.com* (2003). http://www.salon.com/ books/2003/06/27/black_geeks/. Accessed 25 July 2009.

Dow, Bonnie J. "Feminism, Miss America, and Media Mythology." *Rhetoric and Public Affairs* 6, no. 1 (2003): 127–60.

———. "Fixing Feminism: Women's Liberation and the Rhetoric of Television Documentary." *Quarterly Journal of Speech* 90, no. 1 (February 2004): 53–80.

English, James F. *The Economy of Prestige: Prizes, Awards, and the Circulation of Cultural Value*. Cambridge, MA: Harvard UP, 2005.

Fellman, Anita Clair. "'Don't Expect to Depend on Anybody Else': The Frontier as Portrayed in the Little House Books." *Children's Literature* 24 (1996): 101–16.

Fleming, Michael. "'True' Tale on Deck for DeVito." *Variety*, 16 July 2008, 1. Available online through Lexis/Nexis. Accessed 7 December 2008.

Friedan, Betty. *The Feminine Mystique*. 1963. New York: Dell, 1984.

Gerhardt, Lillian N. "Watson, Sally. *Jade*." *Library Journal* 94 (15 February 1969): 889.

Goodwin, Polly. "*Jade*. By Sally Watson." *Chicago Tribune*, 6 July 1969, K10. Available online through ProQuest Historical Newspapers. Accessed 9 June 2008.

Greven, Philip. *The Protestant Temperament: Patterns of Child-Rearing, Religious Experience, and the Self in Early America*. Chicago: U of Chicago P, 1977.

Jackson, Charlotte. "Child's Book Shelf: Ancient Game with a Happy Ending." *Los Angeles Times*, 24 February 1963, B15. Available online through ProQuest Historical Newspapers. Accessed 9 June 2008.

"Jade by Sally Watson." *Young Readers Review* (1969): n. pag.

Kidd, Kenneth. "Prizing Children's Literature: The Case of Newbery Gold." *Children's Literature* 35 (2007): 166–90.

MacLeod, Anne Scott. *American Childhood: Essays on Children's Literature of the Nineteenth and Twentieth Centuries*. Athens: U of Georgia P, 1994.

Mills, Claudia. "From Obedience to Autonomy: Moral Growth in the Little House Books." *Children's Literature* 24 (1996): 127–40.

Mintz, Steven. *Huck's Raft: A History of American Childhood*. Cambridge, MA: Harvard UP, 2004.

P. M. "Blowing the Dust off History." *Christian Science Monitor*, 2 May 1968, B10. Available online through ProQuest Historical Newspapers. Accessed 9 June 2008.

"Sally (Lou) Watson." *Contemporary Authors Online*. Entry updated 15 June 2001. Gale Literary Databases, 2002. Online at http://galenet.galegroup.com. Accessed 25 July 2008.

Sammond, Nicholas. *Babes in Tomorrowland: Walt Disney and the Making of the American Child, 1930–1960*. Durham, NC: Duke UP, 2005.

Sawyer, Ruth. *Roller Skates*. 1936. New York: Dell, 1980.

Segel, Elizabeth. "Tomboy Taming and Gender Role Socialization: The Evidence of Children's Books." In *Gender Roles through the Life Span: A Multidisciplinary Perspective*, edited by Michael R. Stevenson, 47–61. Muncie, IN: Ball State UP, 1994.

Snedeker, Caroline Dale. *Downright Dencey*. Garden City, NY: Doubleday, 1927.

Sutherland, Zena. Review of *Jade*. By Sally Watson. *Saturday Review* 52 (22 February 1969): 47.

Watson, Sally. *Jade*. New York: Holt, Rinehart & Winston, 1969.

———. Personal communications with Claudia Nelson, 8–9 July 2008. By email.

"Watson, Sally. *Jade*." *Center for Children's Books Bulletin* 22 (April 1969): 135.

Wilder, Laura Ingalls. *Little House in the Big Woods*. 1932. New York: Harper, 1994.

———. *Little Town on the Prairie*. 1941. New York: Harper, 1971.

———. *These Happy Golden Years*. 1943. Rev. ed. 1953. New York: Harper, 1971.

FURTHER READING

Butler, Judith. *Gender Trouble: Feminism and the Subversion of Identity*. New York: Routledge, 1990.

Epstein, Julia, and Kristina Straub, eds. *Body Guards: The Cultural Politics of Gender Ambiguity*. New York: Routledge, 1991.

Halberstam, Judith. "Oh Bondage Up Yours! Female Masculinity and the Tomboy." In *Sissies and Tomboys: Gender Nonconformity and Homosexual Childhood*, edited by Matthew Rottnek, 153–79. New York: New York UP, 1999.

Levstik, Linda S. "'I am no lady!' The Tomboy in Children's Fiction." *Children's Literature in Education* 14, no. 1 (March 1983): 14–20.

CHAPTER 25

HAPPILY EVER AFTER: *FREE TO BE . . . YOU AND ME,* SECOND-WAVE FEMINISM, AND 1970S AMERICAN CHILDREN'S CULTURE

LESLIE PARIS

MARLO Thomas (born Margaret Julia Thomas, 1937–), an American actress and writer, has worked in television, film, and stage productions from the late 1950s onward. Best-known as the star of That Girl, *an ABC television comedy (1966–71), she has also collaborated on several album projects, books, and television specials.* Free to Be . . . You and Me *was created with coeditors Letty Cottin Pogrebin, Mary Rodgers, and Carole Hart.*

Every boy in this land grows to be his own man.
In this land, every girl grows to be her own woman.
Take my hand. Come with me, where the children are free.
Come with me. Take my hand, and we'll run . . .
To a land where the river runs free—
(To a land) through the green country—
(To a land) to a shining sea—
(To a land) where the horses run free—
(To a land) where the children are free.
And you and me are free to be you and me.
(Hart and Lawrence 17)

On a winter day in the mid-1970s, a group of fifth-grade girls in Torrance, California, a city on the outskirts of Los Angeles, spent their "free period" at school writing to actress and feminist Marlo Thomas. The girls were fans of an album, *Free to Be . . . You and Me* (hereafter *Free to Be*), which Thomas had produced as an alternative to traditional children's stories and songs. Released in November 1972 by Bell Records, *Free to Be* was designed to emancipate girls and boys from harmful gender stereotypes. Wrote Leslie F., "I want to tell you what a great record you put out, 'Free to be, You and me.' It really goes deep in to things like womans lib, and its okay, for a boy to play with a doll." Her classmate Karen M. concurred: "I'm only in the fifth grade but I feel I can understand these songs. They are so meaningful and sensitive." Christina F. related that "our class plays it everday and they all enjoy it! The songs in it are farout because they all tell a little story by themselves" (Leslie F., Karen M., Christina F., original spelling preserved).

The songs, stories, and sketches that constituted *Free to Be* reflected the collaboration of a diverse, all-star cast. Thomas recruited as collaborators in development and editing widely published feminist authors and *Ms.* magazine founding editors Gloria Steinem and Letty Cottin Pogrebin; Mary Rodgers, a successful Broadway composer and author of the 1972 youth novel *Freaky Friday*; and Carole Hart, one of the original writers for the children's public television show *Sesame Street* (1969–). The larger group contributing to *Free to Be* included lyricist Sheldon Harnick, best-known for the Broadway hit *Fiddler on the Roof*; composer Bruce Hart, who had written the theme song for *Sesame Street*; singers including Diana Ross and the folk group The Seekers; and a range of other entertainers, including talk-show host Dick Cavett and actor Alan Alda, both of whom had speaking parts. Each of the album's eighteen tracks encouraged young children to feel free to express their feelings, to seek success on their own terms, and especially to move beyond sexist assumptions about girls' and boys' potential.

The album met with an enthusiastic national reception. Indeed, the *Free to Be* enterprise was one of the most financially and culturally successful feminist projects of the 1970s. Nominated for a Grammy the year it was released, the album sold a very respectable 150,000 copies by March 1974, when Thomas simultaneously released a book version of *Free to Be*, which included additional poems and stories, and a one-hour television prime-time special on ABC (Grant 149). The book was for several weeks a *New York Times* bestseller and won an American Library Association Award. The television special drew a large audience (a 18.6 rating/27 share) and won both an Emmy award for children's prime-time entertainment and a Peabody Award for excellence in broadcasting. These three convergent media assured widespread dissemination of the *Free to Be* message.

In the early 1970s, the success of the *Free to Be* series reflected both the aspirations of a liberal cohort of adults who wished to socialize children less traditionally than their own parents had socialized them and children's own delight in the songs, stories, and sketches. *Free to Be*, aimed primarily at elementary-school-aged children, was playful and entertaining. Some sections of the project were explicitly moralizing; Sheldon Harnick's "Housework," for instance, was an invective against television advertisements that suggest women find enormous joy in cleaning their homes. But overall, the tone of the album, book, and television special was variously inspiring, funny, and joyful, an approach that appealed to parents, teachers, and children alike.

At the same time, *Free To Be* worked to teach children ways of reading more traditional children's texts ironically, against the grain. By playing with the conventional tropes of children's culture, such as fairy tales in which brave princes rescue passive maidens, *Free to Be* helped produce a cohort of media-savvy children whom it encouraged to critique and rework that culture. Emphasizing the political possibilities of children's culture, *Free to Be* was at once entertaining and a call to action. And while *Free to Be* did not in and of itself radically transform children's culture, its vision of a land "where the river runs free" was compelling to many children and adults. An important document of liberal feminism, *Free To Be* vividly illustrates the widening parameters of mainstream American children's gender socialization.

This essay begins by setting the *Free to Be* series into the broader context of second-wave feminist activism. *Free to Be* is very much a document of liberal feminism, which was by the early 1970s the most mainstream and visible expression of the larger feminist movement. Liberal feminists advocated for equal opportunity and gender equity. They acknowledged physical differences between the sexes but perceived most gender differences to be grounded in cultural and environmental factors, including the socialization of children. As liberal feminists saw the matter, children's "sex roles" were socially constructed and mutable to important degrees. A call to action, *Free to Be* reflected liberal feminists' enthusiasm for new and more creative ways of socializing children and their efforts to reach young girls and boys at a critical state in their acculturation.

The central sections of this essay explore three of the specific texts featured in *Free to Be*. The range of materials included in the album, book, and television special is considerable and somewhat daunting to summarize. This range includes short stories, poems, songs, and spoken dialogue, as well as photographs, illustrations by adults and children, documentary footage, and animated cartoons. Thematically, *Free to Be* also has a wide scope, from ruminations on gender difference to stories about friendships and sibling relations. I have singled out several stories and songs for particular attention: "Ladies First," the story of a girl who insists on traditional notions of femininity; "Atalanta," a rewriting of a traditional Greek tale in which male suitors vie to marry a princess; and "William's Doll," a song about a boy who challenges traditional masculine stereotypes. These three texts showcase different thematic aspects of the *Free to Be* project. Because all three appeared on the album, book, and television special, they are among the best known. I use these texts to consider how feminists worked to reconfigure children's culture in the 1970s: redefining the meaning of a "bad" girl in feminist terms, offering up new feminist heroines and heroes, and most controversially, positing new options for boys in an era of gender transformation.

Last, I consider the politics of *Free to Be* from the perspective of the present day. In 2008, the *Free to Be* book was reissued in a thirty-fifth-anniversary edition (Thomas). *Free to Be* very much reflects the moment of its inception, and feminist debates about gender relations and sex roles have shifted in important ways since the 1970s. Yet the continued popularity of the *Free to Be* message suggests that the series' emphasis on personal emancipation remains compelling for many contemporary children and parents.

While my own discussion of *Free to Be* focuses on the series' feminist politics, the text is open to other kinds of readings. Inasmuch as *Free to Be* was designed to be inclusive of a range of contributing artists and to tell stories about a diverse array of children, it speaks eloquently to the impact of the civil rights movement and antipoverty activism in mainstream children's culture. One could also read *Free to Be* as emblematic of the new children's rights activism, exemplified by images of bold youth who take risks, defy patriarchal authority, and claim their freedom. The series is of interest both visually and aurally; the book's cover art, for instance, signals its do-it-yourself mandate with a title made of hand-stitched felt letters. One could further situate *Free to Be* in the context of 1970s self-help literature and the era's focus on human development.

Free to Be also offers a valuable example of the reach of children's consumer culture. The impact of *Free to Be* in mainstream American children's lives was significantly greater than the number of albums or books sold might suggest. A single copy of the album often reached twenty or thirty children in a classroom where a sympathetic teacher played it, and individual children commonly memorized the songs and taught them to their friends (A.B.). A number of the songs and skits also became "talent night" standards at American summer camps and youth groups, sometimes far outside feminist circles.

Given its influence, it is striking that *Free to Be* has been the subject of so little critical scholarship ("Still Free to Be," Braun, Martin, Schecter, Tucker). This paucity suggests the importance of bringing histories of the American 1970s, second-wave feminism, and children's literature and culture into closer conversation. Nineteen-seventies historiography has until recently tended to emphasize stories of decline and disillusionment among both mainstream Americans and radical activists. As a newer generation of scholarship suggests, the standard declension narrative, which emphasizes how various rights movements of the 1960s were beset by apathy or factionalism in the 1970s, may be overstated (Carroll, Braunstein and Doyle, Gosse and Moser, Bailey and Farber, Jenkins, Binkley). A number of recent commentators, for example, argue that in the 1970s countercultural ideas profoundly influenced the middle-class quest for more sincere and authentic "lifestyles" (Binkley 6, Braunstein and Doyle 12). The popularity of the *Free to Be* project similarly highlights the continued relevance of rights activism and countercultural liberation ideals in 1970s American culture (and beyond).

The relative dearth of writings on *Free to Be* also reflects the fact that children have generally remained on the periphery in the scholarship on second-wave feminism: they appear as objects of some adult activism around day care and divorce, but rarely as central actors or even central motivating factors for feminist activism. The story of *Free to Be* suggests the importance of children's socialization to adult second-wave feminists, many of whom were mothers eager to raise their children in new ways. This project was increasingly visible both in feminist and mainstream media: the new *Ms.* magazine (1972 onward) regularly published "Stories for Free Children"; more traditional and established women's magazines such as *Ladies' Home Journal* explored the impact of feminism on child-rearing; and popular books such as Dr. Benjamin Spock's *Baby and Child Care* were revised to address feminist parenting goals.

Scholars of 1970s children's literary history, meanwhile, have tended to emphasize gritty "young adult" fiction (although this title is somewhat misleading, as such books are generally read by young adolescents). Anne Scott MacLeod argues that the period from the beginning of the twentieth century through the mid-1960s represented an era of consensus in the children's book industry; for decades, children's literature represented a small and relatively uncontroversial publishing niche that rarely dealt explicitly with questions of racial difference, sexuality, or family dysfunction. Thereafter, MacLeod suggests, in the wake of the civil rights movement, feminist activism, the failure of the American presence in Vietnam, rising economic insecurities, and a culture that emphasized individual fulfillment to a greater degree, numerous "young adult" books challenged the boundaries of acceptable topics in children's books (MacLeod 180–82). Many of the more successful new books aimed at preadolescents and adolescents explored themes such as drug use and violence (Beatrice Sparks's 1971 *Go Ask Alice* and M. E. Kerr's 1972 *Dinky Hocker Shoots Smack*), peer alienation (Robert Cormier's 1974 *The Chocolate War*), and sexual initiation (Judy Blume's 1975 *Forever*), as well as children living outside of traditional nuclear arrangements (Norma Klein's 1974 *Mom, the Wolf Man and Me*). *Free to Be* makes visible a different side of 1970s children's popular culture. Aimed primarily at younger children, it was playful, even utopian. *Free to Be* did not always offer traditional "happy endings," but the series promised a different kind of happiness: personal fulfillment through self-affirmation.

"A SOCIAL POISON": FEMINISTS AND CHILDREN'S BOOKS

The inspiration for *Free to Be . . . You and Me* first came to Marlo Thomas while shopping for a good book of bedtime stories to give to her young niece, Dionne. In the early 1970s, Thomas was a nationally known actress, the star of *That Girl*, an ABC comedy. Her character, a modern aspiring actress in New York City, was groundbreaking for prime-time television, if somewhat daffy: a career woman happily living alone, with a steady boyfriend, unmarried although eventually engaged. During the show's run, Thomas became active in feminist circles. She met journalist Gloria Steinem after the publication of Steinem's first-person exposé of working conditions at Playboy Clubs, and the two women formed a close friendship (Stern 308–10). By the early 1970s, at Steinem's behest, Thomas was regularly speaking to groups of women on feminist issues. Thus, when she shopped for her niece, she had in mind books that would not repeat old-fashioned gender tropes. As she later recalled, "I was shocked to find that all the children's books I found reinforced old gender stereotypes of what girls and boys were supposed to be or ought to be. None of them talked about all the possibilities of what girls and boys could be" (Free to Be Foundation).

From the mid-1960s onward, children's books were the subject of new political scrutiny. In a changing cultural climate, civil rights and feminist activists contended that children's books did not represent the full range of the American experience. Civil rights activists challenged the relative number and quality of images of racial minorities in children's literature.[1] Feminist activists raised similar concerns about the underlying sexism of many children's books, which, they claimed, socialized girls and boys in traditional and even repressive ways. A number of mainstream women's organizations, consciousness-raising groups, and feminist scholars set out to research the ways in which children's books represented girls and boys. As these studies generally concluded, standard "sex roles" in mainstream children's literature reinforced traditional gendered stereotypes and limited young people's aspirations.

Feminists first made their presence known on the national children's publishing scene in mid-October 1970, when two New York–area feminist groups presented a talk and slideshow to book editors at the annual meeting of the Writers' Guild and the Children's Book Council. The Feminists on Children's Media, a group founded in mid-1970 by a consortium of New York City–area mothers, teachers, and book editors, presented one study, "Sexism in Children's Books." In 1971, they would publish a bibliography of nonsexist readings, *Little Miss Muffet Fights Back*. The members of a second group, Women on Words and Images, an offshoot of the New Jersey Council of the liberal feminist advocacy group National Organization for Women (NOW), had spent a year analyzing 144 school textbooks for evidence of sex discrimination. In 1972, they would publish their research as *Dick and Jane as Victims*.

Reading visibility as an important measure of gendered power, both groups had begun by tallying the numbers of boys and girls appearing in children's books. The results were striking. Feminists on Children's Media focused on recipients of an important prize in children's publishing, the Newbery Award. Books with the Newbery imprimatur tended to sell well and to be purchased by schools and public libraries. Among forty-nine Newbery winners, the group reported, stories about boys outnumbered those about girls by a ratio of about three to one. The American Library Association's *Notable Books of 1969*, the group noted, listed twice as many stories about boys as those concerning girls (Feminists on Children's Media 235). Women on Words and Images reported similarly: in the 144 schoolbooks they analyzed, 881 stories focused mainly on boys while only 344 focused mainly on girls (Miles "Harmful Lessons" 168). Other more scholarly studies completed during the 1970s came to the same conclusion: girls were far less visible in children's stories than were boys.[2]

More to the point, feminist activists contended, the actual content of children's books was often insulting to girls and women. Boys and girls, men and women were portrayed and described quite differently in these stories. Visual images showed boys on adventures or climbing trees, while girls were often homebound, watching admiringly from the porch as the boys played and explored. In written texts, girls also generally demonstrated less independence. In one notorious and oft-cited book, Whitney Darrow Jr.'s *I'm Glad I'm a Boy! I'm Glad I'm a Girl!* (1970), children were informed that "Boys invent things. Girls use what boys invent" (Darrow no page number). Less overtly sexist but more typical, Women on Words and Images reported, were stories in which girls appeared to require male direction in order to complete basic tasks. The group cited a story published in a first-grade school reader, in which a girl named Sue is allowed to choose a duck as a present but remains indecisive. "Oh, my!" she says. "Ducks and ducks and ducks. What will I do?" Her friend Jimmy intervenes, choosing a duck for Sue that turns out to be just the one she wants (Miles "Harmful Lessons" 168).

Feminists further argued that while children's books represented men pursuing a wide range of career options, they tended to depict women in exclusively domestic terms. This was the case even though increasing numbers of women were entering the paid workforce; by 1970 almost 40 percent of American women working outside the home were mothers of children under the age of eighteen. As feminists contended, the dearth of salaried women in children's books (outside of a few stereotyped fields, such as teaching and dancing) made it difficult for girls to imagine futures for themselves outside of marriage and motherhood. Citing studies indicating that children established strong gender identities before they went to kindergarten, feminists argued for the importance of better "sex role" models for the youngest children.

Feminists on Children's Media noted a particular source of feminist frustration, what they termed the "Cop-Out" genre. In too many books, the group contended, girls who were initially introduced as strong and spunky heroines ultimately gave up their "tomboy" ways as a sign of a more mature adolescence. This narrative turn had occurred in earlier popular novels such as Louisa May Alcott's 1868 *Little Women* and Carol Ryrie Brink's 1935 *Caddie Woodlawn*. As Feminists on Children's Media reported, this scenario persisted in contemporary children's fiction. In Constance Green's *A Girl Called Al* (1969), for instance, Al, a girl with a "tomboy" identity, suddenly gives up her pigtails and an interest in carpentry in favor of a more feminine style (and ensuing popularity). These last-minute transformations, Feminists on Children's Media contended, served to reinforce traditional sex-role dictates while stunting the heroines' character development. As the group concluded,

"Books that outline a traditional background role for women, praising their domestic accomplishments, their timidity of soul, their gentle appearance and manners, and—at the same time—fail to portray initiative, enterprise, physical prowess, and genuine intellect deliver a powerful message to children of both sexes. Such books are a social poison" (236).

To some degree, publishers did respond to feminist concerns. Over the course of the 1970s, working mothers and active girls appeared more often in mainstream children's books and school readers. But the pace of change would remain slow. Older and more traditional books often lingered on library and classroom shelves for many years, remaining part of the officially sanctioned curriculum; not only was the publication of a new edition of a school reader a years-long process, but in uncertain economic times local school boards were often reluctant to pay for new editions or for supplementary nonsexist books (Scofield 214, 216).

To fill the gap, a few feminist groups established collective presses to publish the kinds of children's stories they wanted to see in print. The Feminist Press, founded in 1970 by two university professors, published a number of children's books in the 1970s, including the Barbara Danish picture book *The Dragon and the Doctor*, which featured a female doctor and male nurse; an ABC coloring book; and Inez Maury's bilingual *My Mother the Mail Carrier/Mi Mami la Cartera* (Wigutof 57–58, Scofield 216). A sister collective press, Lollipop Power, had its origins in a consciousness-raising group founded by Chapel Hill, North Carolina–area feminists in the late 1960s (Castro and Loverde-Bagwell 238). The books published by Lollipop Power, which were aimed at young audiences from two to eight years of age, highlighted racial and class diversity as well as expanded opportunities for girls. In Lynn Phillips's *Exactly Like Me* (1972), a young girl discovers that she can be a girl without wearing frilly dresses; in Carol De Poix's *Jo, Flo, and Yolanda* (1973), a set of Latina triplets considers their varied career ambitions. By 1975, Lollipop Power had sold over twenty-five thousand copies of ten books, while working from (and storing books in) members' own homes (Slifkin 18).

Free To Be, which emerged out of this "do-it-yourself" mandate, was also part of a larger political project. Thomas planned from the outset to use the album's proceeds (and later those of the book and television special) to support feminist causes through a new feminist philanthropic foundation, the fledgling Ms. Foundation for Women. Founded in 1972, the foundation was originally expected to draw 10 percent of the profits from *Ms.* magazine, founded the same year, and to disperse grants to grassroots feminist groups across the country. But the magazine was never profitable (Stern 307). *Free to Be*, however, was a commercial success. In 1977, when the foundation gave $180,000 in grants to various women's groups and feminist causes nationwide, royalties from *Free to Be* accounted for over $120,000 of the Ms. Foundation's budget (Quindlen A16).

As compared to other feminist media efforts on behalf of children, *Free to Be* was unique in achieving a high degree of mainstream popularity. At the intersection of elite feminist circles and the entertainment industry, Marlo Thomas was well placed to make a significant impact. She also had a knack for publicity and an attractive public presence based on the wide appeal of her character on *That Girl*. Deploying these tools to full political advantage, she reached a large and broad audience drawn to her and to the diverse performers with whom she collaborated, as well as to the *Free to Be* message of equal opportunity for girls and boys.

Ladies First: The Death of Traditional Femininity?

Did you hear the one about the little girl who was a "tender sweet young thing?" Well, that's the way she thought of herself. And this tender sweet young thing spent a great deal of time just looking in the mirror, saying "I am a *real* little lady, anybody could tell that: I wear lovely starched cotton dresses with matching ribbons in my lovely curly locks; I wear clean white socks and shiny black patent leather shoes; and I always put just a dab of perfume behind each ear" (Silverstein and Rodgers 39–40).

So begins "Ladies First," Mary Rodgers's elaboration of a Shel Silverstein poem about a girl who insists on the prerogatives of femininity. In the Silverstein version, "Pamela Purse yells 'Ladies First,'" demanding special rights, until she ends up as lunch for hungry cannibals. Rewritten for *Free to Be*, most likely to eliminate the racial connotations of what Silverstein had termed a "wild savage band," the now-nameless girl loses her life to a group of hungry tigers instead. In both versions, the girl insists on the dictum "Ladies First" at all moments in order to attain special privileges. When the group with which she is exploring the jungle is captured by tigers, she sets herself up to be the first captive eaten.

This *Free to Be* story, narrated on the album and the television special by Thomas herself, playfully considers the advantages and costs of traditional femininity. The girl (drawn in the book and the television special in cartoon form, dressed in pink, with blonde fluffy hair) derives enormous pleasure from her own beauty. In the book and the television special, we first see the girl staring lovingly at herself in a mirror, preparing herself for the outside world. The sight of her hair, her soft skin, her starched dress, and her shiny black shoes worn with sparkling white socks all provide her with confidence and power. At school, the other students seem baffled by her, but they acquiesce nonetheless to her selfish demands for special treatment based on her status as a "lady," whether she is stepping to the front of the lunch line or eating more than her fair share of mangoes on a class trip.

Having established the perks available to a girl who insists on special privileges, *Free to Be* then offers her up as a ritual sacrifice. At first the girl is merely an object of curiosity to the tigers, but her vanity compels her to flaunt her softness and sweetness at just the wrong moment. When she insists on "Ladies first," she is first to be eaten, "and mighty tasty too," as Thomas concludes. Here, the girl's "special privileges" are revealed to be not only ridiculous but also dangerous. So greedy and narcissistically engaged with her own femininity that she is unable to see the world as it is, this girl is both deserving of punishment and too "soft" to survive.

"Ladies First" asks children to contemplate questions central to second-wave feminism. What are the attractions and costs of traditional gender roles? From what internal sense of self should girls gain a healthy sense of power and entitlement? What is the role of beauty in girls' and women's culture? Epitomizing *Free to Be*'s mixture of didactic humor, playfulness, and serious intent, "Ladies First" answers these questions primarily through an inversion of traditional literary conventions. In a challenge to stories in which girls' physical beauty functions as a sign of their innate charm (and, conversely, in which "ugly stepsisters" are repugnant both in looks and in action), here a conventionally attractive exterior hides an unpleasant personality, stunted by narrow ambitions.

In *Free to Be*, the "ladylike" girl represents an object lesson for "free" girls. In 1974, while promoting the new book, Thomas told the teenage readers of *Seventeen* magazine about her own misguided adolescent efforts to behave like a "lady": "all through my teens, I tried to conform—to be a good listener, to sit with my hands folded, my legs crossed at the ankle, not to compete with boys. In short, to be a lovely decoration. Thank heavens, I was a terrific failure at all of this because the real me—the joker and chatterbox—kept popping out" (qtd. in Grant 149). As "Ladies First" similarly concludes, a girl whose confidence depends upon performing traditional femininity will lose sight of the real perils and opportunities of the world around her.

This "bad" female subject is somewhat unusual for the *Free to Be* series, which tends to celebrate inspirational images of bold and adventurous girls rather than to condemn conventional ones. More typical of *Free to Be* is a heroine who overcomes adversity through bold action. This heroine might well be a beautiful princess—like the princess Atalanta—who prioritizes her own needs but makes choices based on her strengths as a person, rather than any generic sense of her entitlement as a "lady."

OUTRUNNING THE COMPETITION: ATALANTA

Once upon a time, not long ago, there lived a princess named Atalanta, who could run as fast as the wind.

She was so bright, and so clever, and could build things and fix things so wonderfully, that many young men wished to marry her.

"What shall I do?" said Atalanta's father, who was a powerful king. "So many young men want to marry you, and I don't know how to choose."

"You don't have to choose, father," said Atalanta. "I will choose. And I'm not sure that I will choose to marry anyone at all."

"Of course you will," said the king. "Everybody gets married. It is what people do."

"But," Atalanta told him, with a toss of her head, "I intend to go out and see the world. When I come home, perhaps I will marry and perhaps I will not." (Miles 128)

"Atalanta," Betty Miles's modern feminist rewriting of a Greek myth, considers girls' personal power by engaging with mythic traditions and fairy tales. Like "Ladies First," it offers a challenge to traditional narrative conventions. Should girls aspire primarily to meeting and marrying their "prince"? Should women be judged primarily on their beauty and purity? What right do fathers have to determine their daughters' choice of romantic partners? Whereas the traditional princess genre generally presents young women as prizes for brave and adventurous men, "Atalanta" substitutes in its place a parable of individual fulfillment for both women and men.

In the original myth, King Schoeneus exacts a promise from his daughter, Atalanta, that she will marry anybody who can beat her in a footrace. Atalanta, a fast runner, outruns many suitors, until a man she admires is able to distract her with the help of the goddess Aphrodite. This suitor ultimately wins a race and Atalanta's hand. In the *Free to Be* version of the story, Atalanta is a skilled athlete and astronomer with no present interest in marriage. While she complies on the surface with her father's demand that she submit to marriage with any man who can run faster than she can, she trains secretly to avoid this fate. "Young John," who also trains alone, is a perfect match for her, both athletically and emotionally. After they complete the race "side by side," as equals, John insists that he merely wants to talk to Atalanta, not to force her hand in marriage. The two become friends and then set off on their own individual voyages of exploration. "Perhaps someday they'll be married," the fable ends, "and perhaps they will not. In any case, they are friends. And it is certain that they are both living happily ever after" (Miles 135).

For second-wave feminists, fairy tales and princess stories represented a central if vexed genre of children's literature. In 1970, Alison Lurie argued that fairy-tale heroines could be recuperated for feminism, as competent and resourceful models of female liberation (42). Many other feminists disagreed, describing the stories of male adventure and female passivity that were typical of many popular fairy tales (and their animated Walt Disney renditions) as troubling models for young children (Lieberman, Stone, Rowe). In revisiting these tales, a new generation of feminist writers (mostly, but not exclusively women) challenged the genre's conventions, often using humor to redefine gendered power relations and to reconsider girls' and boys' options (Zipes 138, Haase 1–36). Tales such as "Atalanta" suggested that there were fates more exciting for girls than being selected by princes, just as there were projects of self-discovery more important for boys than acquiring royal spouses.

Reframing the traditional princess story constituted a new form of feminist cultural production.[3] In this new genre, liberal feminist values prevail; girls have to work to gain their freedom, but this work (which often involves girls' efforts to outwit the forces of patriarchy as represented by their fathers or prospective husbands) is shown to be achievable. Fathers (and by implication, patriarchal law) are often portrayed as ridiculously old-fashioned, so the heroines must circumvent their fathers in order to pursue their goals.

John, a sympathetic young man, also has to work hard in order to achieve his goal of meeting and befriending Atalanta. He represents a new kind of hero who does not require the heroine's submission as a measure of his own masculinity. The fact that this well-matched pair do not marry is presented as a necessity, not a tragedy. Respectful companionship and self-knowledge, not romance, are the main characters' primary goals; while marriage to an equal remains a possibility, it is secondary to the necessary journey of individual achievement and self-discovery that must precede it. In this new kind of fairy tale, the "happy ending" is resolved unconventionally, with important consequences for men as well as for women.

William's Doll: Feminism for Boys

> William wants a doll
> so when he has a baby someday
> he'll know how to dress it, put diapers on double,
> and gently caress it to bring up a bubble,
> and care for his baby as ev'ry good father
> should learn to do.
> William has a doll! William has a doll!
> 'cause some day he may want to be a father, too.
>   (Harnick and Rodgers 83–85)

The song "William's Doll" was adapted for *Free to Be* from a 1972 book by Charlotte Zolotow. The story, which would win acclaim for Zolotow as a *New York Times* Outstanding Book of the Year and as the *School Library Journal* Best Book of the Year, concerns the desire of William for a doll of his own to care for. Despite the taunts of other children (on the *Free to Be* album, his peers sing "A doll! A doll! William wants a doll!"), and the displeasure of his father, who prefers to buy him sports equipment and other more traditionally "masculine" toys, William remains determined to have a doll. He is an able and enthusiastic athlete, *Free to Be* makes clear. But as William tells his visiting grandmother, "I'd give my bat and ball and glove to have a doll that I could love" (82). Finally, the grandmother intervenes. Validating her grandson's tenderness toward a doll as preparation for modern manhood, she convinces William's father that her grandson needs to learn childcare skills that will help him in adulthood. After all, the grandmother suggests, "Some day he may want to be a father too" (85).

"William's Doll" reflected second-wave feminists' efforts to promote more nurturing, sensitive, and expressive models of boyhood and manhood. Gender hierarchy, liberal feminists argued, hurt boys and men just as it hurt girls and women, forcing males into rigid "sex-role" stereotypes and forbidding them the pleasures of caregiving and tenderness. As Sandra Scofield, author of a *Redbook* magazine article about sexism and children's books, contended in 1977, "the myths hurt boys too. Unfortunately, there is little support for the boy who expresses emotion—especially fear or sadness—or for the boy who wants to be a dancer or an artist instead of a fireman or an inventor" (214). The *Free to Be* project encouraged boys to share their feelings. The album, book, and television special all included the song "It's Alright to Cry," sung by a contemporary icon of athletic masculinity, popular former National Football League star Roosevelt "Rosey" Grier. The book also included Linda Sitea's poignant "Zachary's Divorce," the story of a boy coming to terms with his sadness after his parents separate.

While the parameters of American girlhood were rapidly expanding in the 1970s, the question of boys' right to take on more traditionally nurturing roles remained the subject of significant cultural contestation. The chorus of voices discouraging boys from participating in so-called feminine activities was real and sometimes insistent. One New York City feminist mother, radio program director Nanette Rainone, later recalled the men who directly criticized her three-year-old son as he wheeled his doll carriage around their neighborhood, including a fireman who said, "Tell your mommy boys should have guns, not dolls!" and a storekeeper who told him, "Your mother should give you a little sister if she wants a girl that badly" (qtd. in Pogrebin 52).

Children themselves also participated in policing gender boundaries. In the mid-1970s, one student teacher visiting a classroom of fourth-graders asked the students to respond to an invented "Dear Abby"-style letter, ostensibly written by a mother concerned because her son wants a doll. Most of the girls and boys advised that the mother should not give her son a doll. When the student teacher then began reading Zolotow's *William's Doll*, scholars Myra and David Sadker later reported, "giggles and snickers erupted from the class, and then a contingent of boys expressed active hostility by booing and hissing. It was only with frequent reprimands to keep the noise down that the teacher was able to finish" (257).

When *Free to Be* was first imagined as a television special, ABC executives asked Marlo Thomas, in her role as producer, to cut "William's Doll." As Thomas later recalled, the executives felt that the segment "would turn every American boy into a homosexual." She insisted and the segment remained ("Still Free to Be"). But the ABC executives' concern speaks to a central reason why "William's Doll" was so controversial; anxiety about homosexuality was often implicit (and sometimes explicit) in twentieth-century American child-rearing advice, which generally promoted separate cultural spheres for girls and boys.

The postwar era's foremost child guidance author, Dr. Benjamin Spock, for example, was among many professionals to insist that parents should treat boys and girls differently in order to support their emerging sexual and gender identities. Through the early 1970s, Spock was leery of idealistic parents' efforts to reduce gender distinctions to a minimum, on the grounds that ambiguity might deprive children of an adequate sense of sex distinction. He encouraged parents to dress girls and boys differently and to allow them different kinds of toys. In his 1970 book *Decent and Indecent*, for instance, he argued that

> A boy should know that his father enjoys his company in a special way because they can talk about cars or carpentry or sports. Even a small boy should feel that his mother appreciates his manly help in carrying things for her, opening doors, running errands, fixing things.
>   A girl needs from her father compliments on the attractiveness of her appearance, on her skill in feminine occupations, and particularly on her thoughtfulness and helpfulness. (57–58)

In the face of heated feminist critique, Spock had a change of heart in the early 1970s. As he explained in 1972, "though I still believe a definite sex identity is important, I don't think it needs to be built through an emphasis on differences in clothes or playthings, or on parental reminders of what little boys are meant to do and what little girls are meant to do." Playing with toys that were traditionally gendered for the other sex might, Spock claimed, actually help children "work through and digest the partial identification with the other sex that is an aspect of every human being" ("Should Girls" 24, 26, 28). By the mid-1970s, Spock wrote a more gender-neutral edition of his classic *Baby and Child Care* (Hulbert 254–56).

Underlying this conversion was an important caveat. As Spock made clear, he had initially understood play as a key vehicle for the development of appropriately heterosexual (or inappropriately homosexual) identification. Now, he saw the origin of homosexuality elsewhere, in "off-kilter" relationships between parents and their children ("Should Girls" 26). If Spock was now less worried about the effects of specific clothes and toys on children's gender development, he continued to represent heterosexual development itself as a pressing concern.

"William's Doll" is written to minimize such anxiety. William is well-adjusted and an excellent athlete, the reader is repeatedly told; his desire for a doll does not make him odd, even if he is scorned and ignored. He remains hopeful and persistent in the face of immense social pressure, until his grandmother finally intervenes. Yet the story's careful framing suggests the anxiety it is meant to allay: that a boy who wants a doll might not be "normal." Indeed, as Ricky Herzog points out in a discussion of the original Zolotow text, William himself never explains his interest in the doll as preparation for fatherhood; perhaps his desire cannot fully be recuperated into a heteronormative narrative (68–69). Certainly, as the response of ABC executives suggests, the story could be read as sexually subversive, even potentially dangerous for boys. The reception of "William's Doll" suggests that the stakes of heterosexual masculinity remained particularly anxious, even as feminists succeeded in challenging many aspects of children's traditional gender socialization.

Where the River Runs Free: *Free to Be . . . You and Me* in Retrospect

Today, the *Free to Be* series represents a foundational text of 1970s liberal feminism. For a particular generational and cultural cohort—adults who were children in liberal (and sometimes radical or apolitical) homes of the 1970s—*Free to Be* is also a nostalgic touchstone of their younger days. In a recent memoir, for instance, writer Susan Jane Gilman recalls her youth as the daughter of white hippies living in a racially and economically diverse New York City neighborhood. Gilman comments that having been "born just as the women's movement was catching fire, my classmates and I were being raised by mothers who would be the first on line to buy copies of *Free to Be . . . You and Me* and multiracial, anatomically correct baby dolls . . . Every kid's Fisher-Price phonograph had "Free to Be . . . You and Me" spinning around on its turntable" (Gilman 26, 43). For many adults of this cohort, the *Free to Be* project has retained its emotional resonance. As one father relates, he and his wife, both children of the 1970s, rediscovered the album as new parents; "not only did we remember the words but we also came to realize how important of a role the album played in our lives. Thinking about it wistfully almost brings a tear to my eye" (Metrodad). Or, as a woman recalls of her 1970s girlhood, "I was free to be me, and I took that message seriously" (Soderlind 9).

Children of the 1970s learned new lessons from the *Free to Be* series. In its unconventional "happy endings," the girl who has no redeeming qualities other than her physical beauty is punished, the women and man who are well matched do not immediately marry, and the boy who plays every sport well remains unsatisfied by traditional gender roles. However, *Free to Be* is also consonant with long-standing American narratives of tenacity and individual achievement. Even where girls' and boys' aspirations are unpopular, the series proposes, those who are determined can access equality of opportunity. Where 1970s "young adult" fiction expresses conflicts but does not always fully resolve them, the *Free to Be* series emphasizes success.

Whether this is a fair or realistic message has been the source of some feminist controversy since the 1970s. For those feminists who emphasize (rather than minimize) the power of structural inequities, the *Free to Be* series' stories and songs inaccurately represent the project of self-actualization in personal rather than collective terms; the texts' emphasis on individual accomplishment and equality of opportunity underplay the ways in which structural categories such as race, class, and gender foreclose individuals' opportunities (Braun 137, 142, Tucker no page number). In a similar vein, Angela Hubler indicts 1970s feminists' critique of the

"Cop-Out" literary genre, calling it an unfair critique given the realities of the time periods in which these texts were written. To say that girls should be stronger and more assertive, Hubler argues, "implies that sexism persists because women individually have not been strong enough in the past." This, she suggests, is victim-blaming, when capitalist patriarchy rather than personality is truly at issue (89). And while *Free to Be* is consciously multicultural, numerous feminists have noted that the kind of female individualism celebrated in *Free to Be* is most available to white, middle-class girls and women (Marshall 260).

These critiques reflect shifts in emphasis in feminist scholarship since the 1970s. *Free to Be* was conceptualized at the height of feminist enthusiasm for sex-role theory, an approach that has come under assault since the early 1980s. As later scholars have contended, early second-wave feminist research on children's books tended to be methodologically uneven; researchers' categories of analysis were often fuzzy, and it was unclear how consistent they were when coding such attributes as "courage" or "adventure."[4] The concept of cultural reception that under-girded this research itself underwent significant revision. Early "sex-role" studies often cast listeners, readers, and television viewers as the passive recipients of dominant cultural texts. Today, scholars see audiences in more active terms as agents producing "negotiated" responses to cultural forms. There has also been an upsurge of feminist research on gender's biological underpinnings, a turn from the liberal feminist emphasis on the social constructedness of gender. Finally, while *Free to Be* (and a later project, Thomas's 1987 *Free to Be . . . A Family*) explored variations on family life including single-parent, multicultural, and blended families, neither of these texts included representations of families headed by lesbian or gay parents, which have been the subject of much feminist attention in recent years.

Yet if *Free to Be* is a document of its time, it is one that remains compelling for many adults and children today. Sexism and traditional gender codes in children's culture have diminished, but by no means have they disappeared. The *Free to Be* project's emphasis on sensitive boys and adventurous girls continues to resonate. At the same time, what were once bold feminist ideas have to a significant degree been integrated into the American mainstream.

NOTES

1. On civil rights and children's books, see, for example, Larrick, Cornelius, Tanyzer and Karl, and Banfield.

2. The classic feminist scholarly study of the period was Weitzman, Eifler, Hokada, and Ross. See also Stewig and Higgs.

3. For an early example of the genre, see Williams, *Practical Princess*.

4. For examples of this critique, see Williams, Allen, Vernon, Williams, and Malecha; and Clark, Kulkin, and Clancy.

WORKS CITED

Anonymous. "Little Miss Muffet Fights Back." *Library Journal* 95, no. 20 (5 November 1970): 3947.

Anonymous. "Still Free to Be." *Lilith*, 1 July 2004. http://www.jccmanhattan.org/category. aspx?catid=1796. Accessed April 9, 2009.

B., A. Letter from teacher to Marlo Thomas. n.d., collection of the Free to Be Foundation, Inc., New York City.

Bailey, Beth, and David Farber, eds. *America in the 1970s*. Lawrence: UP of Kansas, 2004.

Banfield, Beryle. "Commitment to Change: The Council on Interracial Books for Children and the World of Children's Books." *African American Review* 32, no. 1 (Spring 1998): 17–22.

Binkley, Sam. *Getting Loose: Lifestyle Consumption in the 1970s*. Durham, NC: Duke UP, 2007.

Blume, Judy. *Forever*. Scarsdale, NY: Bradbury Press, 1975.

Braun, Kara Lynn. "*Free to Be . . . You and Me*: Considering the Impact of Feminist Influences in Children's Literature from the 1970s." *Journal of the Association of Research on Mothering* 1, no. 1 (Spring-Summer 1999): 137–44.

Braunstein, Peter, and Michael William Doyle, eds. *Imagine Nation: The American Counterculture of the 1960s and '70s*. New York: Routledge, 2002.

Carroll, Peter N. *It Seemed Like Nothing Happened: America in the 1970s*. New Brunswick: Rutgers UP, 1982, 1990.

Castro, Ginette, and Elizabeth Loverde-Bagwell. *American Feminism: A Contemporary History*. New York: New York UP, 1990.

Clark, Roger, Heidi Kulkin, and Liam Clancy. "The Liberal Bias in Feminist Social Science Research on Children's Books." In *Girls Boys Books Toys: Gender in Children's Literature and Culture*, edited by Beverly Lyon Clark and Margaret R. Higonnet, 71–82. Baltimore: Johns Hopkins UP, 1999.

Cormier, Robert. *The Chocolate War*. New York: Pantheon Books, 1974.

Cornelius, Paul. "Interracial Children's Books: Problems and Progress." *Library Quarterly* 41, no. 2 (April 1971): 106–27.

Danish, Barbara. *The Dragon and the Doctor*. Old Westbury, NY: Feminist Press, 1970.

Darrow, Jr., Whitney. *I'm Glad I'm a Boy! I'm Glad I'm a Girl!* New York: Windmill Books, 1970.

De Poix, Carol. *Jo, Flo and Yolanda*. Chapel Hill, NC: Lollipop Power, Inc., 1973.

F., Christina. Letter to Marlo Thomas, n.d., collection of the Free to Be Foundation, Inc., New York, NY.

F., Leslie. Letter to Marlo Thomas, n.d., collection of the Free to Be Foundation, Inc., New York, NY.

Feminists on Children's Media. "A Feminist Look at Children's Books." *Library Journal* 96, no. 2 (15 January 1971): 235–40.

———. Little Miss Muffet Fights Back: Recommended Non-Sexist Books about Girls for Young Readers. New York: Feminists on Children's Media, 1971.

Free to Be Foundation. http://www.freetobefoundation.org/history.htm. Accessed April 9, 2009

Gilman, Susan Jane. *Hypocrite in a Poufy White Dress: Tales of Growing Up Groovy and Clueless*. New York: Warner Books, 2005.

Gosse, Van, and Richard Moser, eds. *The World the Sixties Made: Politics and Culture in Recent America*. Philadelphia: Temple UP, 2003.

Grant, Annette. "Free to Be . . . You and Me" *Seventeen* 33 (June 1974): 149.

Green, Constance C. *A Girl Called Al*. New York: Viking, 1969.

Haase, Donald, ed. *Fairy Tales and Feminism: New Approaches*. Detroit: Wayne State UP, 2004.

Harnick, Sheldon. "Housework." In *Free to Be . . . You and Me*, edited by Carole Hart, Letty Cottin Pogrebin, Mary Rodgers and Marlo Thomas, 54–59. New York: McGraw-Hill, 1974.

Harnick, Sheldon (lyrics), and Mary Rodgers (music). "William's Doll." In *Free to Be . . . You and Me*, edited by Hart et al. 78–85.

Hart, Bruce (lyrics), and Stephen Lawrence (music). "Free to Be . . . You and Me." In *Free to Be . . . You and Me*, edited by Hart et al. 16–23.

Hart, Carole, Letty Cottin Pogrebin, Mary Rodgers, and Marlo Thomas. *Free to Be . . . You and Me*. New York: McGraw-Hill, 1974.

Herzog, Ricky. "Sissies, Dolls, and Dancing: Children's Literature and Gender Deviance in the Seventies." *The Lion and the Unicorn* 33 (January 2009): 60–76.

Hubler, Angela E. "Beyond the Image: Adolescent Girls, Reading, and Social Identity." *NWSA Journal* 12, no. 1 (Spring 2000): 84–99.

Hulbert, Ann. *Raising America: Experts, Parents, and a Century of Advice about Children*. New York: Alfred A. Knopf, 2003.

Jenkins, Philip. *Decade of Nightmares: The End of the Sixties and the Making of Eighties America*. New York: Oxford UP, 2006.

Kerr, M. E. *Dinky Hocker Shoots Smack*. New York: Harper & Row, 1972.

Klein, Norma. *Mom, the Wolf Man and Me*. New York: Avon, 1974.

Larrick, Nancy. "The All-White World of Children's Books" *Saturday Review* 48 (September 1965): 63–64, 83–85.

Lieberman, Marcia R. "'Some Day My Prince Will Come': Female Acculturation Through the Fairy Tale." *College English* 34 (1972): 383–95.

Lurie, Alison. "Fairy Tale Liberation." *New York Review of Books*, 17 December 1970, 42.

M., Karen. Letter to Marlo Thomas, n.d., collection of the Free to Be Foundation, Inc., New York, NY.

MacLeod, Anne Scott. *American Childhood: Essays on Children's Literature of the Nineteenth and Twentieth Centuries*. Athens: U of Georgia P, 1994.

Marshall, Elizabeth. "Stripping for the Wolf: Rethinking Representations of Gender in Children's Literature." *Reading Research Quarterly* 39, no. 3 (July–September 2004): 256–70.

Martin, Karin. "William Wants a Doll. Can He Have One? Feminists, Child Care Advisors, and Gender-Neutral Child Rearing." *Gender & Society* 19, no. 4 (2005): 456–79.

Maury, Inez. *My Mother the Mail Carrier/Mi Mami la Cartera*. Old Westbury: Feminist Press, 1976.

Metrodad. "Free to Be You and Me" (A MetroDad Recommendation). 15 November 2005. http://metrodad.typepad.com/index/2005/11/free_to_be_you_.html. Accessed April 2009.

Miles, Betty. "Atalanta." In *Free to Be . . . You and Me*, edited by Hart et al. 128–35.

———. "Harmful Lessons Little Girls Learn in School" *Redbook* 136, no. 5 (March 1971): 86, 168–69.

Phillips, Lynn. *Exactly Like Me*. Chapel Hill, NC: Lollipop Power, 1972.

Pogrebin, Letty Cottin. "Toys for Free Children" *Ms.* 2, no. 6
     (December 1973): 49–53.

Quindlen, Anna. "Women for Women Only." *New York Times*, 13 March 1978, A16.

Rowe, Karen E. "Feminism and Fairy Tales." *Feminist Studies* 6 (1979): 237–57.

Sadker, Myra Pollack, and David Miller Sadker. *Now Upon a Time: A Contemporary View
     of Children's Literature*. New York: Harper & Row, 1977.

Schecter, Therese. *I Was a Teenage Feminist*. New York: Trixie Films, 2005.

Scofield, Sandra. "Is It True Boys Have More Fun? What Every Parent Should Know
     About Children's Books." *Redbook* 149, no. 1 (May 1977): 214, 216.

Silverstein, Shel, adapted by Mary Rodgers. "Ladies First." In *Free to Be . . . You and Me*,
     edited by Hart et al. 39–45.

Sitea, Linda. "Zachary's Divorce." In *Free to Be . . . You and Me*, edited by Hart et al.
     124–27.

Slifkin, Naomi. "Lollipop Power." *Seventeen* 34 (January 1975): 18.

Soderlind, Lori. *Chasing Montana*. Madison: Terrace Books, 2006.

Sparks, Beatrice (published as Anonymous). *Go Ask Alice*. Englewood Cliffs, NJ:
     Prentice-Hall, 1971.

Spock, Benjamin. *Decent and Indecent*. New York: McCall Publishing Co., 1970.

———. "Should Girls Be Raised Exactly Like Boys?" *Redbook Magazine* 138 (February
     1972): 24, 26, 28.

Stern, Sydney Ladensohn. *Gloria Steinem: Her Passions, Politics, and Mystique*. Secaucus,
     NJ: Birch Lane Press Book, 1997.

Stewig, John, and Margaret Higgs. "Girls Grow Up to Be Mommies: A Study of Sexism in
     Children's Literature." *Library Journal* 98 (15 January 1973): 226–41.

Stone, Kay. "Things Walt Disney Never Told Us." *Journal of American Folklore* 88, no. 347
     (January–March 1975): 42–50.

Tanyzer, Harold, and Jean Karl, eds. *Reading, Children's Books, and Our Pluralistic Society*.
     Newark, DE: International Reading Association, 1972.

Thomas, Marlo. *Free to Be . . . A Family*. New York: Bantam Books, 1987.

——— and Friends. *Free to Be . . . You and Me* (The 35th Anniversary Edition).
     Philadelphia: Running Press Kids, 2008.

Tucker, Judith Stadtman. "Mommies Are People: Revisiting Free to Be . . . You and Me,"
     June 2007. http://www.mothersmovement.org/features/07/06/f2b_prn.html. Accessed
     April 2009.

Weitzman, Lenore J., Deborah Eifler, Elizabeth Hokada, and Catherine Ross. "Sex-Role
     Socialization in Picture Books for Preschool Children." *American Journal of Sociology*
     77, no. 6 (May 1972): 1125–50

Wigutoff, Sharon. "The Feminist Press: Ten Years of Nonsexist Children's Books." *The
     Lion and the Unicorn* 3, no. 2 (Winter 1979–80): 57–63.

Williams, Jr., J. Allen, JoEtta A. Vernon, Martha C. Williams, and Karen Malecha. "Sex Role
     Socialization in Picture Books: An Update." *Social Science Quarterly* 68, no. 1 (March
     1987): 148–56.

Williams, Jay. *The Practical Princess*. New York: Parents' Magazine Press, 1969.

Women on Words and Images. *Dick and Jane as Victims: Sex Stereotyping in Children's
     Readers, an Analysis*. Princeton, NJ: National Organization for Women, 1972.

Zipes, Jack. *Relentless Progress: The Reconfiguration of Children's Literature, Fairy Tales, and
     Storytelling*. New York: Routledge, 2007.

Zolotow, Charlotte. *William's Doll*. New York: Harper & Row, 1972.

FURTHER READING

Douglas, Susan J. *Where the Girls Are: Growing Up Female with the Mass Media*. New York: Three Rivers Press, 1994, 1995.

Greever, Ellen A., Patricia Austin, and Karyn Welhousen, "William's Doll Revisited." *Language Arts* 77, no. 4 (March 2000): 324–30.

Mintz, Steven. *Huck's Raft: A History of American Childhood*. Cambridge, MA: Harvard UP, 2004.

Pogrebin, Letty Cottin. *Growing Up Free: Raising Your Child in the 80's*. New York: McGraw-Hill, 1980.

Stacey, Judith, Susan Béreaud, and Joan Daniels, eds., *And Jill Came Tumbling After: Sexism in American Education*. New York: Dell Publishing Co., 1974.

CHAPTER 26

PARADISE REFIGURED: INNOCENCE AND EXPERIENCE IN *HIS DARK MATERIALS*

NAOMI WOOD

PHILIP *(Nicholas) Pullman was born in Norwich, Norfolk, England, on October 19, 1946. During childhood, he lived in Rhodesia (now Zimbabwe), Australia, England, and Wales. Both his father and stepfather were pilots in the Royal Air Force. After the accidental death of Pullman's father in Kenya, his mother worked in London while he and his brother lived in Norfolk with their grandparents. Pullman credits his grandfather, a Church of England minister, with instilling in him a love of story and language. As a youth, Pullman had catholic tastes in literature: he loved comic books and the poetry of Milton and Coleridge. The first of his family to attend university, Pullman won a scholarship to Oxford, where he earned a B.A. in 1968. Pullman married in 1970 and has two sons. After trying various occupations and publishing two novels for adults, Pullman became a teacher. As a teacher, he learned to tell stories effectively; he also wrote plays performed by his students. Pullman's experience teaching alerted him to the field of young adult literature, and he has published many well-received YA books, including gothic-suspense, graphic novels, and the Sally Lockhart trilogy, set in Victorian England. Pullman's* His Dark Materials *trilogy is his best-known work;* The Amber Spyglass *won the Whitbread Book of the Year Award in 2002, the first children's book to do so.* His Dark Materials *was staged at the National Theatre in 2003, and a film made of* The Golden Compass *was issued in 2007. In March 2005, Pullman was awarded the Astrid Lindgren Memorial Award for children's literature.*

Philip Pullman's trilogy, *His Dark Materials* (1995–2000),[1] meditates on the continuum between innocence and experience, ignorance and knowledge, purity and fecundity, and, not coincidentally, children and adults. Self-consciously revolutionary, *His Dark Materials* builds on and distinguishes itself from previous works of fantasy for children by using them as an occasion to reimagine one of the foundational myths of Western culture, the story of humanity's fall from Paradise. It does so in three ways. First, *His Dark Materials* dismantles the Romantic myth of childhood innocence and erects in its place a narrative about experience, to emancipate both children and adults from the myth's dark implications. Second, the series employs traditional genres and tropes to highlight and question the values and ideology that formed them. It attempts to imbue myth with realism without relinquishing either the archetypal resonance of the first or the mimetic precision of the second. Third, because it uses epic form to assault the structures of religious orthodoxy, *His Dark Materials* invites critical assessment of its own structures and modes, as well as its new mythology of childhood and coming of age. While the reach of *His Dark Materials* may occasionally exceed its grasp, it nonetheless provides a powerful and critical account of children, adults, and the stories that make them human.

Conceived as *Paradise Lost* for young adults, *His Dark Materials* retells the story of humanity's fall from innocence to experience via two children—Lyra "Silvertongue" Belacqua and Will Parry. Using the many-worlds hypothesis of quantum mechanics, Pullman posits parallel worlds in which the same things happen, similar people and places exist, but with variations. In Lyra's world, all humans are born with animal-shaped "daemons," who function as companions and souls. Having a daemon defines humans so categorically that humans without daemons are considered either oxymoronic or hideously mutilated. Lyra's world is ruled by a totalitarian theocracy, the Magisterium (also called the Church), which serves a deity called the Authority and controls the production and dissemination of scientific research, called "experimental theology." Of concern to the Church is a substance called Dust, which has been defined as evidence of Original Sin because it collects around children as they attain puberty and continues to accrete in adulthood. As the narrative unfolds, Dust is revealed to be much more than "sin": Dust is comprised of elementary particles attracted to consciousness; angels are made of Dust; and Dust influences and is influenced by human thought. Vulnerable to indifference and inattention, Dust is particularly at risk over the course of the novels. The Church's insistence upon Dust's sinfulness sets the stage for a cosmic conflict between those who embrace and those who reject it.

Lyra is the illegitimate child of two powerful and charismatic individuals, Lord Asriel and Mrs. Marisa Coulter. She has been identified as a second Eve, one who will be tempted to recapitulate the fall of her foremother. If she falls, the direction of the universe will shift, compromising the ability of the Church to dictate morality in terms of purity and obedience. After she witnesses the perverse consequences of the Church's fear of Dust and the death of her best friend Roger (respectively, the results of actions by her mother and her father), Lyra determines that she will seek out Dust as a power for good. Lyra's journey is aided by her daemon, Pantalaimon (or "Pan"); by a device called the alethiometer, a "truth-measure"; and by Will Parry, a boy from a world like ours. From the same world comes the "serpent" Mary Malone, a nun-turned-physicist. In addition to angels, supporting characters include Gyptians, armored bears, witches, minute fighter-spies called Gallivespians, Harpies, wheeled creatures called *mulefa*, and ghosts. On the way to fulfilling their destiny, Lyra and Will cross several universes and multiple worlds, invade the Land of the Dead and liberate its ghosts, facilitate the death of God and his Kingdom, and fall—in love. Their actions save Dust from extinction, thereby rescuing consciousness and humanist ideals. However Lyra and Will are not permitted to remain together; they learn that the consequences of living in a world not their own are deadly and that they must "build the Republic of Heaven" where they were born.

INNOCENCE AND ITS DISCONTENTS

Of particular concern in *His Dark Materials* is the transition between childhood and adulthood. Throughout the series, Pullman engages a long-standing conversation about the moral status of children, a conversation that gained particular strength during the Romantic era in late eighteenth- and early nineteenth-century Europe and America. *His Dark Materials* addresses two strands of Romantic thought: rebellious challenges to religious and state authority and the Romantic "cult of childhood," which indulged in an orgy of child worship that prized children's innocence over adults' experience.[2] The cult of childhood combined the Genesis story of humankind's fall from grace with classical mythology's Golden Age and situated, in the figure of the child, goodness, hope, creativity, and imagination (Boas 11). At the same time, it posited the child's inevitable fall into dreary conventional reality as "maturity," a tragic effect of childhood's transience.

Wordsworth's "Intimations" ode encapsulates these notions about childhood by imagining infants "trailing clouds of glory" but "shades of the prison-house clos[ing]" in as they move toward adulthood. This Romantic definition of idealized childhood did confer some benefits upon children as a class in that it stimulated labor and education reform. However, Alan Richardson, citing Hugh Cunningham's historical study of children of the poor, notes that the notion of Romantic childhood may have removed the burden of "productive labor" from some children only to replace it with

> a different, perhaps no less demanding, role within the capitalist economy as
> bearers of moral and religious value and as obligatorily blithe denizens of a

> domestic sphere in which economic man could find respite and emotional
> renewal (Cunningham 152). Cut off from the productive sphere and expected
> to enact an impossible fiction, the innocent child experiences a kind of social
> death. . . . (Richardson 27)

Innocence is "a kind of social death" because it denies children a part of their
humanity. This "obligation" to be "blithe" and to offer adults "respite and emotional renewal" elevates children to supernatural status at the cost of removing
them from an earthly sphere—the sphere of life and growth. As the commonly used
adjective "angelic" perhaps unintentionally suggests, the only truly innocent child
may be a dead one.[3] The construction of childhood as innocent too easily masks
adults' exploitive and self-serving use of children through a mystical rhetoric that
"seems deliberately formed to underwrite the wishful autonomy, the privileging of
consciousness, and the devaluation of bodily experience" idealized by certain male
Romantics (Richardson 28). Judith Plotz's study of the Romantic "vocation of
childhood" demonstrates that the Romantic "fixation on a child as the embodiment of eternal youth and fullness of being" attempts to "fix" all children in their
most volatile and amorphous state (xiii). Doing so "arrests, eternalizes, and destroys
the living child for any productive human purpose" (xiv). In making this argument,
Plotz references Goethe's "Erl King,"[4] but a similar goal motivates Pullman's Mrs.
Coulter in *The Amber Spyglass* as she drugs Lyra into Sleeping-Beauty-like submission in order to "protect" her from her own maturity. That children themselves do
not wish to be fixed in childhood is confirmed by the dreaming Lyra, who testifies
to Roger's ghost that "I'm just trying to wake up—I'm so afraid of sleeping all my
life and then dying—I want to wake up first! I wouldn't care if it was just for an
hour, as long as I was properly alive and awake" (*AS* 54). Thus, fanatical Father
Gomez's quest to kill Lyra as a means to preserve her innocence, coupled with his
"horror of harming an innocent person" (*AS* 463), perfectly captures the oxymoronic implications of valuing innocence more than development, experience, even
life itself.

The construction of childhood as innocent, with the corollary that children's
innocence must be fixed, or at least sheltered as long as possible, forms an integral
part of contemporary Anglo-American discourses about childhood and about
educational and public policy. Neil Postman's 1982 work, *The Disappearance of
Childhood*, laments the degree to which modern technologies (even before the
advent of the personal computer and the cell phone) destroy the experiential and
informational boundaries that separate children from adults. Countering these
laments, critics such as Henry Giroux observe that the "myth of innocence" and
fears about the "disappearance of childhood" serve a paradoxical ideological
function: constructing the child as essentially Other "allow[s] adults to believe
that children do not suffer from their greed, recklessness, perversions of will and
spirit" (31). For Giroux, "while the concept of innocence may incite adults to
publicly proclaim their support for future generations, it more often than not
protects them from the reality of society and the influence they have in contributing to the ever increasing impoverishment of children's lives" (37).[5] Removing

"the child" from time and placing it in myth, thus, obscures history's *children* who may have desires, orientations, and needs not countenanced by the adult-generated ideal.

Like these other critiques of the exploitive and mystifying aspects of Romantic childhood, *His Dark Materials* depicts innocence as a negative quality—as a *lack*. As the prefix "in-" suggests, innocence is defined by what it is not rather than what it is. Derived from *in-nocere*, innocence is "not harmful," "innocuous," rather than being a positive, active virtue. In *His Dark Materials*, Pullman's narrator acknowledges adults' pleasure in the spectacle of children's innocence but challenges the notion that children's difference from adults is absolute or something to be preserved at all costs. In *The Golden Compass*, the narrator ironically voices the sentimental attitude toward children taken by those who have no direct contact with them:

> [T]he Scholars, for their part, would have been unable to see the rich seething stew of alliances and enmities and feuds and treaties which was a child's life in Oxford. Children playing together: how pleasant to see! What could be more innocent and charming?
>
> In fact, of course, Lyra and her peers were engaged in deadly warfare.
> (*GC* 35)

Adults' construal of children's play as "innocent" betrays their ignorance (or amnesia) about children's naked pursuit of power and prestige through play—the same activities that will engage them as adults. "Of course" children's social organization mimics that of adults—the stakes and consequences of "deadly warfare" may change, but the emotions and strategies are similar. Adults' sentimentality about children may seem innocuous, but *His Dark Materials* shows its toxic consequences. The overvaluing of children's innocence not only ignores evidence that children, like adults, engage in "alliances and enmities and feuds and treaties" but also is used to justify terrible mutilation to prevent them from maturing into physical, and especially sexual, adulthood. As already noted, in Lyra's world everyone has a daemon—an external manifestation of the soul. In childhood, the daemon is a shape-shifter who experiments with many different bodies; however, in puberty it "settles" into a fixed body, an indication that child and daemon have begun the transition to adulthood. "Settling" happens as children become conscious of their sexuality; by discovering the pleasures of the flesh, they establish their identity as embodied and conscious beings. The Church's experimental theologians have noticed Dust begins to collect more thickly around children after their daemons have settled and have determined that it is physical evidence of Original Sin.

In a twisted effort to "protect" children from Dust, Lyra's mother, Mrs. Coulter, has instituted the General Oblation Board, which abducts impoverished and lower-class children for theologico-medical experiments in the far North. There, researchers attempt to stop the developmental process altogether by severing children from their daemons. *The Golden Compass* starkly depicts the consequences of "intercision," the clinical term obscuring the horrific consequences. One "severed child," Tony Makarios, has somehow escaped the Nazi-like experimental station Bolvanger, where such atrocities are committed; cast from human society, Lyra and Pan find him clinging to a piece of dried fish as a pathetic replacement for his daemon. Like other victims of this process, Tony soon dies from the trauma of being severed from his soul. Using paternalistic justifications about how adults want to prevent children from being "infected" with Dust, from becoming aware of the "bothersome" feelings of adolescence, Mrs. Coulter attempts to persuade Lyra that

> "the doctors do it for the children's own good, my love. . . . [A] quick operation on children means they're safe. . . . All that happens is a little cut, and then everything's peaceful. Forever!" (*GC* 282–83)

But Lyra is not convinced, especially since Mrs. Coulter prevented Lyra and Pan from being subjected to the process. Lyra "hate[s] it with a furious passion. Her dear soul, the darling companion of her heart, to be cut away and reduced to a little trotting pet?" (*GC* 284).

Preserving this "peacefulness" (however imaginary) may seem desirable by adults in power—no worries about sexual impurity in word or deed. However, Pullman emphasizes that innocence by itself is no guarantor of moral virtue in children or adults. Victims of intercision in Africa become "zombis" with no will of their own, totally under the control of their masters (*GC* 375). Lyra's childhood is punctuated by such innocent acts of cruelty as catching an injured rook, killing it, and then roasting it—innocent because she does not intend to cause pain, but cruel nonetheless. The narrator characterizes Lyra as "a coarse and greedy little savage" (*GC* 36). The "Children's World" in *The Subtle Knife* is by no means peaceful; it is reminiscent, rather, of William Golding's *Lord of the Flies*. When Will and Lyra in Cittàgazze come upon a crowd of "twenty or so children" cornering and stoning a cat, Lyra expresses astonishment: "I never seen kids being like that," but Will responds tersely, "I have" (*SK* 108; *SK* 111). In the Land of the Dead, the "jeering, hate-filled sound" of the Harpies' voices "remind[s] Will of the merciless cruelty of children in a playground" (*AS* 290). Thus, by showing some of the negative consequences of innocence's inability to imagine the pain of the other or to take responsibility, Pullman depicts children's innocence as potentially amoral, even immoral.

Apart from his fiction, Pullman most explicitly critiques the fetishization of innocence in his review of Blake Morrison's *As If*, a nonfiction account of the 1993 murder of toddler James Bulger by preteens Robert Thompson and Jon Venables. Published in the same year as *The Subtle Knife*, the review recounts Pullman's trip to the zoo, his enjoyment of the gibbons, and the sudden turn his enjoyment took when he saw one of the gibbons catch a starling and "beg[i]n to pull it to pieces. I can't forget the crackings and snappings, the tough white sinews, the lolling shrieking head, and most of all the curious innocent concentration of the ape" (Pullman, "Understand" 6).[6] Pullman's description of the gibbon as "innocent" invites us to understand that the consequences of one's actions may be simultaneously innocent and yet utterly culpable. To Pullman, idolizing innocence prevents developing children from becoming conscious and, therefore, from becoming fully moral beings. It is better to "go forward, into deeper knowledge, painful though that is" (Pullman, "Understand" 6)[7]

The child protagonists of *His Dark Materials* chafe at the restrictions imposed by their status as children. Lyra is distinguished by her rebellious attitude toward adults' proscriptions from the very beginning. Caught in an act of disobedience as the series opens, Lyra's pursuit of forbidden knowledge establishes a central theme of the trilogy. Will, introduced in the second volume, demonstrates considerable resolve and resourcefulness at the same time that he too is vulnerable to the threat of adult intervention—he must hide the fact of his mother's mental illness to prevent their separation and institutionalization. Lyra and Will each have exceptional qualities *as children* at the same time that their development toward adulthood is celebrated. They exhibit both the abilities and weaknesses of childhood; both must relinquish the intuitive grace of childhood for the arduous but rich understanding of mature experience. Lyra begins her quest as a good liar—someone who generates romantic stories for the entertainment or befuddlement of her listeners—and ends by discovering the value of "true stories." She becomes, in effect, an Apollonian lyre for stories that partake of the earth, of human materiality, and of the joy of existence. Initially, Will exists alone, focused entirely on hiding his mother's disability, characterized primarily by his desire to protect her. By the end, he has gained a true love, Lyra, and a true friend, Mary Malone. With the latter, Will can begin to live his life in anticipation of greater scope for action than his stunted and secretive childhood permitted. Pullman stages Lyra's and Will's "fall" into adulthood as a positive gain in contrast with the Romantic discourse of childhood that emphasizes loss and diminishment as essential components of maturation.

Depicting the child's "fall" from innocence as not only inevitable but desirable, *His Dark Materials* finds hope not in the negative values of *in*nocence, *in*experience, and *i*gnorance ("not knowing") but rather in the positive values of curiosity, connection, action, and imagination.

"Passing through Infinity": Remythologizing Experience

> "You will not die. For God knows that when you eat of it [the fruit] your eyes will be opened, and you will be like God, knowing good and evil. . . . Then the eyes of both were opened, and they knew that they were naked; and they sewed fig leaves together and made themselves aprons." (Genesis 3:4b–5, 7, RSV)

"[N]ow that we've eaten of the tree of knowledge . . . Paradise
is locked and bolted, and the cherubim stands behind us. We
have to go on and make the journey round the world to see if
it is perhaps open somewhere at the back." (Kleist 201–2)

Pullman's revised myth of innocence and experience draws explicitly upon old
mythology, especially the story of Adam and Eve. As the story goes, after eating the
apple of knowledge, Adam and Eve lose their innocence, become aware of their
nakedness, and are expelled from the Garden of Eden. However, even the biblical
account confirms that the Serpent's promise was true: eating the fruit did make
Adam and Eve god-like and, therefore, rivals to God himself: "Then the Lord God
said, 'Behold, the man has become like one of us, knowing good and evil; and now,
lest he put forth his hand and take also of the tree of life, and eat, and live for
ever'—therefore the Lord God sent him forth from the garden of Eden" (Genesis
3:22–23, RSV). This story of Adam and Eve defines human identity as culpable
(they disobeyed a simple order), incomplete (they must be covered), subject to
pain and toil, and marred by knowledge.[8] At the same time, it acknowledges the
god-like nature of moral consciousness and raises questions about God's motives
in punishing the couple so harshly. Were they expelled from Paradise for their disobedience or in order to defend a vulnerable boundary between God and creation?
These questions have been debated and answered variously in the long history of
biblical hermeneutics and retold in epic form by John Milton, William Blake, and
others.[9]

His Dark Materials retells the Genesis story four times, each time shifting the
point of view. In The Golden Compass Lord Asriel reads: "And the serpent said. . . .
For God doth know that in the day ye eat thereof, then your eyes shall be opened, and
your daemons shall assume their true forms, and ye shall be as gods, knowing good and
evil" (372, italics in the original). This account, most similar to the account and
language found in the King James Bible, emphasizes knowledge—of self ("your
daemons shall assume their true forms") and of ethics, of responsibility ("knowing
good and evil")—as central to Eve's and Adam's temptation to eat the fruit. Likewise, in The Amber Spyglass, the mulefas' "Eve" is told to "Put your foot through the
hole in the seedpod where I was playing, and you will become wise" (224, italics in
original). Here, wisdom is the temptation, but there is no mention of rivalry with a
god or gods. Indeed, the mulefa have no concept of a god, only a symbiotic relationship with the trees whose seedpods enable them to see "sraf," their word for Dust,
which they associate with wisdom. By contrast, the human-divine rivalry implied in
the Genesis account is emphasized in the terse exchange between ex-nun physicist
Dr. Mary Malone and Dark Matter in The Subtle Knife. Mary discovers that the
elementary particles she has been researching are conscious and able to communicate with humans; they reveal that they played a role in the story of how humans
separated from animals to become conscious in their own right. Mary asks:
"And did you intervene in human evolution? — YES. —Why? — VENGEANCE.
—Vengeance for—oh! Rebel angels! After the war in Heaven—Satan and the Garden

of Eden—" (249–50). Even as the fall from innocence into experience condemns humanity to toil and want, it also begins the process by which humans become like gods.

These accounts relate a fall that is immediate and irrevocable; Adam and Eve instantly become aware of their nakedness and seek to clothe themselves. Knowledge of good and evil brings self-consciousness and shame. In Lyra's Bible, following the eating of the fruit, the man and woman also change: "*But when the man and the woman knew their own daemons, they knew that a great change had come upon them, for until that moment it had seemed that they were at one with all the creatures of the earth and the air, and there was no difference between them*" (GC 372). In the *mulefa* account, "Eve" and her mate "*knew who they were, they knew they were mulefa and not grazers. They gave each other names. They named themselves mulefa. They named the seed tree, and all the creatures and plants*" (AS 224). As in the Genesis account, Pullman's myths of the Fall emphasize coming to knowledge and experience as separation from the world; however, in Pullman's version, that split is linked with enhanced knowledge of the soul (the man and the woman "*knew their own daemons*") and the power of the word, the ability to name and to master the world through naming.[10]

When the time comes for Lyra and Will to reenact the Fall, Mary Malone, in her role as serpent, tempts them by "tell[ing] them stories" (AS 864). Unlike other accounts of the Fall, Mary's narrative emphasizes connection and recovery of the lost paradise. Mary tells of sharing food and falling in love and thereby reentering paradise: "it was like a quantum leap, *suddenly*—we were *kissing* each other, and oh, it was more than China, it was paradise" (AS 444). Eden's gate reopens not through disconnection, self-consciousness, but through the senses—taste, touch—and sexual merging. Lyra and Will are not slow to follow Mary's example, sharing "little red fruits" and confirming their mutual love (SK 465–66). Mary's stories, however, do not end with the bliss of romantic love. Instead, Mary's sensual experience deconverts her: she ceases to be motivated by belief in a God that prohibits the "treasures and strangeness and mystery and joy" of sexuality (SK 445). Having rediscovered her body, Mary's mind is liberated: "I stopped believing that there was a power of good and a power of evil that were outside us. And I came to believe that good and evil are names for what people do, not for what they are" (SK 447). Yet Mary still "misses" God: "the sense of being connected to the whole of the universe," and her sexual relationships, though intensely satisfying, are not lasting—she lives alone (SK 447). Moreover, Lyra and Will's fall is by no means cerebral, but highly emotional and sexual. Initially this new "Fall" appears to recapture Eden's bliss, to rejoin the body with the spirit, and the individual with the universe.

Despite its lyrical celebration of human sexuality and love as paradisiacal, however, *His Dark Materials* concludes not with marriage but with separation, not with rest but with labor. Experience, it seems, still necessitates pain and toil, just as the God of Genesis 3 decrees. For Pullman, though, labor in and of itself is a reward, allowing the laborer to transcend her natural limits, pushing toward the lost transcendence of Eden. Once her daemon "settles" and she declares her love for Will, Lyra loses her ability to read the alethiometer intuitively. However, she is promised the opportunity to begin studying its workings "systematically" (*AS* 515). As David Gooderham has noted in his analysis of this austere conclusion, Pullman's "closure endorses . . . no 'libidinous civilization' here; rather, . . . one powered by young people who, after the first blush of sexual experience, settle for the realism of their mentor's [Mary Malone's] single, sublimated, socially responsible, and hardworking way of life" (172). For many readers, the tragedy of Will and Lyra's separation—the diminishment implied by their being forced to return to school and domestic life after adventures in multiple worlds, the rejection of utopian bliss and a return to Eden—is not allayed by a triumphal celebration of work, no matter how gallantly Lyra and Pantalaimon declare their readiness to begin building the Republic of Heaven through their self-discipline, charity, and scholarship. What does Pullman hope to accomplish by this ending?

In offering labor and effort as the evidence and reward of experience, Pullman frequently cites German Romantic writer Heinrich von Kleist's 1812 essay "On the Marionette Theatre" (Nicholson and Parsons 117). In this essay, Kleist writes of meeting a dancer-friend in the park admiring a marionette show. The dancer asserts that marionettes are far more graceful than the best human dancer because their souls are never at odds with their bodies; human self-consciousness, by contrast, kills such grace. Kleist's speaker then recalls the moment a graceful boy he knew became awkward, a result of becoming self-conscious, aware of his resemblance to a beautiful statue. The dancer tells of a bout of fencing with a bear, whose instinct frustrates the man's most calculated feints. The men agree that the artless and intuitive grace of animals and children is superior to the conscious efforts of the artist. Yet that is not all:

> [I]n the organic world, as thought grows dimmer and weaker, grace emerges more brilliantly and decisively. But just as a section drawn through two lines suddenly reappears on the other side after passing through infinity, or as the image in a concave mirror turns up again right in front of us after dwindling into the distance, so grace itself returns when knowledge has as it were gone through an infinity. Grace appears most purely in that human form which either has no consciousness or an infinite consciousness. That is, in the puppet or in the god. (Kleist 206–7)

This characterization of the state of artistic grace suggests that consciousness and self-awareness must inevitably destroy grace. Art is an adult's attempt to recapture what childhood once freely had, and both men reference Genesis as a way of explaining the paradox that consciousness and wisdom appear to be antithetical to grace. Thinking about the circle of experience connecting puppet with god, Kleist's speaker asks, "in some bewilderment," "Does that mean [. . .] we must eat again of the tree of knowledge in order to return to the state of innocence?" His companion replies, "Of course, [. . .] but that's the final chapter in the history of the world" (Kleist 207). Kleist provided Pullman not only with an image—that of a bear fencing with a human—but also with his theme. As Pullman related in a 1999 interview:

> We lose this state of being, but [. . .] this is not something to lament because there's a sort of spectrum here. At one end, there is the inanimate grace of the puppet; at the other end, however, is the fully conscious, fully animate grace of the god. Between, there is human life. We lose the innocence that we were born with, and we then go on through life. But if we work hard, and if we train ourselves like the dancer, if we undergo all kinds of discipline, pain, suffering, and so forth, then the point is that we can regain grace (qtd. in Nicholson and Parsons 118).

Pullman's interpretation is more optimistic than Kleist's actual words would suggest: Kleist does not promise *fulfillment* of the wish to achieve the conscious grace of gods. As the dancer says, "now that we've eaten of the tree of knowledge [. . .] Paradise is locked and bolted, and the cherubim stands behind us. We have to go on and make the journey round the world to see if it is *perhaps* open somewhere at the back" (Kleist 201–2, emphasis mine). Such an accomplishment would be "the final chapter in the history of the world," at the very end of history and no more achievable than the reversal of the Fall, according to Kleist. However, Pullman uses Kleist's image of grace to offer a substitute myth. In setting "the fully conscious, fully animate grace of the god" as the goal of experience, Pullman echoes the promise the Serpent made to Eve, that "when you eat of [the fruit] your eyes will be opened, and you will be like God, knowing good and evil" (Genesis 3:5, RSV). Consciousness does not come without cost, as both Will and Lyra learn, but their unconscious restaging of the Fall overthrows the Kingdom of Heaven in order to begin building its Republic. A crucial aspect of this reconstruction is the invention of new, true stories. According to Lord Asriel, the original story of Adam and Eve is "like an imaginary number, like the square root of minus one: you can never see any concrete proof that it exists, but if you include it in your equations, you can calculate all manner of things that couldn't be imagined without it" (*GC* 372); now other stories must provide opportunities for imagining new paradigms.

The new myth Pullman has constructed is realistic in its adherence to the physical matter that makes up life. Santiago Colás has brilliantly shown how *His Dark Materials* engages with ancient and modern philosophical discourses about spirit and matter, the universe, the self, and the good. Colás argues that a "true story," such as the one that Mary tells Lyra and Will, is simultaneously "perfectly innocent" in that it does not deliberately "tempt," and also "perfectly experienced" (61) in that it tells, as clearly and as honestly as possible, what it means to live in a body in the world. Such is the story Lyra learns to tell in response to the Harpies (who are prison guards of the Land of the Dead), where she and Will have gone to see the ghost of her childhood friend Roger. For most of the series, Lyra's primary weapon has been her ability to lie, a gift that earns her the epithet "Silvertongue" from Iorek Byrnison, the armored bear who becomes Lyra's friend and protector. Lyra lies to entertain and intimidate her peers, to misdirect her enemies, to manipulate others' perception and desire. Lyra's grandiloquent storytelling casts her as the hero(ine) of her own drama in both preposterous and apposite ways—sometimes unwittingly anticipating the outlines of her own romantic saga as when she imagines (before she learns they are her biological parents) Lord Asriel and Mrs. Coulter falling in love and adopting her (*GC* 75). Lyra glories in combining and recombining the classic elements of romance: "*parents dead; family treasure; shipwreck; escape . . .*" (*AS* 292); such confabulation infuriates the Harpies, who attack her for telling "lies and fantasies" (*AS* 781). Lyra's imaginative breakthrough occurs when she discovers that even the Harpies can be nourished by "true stories" about "the world and the sun and the wind and the rain" (*AS* 317). Fittingly, the story with which Lyra enthralls the Harpies is about clay, when she and Roger played war with the clay-burners' children. Thenceforth, the dead will be able to free themselves from their prison and mingle their particles with the world of the living by telling the Harpies "true stories . . . that integrate their experience of life . . ., their experience of senso-rial ('seen and touched and heard'), affective ('loved'), and intellectual ('known') existence" (Colás 62). No longer will the dead be plagued by the Harpies' knowl-edge of the evil and vile things they experienced or felt[11]; if they have truly lived in the world and remember it, they will possess the passport to rejoin it, their dae-mons, and their loved ones. Telling true stories becomes the key to reintegration with the cosmos, consciously using experience to reassert continuity between the self and the world.

  His Dark Materials, through multiple accounts, reinvents the story of Adam and Eve as a story about humanity's accession to wisdom and refocuses attention on alternate points of view, motivations, and effects. Although the Genesis account interprets the Fall as "sin" and diminishment, Pullman's new versions shift the focus onto the desire for wisdom: in Pullman's Bible Eve wants to understand her daemon's true form; the *mulefa* desire wisdom; angels desire revenge against a tyrannical usurper who prohibits self-understanding and consciousness. This thematization (with variations) of what happens when innocence turns into expe-rience shifts the value of experience from the negative side of the binary to the positive. Yet, as Kleist laments, the only way to recover Eden's bliss is to engage in another imaginary journey—past innocence and through to the outside edge of experience (202). *His Dark Materials* opens the "back door" of Eden by retelling the myth to revalue experience, matter, and physical pleasure; yet it ends, as does the original Eden story, with an injunction to toil. As David Gooderham quips, Pullman "determin[es] to bend the old myth to his new secular purposes—and the old myth bit[es] back!" (170). Myth can subvert efforts to graft realism (as historicity and particularity) onto its structure as easily as realism can be used to subvert myth.

Democratizing the Grand Narrative

> I think the grand narratives aren't so much played out or
> exhausted in contemporary writing, as abandoned for ideo-
> logical reasons, because they're felt to be somehow impure or

improper. Maybe the whole thing is weakened by a fatal lack
of ambition.

(Pullman, qtd. in Nicholson and Parsons 117)

In the speech with which he accepted his first Carnegie award for *Northern Lights*
(the U.K. title of *The Golden Compass*), Philip Pullman gained some notoriety by
claiming that the only good storytellers in contemporary fiction were writers for
children—adult writers, he asserted, are "embarrassed" by plot and would do without it if they could ("Why Modern Literary Culture Has Lost the Plot"). By contrast, Pullman glories in classic narratives, unabashedly appropriating good ideas
and motifs from his broad reading and undertaking to put a new spin on the grand-
est narrative in Western culture: the Fall of Man. Pullman calls himself "a 1662
Book of Common Prayer atheist," which perfectly evokes the ambivalent and productive relationship *His Dark Materials* has to the Christian fantasy tradition on
which it draws (Odean 50). *His Dark Materials* self-consciously uses literary
accounts of the Fall such as John Milton's epic *Paradise Lost* and C. S. Lewis's
Chronicles of Narnia (1950–56) and *Perelandra: Voyage to Venus* (1943). It also references William Blake's subversive mythology, which reverses the values of orthodox Christianity, critiques institutional religion, and, as Carole Scott writes,
constructs "a realm where creativity knows no bounds, where heresy is laughable,
where emotions and intuition rise above reason, and where all that is emotional,
sensuous, and joyful is an aspect of 'the body divine'" (102). Pullman makes those
connections explicit with epigraphs, allusions, and even parallel plot elements.
Many correspondences exist between Pullman's trilogy and Lewis's series: Pullman
begins his fantasy epic with a child's surreptitious entrance into a wardrobe and
makes one of the chief antagonists a coldly ambitious, beautiful woman in furs;
talking animals and animal-daemons provide companionship and insight; doors
exist between worlds; and human actions have cosmic significance. Pullman also
employs the magnificent imagery of Milton's epic: an impregnable citadel, an unfathomable abyss, larger-than-life combatants, angels both good and evil, powers
and principalities. He employs epic style: epic simile to describe, for example, the
single combat between the armored bears Iorek and Iofur for the throne at Svalbard
in *The Golden Compass*, and Will Parry's realization of the incommensurability of
his desire with fate and necessity at the end of *The Amber Spyglass* (*GC* 353, *AS* 493).
Like C. S. Lewis a student of English literature and an admirer of Miltonic language,
Pullman honors the language and themes of *Paradise Lost* in the form of a children's fantasy.

Unlike Lewis, however, and in fellowship with William Blake, who memorably
declared Milton to be "of the Devil's party"(*The Marriage of Heaven and Hell*, plate
6), Pullman's characters cast their lot with seekers after forbidden knowledge, rebels, revolutionaries, and republicans. In contrast with the Platonic premise of
Lewis's *Narnian Chronicles*, which celebrates release from this world in favor of a
"Real" world beyond, *His Dark Materials* embraces the material, mortal world with

all its imperfections.[12] Like Blake's *The Marriage of Heaven and Hell*, *His Dark Materials* attempts to deconstruct the grand narrative Milton used to "justify the ways of God to Man" by reversing the poles—what was good becomes evil, and evil good; obedience to the Authority's arbitrary commands is shown to be evil, while challenging power in the pursuit of wisdom and justice is shown to be good.

Pullman says he learned to tell stories when he was a middle-school teacher seeking to engage his students' interest in fairy tales, legends, Greek myths, and epic poetry such as the *Iliad* and the *Odyssey* (Odean 50). Reworked legend and myth become "high fantasy" and clearly inform the design of *His Dark Materials*. High fantasies embody the traits of Lord Raglan's archetypal hero tale, including a child of ambiguous (unknown, frequently royal) parentage, frequently the subject of a prophecy, who, raised by foster parents, is "called" to embark on a quest, during which he or she encounters dangers and overcomes them, descends into hell, participates in a conflict of cosmic proportions, and establishes his heroism and right to kingship and immortal fame (Raglan 174–75). Though Raglan's archetypes figure in *His Dark Materials*, Pullman's narrative deliberately reverses them, critiquing the "grand narrative" of the establishment of divine kingship as inherently undemocratic and irrational: what is wanted is not the "Kingdom of Heaven," but the "Republic of Heaven" (*AS* 814).

Use of the grand narrative, however, can threaten the whole idea of a "Republic of Heaven," if "republic" means power lodged in the hands of the people and their elected officials. The stock elements of mythic romance threaten to overwhelm the goals of the trilogy by recapitulating the very patterns it claims to challenge. At the same time that it protests the unreality of romance—as when the Harpies attack Lyra for telling "lies" couched as romance—*His Dark Materials* follows romance's pattern. Lyra's central role as a child of destiny, set apart by parentage and by nature, is repeatedly confirmed by higher powers: angels and the Dust that moves the needles on the alethiometer. From the first, the Master of Jordan College knows that Lyra "has a part to play in all this, and a major one" (*GC* 31). The witches recognize her as mother of life, disobeyer, "Eve again" (*SK* 314). Angels surround Will and Lyra as they sleep, reminiscent of another nativity (*SK* 499). Stephen Thomson convincingly demonstrates that Lyra's exceptionality, her aristocratic parentage, and her noble attributes reinforce ideas that birth and breeding define one, even as characters attempt to establish a more democratic order (154). Thomson exposes the "tricky double shuffle" that exhibits Lyra as "at once only one individual child and representative of all children. Following the odd logic of the exemplary, [Lyra] represents 'the child' *better* than other children" (153). This logic tacitly recapitulates the same essentialist errors of the cult of childhood innocence. Observing the narrative arc of the romance (even while ironizing it), *His Dark Materials* actually naturalizes feudal social relations (Thomson 152–54). Lyra is destined by birth and breeding to liberate her world.

One of the series' solutions to the problem presented by predestination in a book about the end of destiny is to make Lyra *unconscious* of what she is *supposed* to do.[13] The Master says "she must do it all without realizing what she's doing"

(*GC* 24), and in the first two volumes, Lyra does fulfill her destiny through a combination of willful disobedience—recapitulating the example of her foremother Eve—and a strong, if frequently irregular, sense of accountability. Especially in *The Golden Compass*, Lyra's disobedient spirit propels the action: forbidden to enter the males-only Retiring Room, she there observes the Master of Jordan College pouring poison into Lord Asriel's wine and so saves Lord Asriel's life and his mission; she resists Mrs. Coulter's instruction in properly seductive femininity while discovering important information about the Church's activities; at the book's conclusion, she determines to work against both her father and her mother by seeking out Dust in order to "cherish" it. Yet Lyra is not motivated only by contrarity; she actively seeks justice and reparation for those who have been dispossessed—of liberty, of status, or of life. She desires to go North in the first place to save her friend Roger and the other kidnapped children, and through a brilliant trick she provides the opportunity for a dispossessed king to come into his own. Lyra convinces the usurper Iofur to fight Iorek in single combat by concocting a story calculated to appeal to her antagonist's psychological vulnerability. After Roger's death, Lyra resolves to aid all who fight the Church and its representatives and to rescue Roger from the Land of the Dead.

In *The Subtle Knife*, however, the disobedient willful spirit that has up until this point served Lyra so well begins to dissolve. Chastened by her inexperience and ignorance, and particularly pained by the temporary loss of the alethiometer, Lyra becomes uncharacteristically docile in Will's Oxford, promising only to consult the alethiometer to aid Will, obedient to its command (*AS* 259–60). From here, Will, as suits his name, becomes the agent who disobeys angels, fights to the death, and earns the right to bear the subtle knife. Settling into conventional gender roles (Will as protector and heir of his father's "mantle," Lyra as protected one and faithful friend), the children succumb, as do their daemons, to a script mandated by their predetermined roles. By the end of the series, even after demolishing the theocratic structure of her world and establishing the Republic of Heaven, Lyra's desire cannot move, any more than Will's can, "the iron-bound coast of what had to be" (*AS* 493). Neither can they make a story in which their desire is fulfilled.

In a narrative ostensibly about the reinstatement of free will in a world usurped by an imposter-god, Lyra and Will must nonetheless submit to the grander narrative. As messiah of her world, Lyra liberates it, and legions of the dead, from the Authority's prison, yet almost immediately her self-determination, power, and desire are baulked. As Lyra and Will puzzle over John Parry's final message to his son, that "we have to build the Republic of Heaven where we are [, because] . . . for us there isn't any elsewhere" (*AS* 488), Lyra realizes that she has lost her ability to read the alethiometer. The rebel angel Xaphania, an embodiment of wisdom and testimony to the limitations of the reality principle, confirms that along with destiny, grace has disappeared or been postponed in Lyra's world. What is left is "a lifetime work," which may recapture in some part the fullness of understanding, the connection with the universe, and the perfect love that, until now, Lyra and Will had experienced freely, through childhood's grace. Xaphania affirms that they are both assigned "other work," and Will realizes he would rather not know what it is, to give himself the illusion, if not the reality, of choice:

> "What work have I got to do, then?. . . . No, on second thought, don't tell me. *I* shall decide what I do. If you say my work is fighting, or healing, or exploring, or whatever you might say, I'll always be thinking about it. And if I do end up doing that, I'll be resentful because it'll feel as if I didn't have a choice, and if I don't do it, I'll feel guilty because I should. Whatever I do, I will choose it, no one else."
> (*AS* 496)

Xaphania tells him, "Then you have already taken the first steps toward wisdom" (*AS* 496). In this context, it appears that wisdom seeks *not to know* one's predestined fate, a paradoxical turn in a narrative celebrating Eve's pursuit of knowledge. Rather, the wise understand life to be a series of choices, each of which opens up other possibilities and challenges, something Lyra and Will have intuitively understood. Grace now is only attainable through work and choice.

What author's logic insists upon this end? Lyra's realistic and mundane resolution to be "all those difficult things like cheerful and kind and curious and patient, . . . to study and think and work hard" (*AS* 518) fails to negate the text's use of the marvelous and mysterious registers of destiny: how *does* Lyra come to be chosen as "Eve, again"; does her flawless execution of the prophecy to bring about the "end of destiny" undercut or validate the notion of fate? What remains is an unanswered question about the motive force behind destiny, a question that might be answered by Tolkien's notion that the story is independent of the individual author (Tolkien 127). Thus, the death of one god in *His Dark Materials* only buries the question of destiny, which is now removed from the purview of an individualized deity and becomes instead an effect of matter's desire "to know more about itself" (*AS* 31–32). In Pullman's humanist transcendentalism, humanity fell not because it pursued knowledge but because it feared it. As Dark Matter or Dust, individual consciousness becomes reified into collective consciousness. Dust—or clay or matter—now is understood as constitutive of human identity, and to know more about Dust is to know more about the self.

This more diffuse rendition of destiny potentially remains deterministic, albeit at a remove. Pullman's epic inveighs against predestination, but the trilogy palimpsestically reinscribes the epic formula, organizing its materials so that predictions come true. However, as the mechanisms become clear, the trilogy shows that a single ordering intellect is unnecessary—there is no guiding deity, and characters act as if they are destined as they step into the roles they play, becoming versions of Asriel's imaginary numbers. By placing heaven within Lyra's and, by extension, every reader's grasp, *His Dark Materials* reinvents, makes republican, a heaven as it demolishes the Kingdom of Heaven. As Anne-Marie Bird has shown, positioning Dust as the mechanism behind destiny does not reduce destiny to a single totalizing narrative in the style of previous grand narratives. Dust is "a system characterized by contingency and uncertainty," which permits "an open, more egalitarian vision" of conscious endeavor (197). Dust—us—feeds and is fed by consciousness and can act only through the will of sentient beings and their determination to interpret the world by making stories about it. Will and Lyra, despite their separation, can still resolve and evolve to bridge the distance between worlds by means of love and imagination (*AS* 912) by remembering their childhoods as fraught with earthly conflict and joy rather than succumbing to the Romantic amnesia that misremembers childhood as innocent and bodiless.

CONCLUSION

His Dark Materials poses answers to long-standing questions about the best way to teach children to understand themselves, their bodies, and their place in the world. Using the story of Adam and Eve but reimagining and recombining individual characters, motives, and actions, *His Dark Materials* encourages critical engagement with foundational myths of Western culture. Rather than obeying myths blindly, storytellers and readers might tease out possible meanings, other ways of interpreting truth. To become conscious of myth in the context of history as an evolving and changing means of understanding one's self in relation to the cosmos, to others, and to self—rather like Dust—is to become critically aware of the ways in which stories define children and adults, as subjects and objects in great dramas. Changing a story can change the course of history. Yet stories exert their own power upon the imagination, as testified by *His Dark Materials'* challenge in making a grand narrative do something . . . different. With its gestures toward self-conscious self-determination and the achievement of grace through hard work and sacrifice, *His Dark Materials* places the fate of free will and consciousness in multiple worlds in the hands of a boy and a girl—children. Pullman thus expresses faith in his young readers, in children's ability to "begrace" themselves, to begin the arduous process of achieving grace through experience.

His Dark Materials legitimately and usefully challenges deeply entrenched notions that children are best kept innocent and that one's physical, material, and sexual existence is less significant than the spiritual. Sexuality is a fitting site for the contest between forces of innocence and experience because of its inescapably material, physical aspect and its role as the mechanism of natural selection's rich variety. Against a totalitarian narrative that privileges the One, the Pure, the Almighty, sexuality (with its anarchic subversion of intention, its messiness, its ability to overwhelm judgment and morality, even its unexpected and uncontrollable combinations of DNA) challenges the simple binary value system that decrees one thing naturally good and another naturally bad. As storytellers make new choices, and as their listeners in turn reproduce and recombine the old tales, perhaps "natural selection," combining imagination and knowledge, may evolve ways of telling new stories about the transition from innocence to experience.

NOTES

1. References to individual volumes of *His Dark Materials* are complicated by differences between U.K. and U.S. editions. This essay cites the first U.S. editions by Knopf: *The Golden Compass* (*GC* in text), *The Subtle Knife* (*SK* in text), and *The Amber Spyglass* (*AS* in text). It's important to note, however, that the first U.K. volume was entitled *Northern Lights* and that the first U.K. edition of *Amber Spyglass* included epigraphs not printed in the first American edition.

2. Although the origin of the concept that the child is essentially separate from adult modes of being is generally attributed to Jean-Jacques Rousseau, the English Romantics, especially Wordsworth, Coleridge, Lamb, and de Quincey, disseminated the principles of Romantic childhood in England (Plotz 3–4). This cult not coincidentally produced the first "golden age" of children's literature; the impossible and imaginary construction of the Romantic child through children's literature has been admirably analyzed by Jacqueline Rose.

3. Peter Coveney's landmark study, *Poor Monkey: The Child in Literature* (1957), first made this observation, which has been taken up more recently by such writers as Laurence Lerner in *Angels and Absences: Child Deaths in the Nineteenth Century* (1997) and by Judith Plotz in *Romanticism and the Vocation of Childhood* (2001). Similar observations have been made of constructions of Victorian domesticity and womanhood, beginning with Virginia Woolf's recommendation that women kill the angel in the house (Barrett 60).

4. Goethe's 1782 poem by that name recounts the story of an uncanny supernatural being who tries to tempt a beautiful boy away from the protection of his father during their journey through a dark forest. At the end of the journey, the boy is dead, taken by the Erl King.

5. The works of Jacqueline Rose and James Kincaid provide important interventions into this topic: Rose's 1984 *Case of Peter Pan, or, The Impossibility of Children's Literature*, points out that the "childhood" premised by children's literature is more of an order—or at least a "seduction"—to children who may or may not value the image thus promoted (2). Kincaid's *Child-Loving: The Erotic Child and Victorian Culture* (1992) also targets adult desire as the key component of the construction of the innocent child, not least because it allows adults a blank canvas upon which to paint their fantasies (13). George Boas, in *The Cult of Childhood* (1966), traces the history of the apotheosis of childhood in pictorial art from medieval depictions of Christ as an infant to the establishment of the artist-child as the pinnacle of authentic, unrepressed humanity at the turn of the nineteenth and twentieth centuries. Childhood innocence, which Boas demonstrates to be an ambiguous term at best, no more serves children than does the notion of original sin.

6. "Understand a Little More"; Pullman's review advocates Morrison's attempt to understand *how* such things can happen rather than simply condemning the perpetrators. In chapter 4 of *The Amber Spyglass*, Pullman makes use of the gibbon incident when Mrs. Coulter's golden monkey daemon—surely the very opposite of innocent—similarly rends a bat. I discuss this connection and expand upon its implications in "Dismembered Starlings and Neutered Minds."

7. Further critiquing thoughtless valuations of innocence, the Authority himself is described in his doddering senility as "innocent"; "demented and powerless," he has "no will of his own" and responds "to simple kindness like a flower to the sun" (*AS* 410).

8. For a full account of this interpretation, see C. S. Lewis, *A Preface to Paradise Lost*.

9. C. S. Lewis, in *A Preface to Paradise Lost*, follows St. Augustine's interpretation and uses the same ideas in his adult fantasy *Perelandra: Voyage to Venus* (1943). For alternate histories, see Elaine Pagels's account of gnostic interpretations in *Adam, Eve, and the Serpent*. For a discussion of Milton and Blake in relation to Pullman, see Carole Scott's "Pullman's Enigmatic Ontology: Revamping Old Traditions in *His Dark Materials.*"

10. Rose's analysis of the problem of language in children's literature argues that this utopian view of language cannot hold. Lacan's theorization of the alienated effect of the split consciousness provides a tragic counternarrative to most children's literature's more optimistic treatment of language. Lacan highlights language's role in mastering, dominating, and fragmenting the self (Rose 12ff). For more on the relationship between Lacanian theory and children's literature, consult the work of Karen Coats, particularly *Looking Glasses and Neverlands; Lacan, Desire, and Subjectivity in Children's Literature* (2004).

11. In this prison camp of the afterlife, the Harpies torture ghosts with stories of their darkest secrets, a privilege granted them by the Authority.

12. For a compelling and illuminating discussion of the philosophical bases for *His Dark Materials*, including the ideas about materiality and spirituality proposed by Plato, Hume, Heidegger, and others, see Colás.

13. This prophecy, clearly linked to the notion of innocence, encodes both the childlike grace that Lyra embodies and its transience—she will have one opportunity to subvert the wrongful enshrining of innocence as an ultimate virtue. As I show in the following discussion, Lyra's innocent confidence of action is muted by experience in the second book of the series and both undercuts and reinforces the superiority and inevitability of experience. The task presented to both protagonists at the series' end is to accept innocence's death and meet experience with the knowledge that grace *might* be recoverable with sufficient effort.

WORKS CITED

Barrett, Michèle, ed. *Virginia Woolf on Women & Writing.* London: Women's Press, 1979.

Bird, Ann-Marie. "Circumventing the Grand Narrative: Dust as an Alternative Theological Vision in Pullman's *His Dark Materials.*" In Lenz and Scott, *His Dark Materials Illuminated* 188–98.

Blake, William. *The Marriage of Heaven and Hell.* Reprinted in *The Norton Anthology of English Literature*, vol. 2, 7th ed., edited by M. H. Abrams, 72–82. New York: W.W. Norton & Co., 2000.

Boas, George. *The Cult of Childhood.* London: The Warburg Institute, 1966.

Coats, Karen. *Looking Glasses and Neverlands; Lacan, Desire, and Subjectivity in Children's Literature.* Iowa City: U of Iowa P, 2004.

Colás, Santiago. "Telling True Stories, or the Immanent Ethics of Material Spirit (and Spiritual Matter) of Philip Pullman's *His Dark Materials.*" *Discourse* 27, no. 1 (2005): 34–66.

Coveney, Peter. *Poor Monkey: The Child in Literature.* London: Rockliff, 1957.

Cunningham, Hugh. *The Children of the Poor: Representations of Childhood Since the Seventeenth Century.* Oxford: Blackwell, 1991.

Giroux, Henry. "Nymphet Fantasies: Child Beauty Pageants and the Politics of Innocence." *Social Text* 57 (Winter 1998): 31–53.

Gooderham, David. "Fantasizing It As It Is: Religious Language in Philip Pullman's
     Trilogy, *His Dark Materials.*" *Children's Literature* 31 (2003): 155–75.
Kincaid, James. *Child-Loving: The Erotic Child and Victorian Culture.* New York:
     Routledge, 1992.
Kleist, Heinrich von. "On the Marionette Theatre." Translated by Idris Parry. In *Essays on
     Dolls.* London: Penguin/Syrens, 1994. Reprinted in *Darkness Visible: Inside the World of
     Philip Pullman,* by Nicholas Tucker, 197–207. Cambridge: Wizard Books 2003.
Lenz, Millicent, and Carole Scott, eds. *His Dark Materials Illuminated: Critical Essays on
     Philip Pullman's Trilogy.* Detroit: Wayne State UP, 2005.
Lerner, Laurence. *Angels and Absences: Child Deaths in the Nineteenth Century.* Nashville:
     Vanderbilt UP, 1997.
Lewis, C. S. *Perelandra: Voyage to Venus.* London: John Lane, 1943.
———. *A Preface to Paradise Lost.* London: Oxford UP, 1961.
Nicholson, Catriona, and Wendy Parsons. "Talking to Philip Pullman: An Interview." *The
     Lion and the Unicorn* 23, no. 1 (January 1999): 116–34.
Odean, Kathleen. "The Story Master." *School Library Journal* 46, no. 10 (October 2000): 50.
Pagels, Elaine. *Adam, Eve, and the Serpent.* New York: Random House, 1988.
Plotz, Judith. *Romanticism and the Vocation of Childhood.* New York: Palgrave, 2001.
Postman, Neil. *The Disappearance of Childhood.* New York: Delacorte Press, 1982.
Pullman, Philip. *The Amber Spyglass.* New York: Knopf, 2000.
———. *The Golden Compass.* (Published in the U.K. by Scholastic as *Northern Lights,* 1995)
     New York: Knopf, 1996.
———. *The Subtle Knife.* New York: Knopf, 1997.
———. "Understand a Little More." Review of *As If,* by Blake Morrison. *The Independent*
     (London) 1 February 1997: Books. Lexis-Nexis. Hale Library, Manhattan KS. Accessed
     18 December 2008. http://www.lexisnexis.com.
Raglan, FitzRoy Richard Somerset. *The Hero.* New York: Vintage Books, 1956.
Richardson, Alan. "Romanticism and the End of Childhood." In *Literature and the Child:
     Romantic Continuations, Postmodern Contestations,* edited by James Holt McGavran,
     24–43. Iowa City: U of Iowa P, 1999.
Rose, Jacqueline. *The Case of Peter Pan, or, The Impossibility of Children's Fiction.* London:
     Macmillan, 1984.
Scott, Carole. "Pullman's Enigmatic Ontology: Revamping Old Traditions in *His Dark
     Materials.*" In Lenz and Scott, *His Dark Materials Illuminated* 95–105.
Thomson, Stephen. "The Child, the Family, the Relationship. Familiar Stories: Family,
     Storytelling, and Ideology in Philip Pullman's *His Dark Materials.*" In *Children's
     Literature: New Approaches,* edited by Karin Lesnik-Oberstein, 144–67. London:
     Palgrave Macmillan, 2004.
Tolkien, J. R. R. "On Fairy Stories." In *The Monsters and the Critics and Other Essays,*
     edited by Christopher Tolkien, 109–61. London: George Allen and Unwin, 1983.
"Why Modern Literary Culture Has Lost the Plot." *The Independent* (London), 18 July
     1996: Leader. Lexis-Nexis. Hale Library, Manhattan, KS. Accessed 28 February 2009.
     http://www.lexisnexis.com.
Wood, Naomi. "Dismembered Starlings and Neutered Minds: Innocence in *His Dark
     Materials.*" In *Navigating the Golden Compass,* edited by Glen Yeffeth, 15–24. Dallas:
     BenBella Books, 2005.
Wordsworth, William. "Ode: Intimations of Immortality from Recollections of Early
     Childhood." Reprinted in *The Norton Anthology of English Literature,* vol. 2, 7th ed.,
     edited by M. H. Abrams, 287–92. New York: W.W. Norton & Co., 2000.

FURTHER READING

Bird, Anne-Marie. "Dust, Dæmons and Soul States: Reading Philip Pullman's His Dark
   Materials." *British Association of Lecturers in Children's Literature Bulletin* 7 (2000):
   3–12.

Brooke-Rose, Christine. *A Rhetoric of the Unreal: Studies in Narrative and Structure,
   Especially of the Fantastic*. Cambridge: Cambridge UP, 1981.

Gilead, Sarah. "Magic Abjured: Closure in Children's Fantasy Fiction." *PMLA* 106, no. 2
   (March 1991): 277–93.

Gray, William. *Fantasy, Myth and the Measure of Truth: Tales of Pullman, Lewis, Tolkien,
   MacDonald and Hoffman*. Palgrave MacMillan, 2009.

Hopkins, Lisa. "Dyads or Triads? His Dark Materials and the Structure of the Human." In
   Lenz and Scott, *His Dark Materials Illuminated* 48–56.

Jackson, Rosemary. *Fantasy: The Literature of Subversion*. London: Methuen, 1981.

Keane, Beppie. "Of the Postmodernists' Party Without Knowing It: Philip Pullman,
   Hypermorality and Metanarratives." *Papers: Explorations into Children's Literature* 15,
   no. 1 (2005): 50–58.

Rutledge, Amelia. "Reconfiguring Nurture in Philip Pullman's *His Dark Materials*."
   Children's Literature Association Quarterly 33, no. 2 (Summer 2008): 119–34.

Shohet, Lauren. "Reading Dark Materials." In Lenz and Scott, *His Dark Materials
   Illuminated* 22–36.

Index

Abate, Michelle, on tomboyism, 498, 503, 508, 514n9
Aberson, Helen, 151
abolitionism, 505
Ackerley, J.R., 461
activism, 288, 521–22
Adam/Eve, 417–18, 555
    fall of, 546–47, 549, 551
    reinventing, 550
Adams, James Eli, 468
Adams, Maude, 485–87, 489
Adams, W. Davenport, 477
Addams, Jane, 149
adolescent crush, 456
adolescent literature, 16, 381, 383, 505, *See also*
        young adult literature
    of 1970s, 522, 523
adoption
    discourses of, 28, 336, 344
    laws on, 320, 325n12, 342
    promotion of, 330
    public discourse on, 331–32, 343
    suitability for, 344–45
adult(s)
    children v., 39
    comics as, 168–69
adult audiences
    child audiences v., 9. *See also* cross-writing,
        reader, readership, reading.
    comics for, 168–69
adulthood, as concept, 41
adult literature, children's literature v., 24
Adventures of Bill and Tom with their Dog Jack
        (Hale, Charles), 448–49
Adventures of Huckleberry Finn (Twain), 293, 295
The Adventures of Tom Sawyer (Twain), 27,
        293–95, 296–307
affection, 423–24, 456
African American(s), 160, 163n23, 367, *See also*
        Harlem Renaissance
    as primitive, 140
    black art, 134
    children's literature, 130, 132, 372, 376, 385–86
    music, 140
    Taylor on, 372
    Twain on, 298
age
    coming of, 280–85
    of consent, 423
    of menarche, 46

agency, 30
    denial of, 172
    innocence and, 15–17
The Agony in the Kindergarten (Steig), 183
Aladdin and the Wonderful Lamp (Mackinstry), 123
Alberghene, Janice M., 504
Alcott, Louisa May, 295, 297, 324n9
Alda, Alan, 520
Aldrich, C. Anderson, 156
Aldrich, Mary, 156
Aldrich, Robert, 463
Alger, Horatio, 314–16, 322
Alice and Other Fairy Plays for Children
        (Freiligrath-Kroeker), 481
Alice's Adventures in Wonderland (Carroll), 23,
        35–36, 39–43, 45, 47, 48
    books of analysis of, 38
    as classic, 37–38
    as reflection of tormented soul, 44
    review of, 484
    translations/representations of, 37–38
Alice to the Lighthouse (Dusinberre), 178
alternative comics, 178. *See also* comics
The Amateur Emigrant (Stevenson, R.), 275
The Amber Spyglass (Pullman), 542, 546
American Born Chinese (Yang), 14, 26, 231, 234, 235,
        236f–237f, 237–8, 239f, 240f, 241–42, 245–46,
        245f–246f. *See also* Monkey King story
    audience for, 244
    awards for, 247n4
    genre blending in, 243
    storylines of, 232
    success of, 232, 245
American Character, 353
American Indians, 27, 428n9
    burials of, 302
    difficulties faced by, 306
    literary image of, 300
    as objects of study, 299
    Puritan fears about, 301
    Scheckel on, 297
    skulls of, 299
    stereotype of, 297
    subtextual discourse on, 303–4
    as trope, 301
    Twain on, 297–306
American individualism. *See* individualism
American Library Association's *Notable Books of
        1969*, 524–25

anapestic tetrameter, 189
Anderson, Benedict, 331, 423
Anderson, Celia, 190, 206
anger, 213, 219, 221–22, 227n7
The Animal Family (Jarrell), 53
Animal Life in the Alpine World (von Tschudi), 224
Animals, 59, 546, 548
    as characters, 55, 57, 61, 63, 64, 66, 71, 73, 75–88,
        88n6, 151–55, 163n14, 194, 197–99, 202, 203,
        233, 235–37, 244, 540, 551
Anne of Green Gables (Montgomery), 28, 332,
        334–42, 344–45
    adoption promotion by, 330
    context of, 330–31
    criticism of, 330
    gender in, 330
    history in, 333
    iconic status of, 345
    plot of, 343
    success of, 329
Anstey, F., 284
anti-Chinese sentiment, 243
Apollonian, Dionysian and, 82–83
Apseloff, Marilyn, 190, 206
Ardizzone, Edward, 44–45, 124
Arendt, Hannah, on Jarrell, 58
Are You There, God? It's Me, Margaret (Blume),
        28, 351, 353, 355, 357–67
    criticism of, 352
    opening of, 352, 354
    social change in, 356
Ariès, Philippe, 15
Arno, Peter, 123
Arnold, Thomas, 468, 470n8, 471n11
art comics, 181
asexuality, 468
Asian American children's literature, 241–43
Asian American literature, 234, 241
Asian Americans, 367, 404n5
asylums, reputations of, 341–42
"Atalanta," 528, 530
    original myth of, 529
Atwood, Margaret, 276, 343
Auden, W.H., on children's books, 106
audience, 64–65, 294–295, 476, 479 *See also* reader
        /readership/reading
    adult v. child, 9, 45
    of *American Born Chinese*, 244
    Chicano, 394
    of *The Circuit: Stories from the Life of a Migrant
        Child*, 390, 404n2
    crossing, 93–108, 297
    of *The Dream Keeper*, 131
    of *Free to Be...You and Me*, 520
    of *Harry Potter* series, 95–97, 105–106
    interracial, 131
    of *Peter Pan*, 483–84
    of *Tom Sawyer*, 294–97
Austen, Jane, 95–96, 108n4

authority figures, 422–23, 509
autobiography,
    and Blume's *Are You There God*, 353
    and Jiménez, 392–93, 404n1
    and Taylor's Logan trilogy, 372–73
Avi (pen name), 512
Ayres, Bill, 506

Babies are Human Beings (Aldrich, M. & Aldrich,
        C.), 156
Bader, Barbara, 212–13
    on *Kenny's Window*, 219
Bakhtin, Mikhail, 190
    on carnivalesque setting, 192–94
Ball, John Clement, 222
"Ballad of a Thin Man" (Dylan), 199–200
Ballet Shoes (Streatfeild), 109n8
Balmoral Castle, 286
Bambi (Disney), 151
Barks, Carl, 168
Barmby, J., 480
Barnaby (Johnson, C.), 171
Barnardo, Thomas, 333–34
Barnardo children, 332–33, 335, 337–39, 341
Barnardo homes, 333, 337–38, 344
Barrie, J.M., 30, 48
    on acting of a fairy play, 482
    casting choices by, 486–87
    extreme opinions of, 475–76
    habit of attributing authorship to children,
        482–83
    praise for, 482
Bartholomew and the Oobleck (Seuss), 191
    controversy of, 195–96
Baruch, Dorothy, 213–14
    case study by, 219
    on child-rearing, 157–58, 161–62
Batey, Mavis, 43
The Bat-Poet, 13, 23, 53–55, 57, 59, 62–66
    Nodelman on, 60–61
    Thomas, Joseph on, 56, 58, 61
Baxter, Charles, 282
Baym, Nina, 320
Beerbohm, Max, 487–88
bee reading, 420–21
Beginner Books, 74
behaviorism, 151, 156
Bell, Ian, on *Kidnapped*, 285
Belladonna: A Lewis Carroll Nightmare (Thomas,
        D.), 38
Bennett, John, 119
Berlant, Lauren, 403, 405n10
Bettelheim, Bruno, 225, 227n9
*Between Men: English Literature and Male
        Homosocial Desire* (Sedgwick), 85
Bible
    incarnations of, 417
    progressive reading of, 420–21

bibliotherapeutic texts, 219–20

bildungsroman
    Harry Potter series as, 24, 94–97, 100, 103
    Kidnapped as, 280
    principal elements of, 95, 108n3
Bird, Anne-Marie, 554–55
Birkin, Andrew, 481–82
The Birth of Tragedy (Nietzsche), 82
Bishop, Elizabeth, on Jarrell, 57
Blackbeard, Bill, 170
black children. *See also* African American(s) and
        African American children
    cultural position of, 138
    educational pressures on, 139
Black Misery (Hughes, L.), 129
Black Panthers, 201
Black Student Alliance, 374
Blake, William, illustrated work of, 75
Blanchard, E.L., 477
Bleak House (Dickens), 267–68
*Bloody Jack: Being an Account of the Curious
        Adventures of Mary "Jacky" Faber, Ship's Boy*
        (Meyer), 515n20
blues poetry, 133–37
blues songs, 136
Blume, Judy, 28, 45, 353–67
    awards of, 351–52
    censorship of, 351
    taboo topics of, 351
Blyton, Enid, 97, 99–100, 109n8
Boas, George, 541, 556n5
Bobby Make-Believe (King), 169
Bontemps, Arna, 129–30
book
    as beloved object, 412, 416, 422, 425
    as child creation, 438–51
Book-of-the-Month Club, 498
Books, Children, and Men (Hazard), 7
Boone, Troy, 14
Boop, Betty, 149
Booth, Wayne, 95
Borges, Jorge Luis, 276
Bosmajian, Hamida, 378, 380–81
Boucicault, Nina, 487
Bourdieu, Pierre, 223, 317
boy book, 296, 306n1, 306n4 *See also* school story
boyhood, parameters of, 531
boyology, 3, 212
boys' school story. *See* school story
Bradbury, Charles, 337
Bram, Christopher, 86
Bratton, Jacqueline, 478
Breaking Through (Jiménez), 389–90
breeding, 322–23
    poverty v., 316
Brenda (pseud. of Georgina Castle Smith), 14,
        255, 257–59, 260, 267–68
    agenda of, 262
Brink, Carol Ryrie, 498

Britain, nineteenth century
    children in, 256–57
    city composition in, 271
    poverty in, 257, 334
    and race, 101
    and social class, 101
British Invasion, 193
British North America Act, 330
British public schools, 469n1
    homosocial environment of, 458
    Reed on, 456–57
    Sedgwick on, 458
Brode, Douglas, 84, 86
Brodhead, Richard, 316
bromance, 88n9
Brooks, Cleanth, 65, 67n5
Brown, Margaret Wise, 183, 214
Brown, Matthew P., 417, 420–21
Brown, Sterling, 135
Brown, William Wells, 302
Browne, Anthony, 74
Brownmiller, Susan, 506
de Brunhoff, Jean, 124
Burke, Martin J., 317
Burnett, Frances Hodgson, 284
Burt, Stephen, 58–59, 62, 68n14
Burton, Virginia Lee, 123
Busch, Wilhelm, 169–70
Buster Brown (Outcault), 169
Butler, Judith, on sexuality, 511
The Butter Battle Book (Seuss), 193
Byatt, A.S., 105, 107, 108n2

Caddie Woodlawn (Brink), 498, 503, 525
    heroine of, 507
    MacLeod on, 501–2
    punishment in, 511
Caldecott, Randolph, 124
Caldecott Medal, 8, 212
Calder, Jenni, 286
Calico Bush (Field), 498, 502, 508
    heroine of, 507, 514n10
Calvin and Hobbes (Watterson), 171
Calvinism, 285
    Jacobitism and, 286
Calvino, Italo, 276
Campe, Joachim Heinrich, 435–36
Canada, 330–31, 333–34, 336, 339, 345
    and national identity, 332–33, 345
canonicity, 6, 31, 54–55, 498, 512
capitalism, 191
    industrial, 24
di Capua, Michael, 53, 57
Carlyle, Thomas, 469
    on hero worship, 470n3
Carnegie Medal, 8
carnivalesque, 190, 192–194, 196, 197, 206
    Bakhtin on, 192–94

carnivalesque(*Continued*)
  function, 196
  humor, 192
  traditions, 194–95
Carroll, Lewis, 23, 35–37, 39–44, 48–49, 477
  Cohen on, 45–46
  as infamous/controversial, 36, 44, 47
Carson, Norma Bright, 314–15
*The Case of Peter Pan, or The Impossibility of
    Children's Fiction* (Rose), 45, 476, 556n5
Castañeda, Claudia, 13
castaway
  concept of, 434–35
  playing, 442
  stories, 439
The Cat in the Hat Comes Back (Seuss), 191, 193
The Cat in the Hat for President (Coover), 198–99
The Cat in the Hat (Seuss), 26, 74, 189, 193, 196,
    199, 202f, 203–4.
  animated version of, 199
  children in, 200, 205–6
  as overtly political, 197–98
  as response to Dick and Jane books, 198
Catriona (Stevenson, R.), 276
Cavett, Dick, 520
Cech, John, 212
*Centuries of Childhood: a Social History of Family
    Life* (Ariès), 15
Chao, Patricia, 234
character development, 94–97, 284
Charlieshope Library, 439, 441f, 445, 450
Chase, Pauline, letters to, 485
Chavez, Leo, 391–92, 395
Chen, Debby, 235
Chesterton, G.K., 276
Chicano
  literature, 394, 399, 404n4
  movement, 394
  studies, 404n2
Child, Lydia Maria, 302, 424–25
child-centered model, of childhood. *See*
    permissive model, of childhood
child characters, in comics, 169–70
child/children. *See also* street children, child
    development, childhood
  adults v., 39
  African American, 130–34, 138–42, 372, 373
  authorship by, 482–83
  as blank slates, 418, 428n10
  in Britain, nineteenth century, 40, 256–57
  cruelty among, 174
  drawing, 214–15, 441, 446
  as emotionally priceless, 16
  in Harlem Renaissance, 130labor
  in Canada, 334–36, 344
  meaning of, 10, 14
  orphaned, 337–38, 340
  pantomimes and, 477
  as performers, 486

  protection of, 175–76
  rights of, 325n12
  Sánchez-Eppler on, 13–14
  as savage, 13–14, 258–259, 265–266
  second-wave feminism and, 522–23
  Seuss on, 191, 200, 205–6
  as theater reviewers, 489
  theatricals by, 480
  as vehicles for social change, 25, 134, 142, 143,
    285, 374, 375, 381
child development
  in *Kidnapped*, 280–81
  movies and, 148–50
child emigration schemes, 333–36
childhood. *See also* child/children
  as category of analysis, 3
  cult of, 541
  as dependent state, 81
  disappearance of, 16, 542
  innocence, *See* innocence
  meanings of, 10, 14, 16
  "New Negro," 131, 134–135, 141–42
  permissive model of, 151, 157
  popular ideas of, 173–74
  reading, *See also* audience, reading, child
    reader
  romantic, 48, 556n2
  Schulz on, 183
  and segregation, 135
  of Sendak, 211, 223
  studies, 6, 232
  Twain on, 296–97
*Childhood, Culture and Class in Britain: Margaret
    Macmillan* (Steedman), 16
*Child-Loving: The Erotic Child and Victorian
    Culture* (Kincaid), 556n5
child placement, 321
child reader, 39–41, 62, 80, 105, 106, 130, 262,
    266–67, 415–16, 435. *See also* reader.
  African-American, 136, 139–40, 143, 379, 382,
    426
  as hybrid, 415
  self-creation of, 416
  white, 450.
child-rearing, 9, 220–21, 524
  Baruch on, 157–58, 161–62
  Dixon on, 159, 161
  in early America, 428n15
  gender distinct, 504
  Hulbert on, 213
  management-oriented, 156–57
  Mead on, 157, 162
  permissiveness, 151, 157
children's books. *See* children's literature
*Children's Books in England: Five Centuries of
    Social Life* (Darton), 7
children's culture, 5, 10
  dismissive attitudes towards, 182
  political possibilities of, 521

children's culture (*Continued*)
  popular, 523
  tropes of, 521
  visual imagery in, 12
children's labor, 335–36, 341
  demand for, 334
  legal restrictions to, 334
  productive, 541–42
children's literature, 36, 41, 45, 49, 94, 103, 104,
    106–8, 294–96. *See also*, African American,
    Asian American, Mexican-American
  adult literature v., 24
  African American, 130–143, 372, 376, 385–86
  Asian American, 401–3
  approaches to, 5, 7–8, 456
  boundaries of, 103–4
  censorship of, 45
  Chicano, *See* Mexican American
  critical study of, 7, 37
  critics, 44–47
  cross-written nature of, 9, 104, 130
  definition of, 9, 47–49
  development of, 8
  and ethnicity, 242. *See also* African Ameri-
    can, American Indians, Asian American,
    Chicano
  financial success of, 104
  formative effects of, 9
  genres of, 94–108, 276. *See also* genre.
  history of, 7–8
  Hunt on, 108n1
  as impossible, 3–4
  legitimacy of, 104–5, 107
  Mexican American, 394, 399, 404n.4
  movies as, 148, 150, 162
  multi-racial, 14 *See also* African American,
    American Indians, Asian American, Chicano
  queer theoretical approach to, 456
  sexuality in, 83–88. *See also* sexuality
  slavery in, 139
  study of, 7–10, 57, 72, 294
  teaching of, 38, 54–55, 60, 65, 72, 73, 78, 87, 242,
    245
*Children's Literature: Criticism and the Fictional
  Child* (Lesnick-Oberstein), 18n3
Children's Literature Association, 7–8
children's literature criticism, 4, 18n3
  fundamentals of, 35–49
  possibilities of, 5
  protective impulse in, 72–73
children's needs, assumptions about, 4
children's play, pedagogical value of, 16
children's rights activism, 522
children's theater, 476–77. *See also* theater.
  criteria for, 478–79
  history of, 490
  intertheatrical approach to, 478–80
  subversion of, 487–88
  Twain and, 481

children's writing, scavenging and, 434–35
child-rescue discourse, 343
A Child's Garden of Verses (Stevenson, R.), 275
The Child That Books Built (Spufford), 9
Chinese Exclusion Act, 242
The Chinese Siamese Cat (Tan & Schields),
  240–41
Chrisman, Arthur Bowie, 119
Christian Socialism, 455
The Christmas Gift/El Regalo de Navidad
  (Jiménez), 390
Chubb, Percival, 160
Cichetti, Dante, 401
*The Circuit: Stories from the Life of a Migrant
  Child* (Jiménez), 14, 29, 389, 391, 395–403
  audience of, 390, 404n2
  as autobiographical, 392–93, 404n1
  confessional writing style of, 390
  social/political issues in, 402
  Spanish in, 393–94
The City (Masereel), 123
Civil Rights Act, 375
civil rights movement, 191, 193, 196, 372, 386
  Free to Be. . .You and Me and, 522
  Taylor, M., and, 373–74
*Clara Andrews and Her Friend who Lived in a
  Tree*, 450
Clarence and Corinne (Johnson, A.), 385
Clark, Beverly Lyon, 13, 27, 104
Clark, Kenneth, 160
Clark, Mamie, 160
Clarke, Henry Savile, 477
class/classes, 13–14, 28, 97, 315, 316, 320
  behavior and, 157
  and caste, 101
  family and, 323
  sociological studies of, 317
  tensions between, 262–63
classism, 335
The Class Structure of the Advanced Societies
  (Giddens), 317
Clemens, Samuel Langhorne. *See* Twain, Mark
Clever Bill (Nicholson), 124
Clotel (Brown, W.), 302
Cohen, Donald, 401
Cohen, Morton N., on Carroll, 45–46
Colás, Santiago, 549
Collins, Bernard, 489–90
colonization, 449
  colonial encounters, 405n6
  legitimization of, 257
  power and, 257, 451
Colvin, Sidney, 288
Comedy (Stott), 83
comedy duos, 82
  as same sex, 83–85
Comenius, 10–11
comic books. *See* comics
comics. *See also* graphic novel.

comics (*Continued*)
  accomplishments for, 181–82
  as adult, 168–69
  alternative, 178
  American, 170–71
  art, 181
  child characters in, 169–70
  critical study of, 168
  cross-writing and, 169
  emergence of, 243
  as extension of popular journalism, 170
  psychiatric language in, 175
  as reclamation project, 178
comic-strip child. *See also* strip kid
  historical development of, 25
  lasting angst of, 175
The Commonsense Book of Baby and Child Care
  (Spock), 157
community, 142–43
competition, friendship and, 79–80
Complete Peanuts (Seth), 178–79
Condition of the Working Class in England
  (Engels), 262–63
conformity, 367
  individualism and, 155–56, 352, 354–55
  Riesman on, 353–54
A Connecticut Yankee in King Arthur's Court
  (Twain), 293
Conroy, Pat, 303
Constructing the Canon of Children's Literature
  (Lundin), 104
consumerism, 191
contact zones, 405n6
contextualization, as interpretive tool, 277
A Contract with God and Other Tenement Stories
  (Eisner), 246n3, 248n18
The Conundrum of Class (Burke), 317
conversion narratives, 419, 427n4
Coover, Robert, 198–99
"Cop-Out" genre, 526, 533–34
  tomboy tradition and, 525
Cott, Jonathan, 223–24
The Country Bunny and the Little Gold Shoes
  (Heyward), 215
Cox, James M., 305
Cox, Richard, 121
Cradle of Liberty: Race, the Child, and National
  Belonging from Thomas Jefferson to W. E. B.
  DuBois (Levander), 14
Craft, Ellen, 138
Craft, William, 138
critical literacy, 10. *See also* literacy
  improvement in, 75
  primer for, 71–88
critical reading practices, 24. *See also* reading
  McGillis on, 72
  resistance to, 72–73
critical theory, prestige of, 55
criticism, 55, 73. *See also* children's literature criticism

Crockett, Lucy Herndon, 123
Crofters' Holdings Act, 288
Crofters' War, 287–89
Crosby, Percy, 171, 176
cross-writing, 9–12, 61, 104
  comics and, 169
  definition of, 68n10, 169
  The Dream Keeper as, 130
  Harry Potter series and, 107
  influence of, 178
  Knoepflmacher on, 61, 169
  Myers on, 61, 169
  Peter Pan as, 489–90
  in poetry, 62, 142
  by Schulz, 178, 184–85
  by Twain, 295
Cruse, Howard, 176
crush(es), 459, 460–3,
  467, 470n5
  adolescent, 456, 459–60
  broader implications/uses of, 460–61
  on officers/administrators, 463–64
  spiritual salvation and, 467–69
Cuban Missile Crisis, 193
Cullen, Countee, 131, 135, 140
Culloden, Battle of, 278
The Cult of Childhood (Boas), 541, 556n5
cultural relativism, 300
cultural status, 392
cultural studies, 10. *See also* children's culture
cultural transformation, 232
culture. *See also* children's culture; mass culture;
  popular culture
  boy, 296
  complexity of, 339
  consumer, 10, 522
  dominant, 340
  folk, 138
  formation of, 451
  gendered, 504
  ideological constructions of, 87
  nature and, 330
  production of, 223
  religious, 415, 421
  sixties, 192–93
Cultures of Letters (Brodhead), 316
Cummins, June, 13, 28
Cunningham, Hugh, 541–42

Dahl, Roald, 277
Dalgliesh, Alice, 121–22
Danish, Barbara, 526
Danny the Champion of the World (Dahl), 277
Darrow, Whitney, Jr., 525
Darton, F.J. Harvey, 456
  on *Peter Pan*, 476
Darton, Harvey, 7
Davidson, Donald, 67n5

Davies, Arthur Llewelyn, 475
  sons of, 48
Davin, Anna, 271
Davis, Desmond, 38
Davis, Grania, 235
Davis, Whitney, 224
Days with Frog and Toad (Lobel), 72, 85f
death
  "good," 268–69
  jokes about, 43
Decent and Indecent (Spock), 532
Declaration of Independence, 402–3
declension narrative, 522
Deenie (Blume), 351
Defoe, Daniel, 433, 435–37, 440, 449, 451
democracy, founding principles of, 314
demon child, 170
demonic adult, 420
Dennis the Menace (Ketcham), 171
*Dependent States: The Child's Part in
    Nineteenth-Century American Culture*
    (Sánchez-Eppler), 13–14
development, physical, 98, 355–56
Devereux, Cecily, 335
Dick and Jane books, 74, 75, 88n2
  responses to, 198
Dickens, Charles, 267–70
diction
  of Dick and Jane books, 75
  of *Frog and Toad Together*, 75
Did I Ever Tell You How Lucky You Are? (Seuss),
    193, 201
Dimock, Wai Chee, 314
Dionysian, Apollonian and, 82–83
Dirks, Rudolph, 169–70
The Disappearance of Childhood (Postman), 542
disciplinary intimacy, 316
discipline, excessive, 425
Disney, Walter Elias, 25, 147–62. *See also* Walt
    Disney Productions
  as disingenuous, 150–51
  hands-off approach of, 147
Disney stories, plots of, 150–52
Distinction (Bourdieu), 317
*Disturbing the Universe, Power and Repression in
    Adolescent Literature* (Trites), 381
Dixon, Madeleine, on child-rearing, 159, 161
doctrine of free grace, 418
doctrine of harmony, 317–18
Dodge, Mary Mapes, 324n9
Dodgson, Charles Lutwidge. *See* Carroll, Lewis
domestic novels, 507
domestic orientalism, 258
  power of, 257
domestic role, of women, 525
domestic spaces, construction of, 447–48
Dong, Lan, 12, 26
Donnelly, Jennifer, 106
double spreads, 122–23

Douglas, Aaron, 141
Douglass, Frederick, 138
Dow, Bonnie, 506
Downright Dencey (Snedeker), 498, 502–3
  friction in, 508
  publication of, 504
  punishment in, 510–11
Dr. Seuss's ABC (Seuss), 193, 196
The Dragon and the Doctor (Danish), 526
Drain, Susan, 331
drama, 478, 555
  of exclusion, 319
Drawing the Dream of the Wolves (Davis, W.), 224
The Dream Keeper (Hughes, L.), 12, 25, 129,
    135–36, 139–43
  audience of, 131
  cross-writing and, 130
  emotions explored in, 132
  final section of, 137–38
  first section of, 132–33
  interracial audience of, 131
  recent edition of, 131
  second section of, 133
  third section of, 133–34
Dreams of Authority (Thomas, R.), 217
Duane, Anna Mae, 415
Du Bois, W.E.B., 131, 134–35, 138, 140–41
Dumbo (Disney), 25, 149–50, 153–55, 162
  animator's strike during, 147
  as children's literature, 148
  crows in, 155f, 158–61
  military motifs in, 152f
  obstacles faced in, 158
  plot of, 151–52
  production of, 157
  release of, 156
  as warning to children, 160
Dunbar, Paul Laurence, 133
Duncan's Kingdom (Yang), 231
Durivage, Robert, 450
Dusinberre, Juliet, 178, 181
Dusk of Dawn (Du Bois), 140
Dylan, Bob, 199–200

Eagleton, Terry, on New Criticism, 75
Eco, Umberto, 176
economic identity, 317
Eddy, Jacalyn, 216
education,
  children's books as, 245, 412–14
  for African American children, 138–39, 372, 374–75
  British, 256, 270
  and citizenship, 342
  for the poor, 264
  Progressive, 214, 226n2
  sexism and, 524–27
Education: Intellectual, Moral, and Physical
    (Spencer), 13

Edwards, Cliff, 155, 163n17
egocentrism
    deconstruction of, 394
    transcendence of, 401
Eisenstein, Sergei, 153
Eisner, Will, 246n3, 248n18
Elliott, Michele, 46–47
Ellis, Havelock, 459–60
Elster, Charles, 98
Emile (Rousseau), 443
Emma (Austen), 95–96
emotional self-awareness, 156–57
employment discrimination, 375
Engels, Friedrich, 262–63
English Victorian child, conceptualization of, 40
Epstein, Lawrence J., 84
Eric, or Little by Little (Farrar), 457, 464–67
    dangerous crush in, 461–62
The Eternal Smile: Three Stories (Yang & Kim), 231
ethnic children's literature, 242. *See also* African
    American children's literature, Asian
    American children's literature, Mexican
    American children's literature
ethnicity, 368n8
    as problematic, 81
    study of, 232, 241
ethnic purist, 364
ethnic stereotypes, 26
Ets, Marie, 213
evangelical writers, 267–71
Evans, Ernestine, 117
Exactly Like Me (Phillips), 526
existentialism, 202–4

Fables (Lobel), 71
fag, as term, 470n9
fairy tales, 79
fairy-tale formula, 118
    traditional period close for, 440
Fame and Fortune (Alger), 315
family
    biological, 323
    class and, 323
    in *Froggy's Little Brother*, 263–64
    ideal, 321–22
    notions about, 28
    surrogate, 320
Family Circus (Keane), 171
family instruction, 436
family lore, 384–85
family story, 316
fantasy, 94, 100, 102–3, 109n11, 540
    animal, 81
    hybrid, 101
    instrumentalization of, 225
farm labor camp, 396
Farrar, Frederic, 457, 464–65
fatherhood, 282, 356, 380, 385

father-son relationship, 276–77, 282–83
Fauset, Arthur Huff, 141
Fauset, Jessie, 131
Feiffer, Jules, 176
Feininger, Lyonel, 169
female adventure story, 507
feminine/masculine
    domains of, 227n5, 511
    female/male v., 84
    others as, 272n8
femininity, traditional, advantages/costs of, 527–28
feminism, 193. *See also* second-wave feminism;
        second-wave feminist activism
    as challenge to gender norms, 31
    increasing, 505
    liberal, 533
    power and, 85
    public image of, 506
    scholarship of/on, 534
feminist parenting goals, 523
The Feminist Press, 526
feminists, presence of, 524
Feminists on Children's Media, 524
feminist studies, 456
feral tales, 212
Field, Rachel, 498
field of cultural production, 223
Field of Nonsense (Sewell, E.), 196–97
The Fifth Form at St. Dominic's (Reed, J.), 457
figuration, of development, 13
Figurations: Child, Bodies, Worlds (Castañeda), 13
film appreciation movement, 499
films. *See* movies
Findlay, Ellen, 335
Finger, Charles, 118
first-person narrative, 238
First Term at Malory Towers (Blyton), 99–100
Fisher, Margery, 88
    on Frog and Toad stories, 73
Fitzhugh, Louise, 74
The 500 Hats of Bartholomew Cubbins (Seuss), 191
Five Little Peppers and How They Grew (Sidney),
        14, 28, 313–23, 324n4
    contemporary reviews of, 314–15
    paradox of, 316
Five Little Peppers Midway (Sidney), 318, 325n14
Fletcher, Robert P., 177
Fliegelman, Jay, 423
Fly By Night (Jarrell), 53
Flynn, Richard, 10, 13, 23
folklore, folktales, folk motifs/expressions, 73,
        115–120, 135–39, 141, 243
follow-up review, 488–89
food scavenging, 397
For Better or for Worse (Johnston), 171
Forever (Blume), banning of, 45
For Freedom (Fauset, A.), 141
formalism, 74–75
Forman, Henry James, 149

foster care, 344
  public discourse on, 331–32
foster parents, 338–39
Fox in Socks (Seuss), 193, 196
Frahm, Ole, 177
The Franklin Circulating Library, 438–42, 446,
  447*f*
Frederick (Lionni), 60, 68n9
Freedom, 29, 375
  denial of, 48–49
  images of, 510
  social, 364
Freedom Summer, 375
Free to Be. . .You and Me (Thomas, M.), 17, 31, 519,
  521, 525, 528–32, 534
  book version of, 520
  civil rights movement and, 522
  Grammy nomination of, 520
  influence of, 522
  inspiration for, 523–24
  as nostalgic touchstone, 533
  politics of, 522
  popularity of, 520, 522, 526–27
  possible readings of, 522
  target audience of, 520
  on traditional children's texts, 521
  writings on, 522–23
free will, reinstatement of, 553–54
Freiligrath-Kroeker, Kate, 481
Freud, Sigmund, 213–14, 216–18, 221, 224–25
  Sendak and, 219
friendship
  competition and, 79–80
  detrimental, 465–66
  romantic, 459, 462, 464, 469n2
  sexual, 464
The Friendship (Taylor, M.), 372
Frog and Toad All Year (Lobel), 72, 76
Frog and Toad Are Friends (Lobel), 72
Frog and Toad stories (Lobel)
  common themes of, 87
  complexity of, 73
  darker side to, 73, 80
  Fisher on, 73
  humor in, 82–83
  illustrations of, 75
  obsessive compulsive disorder in, 73
  paradox of, 76
  skills learned through, 72
  Walsh on, 73
Frog and Toad Together (Lobel), 24, 71–72, 74, 77*f*,
  81–82
  action initiation in, 78
  complexities of, 75–76
  homosexual subtext in, 85–87
  gender/sexuality in, 83–88, 88n8
  genres of, 81–83
  humor in, 78, 82–84
  initial reaction to, 75

irony in, 78–80
Newbery Honor award of, 73
plots in, 78–79
Froggy's Little Brother (Brenda), 14, 27, 261*f*, 265*f*
  agenda of, 262
  appeal of, 260, 265–67
  childhood in, 264–65
  cover of, 256*f*
  family depiction in, 263–64
  honorable characters in, 261–62
  postcolonial perspective on, 258
  readership of, 257–58
  religious symbolism in, 269
Fromm, Erich, 220
The Frumious Bandersnatch (McBain), 38
full animation, 153, 163n16
Fussell, Paul, 460–61, 463–64

Gág, Wanda, 24, 118
  author/illustrator reputation of, 115, 124
  black/white illustrations of, 123
  commercial opportunities of, 116
  exhibitions of, 117
  hardships of, 119
  idealism of, 125
  influences of, 123
  passions of, 126n9
  pastoralism of, 119
  as quintessential modernist, 116–17
  roots of, 115, 119
  vision of, 122
gag cartoons, 123
Gaines, Kevin K., 134
Gammel, Irene, 330, 332
Gardner, Howard, 214
Gardner, Martin, 46
Garner, Alan, 277
Geisel, Theodore Seuss. *See* Seuss, Dr.
gender
  in *Anne of Green Gables*, 330
  child-rearing and, 504
  cultural constructions of, 84
  distinctions of, 445
  equality/equity, 505–6, 521
  in *Frog and Toad Together*, 83–88
  identity, 525, 532
  politics of, 301–2
  social constructedness of, 534
  socialization, 521
  tropes, 524
gendered power, visibility and, 524–25
gender norms, 511
  feminism as challenge to, 31
  loosening of, 450
  in *The Swiss Family Robinson*, 445
  in visual imagery, 525
gender roles, 84, 509–10
gender stereotypes, 520, 524

gender studies, 87–88
Genesis, story of, 546–47
genre, 6
    blending, 93–108, 243
    "Cop-Out," 525–26, 533–34
    criticism, 81, 87–88
    emphasis on, 56
    fiction, 107
    of *Frog and Toad Together*, 81–83
    multiple, 419
    strip, 171
Gerhardt, Lillian, 505
Giddens, Anthony, 317
Gillis, John, 451
Gilman, Susan Jane, 533
The Gingerbread Rabbit (Jarrell), 53
A Girl Called Al (Green, C.), 525
girlhood, parameters of, 531
girls' canon, adult-approved, 498–99
Giroux, Henry A., 272n5, 542
Glass, Buddy, 44
Glorious Revolution, 278, 284, 286–87
God
    contact with, 412
    divine law of, 414
God's Man (Ward), 123
Godwin, Mary, 437
Godwin, William, 437
The Gold Cadillac (Taylor, M.), 372
The Golden Compass (Pullman), 539, 543–44, 546,
    553
    award for, 551
Goldschmidt, A.M.E., 46
Goldstein, Philip, 294
Gooderham, David, 548
Goodnight Moon (Brown, Margaret), 183
Goodwin, Polly, 506
Gordon Yamamoto and the King of the Geeks
    (Yang), 231
Gore, Arthur Jocelyn Charles, 266–67
Governor General's Literary Award for Chil-
    dren's Literature and Illustrators, 8
Grahame, Elspeth, 48, 86
grandmother, role of, 357–58
grand narrative
    democratizing, 550–55
    use of, 552
Grant, Joe, 147
graphic novel, 12, 26, 245. *See also American Born
    Chinese*
    definition of, 246n3
    educational value of, 248n17
    popularity of, 243
    reconfiguration of, 244
Gray, Harold, 171
Great Depression, 148, 156, 161, 378–79
Great Migration, 136
Green, Constance, 525
Green, Roger Lancelyn, 476

Greenacre, Phyllis, 46
Greenaway, Kate, 124
Green Eggs and Ham (Seuss), 189, 193–94, 196
Greenwich Village folk scene, 193
Grenby, M.O., 13, 17, 25
Griever, An American Monkey King in China
    (Vizenor), 234
Groensteen, Thierry, 184
Gross, Milt, 123
*Growing Up Poor: Home, School and Street in
    London 1870–1914* (Davin), 271
Gubar, Marah, 16, 30

habitus, 223
Hacker, Marilyn, 56
Hader, Berta, 123
Hader, Elmer, 123
Hager, Kelly, 13–14, 28
Halberstam, Judith, on sexuality, 511
Hale, Charles, 446, 448–49
Hale, Edward Everett, 445–46
Hale, Ellen Day (Nelly), 439, 441–42, 441f, 445
Hale, Nathan, 438
Hale, Sarah, 438
Hale families, 440, 443
    papers of, 447f
half-breed, *See* individuals
Halfway Covenant, 415
Hall, David D., 412
Hans Brinker (Dodge), 324n9
Harlem Renaissance, 131
    aesthetic energies of, 134–35
    child's place within, 130
    context of, 141
    power during, 139
    spirit of, 143
Harnick, Sheldon, 520
Harold and the Purple Crayon (Johnson, C.), 215
Harriet the Spy (Fitzhugh), 74
Harris, Benjamin, 411
Harry Potter series (Rowling), 24, 93, 98–99,
    101–2, 107–8
    audience, 103–106
    as *bildungsroman*, 24, 94–97, 100, 103
    educational setting of, 97
    Hunt on, 106
    popularity of, 94
    Ratzinger on, 45
    reviews/criticisms of, 104–5
Harry Ransom Center, 38
Hart, Bruce, 520
Hart, Carole, 520
Hartman, Charles, bibliography of, 415
Haskin, Sara Estelle, 141
Hatfield, Charles, 12, 25
Hays Office, establishment of, 149
Hazard, Paul, 7
Heaney, Seamus, 105

heart
    as seat of knowledge, 414, 427n6
    as site of change, 422
heart-piety, 420
He Done Her Wrong (Gross), 123
Heer, Jeet, 178
Heins, Marjorie, 15
Hendler, Glenn, 301–2, 315–16
Hensher, Philip, 105–6, 108n2
Hentoff, Nat, 136
Hergé, 168
hero worship, 456, 469
    benefits of, 462–63
    Carlyle on, 470n3
heteronormative narrative, 532
heterosexuality, 459
Heyward, Du Bose, 215
The Hidden Adult, Defining Children's Literature
    (Nodelman), 47, 223
Hidier, Tanuja Desai, 243
high culture, mass culture and, 62
Highland Clearances, 287
Highland Rebel (Watson, S.), 497
Highland Scotland dialect, 277–78
Highland v. Lowland Scotland, 285–86
His Dark Materials (Pullman), 17, 31, 106–7, 539,
    542, 546, 548, 552–55
    characters in, 540–41
    destiny in, 554
    plot of, 540–41, 543–44, 547, 549–50, 552–54
    protagonists in, 545
    tradition of, 551
historical fiction, 276–78, 372, 376, 385, 507
history,
    African American, 372, 375–76, 385
    biases of, 138
    as context for interpretation, 276
The Hobbit (Tolkien), 277–78
Hobomok (Child), 302
Hoffman, Abbie, 198
Hogan's Alley (Outcault), 169
A Hole Is to Dig (Krauss), 211
Hollinger, David, 365–66
Hollingshead, John, 262–63
Holm, Anne, 276
Homecoming (Voigt), 276
homelessness, depiction of, 395–96
homemade toy book, 117–18
home theatricals, popularity of, 480–81
homoeroticism, 84–85
    in schools/school stories, 458–59
homophobia, 85
    Sedgwick on, 87
homosexuality, 84–86, 471n11, 515n17
    anxiety about, 531–32
    and boys' boarding schools, 456, 458, 459, 461
    language of, 458–59
    latent, 225
    Lobel and, 85–86

Sendak and, 223, 226
    Spock and, 532
homosocial, 85–87, 458
homosocial desire, 30, 458
homosocial networks, 30
*Hooligans or Rebels? An Oral History of
    Working-Class Childhood and Youth
    1889–1939* (Humphries), 271
Hop on Pop (Seuss), 193, 196
The Horn Book, 8
Horton Hears a Who! (Seuss), 189, 191,
    193, 196
Howey, Ann, 416
How the Grinch Stole Christmas (Seuss), 189, 191,
    193, 196–97
Hubler, Angela, 533–34
Huemer, Dick, 147, 160–61
Hughes, Langston, 12, 25, 129, 131–32, 134, 136, 138–43
    assumptions about, 135
    Communist leanings of, 143
    literary elite on, 134
    musical interests of, 137
    popularity of, 130
    world travels of, 133
Hughes, Thomas, 97
    education of, 455
Hulbert, Ann, 213
human development, biological history of, 13
Humble Comics, 231
Humphries, Stephen, 271
Hunt, Peter, 8–10, 23, 104
    on children's literature, 108n1
    on Harry Potter series, 106
The Hunting of the Snark (Carroll), 36, 41
Hurston, Zora Neale, 131, 135
hybrid fantasy, 101

I Am David (Holm), 276
I Can Read books, 74, 86, 88
iconography, attention to, 12
identity
    American, 352, 360–61, 367, 402
    black, 137
    categories of, 101
    consent-based, 360, 367
    as culpable, 546
    economic, 317
    ethnic, 360
    formation, 245
    gender, 525, 532
    group, 367
    liberty and, 297
    national/racial, 13–14, 360, 365–67, 368n2
    post-ethnic, 28
    pursuit of, 242
    of reader, 40–41
    religious, 28, 355–56, 358–59, 361–65, 367, 414
    Sollors on, 360–61

identity politics, 232
ideologies of difference, 101–2
I Had Trouble in Getting to Solla Sollew (Seuss), 196
illegal immigrants, 391
    status of, 403
illustrated folktale collections, popularity of, 118–19
illustration(s), 10–13. *See also specific illustrators/ stories*, children (drawing), picture books. style of, 116
image, as structuring category, 12
imaginative work, construction efforts and, 446–47
Imagined Communities (Anderson, B.), 423
I'm Glad I'm a Boy! I'm Glad I'm a Girl! (Darrow), 525
immigrant realities, 400. *See also* Mexican immigrants
immigration discourse, 403
immigration history, 29
imperialist nostalgia, 301
Indians. *See* American Indians
individualism, 148, 161–62, 367
    celebrating, 151, 155–56
    conformity and, 155–56, 352, 354–55
    patriarchalism and, 413
infant depravity, 15
infantilization, 281
informed consent, 423
Injun Joe (character), 27, 299–306
inner-directed society, 353, 362, 364
    Riesman on, 356, 359
Inness, Sherrie A., 460
innocence, 557n13
    adult investment in, 478
    agency and, 15–17
    as boundary, 17
    challenges to, 555
    in childhood, 15, 42
    children's books and, 41–42
    discontents of, 541–45
    experience and, 540, 555
    fall from, 545
    fetishization of, 544–45
    as myth, 542
    as negative, 543
    privilege of, 31
    revised myth of, 546
    Romantic ideal of, 257, 264–65
    Schulz on, 173–74
innocence profiling, 272n5
The Innocents Abroad (Twain), 295
institutions
    adult, 174–75
    children and, 342
    reputations of, 341–42
integrity, value of, 378–79
intent by author, affect on reader v, 36–37
intermarriage, 360–61, 368n7

The Interpretation of Dreams (Freud), 216
irony, in *Frog and Toad Together*, 78–80
It's a Good Life, If You Don't Weaken (Seth), 179
Iwerks, Ub, 147

Jabberwocky (Carroll), 38
Jack, R.D.S., 475–76
Jackson, Helen Hunt, 306
Jack Tokera, 446, 448f
Jacobite Rising/Rebellion, 278, 281, 286–88
Jacobitism, 287
    Calvinism and, 286
Jade (Watson, S.), 16–17, 31, 497–98, 502–4, 507–9
    dominant image pattern of, 510
    lack of recognition for, 499, 515n20
    negative review of, 505
    as new tomboy model, 512
    punishment in, 511
    as romantic, 505–6
    summary of, 500–501
Jager, Eric, 414
James, Henry, 276
Janeway, James, 15, 419
Jarrell, Randall, 55–66
    Arendt on, 58
    awards of, 54, 57
    Bishop on, 57
    on dialectical theory of poetry, 58, 67n7
    education of, 53, 57, 67n5
    Lowell on, 54, 64
    marriages of, 53–54
    McCarthyism and, 59
    Nodelman on, 61
    poetic structure theories of, 62
    on poetry, 60
    on poets, 54
    postwar aesthetic of, 58–59
    postwar subject matter of, 59
    on reading, 62
    Sendak on, 54
Jehlen, Myra, 314
Jenkins, Henry, 191, 199, 206
Jewish identity, 358, 359, 361–66
Jiménez, Francisco, 14, 29, 396–403
    autobiographical work of, 392–93, 404n1
    background of, 389–91
    education of, 389
    linguistic choices of, 394
    publications of, 389–90
Jimmy Corrigan: The Smartest Kid on Earth (Ware), 179–81, 180f
Jo, Flo, and Yolanda (De Poix), 526
Johnson, Amelia E., 385
Johnson, Crockett, 171, 183, 211, 215
Johnson, Dianne, 134
Johnson, Georgia Douglas, 131
Johnson, James Weldon, 138, 143
Johnston, Lynn, 171

Jones, Katherine, 416
Jones, Lois Mailou, 141
The Journey to the West (sixteenth century Chinese novel), 233–35, 247n10, 247n11. *See also* Monkey King story
Junior Literary Guild, 498
Juvenile Miscellany (Child), 424–25

Kannenberg, Gene, 181
Kate Greenaway Medal, 8
The Katzenjammer Kids (Dirks), 169
Keane, Bil, 171
Kellogg, Susan, 220
Kelly, Eric P., 119
Kelso, J.J., 337, 341, 344–45
    appointment of, 335–36
Kempler, Anita, 71
Kenny's Window (Sendak), 213–18
    Bader on, 219
Ketcham, Hank, 171
Kidd, Kenneth, 11, 26, 86, 279
    on Newbery Medal, 499, 513n3
Kiddie Lit (Clark, B.), 104
Kidnapped: Being Memoirs of the Adventures of David Balfour in the Year 1751 (Stevenson, R.), 27, 275
    Bell on, 285
    as *bildungsroman*, 280
    character development in, 284
    child development in, 280–81
    coming of age and, 280–85
    context of, 277, 285–90
    as historical/national novel, 286
    motifs/themes of, 277, 282–83
    plot of, 282
    problems of, 276–80
    as propaganda, 288–89
    setting of, 278
    strengths of, 279–80
    structure of, 279
    tone of, 277
Kidscape, 46
The KIDS Fund, 351
Kim, Derek Kirk, 231
Kincaid, James, 556n5
The Kinder-Kids (Feininger), 169
King, Frank, 169
Kingsley, Charles, 468
The King's Stilts (Seuss), 191, 196
Kingston, Maxine Hong, 234
Kingston, William Henry Giles, 438
Kipling, Rudyard, 457, 465
Kissell, Mary, 120, 126n8
KKK. *See* Ku Klux Klan
Klein, Melanie, 214, 219
Klein, Norman, 153
von Kleist, Heinrich, 548–49
Knoepflmacher, U.C., 9–10
    on cross-writing, 61, 169

knowledge
    book, 443
    heart and, 414, 427n6
    mutual respect for, 98
    school, 243
Krasner, David, 134
Krauss, Ruth, 211, 214–15
Ku Klux Klan (KKK), 379, 384–85
Kushner, Tony, 212, 226, 227n11
Kyle, Richard, 246n3

labor, cheap, need for, 335–36. *See also* children's labor
"Ladies First," 527–28
Laing, R.D., 202
land, back to the (movement), 354
land ownership, 372–73, 376, 378
    commitment to, 379–80
    importance of, 374
    protection of, 378–79, 381
    sacrifice for, 377
    sharecropping and, 386n3
    transfer of, 379
The Land (Taylor, M.), 372, 376
Lang, Amy Schrager, 317
Lark Rise to Candleford (Thompson, F.), 270
Larsen, Nella, 302
learning
    as collaborative endeavor, 99
    lifelong, 98
    race/class, 13–14
Legion of Decency, 149
Legitimist Jacobite League, 287
Lehmann-Haupt, Hellmut, 124
Lennon, Florence Becker, 46
Lesnick-Oberstein, Karín, 18n3
Let the Circle Be Unbroken (Taylor, M.), 372
Levander, Caroline F., 14
Lewis, C.S.
    on children's books, 41, 106
    Pullman and, 551–52
Licensed to Hug, 45
Liddell, Alice, 35, 38, 42
Life and Correspondence of Thomas Arnold (Stanley), 468
Life in Search of Readers: Reading (in) Chicano/a Literature (Martín-Rodríguez), 394
Life on the Mississippi (Twain), 293
limited omniscient point of view, 95–96
Lindner, Robert, 159–60
Lionni, Leo, 60
literacy, 72, 74, 384, 428n9. *See also* critical literacy
literary fiction, future of, 93–108
literary salvaging, 439
literary theory, 332
literature, 352, 435 *See also* children's literature, African American, Asian American, Chicano, Mexican American

literature (*Continued*)
    adolescent, 16, 505, 523,
    adult v. children's, 24. *See also* cross-writing.
    movies as competition to, 148
    as vehicle for social change, 25
    visual-verbal, 124. *See also* picture books.
Little Bear (Minarik), 74
A Little Book for Little Children (White), 419
Little Friend, Little Friend (Jarrell), 53
Little Golden Books, 8
Little Goody Two Shoes: or, Harlequin Little Boy Blue (Blanchard), 477, 480, 488
Little House series (Wilder), 498, 501, 503
    friction in, 508
    heroine of, 507
    punishment in, 510
Little Jimmy (Swinnerton), 169
Little Lord Fauntleroy (Burnett), 284, 295
Little Nemo in Slumberland (McCay), 169, 217
Little Orphan Annie (Gray), 171
Little Red Hen Makes a Pizza (Sturges), 11–12
Little Strangers (Nelson), 325n12
The Little White Bird (Barrie), 475
Little Women (Alcott), 295, 324n9
    Christmas playacting scene in, 480
    as "Cop-Out" genre, 525
Lobel, Arnold, 24, 71–88
Locke, Alain, 135, 138–39
Lofting, Hugh, 118–19
Logan, Taylor, 29
Logan family novels, 29, 371–86
Lollipop Power, 526
The Lonely Crowd (Riesman), 352, 364
    popularity of, 353
    preface to, 359
The Lorax (Seuss), 191, 193, 205–6
Losses (Jarrell), 53
The Lost World (Jarrell), 54, 61–63, 66n2
Lothrop, Harriett Mulford Stone. *See* Sidney, Margaret
Lowell, Robert, 56, 67n5
    on Jarrell, 54, 64
Loyola Chin and the San Peligran Order (Yang), 231
Lucas, Audrey, 484
Lucio and His Nuong (Crockett), 123
Lucy Brown and Mr. Grimes (Ardizzone), 44–45
Lundin, Anne, 104
Lurie, Alison, 529

MacDonald, George, 74
MacDonald, Ruth, 191, 198–99, 205–6
Macherey, Pierre, 332
Machor, James L., 294
Mackail, Denis, 483–84
Mackinstry, Elizabeth, 123
MacLeod, Anne Scott, 505
    on children's literature, 523
    on tomboy tradition, 501–2

Macmillan Publishers, 8
Making American Boys: Boyology and the Feral Tale (Kidd), 212
manhood, 446
    sensitive/expressive models of, 531
The Manliness of Christ (Hughes, T.), 455
maple-sugar child, 132–33
Marcus, Leonard S., 212–13, 215–16
La Mariposa (Jiménez), 390
Marqusee, Mike, 200–201
Marshall, James, 226
Martin, Alice, 134
Martin, Michelle, 13, 29
Martín-Rodríguez, Manuel, 394, 405n9
Marvin K. Mooney Will You Please Go Now! (Seuss), 194
Marxism and Literature (Williams, R.), 339–40
Masereel, Frans, 123
Maslow, Abraham, 220
mass culture, 59
    high culture and, 62
    movies as, 149
Massee, May, 122
Masterton, Graham, 38
masturbation, 351
Mather, Cotton, 418–19, 427n7
Matthews, Gareth B., 80
maturation, in children's literature, 401
du Maurier, Angela, 484–85
Maury, Inez, 526
Max und Moritz (Busch), 169
Mayhew, Henry
    articles by, 259, 262–64
    diatribe by, 260
    taxonomy of, 259
Mayne, William, 46
McAleavey, David, 56
McBain, Ed, 38
McCarthy, Cormac, 277
McCarthyism, Jarrell and, 59
McCay, Winsor, 169, 217
McCrum, Robert, 105
McFadden's Row of Flats (Outcault), 169
McGillis, Roderick, 213, 221
    on Blake, 75
    on critical reading, 72
    on Oedipal experience, 222–23
McManus, George, 169
McNutt, James C., on Twain, 300, 306n7
Mead, Margaret, on child-rearing, 157, 162
media. *See also* children's literature, comics, literature, movies
    influence of, 359
    production of, 402
    visual, 12
Meigs, Cornelia, 122–23
melting pot, 361
The Melting Pot (Zangwill), 361
menarche, age of, 46

Menefee, Joan, 215
Menikoff, Barry, 282
menstruation, 351
Messent, Peter, 305
meter, 56
Mexican American children's literature, 394, 399, 404n.4
Mexican immigrants, 391, 403, 404n5, 405n10
  perceived as opportunistic, 395
Meyer, L.A., 515n20
Michaelis, David, 174, 184
Michaelsen, Scott, 303
Mickenberg, Julia, 5, 226n2
Middle Earth, 277
migrant families
  emotional toll on, 397–98
  experiences of, 393, 395
  living conditions of, 396–97
  social invisibility of, 402
  status of, 392
  struggles/resiliency of, 391, 397, 399–400, 403, 405n11
Mike Mulligan and His Steam Shovel (Burton), 123
Miki: The Book of Maud and Miska Petersham (Petersham, M. & M.), 118, 123
Miles, Betty, 529
Miller, Flournoy, 155
Miller, J. Hillis, 434, 437
Miller, Kelly, 143
Million, Elmer M., 303
Millions of Cats (Gág), 24, 115–16, 122–23
  archetypes in, 121
  as canonical text, 125
  as commentary on violence, 121
  originality of, 118
  origin of, 117–18
  plot of, 119–21
  reputation of, 124
  setting of, 118
Minarik, Else, 74
mind, development of, 98
Minear, Richard, 191
Mintz, Steven, 213, 220, 514n11
  on gender distinct child-rearing, 504
Mirror (Masterton), 38
mise-en-scène, 278
Mississippi Bridge (Taylor, M.), 372
Mitchell, Lucy Sprague, 214, 216
mixed-race individuals. 302–3 See also mulatto
Mo, Timothy, 234
modern/modernist cultural production, 24, 116, 125, 148
modern subjectivity, 412
Monkey King (Chao), 234
The Monkey King: Legend of a Wise and Brave Leader (Davis, G.), 235
Monkey King story, 236–37. See also The Journey to the West

children's books of, 234–35, 248n12
illustration of, 234f
position of, 234–35
rewriting of, 232–33, 243–44
The Monkey King (Mo), 234
Monkey King Wreaks Havoc in Heaven (Chen & Ma, W.), 235
Montgomery, L.M., 28, 331–45
  depression of, 330
  works of, 329–30
Moon, Michael, 315
Moore, Anne Carroll, 122, 216
More About Froggy (Brenda), 255
Morgan, Judith, 190, 197
Morgan, Neil, 190, 197
Morgan, Peter E., 244
Mother Goose, 440
Motion Picture Production Code, 149, 498–99
movies
  child development and, 148–50
  childlike characters in, 150
  as children's literature, 148, 150, 162
  dichotomous view of, 149
  as literature's competition, 148
  as mass entertainment, 149
  movie industry, 148–49
  regulation of, 149
Ms. Foundation for Women, 526
mulatto, 302, See also mixed-race individuals
Munsterberg, Hugo, 149
muscular Christianity, 455, 468
music, as freeing, 133–34
Must We Conform? (Lindner), 159–60
Myers, Mitzi, 9–10
  on cross-writing, 61, 169
My Mother the Mail Carrier/Mi Mami la Cartera (Maury), 526
The Mysterious Stranger (Twain), 293

Na, An, 243
narrative
  art, aesthetic test for, 105, 108n2
  flexibility, 107
  misdirection, 95
  structure, 243
National Board of Review, 149
national identity, 13–14, 332–333, 345, 360, 365–67, 368n2
nationalism, 29, 403
National Organization for Women (NOW), 524
national reconciliation, 286–87
Native Americans. See American Indians
Nazi Party, power of, 156
Negro History Week, 140
The Negro Slave (Durivage), 450
"The Negro Speaks of Rivers" (Hughes, L.), 140–41
Nelson, Claudia, 16–17, 31, 321, 325n12, 330, 339, 464, 468

Neumeyer, Peter, 60
Newbery, John, 8
Newbery heroines, 507,
    511–12
    household friction with, 508
Newbery Honor award, to *Frog and Toad*
    Together, 73
Newbery Medal, 8, 118
    importance of, 513n3
    Kidd on, 499, 513n3
    as shorthand cultural approval, 499
New Criticism, 56, 80–81, 87–88
    Eagleton on, 75
    hegemony of, 57
    politics of, 23
    prestige of, 74
    return to, 65
New England Primer, 29, 411, 413–15, 417, 419–22,
    424–426
    on affection, 423–24
    book-heart couplet in, 412, 416, 422, 425
    evangelical revisions of, 418
    extant copies of, 426n1
    multiple verions of, 419, 422, 425
    pedagogy of, 412
    religious identity and, 414
New Left ideal, 26, 190, 205
Newman, Andrew, 426
"New Negro" childhood, 134, 141–42
Newsome, Effie Lee, 132
Newton, Huey, 201
Nibsy the Newsboy in Funny Fairyland
    (McManus), 169
Nicholson, William, 124
Nietzsche, Friedrich, 82
night men. *See* Ku Klux Klan
"The Noble Red Man" (Twain), 299–300,
    305
Nodelman, Perry, 11, 45, 47
    on *The Bat-Poet*, 60–61
    on Bourdieu, 223
    on Jarrell, 61
    on *Where the Wild Things Are*, 220
The Noisy Book (Brown, Margaret Wise), 183
nonsense, 37, 202
    anarchic, 26, 199
    definition of, 191–92
    literary, 190, 206
    politics of, 13
Nonsense Literature for Children: Aesop to Seuss
    (Apseloff & Anderson, Celia), 190, 206
The Norton Anthology of Children's Literature, 8
nostalgia, 107, 296, 301
Not in Front of the Children: "Indecency," Censorship,
    and the Innocence of Youth (Heins), 15
novel of formation. *See* bildungsroman
NOW. *See* National Organization for Women
nuclear war, 191
The Obscurity of the Poet (Jarrell), 61

Oedipal experience, 222–23
Oh, the Places You'll Go! (Seuss), 189, 193
Oliver Twist (Dickens), 268
"Onawandah" (Alcott), 297
On Beyond Zebra (Seuss), 193, 201
One Fish Two Fish Red Fish Blue Fish (Seuss), 191,
    193, 202, 203f, 204f
On Heroes, Hero-worship, and the Heroic in His-
    tory (Carlyle), 469
op de Beeck, Nathalie, 11, 24
Opper, Fred, 170
oral history, 373, 375–76
oral tradition, 115, 117, 121, 122, 125, 138, 243
Orbis Sensualium Pictus (Comenius), 10–11
Orientalism, 241
    domestic, 257–58
Orientalism (Said), 257
original sin, 15
Ormond, Leonée, 475–76
orphaned children, 256, 260, 264, 334, 337–38, 340
other-directed society, 353, 356, 357
    Riesman on, 356, 359
other/others
    childhood as, 184
    as feminine, 272n8
    self v., 31
    taxonomy of, 259
Oulton, Carolyn, 458
Outcault, Richard, 169–70
outsider, perspective of, 136

Paine, Albert Bigelow, 303
Pankejeff, Sergey. *See* Wolf Man
pantomimes
    all-child, 477, 480
    as inappropriate for children, 477
paraphrase
    forms of, 66
    inadequacy of, 65
parental anxiety, 150
Paris, Leslie, 12, 17, 29
Parker, Roy, 334
Parkman, Francis, 302
Parr, Joy, 333–34
participatory democracy, 26, 190, 205
Passing (Larsen), 302
Passionate Journey (Masereel), 123
pastoralism, 81–82, 119
paternal authority, 509
patience, benefits of, 383
patriarchy (patriarchal subject), 412–13
patriotic nationalism, 403
Payne Fund Studies, 149
Peanuts (Schulz), 12, 25, 167, 168, 169–70, 172f,
    173f, 174f, 175–77, 179–83
    appeal of, 177–78
    as about children v. children's strip, 171–72
    complete history of, 167

as cross-writing, 178, 184–85
early to mid-period years, 175
early years of, 172–74
humor of, 182–84
as innovation/groundbreaking, 168, 183–84
licensing of, 167
pedagogy, *See also* education, progressive education.
in *New England Primer*, 413
shared, 98–99
pedophilia, 46
peers, influence of, 359
Penguin, 8
performance, as transient, 478
Perl, Harold, 151
permissiveness *See* child rearing
personhood, boundaries of, 14
Peter Pan (Barrie), 30, 475, 476–82, 486–88
audience of, 483–84
children's opinions of, 489
as cross-writing, 489–90
Darton on, 476
early productions of, 485
formal hybridity of, 481
origins of, 481
reenacted in homes, 485
Petersham, Maud, 118, 123
Petersham, Miska, 118, 123
phallocentric world, 45
Phillips, Lynn, 526
The Photoplay: A Psychological Study
(Munsterberg), 149
Phronsie Pepper's New Shoes (Sidney), 313, 325n14
pictorial narratives, 125
picture-book psychology, 213–14, 225
picture books, 11, 116–117. *See also* comics, graphic
novel.
classic, 220
close reading of, 75
dreamwork in, 214, 220
Frog and Toad as, 75
sequential, 123
pictures
as mode of communication, 11
poetics and, 10–13
Pictures from an Institution (Jarrell), 60
The Pigtail of Ah Lee Ben Loo (Bennett), 119
"Pink Elephants on Parade," 152–54, 153f, 154f
Pinkney, Brian, 131
Pinocchio (Disney), 151
pirates, 508–9
The Pirate Twins (Nicholson), 124
Plays for Young People (Barmby), 480
play, 213–14, 244, 318, 413, 425, 441, 442, 445, 449,
482–83, 520, 525, 532, 543
play therapy, 219
play-acting, 481,
plot of transformation, 331
Plotz, Judith, 56, 67n3, 272n5, 542

poet, plight of, 54
poetic(s)
notions of, 12
pictures and, 10–13
The Poetics of Childhood (Natov), 12
The Poetics of Children's Literature (Shavit), 12
poetry/poetries
African American, 132
blues, 133–37
cross-writing in, 62, 142
emotional resonance of, 57
hostility towards, 65
Hughes and, 129, 130
interpretations of, 65
Jarrell on, 58, 60, 67n7
nonsense and/as, 206
raw/cooked, 56
Poetry's Playground (Thomas, Joseph), 56
Pogrebin, Letty Cottin, 520
De Poix, Carol, 526
political jokes, 43
Polly Pepper's Chicken Pie (Sidney), 313
Poor Law Acts, 268
the poor
conditions of, 262–63
plight of, 267
presentation of, 266, 271
view of, 260
Poppy Seed Cakes (Petersham, M. & M.), 118
popular culture, 59, 241
postcolonial theory, 29–30, 257–258, 271, 271n2, 405n6,
post-ethnic identity, 28
postethnicity, 365–67
Postman, Neil, 542
postmodern reception study, 294
Potter, David, 352
poverty
breeding v., 316
in Britain, nineteenth century, 257
as inspiration, 120
leaving behind, 390
politics of, 27
power, 46–49, 101–103, 191–92, 382–83,
of children's books, 36
colonization and, 257, 451
of domestic orientalism, 257
gendered, 85, 524–25
in Harlem Renaissance, 139
of Nazi party, 156
prejudice and, 381–83
publication as, 139
Power, Effie L., 130
powwow, 304–5, 307n11
preindustrial America, as permissive
environment, 502
prejudice, power and, 381–82
Prevention of Cruelty to Children Act, 270
*Pricing the Priceless Child: The Changing Social
Value of Children* (Zelizer), 16

Prime Baby (Yang), 231
primers, 72, 81, 86, 87, 88n2, *See also New England Primer*
The Prince and the Pauper (Twain), 284, 293, 481
The Princess and the Goblin (MacDonald, G.), 74
princess story, reframing, 529–30
printerly conventions, 446
printing
    reading and, 413–14
    as trope, 414
printmaking, 116
Printz Award, 231
privilege
    distribution of, 400
    of innocence, 31
Production Code, 149, 498–99
progressive education, 214, 226n2
protective impulse, in children's literature criticism, 72–73
Protestant religious culture, 415
psychiatric language, in comics, 175
Psychological Care of Infant and Child (Watson, John), 156
psychological realism, 94, 96
    moral ambiguity of, 99
puberty, 28, 352, 356
publication, as power, 139
public school. *See* British public schools
Pullman, Phillip, 17, 31, 105–7, 109n13, 539
    on adult v. children's writers, 551
    education of, 539
    Lewis and, 551–52
    as storyteller, 552
    style of, 551
punishment
    images of, 510
    in tomboy tradition, 510–11
Puritans, 15
    fears of, 301
purity, 101, 478
    racial, 302

"The Quadroons" (Child), 302
queerness, 225–26. *See also* homosexuality.
queer studies, 456
queer theory, 3, 30
    children's literature and, 223, 456
Quick Henry, the Flit! (Seuss), 189

Rabelais and His World (Bakhtin), 190
race, 13–14
    as dualistic, 297
    politics of, 301–2
    portrayal of, 305–6
    study of, 241
racial caste system, 101
racial essentialism, 240

racial identity, 13–14, 360, 365–67, 368n2
racial purity, boundaries of, 302
racial science, 14
racial stereotypes, 239–41, 243
racism, 134, 241–42, 335, 401, 505
    depiction of, 161
    discourse on, 391
    power and, 381, 383
    resistance to, 382
    in *Roughing It*, 299
    Taylor, M., on, 373
    Twain and, 299–300
Ragged Dick (Alger), 315
Ragged London (Hollingshead), 262–63
Rahn, Suzanne, 372
Rainone, Nanette, 531
Ramona (Jackson), 306
Ransom, John Crowe, 53, 58, 67n5
Ratzinger, Cardinal Joseph, on Harry Potter series, 45
Reaching Out (Jiménez), 390
reader, 38–39, 42, 43. *See also* child reader
    adult readers of children's literature, 36–37, 40–41, 103, 105, 106
    child, 415–16, 434–35, 437, 443, 447
    identity of, 40–41, 450
readership
    flexibility of, 107, 296
    implied, 39–40, 47–48, 80
reading. *See also* critical reading practices
    adult v. child, 62
    as cultural reproduction, 416–17
    experience and, 41
    Jarrell on, 62
    instruction laws on 417, 428n9
    printing and, 413–14
    process of, 41
    purpose of, 40–41
    repetition and, 412
    Sánchez-Eppler on, 414
    as transmission of religious beliefs, 417, 420–422
    value of, 60–61
rebel figures, 298
reception study, 294, *See also* audience, readers, readership, reading
Reed, John, on British public schools, 456–57
Reed, Talbot Baines, 457
Reid, Julia, 278
Reimer, Mavis, 13, 28
religious identity, 28, 355–56, 358–59, 361–64, 367
    New England Primer and, 414
    inculcation of, 269
    search for, 365
religious symbolism, in *Froggy's Little Brother*, 269
Religious Tract Society (RTS), 269
replication, theme of, 411
respectability, rhetoric of, 260

Revard, Carter, 299, 302
Reynolds, Kimberley, 13–14, 27
The Rhetoric of Fiction (Booth), 95
Richardson, Alan, 541–42
Riesman, David, 28, 352–53, 357, 361, 364
    on children, 353, 359–60
    on conformity, 353–54
    on inner- v. other-directed, 356, 359
Ritterhouse, Jennifer Lynn, 134
The Road (McCarthy), 277
The Road to Memphis (Taylor, M.), 372
Robinson Crusoe
    appreciation of, 445
    formative appeal of, 435–36
    manhood in, 446
    publication of, 435
    Seidel on, 446
    setting of, 444
Robinson der Jungere (Campe), 435
Rodgers, Mary, 520
Rogers, Carl, 220
Rogers, John, 416, 419, 426
Roiphe, Katie, 38
Roller Skates (Sawyer), 498, 501–2
    heroine of, 507
Roll of Thunder, Hear My Cry (Taylor, M.), 14, 371–72
romantic friendships, 459, 462, 469n2
    dangers of, 464
Romanticism and the Vocation of Childhood (Plotz), 272n5
Rooke, Patricia, 336
Rosaldo, Renato, 301
The Rosary Comic Book (Yang), 231
Rose, Jacqueline, 3, 45, 476
Rosenberg, Teya, 10, 24
Ross, Diana, 520
Ross, Harold, 123
Roth, Rita, 191–92
Rotundo, E. Anthony, 296
Roughing It (Twain), racism in, 299
Rousseau, Jean-Jacque, 443
Rowlandson, Mary, 301, 421
Rowling, J.K., 93, 97–102, 105–8
    on adult books, 103–4
    criticism of, 95–96
    literary influences of, 94
    narrative style of, 95–97
RTS. *See* Religious Tract Society
Rubin, Jerry, 198
Rudd, David, 81
Rugby, Tennessee, 455–56
Rugby School, founding of, 457
Runton, Andy, 243

Sadker, David, 531
Sadker, Myra, 531
Said, Edward, 257

Salinger, J.D., 44
salvation, 262
    spiritual, 467–69
same-sex crushes. *See* crush(es)
Sammond, Nicholas, 12, 25, 504
Sánchez-Eppler, Karen, 30
    on children, 13–14
    on reading, 414
Sandars, T.C., 468
satire, 94
    of Twain, 296
savage, 449
Sawyer, Ruth, 498
scapegoat, function of, 303
scavenging, children's writing and, 434–35
Schechner, Richard, on drama/script/theatre/performance, 478
Scheckel, Susan, on American Indians, 297
Schields, Gretchen, 240–41
schizophrenia, study of, 202
Schlesinger, Leon, 149–50
Schnell, R.L., 336
schoolboy/schoolgirl crush. *See* crush(es)
school knowledge, 243. *See also* education.
school story, 94, 97–100, 108n7, 457. *See also* Harry Potter series; *Tom Brown's Schooldays*
    boy book and, 294–95
    homoeroticism in, 458–59
    same-sex relations in, 459
Schroeder (character), 172–73
Schulz, Charles M., 25, 168–72, 181–84
    childhood of, 173
    on childhood, 176–77, 183
    cross-writing of, 178, 184–85
    fictive kids of, 174–75
    formula of, 181–82
    on innocence, 173–74
    influence of, 179–181
    work ethic of, 167
Schwartz, Ben, 173
Schwartz, Eugene, 220
Scofield, Sandra, 531
Scotland
    dialects of, 277–78
    division of, 287
    Highland v. Lowland, 285–86
SDS. *See* Students for a Democratic Society
Seale, Bobby, 201
second-wave feminism, 529
    children and, 522–23
    on manhood, 531
second-wave feminist activism, 521
Sedgwick, Eve Kosofsky, 85
    on avunculate, 225
    on homophobia, 87
    on public schools, 458
    on sexuality, 511
Seduction of the Innocent (Wertham), 124
The Seekers, 520

Segel, Elizabeth, 505
segregation, 135, 161–62, 373
Seidel, Michael, on *Robinson Crusoe*, 446
Selected Poems (Jarrell), 54
self-determination, 413
Self-Help (Smiles), 260
Selznick, Brian, 212
Sendak, Maurice, 26, 66n1, 74, 124, 211, 224–26
    awards of, 211
    childhood of, 211, 223
    as child psychologist, 212
    depression of, 223
    dreamwork of, 214, 220
    education of, 216
    Freudian influence on, 219
    illustrations by, 53, 57
    on Jarrell, 54
    on Seuss, 195
    sexuality of, 211, 222–26
    Tatar on, 225
    training of, 215–16
sentimental identifications, 301–2
"separate but equal," 160, 163n22
Serlin, David, 212
Serraillier, Ian, 276
Serrato, Phillip, 13, 29
Seth (Canadian cartoonist), 178–79
Seuss, Dr., 26, 74, 191, 193, 197, 205, 206
    on children, 191, 200, 205–6
    crucial period of, 193
    education of, 189
    Sendak on, 195
    Spock and, 213
    as subversive, 190, 197
The Seven Lady Godivas (Seuss), 195
The Seven-League Crutches (Jarrell), 54
Sewell, Anna, drawings by, 131
Sewell, Elizabeth, 196–97
sex, war and, 461
sex identity, Spock on, 532
sexism, persistence of, 534
sex roles, 521, 524, 531. *See also* tomboy
    acceptance of, 505
    models for, 525
    studies of, 534
sexual friendship, dangers of, 464
Sexual Inversion (Ellis), 459–60
sexuality, 555
    attitudes toward, 46
    Butler on, 511
    celebration of, 547–48
    in children's literature, 83–88, 477, 478, *See also*
        homosexuality
    In *Peter Pan*, 487
    discursive formations of, 456
    in *Frog and Toad Together*, 83–88, 88n8
    Halberstam on, 511
    historians of, 458
    of Lobel, 85–86

as problematic, 81
    Sedgwick on, 511
    of Sendak, 211, 222–26
sexual revolution, 193
sexual symbols, 46
Seymour--an Introduction (Salinger), 44
Shaddock, Jennifer, 222
*Shadowed Lives: Undocumented Immigrants in
    American Society* (Chavez), 395
Shannon, George, 82
sharecropping, 386n3
Sharpsteen, Ben, 147
Shavit, Zohar, 12
Shaw, Bernard, 488
Shaw, John F., 269–70
Sheng-mei Ma, 240–41
Shen of the Sea (Chrisman), 119
Shortsleeve, Kevin, 13, 26
Sidney, Margaret, 14, 28, 313–23
Signal, 7
The Sign on Rosie's Door (Sendak), 215
The Silver Sword (Serraillier), 276
Skippy (Crosby), 171, 176
skulls, scientific study of, 299
slavery, 382, 426
    as business, 384–85
    in children's literature, 139
    defining liberty through, 297
    politics of, 302
    sharecropping and, 386n3
Smashing Time (Davis, D.), 38
Smiles, Samuel, 260
Smith, Georgina Castle. *See* Brenda
Smith, Henry Nash, 296
Smith, Katharine Capshaw, 12–13, 25
Smolderen, Thierry, 171
Snedeker, Caroline Dale, 498
The Sneeches (Seuss), 191, 193
Snow White (Disney), 151
social change/reform, 269, 504
    in *Are You There God? It's Me, Margaret*, 356
    children/literature as vehicles for, 25
    progress and, 141
social class, *See* class
social cohesion, 156
social order, 155–56
Society for Promoting Christian Knowledge
    (SPCK), 269
solitary reverie, reading and, 412
Sollors, Werner, 364, 366
    on hardness, 361
    on identity, 360–61
Song of the Trees (Taylor, M.), 371–72, 376
The Souls of Black Folk (Du Bois), 135
*South and Central American Tales from Silver
    Lands* (Finger), 118
*The Soveraignty and Goodness of God, Together
    with the Faithfulness of His Promises
    Displayed; Being an Account of the Captivity*

and Restauration of Mrs. Mary Rowlandson
(Rowlandson), 301, 421
SPCK. *See* Society for Promoting Christian
Knowledge
Speare, Elizabeth George, 498
Spencer, Herbert, 13
Spiegelman, Art, 181
spiritual salvation, crush and, 467–69
Spitz, Ellen Handler, on classic picture books,
220
Spock, Benjamin, 157
homosexuality and, 532
Seuss and, 213
on sex identity, 532
Spring of Prague, 193
Spufford, Francis, 9
Stalky and Co. (Kipling), 457, 465
Stanley, A.P., 468
Steedman, Carolyn, 16
Steig, William, 183
Steinem, Gloria, 520, 524
stereotypes, *See also* prejudice
of American Indians, 297
discomfort produced by, 239–41
ethnic, 26
gender, 520, 524
racial, 239–41, 243
Stevenson, Deborah, 7
Stevenson, Robert Louis, 27, 276–77, 279–87, 290
as educator, 278, 289
illness of, 275
political opinions of, 288–89
Still She Haunts Me (Roiphe), 38
Stone Book Quartet (Garner), 277
Stoneley, Peter, 316, 319–20, 323, 324n9
story, vitality of, 107
storytelling
as caring act, 48
importance of, 385
of Pullman, 552
traditional, 116
Stott, Andrew, 83
straight man role, 82, 84–85
Strange Case Dr Jekyll and Mr Hyde (Stevenson,
R.), 275
Streatfeild, Noel, 109n8
street arab fiction, 256–67
conventions of/in, 266–67, 270
"good" death in, 268–69
lessons of, 262
writers of, 269
street arab novel, 27
street arabs, 256–57, 332, 335, 339–340
street children, 256–59, 262–68, 270
strip genre, 171
strip kid, 171, 177. *See also* comic-strip child
Strong-Boag, Veronica, 342
structures of feeling, 331
Struggling Upward (Alger), 315

Struthers, E.A., 334, 338
Students for a Democratic Society (SDS), 190
Sturges, Philomen, 11–12
subjectivity, p. 412
subtextual discourse, 299
on American Indians, 303–4
in *Frog and Toad Together*, 85–87
The Subtle Knife (Pullman), 546, 553
subversion
of children's theater, 487–88
of xenophobia, 393
Sundquist, Eric J., 298, 302
Superfudge (Blume), 351
Surrealism, 169
surrogate family, 320
survival narrative, 434
*Swift and Carroll: A Psychoanalytical Study of Two
Lives* (Greenacre), 46
Swinnerton, James, 169
The Swiss Family Robinson, 30, 444f
adaptations of, 437–38
colonizing stance of, 449
as domestic celebration, 451
as family endeavor, 436–37
gender norms in, 445
plot/form of, 437
preface to, 442
publication of, 434
as reference book, 443–44
setting of, 444
Sylvie and Bruno (Carroll), 36

Tales of a Fourth-Grade Nothing (Blume), 351
Tan, Amy, 240–41
Tang Monk Disciples Monkey King (Chen & Ma,
W.), 235
Tatar, Maria, on Sendak, 225
Tate, Allen, 58, 68n7
Taylor, Charles, 105
Taylor, Henry, 56
Taylor, Mildred, 14, 377–84
on African America, 372
Black Student Alliance activity of, 374
career of, 385–86
civil rights movement and, 373–74
education of, 371
Ethiopia and, 374–75
Peace Corps service of, 374–75
publication of, 376
on racism, 373
teachers, influence of, 359
teaching. *See* children's literature (teaching of).
technology, absence of, 81
Tenniel, John, 39
Tent City, 396
Terriss, Ellaline, 487
Tezuka, Osamu, 168
Thacker, Deborah, 227n5

theatre, 478. *See also* children's theater
Their Eyes Were Watching God (Hurston), 131
Then Again Maybe I Won't (Blume), 351
There's a Wocket in My Pocket! (Seuss), 193
third force psychology, 220
Thomas, Donald, 38, 46
Thomas, Isaiah, 416
Thomas, James, 104
Thomas, Joseph, on *The Bat Poet*, 56, 58, 61
Thomas, Marlo, 519–22, 525, 528–34
    career of, 523–24
    impact of, 526–27
Thomas, Ronald R., 217
Thompson, Flora, 270
Thompson, Michael, on *Where the Wild Things
    Are*, 221–22
Thomson, Shawn, 445
Through the Looking-Glass (Carroll), 23, 35–36,
    39–45
    as bound by time, 48–49
    as classic, 37–38
    as love letter, 47
    pedophilia and, 46
    translations/representations of, 37–38
Till, Emmett, 379–80
    murder of, 374
de Tocqueville, Alexis, 352
togetherness, idea of, 76, 79
*A Token for Children: Being an Exact Account of
    the Conversion, Holy and Exemplary Lives
    and Joyful Deaths of Several Young Children*
    (Janeway), 15
Tolkien, J.R.R., 277
tomboy tradition/phenomenon, 497, 500, 504,
    506–7, 509
    Abate on, 498, 503, 508, 514n9
    "Cop-Out" genre and, 525
    haircuts of, 513n6
    as historical fiction, 501
    MacLeod on, 501–2
    new model of, 512
    parameters of, 499
    prevalence of, 505
    punishment in, 510–11
Tom Brown at Oxford (Hughes, T.), 455
Tom Brown's Schooldays (Hughes, T.), 16, 30,
    97–99, 455–56, 458–60, 462–69
    central narrative arc of, 457
    crush dynamic in, 461
    as model for boys' school stories, 457
Tom Sawyer, Detective (Twain), 295
Tom Sawyer Abroad (Twain), 295
Töpffer, Rodolphe, 123
topoi, 321
Toronto Children's Aid Society, 343–44
And to Think That I Saw It on Mulberry Street
    (Seuss), 189, 193
Tracy, Steven, 137, 143
The Tragedy of Pudd'nhead Wilson (Twain), 293

Trail of Tears, 297
transnational mythology, 245
Travisano, Thomas, 58
Treasure Island (Stevenson, R.), 275, 282
tree motif, 227n8
Tribunella, Eric L., 16, 30
Tripmaster Monkey: His Fake Book (Kingston,
    M.), 234
Trites, Roberta Seelinger, 381
trope(s)
    of American Indian burials, 302
    of American Indians, 301
    of children's culture, 521
    gender, 524
    printing as, 414
The True Confessions of Charlotte Doyle (Avi),
    512, 515n20
The Trumpeter of Krakow (Kelly), 119
von Tschudi, Friedrich, 224
Tubman, Harriet, 138
Twain, Mark, 27, 284
    on African Americans, 298
    on American Indians, 297–307
    bankruptcy of, 293
    on childhood, 296–97
    cross-writing by, 295
    first novel of, 293–94
    McNutt on, 300, 306n7
    racism and, 299–300
    satire of, 296
    as supporter of children's theater, 481
Two Years Ago (Kingsley), 468

undocumented immigrants, 391
    status of, 403
*The Upward Climb: A Course in Negro
    Achievement* (Haskin), 141*upward climb,
    metaphor of*, 141–42
Uses of Enchantment (Bettelheim), 225

Vallone, Lynne, 5, 43
Varty, Anne, 476
A Very Special House (Johnson, C.), 215
Vice Versa: A Lesson to Fathers (Anstey), 284
Vicinus, Martha, 460
*Victoria Through the Looking Glass: The Life of
    Lewis Carroll* (Lennon), 46
Vietnam War protests, 193, 206
visibility, gendered power and, 524–25
visual coherence, 122
visual imagery. *See also* comics, illustration.
    graphic novels, movies, picture books,
    in children's culture, 12
    gender norms in, 525
    and literature/language 124, 216
    resonance of, 10–11
    verbal incongruities with, 183

Vizenor, Gerald Robert, 234
Voices in the Park (Browne), 74
Voigt, Cynthia, 276
Voting Rights Act, 375
The Voyage of Doctor Doolittle (Lofting), 119
A Voyage to Patagonia (Hale, Charles), 446

Wall, Barbara, 48
Walrod, Amy, 11
Walsh, Jill Paton, on Frog and Toad stories, 73
Walt Disney Productions, 147, 162n2
  feature films, 150
  plot template of, 150–52
  reputation of, 148, 150
Walter, Natasha, 107–8
war
  Crofters', 287–89
  exigencies of, 156–57
  nuclear, 191
  sex and, 461
  Vietnam, 193, 206
Ward, Lynd, 123
Ware, Chris, 179–80
Warner, Marina, 106
Warner, Michael, 423
Warner Brothers' Looney Tunes & Merry Melodies, 149–50
Watergate scandal, 193
Watson, John B., 156
Watson, Julia, 392
Watson, Sally, 31, 498–500, 502–5, 507–12, 512n1
  popularity of, 497
  swashbuckling plots of, 506
  on writing in a tradition, 501
Watson, Victor, 48
Watters, David H., 417
Watterson, Bill, 171
Webster, Noah, 423–24
Wee Willie Winkie's World (Feininger), 169
Weikle-Mills, Courtney, 15, 29
Weinstein, Cindy, 322–23, 325n12
Welfare State, modern, 270
The Well: David's Story (Taylor, M.), 372
The Well-Wrought Urn (Brooks), 65
Wenhai Ma, 235
Wertham, Fredric, 124
Westman, Karin E., 10, 24
"What Was I Scared Of?" (Seuss), 204–5
Wheatley, Phillis, 138
Where the Wild Things Are (Sendak), 26, 74, 211, 214–19, 224–26
  Caldecott Medal of, 212
  colonialist echoes of, 222
  Nodelman on, 220
  Oedipal experience in, 222–23
  as psychological primer, 213
  Thompson on, 221–22
Whistler, James Abbott McNeill, 116

White, Thomas, 419
Whitman, Walt, allusion to, 142
Whitney, Marian, 320–21
Wilder, Laura Ingalls, 131, 498
Willard, Nancy, 66
Williams, Garth, illustrations by, 53
Williams, Martin, 170
Williams, Raymond, 331, 339–40
"William's Doll," 530–33
Wind in the Willows (Grahame), 86
witchcraft, as abomination, 45
The Witch of Blackbird Pond (Speare), 498, 501–3, 514n16
  heroine of, 507
Witch of the Glens (Watson, S.), 499
Wojik-Andrews, Ian, 12
Wolf Man, 213–14, 216–18, 221, 224–25, 227n3
Womack, Peter, 286
The Woman at the Washington Zoo (Jarrell), 54, 68n13
women, domestic role of, 525
Women on Words and Images, 524–25
The Wonderful Locomotive (Meigs), 123
wonderland, meaning of, 38
Wood, Naomi, 17, 31
Wood, Samuel, 424
Woodson, Carter G., 140
Words about Pictures (Nodelman), 11
The World of Alice (Batey), 43
worthy lives, 392–93
Wounded Knee massacre, 297
Wright, Terence, 465
writers, lives of, 44
  children as, 438–42
Wyss, Johann David, 433, 436
Wyss, Johann Rudolf, 433, 436, 442

xenophobia, 333, 401
  intensification/proliferation of, 391
  subversion of, 393
Xeric Grant, 231
Xuanzang's historical journey, 233–34

Yamate, Sandra S., 242
Yang, Gene Luen, 14, 26, 232–36, 239–46, 248n20
  alias of, 231
  Monkey King interest of, 237–38
The Year of Jubilo (Sawyer), 498, 502
  friction in, 508
Yellow Kid, 169–70
Yep, Laurence, 242
Yertle the Turtle (Seuss), 191, 193, 195
Yippies, 198
Yonge, Charlotte Mary, 258
Yoo, David, 243
You Don't Look 35, Charlie Brown! (Seth), 179
Young Adult literary realism, 383

Young Adult literature, 539, *See also* adolescent
    literature
  Asian American, 243–4
  Of the 1970s, 533
"Youth" (Hughes, L.), 142–43
youth, crushes in, 456,
    459–60

youth leadership, 141–42
*Youth of Darkest England: Working-Class Children
    at the Heart of Victorian Empire* (Boone), 14

Zangwill, Israel, 360–61
Zelizer, Viviana, 16, 339, 343–44
Zipes, Jack, 45, 108n2
Zolotow, Charlotte, 530–31